The Global Coffee Economy in Africa, Asia, and Latin America, 1500–1989

Your cup of coffee comes from far away. It was grown in Brazil, Colombia, Vietnam, or one of the hundred other coffee-producing lands on five continents. It is a palpable and long-standing manifestation of globalization. For 500 years coffee has been grown in tropical countries for consumption in temperate regions.

This volume brings together scholars from nine countries who study coffee markets and societies over the last five centuries in fourteen countries on four continents and across the Indian and Pacific oceans, with a special emphasis on the nineteenth and early twentieth centuries. The chapters analyze the creation and function of commodity, labor, and financial markets; the role of race, ethnicity, gender, and class in the formation of coffee societies; the interaction between technology and ecology; and the impact of colonial powers, nationalist regimes, and the forces of the world economy in the forging of economic development and political democracy.

William Gervase Clarence-Smith is Professor of Economic History of Asia and Africa, University of London. He is the author of *Slaves, Peasants and Capitalists in Southern Angola, 1840–1926* (1979), *The Third Portuguese Empire, 1825–1975* (1985), and *Cocoa and Chocolate* (2000).

Steven Topik is Professor of History at the University of California, Irvine. He is the author of *The Political Economy of the Brazilian State, 1889–1930* (1987), *Trade and Gunboats* (1996), and the coauthor (with Kenneth Pomeranz) of *The World That Trade Created* (1999) and (with Allen Wells and Jonathan Brown) of *The Second Conquest of Latin America* (1998).

The Global Coffee Economy in Africa, Asia, and Latin America, 1500–1989

Edited by

WILLIAM GERVASE CLARENCE-SMITH

School of Oriental and African Studies, University of London

STEVEN TOPIK

University of California, Irvine

CAMBRIDGE UNIVERSITY PRESS

CAMBRIDGE UNIVERSITY PRESS
Cambridge, New York, Melbourne, Madrid, Cape Town, Singapore, São Paulo

Cambridge University Press
40 West 20th Street, New York, NY 10011–4211, USA

www.cambridge.org
Information on this title: www.cambridge.org/9780521818513

First published 2003
Reprinted 2005
This digitally printed first paperback version 2006

A catalogue record for this publication is available from the British Library

Library of Congress Cataloguing in Publication data
The global coffee economy in Africa, Asia and Latin America, 1500—1989 / edited by
William Gervase Clarence-Smith, Steven Topik.
p. cm.
Includes bibliographical references and index.
ISBN 0-521-81851-6
1. Coffee industry — Africa — History. 2. Coffee industry — Asia — History. 3.
Coffee
industry — Latin America — History. I. Clarence-Smith, W.G., 1948— II. Topik,
Steven.
HD9195.A3512 G58 2003
338.1'7373—dc21 2002073472

ISBN-13 978-0-521-81851-3 hardback
ISBN-10 0-521-81851-6 hardback

ISBN-13 978-0-521-52172-7 paperback
ISBN-10 0-521-52172-6 paperback

To Keiko and Sarah

and

To my mother Trudy. Raised in a Viennese coffeehouse, she dedicated her life to helping others.

Contents

World coffee production

Very approximate major areas of coffee production in the 19th and early 20th century

BRAZIL Country/region for which coffee is a major crop at some point

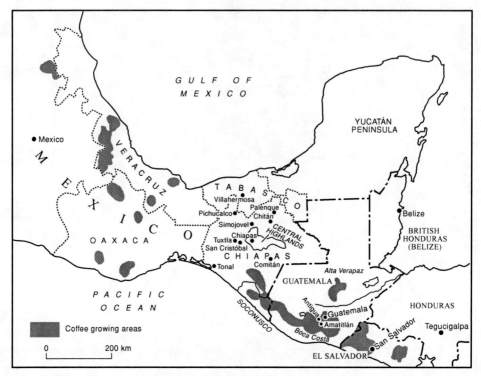

Guatemala and Mexico

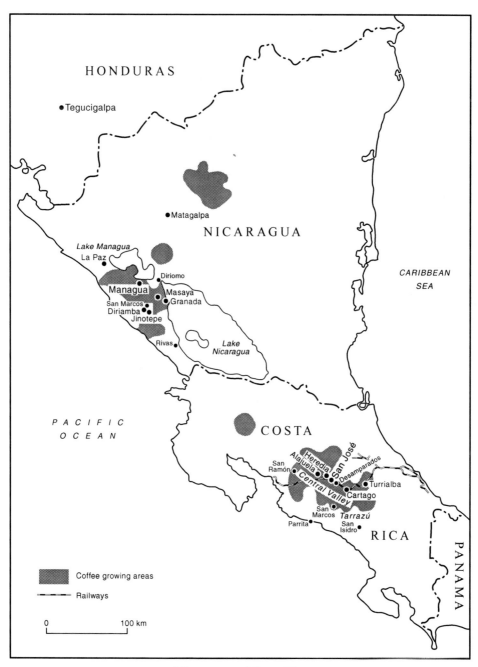

HONDURAS

● Tegucigalpa

NICARAGUA

● Matagalpa

CARIBBEAN
SEA

Lake Managua
La Paz ●

Diriomo
Managua ●
Masaya
San Marcos ● Granada
Diriamba ●
Jinotepe ●

Rivas ●

*Lake
Nicaragua*

PACIFIC
OCEAN

COSTA

San
Ramón ●
Alajuela
Heredia
San José
Desamparados
Central Valley
Cartago
Turrialba

San
Marcos ●
Tarrazú
Parrita ●
San
Isidro

RICA

PANAMA

Coffee growing areas

Railways

0   100 km

Nicaragua and Costa Rica

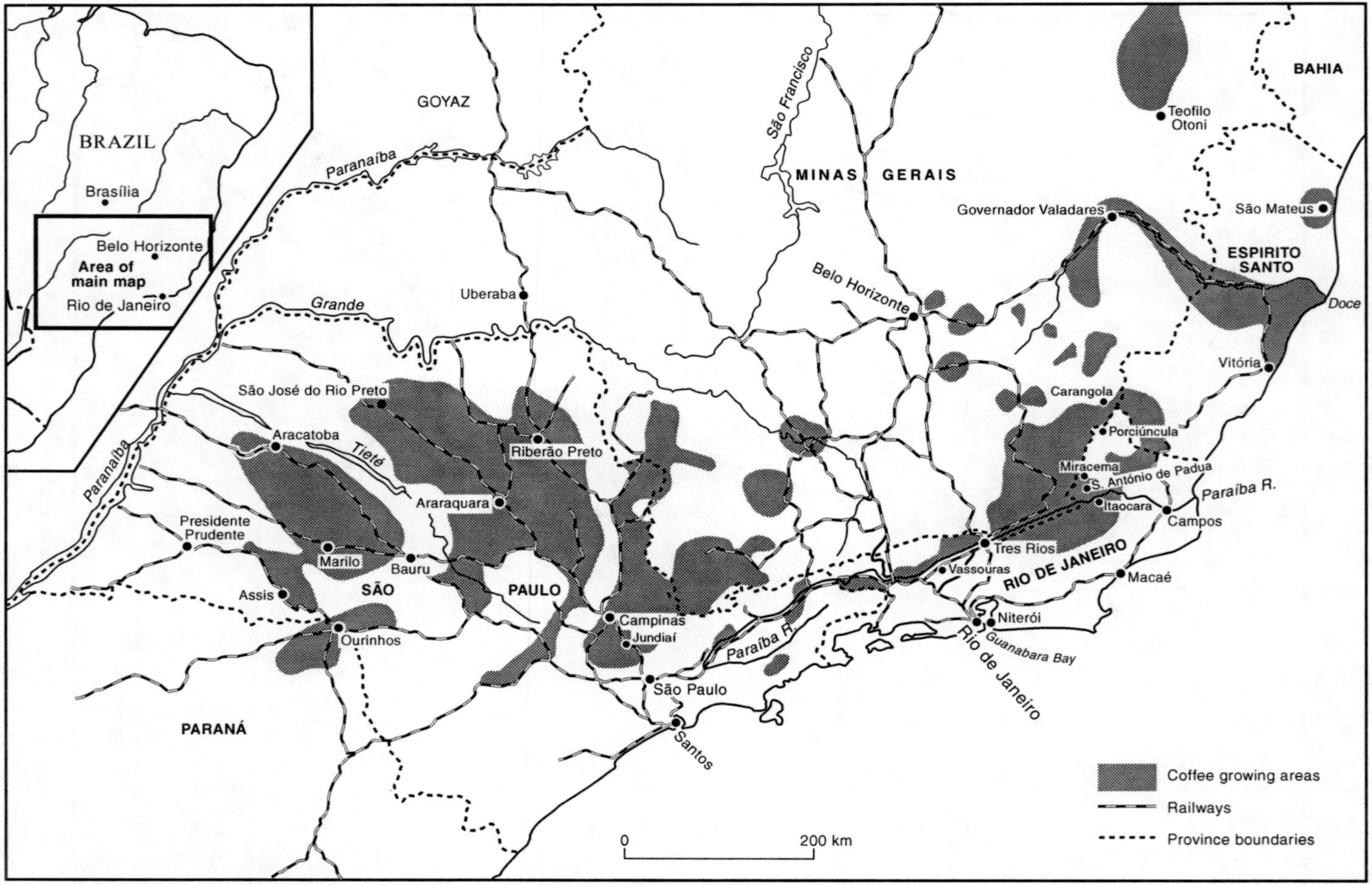
BRAZIL
Brasília
Belo Horizonte
Area of main map
Rio de Janeiro
GOYAZ
Paranaíba
São Francisco
MINAS GERAIS
BAHIA
Teofilo Otoni
São Mateus
Governador Valadares
ESPIRITO SANTO
Doce
Vitória
Belo Horizonte
Uberaba
Grande
São José do Rio Preto
Aracatoba
Tietê
Riberão Preto
Araraquara
Carangola
Porciúncula
Miracema
S. António de Padua
Itaocara
Paraíba R.
Campos
Tres Rios
Vassouras
RIO DE JANEIRO
Macaé
Niterói
Guanabara Bay
Rio de Janeiro
Presidente Prudente
Marilo
Bauru
Assis
SÃO
PAULO
Campinas
Jundiaí
Paraíba R.
Ourinhos
São Paulo
Santos
PARANÁ
Coffee growing areas
Railways
Province boundaries
0
200 km

Brazil

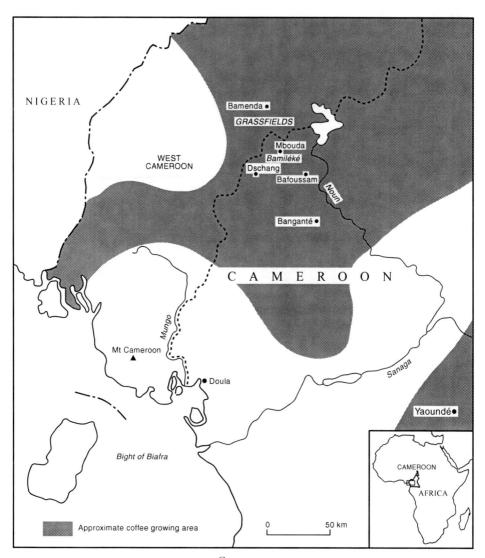

NIGERIA

WEST
CAMEROON

Bamenda •
GRASSFIELDS

Mbouda
•
Bamiléké
Dschang •
Bafoussam

Noun

Banganté •

C A M E R O O N

Mungo

Mt Cameroon
▲

• Doula

Sanaga

Yaoundé •

Bight of Biafra

CAMEROON
AFRICA

Approximate coffee growing area

0   50 km

Cameroon

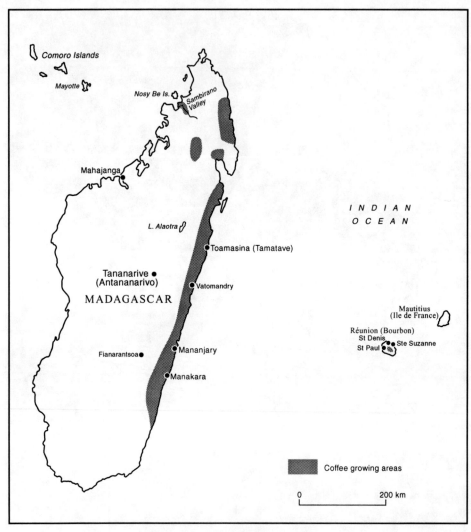

Madagascar and Réunion

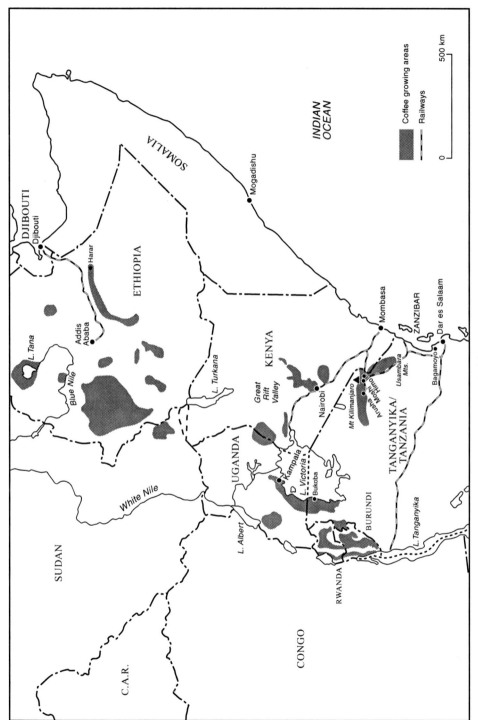

INDIAN
OCEAN

SOMALIA

Mogadishu

DJIBOUTI

Djibouti

Harar

ETHIOPIA

Addis
Ababa

L. Tana

Blue Nile

L. Turkana

KENYA

Great
Rift
Valley

Nairobi

Mombasa

ZANZIBAR

Dar es Salaam

Usambara
Mts.

Arusha

Mt Kilimanjaro

Moshi

Bagamoyo

TANGANYIKA/
TANZANIA

UGANDA

Kampala

L. Victoria

Bukoba

BURUNDI

RWANDA

L. Tanganyika

White Nile

L. Albert

SUDAN

CONGO

C.A.R.

East Africa

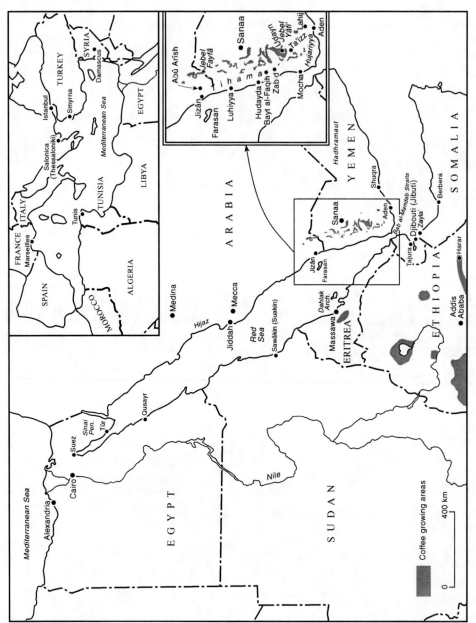

Red Sea

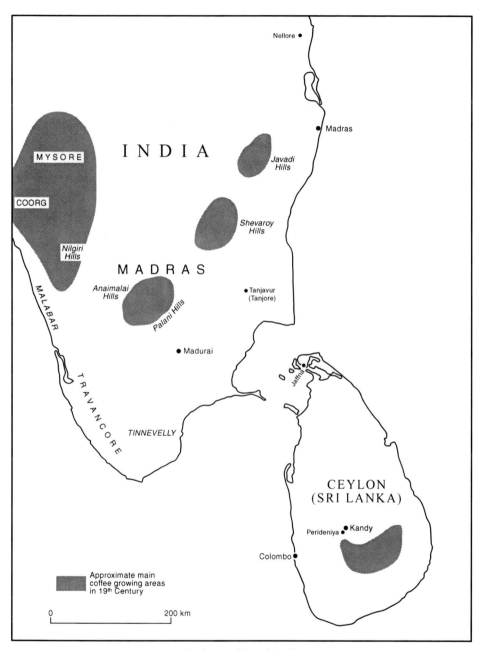

Ceylon and South India

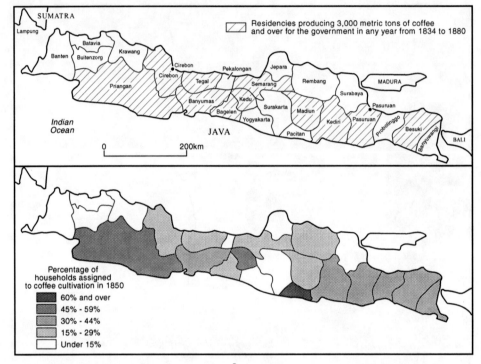

Java

Introduction

Coffee and Global Development

Steven Topik and William Gervase Clarence-Smith

That cup of coffee you sip at your breakfast table, desk, or café comes from far away.[1] It was grown in Brazil, Colombia, Vietnam, the Ivory Coast, or one of a hundred other coffee-producing lands on five continents. It is a palpable and long-standing manifestation of globalization. For 500 years coffee has been grown in tropical countries for consumption in temperate regions, linking peoples of different lands and continents by trade, investment, immigration, conquest, and cultural and religious diffusion. There is a world of history in your cup.[2]

An increasingly sophisticated study of world history is a means of understanding these processes. We have thus brought together scholars from nine countries, who cover coffee markets and societies over the last five centuries in fourteen countries on four continents and across the Indian and Pacific oceans, with a special emphasis on the nineteenth and early twentieth centuries. We analyze a wide variety of issues, related to economic, political, and cultural development, to see how they have played out over the last centuries in different parts of the globe, under different political arrangements: the creation and function of commodity, labor, and financial markets; the role of race, ethnicity, gender, and class in the formation of coffee societies; the interaction between technology and ecology; and the impact of colonial powers, nationalist regimes, and the forces of the world economy in the forging of economic development and

---

[1] Parts of Topik's contribution here were previously published in "Coffee Anyone? Recent Research on Latin American Coffee Societies," *Hispanic American Historical Review* (May 2000): 225–66.

[2] Steven C. Topik, "Coffee," in K. Kipple, ed., *The Cambridge History of Food and Nutrition* (New York: Cambridge University Press, 2000), pp. 641–53.

political democracy. Our goal is that this volume should contribute not only to an understanding of global coffee economies, but also to world history and postcolonial perspectives.

Why Coffee?

Studying larger theoretical trends through the lens of coffee might seem to cloud the issue, but this is not an exercise in "coffee fetishism," nor a trendy effort to cash in on the "Starbucks Revolution." Coffee is a commodity worthy of serious attention because of the central and long-standing place it has held in the world economy and in the lives of millions of people. One of the few holdovers from the era of the spice trade and mercantilism, coffee has been a major traded good since the sixteenth century. Indeed, it is one of the most valuable internationally traded agricultural commodities in history. Spreading out from Sub-Saharan Africa, it is now produced in over a hundred countries, on five continents and many islands. Whereas sugar comes in part from temperate regions, derived from sugar beet, coffee-producing countries have always been in the tropics, while consumption has been concentrated in temperate areas. Essentially, poor countries have grown coffee for rich ones.

Coffee cultivation involved many colonial powers, and yet much of the literature has not treated it as a colonial product. From Yemen, fitfully and partially part of the Ottoman Empire, it spread to the overseas possessions of the Dutch (Java, Surinam), French (Réunion, Martinique, Guadeloupe, Saint Domingue, Madagascar, Côte d'Ivoire, Vietnam, New Caledonia), British (India, Ceylon, Jamaica, Kenya, Tanganyika, Uganda), Portuguese (Brazil, Angola, São Tomé), Spanish (New Spain, Cuba, Puerto Rico, Philippines), Italians (Eritrea), Belgians (Congo), Germans (Tanganyika, Cameroon, New Guinea), and North Americans (Puerto Rico, Hawai'i).[3]

Despite this colonial spread, most coffee has been grown in independent countries of Latin America since the middle of the nineteenth century, and the predominance of independent states, counterintuitively, allowed politicians in such countries to take partial control of the world coffee

---

[3] Frédéric Mauro, *Histoire du café* (Paris: Editions Desjonquères, 1991); A. E. Haarer, *Modern Coffee Production* (London: Leonard Hill, 1956), ch. 1; G. Wrigley, *Coffee* (Harlow: Longman, 1988).

market. World coffee output, which grew vertiginously in the nineteenth century, was transformed by Brazil's valorization program from 1906, which deeply affected the market up to the late 1930s, and gradually involved other Latin American states. The 1960s saw the emergence of the International Coffee Organization (ICO), a cartel of producing and consuming states from all over the globe, which attempted to influence the world price of coffee until 1989.[4]

Latin America continues to produce more than twice as much coffee as the rest of the world combined, but Africa and Asia are catching up. Even once its relative output had diminished by the mid-1980s, coffee was the principal export of seven Latin American countries, and the second export of another two, making it by far the most important agricultural export for the continent, and second overall in value to petroleum.[5] However, Africa is now approaching Latin America in terms of acres planted in coffee, and many African countries are more dependent on coffee for their exports. Ethiopia is the world's fifth largest producer, and Côte d'Ivoire, Cameroon, Uganda, Kenya, Tanzania, Rwanda, Burundi, Congo, and Madagascar are among the largest producers. Parts of Asia are also rapidly gaining ground, notably, Vietnam, India, Thailand, Indonesia, and the Philippines. That said, African and Asian countries place a greater emphasis on *robusta* (*Coffea canephora*) varieties, less valuable than the *C. arabica* varieties typical of Latin American producers.[6] This book reflects the extension of coffee production across the Southern Hemisphere by considering case studies from Latin America, Africa, and Asia, including the Indian and Pacific oceans.

But why compare coffee countries? Why should one assume that there would be any similarity between them? How might this provide valuable insights into world history? Following a new interest in "commodity chains," we have both recently argued for the utility of such an approach,

---

[4] Robert H. Bates, *Open-Economy Politics: The Political Economy of the World Coffee Trade* (Princeton: Princeton University Press, 1997); V. D. Wickizer, *The World Coffee Economy, with Special Reference to Control Schemes* (Stanford: Food Research Center, 1943); Edmar Bacha and Robert Greenhill, *Marcellino Martins and E. Johnston, 150 anos de café* ([Rio de Janeiro]: Marcellino Martins and E. Johnston Exportadora Ltds., 1992); Topik Chapter 1.

[5] Victor Bulmer-Thomas, *The Economic History of Latin America since Independence* (Cambridge: Cambridge University Press, 1994), p. 9.

[6] Gregory Dicum and Nina Luttinger, *The Coffee Book: Anatomy of an Industry from Crop to the Last Drop* (New York: New Press, 1999), pp. 41, 42; J. de Graaff, *The Economics of Coffee* (Wageningen: Pudoc, 1986).

as opposed to more common nation-centered perspectives.[7] This stems from a central observation of Karl Marx:

> [Man] begins to distinguish himself from the animal the moment he begins to *produce* his means of subsistence, a step required by his physical organization. By producing food, man indirectly produces his material life itself. . . . What they [individuals] are, therefore, coincides with *what* they produce and *how* they produce. The nature of individuals thus depends on the material conditions which determine their production.[8]

Rather than produced for just subsistence, coffee production soon became an activity of local and then international exchange. Export products became "social motors" that sucked peripheral areas into the world economy, especially beginning in the mid-nineteenth century.

Although modernization and dependency theorists both rightly stress that the nature of the export sector shaped the national systems that emerged, similar impulses did not dictate that all societies would come out the same. The motor was not driving a social steamroller, flattening all participants into homogeneous pieces of a puzzle. Local social relations, prior histories, cultural understandings, and political power all mediated the impact of coffee. Indeed, the comparative study of coffee societies is useful precisely because it allows us to understand the extent of the freedom of action enjoyed by local producers, and the diversity of institutions and social relations in play.

Early Views and Policies Concerning Coffee

The first literate agents involved in coffee considered it purely as a commodity for commercial exchange. Cultivation for a century and a half was restricted to small terraced gardens in the mountains of Yemen, rarely, if ever, visited by merchants. Systems of production were thus little considered by Arab, Jewish, Indian, or European traders. Coffee was simply

---

[7] G. Gereffi and M. Korzeniewicz, eds., *Commodity Chains and Global Capitalism* (Westport: Greenwood Press, 1994); A. Appadurai, ed., *The Social Life of Things: Commodities in Cultural Perspective* (Cambridge: Cambridge University Press, 1988); Steven Topik and Allen Wells, eds., *The Second Conquest of Latin America: Coffee, Henequen, and Oil during the Export Boom, 1850–1930* (Austin: University of Texas Press, 1998); William G. Clarence-Smith, *Cocoa and Chocolate, 1765–1914* (London: Routledge, 2000); William G. Clarence-Smith, *Cocoa Pioneer Fronts since 1800: The Role of Smallholders, Planters, and Merchants* (New York: St. Martin's Press, 1996).

[8] Karl Marx, "The German Ideology," in Loyd D. Easton and Kurt H. Guddat, eds., *Writings of the Young Marx on Philosophy and Society* (Garden City, N.J.: Anchor Books, 1967), p. 409.

a resource from which they could profit, and from which governments could extract taxes. To the extent that there was discussion about the social or political consequences of coffee, they were directed at consumption. Since Muslims played the largest part in diffusing coffee in its first three centuries, a burning issue was whether coffee drinking was permitted by the Sharia or whether it should be prohibited, like alcohol. The issue was resolved fairly quickly in favor of coffee. A related and more persistent question was whether coffeehouses, as centers of intrigue and subversion, should be closed down.[9] The latter question also surfaced in Europe, but Western doubts about consumption were related more to concerns about health and politics than to religious issues.[10]

Despite the common assumption that European merchants and bureaucrats were the engine that powered the growth of the world coffee economy, they were not alone in spreading the crop. *Arabica* beans were planted in India by Muslim pilgrims in the seventeenth century, long before the British took any interest in the crop. Dutch imports of seedlings into Java in the 1690s have been much trumpeted as the "origins" of coffee cultivation in monsoon Asia, but the seedlings came from India via Muslim traders, not from Yemen. Moreover, Dutch efforts at growing coffee in Indonesia may well have been preceded by those of Muslim travelers, especially in Sumatra. An Islamic expertise in early coffee cultivation certainly ran parallel to that of Europeans. When Europeans did introduce the crop in Asia and the Pacific, they were often Roman Catholic missionaries, rather than personnel of the Dutch East Indies Company.[11]

Sub-Saharan Africa was the original home of wild coffee, with a great diversity of species and subspecies, so that an intimate knowledge of the environment, transmitted orally, proved an advantage for indigenous peoples in the early phases of the exploitation of coffee. Indeed, well before the spread of the beverage made from roasted beans, wild green robusta beans were chewed as part of ceremonial rituals of alliance in what later

---

[9] Tuchscherer, Chapter 2; Ralph Hattox, *Coffee and Coffeehouses: The Origins of a Social Beverage in the Medieval Near East* (Seattle: University of Washington Press, 1985); Antoinette Schnyder-von Waldkirch, *Wie Europa den Kaffee Entdeckte* (Zurich: Jacobs Suchard Museum, 1988).

[10] Wolfgang Schivelbusch, *Tastes of Paradise: A Social History of Spices, Stimulants, and Intoxicants*, trans. by David Jacobsen (New York: Vintage Books, 1993); Andrew Barr, *Drink: A Social History* (London: Pimlico, 1998).

[11] William G. Clarence-Smith, "The Spread of Coffee Cultivation in Asia, from the Seventeenth to the Early Nineteenth Century," in Michel Tuchscherer, ed., *Le Commerce du café avant l'ère des plantations coloniales* (Cairo: Institut Français d'Archéologie Orientale, 2001), pp. 371–84.

became Uganda.[12] Angola's first robusta exports, in 1822, were picked from wild trees and brought to the coast by Africans.[13] As the rush to coffee developed, Angolan Africans took part in clearing and ameliorating wild stands in the hinterland of Luanda.[14]

As Westerners gradually came to dominate international trade and consumption, coffee became an object of the mercantilist analyses and policies developed in Early Modern Europe. Heavy taxation of "luxuries" ensured that European and North American consumption levels remained quite limited until the end of the eighteenth century, but they were sufficient to nourish a lucrative trade. As coffee could not be cultivated in cold northern latitudes, it was a natural product for the colonial division of labor, entirely produced in tropical colonies, transported on metropolitan ships, reexported to countries without colonies of their own, and mainly consumed in the West.[15] As Europeans spread coffee cultivation to their Caribbean possessions, and later to Portuguese and Spanish America, the French initially took the lion's share of the trade from the New World, even selling Caribbean beans in the Near East by the eighteenth century. However, the Dutch retained a near monopoly of imports from Asia.[16]

Once coffee cultivation had become established in their colonies, Europeans showed a growing interest in production, focused mainly on coercive methods of labor recruitment and control. The Dutch East Indies Company imposed forced coffee cultivation in West Java, combined with the occasional uprooting of trees if prices in Europe fell too low. They concluded delivery contracts with local "regents," who forced their subjects to produce the required amounts. The Dutch thus transferred seventeenth-century methods developed in the spice islands to the coffee "gardens" of West Java.[17] In contrast, European settlers in the New World and the

---

[12] Haarer, *Modern Coffee Production*, p. 1.

[13] Joaquim António de Carvalho e Menezes, *Memória geográphica e política das possessões portuguezas n'Africa occidental* (Lisbon, 1834), p. 20.

[14] David Birmingham, "The Coffee Barons of Cazengo," *Journal of African History* 19, no. 4 (1978): 523–38, reprinted in David Birmingham, *Portugal and Africa* (Basingstoke: Macmillan, 1999).

[15] Simon Smith, "Sugar's Poor Relation: Coffee Planting in the British West Indies, 1720–1833," *Slavery and Abolition* 19, no. 3 (1998): 68–9.

[16] Tuchscherer, Chapter 2; Clarence-Smith, "The Spread of Coffee Cultivation."

[17] M. R. Fernando and William O'Malley, "Peasants and Coffee Cultivation in Cirebon Residency," in Anne Booth et al., eds., *Indonesian Economic History in the Dutch Colonial Era* (New Haven: Yale University Press, 1990), pp. 171–86; Peter Boomgaard,

Indian Ocean turned to African slaves, already tried and tested for sugar production. Most Africans who grew coffee thus did so in the Americas, at least until Brazil abolished slavery in 1888.[18] This myopic duplication of earlier labor systems may well have hampered production, as coercion offered no real advantages in a system of cultivation without labor gangs, while the demoralization and resentment of workers probably lowered productivity.

The explosion of coffee cultivation beginning in the mid-nineteenth century reflected sharp tax reductions in the West, as free trade spread, and towns, industry, and population grew rapidly. This helped to make coffee a staple part of the diet of North America and much of Europe, especially France and the Germanic lands.[19] Tea-drinking Britain and Russia and chocolate-drinking Spain were the main countries to resist the addictive allures of coffee, and that only partially. Moreover, coffee consumption made great strides in less developed countries, notably, in parts of Latin America, where it pushed aside chocolate, *guaraná*, *maté*, and other traditional local beverages.[20]

Brazil was the greatest long-term beneficiary of this tremendous boom. The destruction of Haiti's *arabica* plantations after the slave insurrection of 1791 left a gaping hole in the market.[21] Initially, there were other contenders for Haiti's position as the world's leading exporter. In Asia, Indonesia was at the fore, with Ceylon, India, and the Philippines showing great promise. However, the *Hemileia vastatrix* fungus epidemic in the 1870s played havoc across the Old World, compounding problems originating in shortages of well-placed forested land.[22] Among Hispanic American producers, Puerto Rico's early success was limited by the small size of the island.[23] However, Venezuela's speedy reallocation of labor

Children of the Colonial State; Population Growth and Economic Development in Java, 1795–1880 (Amsterdam: Free University Press, 1989), pp. 19, 30–1; F. de Haan, *Priangan: De Preanger-Regentschappen onder het Nederlandsch bestuur tot 1811* (Batavia: Bataviaasch Genootschap van Kunsten en Wetenschappen, 1910–12).

[18] Mauro, *Histoire*, chs. 5 and 10.
[19] Topik, Chapter 1; Barr, *Drink*, pp. 5–6; John Burnett, *Liquid Pleasures, a Social History of Drinks in Modern Britain* (London: Routledge, 1999).
[20] Clarence-Smith, *Cocoa and Chocolate*, chs. 2–3.
[21] Michel-Rolph Trouillot, "Motion in the System: Coffee, Color, and Slavery in Eighteenth-Century Saint-Domingue," *Review* 3 (Winter 1982): 331–88.
[22] Clarence Smith, Chapter 4.
[23] L. W. Bergad, *Coffee and the Growth of Agrarian Capitalism in Nineteenth Century Puerto Rico* (Princeton: Princeton University Press, 1983).

from cocoa to coffee was a taste of things to come, even if postindependence political chaos slowed the adoption of coffee in Colombia and Central America.[24]

The prominence of Brazil's coffee exports, together with improvements in Western agronomy and the spread of free trade, provoked no more than a limited, and sometimes simplistic, interest in the crop's place in economic development. Labor was the main focus of analysis, with debates centering on the morality and efficacy of slavery.[25] Southern European immigrants replaced slaves after 1888, making questions of immigration central to the coffee economy, notably, the refusal to allow Africans or Chinese to enter the country.[26]

The scientific analysis of Brazilian cultivation methods faced formidable obstacles. There was only one fairly reliable census in the nineteenth century, that of 1872, and planters often did not know how many hectares of land they owned, nor how many trees they had planted to the hectare. Although a few planters' manuals were published, there were no schools of agronomy, and the first experimental station was founded only in 1887. The success of coffee was evidence of the truth of the popular proverb, "God is Brazilian," demonstrated by the natural wealth of the country's soil and climate. There was little institutionalization of credit, land, or labor markets, and individual growers adapted to local conditions on an ad hoc basis, for the Brazilian elite was much more interested in modernizing the cities than in developing the countryside. Indeed, overwhelming the world coffee market was proof that their trial-and-error methods sufficed.[27]

---

[24] R. Cartay, *Historia económica de Venezuela, 1830–1900* (Valencia: Vadell Hermanos, 1988); William Roseberry, *Coffee and Capitalism in the Venezuelan Andes* (Austin: University of Texas Press, 1983); Marco Palacios, *El Café en Colombia, 1850–1970* (Mexico City: El Colegio de Mexico, 1983); United States, *Cultivation of, and Trade in, Coffee in Central and South America* (Washington, D.C., 1888); 50th Congr., House of Representatives, 1st sess., Consular Reports on Commerce etc., no. 98.

[25] Joaquim Nabuco, *O abolicionismo* (London: Kingdon, 1883).

[26] Thomas Holloway, *Immigrants on the Land: Coffee and Society in São Paulo, 1886–1934* (Chapel Hill: University of North Carolina Press, 1980); George Reid Andrews, *Blacks and Whites in São Paulo Brazil, 1888–1988* (Madison: University of Wisconsin Press, 1991).

[27] Franz W. Dafert, *Über die Gegenwartige Lage des Kaffeebaus in Brasilien* (Amsterdam: J. H. de Bussy, 1898), and *Principes de Culture Rationnelle du Café au Brésil* (Paris: Augustin Challand, 1900). See also Warren Dean, *Rio Claro: A Brazilian Plantation System, 1820–1920* (Stanford: Stanford University Press, 1976); Warren Dean, *With Broadax and Firebrand* (Berkeley: University of California Press, 1995); Stanley Stein, *Vassouras* (Cambridge, Mass.: Harvard University Press, 1958); Steven Topik, "Representações nacionais do cafeicultor: Ze Prado e Juan Valdez," *Revista Brasileira de História* 15, no. 29 (1995): 157–72.

Hispanic America displayed a similar lack of agronomic enthusiasm, combined with a focus on labor issues. In the preface to a later edition of his manual on coffee production in Mexico, Matias Romero noted that when he first published it in 1878, he sold only two or three copies.[28] Indeed, such manuals were often published in Europe and exported to Latin America.[29] Central American governments participated in the coffee economy mainly by enforcing debt peonage, although local elites were most influential in shaping local labor systems. Mayans were forced into the coffee fields of Guatemala and Mexico, whereas in Nicaragua, market forces proved stronger than coercion in coaxing Amerindians and others to participate in the coffee economy.[30]

Labor was again the main center of attention in colonial Asia and Africa, for coffee was the key to the Dutch "Cultivation System" of obligatory deliveries to the state in Indonesia from 1832, "the cork on which the Netherlands float." Coffee alone provided 82 percent of government revenues from the iniquitous system up to 1860, whereas sugar was a loss-making crop to the mid-1840s.[31] Debates about the morality and efficacy of this modernized and intensified system of forced cultivation raged until the 1870 decision to engender a gradual transition to European estates. Even then, the winding down of forced coffee cultivation lasted up to the First World War. By this time the devastation of *Hemileia vastatrix* had greatly reduced the economic significance of coffee, and smallholder success was raising awkward questions about the choice of estates to achieve economic growth.[32]

Portuguese and French colonies relied more on coercing labor for European estates, although the Portuguese in Timor also copied the forced cultivation methods of their Dutch neighbors until the 1920s.[33] The problem of slavery was most acute in Angola, as late as the 1910s. Moreover,

[28] Matias Romero, *Coffee and India-Rubber Culture in Mexico* (New York: G. P. Putnam's Sons, 1898), p. v.
[29] Mario Samper Kutschbach, "Modelos vs. practicas: Acercamiento inicial a la cuestión tecnológica en algunos manuales sobre caficultura, 1774–1895," *Revista de Historia* (Costa Rica) 30 (July-December 1994): 11–40; Carlos Naranjo G., "La Primera modernizacion de la caficultura costarricense, 1890–1950," *Revista de Historia* (Costa Rica) 36 (July-December 1997): 79–106.
[30] Rus, McCreery, Dore, and Charlip, Chapters 8–11.
[31] Cornelis Fasseur, *The Politics of Colonial Exploitation: Java, the Dutch and the Cultivation System* (Ithaca: Cornell University, 1992), pp. 32–6, 151, and 221.
[32] William G. Clarence-Smith, "The Impact of Forced Coffee Cultivation on Java, 1805–1917," *Indonesia Circle* 64 (1994): 241–64.
[33] William G. Clarence-Smith, "Planters and Smallholders in Portuguese Timor in the Nineteenth and Twentieth Centuries," *Indonesia Circle* 57 (1992): 15–30.

the Portuguese replaced slavery with forced labor, causing major international scandals until the system was finally wound up as late as 1962.[34]
French coffee planters in Madagascar and Côte d'Ivoire did not have the
same recourse to slavery, but they depended on labor coerced by the state
until 1946.[35]

The British, the standard-bearers of liberal colonialism, were loath
directly to coerce workers, even though they briefly applied forced coffee
cultivation in Ceylon in the early nineteenth century. The main problem
lay in persuading Tamils from southern India to migrate seasonally to
Ceylon's coffee estates, and the authorities in both India and Ceylon long
turned a blind eye on various abuses in this formally free labor system.[36]
In Kenya, the British banned African cultivation of *arabica* to protect
European settlers, although this was not extended to other territories.[37]

For all their overriding concern with labor, some colonial elites in the
Old World showed a greater interest in techniques of coffee cultivation
than that displayed by their counterparts in independent Latin America.
Nowhere was tropical agronomy more developed than in Indonesia,
where the Dutch carried out research for indigenous smallholders, while
European planters banded together to create their own institutes for
each of the major crops.[38] This work revolutionized sugar cultivation
around the world, through the development of new strains of cane.[39]
However, there seems to have been no parallel breakthrough with coffee,
despite some worthy publications.[40] Investigations into tropical agriculture were carried out by other colonial powers, with the results finding

---

[34] James Duffy, *A Question of Slavery* (Cambridge: Harvard University Press, 1967);
Birmingham, "The Coffee Barons"; [William] G. Clarence-Smith, *The Third Portuguese
Empire, 1825–1975, a Study in Economic Imperialism* (Manchester: Manchester University
Press, 1985), pp. 107–8, 139–41, 183, 215.

[35] H. Fréchou, "Les Plantations européennes en Côte d'Ivoire," *Cahiers d'Outremer* 8, no. 29
(1955): 56–83; Campbell, Chapter 3.

[36] Kurian, Chapter 7.

[37] Paul Mosley, *The Settler Economies: Studies in the Economic History of Kenya and Southern
Rhodesia, 1900–1963* (Cambridge: Cambridge University Press, 1983); C. C. Wrigley,
Crops and Wealth in Uganda: A Short Agrarian History (London, 1959); Curtis and Eckert,
Chapters 12 and 13.

[38] C. J. J. van Hall and C. van de Koppel, eds., *De Landbouw in de Indische archipel* (The
Hague: W. van Hoeve, 1946–50).

[39] William K. Storey, *Science and Power in Colonial Mauritius* (Rochester, N.Y.: University of
Rochester Press, 1997).

[40] J. Hagen, *De Koffiecultuur* (Haarlem: H. D. Tjeenk Willink and Zoon, 1932); A. J. Ultée,
"Koffiecultuur der ondernemingen," in Hall and Koppel, eds., *De landbouw*, vol. 2b,
pp. 7–88; B. H. Paerels, "Bevolkingskoffiekultuur," in Hall and Koppel, eds., *De
Landbouw*, vol. 2b, pp. 89–119.

their way into the *Bulletin of the Imperial Institute* and the proceedings of various international congresses of tropical agriculture. For all this, an eminent authority noted in 1951 that "it is sometimes said that no important changes have been made in the coffee production methods in the last 150 years."[41]

Ten Propositions on Coffee from Postwar Developmental Economics

World sales of coffee took a quantum leap after the Second World War, as the spread of instant forms of the beverage opened up new markets, and the long capitalist boom increased incomes.[42] Instant coffee also allowed for a greater utilization of *robusta*, opening new niches for African and Asian producers of low-quality beans.[43] A small number of large Western roasting companies simultaneously tightened their grip on the coffee market, dictating the types of coffee that they required.[44]

In colonial and postcolonial Africa and Asia, the stranglehold of the state over smallholder economies increased markedly. Almost everywhere, the purchase and export of beans fell into the hands of state marketing boards. After independence, these institutions were not only maintained but also often expanded. Particularly influential was the Caisse de Stabilisation in Côte d'Ivoire, rapidly emerging as one of Africa's largest coffee producers. While providing short-term price stability for smallholders, marketing boards rapidly turned into mechanisms for harsh taxation and extensive corruption.[45] At the same time, many newly independent governments nationalized plantations, as in Indonesia and North Vietnam, generally leading to a sharp fall in the output of estate coffee.[46]

In this context, developmental economics arose as a global body of scholarship. It was much marked by independence struggles in Africa and Asia, nationalist and populist social movements in Latin America, the authoritarian thrust of Communist and Fascist regimes, state-led Western responses to the Great Depression, and the extension of state power

---

[41] V. D. Wickizer, *Coffee, Tea and Cocoa* (Stanford: Food Research Institute, 1951), p. 36.

[42] Jean Heer, *World Events, 1866–1966: The First Hundred Years of Nestlé* (Lausanne: Imprimeries Réunies, 1966), ch. 19.

[43] Graaff, *The Economics of Coffee*, p. 49.

[44] Topik, Chapter 1.

[45] Robert H. Bates, *Markets and States in Tropical Africa: The Political Basis of Agricultural Policies* (Berkeley: University of California Press, 1981).

[46] Robert McStocker, "The Indonesian Coffee Industry," *Bulletin of Indonesian Economic Studies* 23, no. 1 (1987): 40–69.

around the world during the world war. The emphasis was thus on the state as a tool for economic improvement. At the same time, there was growing concern with the consequences of focusing on particular crops, initiated by Harold Innis and the staples school in Canada.[47]

Albert Hirschman took off from staples theory by stressing linkages. Different commodities had different spread effects and social consequences, and could even have different economic consequences. He thus recognized that coffee had its own life and possibilities. These inhered in the commodity's botany and production process, rather than being imposed by the world economy and economic laws in general. Indeed, Hirschman argued that the nature of coffee production and processing may have stimulated native entrepreneurship and industrial development, not just colonial or neocolonial exploitation.[48] The nature of the crop and its internal demands and linkages thus became central tenets of development economics and government programs.

A number of students of Latin American development applied these new theories to coffee export economies, and a body of generalizations emerged. Because Latin America still produced more than three-quarters of the world's coffee at the time, authors tended to ignore the Old World. Moreover, as independence spread in Asia and Africa, the elites of new countries often adopted ideas elaborated with reference to Latin America, especially dependency theory. Although such studies did not necessarily systematically explore the relationship between coffee and development, ten implicit propositions can be drawn from them.

1. Coffee was chiefly grown on large landholdings. These were in turn conceptualized either as a colonial legacy or as a consequence of nineteenth-century Liberal distribution of public "waste" land and indigenous corporate property. Large rural proprietors, or *latifundiários,* were thus the most important producers of coffee, with cultivation usually directed by the planter and his overseers on demesne lands.

2. Even when the forces producing an unequal social distribution of land weakened or disappeared, economies of scale explained the persistence of large units of production. Although the technology of coffee cultivation was not especially sophisticated, it was still beyond the reach

---

[47] John Richards, "The Staple Debates," in Cameron Duncan, ed., *Explorations in Canadian Economic History: Essays in Honour of Irene Spry* (Ottawa: University of Ottawa Press, 1985), pp. 45–72.

[48] Albert Hirschman, "A Generalized Linkage Approach to Development, with Special Reference to Staples," *Economic Development and Cultural Change* 25 (1977, supplement): 67–98.

of peasants. Some national studies associated coffee with smallholdings, as in the cases of Antioquia (Colombia), Costa Rica, and the Dominican Republic. However, even in these cases, there were authors who stressed the optimal character of large-scale coffee cultivation.

3. Coffee was a frontier crop that expanded into "virgin" lands, and hence had no opportunity costs. Indeed, the onward march of the frontier had the added benefit that "vacant" land was incorporated into the civilized world.

4. The export drive brought monocultural specialization in its wake. Foodstuffs had to be purchased from others, and malnutrition among workers was rife. Monoculture also increased vulnerability to world market fluctuations.

5. Agricultural workers were assumed to be male and culturally part of the majority group, at least after the end of slavery. Little attention was paid to gender, culture, or race. Indigenous populations were deemed to be either marginalized or acculturated by the advance of coffee.

6. Coffee workers were often visualized as potential revolutionaries. They were coerced, initially through slavery and later through government imposition, but involvement in growing a cash crop brought them into the national economy, and more broadly into national life, as a rural proletariat. However, some authors recognized that effective land reform could blunt revolutionary zeal.[49]

7. Little attention was paid to the role of intermediaries, in part because large units of production "internalized" many more commercial and service functions than did small farms. To the extent that intermediaries were considered, they were conceptualized as foreigners, and, as such, conspirators against the true development of the national economy. This underpinned the extension of marketing boards across most of the tropics, even when such organizations were not legally public bodies, as in the case of Colombia's Federación Nacional de Cafeteros.

8. Technically sophisticated coffee planters and traders were believed to be more progressive than internally oriented *hacendados* and subsistence farmers, tied to the precapitalist colonial heritage. Exporters were progressive because of their interest in a legal framework to protect property rights and capital accumulation and their role in creating a transportation infrastructure and, eventually, a wage labor force.

9. As a particularly significant instance of this progressive economic role, coffee producers were thought to be those most likely to foment

---

[49] Charles Bergquist, *Labor in Latin America* (Stanford: Stanford University Press, 1986).

industrialization, considered to be the touchstone of development. This was evidenced by the cases of São Paulo (Brazil), Antióquia (Colombia), and El Salvador. However, there was a difference of opinion here, with extreme Dependentistas arguing that "true" industrialization was precluded in such cases.

10. Extending out from the economic sphere, coffee planters were also credited with creating Liberal national states, and bringing political peace to the squabbling factions of the elite. However, because "coffee republics" were run by a planter class that favored laissez-faire and free trade, governments played a small direct role in coffee economies. Because of the focus on Latin America, the colonial state lay outside this analysis.

To be sure, there were disagreements about all these propositions, based on political perspectives, the time period examined, and the areas concerned. Nonetheless, it is our contention that most students of Latin America would have broadly agreed with these characterizations, and that many of these ideas were then taken up by students of the rest of the tropics.[50]

New Directions

In the last two decades, and particularly the last few years, these ten propositions have been questioned from many quarters.[51] Current conceptions of export societies in general, and coffee societies in particular, have refined, qualified, or even cast out most of the preceding ten propositions. In a Latin American context, many of the earlier generalizations came to be seen as more applicable to sugar and bananas than to coffee, and some of the leading authors of this reappraisal have contributed to this volume. In particular, the focus of discussion has shifted from national economic growth and political structures, which concentrated on elites and capital accumulation, to a much greater emphasis on the social conditions of primary producers.

The integration of studies of coffee societies in the Old World has extended the process of reappraisal. This is the first volume to attempt such a synthesis within a clearly historical framework, and comparisons of

---

[50] George Beckford, *Persistent Poverty: Underdevelopment in the Plantation Economies of the Third World*, 2nd ed. (London: Zed Press, 1983).
[51] Steven Topik, "Coffee, Anyone? Recent Research on Latin American Coffee Societies," *Hispanic American Historical Review* 80, no. 2 (2000): 225–66.

African and Asian experiences in the social sciences have also thrown new light on Latin America.[52] The resilience and productivity of African and Asian smallholders have challenged models based on alleged economies of scale and the normative nature of large estates.[53] Widespread polyculture, of both cash and food crops, suggests that monoculture is more a choice than a natural progression, and challenges the view of the great planter as a progressive agriculturalist. A stress on indigenous populations undermines assumptions that forests were empty prior to the advance of the coffee frontier. Warnings about the ecological consequences of chopping down primary forests are assuming apocalyptic tones, and interest in agroforestry methods is growing. Complex labor systems indicate that wage work is not standard, and turn the spotlight on sharecropping and tenancy as flexible and effective contracts. Many women and children labor in coffee, helping to sustain and develop cultures other than those of ruling elites. Commercial intermediaries have forced their way to the forefront of the analysis, following the catastrophic failure of most state marketing boards in Africa. Industrialization based on the coffee profits of large landlords has been verified in cases such as Angola and Kenya, but distinct models are needed for smallholder economies. Finally, Old World colonialism and its aftermath have presented political contexts divergent from those studied in Latin America.

Smallholder agency has thus become the new watchword, contrasting with earlier visions of backwardness, repression, and victimization. Women and children simultaneously receive more attention. Thus, in Nicaragua, the rising value of property led municipalities to legislate about morality, to determine who had a right to own, inherit, or cede property.[54] Since resistance and power are not necessarily structural and overtly political but, rather, take everyday forms, local culture has become a key concern, and microstudies of local resistance reveal a more complicated and varied story than eagle's-eye structuralist approaches. Generalization has certainly become more difficult.

At the same time, historians have turned to seeing peasants not only resisting and creating their own social spaces at the local level, but also participating in state formation and regional and national identity creation, as

---

[52] J.-C. Tulet et al., eds., *Paysanneries du café des hautes terres tropicales* (Paris: Karthala, 1994); Ministère de la Coopération, *Cafés, études de cas sur la compétitivité des principaux pays producteurs* (Paris, 1994); Wrigley, *Coffee.*

[53] John Tosh, "The Cash-Crop Revolution in Tropical Africa: An Agricultural Reappraisal," *African Affairs* 79 (1980): 79–94.

[54] Dore, Chapter 9.

issues of nationalism and regionalism draw renewed attention.[55] In northern Central America, where the indigenous population was long treated as marginal, there is a novel interest in non-ladino culture.[56] Cash-cropping farmers were crucial to anticolonial mobilization in Asia and Africa, even if they were often the main victims of postcolonial governments.[57]

By bringing to bear the erudition of our international and interdisciplinary contributors on such problems, we hope to have furthered the process of provoking reassessments of received wisdom, proposing new bounded generalizations and categories of analysis, and setting out new agendas for future study. Our tentative revisions of the ten propositions delineated above are put forward in the conclusion to this volume, expanding on the brief critique above and incorporating more of the contributions of our authors.

Acknowledgments

The fifteen chapters that follow originated at the first international conference to examine the history of the social and developmental impact of coffee world-wide, held at St. Antony's College, Oxford, September 10–12, 1998. It brought together twenty-five historians, anthropologists, economists, agronomists, and political scientists from twelve countries on five continents. They pooled their expertise on some two dozen of the world's most important coffee-growing countries and scrutinized various theories applied to the world coffee economy.[58]

[55] Aviva Chomsky and Aldo Lauria-Santiago, eds., *Identity and Struggle at the Margins of the Nation-State: The Laboring Peoples of Central America and the Hispanic Caribbean* (Durham, N.C.: Duke University Press, 1998); Aldo A. Lauria-Santiago, *An Agrarian Republic: Commercial Agriculture and the Politics of Peasant Communities in El Salvador, 1823–1914* (Pittsburgh: University of Pittsburgh, 1999); Florencia Mallon, *Peasant and Nation: The Making of Postcolonial Mexico and Peru* (Berkeley: University of California Press, 1995); Jeffery Paige, *Coffee and Power* (Cambridge, Mass.: Harvard University Press); Mario Samper K., *Producción cafetalera y poder político en Centroamérica* (San José, C.R.: Colección Ruedo del Tiempo, 1998); Robert Williams, *States and Social Evolution: Coffee and the Rise of National Governments in Central America* (Chapel Hill: University of North Carolina Press, 1995). Also see Steven Topik's review of four regional studies, "Mexico's Southern Liberals in the Post-Independence Decades," in *Mexican Studies/Estudios Mexicanos*, in press.

[56] Rus and McCreery, Chapters 8 and 11.

[57] Bates, *Markets and States*.

[58] In addition to contributions from the authors in this volume, we benefited from the insightful presentations and comments at the Oxford meeting from Abdussamad H. Ahmad, Robert Greenhill, Birgitte Holten, Nancy Naro, Jeffrey Paige, Renato Perissinoto, François Ruf, Charles Schaeffer, and Robert Williams.

We gratefully acknowledge funding and other material support from the CANA Foundation; the School of Oriental and African Studies, University of London; the University of California, Irvine, especially Dean of Humanities Karen Lawrence; the British Academy; the Rhodes Chair Travel Fund, Oxford, and Professor William Beinart; and the Centre of Brazilian Studies, Oxford, and its director, Professor Leslie Bethell. We also received helpful encouragement from the International Coffee Organization, London, and its director, Celsius Lodder.

PART I

ORIGINS OF THE WORLD COFFEE ECONOMY

The Integration of the World Coffee Market

Steven Topik

Studies of coffee too often reify the international market. It is seen as an exogenous force that imposes itself on local producers who are powerless to do anything but obey its dictates. The "law of supply and demand" is seen as a structural dictator. There has been a substantial debate on the extent to which changes have been occasioned by changes in production processes (the creation of surplus) or in demand induced by changing consumption patterns or caused by commercial intermediaries. Who in the commodity chain is in control of prices, and has this changed over the centuries?[1]

A second issue, which may appear only a technical subsidiary of the first two but is in fact central, is the creation of international standards and grades. How homogeneous is the commodity and how uniform internationally are the definitions? Do people mean the same thing when they say "coffee"?

This chapter analyzes the transformation of coffee from Arab monopoly to European colonial product to the sustenance of Latin American national states to, finally, a globally produced multinational commodity by asking the following questions: (1) What was the relative importance of changing patterns of demand and production in transforming the market, or, to put it another way, what were the relative roles of culture and technology in driving change? (2) What were the relative roles of private

---

[1] An earlier and briefer version of this essay appeared as "The Integration of the World Coffee Market," in *Integration of Commodity Markets in History*, Proceedings of the Twelfth International Economic History Congress, edited by Clara Eugenia Núñez (Sevilla: Universidad de Sevilla, 1998), pp. 55–65.

and public actors in creating the market? (3) What forces drove standard-ization, grading, and other market conventions? (4) To what extent was coffee caught up in a true international market in which price was deter-mined by supply and demand? (5) What was the relative role of producers, consumers, and intermediaries in the commodity chain?

Coffee has been one of the world's most valuable internationally traded commodities for several centuries. One of the few commodities that was already important under Early Modern luxury long-distance trade, it con-tinues today as a key trade good. But one should not reify the "coffee market." Rather than a continuous, homogeneous institution, the inter-national mart has been marked by radical disjunctures and essential trans-formations. Coffee continues to enjoy great international importance be-cause the nature of its appeal to consumers has shifted to conform to remarkable changes in the societies of the dominant buyers over the last four centuries. The "social life" of coffee, its meaning to producers and consumers, changed also. Over time, coffee consumption became increas-ingly segmented, balancing between a luxury and a necessity. Production has also markedly shifted geographically from the Middle East to Asia to Latin America and now, increasingly, to Asia and Africa again.

The nature of the international coffee market has changed dramati-cally over its five centuries of existence. So has control of that market, which moved in the sixteenth century from the producer to the exporter, in the nineteenth century to the importer, in our century to the roaster and to national and international government institutions, and finally today to a few vertically integrated multinational firms. To simply speak of "the market" or "market forces" is to ignore the evolving nature of that market and the role of human agency in creating it. But the central fact continues to be that over 90 percent of all coffee is exported by rela-tively poor tropical countries and a similar percentage is imported by rich, temperate countries. (The one significant change is that producing coun-tries are consuming an ever greater share of their crop, especially in Latin America.)

The very many histories of coffee that have been written all treat coffee as an essential unity, an unproblematic commodity. Indeed, the most com-mon story of coffee's development has it originating in Ethiopia, where it was passed to Yemen. A Yemeni seedling supposedly was spirited out by Dutchmen who began cultivating in Java. A Yemeni by-way-of-Java seedling then went to Amsterdam, from there to Paris and from there to Martinique. The Martinique tree is argued to be the mother of all Latin American coffee, a direct descendant of Ethiopian coffee. Purveyors of this neat story are unwitting assistants of international traders and mass roasters who had a vested interest in positing a monolithic sort of coffee. Frank Perlin, discussing cotton, points out that although there was an "astonishing variety" produced in the fields, the demands of the market-place reduced the varieties to a much smaller number:

> thousands of names for field cultivars, a much smaller (yet still striking) number in the local market, and by the time the as yet unspun cotton reached London, Bordeaux or Amsterdam, a relatively small number of highly generalized, often regional names and ordinal grading symbols...would be recorded in price quotations in 18th and early 19th century newspapers.[2]

Coffee faced a similar situation in that the market created a small number of categories and grades; however, its trajectory over time was different in that the number of commercial cultivars and market categories grew rather than diminished, as is the usual case. That is, rather than reflecting convergence, coffee production and consumption were characterized more by dispersal. This is because, unlike most staples, coffee was a semitropical luxury good grown much more for export than for home use. Hence distinction, especially in its first histories, was more important than homogeneity.

Its diffusion was much messier than the official story lets on. As Campbell and Clarence-Smith discuss in this volume, India, the islands of Réunion (formerly Bourbon), Mauritius, and Dutch Guiana (today Surinam) played important roles in coffee's early spread. New African species (*robusta* and *liberica*) were introduced at the end of the nineteenth century, and new *arabica* cultivars as well as hybrids were planted in the twentieth century.

These changes were not just the result of human ingenuity and will. Botany prevented the international homogenization that many traders would have preferred. The coffee tree is very sensitive to soil and climatic conditions, so even the same species can vary greatly in taste or appearance in neighboring areas and, as with grapes, yearly vintages from the same trees differ considerably. And since coffee trees were grown from seedlings, that is, were sexually reproduced, mutations occurred. These were less common among *arabica* trees, which self-pollinated, than among *robusta* trees, which cross-pollinated. Peasants, in choosing the seeds to plant in their nurseries, further extended change.

---

[2] Frank Perlin, "The Other Species World," in *Unbroken Landscape: Commodity, Category, Sign and Identity; Their Production as Myth and Knowledge from 1500* (Aldershot: Variorum and Brookfield, Vt.: Ashgate, 1994), pp. 206, 209.

The market was not just constituted by the supply of objectively different coffee beans. Reception, that is, the subjective perceptions of merchants and consumers, put its stamp on the commodity. The process of grading and standardizing was an intellectual one of people, mostly traders, creating categories and coffee drinkers responding to them. The creation of international standards of just what one meant by "coffee" was a slow and complicated process. Variation was commercially important because consumers were more aware of differences in coffee types than in other raw materials and foodstuffs (grains and sugar come immediately to mind). No mechanical tests of coffee's essence could be conducted as with sugar (sweetness), metals (assay), or cotton (fiber strength and length).[3] Appearance and taste were the keys. As a beverage that used few additives, consumers were quite aware of quality and often discriminating in taste. This was particularly true in the more lucrative luxury market – which was the principal European market for some two centuries – in which "high quality" coffee was used as a sign of social distinction. But as Samper points out in this volume, quality is a historically and regionally contingent category. Over the centuries it has varied and changed markedly.

The Beginning

It is generally assumed that coffee entered into human history only when Yemenis of a Sufi Muslim order began creating the drink. Although native to what is today Ethiopia and Central Africa, Christian Abyssinians did not drink coffee in any appreciable amount until the twentieth century. Clearly, the ability to produce coffee was not the key to transforming it into a commodity. Culture was equally important. Muslims, however, introduced the beverage into Harar (today part of Ethiopia) probably in the fifteenth century. As Tuchscherer explains in his chapter, *arabica* coffee continued to grow wild in Abyssinia (*liberica* in Liberia and *robusta* in the Congo), but with a small market economy and great hostility to neighboring Muslims who became associated with the drink, Abyssinians neither picked nor drank the berries.[4]

---

[3] As late as March 1916, *The Tea and Coffee Trade Journal*, p. 253, confessed, "Little is known of the chemical nature of coffee. The government is now looking after coffee with a view to standardizing grades."

[4] Father Jerome Lobo, *A Voyage to Abyssinia*, trans. by Samuel Johnson (London: Eliot and Kay, 1789), does not mention coffee. Jean Poresse, *La Vie quotidienne des Ethiopiens Chrétiens aux XVIIe et XVIIIe siècles* (Paris: Hachette, 1972), p. 268. Charles Beke, *Letters*

A taste for coffee was also not necessary to become a major exporter. Coffee was rather unusual because it was produced for exchange rather than use very soon after gaining human favor in the fifteenth century. Normally, foods have been consumed first by their cultivators or gatherers, who proceeded to trade surplus and only later produced a commodity with the intention of exchanging with others. Coffee, however, quickly became an export commodity. Fortunately for the export trade, Muslims in the Middle East liked to make the caffeine-rich drink out of the hard and relatively imperishable beans in the core of the plant, for these could easily weather long journeys.[5] The people of Yemen preferred to brew a tea from the much more perishable pulp of the *Coffea* plant, rather than the bean. In fact, it is likely that the Yemeni, who today prefer qat to coffee, were never particularly fond of coffee, setting the precedent from the beginning of producers in the south and consumers in the north. This was quite unlike most other food crops, which were consumed in large part in the producing countries and were, unlike coffee, nutritious. Even the principal beverages – wine, beer, and milk – were nutritious.[6] In this sense, coffee was an especially export market–oriented commodity from early in its history. Initially, coffee had a relatively uniform production price that was largely set in the producing country, because it was almost all comercially produced in Yemen and Ethiopia for the first three centuries of its life as a commodity. Although there are in fact three different subspecies of *Coffea arabica* in Yemen, these differences apparently were not reflected in the market. Ethiopian and Harar coffee were often sold as Yemeni "mocha."

But prices in consuming countries varied greatly. Partly this was for botanical reasons: *Arabica* plants are prone to great variations in yield. Not only do year-to-year differences in rainfall, land fertility, and sunshine translate into variable yields, as with all plants, but coffee trees for unknown reasons occasionally have exceptionally large crops, which are followed by several below average ones while the trees "rest." They

---

on the Commerce and Politics of Abessinia and Other Parts of Eastern Africa (London: printed for private use, 1852), pp. 3, 19, 184.

[5] Coffee "beans" are not legumes but actually similar to the pits of cherries, which explains why the ripe coffee fruit is called the "cherry" in many producing countries.

[6] Only tea rivaled coffee's nutritional uselessness. Cacao, the other competitor in the hot leisure beverage market, was nutritious. Since few Middle Easterners added sugar in the first centuries after coffee's introduction, even that avenue for calories was lacking. It is true, according to F. Hulton Frankel, in *The Tea and Coffee Trade Journal* (Feb. 1917), that coffee has more protein than wheat, 14 percent versus 11 percent, but the protein is insoluble and remains in the grounds rather than passing into the drink (p. 142).

undergo two- and seven-year cycles. So there were great fluctuations in production levels.

This could have been overcome, as it would be in the late nineteenth century, with warehouses because coffee can long be held off the market, but production and intermediation was still small and scattered, capital insufficient, and transportation rudimentary and expensive. More relevant, the early traders hoped to make monopoly rents by taking advantage of the spasmodic nature of supply rather than seek a mass market by dampening the oscillations. Even had they wanted to control the small market – only 12 to 15 tons a year were produced in Yemen in the eighteenth century – merchant capital was subject to the whims of producing peasants, who brought small amounts to market as the price or their need for money demanded.[7] Yemeni coffee was produced in small garden plots by farmers who grew subsistence crops between and alongside their coffee. Despite having a virtual world monopoly on one of the ancient world's more valuable commodities, growers were not converted into commodity producers. The king planted some trees, and slavery was known, but neither state farms nor slave production had much of an impact on the overall crop. Indeed, slaves seem to have been used more in processing than in cultivation. Aside from taxing the trade, the state appears to have had almost no role in coffee. Merchandizing was controlled by a trading diaspora of Banyans from the Indian port of Surat and Cairo merchants.[8] Although, as we see below, production was later revolutionized, producers were buffered from world market forces for coffee's first three centuries as a world commodity. Thus, Yemeni coffee *was* integrated into the world economy in the sense that Indian merchants acting for Middle Eastern, Indian Ocean, North African, and European exporters purchased the Arabian product with Mexican silver. On the other hand, production levels and technology were relatively unaffected by world demand, and the price of coffee in consuming countries probably varied according to local merchants' ability to monopolize and the willingness of the elite and urban middle class to pay.

Transaction costs were very high. Transportation within Yemen remained so rudimentary that even 300 years later the barest mule paths connected the mountain gardens to the lowland markets. Jean de la Roque, the

---

[7] Tuchscherer, Chapter 2.
[8] Balkrishna Gouind Gokhale, *Surat in the Seventeenth Century* (Bombay: Scandinavian Institute of Asian Studies, 1979), pp. 97, 106; Tuchscherer Chapter 2. An excellent source for understanding trading diasporas in Phillip Curtin's *Cross-Cultural Trade in World History* (Cambridge: Cambridge University Press, 1984).

first Frenchman to directly buy in Yemen, reported that it took six months to buy enough coffee to fill his ship's hold. Acting through an Indian intermediary, he was more a gatherer than a buyer.[9] His demand drove prices sharply up, demonstrating how shallow the market was, but the coffee still trickled to market, reflecting peasants' limited market orientation. Muslims, who consumed the great majority of coffee until well into the eighteenth century, faced the additional burden of the taxes of the Ottoman Turks and enormous transportation prices for the large caravan trade. The market was wide, spreading from Morocco to Turkey in the Levant, west along northern Africa and the Balkans, east to India, and, beginning in the middle of the seventeenth century, north to Eastern and Western Europe. But it was a shallow market because consumption was largely confined to urban coffeehouses where it served as both secular drug and religious drink closely tied to Islam.[10] Indeed, the hajj pilgrimages to Mecca were a major market and source for the spread of the beverage to new lands.

The Dutch were the first European colonial power to enjoy much success in planting coffee in their colonies when they brought it to Java in the 1690s, though no doubt Muslim pilgrims had earlier introduced some coffee into Indonesia. (Earlier British efforts to grow coffee in Madras, India, failed.) This was not a mercantilist effort to keep consumer and producer within the empire, since neither the Javanese nor the Dutch were great coffee consumers. Indeed, for the first century most of the coffee appears to have been exported to Muslim countries. For example, coffee became popular in Siam only after lower-priced Javanese production reached it in the eighteenth century.[11] Interestingly, the burger Dutch, who, unlike foreign traders in Yemen, did indirectly control production, did not change the essentially peasant nature of production as Fernando's Chapter 6 demonstrates. Peasants were forced to grow coffee and sell the exotic crop at a set price to Dutch East Indian stores. Peasants were not economically integrated into the market in the sense that they were not

---

[9] Jean de La Roque, *A Voyage to Arabia the Happy* (London: G. Strahan, 1726), passim. "Some Late Facts about the Mocha Coffee Industry," *Spice Mill* (Oct. 1910): 729.

[10] For more on Muslim consumption, see Ralph Hattox, *Coffee and Coffeehouses: The Origins of a Beverage in the Medieval Near East* (Seattle: University of Washington Press, 1985), and Rudi Matthee, "From Coffee to Tea: Shifting Patterns of Consumption in Qajar Iran," *Journal of World History* 7, no. 2 (1996): 199–229; Omar Carlier, "Le Café maure: Sociabilité masculine et effernescence citoyenne (Algérie XVIIe–XXe siècles)," *Annales Économies, Sociétés, Civilisations* 45, no. 4 (July–Aug. 1990): 975–1003.

[11] Anthony Reid, *Southwest Asia in the Age of Commerce, 1450–1680*, vol. 1 (New Haven: Yale University Press, 1988), p. 38.

responding to market impetuses. Each villager was required to tend and harvest several hundred trees. Since his concern was only meeting an obligation, he often chose inappropriate lands for planting and productivity was very low. But since the Dutch paid an extremely low price, this system was profitable to the V.O.C. (the Dutch East India Company). This was essentially state commercial capitalism. Production levels did respond to market forces because the Dutch East Indies Company varied the pressure it put upon peasants according to international prices; but the V.O.C.'s heavy hand was not very capable at fine tuning. Production levels swung wildly.[12]

The market became yet more complicated when thirty years after the Dutch began *Coffea arabica* cultivation in Java, it spread to the Americas. The Dutch and French states participated in this hemispheric transfer by nurturing *Coffea* seedlings in their home botanical gardens. But the expenses of *Coffea*'s transfer and cultivation in the New World were borne by private individuals. Climate and soil differences translated into marked taste differences. Combined with mutations into numerous subspecies, *Coffea arabica* ceased to be a homogeneous product by the nineteenth century. Nonetheless, for at least the first half of the eighteenth century, many Latin American beans were designated "Mochas," "Bourbons" (from Réunion), or "Javas" because they were theoretically genetically related to those of the first coffee-producing areas (and, not coincidentally, the areas whose coffee fetched the highest prices on the market).

The Dutch were able to overtake the port of Mocha and those of the Mediterranean to transform Amsterdam into the world's leading coffee entrepot for over a century. By 1730, Amsterdam was trading in coffee from three continents: Asian Java and Réunion, Middle Eastern Yemen, and American Dutch Guiana, St. Domingue (today Haiti) and Martinique. Although Europe was still a small luxury market, its demands outstripped Mocha's possibilities. Whereas 90 percent of Amsterdam's imports in 1721 were from Mocha, by 1726, 90 percent were from Java. But the Dutch were not driven just by mercantilist logic. They were perfectly willing to import cheaper coffee from elsewhere and sell Java's product in Asia. By 1750, Amsterdam's imports of American production almost matched its purchases of Javanese coffee. Initially, the American

---

[12] A. S. Kok, *Colonial Essays* (London: Sampson Low, Son and Marson, 1864), pp. 250, 266, 271; J. W. B. Money, *Java; or, How to Manage a Colony* (London: Hurst and Blackett, 1861), vol. 1, p. 79; C. G. F. Simkin, *The Traditional Trade of Asia* (London: Oxford University, 1968), pp. 231–2. For more on Java, see Fernando, Chapter 6.

good was mostly colonial production from Dutch Guiana. But soon the price of French production from St. Domingue made that island more attractive. Already before the French Revolution over 80 percent of the world's production originated in the Americas. By 1820, Java supplied only 6 percent of Europe's consumption and the Dutch imported mostly non-Dutch coffee, though later in the century Java and Ceylon would enjoy a three-decade-long renaissance.[13] Decline also occurred in the Middle East. Already by the 1770s, French coffee from St. Domingue was replacing Yemeni competitors in the Ottoman market of Cairo because it was cheaper, even it had to cross the Atlantic and the Mediterranean.[14] This demonstrates that shipping rates were sufficiently low well before the steam transportation revolution to remove distance as a major barrier to market integration. By 1840, Yemen supplied only 2 to 3 percent of world consumption.

Prices in the Amsterdam market demonstrated the extent to which the world coffee economy had become integrated by the second half of the eighteenth century. Rather than the spasmodic prices of a century before, which fluctuated with the arrival of each rare coffee-laden ship, prices now were quite stable from month to month and fairly comparable between Java and the Americas. Improved warehouse capacity, port facilities, bulk freight, and predictable freight lines reduced intermediation costs. Yemeni prices followed competitors less steadily but by the end of the century were close. When the French Revolution provoked a slave rebellion in St. Domingue, greatly reducing the production of what had been the world's premier producer, prices in Java and the Americas jumped to take advantage (see Table 1.1).

Complexity was compounded in the late nineteenth and early twentieth centuries when other African coffee species, *robusta* and *liberica*, were discovered by European imperialists eager to export something from their newly won colonies. However, it should be emphasized that except for the Dutch, who played a key role in coercing the Javanese to grow coffee in their colony, and rather unsuccessful British, French, and Portuguese efforts in Ceylon, India, and Africa, European states did not play a major

---

[13] John Crawford, *History of the Indian Archipelago* (Edinburgh: Archibald Constable, 1820), vol. 3, p. 374; Niels Steensgaard in James D. Tracy, ed., *The Rise of Merchant Empires* (Cambridge: Cambridge University Press, 1990), pp. 129–30. Calculated from José Antonio Ocampo, *Colombia y la economía mundial, 1830–1910* (Bogotá: Siglo Ventiuno, 1984), p. 303. Also see Fernando and Clarence-Smith, Chapters 4 and 6.

[14] Paul Butel, "Les Ameriques et l'Europe," in Pierre Leon, ed., *Histoire Economique et Social e du Monde*, vol. 3 (Paris: A. Colin, 1978).

TABLE I.I. *Amsterdam Coffee Prices (in gulden per pound, January of each year)*

	Mocha	Java	Dutch Guiana	St. Domingue (Haiti)
1735	1.06	.79	.74	
1740	.70	.48	.40	
1745	1.10	.51	.50	
1750	.90	.73	.50	
1755	.83	.59	.44	
1760	.80	.50	.36	.36
1765	.93	.63	.38	.43
1770	.76	.61	.54	.53
1775	.81	.41	.31	.28
1780	.74	.40	.35	.33
1785	1.13	.58	.53	.49
1790	.78	.70	.57	.53
1795	.71	.65	.60	.54
1800	–	1.20	1.03	.99
1805	1.10		1.06	1.03
1810	1.50		1.10	1.05
1815	2.48	.77	.84	.78

Source: N. Posthumus, *Inquiry into the History of Prices in Holland* (Leiden: E. J. Brill, 1946), pp. 181–9.

role in the development of world coffee production. They relied instead on comparative advantage in the world coffee market. Unlike the case of sugar, the first age of colonialism of the sixteenth through eighteenth centuries did not see the development of independent coffee colonies to supply the individual metropolises. On the contrary, the French at first attempted to prohibit production in their colony of St. Domingue because of the Levant Companies' interest in its Middle Eastern monopoly. True, French colonies supplied two-thirds of the world's coffee in the years immediately before the French Revolution. But once Haiti gained its independence, the French did not turn to other of their colonies until African coffee became prominent in Le Havre in the twentieth century.[15] The British, who saw the mercantilist possibilities in exploiting the Chinese and then the India tea trade, were the only Western European power to reduce per capita coffee consumption rather than exploit the coffee-growing potential of Jamaica, Ceylon, or India. The Spanish preferred

[15] Ocampo, *Colombia*, p. 303, and Campbell, Chapter 3.

cacao, so that Latin America had to wait for independence to become a significant coffee producer.[16] Even later, once the United States gained the coffee-producing colonies of Puerto Rico, Hawaii, the Philippines, and effectively Cuba – at a time when the United States was the world's greatest coffee consumer – it continued to import from Brazil in an open market.[17] After the decline of Java toward the end of the nineteenth century, production was dominated by independent nations in a relatively unhindered international market. States in consuming countries did not interfere except to tax imports.

Coffee was treated differently from sugar and rubber in the nineteenth-century Age of Empire, because its low technological demands meant that an independent country richly endowed with the factors of production, such as Brazil, could begin producing on an unprecedented scale. Cheap fertile land and slave labor allowed coffee prices to plummet after 1820 and remain low until the last quarter of the century, creating supply-induced demand. Brazil's exports jumped seventy-five-fold between independence in 1822 and 1899. World consumption grew more than fifteenfold in the nineteenth century.[18] No colonies could compete with Brazil in price nor meet the large new demand in the colonial powers and the United States. By 1850, Brazil was producing over half the world's coffee; in 1906 it produced *almost five times as much as the rest of the world combined*. Indeed, about 80 percent of the expansion of world coffee production in the nineteenth century occurred in Brazil alone.[19] Most of the rest of the growth was in Spanish America, as African and Asian production fell from one-third of the world total in the 1830s to the 1870s down to 5 percent on the eve of World War I.[20] And this was no marginal market. At the dawn of the twentieth century, the value of internationally

---

[16] In 1909, the *Spice Mill* reported on p. 174 that Spanish and Portuguese per capita coffee consumption at 0.7 and 0.5 kilos was one-fifth to one-tenth of that of northern European countries and the United States.

[17] The *Spice Mill* (May 1909) in an article discussing the limited amount of U.S. investment in Mexican coffee fincas (when U.S. capital was flooding into other Mexican areas), explained, "Concerning the increase in the production of coffee, Brazil continues and will continue to have no competitors in the world" (p. 299).

[18] Brazil, Instituto Brasileiro de Geografia e Estatística (IBGE), *Séries Estatísticas Retrospectivas*, vol. 1 (Rio: IBGE, 1986), p. 85.

[19] Calculated from Robert Greenhill, "E. Johnston: 150 anos em café," in Marcellino Martins E. Johnston, *150 anos de café* (Rio: Marcellino Martins and E. Johnston, 1992), p. 308; Ocampo, *Colombia*, p. 303, Brazil, IGBE, *Séries Estatísticas retrospectivas*, vol. 1 p. 84.

[20] Clarence-Smith, Chapter 4.

traded coffee trailed only grains and sugar.[21] Thus, Latin American production helped to redefine the nature of consumption by dropping prices and boosting volume sufficiently to reach a mass market.

The reasons for Brazil's ability to so rapidly expand are complicated. I hesitate to attribute too much of this to technological improvements. There were no revolutions in production techniques; cultivating and harvesting continued to be done by hand – by slaves until 1888.[22] Milling was advanced by steam power only late in the century. The rate of export expansion after the advent of the railroad and the steamship in South America, between 1860 and 1900, was barely greater than it had been with mules and sail between 1830 and 1860.[23] And coffee production grew rapidly despite depending on an increasingly aging and expensive slave labor force until abolition in 1888. Initially, at least, the expansion was due to vast, easily accessible virgin forests (meaning a sparse indigenous population that could be pushed out), proper climate, an export-oriented commercial infrastructure, a large slave force, and relative political peace.

If not key in instigating the export boom, the railroad was important in permitting it to continue to expand. Before the iron horse, transport had been very expensive. By one calculation, 20 percent of the male slave force was used in mule trains, and transport cost one-third of the final price. Moreover, the primitive form of conveyance often damaged the beans.[24] The train reduced tariffs, but not dramatically. Because of relatively little competition and because the richest planters also invested heavily in railroad stocks, bulk discounts and distance rebates were not offered. In fact, coffee rode for a considerably higher price than did domestic staples. By the turn of the twentieth century, rail transport still contributed from 15 to 22 percent of production costs. But if Brazil had not constructed by far the largest rail network in any coffee-producing country, the explosion of exports and the creation of a mass market abroad would have been impossible. The narrow mountain paths would have been jammed with enormous lines of mules and transportation would have been considerably more than 20 percent of the production costs, as it was in rail-deprived countries such as Colombia and Madagascar.

[21] Michael G. Mulhall, *The Dictionary of Statistics*, 4th ed. (London: G. Routledge and Sons, 1899), p. 130.
[22] V. D. Wickizer noted in *Coffee, Teas and Cocoa* (Stanford: Food Research Institute, 1951), p. 36, "It is sometimes said that no important changes have been made in the coffee production methods in the last 150 years."
[23] Ocampo, *Colombia*, p. 302.
[24] Stanley Stein, *Vassouras* (rpt., N.Y.: Atheneum, 1970), pp. 91, 94.

The railroad meant that the quality of coffee was better, and more important, cheaper, since more fertile lands were now accessible in the interior.[25] This also meant that once slavery was abolished in 1888, Brazil could become the only country to attract millions of European immigrants to work in semitropical agriculture.[26]

In addition to the contribution of the iron horse, the shipping revolution meant that swelling Brazilian coffee exports – which grew sixfold between 1850 and 1900 – could be brought to market without shipping bottlenecks. A host of European steamers began regular service to Brazil, where port facilities were slowly improved and hence shipping costs reduced.[27] This allowed growers to receive a greater share of the final wholesale price, while consumers enjoyed lower end prices. Because imports became cheaper, Brazil could enjoy steadily improving terms of trade; that is, the real price of coffee reflected in the imports that coffee income purchased increased more rapidly than did its nominal price, which was fairly steady until the late 1880s.[28] Gudmundson points out that the declining cost of oceanic shipping also increased returns to Costa Rica's growers.[29] In other Latin American countries such as Colombia, Venezuela, Guatemala, Nicaragua, El Salvador, and southern Mexico,

[25] On rail costs, see Franz Dafert, *Uber die Gegenwartige Lage des Kaffeebaus in Brasilien* (Amsterdam: J. H. de Bussy, 1898), p. 49; Centro Industrial do Brasil, *O Brasil: Suas riquezas naturais, suas indústrias*, vol. 2 (Rio: Imp. M. Orosco, 1908), p. 91. For rising land costs near Rio, see Stein, *Vassouras*, p. 229. For a detailed study of Brazilian railroads, see William R. Summerhill, *Order against Progress: Government, Foreign Investment, and Railroads in Brazil, 1854–1913* (Stanford: Stanford University Press, forthcoming).

[26] W. Arthur Lewis in *Growth and Fluctuations* (London: George Allen and Unwin, 1978), p. 181, points out that in receiving European immigrants between 1871 and 1915, Brazil (1.43 million) trailed only the United States (23.4 million) and Argentina (2.5 million).

[27] For a discussion of commercial conditions in Brazil at the end of the nineteenth century, see Steven C. Topik, *Trade and Gunboats, the United States and Brazil in the Age of Empire* (Stanford: Stanford University Press, 1997). Also see Robert Greenhill, "Shipping," in D. C. M. Platt, *Business Imperialism* (Oxford: Clarendon Press, 1977); Paul Bairoch, "Geographical Structure and Trade Balance of European Foreign Trade from 1800 to 1970," *Journal of European Economic History* 3, no. 3 (Winter 1974): 606; Douglass North, "Ocean Freight Rates and Economic Development, 1750-1913," *Journal of Economic History* 18 (Dec. 1958): 537-55.

[28] Nathaniel H. Leff, *Underdevelopment and Development in Brazil*, vol. 1 (London: George Allen and Unwin, 1982), pp. 80-5; C. Knick Harley, "Late Nineteenth Century Transportation, Trade and Settlement," in Harley, ed., *The Integration of the World Economy, 1850-1914*, vol. 1 (Cheltenham, U.K.: Edward Elgar, 1996), p. 236. Edmar Bacha, "Política brasileira de café," in Martins and Johnston, *150 anos de Café*, p. 20.

[29] Gudmundson Chapter 14 citing Jorge León Sanchez, *Evolución del comercio exterior y del transporte maritime de Costa Rica, 1821–1900* (San José: Editorial Universidade de Costa Rica, 1997).

which were slow to build railroads in their coffee-producing regions, the fall in intercontinental shipping costs was crucial to the expansion of exports.

Brazilian coffee planters (*fazendeiros*); slavocrat growers in Haiti, Jamaica, and Puerto Rico; and planters in Ceylon, Java, parts of Africa, Chiapas (Mexico), Guatemala, and Nicaragua who used coerced labor were market-oriented, though the laborers who worked for them had little incentive to concern themselves about the demands of the market. But even the growers were buffered from the market in the interior by the lack of transport and communications until the twentieth century and the existence of a complicated web of intermediaries in which small growers sold to larger growers or mill owners, who sold through factors ("commissarios"), who often sold to sackers, who blended the coffee and then sold to exporters, who initially were consignment merchants.[30] Even in Brazil, the world's pacesetter, there were few coffee markets in the interior and no coffee exchange until the 1920s, so information on prices and supply were very imperfect and favored the intermediaries. Indeed, planters were often virtually innumerate.[31] Moreover, being quite undermonetarized, even the world's largest coffee economy dealt in credits and notes, which relied to a great degree on personal reputation and favors, not just price and other market forces.[32]

In addition, Brazilian currency was usually inconvertible paper money, which fluctuated greatly vis-à-vis the pound sterling, though internal prices remained steady. Spanish American currencies, when not inconvertible, were pegged to silver, which underwent a dramatic decline in the last quarter of the nineteenth century, effectively creating a devaluation. Hence the real price of the crop to someone importing in the port cities

[30] For detailed studies of the Brazilian coffee market, see C. F. Van Delden Laerne, *Brazil and Java: Report on Coffee-Culture in America, Asia, and Africa to H. E. the Minister of Colonies* (London: W. H. Allen, 1885); Joseph Sweigart, *Financing and Marketing Brazilian Export Agriculture: The Coffee Factors of Rio de Janeiro, 1850–1888* (New York: Garland Publishers, 1987); Greenhill, "E. Johnston."

[31] Stein reports in *Vassouras*, p. 83, that "most planters were unwilling to use 'complicated processes of commercial accounting' and preferred to await reports occasionally forwarded by the more zealous comissários." This led to a situation noted by Van Delden Laerne, *Brazil and Java*, p. 212, of comissários "from being the agents of the agriculturalists, became their bankers."

[32] Edward Greene, director of E. Johnston's Santos office reported in his letter to R. Johnston, Rio, Nov. 1, 1899 (Johnston archive, University College library, University of London), that conditions were different in each zone, personal acquaintances were necessary, and that "to induce fazendeiros to sell to a perfect stranger has not been easy work."

was often quite different from its value to someone in the interior, who would use his receipts to buy mostly domestic goods. This again muf- fled the effects of price fluctuations in the interior. For example, between 1875 and 1886, when coffee prices fell by 40 percent, the 33 percent de- preciation of the Brazilian *mil-reís* mostly compensated planters, so that production expanded more than 50 percent.[33]

The four- to six-year gestation period necessary for coffee seedlings to become commercially viable meant production could not be modified quickly to respond to price differences, especially to downturns. When prices fell, planters with land reserves continued to expand output anyway, because productivity was as much as twice as high on new virgin lands as on already planted lands. Hence, to meet declining prices, they expanded output to reduce unit costs but probably helped to further reduce prices by glutting the market. Their salvation was a good frost – if it ruined their neighbor's crops and not their own. The world coffee trade had its eyes on the Brazilian weather reports. Brazil was the major producer furthest from the tropics, hence with the greatest weather variations and the greatest year-to-year variation in yield. Even when planters planned and kept account of the number of trees in production, they had great difficulty predicting their output. Nature came to the rescue in 1887, 1902, 1904, 1912, 1918, 1942, 1953, 1955, 1957, 1966, 1975, 1981, 1985, and 1994 with severe frosts and a drought, driving down production and increasing prices.[34]

This is not to say that planters were completely unable to adjust to market conditions, but that responses were quite slow to reduce output or to catch up with demand. Great price rises led to rapid expansion and geographic diversification. The Haitian Revolution, for example, encour- aged planting in other parts of the Caribbean and in the state of Rio, Brazil. The next rapid jump in prices, in the late 1880s and early 1890s, caused in good part by the leaf rust in Asia, caused a four-fold jump in São Paulo's trees in fourteen years, giving it alone over half the world's production; Colombia, Mexico, and Central America also stepped up pro- duction. High prices in the 1920s after World War I dampened the world market, and the Brazilian federal government began to control exports, pushing Colombia and Central America to much greater output. The price rise after the Korean War encouraged African producers and in the state of Paraná, Brazil. The protective blanket provided by the creation of

[33] Martins and Johnston, *150 anos de Café*.
[34] J. de Graaff, *The Economics of Coffee* (Wageningen: Pudoc, 1986), p. 105.

TABLE 1.2. *Fluctuations in Brazil's Coffee Crops,
1890s–1930s (in millions of bags of 60 kilos)*

Year	Average crop	Upper limit	Lower limit
1890s	7.2	11.2	4.4
1900s	12.6	20.2	9.4
1910s	13.3	16.0	9.7
1920s	14.7	27.1	7.5
1930s	23.5	29.6	16.6

Source: United States Federal Trade Commission, *Economic
Report of the Investigation of Coffee Prices* (Washington,
D.C.: Government Printing Office, 1954), p. 20.

the International Coffee Organization (ICO) and its quota system in the
1960s encouraged new producers, particularly in Africa, for example, the
Ivory Coast and Ethiopia. The collapse of the ICO in 1989 and a precipitous fall in prices, rather than high prices, stimulated a stunning expansion
of production in Vietnam in the 1990s and to a lesser extent in Indonesia
(more Sumatra than Java) and the Philippines.

Reductions in production usually came from sources other than the
market: political unrest such as the Haitian Revolution or Colombia's
War of a Thousand Days; acts of nature like the leaf blight that after 1885
wiped out production in Java and Ceylon; or government interventions
such as the prohibitive tax in São Paulo in 1903 and later eradication
programs. The fluctuation of coffee harvests was large (see Table 1.2).
However, since world coffee demand has been in secular ascent for over
300 years, this relatively short-run inflexibility and unpredictability did
not present a great problem. While unpredictable and awkward, with
many market imperfections, the global coffee production system did allow
the bean to become one of the world's most widely traded commodities
and a mass drink.

Mass Consumption

During its first centuries as a Muslim drink, coffee created a narrow luxury market. It was often traded by pilgrimage caravans and went through
many intermediaries; transport, taxes, and merchant costs were high.
When Europeans spread production to their colonies in Java, Réunion,
St. Domingue, and Jamaica, costs fell somewhat. But mercantilist-minded
colonial governments insisted on high taxes, maintaining coffee as a bourgeois beverage. Peasants and proletarians, if they drank a hot beverage at
all, tended to drink chicory or other substitutes for *Bohnenkaffee*.

Then after the Napoleonic Wars, African slaves and semicoerced indigenous workers and European immigrants in the Americas as well as
coerced migrants in the Indian Ocean made the beverage available to
urban workers and even occasionally to rural residents. Coffee's heroic
nineteenth century occurred not only because of Brazilian production,
but also because of skyrocketing consumption in the United States and
Northern Europe. The transportation revolution and lowered transaction costs fueled the vertiginous trajectory of the Atlantic coffee economy.
Brazil improved transport by constructing railroads and ports and marketing economies of scale in which production costs remained level while
output increased. This combined with the exogenous benefit of greatly
reduced international shipping costs, the world's most efficient internal
transportation system, and an elaborate marketing network in the United
States to stimulate a rapid rise in American per capita consumption. Coffee
became truly a mass product for the first time in the United States.

U.S. government policy also helped. The United States was the only
major market to import coffee tax-free as duties declined from a high
of 10 cents a pound in 1812 to 5 cents in 1814 and free for all but one
decade after 1832. Consequently, per capita consumption grew from one-
eighteenth of a pound in 1783 to nine pounds a hundred years later. U.S.
population's fifteen-fold explosion in that century meant that total coffee
imports grew 2,400 percent! By the end of the nineteenth century, the
United States was consuming thirteen pounds per capita and importing
over 40 percent of the world's coffee. (It would grow to over 60 percent
after World War II.) Half of the growth in world consumption in the
nineteenth century was due to increased United States purchases![35]
Almost all the rest was in Western Europe, especially in Northern Europe:
Belgium, Germany, France, the Netherlands, and Scandinavia. Coffee producers were very fortunate to find such favor in the countries whose gross
national products were among the fastest-growing in the world.[36] The
relationship was not purely coincidental. Caffeine became instrumental
to the regimented time of the urban industrialized societies. U.S. and
Northern European consumption would continue to grow, with some
fits and starts, until the 1960s. Thus the world coffee market, which had
long been a near monopoly (Yemen, then St. Domingue, and finally Brazil)
also became an oligopsony with just a handful of major buyers.

---

[35] Calculated from Greenhill, "E. Johnston," pp. 330–1. A. Wakeman, "Reminiscences of
   Lower Wall St.," *Spice Mill* (March 1911): 193.
[36] Bairoch, "Geographical Structure," pp. 17–18.

Coffee's rapid expansion of the nineteenth century was due to peculiar demand conditions as well as Brazil's and later Spanish America's ability to meet that demand cheaply.[37] Demand in the nineteenth century, in both the United States and Europe, was initially both income- and price-elastic. Surprisingly, this was not the case in the twentieth century, despite better quality, more accessible coffee, and rapidly expanding discretionary incomes. The reason for the change is cultural. Coffee was one of the few major internationally traded commodities in the nineteenth century to enjoy a real price increase in the second half of the century and still experience a per capita consumption increase.[38] Once its status declined in the early twentieth century, its income elasticity did also, though it continued to be a necessity for many.[39]

In the early nineteenth century, coffee was viewed as a luxury item, a sign of bourgeois distinction. As it became available to lower-class urban inhabitants and eventually even to rural populations at a relatively low price, they chose it over the ersatz coffees and teas they had previously drunk. So powerful was this appeal that the income-elasticity in developed countries between 1830 and 1900 has been estimated at 1.3 (that is, coffee purchases grew proportionately faster than income grew). However, as it became an accepted part of the working class's breakfast, and increasingly lunch, afternoon snack, and dinner, coffee became rather price- and income-inelastic. The United States Federal Trade Commission estimated income elasticity in 1954 at only 0.2 percent; almost no additional income was spent on coffee.[40] Effectively, the population had almost entirely satisfied its desire for coffee.

[37] As Jeffrey Williamson has pointed out, "the long-run inducement to augmented staple supply is not met with collapsing prices if foreign demand is elastic. Like the case of expanding demand, price-elastic demand can also be viewed an export engine of growth." J. Williamson, "Greasing the Wheels of Sputtering Export Engines: Midwestern Grains and American Growth," in Harley, ed., *Integration of the World Economy*, vol. 2, p. 411.

[38] Ocampo, *Colombia*, pp. 302–3; Bacha, "Política brasileira de café," p. 20.

[39] Albert A. Okunade, in "Functional Former Habit Effects in the U.S. Demand for Coffee," *Applied Economics* 24 (1992): 1203–12, found for the 1957–87 period that per capita consumption was own-price inelastic and income inelastic for individuals. Habits inhibited responses to changes in relative prices. *The Tea and Coffee Trade Journal* (July 1916) reflected: "It is difficult to explain the continued stagnation in the coffee business with the earning capacity of the masses so much greater than ever before. The reason given by some is that the large amount paid to wage earners is being spent on luxuries [not coffee] and that the living expenses have not been increased materially" (p. 67).

[40] FTC, *Investigation of Coffee Prices* (Washington, D.C.: Government Printing Office, 1954), pp. 39–40.

The central role of U.S. consumption in the world market underlines the fact that British imports did not directly serve as an "engine of growth" for Latin America. Rather, there was a triangular trade. Brazilians sold their coffee in the United States and used the returns to purchase British finished goods. Americans purchased coffee with foreign exchange earned by selling temperate raw materials in Britain, as well as to the Continent.[41] Although the British did not drink much of the coffee that they serviced, they profited from reexports to major consumers and the insurance and carrying trades, which they dominated until the 1930s.[42]

Futures

The freewheeling coffee market began to change in 1870 when a submarine cable tied South America to New York and London by telegraph. Information about prices and demand and supply became internationally homogeneous. Warehouses that held a substantial share of the world's visible stocks were built, strengthening the market position of importers. Exporters ceased being consignment agents, becoming instead agents of importers who controlled the trade and set the prices. Because of speculation, prices fluctuated wildly. The creation of the New York Coffee Exchange in 1882, which was instituted to prevent commercial corners from driving up prices as had happened in 1880, institutionalized access to information. (Hamburg, Le Havre, and London followed with major coffee exchanges.) Although this might seem late for the development of a futures market, since the Chicago wheat market began in 1848, in fact Britain's first futures market started only in 1883.[43] Coffee was a pioneer in global commodity institutionalization.

The telegraph created the possibility of an international commodity market. Prices and grades thereby became more generalized. As long as

---

[41] C. Knick Harley, Introduction, *Integration of the World Economy*, vol. 1, p. xix. For more on Brazil's trade, see Topik, *Trade and Gunboats*, ch. 9. Britain's minimal direct role in the coffee economy can be seen by the fact that while U.S. per capita consumption rose from 6.25 pounds to 13 pounds in the second half of the nineteenth century, German went from 4.5 to 7 pounds, and French rose from 1.3 to 6.4 pounds. British coffee drinking actually fell from the anemic 1.3 pounds to 0.6 pounds; Ocampo, *Colombia*, p. 302.

[42] *Simmons' Spice Mill* quoted a London coffee manager, J. H. Brindley, in June 1914: "Even that great coffee-drinking nation, the United States, has almost all its supplies carried in English bottoms" (p. 576).

[43] A. J. H. Latham, "The International Trade in Rice and Wheat since 1868," in *The Emergence of a World Economy, 1500–1914*, vol. 2, p. 651. For more on commodity and futures markets, see William Cronon, *Nature's Metropolis, Chicago and the Great West* (New York: W. W. Norton, 1991), ch. 3.

all purchases were on the spot, specific beans were judged. With the advent of futures, coffee became a more pure commodity in the sense that rights to coffee shipments were now bought and sold on the market floor without the buyer actually seeing the lot in question. Coffees became commodities possessing a bundle of specific, graded attributes. Indeed, with the advent of futures, buyers purchased coffee not yet blossoming on distant trees. Already in 1880 merchants were buying an idea rather than palpable beans. That year there were 61 million bags bought and sold on the Hamburg futures market when the entire world harvest was less than 7 million bags!

The establishment of the New York Coffee Exchange had an unexpected and unwanted effect on the trade. Local importers had hoped to corner the U.S. market for themselves, edging out competitors in Baltimore, New Orleans, and San Francisco. Instead, the standardization and accessible information brought about by the exchange undercut the New York merchants' insider information, personal relations, and crafts expertise, allowing the New York Exchange to be dominated by "out-of-towners."[44] The process of agreeing on grades and standards was not an easy one, however.

Grading

The United States was not a market interested in quality coffee. The long transport in carts, trains, and ships often caused damage of beans that were often not especially good quality to begin with because Brazil's slave system emphasized volume rather than quality. A typical 122-pound bag of "Java" coffee in the 1860s not only actually came from Jamaica, but usually had about five pounds of sticks and stones added in.

Coffee categories were largely historical remnants with no consistent naming practice. In general, lots were named after the port from which they were shipped, which assumed a delimited and set hinterland from which to draw. Hence, Mocha, the Yemeni port far from coffee-growing areas, gave its name to a type. This name remained centuries after the actual port of Mocha silted up. In the nineteenth century, "Mocha" came to include coffee grown not in Yemen but in Harar, across the Red Sea. (Only in the late twentieth century did the term come to mean chocolate added to coffee.) Other important ports that lent their names to coffee types were Rio and Santos, Brazil, and Maracaibo, Venezuela. (Only in

---

44 Wakeman, "Reminiscences," *Spice Mill* (Aug. 1911): 636.

the twentieth century did producing areas such as Tres Rios, Costa Rica, Antigua, Guatemala, or Narino, Colombia, give their names to types.)

These names reflected the pre-twentieth century reality of a distant, mysterious hinterland often off-bounds for international merchants, and the entrepot ports, which were satellites of the world economy. The ports served as sorts of shock-absorbers that translated domestic grades, measurements, and currencies into international standards and distributed foreign revenues, capital, and technology to the interior. In some cases such as Rio and later Santos, the ports were more than compradors, agents of the world market; they were creative, active, and somewhat independent players in that market. Edward Greene, of the large British exporting house of E. Johnston, explained why he was purchasing coffee from São José de Campos even though it was lower quality Rio coffee: "However, as every bag received direct from the interior leaves something behind it and as the classification is in our own hands, we have not discouraged the business."[45] Still, ports in the producing countries would gain significant market power only when state governments began to intervene in the twentieth century, as we see below. Before that, when they attempted to establish their own coffee exchange in 1882, they became "the laughing stock of the trade" and quickly failed.[46]

Two major problems continued to plague the trade after the establishment of exchanges in New York and Europe: difficulty in determining the quality and origins of shipments and information about the size of annual crops. The former threatened to drive away defrauded customers and the later made longer-term price calculations difficult. The quality problem was rectified not by planters and traders but by government. In 1907, the U.S. Pure Food and Drug Act decreed that imported coffee be marked according to its port of exit. Thus, "Santos" became a specific type of coffee, as did "Java" or "Mocha." There were more than a hundred different types of coffee imported into the United States, the greatest variety in the world. Importers were now less able to adulterate and defraud buyers. No longer could Hills Brothers assert that their Santos coffee was "Mocha-Java." Of course, exporters did not give up without a fight. Some enterprising exporters sent Brazilian Santos beans to both Yemen and Java so they could claim them as Mocha and Java, since those were their last

[45] E. Green to E. Johnston, Santos, Jan. 10, 1902, in E. Johnston archive, University College Library, University of London, London.
[46] Wakeman, "Reminiscences," *Spice Mill* (March 1911): 195. Eugene Ridings, *Business Interest Groups in Nineteenth Century Brazil* (Cambridge: Cambridge University Press, 1994), p. 116.

ports of embarkation. That this was even attempted demonstrated both the low price of ocean freight, the differential between the various types, and a belief that the Federal Department of Agriculture would enforce the law – which it did.

The reason that the U.S. government intervened in coffee had to do with North American generalized concern with food adulteration (partly driven by European boycotts against U.S. diseased meat exports), drugs then legal such as cocaine and opium, Progressive politics, and the nature of the U.S. coffee market.[47] Social practices in the United States very much affected the nature of demand and the ability of roasters to respond to it and shape it. The fact that in the U.S. coffee was consumed in the home much more than in coffeehouses, as was the case in much of Europe, had important implications for the organization of the trade. Since coffee in the United States was overwhelmingly sold in grocery stores, a few roasting companies such as the Arbuckles and the Woolson Spice Company created brand names. But they could not overtake the thousands of grocers and small roasters who sold green beans or custom roasted until they found a way to prevent ground coffee from quickly losing its flavor, a way to win consumer confidence in the quality of packaged beans they could not see, and a stable price. The first problem was easily solved when vacuum sealing was invented in 1900, though it would require two decades for vacuum packing to gain wide acceptance.

But the second problem required taking command of the market away from importers, who often adulterated coffee stocks. This was largely done through government interventions. In the United States, the Pure Food and Drug Act of 1907, based upon a British pure food law some thirty years earlier, set standards.[48] To protect themselves, roasters created for the first time a national organization, the National Association of Roasters. Under attack from coffee substitute interests who decried coffee on religious grounds (Seventh-Day Adventists and Mormons preached against it), health grounds (John Kellogg claimed it was bad for digestion), and moral grounds (caffeine was seen as an intoxicant), roasters joined

---

[47] For reasons I have not yet ascertained, tea was actually regulated some twenty years before coffee, as the federal government forbade the importation of adulterated tea in 1883 and established a tea testing board (something it never did with coffee). Friedman, *A History of American Law*, p. 403.

[48] Oscar E. Anderson, *The Health of a Nation: Harvey W. Wiley and the Fight for Pure Food* (Chicago: Published for the University of Cincinnati by the University of Chicago Press, 1958); Lawrence M. Friedman, *A History of American Law* (New York: Simon and Schuster, 1973), 400–5.

government agents in enforcing the standards. Although their standards were apparently less demanding, the French, Germans, and Canadians followed suit with coffee purity laws, and international conferences were commenced to establish international standards.[49]

By gaining the confidence of consumers and providing mass-produced roasted coffee due to advances in roasting technology, transport, and marketing, large industrial roasting firms began to control the market.[50] Roasters began to integrate vertically, sometimes even buying plantations in producing countries and sending their agents into the coffee interior to purchase directly from producers.[51] This initially led to segmentation of the market: Costa Ricans mostly exported to the United Kingdom, which reexported to Germany, which paid a higher price for a better quality bean; Guatemalans and Mexicans from Soconusco also produced mainly for the German market; El Salvador for a time sold principally to France; Brazil oriented its trade to the lower-quality U.S. market; and Madagascar producers shipped mainly to France.

There was a growing sophistication of roasting, grinding, and packaging technology in the twentieth century's first decades, so that processes formerly undertaken by the grocer or the housewife became industrial. By 1935, 90 percent of all coffee sold in the United States was sold roasted in packages.[52] As a result, value was increasingly added and an ever greater share of the value was added in consuming countries and by an ever smaller number of companies. Even where the world market allowed coffee growers to obtain over half of the final wholesale price of green coffee, as Gudmundson shows was the case for Costa Rican producers in the first decades of the twentieth century, they received a substantially smaller share of the retail industrialized price.[53] Probably over three-quarters of the retail price of coffee in the grocery store was added in consuming countries before the creation of the International Coffee Organization in 1962.[54] Since roaster profits came from using coffee as a raw material,

[49] *Spice Mill* (Nov. 1909): 702; (Jan. 1911): 30; (Oct. 1912): 857. *Tea and Coffee Trade Journal* (Jan. 1911): 34.

[50] In 1912 the Woolson Spice Company built the world's largest roasting factory in Toledo, Ohio, with 500 employees and a capacity of one million pounds of coffee a week. *Spice Mill* (Jan. 1912): 28.

[51] Goetzinger, *History of the House of Arbuckle*, p. 3; Zimmerman, *Wille*, p. 123; Greenhill, "Brazilian Warrant."

[52] Wm. Ukers, *All about Coffee* (New York: Tea and Coffee Trade Journal, 1935), p. 388.

[53] Gudmundson, Chapter 14, Fig. 14.2.

[54] John M. Talbot calculated the division of total income and surplus in the coffee commodity chain between 1871 and 1995 in "Where Does Your Coffee Dollar Go? The Division

rather than an object of speculation as it had been for many merchants, roasters favored stable, predictable prices.[55] Although the European coffee trade was slower to turn to large mass roasters and retail sales of packaged coffee, brands such as the Pélican Rouge captured large markets in the early twentieth century.[56]

The gradual rise to dominance of industrial capital did not mean that the consumer market was very price-sensitive and susceptible to new coffee product lines and advertising. The expansion of large roasting companies with their superior technology, greater efficiency, more reliable and cheaper product, and marketing sophistication did not expand coffee consumption as one might have expected. On the contrary, just as consolidation was beginning to occur, per capita consumption in the United States was stagnating. It would take forty years for U.S. consumers to again reach the thirteen pound per capita level of 1902.[57]

Consumers were not very price-conscious because they were long buffered from recognizing the price. If they drank in cafes, they were unaware of the type of coffee they were drinking. As the price of one sort rose, cafe owners often blended in cheaper substitute grades rather than raise their prices. The same seems to have been true for grocers. Coffee was very profitable for them before the 1930s. But it occupied an unusual position. As William B. Harris of the U.S. Department of Agriculture lectured: "90 percent of the regular customers of the retail dealer are held to the store by their purchases of coffee and tea."[58] Rather than risk losing their clientele, they competed on blends, not on price. They also sought to keep prices constant. Price rises were often not passed on to the consumer. Instead, cheaper blends were used or grocers reduced their profit margin. Moreover, as coffee sipping became customary and even habit-forming, it was transformed into a necessity for many. As a result, coffee in the twentieth century became price- and income-inelastic. Thus

of Income and Surplus along the Coffee Commodity Chain," *Studies in Comparative International Development* 32, no. 1 (Spring 1997): 66, 67. He found that the value added in consuming countries rose from 47 percent of the retail price in 1975/76 to 83 percent in 1991/92.

[55] Edward Green wrote to R. Johnston from Santos, Oct. 12, 1903 (Johnston archive): "There is no denying the fact that all of us in Santos formerly looked upon our stock of coffee as a speculative thing to lay with or a peg on which to hang larger speculations in Exchange."

[56] The Pélican Rouge company had four factories with just one of them employing 1,000 women sorters. *Spice Mill* (June 1909).

[57] Michael Jiménez, "From Plantation to Cup," in Wm. Roseberry, L. Gudmundson and Mario Samper, eds., *Coffee, Society and Power in Latin America* (Baltimore: Johns Hopkins University Press, 1995), pp. 42–3.

[58] *Tea and Coffee Trade Journal* (Nov. 1916): 427.

we are presented with the irony that the international coffee market at the turn of the twentieth century, one of the world's largest commodity markets, was relatively price-inelastic (within a reasonably large range) at both the production and the consumption end, though profit-driven commercial and industrial intermediaries were extremely conscious of price. In other words, it was a quite imperfect market.

This raises the question of what caused price swings if neither producer nor consumer was very price-conscious. Certainly, on the macro level supply and demand did figure in. Great frosts, world wars, or economic depressions disrupted the trade and affected prices. But within narrower bounds speculation seems to have been very important. Certainly, William Ukers, for over thirty years the editor of the influential *Tea and Coffee Trade Journal*, thought bulls and bears on the New York, Havre, or Hamburg markets were very influential in rapid price shifts.[59]

The most complete study I have found on the influences of coffee prices, done by the U.S. Federal Trade Commission in 1954, concluded that the great price rise "cannot be explained in terms of the competitive laws of supply and demand."[60] The FTC partly blamed "the inadequacy of present crop reporting systems in coffee growing countries." Planters and exporters never had a good idea of the extent of the harvest because of climatic variation; the size of stocks was kept secret; and, moreover, they often tried to manipulate the market with false information. Apparently, "the known existence of world surplus stocks, wherever held, seems to have a more pronounced effect on prices in a particular consuming country than the size of its domestic stocks."[61] Even when producing governments controlled the crops and built warehouses in the interior, information was not forthcoming. Indeed, the Colombian government outlawed the release of information of interior stocks.[62]

The FTC also complained that futures speculation drove up prices out of line with supply and demand. Although the futures market was in fact little used for actual purchases of coffee or even for commercial hedges by roasters – that is, it was dealing in pure speculation rather than real coffee, and the level of speculation was a tenth to a thirtieth of that on the cotton and grain markets – its prices did affect spot prices.[63]

[59] Ukers, *All about Coffee*, pp. 404, 457–8.
[60] FTC, *Investigation of Coffee Prices*, p. xv.
[61] Wickizer, *Coffee, Tea, Cocoa*, p. 87.
[62] FTC, *Investigation of Coffee Prices*, p. 1.
[63] Ibid., p. 311. *Tea and Coffee Trade Journal* (July 1917): 31.

The third culprit, according to the FTC, was the concentration of the trade in a few hands. Ten exporting houses in Brazil sent out between two-thirds to 90 percent of the crops until the 1920s and continued to control over half after that.[64] Since Brazil was exporting between 40 and 80 percent of the world's coffee and these exporting houses operated in other producing areas as well, a few houses dominated world exports. In the United States, the top ten importers (some of whom were also exporters) imported over half the total. And increasingly, a small number of roasters dominated that trade. By the 1950s the five largest roasters in the United States roasted over one-third of all coffee and held 78 percent of all stocks.[65]

The roasters increasingly purchased directly from producers or government agencies rather than on the spot market. Some of them, such as Nestlé, tended to employ the concept of "fair price" rather than what the market would bear, to ensure continued long-term production.[66] Others, such as Philip Morris, apparently wanted to use their market power to lower raw material prices as with any other commodity.

This small number of traders and roasters gave the competitors oligopsonic power not only over prices but over grades. Despite an apparently precise system in which all grades and sorts in New York and Europe were based on discounts or premiums on Rio number 7 and later Santos number 4 coffee, in fact, as the *Tea and Coffee Trade Journal* reported in July 1917 (p. 30): "The commercial classification of coffee is a matter of great complication. The factors which determine the market value of coffee are almost infinite in number." Standards varied widely and were quite artisanal.[67] The companies with the largest market power could assert its standards.

The Valorization of Coffee

Government intervention, which characterized the world coffee market more than any other commodity for most of the twentieth century, worked

[64] Greenhill, "E. Johnston," 389–91.
[65] *Spice Mill* (Jan. 1909): 37; (Feb. 1910): 118. FTC, *Investigation of Coffee Prices*, p. xviii.
[66] Pamphlet published by Nestle, "The Worldwide Coffee Trade," July 1990, p. 9.
[67] The *Tea and Coffee Trade Journal* reported in January 1917 that the complications passed on to roasted coffee: "We do not believe that any two concerns use the same terms in describing their grinds and I do not believe that I have any two salesmen on the road who write up order alike" (p. 32). The FTC, *Investigation of Coffee Prices*, p. xxii, chided the industry's "rule-of-thumb practices."

to further dampen the market's price mechanisms and brought some control back to the producing countries. Beginning in 1906, some of Brazil's states held stocks off the world market to "valorize" them. This led to a federal price support program, the Inter-American Coffee Agreement and, finally, in 1962, the International Coffee Agreement. Since the main objective of these cartels was to stabilize prices rather than corner the market, roasters in the consuming countries gladly joined. They were perfectly willing to accept somewhat higher prices in return for guaranteed production because most of value was added in the consuming countries. The coffee bean itself was a low-cost raw material. After initially strenuously opposing valorization, the governments of the consuming countries signed on. Their reasons were less economic than political, however. Coffee was a pawn in the Cold War. It was no coincidence that the United States came on board two years after the Cuban Revolution. Nor was it a coincidence that the United States abandoned the agreement the year the Berlin Wall came down. Until 1989, when the accord broke down, countries were given annual quotas.

This form of state capitalism provided conditions for rapid consolidation and vertical integration in the consuming countries. As coffee processing became increasingly industrialized, economies to scale grew and an ever larger share of the value was added in consuming countries. Not only were roasting, transporting, weighing, and packaging mechanized and therefore centralized, but new products were created: decaffeinated coffee and, after World War II, instant coffee in which processing added increased value.

Instant coffee consumption grew to the point that it provided a third of all coffee drunk in the United States in its peak year of 1978.[68] This new product had a major impact on the world coffee market. Drinkers of instant coffee were concerned with speed and convenience, not the quality of the brew. Consequently, the small number of roasters who captured this capital-intensive market used low-priced beans, especially *robusta* beans that Africa and Asia began growing. This undercut the price of *arabica* beans, lowered the overall quality of coffee consumed, and increased returns to ever larger processors rather than growers.

---

[68] Pan American Coffee Bureau, *Coffee Drinking in the United States* (New York: Pan American Coffee Bureau, 1970), p. 7; Gregory Dicum and Nina Luttinger, *The Coffee Book. Anatomy of an Industry from Crop to the Last Drop* (New York: New Press, 1999), p. 131.

Marketing played a role in the growth of the industry as important as that of automation. Arbuckle's had become by far the largest coffee roaster in the United States after the Civil War because it sold beans in one-pound paper sacks and awarded gift premiums in exchange for returned labels. The rise of chain stores such as the Great Atlantic and Pacific Tea Company in the early twentieth century, which made coffee their most profitable good, allowed wholesaling concentration, though each chain still roasted its own green coffee blends. This changed in the 1950s, when the supermarket was created. Selling a vastly larger number of goods, the supermarket depended on small margins but large volume. For the first time, coffee companies competed on price rather than the quality of their blend. This was because the supermarket corresponded with two other phenomena at the same time. Giant food conglomerates such as General Foods, Coca-Cola, and Ralston Purina, which bought up smaller successful coffee companies, had less interest in coffee as a family artisanal tradition than had earlier coffee roasters such as Chase and Sanborn or Maxwell House. Moreover, the mechanization of coffee processing had eliminated the human factor in roasting techniques, since constant heat allowed temperature and time measurements to replace the eye of the expert roaster in determining a proper roast. Second, the advent of the automobile led to suburban living, interest in fast foods, and home drinking rather than cafe drinking, so that convenience became the watchword rather than quality. This facilitated the spread of a few very large companies that offered lower quality, ground, roasted canned coffee. Consolidation proceeded to the extent that today four companies control 80 percent of the U.S. coffee market. Worldwide, four or five companies control half the world's instant and roast coffee markets.[69] Thus, although coffee was the world's second most important internationally traded commodity in many years, and it was produced in over 100 countries while being consumed in virtually every country, it has become surprisingly oligopolized and oliopsonized.

Conclusions

The world coffee market was integrated very early on in its history in the sense that the law of one price more or less obtained in the major consuming markets. However, this was not the price-responsive market

---

[69] International Coffee Organization, *Coffee International File, 1995–2000* (London: ICO, 1996).

of neoclassical economists' dreams. Producers were buffered from the market by a host of intermediaries, state monetary and price support policies, the botanical inflexibility of the crop, and the incentives of peasant agriculture. Technological advances had little impact on cultivation until recently with the Green Revolution beginning in the 1960s. Consumers, who at first reacted in a "price rational" manner, became socially and physiologically addicted; their indifference curve was not much affected by price within a fairly broad range. Their love of coffee was also not much affected by technology. Between the hundreds of thousands of coffee producers and the hundreds of millions of coffee consumers were a handful of exporters, importers, and roasters. Over time, the nature of the international market shifted notably. Control went from peasants to local merchants to importers to roasters to, for most of the twentieth century, states. Today the trade is dominated by multinational corporations. Although the market's dynamism came almost entirely from private initiatives, state intervention was necessary to institutionalize and standardize practices once the market's size outstripped the merchants' ability to operate it. Both the ability of producers to meet growing demand without raising prices (by superexploiting natural resources and labor rather than technological improvements) and consumers' tastes and culture explain the rapid and huge expansion of the ever-changing international coffee market.

2

Coffee in the Red Sea Area from the Sixteenth to the Nineteenth Century

Michel Tuchscherer

The southern end of the Red Sea was the cradle of coffee cultivation and consumption in the world. Wild coffee gathered in Ethiopia was already traded at the end of the fifteenth century, but progress was slow. In the second half of the sixteenth century, a true coffee economy emerged. Yemeni peasants began to cultivate coffee intensively on terraces, carved out of the steep mountains rising above the Tihama coastal plain. Effective marketing networks linked Yemeni ports to Jiddah and Cairo. By the seventeenth century, the coffee trade had superseded the declining spice trade. Fed by silver bullion originating in Spanish America, coffee played a major role in commerce between the Indian Ocean and the Mediterranean. To be sure, the development of coffee estates in the Indian Ocean and the New World from the eighteenth century progressively diminished Yemen's share of world coffee output, but the Red Sea trading network remained in place until the end of the nineteenth century.

The Origins of the Coffee Economy

Ethiopian forests, especially to the west of the Great Rift Valley, abound in wild *arabica* coffee, but we know very little about the origins of consumption there.[1] Coffee was probably long picked from the wild, and it was used to an increasing extent from the fourteenth century by the Islamized peoples of southeastern Ethiopia.

[1] C. Schaeffer, "Coffee Unobserved: Consumption and Commoditization in Ethiopia before the Eighteenth Century," in M. Tuchscherer, ed., *Le Café avant l'ère des plantations coloniales: espaces, réseaux, sociétés (XVè–XVIIIè siècles)* (Cairo: IFAO, 2001), pp. 23–34.

The coffee habit diffused to the Rasulid sultanate in Yemen, which had strong commercial and cultural connections with Muslim kingdoms in Ethiopia.[2] The consumption of coffee spread first around Aden, Mocha, and Zabid during the first half of the fifteenth century. The preparation of coffee resembled one of the uses of qat leaves, as coffee leaves or whole cherries were initially brewed. Muslim Sufi brotherhoods, especially the Shâdhiliyya, may have been coffee's initial proponents, for the stimulating properties of the beverage were greatly appreciated by mystics needing to keep awake and alert for their spiritual exercises. From Yemen, the consumption of coffee spread to the Holy Places of Islam, probably around 1475. At the end of the fifteenth century, coffee appeared in Cairo, initially among Yemeni students at the al-Azhar university, and later among other social groups.

From then on, coffee was traded as a commodity, although production was probably restricted to gathering cherries from the wild in Ethiopian forests. Ethiopia certainly remained the only source of coffee, exporting it to the countries bordering on the Red Sea through the port of Zayla'.[3] Both the bean and the husk were used to make a beverage, sometimes together. At the southern end of the Red Sea, coffee was added to the goods coming from India and the Far East and destined for regions to the north. The oldest known written reference to coffee, dated to 1497, occurs in a letter from a merchant of Tûr, at the southern tip of the Sinai Peninsula.[4] Coffee is mentioned in this letter together with pepper and indigo.

The Ottoman conquest of the ancient Mamluk state of Egypt in 1516–17 opened the immense regions under Ottoman rule to the diffusion of coffee. Coffee was drunk in Damascus from 1534.[5] Some twenty years later, it was in Istanbul, for Suleiman the Magnificent introduced a tax on coffee in 1554, to limit the consumption of the new beverage to the well off.[6] Merchants and soldiers, as well as Ulamâ and Sufi brotherhoods,

[2] R. Hattox, *Coffee and Coffeehouses: The Origins of a Social Beverage in the Mediaeval Near East* (Seattle: University of Washington Press, 1988). The only primary source remains Jaziri's sixteenth-century memorandum.

[3] R. Serjeant, *The Portuguese off the South Arabian Coast: Hadrami Chronicles* (Oxford: Clarendon Press, 1963), p. 105.

[4] Mustuo Kawatoko, "Coffee Trade in al-Tûr Port, South Sinai," in Tuchscherer, ed., *Le Café*, pp. 51–65.

[5] J.-P. Pascual, "Café et cafés à Damas: Contribution à la chrologie de leur diffusion au XVIe siècle," *Berytus* 42 (1995–6): 141–56.

[6] Saraçgil (Ayse), "L'Introduction du café à Istanbul," in H. Desmet-Grégoire and F. Georgeon, eds., *Cafés d'Orient revisités* (Paris: CNRS, 1997), p. 32.

contributed to the spread of coffee in the towns of the empire, although it was still restricted to small social groups.

The Development of the Red Sea Coffee Economy, 1540s–1725

As early as the 1540s, southern Ethiopia was probably struggling to meet the modest but growing requirements of the Ottoman Empire. Wars between Christians and Muslims, followed by the expansion of Oromo groups toward the Christian highlands and the Muslim principalities, destabilized Ethiopia for a long time. This undoubtedly affected the output of coffee.

Yemen filled the gap after coffee cultivation was introduced in 1543–44, according to a later Yemeni chronicle.[7] It is possible that this was on the initiative of Özdemir Pasha.[8] He knew Ethiopia well, for he had fought there with the Muslim forces against the Christians and their Portuguese allies, prior to being named governor of the new Yemeni province, where the Ottomans were still extending their control. That said, Yemeni production probably took off only after 1571, following the crushing of the Zaydi Imam's rebellion against the still fragile Ottoman regime. Significantly, coffee appeared with any frequency only from the 1560s on lists of goods traded by Cairo merchants.[9]

Other factors contributed to economic prosperity in the Red Sea area. Around 1570, the streams of New World silver, which initially flowed over Europe from Spain, reached the eastern Mediterranean. From there silver was irresistibly attracted to the Mughal Empire in India, and to China, filling the constant deficit in the balance of trade with Asia. The Red Sea was one of the conduits for this flow of money, which, in passing, contributed to invigorating the coffee trade.

During the first quarter of the seventeenth century, the shipment of spices up the Red Sea suffered from the arrival of the Dutch and British East India Companies in the Indian Ocean. Unlike the Portuguese, the newcomers managed to divert the spice trade to Europe out of the hands of Arab and other Muslim traders on a permanent basis. An irremediable

---

[7] Yahya b. al-Husayn b. al-Qâsim, *Ghâyat al-amânî fi akhbâr al-qutr al-yamânî* (Cairo: Dâr alKâtib al-'Arabî, 1968), vol. 2, p. 689.

[8] E. van Donzel, B. Lewis, and Ch. Pellat, *Encyclopédie de l'Islam* (Leiden: Brill, 1978), vol. 4, p. 470, article on "Kahwa."

[9] M. Tuscherer, "Production et commerce du café en Mer Rouge au XVIe siècle," in Tuchscherer, ed., *Le Café*, pp. 69–90.

decline would have affected Jiddah and Yemeni ports, as well as the Cairo bazaar, if there had not been a corresponding and very marked progress in the coffee trade. This not only saved commerce in the Red Sea, but also made it more prosperous than it had ever been before.

The coffee trade was principally in the hands of merchants resident in Cairo. Some were Egyptians, but others had come to the great city on the Nile from all the major towns of the Ottoman Empire. They redistributed coffee around the Mediterranean, in networks that stretched to Damascus, Smyrna, Istanbul, Salonika, and Tunis. Only the ports of Western Europe escaped them, when coffee consumption picked up in Europe from the mid-seventeenth century. The traders of Marseilles bought coffee in Alexandria, and jealously guarded their quasimonopoly of redistributing it in Europe. In the process, they brought large quantities of European silver coins to Egypt, which Cairo traders used to buy coffee in the Red Sea. In these transactions, the Seville dollar was long favored, before giving way to the famous Maria Theresa dollar of the Austrian empress in the mid-eighteenth century. The latter remained the standard currency of the Red Sea well into the twentieth century.

Cairo traders sometimes obtained coffee directly from Yemeni ports, but usually they drew their supplies from Jiddah. The expulsion of the Ottomans from Yemen in 1638 curtailed the influence of Cairo merchants there and enhanced the role of the Hijaz. However, Jiddah's position was also due to the decision of the Ottoman authorities to make the port an obligatory entrepot for shipping. By allowing the Sharîf of Mecca to share customs duties equally with the Pasha of Jiddah, the Sultan gained both the support of the prestigious Sharîf and the funds necessary to finance his army and administration in the Hijaz. Moreover, the obligatory transshipment of coffee in Jiddah ensured the profitability of cereal exports from Suez to the holy places of Islam. Some ten vessels a year engaged in this trade from the late seventeenth century, out of the forty or so registered in Suez.[10] On the return journey, they loaded coffee and other goods that Egypt imported from the Red Sea region.

Cairo traders, intimately associated with the military caste that ruled Egypt, made considerable fortunes from their activities in the Red Sea. In the late seventeenth and early eighteenth centuries, their agents in Jiddah or, more rarely, in Mocha or Hudayda, annually bought an average of

---

[10] M. Tuscherer, "Approvisionnement des villes saintes d'Arabie en blé d'Egypte d'après des documents ottomans des années 1670," *Anatolia Moderna* 5 (1994): 79–99; M. Tuscherer, "La Flotte impériale de Suez de 1694 à 1719," *Turcica* 29 (1997): 47–69.

some 30,000 loads of coffee, equivalent to about 4,500 tonnes.[11] This represented over half of Yemen's total exports at the time, and was paid partly in goods and partly in European coin.

Yemeni coffee was planted on terraces overlooking the coastal plain, from Jebel Yâfi' in the hinterland of Aden to Jebel Fayfâ in the latitude of Jizân, wherever natural conditions were favorable. The expansion of coffee planting resulted in higher population densities in these mountain districts, attracting peasants from the arid high plateaus. Most families owned their groves, which were usually quite small, producing 0.7 to 2 tonnes a year, on average.[12] A few rural notables, especially members of the family of the Imam, owned larger plantations. Moreover, some lands belonging to *waqf* (charitable trusts) were also planted in coffee. The harvest began at the end of the rainy season in October, and continued until February.

Marketing involved a chain of intermediaries. As the cherries were plucked and dried, producers carried them to the weekly market of the nearest small town, to exchange them for Indian cloth, salt, and hardware. The traders were Arabs or Banyans, the latter usually Hindu or Jain agents of Gujarati firms spread around the Indian Ocean. With hundreds of agents in ports and distant interior markets, these Banyans also controlled the allocation of credit in Yemen. Thus, they probably contributed to financing the cultivation of coffee, albeit in ways that remain to be discovered.

Traders had the dried cherries hulled in small workshops, equipped with millstones. The husks were exported to Egypt and the Ottoman Empire up to the seventeenth century, but were then consumed locally as the raw materials for a peasant beverage. Beans passed through the hands of various intermediaries, who transported them to larger markets, chiefly Bayt al-Faqih. There, they were purchased by merchants, often foreigners, who had them taken to ports. From Luhiyya and Hudayda, coffee generally went to Jiddah on small dhows, whereas Mocha exported more to the Gulf, Iran, and India or, from the end of the seventeenth century, to Europe.

These exports furnished Yemen with substantial revenues, mainly in European coin. Taxes on peasants and customs duties were decisive in

---

[11] A. Raymond, *Artisans et commerçants au Caire au XVIIIe siècle* (Damascus, 1974), vol. 1, p. 133. A tonne equaled 1000 kilos.

[12] N. Bréon, "Mémoire sur la culture, la manipulation et le commerce du café en Arabie," *Annales Maritimes et Coloniales* 2 (1832): 559–67.

consolidating the power of the Zaydi Imams after the withdrawal of the Ottomans. The Qâsimî dynasty was thus able to extend its dominion over the whole of Yemen, from Jîzân to Hadhramaut, politically uniting the country for the first time in history. Under Imam al-Mutawakkil Ismâ'îl (1644–76), the Yemenis also seized the port of Zayla', gaining control of the main maritime export center of southern Ethiopia.

European coin did not remain in Yemen, but served to buy imported Indian goods, mainly cottons that the population used to clothe themselves. Mocha became the entrepot of Indian commerce, not only for Yemen, but also for the whole of the Red Sea. Each year, a large fleet left Surat and other Indian ports during the winter monsoon, bringing cottons, shawls, spices, sugar, and rice. The Indian commercial network stretched up the Red Sea as far as Jiddah, but the northern half of the sea was jealously held by Cairo merchants.

The Survival of the Red Sea Coffee Economy, 1725–1840

From the second quarter of the eighteenth century, Europeans began to threaten the future of the Red Sea coffee economy. They developed plantations in their possessions in Asia, the Indian Ocean, and the Americas, and sold the coffee from these new zones of production in the Middle East as well as in Europe.

The output of Yemeni coffee probably reached its zenith in the first quarter of the eighteenth century, at around 12,000 to 15,000 tonnes a year.[13] This level was probably more or less maintained throughout the eighteenth century, but in a context of rapidly growing world consumption. Whereas Yemen still had a quasimonopoly of supplies in 1720, its share of world production was down to a mere 2 to 3 percent around 1840.[14] From the beginning of the nineteenth century, the absolute level of Yemeni output also began to decline, partly because of political troubles.

Ethiopian production also remained depressed, partly because Coptic Christian highlanders were strongly opposed to drinking coffee, a practice seen as typical of Muslims and Oromo pagans.[15] Coffee cultivation

[13] Raymond, *Artisans*, vol. 1, p. 133, n. 2, citing Hamilton and Parsons. The figure of 22,000 tonnes given here seems exaggerated, as my calculations indicate that a "load" actually only weighed around 140 kilos.
[14] H. Becker et al., *Kaffee aus Arabien* (Wiesbaden: Franz Steiner, 1979), p. 20.
[15] R. Pankhurst, *Economic History of Ethiopia* (Addis Ababa: Haile Selassie University Press, 1968), p. 198.

nevertheless developed slowly in different parts of the country during the nineteenth century. Shoa's coffee exports financed the purchase of firearms, needed to ensure the principality's autonomy and expansion. The port of Massawa exported 40 to 80 tonnes a year, coming from Enarya, Gojjam, and the banks of Lake Tana. Harar's coffee passed through Zayla' and Berbera.[16]

Despite much competition, Yemeni coffee's reputation for high quality enabled it to retain a niche among a clientele of connoisseurs, prepared to pay a markedly higher price. Java coffee soon overshadowed the Mocha article in Amsterdam. The Dutch had bought large quantities of Mocha coffee from 1698, rising from some 350,000 pounds a year to 1,500,000 after 1715. However, they ceased to come regularly to Yemen from 1726, preferring to obtain supplies from Java.[17] At the same time, coffee from the French Caribbean reached the Mediterranean from 1730. Marseilles traders reduced their purchases of coffee in Alexandria, from around 600 tonnes a year at the beginning of the century to under 200 in 1785–89.[18] However, the British East India Company remained a major European customer for coffee in Mocha right through the eighteenth century, reducing its purchases only around 1800. Even then, the withdrawal of the British was countered by the appearance of American ships in the Yemeni port. In 1806, Mocha still exported 13,000 loads of coffee (about 1,800 tonnes), of which 9,000 loads (about 1,250 tonnes) were taken by Americans.[19]

European plantation coffee also began to penetrate Middle Eastern markets. The Ottoman authorities, keen to avoid troubles originating from shortages, facilitated imports of Caribbean coffee by halving duties from 1738. At the end of the eighteenth century, Marseilles exported some 2,000 tonnes to the Levant, mainly to Salonika, Smyrna, and Istanbul. In Syria, and especially in Egypt, Caribbean coffee was less in demand. Despite its markedly lower price, its taste was not greatly appreciated. Above all, it encountered the hostility of powerful Cairo merchants, who

[16] M. Aregay, "The Early History of Ethiopia's Coffee Trade and the Rise of Shawa," *Journal of African Studies* 29 (1988): 19–25.

[17] G. J. Knaap, "Coffee for Cash: The Dutch East India Company and Its Expansion of Coffee Cultivation in Java, Ambon and Ceylon, 1700–1730," in J. van Goor, *Trading Companies in Asia, 1600–1830* (Utrecht: Hes, 1986), pp. 33–49.

[18] A. Raymond, "Les Problèmes du café en Egypte au XVIIIe siècle," in *Le Café en Méditerranée: Histoire, anthropologie, économie, XVIIIe–XXe siècle* (Aix-en-Provence: CNRS, 1981), pp. 57–8.

[19] *Records of the Hijaz, 1798–1925* (Oxford: Archive Editions, 1996), vol. 1, p. 207, Lord Valentia, "Observations on the Trade of the Red Sea."

even obtained a ban on imports of European coffee in 1764.[20] Muhammad Ali renewed this prohibition in 1830.[21]

Further east, competition from another beverage complicated the situation, as the consumption of tea spread in Iran and India from the seventeenth century. Tea eventually overcame its rival in Qajar Iran, probably between 1820 and 1850.[22] The French thus tried in vain to market their Bourbon (Réunion) coffee in Basra.

The commercial networks that linked Yemeni ports to Cairo, via Jiddah and Suez, proved to be remarkably strong, surviving major political upheavals in Egypt, the Hijaz, and Yemen. Cairo merchants suffered from incessant rivalries between rapacious Mamluk factions, and imports of Red Sea coffee fell markedly after 1785.[23] The Wahhabi Muslim reformers severely disrupted the trade of Jiddah from 1803 to 1805. In Yemen, Sharîf Hamûd of Abû Arîsh, temporarily allied to the Wahhabis, conquered all the Tihama coastal plain, except for Mocha. Continuing struggles in the Tihama endangered commercial relations with the mountainous hinterland, where coffee was grown. This area remained under the rule of the Imam in Sanaa, but his power was weakened by the loss of customs revenues. Coffee growers were thus increasingly at the mercy of raids by Zaydi highland tribes, in almost permanent revolt against the Imam.

This troubled political situation was only partially remedied by the consolidation of Muhammad Ali's rule over Egypt from 1810. He crushed the Wahhabi, who had erupted from Nejd to conquer the Hijaz, and he temporarily conquered the whole of the Tihama, including Mocha. Egyptian soldiers returned in 1833 to expel Türkshe Bilmez, an Ottoman officer who had fled to the Tihama after a failed revolt in Jiddah. Then Egyptian troops progressively subjugated Yemen's Red Sea ports. However, by installing themselves in the Tihama, the Egyptians reinforced the isolation of the ports from their mountainous hinterland. Moreover, fearful of Egyptian expansion into Arabia, the British reacted by taking Aden in early 1839.

During these upheavals, warlords and rulers battened on the coffee trade, to secure revenue to shore up their power, especially by buying firearms. Sharîf Hamûd attempted to concentrate all coffee exports in

[20] Raymond, "Les problèmes," p. 58.
[21] Archives de la Chambre de Commerce de Marseille, M.Q 5.2 Egypte 1818–33.
[22] R. Matthee, "From Coffee to Tea: Shifting Patterns of Consumption in Qajar Iran," *Journal of World History* 7, no. 2 (1996): 199–230.
[23] Raymond, *Artisans*, vol. 1, table 23, pp. 146–7.

Luhiyya.[24] In 1804–5, he secretly proposed an exchange of coffee for weapons to both the French and the British.[25] As for Muhammad Ali, he did not conceal that one of his objectives in conquering both shores of the Red Sea was to exert strict control over the coffee trade and to make it into a state monopoly. He tried to buy coffee at a low fixed price, in order to sell it to foreign merchants for much more.[26]

Although Red Sea commercial networks survived for the first forty years of the nineteenth century, they changed in significant ways. Indian ships went more frequently directly to Jiddah, which became their main entrepot. Ships from Calcutta yearly brought rice and cottons, and left with salt from the Sawâkin (Suakin) region on the Sudanese side of the Red Sea.[27] This was to the detriment of Mocha, which thus began to decline long before the British seized Aden in 1839. Hadhrami merchants, rarely encountered before the end of the eighteenth century, extended their network in all the ports of the Red Sea, for reasons that are still largely unclear. In Jiddah, they eventually came to engross most of the port's trade.[28]

Transformations and Continuities, 1840–1880

After 1840, the rate of European penetration into the Red Sea suddenly accelerated, provoking mutations in the coffee economy, but not fundamentally reshaping its ancient foundations. Having seized Aden in January 1839, to serve as a port of call on the sea route between Suez and India and to prevent Muhammad Ali from conquering the whole of Yemen, the British extended their influence by a series of subsequent treaties. The first, in 1843, was with the Abdalî sultanate of Lahij. In 1873, nine neighboring polities signed treaties, this time to ward off the danger of Ottoman expansion.[29] From 1854, measures to build a canal between the Mediterranean and the Red Sea stoked the rivalry between France

[24] Becker et al., *Kaffee*, p. 36, n. 75.

[25] Valentia, "Observations," pp. 210, 220.

[26] *Records of the Hijaz*, vol. 1, pp. 506–7, Letter to Sir Alexander Johnston, June 1, 1837.

[27] *Records of the Hijaz*, vol. 1, pp. 635–7, A. C. Ogilvie, March 26, 1849.

[28] H. von Maltzan, *Reisen nach Südarabien und geographische Forschungen im und über den südwestlichen Theil Arabiens* (Braunschweig: Friedrich Liebeg, 1873), p. 83; J. Ewald and W. G. Clarence-Smith, "The Economic Role of the Hadhrami Diaspora in the Red Sea and the Gulf of Aden, 1820s to 1930s," in U. Freitag and W. G. Clarence-Smith, eds., *Hadhrami Traders, Scholars and Statesmen in the Indian Ocean, 1750s–1960s* (Leiden: Brill, 1997), pp. 281–96.

[29] R. J. Gavin, *Aden under British rule, 1839–1967* (London: C. Hurst, 1975), pp. 63–71, 145–6.

and Britain over the southern Bab al-Mandab Straits, especially on its African shore.

The Ottomans reacted by expanding their possessions after Muhammad Ali's forced departure from Arabia in 1840. They took over direct administration of the Hijaz, and the Sharîf of Abu Arîsh ruled the Tihama for a few years in their name. When he proved unable to restore order, the Ottomans sent in troops and officials in 1848. In the same year, they took Sawâkin and Massawa, on the African side of the Red Sea, from the Egyptians. In a few years, the Ottomans had once again become a major power in the region.[30]

The political disintegration of the Yemeni highlands resulted in a further extension of Ottoman rule. With the Zaydi Imam more or less reduced to the control of Sanaa, the country fragmented into a multitude of principalities, under tribal chiefs or rival Imams. Coffee producers were isolated from the coast and had difficulty taking their crop to the ports. Taxes and tolls increased on the road to Aden through Abdalî lands.[31] The same happened in the Tihama under Ottoman rule, with a tax of 2.5 dollars per load of coffee sent to Hudayda.[32] Frequent famines and epidemics, partly caused by anarchy, further disrupted coffee production.

European interest in the Red Sea focused on the route to the Indian Ocean and the Far East, and the transport of coffee was not immediately affected. As early as 1829, the British launched the first steamer service between Suez and Bombay, but this was for passengers only. From 1843, Peninsular and Oriental, soon followed by a French company, ran a regular steamer line from Suez to India.[33] However, these ships called at Aden only for a few years, and thus had almost no effect on the caravan and dhow trade. It was the completion of a railway linking Cairo to Suez in 1859 that began a new phase. The caravans that had earlier carried coffee on this route soon disappeared. For a similar price, trains had the advantage of transporting goods in a few hours, instead of three or four days, and with greater security and regularity.[34]

Although European steamers began to call at more ports in the Red Sea, especially Jiddah, dhows continued in business by undercutting freight

[30] Ibid., pp. 91–7.
[31] Ibid., p. 119.
[32] *Records of the Hijaz*, vol. 2, pp. 189–239, S. Page, June 1, 1856.
[33] Gavin, *Aden*, p. 106.
[34] Archives du Ministère des affaires Etrangères, Nantes (henceforth AE), Suez, carton 1, correspondance commerciale, letter of March 2, 1862.

rates.[35] In 1868, it cost twelve dollars to ship a quintal of coffee from Jiddah to Suez by steamer, and three to five dollars less by dhow.[36] To be sure, steamers also offered speed, security, and predictability.[37] However, local merchants were the main owners of the dhows that sailed between Red Sea ports.[38] As in preceding centuries, local shippers based in Suez or Qusayr did not venture beyond Jiddah, while those from Yemen, Massawa, or the Dahlak archipelago controlled the coasting trade of the southern part of the Red Sea. Moreover, the gum and coffee sent to Aden from Berbera and Tajura, in the Gulf of Aden, remained a monopoly of Somali shippers.[39]

Other measures kept the bulk of the coffee trade out of European hands until the end of the 1870s, despite the theoretical application of the 1838 Ottoman commercial treaty to the region. From 1859, the viceroy of Egypt set up a steamer service for the coastal trade of the Red Sea. Three years later, Haji Hababi, a rich trader of Maghrebi origins mainly trading between Egypt and Arabia, launched another steamer line. He planned to link up all the Red Sea ports, and to place Algerian agents there.[40] However, it was not until the 1860s that the Egyptian Aziziyya Company managed to establish a truly regular steamer service for the whole sea.[41]

The Rise of Aden as a Coffee Exporter

The British did not immediately manage to develop Aden as an entrepot after 1839. To be sure, the main chief of the Hujariyya tribe, south of Ta'izz, had his coffee harvest taken to Aden for a few months in 1839.

---

[35] W. Ochsenwald, "The Commercial History of the Hijaz Vilayet, 1840–1908," *Arabian Studies* 16 (1982): 57–76; also in W. Ochsenwald, ed., *Religion, Economy and State in Ottoman-Arab History* (Istanbul: Isis Press, 1998), pp. 53–77.

[36] AE, Série A, Consulat de Djedda, carton 1, régistre no. 4, pp. 210–4, Dubreuil, March 31, 1868.

[37] Maltzan, *Reise*, p. 80; AE, Suez, carton 1, correspondance commerciale, letter of March 2, 1862.

[38] *Records of the Hijaz*, vol. 1, pp. 465–81. Campbell, a British Consul in Egypt, in 1836 gave a seemingly exhaustive list of 108 boats from the following harbors: Suez, Qusayr, Tur, Yanbu', and Djedda. See *Records of the Hijaz 1798–1925* 1, pp. 465–481.

[39] Schweiger-Lechenfeld, "Der Kaffeehandel Adens," *Österreichische Monatsschrift für den Orient* 3 (1877): 187–9.

[40] AE, Suez, carton 1, correspondance commerciale, letters of Oct. 7, 1861, March 2, April 10, May 29, and Oct. 17, 1862, and Jan. 22, 1863.

[41] AE, Série A, Consulat de Djedda, carton 1, régistre no. 4, letter of Dec. 17, 1864, p. 22; Ochsenwald, "The Commercial History," pp. 74–5.

This was because of a quarrel with the Egyptians, then in control of Mocha. However, after Muhammad Ali's withdrawal the following year, the coffee of southern production zones went once again to Mocha. As for Yâfi' beans, they were exported through Shuqra, in Fadli territory to the east of Aden. Haines, the first British resident, nevertheless hoped to attract a good part of the coffee business to Aden. Surrounded by local advisers, some of them Mocha coffee merchants, he negotiated with the Imam in Sanaa and the Hujari Shaykhs, offering to swap coffee for arms. He failed, largely because of hostility fostered by Ottoman and Egyptian agents.[42] Throughout the 1840s, Mocha merchants stirred up trouble among the tribes of Aden's hinterland.[43]

However, Aden's customs duties were a more significant obstacle, and the situation changed rapidly after the British had made Aden a free port in 1850. British and American houses immediately moved to Aden from Mocha, soon followed by most Muslim, Jewish, and Banyan traders. Within a few years Aden had secured most coffee exports to Europe and America. The decline of Mocha suddenly accelerated, and within twenty years the town had become an almost abandoned ruin. The lack of customs duties was not the only advantage of Aden, for ships could come directly alongside the quay, cutting out the need for lighters. Coffee was also available in the town's warehouses, whereas in Mocha it was usually necessary to buy beans in Bayt al-Faqih and organize caravan transport to the sea. Now that Yemeni coffee was marginal in world terms, Western buyers could afford to be choosy, imposing the costs and risks of transport to Aden, further from production zones than Mocha, onto local producers and intermediaries.[44]

Aden's coffee trade boomed after 1850, although data remain fragmentary, in the absence of a thorough examination of available sources. In the 1840s, yearly exports averaged around 15 tonnes, but by 1857 they exceeded 1,000.[45] Most beans probably came overland to Aden. Called "Jebeli," this coffee was transported by caravans of producers or brokers.[46] In the 1850s, a significant part came from Udayn, northwest of Ta'izz, but most subsequently originated from the region of Hujariyya, south of Ta'izz.[47] In the early 1860s, prior to the opening

[42] Gavin, *Aden*, pp. 45–51.

[43] Becker et al., *Kaffee*, p. 32.

[44] Ibid., p. 34.

[45] Calculated from Gavin, *Aden*, p. 388, n. 126.

[46] Schweiger-Lechenfeld, "Der Kaffeehandel," p. 187.

[47] Gavin, *Aden*, p. 119.

of the Suez Canal, some coffee was exported from Aden via Zanzibar, notably to Marseilles.[48]

The opening of the Suez Canal in 1869, together with the inauguration of the first telegraph line from Europe to Aden in 1870, gave Aden a great boost.[49] The port's coffee trade doubled in the 1870s, as the British colony captured a large part of the flows of coffee that had earlier reached Europe via Jiddah, Cairo, and Alexandria.

Detailed figures for 1875–76 show that many more beans now arrived by sea for reexport. In that year, Aden received 6,738 camel loads, equivalent to 1,268 tonnes, compared with 2,516 tonnes by sea. Very little of this sea-borne traffic came from Ethiopia, as Zayla' and Berbera provided only 156 tonnes. The main suppliers were Yemeni ports, for, despite all their efforts, the Ottomans were unable to channel all the trade into routes under their control. Hudayda alone, with 1,968 tonnes, was responsible for 63 percent, while Luhiyya sent 16 percent.[50] In contrast, arrivals from Mocha, Jîzân, Farasan, and Shuqra were tiny. France took most of Aden's coffee exports, with 1,403 tonnes, followed by Britain with 792 tonnes, and Austria with 369. The Americans had sunk to a secondary position, with only 208 tonnes. After sorting and cleaning, and sometimes hulling, coffee was purchased by French, Austrian, Swiss, and British houses, which ensured that indispensable Marie-Theresa dollars continued to be minted in Vienna for this purpose.[51]

Jiddah, the Great Entrepot of the Red Sea

Aden was not alone in benefiting from Mocha's decline, as Jiddah also prospered. Traders from Jiddah not only maintained commercial networks that stretched to Istanbul, Syria, Egypt, and India, but also reinforced their regional position, as Jiddah became the chief entrepot within the confines of Red Sea.[52]

As before, traders were especially active from October to May.[53] They remained bound by the ancient rhythms of sail navigation, dependent

[48] L. Bernard, *Essai sur le commerce de Marseille* (Marseilles, 1887), pp. 39, 68.
[49] Schweiger-Lechenfeld, "Der Kaffeehandel," p. 189.
[50] F. Hunter, *An Account of the British Settlement of Aden* (rpt., London: Cass, 1968), pp. 100–3.
[51] Schweiger-Lechenfeld, "Der Kaffeehandel," pp. 187–8. The main houses in 1877 were C. Tian of Marseilles, Wright Newson and Co. from Britain, Bienenfeld and Co. from Austria, and Escher and Furrer from Switzerland.
[52] J.-L. Miège, "Djeddah: Port d'entrepôt au XIXe siècle," in Institut d'Histoire des Pays d'Outre-Mer, *Etudes et documents*, No. 15 (Aix-en-Provence, 1982), pp. 93–108.
[53] Maltzan, *Reise*, p. 82.

on the winds, for steamers carried only a small proportion of the goods passing through Jiddah. Commercial relations were stronger than ever with India, whence about fifty large sailing ships came every year. They brought mainly rice and cottons, but also indigo, much of it sent on to Egypt, and spices. They returned with Sawâkin salt as well as coffee.[54] A large community of Muslim merchants, some 250 people in all, resided throughout the year in the town's bazaar.[55] As Mocha declined, Indian ships increasingly went straight up the Red Sea to Jiddah, which became their main base in the Red Sea. They ceased to call at any Yemeni ports, and most Banyans deserted inland Yemeni towns and markets, wracked by political upheavals and economic problems.

Ancient ties with Egypt persisted, for the Nile Valley still provided the Hijaz with cereals and other foodstuffs. As the cultivation of cotton developed in Lower Egypt, a growing proportion of wheat came from Upper Egypt, via the port of Qusayr. Returning dhows shipped not only Indian cottons and spices, but also large amounts of coffee. Despite the opening of the Suez Canal, the Hijaz did little direct trade with Europe. Goods continued to pass through Cairo and Suez, and sometimes Istanbul.

The strength of existing commercial networks, Hadhrami Arab as well as Indian, explained much of this. According to Maltzan, of the 200 traders in Jiddah in 1870, fully 150 were Hadhramis.[56] From the middle of the nineteenth century, Hadhramis were also influential in Cairo, where they dominated trade with the Red Sea and India. Working on low margins and living frugally, they were able to supply Jiddah with Western goods more cheaply than the few locally established European houses, which imported directly from Europe. Hadhramis and Indians also benefited from lending money and advancing trade goods. In a region where coin was always short, and banks did not exist, liquidity and trust played a decisive role in business dealings. Hadhramis and Indians were well equipped for such roles by their tight-knit networks, covering much of the Indian Ocean.[57]

Together with British and Indian cottons, coffee was the major commodity traded in Jiddah. Through Hudayda especially, but also Luhiyya or Jîzân, coffee reached Jiddah from all over the production zones of

---

[54] AE, Série A, Consulat de Djedda, carton 1, régistre no. 4, pp. 210–14, letter of March 31, 1868; AE, Série A, Consulat de Suez, carton 1, letter of March 29, 1869.

[55] Maltzan, *Reise*, p. 83–4.

[56] Ibid., p. 83.

[57] Ibid., pp. 80–5; Freitag and Clarence-Smith, eds., *Hadhrami Traders*.

northern Yemen. A little coffee also came from Massawa, and then from the 1850s from Sawâkin as caravans began to reach this Sudanese port from western Ethiopia via Kassala.[58] Jiddah received some 3,000 to 4,000 tonnes of coffee a year all told, probably about the same amount as at the peak of the trade in the preceding century.

Coffee was carefully prepared for export in Jiddah, a process well described by French vice-consul Dubreuil in 1868:

Each bale of coffee receives special care. The beans are spread on the ground, and slaves kneel around. They examine them slowly and thoroughly, picking up each bean. The purpose of this operation is to eliminate all beans without the translucence and greenish colour that ensure the superiority of Yemeni coffee over that from Ethiopia, India and even the Americas. The bales that are exported are thus of great purity and quality, but, unfortunately, they are affected by numerous changes during their long voyage. Firstly, the sea influences the beans, which turn brown, and lose some of their aroma and strength. Then, in Suez, Cairo and Alexandria, they are mixed with equal quantities of inferior beans. Thus, the further Arabian coffee is from its point of origin, the less it resembles pure Mocha. Even in Jiddah, a few traders mix Yemeni beans with Ethiopian coffee, recognisable by its larger bean. It has less aroma, and is inferior. As for Indian beans, they are opaque, dark, and irregular in shape, and are generally little appreciated.[59]

Yemeni coffee retained a following among connoisseurs in the second half of the nineteenth century, and for them Jiddah was the main source. These lovers of Mocha were first and foremost Egyptians, Syrians, and Turks, as well as peninsular Arabs, who were supplied by caravan from Jiddah. In these regions the consumption of tea remained quite marginal, with Jiddah importing considerably less tea than cloves in 1872.[60] Indian ships took small quantities to Bombay and Calcutta, but most coffee was loaded onto dhows bound for Suez. The French vice-consul in Suez estimated that coffee made up over two-thirds of imports by value in 1861 and 1862.[61]

Some of the Mocha beans that reached Egypt were reexported via Alexandria, with quantities fluctuating between 400 and 1,000 tonnes a year. After the abolition of Muhammad Ali's system of monopolies,

[58] *Annales du Commerce Extérieur, Afrique (faits commerciaux)*, vol. 1: *Egypte, Mer Rouge, Abyssinie (1843–1866)*, *Avis divers* No. 1361, Feb. 1867, pp. 19–24.

[59] AE, Série A, Consulat de Djedda, carton 1, régistre no. 4, pp. 210–14, Dubreuil, March 31, 1868.

[60] Maltzan, *Reise*, p. 81.

[61] AE, Série A, Consulat de Suez, carton 1, "Etat des marchandises importées à Suez en 1861," and letter of March 24, 1863.

this port recovered its former role as distributor of Arabian coffee in the Mediterranean. Marseilles merchants were still major buyers.[62]

Up to around 1875, Jiddah was able to maintain its dominant position in the coffee trade of the Red Sea, due to the efficacy of its established merchant networks. About a third of Yemen's yearly output, which can be estimated at around 10,000 tonnes, passed through the port. In the 1870s, however, Aden managed to raise its share to about the same as Jiddah's.

Numerous and profound changes occurred in the ancient coffee economy of the Red Sea during the last two decades of the nineteenth century. Near Eastern coffee imports from the New World rose after 1880, as seen in Marseilles trade figures.[63] Mocha, long a synonym with quality, was challenged by several other kinds of coffee, notably those from Venezuela, India, Haiti, and Puerto Rico.[64] Yemeni smallholders, producing beans on narrow terraces, found it increasingly hard to compete with low-cost producers around the world. Even the Hijaz eventually imported some cheaper coffee from Java or India.[65] However, Yemen remained a source of esteemed planting material, both to renovate old coffee groves and to develop new regions of production. Within the French colonial empire, in the single year of 1883, the authorities of both New Caledonia and Indochina requested that Mocha seed be sent to them.[66]

In the Red Sea, the Ottomans again controlled the whole of Yemen from 1872, and they upgraded the port facilities of Hudayda. The port then managed to claw back a significant proportion of Aden's direct trade with Europe.[67] Hudayda's growth was also to the detriment of Jiddah's role as regional entrepot. The coffee trade of Hudayda was in the hands of Bombay Indian firms, and of a few Greeks who arrived with the returning Ottoman authorities, for the ancient Arab commercial networks had largely vanished by that time.

Ethiopia, with much more forested land suitable for coffee cultivation than Yemen, increased its output considerably in the final decade of

[62] J. Julliany, *Essai sur le commerce de Marseille* (Paris: Renard, 1842), p. 317; Archives de la Chambre de Commerce de Marseille, "Compte-rendu de la situation industrielle et commerciale de la circonscription de Marseille," 1871–80.

[63] Bernard, *Essai*, p. 176.

[64] *Encyclopédie des Bouches-du-Rhône*, vol. 9, 1922, p. 280.

[65] Gavin, *Aden*, p. 131; W. Ochsenwald, *Religion, Society and State in Arabia: The Hijaz under Ottoman Control, 1840–1908* (Columbus: Ohio University Press, 1984), p. 96.

[66] AE, Série A, Consulat d'Aden, carton 4, correspondance avec les autorités françaises 1865–89.

[67] *Moniteur maritime, industriel, commercial et financier*, 374, July 13, 1902.

the nineteenth century. In the north, the old Coptic Christian prejudices against coffee eroded, and much of the crop was locally consumed. In the south, after the conquests of Menilik, a few Europeans acquired vast domains and developed estates of a colonial type. Together with Ethiopian landlords and southern Ethiopian smallholders, they exported a growing quantity of beans on the new railway to the French port of Djibouti, which came fully into service in the 1910s.[68] The production of coffee in the Red Sea region thus swung back decisively to Ethiopia during the course of the twentieth century.

Conclusion

The history of coffee is closely bound up with the lands of the Red Sea. It was in the southern forests of Ethiopia that botanists found wild species of *arabica* coffee. It was in these same forests that humans acquired a taste for the caffeine in the beans. From there, the habit spread to the whole of the Ottoman Empire, and also to India and the Malay World.[69] The smallholders of Yemen and Harar patiently developed the cultivation of the coffee tree on their little terraced fields for centuries. Arab, Turkish, and Indian merchants held the export trade, and Westerners were never able to eliminate them.

However, it was also Yemen that involuntarily furnished grains and seedlings for the spread of *arabica* coffee across the world from the seventeenth century, thus losing its quasimonopoly over supplies. Yemen then appears to have lost its capacity to adapt to the new conditions on the world market, in a long, slow, but irreversible decline. Today, its production is reduced to insignificant amounts, contrary to that of Ethiopia, which has been able to keep its position as a supplier of quality coffee and maintain the reputation of the Mocha brand.

---

[68] Pankhurst, *Economic History*, pp. 199–201.
[69] S. Gopal, "Coffee Trade of Western India in the Seventeenth Century," and W. G. Clarence-Smith, "The Spread of Coffee Cultivation in Asia, from the Seventeenth to the Early Nineteenth Century," in Tuchscherer, ed., *Le Café*, pp. 297–318, and 371–84.

3

The Origins and Development of Coffee Production in Réunion and Madagascar, 1711–1972

Gwyn Campbell

Introduction

Coffee production on Réunion (Bourbon), a small island near Madagascar off the coast of Africa, was significant in the eighteenth century, but declined rapidly thereafter. Réunion Creoles then carried the coffee frontier to Madagascar, conquered by France in 1895. Colonial policies made coffee the major Malagasy export by the 1930s and, inadvertently, promoted indigenous smallholder production. The subsequent battle over resources between Réunion Creoles and their Malagasy competitors on the East Coast was a major cause of the 1947 uprising, one of the most bloody episodes in French colonial history. The revolt effectively squeezed small Creole planters out of coffee, leaving a handful of large metropolitan French concerns and numerous small indigenous cultivators. The 1972 revolution led to the demise of large French companies and ushered in a period of mismanaged nationalization that undermined the entire economy, including the coffee sector.

Réunion, 1711–1895

Wild Mauritiana coffee was discovered, growing at an altitude of over 600 meters, near St. Paul on Réunion in 1711. Popularly termed "*café marron*," it was said that "the most subtle connoisseurs can in no way distinguish [it] . . . from Mocha coffee." From 1720, English and Dutch ships purchased Mauritiana coffee, and it was well received in France in 1721. However, Mauritiana prospered only at high altitude and was pronounced less smooth, less perfumed, and more bitter than Mocha, favored by the French East India Company, which governed Réunion from 1708 to 1758.[1]

The company thus focused its efforts on Mocha coffee, introduced in 1715. In 1718, the company ordered each concessionaire on Réunion to cultivate a minimum of ten coffee bushes per worker. Within two years there existed 7,000 Mocha trees, and by 1723, 100,000, concentrated in "Sous le Vent" near St.-Paul. At maturity, they produced an average 3 to 5 pounds of beans per annum.[2] In France in 1718, Réunion Mocha was described as "a coffee, the small defects of which will be corrected through properly practiced cultivation."[3] However, it soon came to be considered as second only to Yemeni *arabica* in quality, as world demand for coffee soared in the early eighteenth century.[4]

Coffee quickly became the dominant crop on Réunion. Profits were considerable, the "ball" of Mocha became a standard money locally, and hopes were raised that it would dominate the European market.[5] The company in 1723 granted France a monopoly of all Réunion coffee, and declared the next year that it would repossess all concessions on which coffee was not grown. There was even a debate over the imposition of the death penalty for the voluntary destruction of coffee trees. By 1735, some 95 percent of Réunion's 345 planters grew coffee. It was mostly associated with food crops, although 71 producers grew only coffee.[6]

Although competition increased, especially from Java, European demand ensured that Réunion coffee did well, notably in the Ste. Suzanne and St. Denis regions, responsible for 72 percent of coffee production by 1735. From 1726, Governor Pierre Dumas instructed planters to improve

[1] Albert Lougnon, *L'Ile Bourbon pendant la Régence; Desforges-Boucher; Les débuts du café* (Nevac: Imprimérie Couderc, 1956), pp. 57–8, 61, 69, 148–51; Charles Buet, *Madagascar, la reine des Iles Africaines* (Paris: Société Générale de Librarie Catholique, 1883), p. 328; Claude Mazet, "L'Ile Bourbon en 1735: Les Hommes, la terre, le café et les vivres," in C. Wanquet, ed., *Fragments pour une histoire des économies et sociétés de plantation à la Réunion* (St. Denis: Université de la Réunion, 1989), p. 28.

[2] Lougnon, *L'Ile Bourbon*, pp. 72–3, 114–15, 151, 329, 340; Buet, *Madagascar*, p. 328; C. Robequain, *Madagascar et les bases dispersées de l'union française* (Paris: Presses Universitaires de France, 1958), p. 381; C. Wanquet, "Le Café à la Réunion, une 'civilisation' disparue," in Wanquet, ed., *Fragments pour une histoire*, p. 57. The pound was the French livre, slightly different in weight from the English pound.

[3] Quoted in Lougnon, *L'Ile Bourbon*, p. 116; see also Buet, *Madagascar*, pp. 328, 331.

[4] Mazet, "L'Ile Bourbon," p. 28.

[5] F. Ciolina, "Café," in Marcel de Coppet, ed., *Madagascar* (Paris: Encyclopédie de l'Empire Français, 1947), vol. 1, p. 299; Robequain, *Madagascar*, p. 381.

[6] Mazet, "L'Ile Bourbon," pp. 28–9; Wanquet, "Le Café," p. 57.

techniques, notably in drying and packaging.[7] In reaction to a halving of the purchase price per pound of coffee paid by the monopolistic company between 1730 and 1744, some planters defied the monopoly and sold beans clandestinely. In 1725, the entire harvest, some 40,000 pounds, was sold to interlopers, an indication that total sales were considerably higher than official exports to France, registered at 3,400 pounds in 1724. The volume of exports to France rose rapidly thereafter, to 23,800 pounds in 1726, 120,000 in 1727, 500,000 in 1735, and 2,500,000 in 1745.[8]

Coffee production was labor-intensive, and thus intimately linked to slave imports. It was estimated that each coffee planter required a minimum of twelve slaves, and large planters had over twenty. By 1735, when some 80 percent of the total population of 10,000 were slaves, large producers held 68 percent of all concessions under coffee and produced 83 percent of all officially declared coffee. However, the monoculture of coffee was characteristic of smaller farms. Although the six largest planters owned 17 percent of plantations slaves and produced 47 percent of all coffee, they mixed coffee with food crops and livestock.[9]

From around 1740 until the 1790s, Réunion's share of world coffee exports fell steadily, despite a surge in production following the end of the company monopoly in 1769. By 1787, the island was exporting between 2,000 and 3,000 tons of coffee a year, compared with 38,000 tons from St. Domingue (Haiti).[10] Nevertheless, coffee so dominated Réunion's exports that it formed virtually the only cash economy, and became an important medium of exchange in its own right. During the revolutionary era from 1793, paper notes in circulation became so devalued that coffee became the standard money. There was also considerable local opposition to the change in the island's name from Bourbon to Réunion, lest it damage the image of the island's coffee, notably, on the important new North American market.[11]

There were several reasons for this relative decline. Wanquet argues that government insistence from 1789 that Réunion planters should also cultivate food crops undermined international competitiveness, as other producers opted for coffee monoculture. The government did this to

[7] Mazet, "L'Ile Bourbon," pp. 30–31.
[8] Ciolina, "Café," p. 299; Lougnon, *L'Ile Bourbon*, pp. 329, 340–2; Wanquet, "Le Café," pp. 57, 61.
[9] Mazet, "L'Ile Bourbon en 1735," pp. 32–3, 47.
[10] Wanquet, "Le Café," pp. 61–2.
[11] Robequain, *Madagascar*, p. 381; René Coste, *Les Caféiers et les cafés dans le monde*, vol. 1: *Les Caféiers* (Paris: Editions Larose, 1955), p. 1; Wanquet, "Le Café," pp. 57, 59–60.

provision neighboring Ile de France (Mauritius), where passing ships mainly called.[12] Poor production techniques reduced soil fertility and coffee yields, which between around 1730 and 1775 in the St. Paul district fell from 1.5 or 2 pounds per tree to between 0.33 and 0.5. The drying of beans was also often inadequate. Observers associated such faults with the size of plantations, which, due to the tradition of equal inheritance, tended to fragment as the eighteenth century progressed, placing coffee production increasingly in the hands of small planters. Whereas in 1732 the average coffee plantation covered 200 hectares, by 1775, only 2.5 percent of plantations exceeded 100 hectares.[13] Réunion also lay in the path of cyclones, which created famine conditions in 1730–32 and 1734. Storm damage particularly affected small planters, because of the long five- to six-year gestation period for coffee.[14] Cyclones also worsened a poor internal transport network, which accounted for as much as 10 percent of the price of coffee in the ports of St. Denis and St. Paul.[15]

The traditional explanation for the accelerated decline of Réunion coffee in the nineteenth century is that a devastating cyclone in 1806 led planters to diversify into tobacco, cotton, spices, and especially sugar.[16] However, coffee production in 1817 was some 3,000 to 3,500 tons, close to the peak figures of the first years of the nineteenth century. Production fell precipitously only from the 1820s, to 928 tons in 1836, 665 tons in 1845, and 368 tons in 1865. Other explanations have thus been advanced, in particular, the limited size of coffee plantations, which now comprised mainly two- to three-hectare plots worked by family members. In contrast, 58 percent of sugar plantations were over 100 hectares in size by 1848. The more capital-intensive nature of sugar, which was also more cyclone-resistant, ensured the dominance of the latter. Thus, even when the rise in the world price of coffee revived interest on Réunion in the 1870s and 1880s, the structure of land holding limited the expansion of coffee.[17] However, coffee was still the second cash crop behind sugar in 1883.[18]

Hemileia vastatrix, introduced from Ceylon in 1878, proved the death blow. The fungus ravaged Réunion Mocha, notably from 1880–82

[12] Wanquet, "Le Café," p. 62.
[13] Mazet, "L'Ile Bourbon," p. 30; Wanquet, "Le Café," pp. 58, 63, 65.
[14] Mazet, "L'Ile Bourbon," pp. 35–6; Wanquet, "Le Café," p. 65.
[15] Wanquet, "Le Café," pp. 63–4.
[16] Robequain, *Madagascar*, p. 381; Louis Cros, *Madagascar pour tous* (Paris: Albin Michel, [1922]), p. 104.
[17] Wanquet, "Le Café," pp. 58, 67.
[18] Buet, *Madagascar*, p. 326.

onward. Exports fell from an annual average of 407 tons in the period 1871–80 to 379 tons in 1881–90, 103 tons in 1891–1900, and 47 tons in 1901–7.[19] Some wealthier planters experimented with *liberica*, a West African variety introduced from the Buitenzorg Botanical Gardens in Java, but it took four years to produce a reasonable harvest, and quality was poor.[20]

Réunion coffee for a time retained a niche on the French market. By the 1920s, indigenous varieties were again favored, and it was reported: "Bourbon coffee, grown on the island of Réunion, commands a high price in the French market, where practically all exports go. It is a small, flinty bean, and gives a rich cup and fragrance."[21] Later, seedlings from experimental agricultural stations in Madagascar were tried on Réunion, but even local demand had to be supplemented by Malagasy imports.[22] Meanwhile, the rise of new producers within the French empire, in New Caledonia, Indo-China, and especially in Madagascar in the 1930s reduced the market in France for Réunion coffee. Cultivation thus fell to insignificant levels after 1945.[23]

Madagascar under the Hegemony of the Merina Empire

Many poor planters abandoned Réunion in the nineteenth century, and carried the coffee frontier to regions where cheap land and labor were available. The abolition of slavery on Réunion in 1848 provoked a particularly severe crisis. The 60,161 liberated slaves rejected plantation work, while contract labor from Africa and India proved unsatisfactory, as did Vietnamese prisoners of war.[24] Réunion planters first went to the Comoro Islands and Nosy Be, French colonies from the mid-nineteenth century. However, coffee did not prosper on the Comoros, where planters largely switched to perfume plants, sisal, and vanilla after 1900.[25] Coffee did better on the small island of Nosy Be, just off the northwestern coast of

---

[19] Wanquet, "Le Café," p. 68.
[20] B. B. Keable, *Coffee from Grower to Consumer* (London: Isaac Pitman, [1924/25]), p. 13; see also A. de Faymoreau d'Arquistade, "Les Grandes cultures à Madagascar," in E. Caustier et al., eds., *Ce qu'il faut connaître de Madagascar* (Paris: Paul Ollendorf, [1893/94?]), p. 65.
[21] William H. Ukers, *Coffee Merchandising* (New York: Tea and Coffee Trade Journal Co., 1930), p. 98; Cros, *Madagascar*, p. 103; Wanquet, "Le Café," p. 68.
[22] Robequain, *Madagascar*, pp. 337, 38, 386, 389.
[23] Wanquet, "Le Café," p. 68.
[24] Buet, *Madagascar*, pp. 343–4, 347–9, 351.
[25] *La Revue de Madagascar* 6 (1934): 128, 131.

Madagascar, but remained limited to 300 kilos in 1857 and 15,000 kilos in the late 1870s.[26]

Réunion Creoles thus concentrated their efforts on Madagascar.[27] Coffee emerged as a significant crop from the mid-1820s, after the adoption of economic autarky by Merina rulers, who subsequently monopolized all major exports. The Merina court formed an association for plantations on the East Coast with the Réunion firm of de Rontaunay.[28] The Crown provided land and labor, the latter consisting of war captives from the southeast of the island, supplemented by *fanompoana*, forced and unremunerated labor imposed upon local people. De Rontaunay provided the necessary machinery and "European skills." The produce was split between the two parties.[29] In 1825, de Rontaunay contracted to plant 150,000 trees, and in 1840 another Réunion planter signed an eight-year contract for a coffee plantation. Both were in the Mananjary region.[30] By mid-century, de Rontaunay was annually exporting some 500 kilos of Malagasy Mocha from the East Coast.[31] He also introduced coffee to the plateau interior in the 1840s.[32]

The liberalization of foreign trade from 1862, combined with a rise in the price of tropical products, led to a rush of foreigners to the East Coast

[26] Alfred and Guillaume Grandidier, *Histoire de Madagascar* (Tananarive: Hachette, 1928), series 4, vol. 1, p. 580; Cros, *Madagascar*, p. 104; Robequain, *Madagascar*, pp. 365, 367.

[27] M. Fridmann and J. Vianney-Liaud, "Les Caféiers sylvestres de Madagascar," *Café, Cacao, Thé* 10, no. 3 (1966): 207.

[28] Grandidier, *Histoire*, series 4, vol. 5, pp. 70, 228; J. H. Galloway, *The Sugar Cane Industry: An Historical Geography from Its Origins to 1914* (Cambridge: Cambridge University Press, 1989), p. 131.

[29] Archives Historiques de la Vice-Province de la Société de Jésus de Madagascar (henceforth AHVP), Carton dossier 11e, Tentor de Ravis, "Projet de système de conquête, colonisation et civilisation de l'Île de Madagascar," St. Denis, Aug. 15, 1852; Charles Robequain, "Une capitale montagnarde en pays tropical: Tananarive," *Revue de géographie alpine* 37 (1949): 288; Grandidier, *Histoire*, series 4, vol. 5, pp. 70, 228.

[30] Manassé Esoavelomandroso, *La Province maritime orientale du "Royaume de Madagascar" à la fin du XIXe siècle (1882–1895)* (Antananarivo: n.p., 1979), p. 87; Simon Ayache, *Raombana l'historien (1809–1855)* (Fianarantsoa: Librarie Ambozontany, 1976), pp. 321, 323; Public Record Office, Colonial Office (henceforth PRO, CO), 167/78 pt. II, Hastie, "Diary," April 2, 1825; Grandidier, *Histoire*, series 4, vol. 5, p. 171; Gwyn Campbell, "The Role of the London Missionary Society in the Rise of the Merina Empire 1810–1861," Ph.D. thesis, University of Wales, 1985, p. 296.

[31] Chapelier, "Lettres adressées au citoyen préfet de l'Ile de France, de décembre 1803 à mai 1805," *Bulletin de l'Académie Malgache* 4 (1905–6): 3, 16–18, 20, 23; Grandidier, *Histoire*, series 4, vol. 5, pp. 105, 314–5; Cros, *Madagascar*, p. 106.

[32] Robequain, *Madagascar*, p. 217.

of Madagascar, to produce coffee, tobacco, and sugar.[33] It was claimed in 1883 that "coffee grows marvellously there."[34] Production was dominated by Creoles, but trade was in the hands of substantial Western firms, exporting to Mauritius, Britain, and the United States.[35]

However, the Merina court's continued monopoly over land and labor was an obstacle to further growth. Treaties in 1865 and 1868 acknowledged the principle of freehold ownership for foreign nationals, but omitted details as to procedure. In subsequent treaties, the traditional policy of inalienability of land was reasserted. Creoles bypassed these restrictions by forming liaisons with local women, in whose names they purchased houses, land, and slaves. As was noted in 1884, "Frenchmen could not do business in Madagascar without living with native women."[36] Nevertheless, few planters were thereby able to procure sufficient labor, and Merina manipulation of *fanompoana* created insecurity among Creoles:

> Though it is the ostensible policy of the Malagasy Government to conciliate and facilitate the foreigners on the island, much capital will not be invested, until clause 21d of Am treaty will have been repealed, or coolies be brought here, inasmuch as the Queen reserves to herself the right thereby to withdraw at any time labourers engaged without due notice, endangering thereby the Capital invested by the withdrawal of the requisite labour.[37]

In addition, slave and *fanompoana* workers constantly fled the plantations, and had to be supplemented by migrant wage labor, chiefly from the more densely populated regions of the southeast.[38]

---

[33] National Archives of the United States, Washington D.C., United States Consul to Madagascar (henceforth NAUS), Finkelmeier to Secretary of the U.S. Treasury, Tamatave, Jan. 5, 1870; idem to Davis, Oct. 5, 1870; 7th Annual Report on Commercial Relations with Madagascar, Oct. 1872; 8th Annual Report, Oct. 24, 1873; Finkelmeier to Hunter, Dec. 30, 1874; Robinson to Hunter, Oct. 1, 1877.

[34] Buet, *Madagascar*, p. 214; see also G. Foucart, "L'Etat du Commerce à Madagascar," in Caustier et al., eds., *Ce qu'il faut connaître*, p. 87.

[35] Essex Institute, Salem, Ropes Emmerton and Co., Correspondence, Madagascar and Zanzibar Letter Book (henceforth EI), Ropes Emmerton and Co. to Whitney, Salem, Sept. 14 and Nov. 30, 1883; Dawson to Ropes, Emmerton and Co., and Arnold, Hines and Co., Tamatave, Sept. 24, 1885.

[36] *Madagascar Times*, 2, no. 9 (March 5, 1884): 71; see also vol. 2, no. 15, April 16, 1884, p. 133.

[37] NAUS, Finkelmeier to Hunter, Tamatave, Dec. 30, 1874.

[38] Ayache, *Raombana*, p. 323; William Ellis, *History of Madagascar* (London: Fisher, Son, 1838), vol. 1, p. 337, and vol. 2, pp. 521–2; Hubert Deschamps, *Histoire de Madagascar* (Paris: Berger-Levrault, 1972), pp. 191–2; G. S. Chapus, *Quatre-vingts années d'influences européennes en Imerina, 1815–189* (Tananarive: Bulletin de l'Académie Malgache, 1925), p. 33; Samuel Pasfield Oliver, *Madagascar, an Historical and Descriptive Account of the Island and Its Former Dependencies* (London: Macmillan, 1886), vol. 2, p. 810; Gwyn Campbell,

Moreover, *Hemileia* had by 1881 virtually wiped out coffee plantations on land below 270 meters. Coffee exports from Toamasina, which
rose in value from $15,000 in 1877–78 to $63,765 in 1879–80, declined precipitously thereafter. In 1896, only $499 worth of coffee was
exported from the entire island.[39] The fungus, combined with the ravages of a borer, similarly decimated coffee in Nosy Be.[40] Although coffee
grown above 270 meters escaped *Hemileia*, deliberate neglect of the transport network by the Merina court resulted in excessive transport costs.
In the 1890s, it cost 12.5 francs per porter load of 40–50 kg for the
320-kilometer trip from Antananarivo to Toamasina, and 17.5 francs for
the return trip.[41] This meant that domestic Malagasy freight rates were
higher than those for steam ships from Toamasina to Marseilles.[42] In
1884, only 60,000 pounds of coffee, a mere 0.05 percent of the value
of exports, were shipped from Imerina.[43] The 1883–85 Franco-Merina
conflict completed the woes of Creole planters, whose appeals for French
conquest grew increasingly strident.[44]

In contrast, indigenous coffee production expanded. The steady decline
of Merina imperial control from the 1880s enabled individual Malagasy to
establish little groves on swidden slopes on the East Coast and in defensive
ditches surrounding villages on the plateau. They largely escaped *Hemileia*,
because of their isolated and scattered nature and because of altitude in the

"Toamasina (Tamatave) and the Growth of Foreign Trade in Imperial Madagascar, 1862–
1895," in G. Liesegang et al., eds., *Figuring African Trade* (Berlin: Dietrich Reimer Verlag,
1986), p. 534.

[39] Jean Thorel, *La Mise en valeur des richesses économiques de Madagascar* (Paris: Les Presses
Modernes, 1927), pp. 17–18; see also NAUS, Robinson to Payson, Aug. 7, 1880; idem
to Third Assistant Secretary of State, July 3, 1885; Campbell to Porter, Oct. 6, 1888;
idem to Wharton, Dec. 23, 1889; Wetter to Uhl, Oct. 8, 1894; Oliver, *Madagascar,* vol. 2,
pp. 200–3; William Woodruff, *The Rise of the British Rubber Industry during the Nineteenth
Century* (Liverpool: University of Liverpool Press, 1958), pp. 39–40, 63–7.

[40] Cros, *Madagascar,* p. 104.

[41] Foucart, "L'Etat du Commerce," pp. 74, 78–9.

[42] Ciolina, "Café," p. 302.

[43] Campbell, "Toamasina," p. 552.

[44] Noel Deerr, *The History of Sugar* (London: Chapman and Hall, 1949), vol. 1, pp. 21,
28, 241–2; AHVP, vol. 2, p. 1, Lacombe, "Histoire de la mission de Tamatave";
G. S. Chapus and G. Mondain, *Rainilaiarivony: Un homme d'état malgache* (Paris: Editions
de l'Outremer, 1953), pp. 237–8; Manassé Esoavelomandroso, *Problèmes de police et de
justice dans le gouvernement de Tamatave à lépoque de Rainandriamapandry, 1882–1895*
(Antananarivo: Université de Madagascar, 1975), pp. 29, 42–3, 45–6; NAUS, Robinson
to Hunter, Oct. 1, 1877; Robinson to Hankey, Oct. 29, 1879; Finkelmeier to Payson,
May 20, 1880; Robinson to Payson, Oct. 2, 1880; idem to Third Assistant Secretary of
State, Feb. 13, 1882; *Le Courrier de Madagascar* 34, Aug. 23, 1892; *Madagascar Times,*
vol. 2, no. 13, April 2, 1884, p. 115, and vol. 2, no. 24, June 18, 1884, p. 229.

interior. They also survived the vicissitudes of the 1883–85 conflict due to low overheads, reliance on family labor, and the cultivation of subsistence crops alongside coffee.[45] In sharp contrast to Creole plantations, it was noted of indigenous coffee cultivation in the early 1890s:

> The small indigenous plantations in the neighbourhood of some villages on the Tamatave to Tananarive route regularly yield good harvests due to the care taken of them and to the manure they receive.[46]

The ability to sell coffee enabled Malagasy producers, as in Angola, to avoid contract labor on foreign-owned plantations, thus accentuating labor problems on the latter.[47] It also enabled them to pay imperial Merina taxes and meet other financial commitments, thus avoiding the indebtedness that plagued most Malagasy cultivators, many of whom found themselves obliged to mortgage their crop before it had even been sown.[48]

Colonial Protectionism and New Varieties of Coffee, 1896–1947

The French conquest of the island at the end of the nineteenth century created disruption for a time, but then led to a resurgence of European coffee plantations. Coffee exports fell from 117 kg in 1901 to 6 kg in 1904, and 12,506 kg of coffee were even imported in the latter year. Exports then increased steadily to 110 tons in 1910, 1,435 tons in 1919, 2,327 tons in 1923, and 3,359 tons in 1925.[49] This reflected producer optimism following the restoration of security, and the preference given to colonial produce in France. Duties on coffee were traditionally higher in France and Germany than in Britain.[50] However, from January 1892, French import duties were halved on colonial coffees, which thus enjoyed an advantage over "foreign" produce of 0.78 francs per kg.[51] In August 1913, imports from the colonies were declared duty free.[52]

---

[45] *Madagascar Times*, vol. 2, no. 13, April 2, 1884, p. 115.

[46] Foucart, "L'Etat du Commerce," p. 87.

[47] David Birmingham, "A Question of Coffee: Black Enterprise in Angola," in Catherine Coquery-Vidrovitch, ed., *Entreprises et entrepreneurs en Afrique XIXe et Xxe siècles* (Paris: l'Harmattan, 1983), vol. 1, p. 124.

[48] Oliver, *Madagascar*, vol. 2, p. 196.

[49] Robequain, *Madagascar*, pp. 217, 332; E. Leplae, *Les Plantations de café au Congo Belge* (Bruxelles: Falk Fils, 1936), p. 22; Ciolina, "Café," p. 307; Cros, *Madagascar*, p. 106; Thorel, *La Mise en valeur*, pp. 17–18; *La Revue de Madagascar* 2 (April 1933): 125, and 3 (July 1933): 12.

[50] Keable, *Coffee*, p. 70.

[51] D'Arquistade, "Les Grandes culture," p. 65.

[52] Cros, *Madagascar*, p. 106.

In consequence, France absorbed the quasitotality of Malagasy coffee exports until the Second World War, with small quantities shipped to Réunion.[53] From 1919, France constituted the world's second largest coffee market after the United States.[54] Le Havre in 1924 took 37 percent of European coffee imports, and its coffee exchange, alongside those of New York and Hamburg, largely determined the world price of green coffee.[55]

The cultivation of *arabica* in regions above 600 meters remained quite limited. Lower humidity than on the coast helped to combat *Hemileia*, but lack of water during a six-month dry season was often a problem. *Arabica* was thus restricted to "a few rare locations well sheltered from cold winds and particularly blessed with good soil."[56] In 1917, production of *arabica* was estimated at a mere 35 tons.[57] Plateau production was initially restricted to the region around Antananarivo, and thus became known as "Emyrne [Imerina] coffee."[58] Cultivation expanded from the mid-1920s, as the high price compensated for the cost of labor and transport.[59] The colonial administration also promoted *arabica*, in the belief that it could increase the quality and price of other varieties by mixing prior to export.[60] As a result, Malagasy producers established an *arabica* frontier in the Ankaizina region, at 800–900 meters altitude to the north of Mahajanga.[61]

In coastal regions, there was a search for *Hemileia*-resistant varieties. Indigenous coffees, despite their bitter taste and low caffeine content, had by the early 1920s acquired a small market in France, where they were collectively classified alongside other colonial "wild coffees" as Nunez.[62] However, the main impulse was toward alternatives from Africa. This process started in the 1880s with the cultivation of *liberica*, which produced

---

[53] Ciolina, "Café," p. 307.

[54] Keable, *Coffee*, pp. 68, 70; Ukers, *Coffee*, pp. 200–1; Cros, *Madagascar*, p. 106.

[55] Ukers, *Coffee*, p. 77; Keable, *Coffee*, p. 75.

[56] Ciolina, "Café," p. 300.

[57] Ciolina, "Café," p. 299; see also Thorel, *La Mise en valeur*, p. 17. A ton is 1,000 kilos.

[58] André Prunières, *Madagascar et la crise* (Paris: Nouvelles Editions Latines, 1934), p. 100; Ciolina, "Café," p. 299.

[59] Thorel, *La Mise en valeur*, pp. 18–19.

[60] M. Choix, "Le Café," *La Revue de Madagascar* 3 (July 1933): 27–8; Agence Économique du Gouvernement Général de Madagascar et dépendances, *Madagascar à l'Exposition Internationale et Universelle de Bruxelles* (Paris, 1935).

[61] F. Ciolina, "Hydraulique Agricole," in Coppet, ed., *Madagascar*, p. 370.

[62] Cros, *Madagascar*, p. 104; Keable, *Coffee*, p. 100; J. F. Leroy and A Plu, "Sur les nombres Chromosomiques des Coffea malgaches," *Café cacao thé* 10, no. 3 (1966): 217.

TABLE 3.1. *Madagascar: Coffee Prices and Exports, 1926–33 (average price per 50 kg CAF Marseille)*

Year	Price: Kwilu	Price: Liberica	Exports (t)	Value (Francs)
1926	738	708	2,774	27,747,000
1927	513	560	5,032	36,500,000
1928	568	545	4,032	32,930,000
1929	541	437	3,555	24,473,000
1930	334	258	6,670	33,347,000
1931	285	214	11,301	70,000,000
1932	323	236	11,544	84,640,000
1933	319	266	15,236	96,000,000

Source: André Prunières, *Madagascar et la crise* (Paris: Nouvelles Editions Latines, 1934), pp. 86, 100.

an average of 0.5 kg of coffee per tree.[63] However, these plantations suffered from political disturbances, and *liberica* proved hard to market:[64]

it yields considerable harvests, but its irregularly sized bean, its much disputed aroma and its overall lack of appeal render it quite difficult to place on the world market and the planter too often finds difficulty in selling, at a remunerative price, a harvest which cost him years of care and trouble.[65]

Experiments with different types of *robusta* from 1901 were slightly more successful.[66] Types of *robusta* dominated on the East Coast and in the northwest by the 1930s.[67] *Robusta* was valued in France for its strong flavor, and *arabica* for its fine taste, although such small quantities of the latter were exported that it was difficult to judge.[68]

Production responded to artificially increased prices. Brazilian measures to shore up the world coffee price provided Madagascar with a position as a "free rider."[69] However, during the 1930s depression, it was French colonial protectionism that played the major role (see Tables 3.1 and 3.2). In addition, a system of colonial subsidies for coffee producers stabilized coffee prices.

---

[63] Foucart, "L'Etat du Commerce," p. 87; Ciolina, "Café," p. 299.

[64] Foucart, "L'Etat du Commerce," p. 87; Thorel, *La Mise en valeur*, p. 17.

[65] Choix, "Le Café," p. 13.

[66] Leplae, *Les Plantations*, p. 17; Ciolina, "Café," p. 299; Choix, "Le Café," p. 16; Jean Fremigacci, "Les Difficultés d'une politique coloniale: Le Café de Madagascar à la conquête du marché français (1930–1938)," in *Omaly sy Anio* 21–22 (1985): 280.

[67] Thorel, *La Mise en valeur*, p. 17; Agence, *Madagascar*; Robequain, *Madagascar*, pp. 218, 226.

[68] Ciolina, "Café," pp. 307–8; Cros, *Madagascar*, p. 107; Agence, *Madagascar*.

[69] V. D. Wickizer, *Coffee, Tea and Cocoa: An Economic and Political Analysis* (Stanford: Stanford University Press, 1951), pp. 27–8.

TABLE 3.2. *Madagascar: Coffee Production and Exports, 1910–82 (metric tons)*

Year	Production	Exports
1910	n.a	10
1915	n.a	442
1919	n.a	1435
1920	n.a	1221
1921	n.a	1226
1922	n.a	1500
1923	n.a	2327
1924	n.a	2962
1925	n.a	3359
1926	n.a	2774
1927	n.a	5032
1928	n.a	4030
1929	n.a	3022
1930	n.a	6671
1931	n.a	11,354
1932	n.a	13,581
1933	n.a	15,253
1934	n.a	14,336
1935	n.a	15,531
1936	n.a	25,000
1937	n.a	21,205
1938	n.a	41,204
1939	n.a.	30,921
1940	n.a.	20,162
1941	22,320	22,352
1942	140	1,139
1943	12,360	12,369
1944	23,500	45,339
1945	n.a.	26,912
1946	n.a.	22,332
1947	n.a.	29,033
1948	n.a.	19,944
1949	n.a.	25,625
1950	31,500	41,559
1951	29,000	30,521
1952	41,300	41,311
1953	44,700	36,233
1954	44,000	41,486
1955	55,000	47,737
1956	53,040	52,486
1957	49,000	48,207
1958/59	53,700	43,999

TABLE 3.2. *(continued)*

Year	Production	Exports
1959/60	40,900	40,600
1960/61	55,000	43,620
1961/62	55,000	41,900
1962/63	69,600	48,700
1963/64	59,270	47,400
1964/65	74,000	47,800
1965/66	53,300	46,400
1966/67	62,300	43,200
1967/68	82,300	54,100
1968/69	74,700	45,300
1969/70	57,500	49,500
1970/71	90,400	53,200
1971/72	65,700	57,300
1972/73	75,500	57,400
1973/74	84,000	69,200
1974/75	83,100	59,200
1975/76	80,200	70,500
1976/77	65,300	51,300
1977/78	85,500	65,157
1978/79	81,840	63,057
1979/80	84,980	69,470
1980/81	83,880	64,688
1981/82	77,814	58,514

Sources: F. Ciolina, "Café," in Marcel de Coppet, ed., *Madagascar* (Paris: Encyclopédie de l'Empire Français, 1947), vol. 1, p. 306; Lucille Rabearimanana, "La Politique économique coloniale sur la côte est (Madagascar) dans les années 1950," in *Omaly sy Anio* 21–22 (1985): 312, 322–3; Louis Cros, *Madagascar pour tous* (Paris: Albin Michel, [1922]), p. 104; Alphonse Ramilison, "La Production Caféière à Madagascar," in *Omaly sy Anio* 21–22 (1985): 343–4; *Café cacao thé* 1, no. 3 (1957): 159; *Revue de Madagascar* 2 (April 1933): 125, and 3 (July 1933): 9; Louis Chevalier, *Madagascar, populations et ressources* (Paris: Presses Universitaires de France, 1952), pp. 206–7.

Colonial protectionism was even credited with effectively creating the Malagasy coffee sector in the period 1930–38 (see Table 3.3).[70] This was in the context of a collapse in vanilla production and graphite

[70] *Entreprises et produits de Madagascar* 4 (July–Sept. 1950): 125.

TABLE 3.3. *Madagascar: Coffee Exports, 1930–43 (thousands of 60 kilo bags and percentages)*

Year	Exports	% African exports	% world exports	Year	Exports	% African exports	% world exports
1930–34[a]	203	15.21	0.79	1944	756	26.00	2.92
1935–39[a]	455	20.21	1.64	1945	448	13.47	1.64
1940	336	16.39	1.44	1946	372	10.03	1.27
1941	372	15.49	1.76	1947	488	12.39	1.71
1942	19	0.92	0.11	1948	332	7.41	1.03
1943	206	7.89	0.91	1949	427	9.85	1.23

[a] Five-year average.

Source: V. D. Wickizer, *Coffee, Tea and Cocoa: An Economic and Political Analysis* (Stanford: Stanford University Press, 1951), p. 475.

mining.[71] Coffee replaced vanilla as the main cash crop, exports rising dramatically from 3,500 tons in 1929 to 15,236 tons in 1933.[72] By 1938, it accounted for 32 percent of total exports.[73] In 1930, Madagascar was not even listed amongst the leading coffee producers of East Africa, Ukers commenting, "Madagascar produces an insignificant quantity for export, although the coffee is considered fair average, with rich flavor, and considerable fragrance."[74] However, by 1933, Madagascar was the largest coffee producer in the French empire, and there were hopes that it might become a leading world producer.[75] In 1947–48, Madagascar possessed 115,000 hectares of coffee plantation, producing 20,000 tons of beans. This still represented only 1.3 percent of world production, but 42 percent of that of French Africa.[76]

There initially existed a limited local and regional market for Malagasy coffee. Local consumption and stockpiling accounted for 19 percent of coffee output in 1932.[77] In 1933, an attempt was made to stimulate trade with South Africa, the second consumer of coffee in Africa after Algeria, and Madagascar's closest significant coffee market, but this was

[71] Prunières, *Madagascar*, p. 98; Choix, "Le Café," p. 17.
[72] Prunières, *Madagascar*, p. 100; Cros, *Madagascar*, p. 106; Thorel, *La Mise en valeur*, pp. 15, 17–18.
[73] Charles Robequain, *Madagascar et le bases dispersées de l'union française* (Paris: Presses Universitaires de France, 1958), p. 332.
[74] Ukers, *Coffee*, pp. 33, 35, 98.
[75] *La Revue de Madagascar* 3 (July 1933): 9.
[76] *La Revue du Café* 3 (Dec. 1947): 8; Ciolina, "Café," p. 307.
[77] *La Revue de Madagascar* 2 (April 1933): 125.

not backed by a customs agreement nor by the establishment of a regular shipping link.[78]

Scale of Cultivation, 1896–1947

Because of the considerable gestation period between planting and first harvest, coffee cultivation might appear best suited to those with substantial capital.[79] However, the soil most favorable to coffee in Madagascar was in dispersed patches, mostly too limited for the creation of large plantations.[80] By 1912, only eight large territorial concessions were held by French companies, six of which were still operational in 1931, totaling 550,000 hectares. Large concerns in Madagascar generally survived by diversifying from commerce to plantation production, and vice versa. Within agriculture, they adopted other cash crops, such as cocoa, pepper, perfume plants, cinnamon, cloves, and vanilla.[81] Large plantations were limited to areas of volcanic soil, alluvial soils protected from flooding, and laterite soils enriched by artificial fertilizers. They were rare on the East Coast, being mainly confined to the Mananjary and Manakara areas, which enjoyed good transport facilities.[82] In contrast, coffee in the northwest was dominated by large European concerns. These included Lucien Millot, established in 1904, which by 1951 possessed six concessions with seven coffee and cocoa processing factories, 1,300 Malagasy and fifteen European workers, and a steamship and port to ship produce to Nosy Be.[83]

Ciolina claimed that European plantations generally produced 50 percent more than those of Malagasy smallholders, with an average of 375 kilos of *robusta* per hectare and 600 kilos of *liberica*. This was attributed to larger properties, richer soil, and better techniques, notably, better shade and denser planting.[84] Large European plantations on the eve of the 1947 rebellion produced an average of 20–30 tons of beans a year, although some reached 100 tons.[85]

[78] Keable, *Coffee*, pp. 68, 70; Prunières, *Madagascar*, pp. 97–8; Ukers, *Coffee*, p. 198; *Café Cacao Thé* 5, no. 2 (1961): 132.
[79] Choix, "Le Café," p. 25.
[80] Ciolina, "Café," p. 302.
[81] Robequain, *Madagascar*, pp. 211–12, 225.
[82] Ciolina, "Café," pp. 300–2.
[83] *Entreprises et produits de Madagascar* 7–8 (April–Sept. 1951): 103–4.
[84] Ciolina, "Café," p. 304.
[85] Ibid., p. 306.

Gallieni envisaged the formation of a "Franco-Malagasy" race, but potential settlers from France were deterred by malaria and the generally infertile soils of Madagascar, so that most settlers were impoverished Mascarene Creoles. They established coffee plantations of less than 50 hectares, producing 6 to 15 tons of beans annually, along East Coast valleys, where rivers and canals offered ease of transport.[86] From 1925 the completion of a road link attracted Europeans to the Itasy region where they tried *arabica*, but transport and labor costs, *Hemileia*, and indigenous competition caused most of them to abandon coffee.[87]

After the 1895–97 Menalamba revolt, *arabica* was cultivated almost entirely by Malagasy in the high plateau interior and on coastal hills.[88] In contrast to Angola, indigenous operations were essentially small-scale, comprising a few trees tended by family members, although a few families owned several hundred trees.[89] Moreover, unlike most European planters, Malagasy smallholders intercropped subsistence crops, notably manioc and maize, which helped them to survive periods of vicissitude.[90] Lower overhead costs and family labor raised the indigenous share of coffee output from 1944 to 1947, increasing from 68 to 87 percent of the total.[91]

Europeans claimed that Malagasy plots were poorly managed. Trees were planted haphazardly and without shade trees. Whereas Europeans separated different types of coffee, Malagasy on the East Coast indiscriminately mixed Kwilu and other types of *robusta*.[92] On Malagasy plots, the average yield per hectare was 320 kilos of *robusta*, 400 kilos of *liberica*, and 700 to 900 kilos of *arabica*.[93] One typically biased observer wrote:

The indigenous way of farming is in truth very different from that of the European. In the large majority of cases, all work is done by family members – without any capital input. The means of cultivation are rudimentary – without agricultural implements; no processing tool other than the mortar employed to husk the daily rice; it is used to pound the berry, either immediately following the harvest or after having been sun-dried on the ground. These primitive methods are not without their inconveniences for coffee bushes planted without great care and which too frequently are badly maintained, yield poor harvests and can constitute a breeding

---

[86] Ibid., pp. 302, 306.

[87] Ibid., p. 299; Robequain, *Madagascar*, p. 222.

[88] Robequain, *Madagascar*, 136; Ciolina, "Café," p. 300; Agence, *Madagascar*.

[89] Ciolina, "Café," pp. 299, 306; Birmingham, "A Question of Coffee," p. 125.

[90] Keable, *Coffee*, p. 22; Ciolina, "Café," p. 306; Paul Chauffour, "Les Plantes saccharifères," in Coppet, ed., *Madagascar*, p. 331.

[91] Ciolina, "Café," p. 307.

[92] Choix, "Le Café," p. 16; Ciolina, "Café," p. 303.

[93] Ciolina, "Café," p. 304.

ground for diseases. Due to neglecting homogeneity and quality, the indigenous population may in addition be blamed for the devaluation of well prepared produce originating from European property.[94]

High prices for agricultural products in the late 1920s tempted many Malagasy into coffee production, a process reinforced by colonial protection in the 1930s. High monetary taxes were another inducement, especially in times of economic recession.[95] Thus it was commented in 1933:

Only a few years ago, when travelling by palanquin along one of the paths that ascended an east coast river valley, you crossed through a continuous belt of thick bush, broken here and there at lengthy intervals by beautiful settler plantations and by pitiful patches of subsistence crops which surrounded indigenous villages. Today you travel for hours through coffee plantations which occupy much land. Those of the settler and the Malagasy alternate, the one next to the other, almost without interruption. Everywhere that coffee can be grown – whether on alluvial and marshy soil, or in drained river channels – all potentially useful land has been brought into production or soon will be.[96]

Credit and Cooperatives, 1896–1947

Indigenous producers sold unprocessed or semiprocessed beans directly to Creole planters or Chinese shopkeepers, who also provided credit. The first Chinese immigrant to Madagascar probably arrived from Canton in 1862 and set up shop in Toamasina. The Chinese presence in Madagascar remained limited until further immigration occurred in 1891 after which they quickly established a network of retail stores along the East Coast and in Antananarivo. In 1900 they numbered 404, all traders. Further immigrant waves, following political troubles in China, boosted the Cantonese community in Madagascar.[97] They intermarried with local Malagasy and established large extended families, with chains of country stores that served as the first collection point for cash crops.[98]

Governor General Cayla, who responded to the 1934 cyclone by lowering interest rates and prolonging repayment periods, claimed that official provision of credit was one of the main factors sustaining the Malagasy

---

[94] Choix, "Le Café," p. 26.
[95] Ibid., p. 20; Prunières, *Madagascar*, p. 103.
[96] Thorel, *La Mise en valeur*, p. 184; Robequain, *Madagascar*, pp. 136, 263.
[97] Grandidier, *Histoire*, series 4, vol. 1, pp. 518, 563; Robequain, *Madagascar*, p. 116; Virginia Thompson and Richard Adloff, *The Malagasy Republic* (Stanford: Stanford University Press, 1965), pp. 272–3; Maureen Covell, *Madagascar, Politics, Economics and Society* (London and New York: Frances Pinter, 1987), p. 84.
[98] Grandidier, *Histoire*, series 4, vol. 1, p. 562.

coffee industry during the Depression.[99] The Agricultural Credit Union (Crédit Agricole?), established in 1930, extended loans of 5 million francs to planters in 1932.[100] Both indigenous and European producers could obtain finance from this source at 3 percent interest. However, the length of the loan to an indigenous farmer could not exceed the duration of the agricultural operation for which it was intended, and the local collective was made responsible for repayment.[101] In 1933, it was commented that "[t]here already exist groups of [Malagasy] cultivators whose purchase in common of necessary equipment will be facilitated by advances from the Agricultural Credit Union."[102] By 1935 there were forty-three branches, linked to twenty-one European and 292 Malagasy associations, comprising over 8,000 members.[103]

At the same time, the cooperative movement took off. The first Malagasy cooperative, organized in 1933, was for the processing and sale of coffee and cloves at Fenoarivo.[104] It was commented: "Elsewhere, cooperation has enabled the purchase of depulpers, the establishment of stations for the preparation, sorting and classing of coffees, of selection, and of sale in common."[105] During the Second World War, cooperatives organized the stockpiling of coffee that could no longer be shipped to France, furnishing credit to producers on the basis of harvests added to stockpiles from previous years. As a result, the movement spread rapidly. By 1945, there were twenty-four Malagasy cooperatives (with 13,373 members) and by 1952, forty, although some were dormant.[106] Bargues, French High Commissioner in Madagascar in 1950, even attacked cooperatives as the chief means by which the Malagasy came to dominate coffee production.[107]

Technical Assistance and Transport, 1896–1947

Indigenous producers, both individually and through collectives, appear to have gained substantially more than Creole planters from technical

[99] Léon Cayla, "Madagascar en 1934," *La Revue de Madagascar* 9 (Jan. 1934): 8–9.
[100] Prunières, *Madagascar*, pp. 84–5.
[101] André Martin, *Les Délégations économiques et financières de Madagascar* (Paris: Les Presses Modernes, 1938), p. 207; Prunières, *Madagascar*, pp. 137–8; Agence, *Madagascar.*
[102] Choix, "Le Café," p. 26.
[103] Agence, *Madagascar*; Martin, *Délégations*, p. 207.
[104] Robequain, *Madagascar*, p. 263.
[105] Agence, *Madagascar.*
[106] Robequain, *Madagascar*, p. 263.
[107] Guinaudleau, "Madagascar," p. 158.

assistance offered by the administration. From 1931, the authorities imposed quality standards. By 1935 they had established six experimental agricultural stations to train Malagasy in coffee cultivation and sale techniques, and from 1945 they inaugurated a project to develop *arabica* in Ankaizina.[108] In 1934, when exports dipped to 14,336 tons due to the effects of two cyclones, the administration distributed 200,000 coffee seedlings to European settlers and indigenous cultivators on Mayotte.[109] European planters processed beans in their own factories, whereas standardization would allegedly have benefited more from large factories in ports.[110]

Transport costs plagued the marketing of Malagasy cash crops. Lack of finance, combined with rough terrain and a harsh climate, raised internal freight rates, while foreign trade suffered due to the distance between Madagascar and sizable foreign markets.[111] However, the larger European coffee plantations in the Mananjary and Manakara regions were relatively well served by rail, road, and water transport.[112] On Nosy Be and in the Sambirano plain of the northwest, there was a good system of riverine or coastal transport. At Nosy Be's harbor, ships did not have to anchor offshore and use lighters.[113] Producers close to the two rail links from the plateau to the coast were also advantaged. Elsewhere, problems were considerable. In 1927, it cost three francs per ton/per kilometer to send freight by porter from Antananarivo to Toamasina.[114] The French government voted a 735 million franc loan to Madagascar in February 1931, aimed initially at improving the transport infrastructure for planters.[115] However, there were only 4,000 kilometers of road practicable throughout the year as late as 1950.[116]

Moreover, Malagasy port labor was scarce, and characterized by low productivity. Maritime traffic was seasonal, there were no deep-sea quays

[108] Ciolina, "Café," p. 307; Ciolina, "Hydraulique Agricole," p. 370; Agence, *Madagascar*; Choix, "Le Café," p. 26.
[109] Prunières, *Madagascar*, p. 103; Agence, *Madagascar*; *La Revue de Madagascar* 6 (April 1934): 140.
[110] Choix, "Le Café," p. 27.
[111] Robequain, *Madagascar*, pp. 216–20; Cros, *Madagasca*, pp. 385, 410; Coppet, *Madagascar*, vol. 2, p. 328; Campbell, "Toamasina," p. 537.
[112] Thorel, *La Mise en valeur*, p. 143.
[113] Ibid., pp. 154, 156; Robequain, *Madagascar*, pp. 223–4, 230; *Entreprises et Produits de Madagascar* 7–8 (April–Sept. 1951): 103.
[114] Thorel, *La Mise en valeur*, pp. 137–9.
[115] Prunières, *Madagascar*, p. 85.
[116] Guinaudleau, "Madagascar," p. 151.

and no secure storage facilities, so that losses through theft were high. In addition, cyclones regularly hit the island. In 1925, 12 million francs were voted to improve Toamasina harbor, but a severe cyclone in March 1927 destroyed the port, causing damage estimated at 200 million francs.[117] The lack of port facilities ensured Madagascar's exclusion from major international shipping lines, a significant factor in the high price of maritime freight.[118]

Labor, 1896–1947

The dominant view was that the lack of labor was the main obstacle to the development of colonial Madagascar.[119] This was blamed in part on demographic factors. Population densities were generally low and stable until World War II, although there were clusters on the fertile East Coast and on the high plateau.[120] Paucity of capital accentuated Creole reliance on cheap Malagasy labor for the planting, transplanting, weeding, and pruning of trees and harvesting, cleaning, sifting, and packing of beans.[121] Males did most work on European plantations, although women and children also participated in harvesting, gathering an average of 40–60 kilos of beans per person per day.[122] Labor was further required to carry beans from indigenous plantations to collection centers, although coffee from European plantations often traveled by cart or canoe.[123] Whereas small Malagasy plantations used family labor, Europeans required a large work force.

After the abolition of slavery in 1896, the labor available to Europeans was insufficient. Most of the estimated 500,000 liberated slaves remained in their former master's homes, often as unpaid servants, thus supplementing the family labor available to wealthier Malagasy producers.[124] The problem was accentuated for European planters in the Vatomandry

---

[117] Thorel, La Mise en valeur, pp. 150, 153.

[118] Guinaudleau, "Madagascar," p. 149.

[119] Martin, Délégations, p. 195; Robequain, Madagascar, p. 114.

[120] Gwyn Campbell, "The State and Precolonial Demographic History: The Case of Nineteenth-Century Madagascar," Journal of African History 32 (1991): 416; Martin, Délégations, pp. 195–6; Thorel, La Mise en valeur, p. 175.

[121] Chauffour, "Les Plantes saccharifères," p. 331; Keable, Coffee, pp. 22–5.

[122] Ciolina, "Café," p. 304.

[123] Keable, Coffee, p. 35; Ciolina, "Café," p. 306.

[124] Sandra Evers, "Stigmatization as a Self-Perpetuating Process," in Sandra Evers and Marc Spindler, eds., Cultures of Madagascar: Ebb and Flow of Influences (Leiden: IIAS, 1995), pp. 157–85.

region by recruitment for graphite mines. Moreover, labor was of poor quality, due to malnutrition, disease, and alcoholism.[125]

Local coerced and tax-induced labor filled the gap, despite attempts to recruit in China, Java, Japan, Sri Lanka, India, and Mozambique. Contracts were signed with a few Indians and thousands of Chinese, but the latter were considered truculent, and both proved prone to malaria. In 1907 the last immigrant workers were repatriated.[126] Governor General Gallieni imposed the first corvée, fifty days a year for males aged sixteen to sixty, in 1896. He justified it on the grounds that a similar system had existed in the precolonial Merina Empire.[127] Also, from 1901 a tax was imposed of fifteen francs for every male over the age of twenty-five, and of seven francs for every woman aged over twenty-one, payable in days of work.[128]

Corvée impacted immediately and negatively on agricultural production. Thorel noted in 1896:

The corvée system removes labor from agricultural work without consideration of the consequences. Production is affected and it is a cause of ruin for the Malagasy and for the entire country.[129]

The Malagasy thus did their utmost to evade corvée. Exemption could be bought or granted upon proof of private employment with a European.[130] However, European planters generally imposed poor working conditions and appallingly low wages. Thorel commented:

Following this, the settlers abused the system. Speculating on the repulsion for forced labor felt by the indigenous population and on their desire to evade it, settlers offered the Malagasy derisory wages for a work contract that would liberate them from the corvée.[131]

---

[125] André You, *Madagascar, colonie française 1896–1930* (Paris: Société d'Editions Géographiques, Maritimes et Coloniales, 1931), p. 455; Martin, *Délégations*, pp. 195–6; Robequain, *Madagascar*, p. 223; Ciolina, "Café," p. 306; Choix, "Le Café," p. 17.

[126] Martin, *Délégations*, p. 196; Thorel, *La Mise en valeur*, pp. 176–8; Robequain, *Madagascar*, p. 215.

[127] You, *Madagascar*, p. 455; Martin, *Délégations*, pp. 196–7; Robequain, *Madagascar*, p. 214; Gwyn Campbell, "Slavery and Fanompoana: The Structure of Forced Labour in Imerina (Madagascar), 1790–1861," *Journal of African History* 29, no. 2 (1988): 463–86.

[128] Thorel, *La Mise en valeur*, pp. 181, 191; You, *Madagascar*, p. 456; Martin, *Délégations*, p. 197.

[129] Thorel, *La Mise en valeur*, p. 179.

[130] You, *Madagascar*, pp. 457–60; Robequain, *Madagascar*, p. 214; Martin, *Délégations*, p. 197

[131] Thorel, *La Mise en valeur*, p. 179.

European planters also gained access to corvée labor designed for public works. The scandal from these abuses led to the abolition of corvée at the end of 1900, but the resulting labor shortage, accentuated by losses among the 50,000 Malagasy soldiers who fought in France during the 1914–18 war, led to the reintroduction of the system. In consequence, the Malagasy tried to avoid both corvée and wage labor for Europeans. As the governor general noted in 1920:

upon my return to the colony, I was surprised and saddened by the spectacle of a general indolence amongst the Malagasy and a certain resentment of the European. I could detect signs of disaffection on the part of the indigenous population.... The Malagasy no longer wishes to work: He no longer works for the European: he distances and isolates himself from us. The abnormal system of labor conscription is responsible for this – a result which should have been anticipated. If the Malagasy is no longer as confident in coming to us ... it is because badly thought out measures have created, or at least accentuated, the labor crisis.[132]

The labor problems of Europeans were worsened in the late 1920s, when high agricultural prices led many Malagasy into independent cash crop production:

Agricultural products have acquired such value that, on the one hand the difference between salaries, and on the other the revenues of agricultural workers, has become disproportionate. In consequence, a large number of Malagasy have abandoned construction sites or firms where they were before employed and have started working independently. The number of available workers has been considerably reduced at a time when employer demand for them has grown as a result of the expansion of agricultural plantations and the creation of new industries.[133]

As Robequain noted: "They find that they can thus gain in both material profit and moral comfort, escaping the monotonous discipline of work imposed upon them."[134]

In coffee regions on the East Coast, independent Malagasy cultivation of coffee and vanilla prospered.[135] Foreign planters thus sought migrant labor on two-year contracts from recruitment agencies or directly from leaders of migrants from south and southeast Madagascar.[136] By the 1930s, an estimated 6,000 Antaimoro a year traveled to the plantations

---

[132] Ibid., pp. 180–2; see also Robequain, *Madagascar*, p. 215.
[133] Thorel, *La Mise en valeur*, p. 184.
[134] Robequain, *Madagascar*, p. 223.
[135] Chauffour, "Les Plantes saccharifères," p. 331.
[136] Ibid., p. 331; Robequain, *Madagascar*, pp. 215, 233.

of the north and northwest, generally on two- to three-year contracts.[137] Attempts were made to persuade them to settle permanently through offers of farmland. This worked in the Sambirano Valley, where by 1950 large European concerns employed a permanent Malagasy work force of 4,600 on plantations where coffee was the major crop.[138] However, it failed on the East Coast, where local Betsimisaraka violently opposed the settlement of immigrants.[139]

In an attempt to create a sufficient and stable work force, the administration announced a decent wage for Malagasy workers in September 1925. This was backed by a centralized Labor Bureau supervising a network of regional centers and supported by inspectors and an arbitration board.[140] However, private planters again abused the system. In June 1926, the administration established the Public Service Labor Force Scheme (SMOTIG), which from 1927 to 1930 imposed forced labor on 20,000 Malagasy "military conscripts."[141] Private planters were granted access to SMOTIG recruits, and the resulting public outcry led to SMOTIG being abolished in 1936.[142] The departure for France between mid-1939 and June 1940 of 34,000 Malagasy soldiers accentuated the labor crisis.[143]

Forced labor grew worse during the war. Under Vichy, from 1940 to 1942, there was a period of autarky, resulting from the British blockade and a hardening of colonial ideology. Large European concerns gained most from forced labor, leading to rising discontent amongst the small settler-planters of the East Coast. Although colonial archives for the East Coast region during this period are still closed to researchers, it would appear that resentment at forced labor reached new heights under the Free French regime of 1943–44.[144]

---

[137] You, *Madagascar*, p. 478.

[138] Robequain, *Madagascar*, p. 231; *Entreprises et produits de Madagascar* 7–8 (April–Sept. 1951): 105.

[139] Chauffour, "Les Plantes sacchariféres," p. 331.

[140] Thorel, *La Mise en valeur*, pp. 182, 184–7; You, *Madagascar*, pp. 461–3, 471; Martin, *Délégations*, pp. 198, 200.

[141] You, *Madagascar*, pp. 469, 472; Martin, *Délégations*, pp. 199–200.

[142] Robequain, *Madagascar*, p. 215.

[143] Mervyn Brown, *A History of Madagascar* (Ipswich: Damien Tunnacliffe, 1995), p. 255.

[144] Eric Jennings, "Forced Labour in Madagascar under Vichy, 1940–1942: Autarky, Travail Forcé, and Resistance on the Red Island," unpublished paper, International Conference on Slavery, Unfree Labour and Revolt in Asia and the Indian Ocean Region, Avignon, October 4–6, 2001.

In April 1946, forced labor was theoretically abolished in the French Union, but in Madagascar each male of working age continued to be obliged to perform 200 days of wage labor a year. This was the result, in part, of pressure from European coffee growers. The administration could not ignore the fact that coffee represented 32 percent by value of Malagasy exports in 1938 and 34 percent in 1944.[145] By 1950, the Malagasy work force was estimated at 1.5 million, 300,000 of whom were salaried. Many avoided corvée by engaging in sharecropping, notably on the vast rice plantations of the west.[146]

Scale of Cultivation, 1947–1972

There would appear to be a clear correlation between the refusal of the French authorities in Madagascar to apply the 1946 labor law and the outbreak of the 1947–49 revolt. The traditional French and Malagasy nationalist interpretation of the revolt, followed by most historians, is that it was a concerted nationalist uprising against colonial rule. However, the main nationalist organizations were dominated by the Merina intelligentsia, and were strongest in the capital, Antananarivo, and among student groups in France.[147] In contrast, the revolt occurred in the coffee-growing regions of eastern Madagascar among the predominantly rural and uneducated Betsimisaraka. Like other Malagasy peoples subject to Merina rule in the nineteenth century, they harbored an intense enmity for the Merina.[148]

At the same time, the Betsimisaraka were the people most exploited for forced labor by the French, including small settler-planters intent on undermining more efficient coffee smallholders. As Charles Robequain noted of the East Coast:

The coercion exercised by the master and his occasionally abusive management of the work force, would well appear to have contributed to the outbreak of the 1947 rebellion. It was in this eastern region that the revolt was most severe, leading to a sharp decline in European farming.[149]

[145] Ciolina, "Café," p. 308.
[146] Robequain, *Madagascar*, 215–6; *Entreprises et produits de Madagascar* 5 (Oct.–Dec. 1950): 41; see also Pierre Chauleur, *Le Régime du travail dans les territoires d'Outre-Mer* (Paris: Encyclopédie d'Outre-Mer, 1956), p. 44.
[147] Jacques Tronchon, *L'Insurrection malgache de 1947* (Paris: Karthala, 1986); Lucille Rabearimanana, *La Presse d'opinion à Madagascar de 1947 à 1956* (Antananarivo: Librarie Mixte, 1980).
[148] Gwyn Campbell, "The History of Nineteenth Century Madagascar: 'Le Royaume' or 'l'empire'?," in *Omaly sy Anio* 33, no. 6 (1994): 33–6.
[149] Robequain, *Madagascar*, p. 223.

The 1947 revolt squeezed most Creole planters out of coffee, but not large corporations. Settler concessions fell from about 9,000 in 1905 to 2,500 in 1948–49. By 1952, European plantations accounted for only 16 percent of the acreage under coffee production, and 17 percent of coffee exports.[150] French High Commissioner Bargues chiefly blamed the suppression of forced labor for the decline of Creole fortunes, and called for massive immigration of French and other European peasants.[151] Unlike Angola, however, where high coffee prices in the 1940s and 1950s induced many foreign European middlemen to move into production, in Madagascar most small- and medium-sized foreign plantations were abandoned to indigenous producers or absorbed by larger companies. By 1958, one company alone, the Marseillaise de Madagascar, through its subsidiary CAIM, owned 600,000 coffee trees in the Mananjary district.[152] As Robequain noted:

Many settlers will sell or even abandon their plantations, pouring back to the coastal towns, forsaking agricultural production for transport, commerce and the transformation of commodities for export.[153]

Although some "often wretched" Creole planters survived the 1947 revolt, their farms were characterized by family labor, old unproductive trees, and poor cultivation techniques by the late 1950s. Robequain stated that they could survive only if organized into cooperatives and given massive state assistance.[154] By 1958, Creole-owned farms were responsible for 25 percent of production by weight, but they faced "the extremely fierce competition of indigenous planters." Most Creoles became absentee landlords, leaving actual production in Malagasy hands.[155]

On the East Coast, under the pressure of demographic growth, the smallholder coffee frontier moved steadily from the coastal plains to the sparsely populated hinterland hills at the foot of the plateau, where forest land was freely available. The primary concern of small migrant farmers was to clear an area sufficient for a household practicing slash-and-burn agriculture to become self-sufficient in rice. However, climatic factors, such as the risk of drought and cyclone damage, often caused

---

[150] Ibid., pp. 211–14, 217–18, 223, 332.

[151] Guinaudleau, "Madagascar," pp. 154, 159–62.

[152] Robequain, *Madagascar*, p. 224; for Angola, see Birmingham, "A Question of Coffee," pp. 125–6.

[153] Robequain, *Madagascar*, pp. 223–4.

[154] Ibid., pp. 214, 225; see also Lucille Rabearimanana, "La Politique économique coloniale sur la côte est (Madagascar) dans les années 1950," in *Omaly sy Anio* 21–22 (1985): 307–37.

[155] Robequain, *Madagascar*, pp. 136, 224–5, 345.

harvest shortfalls. Thus, mixed plantations of banana and coffee, from cuttings taken from old plantations, were also established. Bananas and rice purchased with money from coffee sales supplemented domestic rice production, proving critical to survival when the latter failed to meet the requirements of the household. When the rice harvest was abundant, coffee production was neglected but never abandoned, as coffee was an integral part of survival strategies. Slash-and-burn cultivation with simple techniques resulted in diminishing yields, to which the small producer responded by clearing more forest, the critically "free" factor of production.[156]

Labor and Quality, 1947–1972

The labor problem eased as Creole producers were squeezed out. Malagasy smallholders used family labor, while large European concerns used migrant labor. Thus, in 1955, some 38 percent of the salaried Malagasy work force in the private sector were engaged in agriculture, most as temporary migrant workers.[157]

Poor farming methods and old trees allegedly resulted in low yields and poor quality: the yield from indigenous coffee plantations is mediocre. It lacks homogeneity. The grower has, without discrimination, used a large variety of strains alongside Canephora [robusta]. Method is much neglected and weeding rarely practiced. In addition, the coffee trees are too old: planted almost exclusively between 1920 and 1935 and for the most part pruned some 12 to 15 years ago, they yield an ever-decreasing harvest.[158]

However, European planters practiced similar cultivation techniques, arguing that only the state could afford to provide new trees of improved strains, and in sufficient numbers to replace old ones.[159]

The 1950 ten-year plan thus envisaged the establishment of an agronomic research station at Lake Alaotra, supported by six experimental stations. Following the example of the British East Africa Institute, coffee research units were established.[160] In 1956, the FSC (Coffee Support Board) financed the distribution, largely to indigenous farmers on the

---

[156] Chantal Blanc-Pamard and François Ruf, La Transition caféière côte est de Madagascar (Montpelier: CIRAD et Centre d'Etudes Africaines, 1992).

[157] Robequain, Madagascar, pp. 136, 230–2, 261–2, 332.

[158] Ibid., p. 136.

[159] Ibid., p. 225.

[160] Entreprises et produits de Madagascar 5 Oct.–Dec. 1950): 29; Coste, Les Caféiers, pp. 5, 329.

East Coast, of 7.7 million coffee seedlings from the nurseries of experimental agricultural stations.[161] Following the decline of Madagascar as a producer of *robusta* from 1959, and a growth in international demand for *arabica*, a major FSC-financed project was initiated to expand production of *arabica*. The authorities distributed 1.72 million seedlings in Antananarivo province, with plans for 5,000 hectares to be planted in Fianarantsoa province by 1966. The Coffee Board, established in 1960–61, was charged with examining how best to market Malagasy *arabica*.[162] To improve quality and save labor, the administration advocated the creation of massive plantations with selected plants, well spaced to facilitate mechanical weeding and transport.[163]

Malagasy producers steadfastly, and probably sensibly, refused such advice. They maintained extensive plantations of old trees, interspersed with other food and cash crops: maize and manioc in the interior and *letchis*, cinnamon, and bananas on the East Coast.[164] The main concern of the small producer was not coffee but rice, which absorbed most of the farmer's land, labor, and capital. Weeding occurred once a year, generally at the time of the coffee harvest. A rice pestle and mortar were used to husk the coffee cherry, and beans were dried on the ground prior to being carried to the local collection center. No significant price incentive was offered for better quality.[165]

Credit, 1947–1972

Following the 1947 revolt, state credit organizations declined in importance.[166] By the 1970s, the Chinese shopkeeper-trader had become the major source of credit for small coffee producers. The Chinese numbered about 5,000 in 1958 and about 10,000 in 1972, mostly on the East Coast and in Antananarivo.[167] These shopkeepers were supplied with considerable credit in goods by European branch managers of major export companies located in Toamasina, Mahajanga, and Zanzibar, and occasionally

---

[161] *La Revue de Madagascar* 1, no. 2 (1957): 43; Robequain, *Madagascar*, p. 136.

[162] *Café cacao thé* 1, no. 2 (1957): 43; *La Revue du café* 1 (1948): 2; Robequain, *Madagascar*, p. 332.

[163] Robequain, *Madagascar*, p. 225.

[164] Blanc-Pamard and Ruf, *La Transition*, pp. 95–214.

[165] Ibid.

[166] Rabearimanana, "La Politique," pp. 315–24.

[167] Grandidier, *Histoire*, series 4, vol. 1, pp. 518, 563; Robequain, *Madagascar*, p. 116; Thompson and Adloff, *The Malagasy Republic*, pp. 272–3; Covell, *Madagascar*, p. 84.

lent canoes and tractors to transport produce.[168] These branch managers largely dictated the purchasing price for crops, which with a profit margin was imposed by the Chinese trader upon the producer. The trader evaluated the worth of the coffee by a system of weights devised by himself and under his control. He extended credit to the producer through short-term cash advances on the harvest, calculated on the anticipated worth of the harvest minus the risk of harvest failure. Goods were advanced immediately prior to the harvest, which ensured that the crop was sold to the creditor. The credit system ensured that most producers were permanently indebted to Chinese middlemen.[169]

Protectionism and Markets, 1947–1972

The damage inflicted by the 1947 revolt and its suppression was one of the major reasons cited, alongside aging trees and poor techniques, for a crisis in the Malagasy coffee industry. Exports fell from a prewar high of 40,000 tons to 25,600 tons by 1949.[170] However, coffee soon recovered, for it accounted for 44 percent of total exports in 1952. By 1955, some 128,000 hectares were under coffee, more than all other crops except manioc (190,000 hectares) and rice (680,000 hectares).[171]

The major problem beginning in 1950 was finding overseas markets. In the few areas where the transport infrastructure was good, as in the vicinity of Toamasina, small producers marketed their coffee directly and thus obtained higher prices. Elsewhere, small producers depended on middlemen and adopted a minimalist strategy geared to ensuring survival.[172] However, coffee was also a domestic beverage, it being commented in 1958 that "coffee has helped to stabilize the Betsimisaraka for whom it has become an everyday drink."[173]

Malagasy coffee faced severe competition on the world market. The ten-year plan for French Overseas Territories, outlined in April 1946 and intended to promote economic development in the interests of both indigenous populations and the French Union, was shelved in Madagascar, due to the 1947–49 disturbances. A new ten-year plan, formulated in 1950, envisaged a major diversification into rice, sisal, peanuts, sugar,

[168] Grandidier, *Histoire*, series 4, vol. 1, p. 562.
[169] Covell, *Madagascar*, p. 19; Blanc-Pamard and Ruf, *La Transition*, pp. 172–3.
[170] Guinaudleau, "Madagascar," p. 154.
[171] Robequain, *Madagascar*, pp. 122, 230–1.
[172] Blanc-Pamard and Ruf, *La Transition*.
[173] Robequain, *Madagascar*, p. 136.

TABLE 3.4. *Madagascar: Export Coffee Production, 1946–60 (metric tons)*

Year	Output	% World total	Year	Output	% World output
1946/47–1950/51[a]	27,180	1.58	1956–57	48,000	2.25
1950/51–1954/55[a]	34,140	1.75	1957–58	49,500	1.78
1954–55	35,160	1.73	1958–59	46,500	1.52
1955–56	53,040	2.02	1959–60	34,500	1.00

[a] Average.

Source: *Café cacao thé* 1, no. 3 (1957): 159; 2, no. 3 (1958): 167; 3, no. 3 (1959): 178.

and tobacco, to avoid dependence on coffee. Nevertheless, it was planned to expand coffee production from 26,000 tons (22,000 tons exported) in 1946 to 45,000 tons (40,000 tons exported) by 1960. There were also plans to improve quality, lower freight costs, and secure markets.[174] See Table 3.4 for actual figures.

The protectionist policies of the European Economic Community (EEC) were considered essential to growth in Madagascar, where five-year plans after independence in 1960 largely failed to induce diversification out of coffee, upon which the economy continued to rely.[175] With other Franc Zone producers, Madagascar argued against the free market, held to be a "system that in reality is fundamentally disadvantageous to primary producer countries, notably the agricultural ones."[176]

Malagasy producers enjoyed continued protection in France, where the National Coffee Purchasing Trust (GNACA), a state monopoly-purchasing agency established in July 1942, bought at fixed prices and stockpiled coffee from overseas territories and resold at world prices. Nevertheless, in 1950 Creole and European coffee producers in Madagascar protested that the GNACA purchasing price was generally below world market prices:

It is undeniable that the state would be undertaking a completely immoral operation if it permitted itself to keep as revenue the money gained through buying the coffee of Overseas Territory producers at lower than market prices.[177]

By mid-January 1950, GNACA had stockpiled 34,670 tons of coffee, 83 percent of which was from overseas territories and purchased at an

[174] *Entreprises et Produits de Madagascar* 5 (Oct.–Dec. 1950): 11–19, 23–5, 29.

[175] Economist Intelligence Unit (Country Report), *Madagascar, Mauritius, Seychelles, Comoros*, vol. 3 (London, 1986), p. 16.

[176] J. Pataut, "L'Evolution des problèmes du Café," *Café cacao thé* 6, no. 2 (1962): 146.

[177] *Entreprises et produits de Madagascar* 4 (July–Sept. 1950): 123–5.

average price of 180 francs per kilo. This was resold at 387 francs per kilo, close to the world price. This entailed a profit for the French government of about 3 million francs. Producer territories campaigned for the government to return these profits to them. This appeal was successful, not least because such sums were seen as assisting European planters to reconstitute plantations devastated during the 1947 rebellion. However, GNACA was dismantled later in 1950.[178]

Coffee from overseas territories continued to enjoy preference from the French government in terms of quantity and price. For instance, whereas the price of *robusta* oscillated considerably on the New York market in 1959, the price in Marseilles remained relatively constant.[179] Malagasy coffee exports rose from 25,624 metric tons in 1949 to 52,500 tons in 1956.[180] They were mostly directed to France, where, from 1950 to 1955, they comprised on average 31 percent of imports from overseas territories, and 20 percent of total coffee imports. At the same time, French Union producers formed the third largest coffee-exporting group in the world after Brazil and Colombia. The major Franc Zone producers also tried to enhance their market share by implementing a coffee standardization code in 1961.[181]

Cyclones and associated floods caused shortfalls in anticipated Malagasy coffee harvests in 1956–57. In March 1959, this amounted to 15,200 tons on a forecast export total of 55,000 tons. The Malagasy share of French imports fell. The 1959 cyclone also reduced production in 1960 and 1961 due to the destruction of leaves and shade trees and the deposition of sand in the soil. Thus, in 1961, Madagascar accounted for 20 percent of Franc Zone coffee imports and 15 percent of total coffee imports into France.[182]

After independence in 1960, Madagascar joined a number of regional and international organizations, set up to stabilize world coffee prices. The International Coffee Organization (ICO), chief among them, imposed production quotas on members. The quota system posed problems for African producers, including Madagascar, on several counts.[183] ICO was dominated by *arabica* producers, who promoted their

[178] Ibid.
[179] *Café cacao thé* 4, no. 1 (1960): 41.
[180] Robequain, *Madagascar*, p. 332.
[181] *Café cacao thé* 1, no. 2 (1958): 39; 1, no. 3 (1957): 49, 153; 6, no. 1 (1962): 61.
[182] *Café cacao thé* 1, no. 2 (1957): 43; 3, no. 1 (1959): 59; 3, no. 3 (1959): 174; 4, no. 1 (1960): 40; 6, no. 2 (1962): 154.
[183] *Café cacao thé* 4, no. 3 (1960): 108, 168; 5, no. 4 (1961): 279–80.

interests over other producers. Second, the early 1960s quota for Franc Zone producers of 254,940 tons was well below production at around 300,000 tons. Third, although *robusta* accounted for only 20 percent of world coffee production, some major *robusta* producers remained outside the ICO:

Robusta producers who are signatories of the agreement, risk undertaking particularly onerous responsibilities in that, in contrast to the Arabica producers of America, they do not possess the quasi-monopoly of world exports.[184]

Associated with this problem was a fall of 50 percent in the price of *robusta* from 1952 to 1962. As Pataut commented:

if, as for example in 1960, the member states of the Franc Zone had not had benefited, in the markets of their own monetary zone, from their particular financial advantage, they would have received in exchange for their combined coffee exports, in real terms, a value considerably below that gained ten years earlier for half as much exported tonnage.[185]

Quotas presented further problems. They were imposed for three-year periods, whereas African *robusta* producers, who witnessed a doubling of their coffee sales in the period 1955–62, would have preferred one-year quotas to react in a more flexible manner to world market trends.[186] *Robusta* producers also faced the problem of dumping. The Brazilian Institute of Coffee used its Trieste depot for this purpose in 1960, and planned to open another depot in West Germany. Unlike South American producers, African producers had limited stocks with which to play the market.[187] The ICO coffee export quota was established for the Franc Zone as a whole, which then established quotas for its members. For the three years 1962/63 to 1964/65, Madagascar was allotted a quota of 49,730 tons, representing 19 percent of the Franc Zone quota, and 1.8 percent of the world total.[188] However, France, a major coffee-consuming country, established its own price for *robusta* of 3.20 new francs per kilo for Franc Zone producers from November 1959, independently of the international market.[189]

---

[184] *Café cacao thé* 5, no. 3 (1961): 188; see also Pataut, "L'Evolution," p. 145.
[185] Pataut, "L'Evolution," p. 146.
[186] Pataut, "L'Evolution," p. 145; *Café cacao thé* 6, no. 3 (1962): 236.
[187] Pataut, "L'Evolution," p. 146.
[188] *Café cacao thé* 4, no. 3 (1960): 168; 6, no. 3 (1962): 235.
[189] *Café cacao thé* 6, no. 2 (1962): 148, and 6, no. 3 (1962): 234; Pataut, "L'Evolution," p. 233.

At the same time, the EEC, under French prompting, resisted U.S. and Latin American pressure to accelerate the lowering of its common external tariff. Established at 16 percent under the Treaty of Rome, it was to fall to 9.6 percent by January 1970.[190] The internal EEC tax on coffee, which included Franc Zone produce, was cut to zero by the start of 1965, at a time when *robusta* constituted about a third of EEC coffee imports. However, Madagascar enjoyed limited European sales outside France. In 1960, it supplied a mere 1,008 tons to Italy (1 percent of total Italian coffee imports) and 538 tons to West Germany (0.3 percent). In that year, 83 percent of Malagasy coffee exports were still directed to the French market.[191]

In addition, Madagascar joined an African bloc, with two major accords signed in Antananarivo in December 1960. In the first, a Coffee Board Liaison Committee was established by the Ivory Coast, Madagascar, Cameroon, and the Central African Republic, jointly responsible for 95 percent of Franc Zone output, to coordinate their policies. They established the goal of respecting their Franc Zone export quotas and obtaining the price authorized by the French government. Outside the Franc Zone, they were to coordinate sales to ensure the highest possible price, and promised to collect and share information. The second accord established the Inter-African Coffee Organization, joined by Cameroon, the Central African Republic, Congo, Ivory Coast, Gabon, Kenya, Madagascar, Uganda, Tanganyika, and Portugal. It was hoped that this would constitute a major coffee producer grouping alongside similar New World organizations. It was further envisaged that other African producers, such as Ethiopia, and other *robusta* producers, such as India and Indonesia, might join this grouping.[192]

Conclusion

The history of coffee production in the southwest Indian Ocean is one of changing frontiers. Commercial production commenced on Réunion, one of the world's most important coffee suppliers in the eighteenth century. Production declined precipitously in the nineteenth century, but the plant was introduced to the East Coast and interior of Madagascar. It

---

[190] Pataut, "L'Evolution"; *Café cacao thé* 6, no. 3 (1962): 234, 236.
[191] *Café cacao thé* 1, no. 2 (1957): 97; 3, no. 1 (1959): 59; 5, no. 4 (1961): 278, 287–8; 6, no. 3 (1962): 244.
[192] *Café cacao thé* 5, no. 1 (1961): 53–4.

achieved modest success before disease wiped it out at altitudes of less than 600 meters in the 1880s. Subsequently, *liberica* and *robusta* were introduced at lower altitudes. Coffee remained a secondary crop until the 1930s, when production was stimulated by colonial protection. An unintended consequence of state measures to assist the cultivation of coffee was the rise of small indigenous producers, who increasingly dominated production. Independent Malagasy production accentuated a chronic shortage of labor, upon which small Creole production depended. Pressure from the latter led to abuses of the colonial corvée system, which in turn contributed to the 1947 revolt. The latter led to the mass exodus from coffee production of Creoles, but protectionism within the Franc Zone assisted larger European concerns and indigenous farmers until the 1972 revolution. However, state credit facilities declined from 1947, and small indigenous producers became increasingly indebted to Chinese middlemen. Moreover, periodic cyclones, a poor transport infrastructure, and restricted markets ensured that rice continued to be the primary concern of small producers. Nevertheless, coffee had become an integral part of the survival strategies of some small producers, providing income to cover shortfalls in household rice production.

4

The Coffee Crisis in Asia, Africa, and the Pacific, 1870–1914

William Gervase Clarence-Smith

The success of New World coffee producers in the late nineteenth century has spawned a large body of writings, whereas stagnation and decline in Asia and Africa have attracted few scholars.[1] Statistics for the early nineteenth century are rare and unreliable, but they suggest that Asia and Africa's share of global coffee exports amounted to around a third in the 1830s.[2] This proportion remained roughly the same in the 1860s and 1870s.[3] However, it then rapidly dwindled to around a twentieth by 1913.[4] Within this broad evolution, there was an additional contrast. Asia was subject to a particularly sharp fall, whereas Africa's small share of the world market remained fairly constant in relative terms. When the focus is further narrowed to particular countries or regions within large and diverse countries such as Indonesia and India, outcomes were even more

---

[1] Portions of this chapter have been perviously published. Permission to reprint has been granted by the publisher.

[2] C. Ratzka-Ernst, *Welthandelsartikel und ihre Preise; Eine Studie zur Preisbewegung und Preisbildung: Der Zucker, der Kaffee, und die Baumwolle* (Munich: Duncker and Humblot 1912), pp. 77, 79; R. Marte, *Estadísticas y documentos históricos sobre Santo Domingo, 1805–1890* (Santo Domingo: Museo Nacional de Historia y Geografía, 1984), pp. 75–6; Edmund Roberts, *Embassy to the Eastern Courts of Cochin-China, Siam and Muscat in the US Sloop-of-War Peacock, during the Years 1832–3–4* (rpt., Wilmington: Scholarly Resources Ltd., 1972), p. 404.

[3] Karl Andree et al., *Geographie des Welthandels* (Stuttgart: J. Engelhorn, 1867–77), vol. 1, p. 595; F. B. Thurber, *Coffee, from Plantation to Cup* (New York: American Grocer Publishing Association, 1881), p. 242; C. F. van Delden Laërne, *Brazil and Java, Report on Coffee-Culture in America, Asia and Africa* (London: W. H. Allen, 1885).

[4] M. L. Bynum, *International Trade in Coffee* (Washington: Department of Commerce, 1926). See also M. Samper and R. Fernando, statistical appendix to this volume.

diverse. This chapter explores both the reasons for the overall downward trend in Africa and Asia's share of world coffee exports and the causes of the extraordinarily uneven nature of that decline.

The evolution of world production took place against a background of increasing volatility in the real price of coffee. The world price rose fairly steadily from the late 1840s to reach a peak in the first half of the 1870s, making coffee the "wonder crop" of tropical farmers around the globe. A sharp slump in the early 1880s was a foretaste of things to come, but it was forgotten by most producers in the feverish boom of the late 1880s and early 1890s. Prices went into free fall in 1896, crashing down to around half their previous level by the turn of the century. They then limped along until the mid-1900s, when they began to rise slowly again.[5]

Against this background, four broad patterns can be distinguished. First, some areas ceased to export, and even became small net importers, notably, Ceylon (Sri Lanka), the Philippines, and a number of Pacific islands. Second, exports to foreign countries declined, but this was partly compensated by rising consumption within the country as a whole, as with Java and West Sumatra, selling within Indonesia, and the princely states of Mysore and Coorg, selling within India. Third, there were opportunist producers, many of them with little or no previous experience of the crop, exporting when the world price was high, but quickly bailing out when the bears began to growl, such as Malaya and Nyasaland (Malawi). The final paradigm represented a long-term commitment to exporting coffee, as in South Sumatra, East Timor, East Africa, Madagascar, and Angola.

Monocausal explanations are of little use in accounting for this complex set of responses, and yet all factors were not equal in their impact. Among possible reasons for decline, scholars have mentioned taxation, prices, quality, pests and diseases, scale of cultivation, shortages of land, methods of cultivation, coercion, scarcity of labor or capital, and competition from alternative crops. Within this long list, the evidence suggests that disease was the main explanation for the overall failure of Africa and Asia, while generous endowment in easily accessible forested land was the key to the relative success of particular producers.

Pests and Diseases

Coffee-leaf blight or rust, caused by the fungus *Hemileia vastatrix*, has long been a popular explanation for the relative decline of Asian and African

---

[5] G. Wrigley, *Coffee* (Harlow: Longman, 1988), p. 532.

producers. *Hemileia vastatrix* apparently originated in Sri Lanka at the end of the 1860s, and by 1914 it had been reported as far east as Samoa, in the South Pacific, and as far west as Cameroon, in western Africa. However, the fungus spared the New World until the 1970s, with the exception of a brief and contained outbreak in Puerto Rico. This differential disease pattern allowed the Americas to forge ahead and consolidate their domination of the world coffee market.[6]

Just how important leaf blight was in the decline of Asian and African producers remains to be ascertained, and the fungus certainly cannot be held responsible for the extraordinary diversity of responses in Asia and Africa. There were striking differences in the evolution of the territories that it spared. Predictably, Angolan and Ethiopian exports increased, and Liberia experienced a great if temporary boom.[7] Conversely, however, production fell to almost nothing in Hawaii, and producers in Nyasaland (Malawi) permanently gave up a crop that had briefly been responsible for over two-thirds of the colony's export revenues.[8] Côte d'Ivoire (Ivory Coast) failed to capitalize on freedom from the fungus, remaining a marginal exporter until the 1920s.[9]

Moreover, territories ravaged by *Hemileia* also reacted differently. "Coffee mania" in Ceylon (Sri Lanka) actually reached new heights for about a decade after the discovery of leaf blight in the island in 1869. Estates changed hands at inflated prices, as buoyant world prices temporarily overrode the impact of the fungus. When prices fell in the early 1880s, however, Ceylon's disenchantment with coffee was as permanent as it was rapid.[10] Indeed, the island was a net importer of coffee by 1913, as were other victims of *Hemileia*, such as the Philippines and Malaya.[11]

---

[6] A. E. Haarer, *Modern Coffee Production* (London: Leonard Hill, 1956); Wrigley, *Coffee*.

[7] J. Mesquita, *Dados estatísticos para o estudo das pautas de Angola; exportação pelas alfândegas do Círculo e do Congo nos anos de 1888 a 1913* (Luanda: Imprensa Nacional, 1918); R. Pankhurst, *Economic History of Ethiopia 1800–1935* (Addis Ababa: Haile Selassie University Press, 1968); M. R. Akpan, "The Liberian Economy in the Nineteenth Century: The State of Agriculture and Commerce," *Liberian Studies Journal* 6, no. 1 (1975): 1–25.

[8] R. C. Schmitt, *Historical Statistics of Hawaii* (Honolulu: University Press of Hawaii, 1977); C. A. Baker, "Malawi Exports: An Economic History," in G. W. Smith et al., eds., *Malawi Past and Present* (Blantyre: CLAIM, 1971), pp. 80–113.

[9] A. J. F. Köbben, "Le Planteur noir," *Etudes Eburnéennes* 5 (1956): 7–190; H. Frechou, "Les Plantations européennes en Côte d'Ivoire," *Cahiers d'Outremer* 8, no. 29 (1955): 56–83.

[10] L. A. Mills, *Ceylon under British Rule, 1795–1932* (rpt., London: Frank Cass, 1964), pp. 245–6.

[11] Bynum, *International Trade*.

Natal began to reduce its production sharply a few years before it was hit by leaf blight.[12] Vanuatu and New Caledonia felt the impact of the blight quite late, around 1910, but while coffee quickly became marginal in Vanuatu, it remained New Caledonia's most important cash crop.[13] In East Africa, Uganda and Kenya shrugged off leaf blight as though it was no more than a minor irritant.[14]

One reason for this diversity of reactions was that *Hemileia* was not consistently devastating in its impact. In the short term, the fungus rarely killed even *arabica* trees, by far the most commonly cultivated variety up to the 1870s, and the most susceptible to infection. Rather, it weakened them and reduced yields. The fungus was less virulent in young and healthy trees and in highland zones with a marked dry season. It could be controlled to some extent by manipulating shade and fertilizers, or by spraying various chemicals, although costs were high. Furthermore, plant breeders in India evolved "Coorg" and "Kent" varieties of *arabica*, to some degree resistant to leaf blight. The latter, discovered in 1911, was widely planted by British settlers in East Africa.[15]

In humid lowlands, the ravages of *Hemileia* were in part averted by substituting more resistant types of coffee for the old *arabica* varieties. *Liberica* from West Africa was initially in great demand, and Liberia cashed in by exporting planting material to destinations as far apart as Costa Rica and Queensland. However, *liberica*'s early reputation for resistance to leaf blight was soon severely dented.[16] Moreover, the beans were disliked by consumers, and were hard to process with machinery developed for *arabica*.[17] *Robusta* varieties from the Congo area were tried from around 1900, with greater success. Yields were higher than for *arabica*, and trees needed less attention, although quality left much to be desired.[18]

[12] A. F. Hattersley, *The British Settlement of Natal: A Study in Imperial Migration* (Cambridge: Cambridge University Press, 1950), pp. 234–5.

[13] B. Weightman, *Agriculture in Vanuatu: A Historical Review* (Cheam: British Friends of Vanuatu, 1989), pp. 185–7; J. Parsons, "Coffee and Settlement in New Caledonia," *Geographical Review* 35, no. 1 (1945): 12–21.

[14] C. C. Wrigley, *Crops and Wealth in Uganda: A Short Agrarian History* (London: Oxford University Press, 1959); Haarer, *Modern Coffee Production*, pp. 342–3.

[15] Haarer, *Modern Coffee Production*, pp. 279–84, 374.

[16] Akpan, "The Liberian Economy," p. 21.

[17] A. J. Ultée, "Koffiecultuur der ondernemingen," in C. J. J. van Hall and C. van de Koppel, *De landbouw in de Indische archipel* (The Hague: W. van Hoeve, 1946–50), vol. 2b, pp. 7–88; A. and G. Grandidier, *Histoire physique, naturelle et politique de Madagascar* (Paris: Hachette, 1928), vol. 4, pp. 73–5.

[18] Wrigley, *Coffee*, pp. 54–8.

More localized pests also need to be taken into account, especially when they acted in concert with leaf blight. Although *Hemileia* appeared in Malaya in 1894, it allegedly did less harm to coffee than the clear-wing hawk moth (*Cephonodes hylas*) after 1899.[19] The joint ravages of a stem borer and *Hemileia* were blamed for the rapid collapse of coffee in both the Philippines and Natal.[20] That said, a combined assault by stem borers and *Hemileia* in India failed to kill off coffee cultivation there.[21]

Elsewhere, ecological factors other than *Hemileia* took the blame. In Malawi, drought and a stem borer were held responsible for planters giving up coffee.[22] Hawaii was ravaged by a plague variously attributed to either an insect or a fungus other than *Hemileia*.[23] Natal and Tonkin (northern Vietnam) were situated at the climatic limits of coffee cultivation. Both territories suffered from bouts of excessively cold weather, with typhoons an added hazard in Tonkin.[24]

Overall, the impact of leaf blight was particularly severe where coffee groves were aging and there was a lack of forested land for new planting. Producers under these conditions gave up coffee with alacrity, as long as they enjoyed attractive alternative uses for their land and labor. Conversely, growers often found ingenious ways around *Hemileia*, when they lacked anything else with which to obtain as attractive a cash income, and disposed of plentiful and cheap forested land close at hand. The high fertility of virgin soils yielded a substantial "forest rent," including few weeds and a lesser susceptibility to disease.[25] The Dutch in Indonesia discovered that the blight devastated young trees planted in land that had already grown coffee, but did less harm to trees planted in virgin soil recently

[19] J. C. Jackson, *Planters and Speculators: Chinese and European Agricultural Enterprises in Malaya, 1786–1921* (Kuala Lumpur: University of Malaya Press, 1968), p. 200.

[20] United States of America, *Census of the Philippine Islands* (Washington: Bureau of the Census, 1905), vol. 4, pp. 82–4; J. Foreman, *The Philippine Islands*, 2nd ed. (Shanghai: Kelly and Walsh, 1899), p. 337; Hattersley, *The British Settlement of Natal*, pp. 234–5.

[21] R. H. Elliot, *Gold, Sport and Coffee Planting in Mysore* (London: Archibald Constable, 1894), pp. 277–9.

[22] Haarer, *Modern Coffee Production*, p. 10.

[23] C. F. van Delden Laërne, *Brazil and Java, Report on Coffee-culture in America, Asia and Africa* (London: W. H. Allen, 1885), p. 426; T. Morgan, *Hawaii: A Century of Economic Change, 1778–1876* (Cambridge, Mass.: Harvard University Press, 1948), p. 162; T. K. Hitch, *Islands in Transition: The Past, Present and Future of Hawaii's Economy* (Honolulu: First Hawaiian Bank, 1992), pp. 113–16.

[24] Hattersley, *The British Settlement of Natal*, pp. 233–4; C. Robequain, *The Economic Development of French Indochina* (London: Oxford University Press, 1944), p. 196.

[25] C. Blanc-Pamard, and F. Ruf, *La Transition caféière, côte est de Madagascar* (Montpellier: CIRAD, 1992), pp. 199–200.

cleared of primary forest, especially if located some distance away from the foci of infestation and at a fair height above sea level.[26]

Shortages of Forest Land and Methods of Cultivation

For Javanese producers, in particular, *Hemileia* simply brought a simmering crisis to a more rapid head. In this densely populated island, complaints that insufficient forests remained for coffee planting were already widespread by the 1850s.[27] Moreover, the clearing of vast tracts of primary upland forest resulted in severe erosion. As lowland irrigation channels for rice and sugar fields silted up, officials and planters argued that further deforestation should be halted. The situation reached a point of crisis at the end of the century, when Java's forest frontier was closed by administrative fiat.[28]

Similar pressure on limited forest resources existed elsewhere. Fears were voiced about the impact of coffee cultivation on the fragile ecology of North Sulawesi as early as in Java.[29] Sri Lanka abandoned coffee a decade or so after the last great reserves of upland primary forest had been cleared in the early 1870s.[30] The short duration of coffee booms in small islands, notably, in the Pacific, was related to shortages of forested land, even when *Hemileia* did not strike.[31]

Cultivation methods magnified the problem. Quick and high yields were obtained by completely clearing and burning the forest and planting coffee without shade trees. However, soils were rapidly exhausted, yields declined, and trees became vulnerable to disease. This led to the constant clearing and burning of more forest. In Sri Lanka, a speculative land market intensified the pressure to adopt such cultivation methods, because of the need to repay loans or obtain a quick return for shareholders.[32] Dutch officials imposed clear-felling and burning on a reluctant Indonesian

[26] W. G. Clarence-Smith, "The Impact of Forced Coffee Cultivation on Java, 1805–1917," *Indonesia Circle* 64 (1994): 241–64.
[27] R. E. Elson, *Village Java under the Cultivation System, 1830–1870* (Sydney: Allen and Unwin, 1994), p. 113; Arsip Nasional Republik Indonesia, Jakarta, Residency Archives, 52, file 1621, Kultuur Verslag, Preanger, 1854.
[28] R. W. Hefner, *The Political Economy of Mountain Java: An Interpretive History* (Berkeley: University of California Press, 1990), p. 51.
[29] M. Schouten, *Minahasan Metamorphoses: Leadership and Social Mobility in a Southeast Asian Society, c. 1680–1983* (Covilhã: Universidade da Beira Interior, 1993), pp. 54–7.
[30] J. Ferguson, *Ceylon in 1903* (Colombo: A. M. and J. Ferguson, 1903), p. 64.
[31] Thurber, *Coffee*, ch. 17.
[32] Mills,*Ceylon*, pp. 235–7; Elliot, *Gold*, p. 278; Thurber, *Coffee*, p. 4.

peasantry, in part because of a desire to receive their "cultivation percentages" (bonuses) as quickly as possible.[33]

Forest land suitable for coffee cultivation was more abundant in Africa, and new railways opened up such lands from the late nineteenth century. The penetration of railways into the interior of British and German East Africa, together with the launching of steamers on Lake Victoria, connected these lands to overseas markets much more effectively than before.[34] The expansion of Ethiopian and Angolan exports were other examples of growth through railways, despite criticisms of the technical deficiencies of the Djibouti and Luanda railways.[35] More than any other factor, the abundance of forested land thrown open to coffee cultivation accounted for East and Central Africa's ability to ignore the ravages of leaf blight. This advantage was all the greater as such lands were generally situated at considerable altitudes and in regions with a marked dry season, lessening the actual or potential impact of *Hemileia*. A well-timed dry season further allowed coffee beans to be cheaply dried in the sun.

Asia had its own vast reserves of forested land, especially in Southeast Asia, but much less of it was situated in regions of high altitude with a marked dry season. There were exceptions, such as the plateau of South-Central Vietnam and Laos, colonized from the 1920s by both French planters and Vietnamese smallholders, growing coffee as their principal cash crop.[36] However, it was *Hevea* rubber that generally emerged as the most suitable cash crop for Southeast Asia's forested land, protected by distance from the pests and diseases that made it impossible to grow it intensively in its Amazon homeland.

Ecologically sensitive forms of cultivation allowed some Asian producers to maintain their coffee output. Javanese farmers preferred to clear only undergrowth and small trees, planting coffee at stake under

---

[33] Clarence-Smith, "The Impact of Forced Coffee Cultivation."

[34] H. Brode, *British and German East Africa, Their Economic and Commercial Relations* (rpt., New York: Arno Press 1977).

[35] E. de Felcourt, *L'Abyssinie: Agriculture, chemin de fer* (Paris: E. Larose, 1911); C. McClennan, "Land, Labour and Coffee: The South's Role in Ethiopian Self-Reliance, 1889–1935," *African Economic History* 9 (1980): 69–83; D. Birmingham, "The Coffee Barons of Cazengo," *Journal of African History* 19, no. 4 (1978): 523–38; W. G. Clarence-Smith, "Capital Accumulation and Class Formation in Angola, c. 1875–1961," in D. Birmingham and P. Martin, eds., *History of Central Africa* (London: Longmans, 1983), vol. 2, pp. 163–99.

[36] Robequain, *The Economic Development of French Indochina*, pp. 67–9, 187–9, 196, 213, 237.

tall jungle trees. The coffee trees took longer to bear, and yields were lower, but they lived longer and soil damage was checked.[37] After some unfortunate experiences, planters in India adopted similar methods. They minimized burning and applied various types of fertilizer, so that their *arabica* trees bore an economic crop for up to fifty years.[38] Planters in Mysore and Java, growing coffee in this way, even claimed that they had achieved a "permanent" system of cultivation.[39] Coffee in Yemen persisted in a marginal environment because of careful terracing, irrigation, and shading.[40] In New Caledonia, where *robusta* was introduced after the damages of leaf blight, coffee was grown in fertile alluvial valley bottoms, rather than on the usual hill slopes.[41] Mixed farming in Tonkin and Kenya allowed planters to apply cattle manure around their coffee trees.[42]

Coffee could also be integrated as a minor crop in wider cultivation systems, notably, *robusta* varieties grown as a catch crop between rubber trees, coconut palms, or oil palms. Coffee was harvested for a few seasons, and then the coffee trees were uprooted when the main crop matured. Estates in East Sumatra, Malaya, and Vietnam all engaged in this type of cultivation.[43] In the poor soils of southern Sumatra, smallholders added a step. Having cleared small plots in the forest and planted *robusta* coffee and *Hevea* rubber, they planted food crops, typically dry rice, for two or three years. The coffee trees, specially selected to mature early, were harvested for another three years or so before being pulled up.[44] The most elaborate crop mixes were to be found among the planters

[37] Hefner, *The Political Economy of Mountain Java*, p. 59; A. van Schaik, *Colonial Control and Peasant Resources in Java; Agricultural Involution Reconsidered* (Amsterdam: Koninklijk Nederlands Aardrijkskundig Genootschap, 1986), pp. 56–8.

[38] Elliot, *Gold*, pp. 277–9, 322–43; S. Playne, *Southern India: Its History, People, Commerce and Industrial Resources* (London: Foreign and Colonial Compiling and Publishing, 1914–15), p. 222.

[39] Wrigley, *Coffee*, pp. 206–8.

[40] Arab Bureau, *Handbook of Yemen* (Cairo, 1917), pp. 33–4.

[41] Parsons, "Coffee," p. 20.

[42] Robequain, *The Economic Development of French Indochina*, pp. 194–6; Great Britain, Admiralty, Naval Intelligence Division, *British East Africa* (London, 1920), p. 405–6.

[43] H. Blink, *Opkomst en ontwikkeling van Sumatra als economisch-geographisch gebied* (The Hague: Mouton, 1926), pp. 118–19; F. W. T. Hunger, *Die oliepalm (elaeis guineensis): Historisch onderzoek over de oliepalm in Nederlandsch-Indië* (Leiden: E. J. Brill, 1924), pp. 268–75; Jackson, *Planters*, pp. 202–4; Robequain, *The Economic Development of French Indochina*, p. 209.

[44] B. H. Paerels, "Bevolkingskoffiecultuur," in C. J. J. van Hall and C. van de Koppel, *De landbouw in de Indische archipel* (The Hague: W. van Hoeve, 1946–50), vol. 2b, pp. 111–12.

of Central Java, on small estates at relatively low altitudes. Originally coffee planters, by the twentieth century they grew an astonishing mix of perennial crops, among which *robusta* coffee had become a minor ingredient.[45]

Estate Owners

Owners of estates, especially large ones, were a group quite inclined to give up on tropical perennials such as coffee during an economic crisis, whether brought about by falling prices, disease, or other causes. Large landowners enjoyed no economies of scale, while suffering from inflated overheads and extravagant salaries paid to European expatriates. This in turn led to high rates of borrowing, further burdening estates with debt. In contrast, smallholders rarely required any capital at all. Waste land was generally free or cheap for them on tropical forest frontier, cheap hand tools constituted a marginal fixed capital outlay, and the recourse to family labor and sharecropping avoided any need for working capital.[46] Large planters were thus opportunistic producers, most likely to turn away from coffee when expenditure was especially high. Ceylon was a good example of this, for planters' costs were grossly inflated by unbridled land speculation in the 1870s.[47]

Labor coercion, the traditional way for estate managers to overcome their relative inefficiency, came under growing international pressure in the nineteenth century. Thus, the slave system that underpinned estate cultivation of coffee in Angola and São Tomé led to a great scandal, and was finally abolished in the early 1910s.[48] However, forced labor then replaced slavery in the Portuguese colonies up to the early 1960s, and persisted in French and Belgian colonies until the 1940s, underpinning the persistence of estate production of coffee.[49] Slavery and coerced labor were also important for coffee planters in Liberia and Spanish Guinea, and international demands for reform in these territories did not build up

---

[45] W. Roepke, *Cacao* (Haarlem: H. D. Tjeenk Willink and Zoon, 1922), pp. 2–4.

[46] W. G. Clarence-Smith, "Cocoa Plantations in the Third World, 1870s–1914: The political Economy of Inefficiency," in John Harriss et al., eds., *The New Institutional Economics and Third World Development* (London: Routledge, 1995), pp. 157–71.

[47] Mills, *Ceylon*, p. 246.

[48] J. Duffy, *A Question of Slavery: Labour Policies in Portuguese Africa and the British Protest, 1850–1920* (Cambridge, Mass.: Harvard University Press, 1967).

[49] D. Birmingham and P. Martin, eds., *History of Central Africa* (London: Longmans, 1983), vol. 2; Chapter 3.

until the League of Nations and the International Labor Office became interested in such matters after 1918.[50]

Where estates continued to produce most of a territory's coffee, it was frequently due to sustained and blatantly discriminatory colonial support for European settlers. This was most obvious in Kenya, where Africans lost huge swathes of land in the White Highlands and were prohibited from growing *arabica* coffee.[51] In the Portuguese colonies of Angola and East Timor, a combination of land alienation and forced labor had the same effect.[52] That said, estates persisted with little official support in India's princely states of Mysore and Coorg, combining a core of permanent workers with a large force of temporary harvesters and producing coffee alongside a multitude of smallholders.[53] Moreover, Brazil's remarkable rise to dominance of the world's coffee economy was achieved despite the predominance of large estates.

In any event, the withdrawal of large planters explains little about the overall decline of coffee in any particular area, for smallholders often took over from them. When German plantation companies in Usambara, East Africa, ceased to plant coffee, African smallholders and small Italian and Greek planters forged ahead in the mountainous hinterland. The completion of the Uganda railway and the establishment of a steamer service on Lake Victoria stimulated the coffee economy further inland, including the harvesting of wild *robusta* beans.[54] Smallholders also gradually took over from coffee planters on the island of Réunion in the course of the nineteenth century.[55] Similarly, Afro-American settlers in Liberia either sold their lands or let them return to forest, but many of their former workers took up coffee production.[56] When the French abolished forced labor in Côte d'Ivoire in 1946, leading to

[50] I. K. Sundiata, "Prelude to Scandal: Liberia and Fernando Po, 1880–1930," *Journal of African History* 15, no. 1 (1974): 97–112.

[51] Paul Mosley, *The Settler Economies: Studies in the Economic History of Kenya and Southern Rhodesia, 1900–1963* (Cambridge: Cambridge University Press, 1983); R. L. Buell, *The Native Problem in Africa* (New York: Macmillan, 1928), pp. 393–4.

[52] Birmingham, "The Coffee Barons"; W. G. Clarence-Smith, "Planters and Smallholders in Portuguese Timor in the Nineteenth and Twentieth Centuries," *Indonesia Circle* 57 (1992): 15–30.

[53] Elliot, *Gold*, pp. 279–88; H. C. Graham, *Coffee Production, Trade, and Consumption by Countries* (Washington: Government Printing Office, 1912), p. 93.

[54] Brode, *British and German East Africa*, pp. 51, 53, 98, 100. See also Chapter 12.

[55] C. Wanquet, "Le Café à la Réunion: Une 'civilisation' disparue," in C. Wanquet, ed., *Economies et sociétés de plantation à la Réunion* (St. Denis: Université de la Réunion, 1989), p. 67.

[56] Akpan, "The Liberian Economy," pp. 23–4.

the collapse of European plantations, smallholders more than filled the gap.[57]

That said, estates were not always replaced by smallholdings producing coffee, even if the following description of parts of the Western Ghats in the 1880s was exaggerated: "the land has now become covered with masses of Lantana (a crawling, climbing thorny plant...), amidst which may occasionally be seen the white walls of unroofed bungalows and dismantled pulping houses."[58] Coffee estates certainly collapsed in southeastern Borneo, Malawi, and Natal without coffee smallholdings emerging to take their place.[59] Moreover, Ceylon's coffee smallholdings shrank more rapidly than estates in the 1870s, and small farmers in Malaya abandoned coffee in tandem with European planters in the rubber boom of the 1900s.[60] In Angola, small producers took the cautious step of ceasing to harvest coffee from their half-wild *robusta* trees when prices fell.[61]

From Coerced to Free Smallholders

Coerced smallholders were another category liable to give up producing coffee, especially in Java, the world's second largest producer in the early nineteenth century. The island was particularly infamous for forced cultivation, the "cork on which the Netherlands floated," and coffee produced the most revenue for the Dutch of all the crops subjected to this system.[62] Coffee was also grown this way in other parts of the Dutch East Indies

---

[57] J. Rapley, *Ivoirien Capitalism: African Entrepreneurs in Côte d'Ivoire* (Boulder: Lynne Rienner, 1993); F. Ruf, "Stratification sociale en économie de plantation ivoirienne," Ph.D. thesis, Paris X (Nanterre), 1988.

[58] Elliot, *Gold*, p. 277.

[59] J. T. Lindblad, *Between Dayak and Dutch: The Economic History of Southeast Kalimantan, 1880–1942* (Dordrecht: Foris, 1988), pp. 30–1; Baker, "Malawi Exports"; Hattersley, *The British Settlement of Natal*.

[60] R. Kurian, "State, Capital and Labour in the Plantation Industry in Sri Lanka, 1834–1984," Ph.D. thesis, University of Amsterdam, 1989, p. 54; Thurber, *Coffee*, p. 92; Jackson, *Planters*, pp. 199–201.

[61] F. Pereira Pimentel, *Investigação commercial na provincia de Angola em 1902–1903* (Porto: Typographia "A Vapor," 1903), p. 115.

[62] C. Fasseur, *The Politics of Colonial Exploitation; Java, the Dutch and the Cultivation System* (Ithaca: Cornell University, 1992); F. van Baardewijk, "Rural Response to Intensifying Colonial Exploitation: Coffee and Society in Central and East Java, 1830–1880," in G. J. Schutte, ed., *State and Trade in the Indonesian Archipelago* (Leiden: KITLV, 1994), pp. 151–76; M. R. Fernando and W. J. O'Malley, "Peasants and Coffee Cultivation in Cirebon Residency, 1800–1900," in A. Booth et al., eds., *Indonesian Economic History in the Dutch Colonial Period* (New Haven: Yale University Press, 1990), pp. 171–86; Elson, *Village Java*; Clarence-Smith, "The Impact of Forced Coffee Cultivation." See also Chapter 6.

(Indonesia), notably, West Sumatra and North Sulawesi.[63] The ending of coercion undoubtedly led some smallholders to give up coffee. As the hated Cultivation System was progressively extinguished in Indonesia between 1870 and 1917, many farmers hastily gave up the crop, notably in East Java, West Sumatra, and North Sulawesi.[64]

Similar dynamics could be observed in Africa. King Leopold aped the Dutch by making coffee cultivation compulsory in 1897 throughout his Congo Free State, resulting in much poorly tended coffee planted near government posts.[65] After Belgium took over the Congo in 1908, temporarily banning forced cultivation, exports of coffee plummeted and the colony briefly became a net importer.[66] Forced cultivation and obligatory harvesting of wild trees lingered on for decades in Ethiopia, but this made rural dwellers averse to the crop, helping to keep production low.[67]

However, there was no clear correlation between the ending of forced cultivation and falling output. While the collapse of Javanese production was striking, it remains unclear whether it caused or followed the abolition of the Cultivation System. Moreover, European estates took up some of the slack, and Javanese smallholders reentered coffee production on a fair scale from the mid-1900s, as prices recovered.[68] In the Luzon Cordillera of the Philippines, the Spanish authorities introduced compulsory growing of coffee in 1881. Emphatically rejected by one group of "tribal" people, the crop was enthusiastically adopted by another. Indeed, this remained one of the few areas where coffee flourished under American rule after 1898.[69] In a similar vein, the British, on taking over from the Germans, obliged the Haya people of East Africa to plant coffee, but the coercive origins of the crop were all but forgotten in the golden years of the 1920s boom.[70]

[63] K. R. Young, *Islamic Peasants and the State: The 1908 Anti-Tax Rebellion in West Sumatra* (New Haven: Yale University Press, 1994), chs. 5–6; Schouten, *Minahasan Metamorphoses.*

[64] Hefner, *The Political Economy of Mountain Java*, pp. 66–7; Young, *Islamic Peasants*, chs. 5–6; Schouten, *Minahasan Metamorphoses*, ch. 4. The cultivation system forced peasants to grow certain crops in specific ways, to be sold to the government alone at a price determined by the government.

[65] A. Poskin, *Bilans congolais: Étude sur la valeur commerciale du Congo par rapport à la Belgique* (Brussels: Société Belge de Librairie, 1900), p. 24.

[66] Great Britain, Admiralty, Naval Intelligence Division, *A Manual of the Belgian Congo* (London, 1920), p. 192; Graham, *Coffee Production.*

[67] Pankhurst, *Economic History*, pp. 199, 203.

[68] Paerels, "Bevolkingskoffiecultuur."

[69] United States of America, 1903 *Census* (1905), vol. 4, pp. 84–6.

[70] Curtis Chapter 13.

Competing Activities and Supplies of Labor

Coffee took some five years to come into full production and could bear for twenty years or more, so that a decision to give up the crop was not taken lightly. Competing claims on supplies of scarce and expensive labor could influence the decision, especially when it was a question of replanting dead trees rather than uprooting live ones. When coffee cultivation involved large inputs of labor, as in efforts to replant coffee in the same land rather than in virgin soil, a switch to another crop became more likely.[71]

However, labor shortages cannot of themselves explain why other crops flourished at the expense of coffee, especially as the supply of free Asian workers to estates increased dramatically in the late nineteenth century, with planters drawing on labor reservoirs from Japan to India.[72] Only in exceptional cases did governments act to stem this influx for political reasons. Thus, the independent Thai authorities were hostile to European planters importing "coolie" labor, and this was presented as a reason for the failure of coffee in the 1890s.[73] Moreover, many competing cultigens were actually more labor-intensive than coffee, so that the availability of labor could even hasten the stampede out of coffee. Other factors intervened, notably, climatic conditions and associated diseases.

Producers in highlands that were humid throughout the year were likely to give up *arabica* coffee, for such conditions favored other crops and accentuated the spread and virulence of *Hemileia*. Coffee's main rival in such areas was tea, which required moisture spread throughout the year, much labor, and complex processing installations. Tea first triumphed over coffee in highland Ceylon, the southern mountains of India, West Java, and Natal.[74] The survival of coffee in Mysore and Coorg was probably due to slightly drier weather, although local labor was also exceptionally abundant and cheap.[75] At a slightly later date, tea also replaced coffee

[71] Blanc-Pamard and Ruf, *La Transition caféière.*
[72] D. Northrup, *Indentured Labor in the Age of Imperialism, 1834–1922* (Cambridge: Cambridge University Press, 1995).
[73] W. Donner, *The Five Faces of Thailand* (London: C. Hurst, 1978), pp. 494–5.
[74] Ferguson, *Ceylon,* ch. 7; P. J. Griffiths, *The History of the Indian Tea Industry* (London: Weidenfeld and Nicolson, 1967), pp. 156–63; G. C. Allen and A. G. Donnithorne, *Western Enterprise in Indonesia and Malaya* (London: George Allen and Unwin, 1962), pp. 101–3; W. G. Freeman and S. E. Chandler, *The World's Commercial Products: A Descriptive Account of the Economic Plants of the World and Their Commercial Uses* (London: Pitman, 1907), pp. 164–6.
[75] Thurber, *Coffee,* p. 106.

in Malawi and neighboring regions of central Mozambique.[76] Cinchona (a tree that is a source of quinine) was a more restricted rival at higher altitudes, as overproduction in Ceylon and Java quickly set in and brought prices crashing down.[77]

At lower altitudes, *Hevea* rubber and cocoa were the chief perennial substitutes for coffee prior to 1914. *Hevea* cultivation was most successful where rainfall was high and well distributed throughout the year. The lowland forests of Southeast Asia and Ceylon were thus turned over to rubber on a huge scale, as rubber prices underwent a phenomenal boom, climaxing in 1909–10.[78] The most direct substitution of rubber for coffee took place in Malaya and Ceylon, but the process could also be observed in many parts of the Dutch East Indies.[79] Cocoa prices were also exceptionally high before 1914, and the crop did better than rubber in areas with a slightly more marked dry season. Cocoa thus pushed coffee aside in much of western Africa, as well as in drier parts of Ceylon and Java.[80] It is rarely remembered that the famous peasant migrants from Akwapim in the Gold Coast (Ghana) were originally as interested in coffee as in cocoa, although they rapidly became the world's main producers of the latter crop.[81]

Transitions from slavery to free labor could change labor costs in ways that favored cocoa over coffee. Thus, São Tomé and Príncipe planters were victims of their own success as cocoa producers, in a context of an increasingly vociferous international campaign against the thinly disguised slave trade to the island colony.[82] Initially, they planned to grow cocoa at lower elevations, while expanding their output of *arabica* coffee above 500 meters, with cinchona at the highest elevations. However, coffee and cinchona were soon neglected, as the little Portuguese colony in the Gulf of Guinea became one of the largest cocoa producers in the world by about 1900, and labor became ever scarcer and more

---

[76] Haarer, *Modern Coffee Production*, p. 10; L. Vail and L. White, *Capitalism and Colonialism in Mozambique: A Study of the Quelimane District* (London: Heinemann, 1980), p. 265.

[77] Mills, *Ceylon*, pp. 248–9.

[78] A. Coates, *The Commerce in Rubber: The First 250 Years* (Singapore: Oxford University Press, 1987); L. G. Polhamus, *Rubber, Botany, Cultivation and Utilization* (London: Leonard Hill, 1962).

[79] Jackson, *Planters*; Mills, *Ceylon*; Ultée, "Koffiecultuur."

[80] W. G. Clarence-Smith, *Cocoa and Chocolate, 1765–1914* (London: Routledge, 2000); C. J. J. van Hall, *Cocoa* (London: Macmillan, 1914).

[81] P. Hill, *The Migrant Cocoa-Farmers of Southern Ghana*, 2nd ed. (Oxford: James Currey, 1997).

[82] Duffy, *A Question of Slavery*.

expensive.[83] When the neo-slave trade to the islands was finally abolished in the early 1910s, coffee output fell more sharply than that of cocoa.[84]

Oil seeds sometimes displaced coffee at lower altitudes, although producers were often discouraged by prices that compared unfavorably to those of rubber and cocoa until just before 1914. Coconut palms needed to be close to the sea to flourish, and the tip of North Sulawesi, in Indonesia, provided a striking example of a rapid shift of labor resources from highland *arabica* coffee to lowland coconuts. This was achieved through both permanent and temporary migration of people from highlands to lowlands.[85] The substitution of coconuts for coffee was also common in South Pacific islands, and occurred in parts of Malaya.[86] Similarly, coffee appears to have declined at the expense of *purgueira* oil seeds in the Cape Verde Islands.[87] In contrast, oil palms rarely appear to have competed with coffee for either labor or land. Indeed, the spread of oil palms in Sumatra and Malaya may have increased the output of *robusta* coffee, which was planted as a catch crop.[88]

Sugarcane was the main annual crop that competed with coffee at lower altitudes. Coffee trees were uprooted to make way for canes in Natal, despite a severe fall in international sugar prices in the late 1880s.[89] Fiji, Mauritius, and Réunion also witnessed something of a switch from coffee to sugar, albeit more in terms of labor use than through direct substitution.[90] Daily wages in Hawaii in the mid-1890s were allegedly three times higher than those paid by coffee planters in Java, making it

---

[83] W. G. Clarence-Smith, "The Hidden Costs of Labour on the Cocoa Plantations of São Tomé and Príncipe, 1875–1914," *Portuguese Studies* 6 (1990): 152–72.

[84] H. Lains e Silva, *São Tomé e Príncipe e a cultura do café* (Lisbon: Junta de Investigações do Ultramar, 1958), pp. 91–3.

[85] Schouten, *Minahasan Metamorphoses*, pp. 59, 165–7.

[86] D. L. Oliver, *The Pacific Islands* (Honolulu: University of Hawaii Press, 1989), p. 63; Jackson, *Planters*, pp. 202–3.

[87] A. Marvaud, *Le Portugal et ses colonies, étude politique et économique* (Paris: Félix Alcan, 1912), p. 202.

[88] W. G. Clarence-Smith, "The Rivaud-Hallet Plantation Group in the Economic Crises of the Inter-War Years," in Pierre Lanthier and Hubert Watelet, eds., *Private Enterprises during Economic Crises: Tactics and Strategies* (Ottawa: Legas, 1997), pp. 117–32.

[89] Hattersley, *The British Settlement of Natal*, p. 235.

[90] I. T. Twyford and A. C. P. Wright, *The Soil Resources of the Fiji Islands* (Suva: Government of Fiji, 1965), vol. 1, pp. 178, 190; Laërne, *Brazil and Java*; p. 512; Wanquet, "Le Café à la Réunion," pp. 66–8.

all the more urgent for Hawaiian planters to concentrate on the most profitable crops, essentially sugar and pineapples.[91]

Cereals were the annuals more likely to replace coffee at higher altitudes, especially in densely populated islands moving into overall food deficit and experiencing rising food prices. Luzon in the Philippines was one such example, with lands formerly devoted to coffee not only turned over to sugar, but also to maize and rice.[92] In thickly populated and urbanized Java, maize was a popular crop to replace coffee in upland smallholdings.[93]

Alternative opportunities that lured producers away from coffee were not necessarily agricultural. Some plantation lands in Malaya were turned over to prospecting for tin, when coffee prices fell to their lowest point around the turn of the century.[94] Similarly, labor demand from the Kimberley diamond fields from the late 1860s drained workers away from Natal's coffee plantations.[95]

Prices and Taxation

The impact of the world price on the relative success of different producers should have been neutral, but governments intervened in markets through differential taxation, quotas, and similar schemes. In the broadly free trading environment prevailing before 1914, such intervention was limited in scale, contrasting with the neomercantilist resurgence triggered by the First World War. Nevertheless, government intervention, broadly defined, did have an impact on the performance of some producers in this period, with the worst consequences being felt in Africa and Yemen.

The clearest results of protectionism were probably exhibited in Hawaii. To be sure, the establishment of preferential trade with the United States in 1876 initially encouraged a switch of scarce labor from coffee to sugar. However, the availability of growing supplies of immigrant labor, together with the intensification of American protectionism, contributed

[91] F. Mauro, *Histoire du café* (Paris: Editions Desjonquères, 1991), p. 190; Hitch, *Islands in Transition*, p. 45.
[92] M. Sastrón, *Batangas y su provincia* (Malabong: Asilo de Huérfanos, 1895), pp. 354–5; United States of America, *Census*, vol. 4, p. 83; Foreman, *The Philippine Islands*, p. 337.
[93] Hefner, *The Political Economy of Mountain Java*, pp. 166–7; Paerels, "Bevolkingskoffiecultuur," p. 95.
[94] Jackson, *Planters*, p. 203.
[95] Hattersley, *The British Settlement of Natal*, pp. 234–5.

to a spurt of coffee exports to the United States after formal annexa-
tion in 1898.[96] Natural protection, afforded by geographical proximity
to California, may also have played its part.

France, the largest coffee importer in the world after the United States,
was far less successful in boosting imports from her colonies. A 50 percent
rebate on duties on colonial coffee was granted in 1892, but it was subject
to quotas for each colony, revised on an annual basis. As planting coffee
was a decision that had economic consequences over decades, the uncertainty generated by the setting of annual quotas probably offset the tariff
advantage. Moreover, the duty on foreign coffee was not yet high enough
to create a truly segmented market in France, with colonial coffee of equal
quality clearly cheaper than its rivals. A paltry 0.7 percent of French imports thus came from the colonies in 1913, with Guadeloupe and New
Caledonia in the lead.[97] The French even provided direct subsidies to
small European coffee planters in Indochina, but the colony remained a
net importer.[98] Madagascar responded sluggishly before 1914, partly because competing commodities were equally protected, and partly because
discriminating French consumers disliked the coarse *liberica* and *robusta*
varieties produced there after the devastations of *Hemileia* in the 1880s.[99]
It was not until the 1930s that more drastic and effective measures were
taken to supply France with colonial coffee, at the expense of the French
consumer.[100]

French protectionism in Vanuatu (New Hebrides) had a curious differential impact, reflecting the peculiar conditions of the Franco-British
condominium agreed for this Pacific archipelago. French landowners persisted with coffee production for the French market, albeit on a small
scale, whereas British planters abandoned the crop altogether. The latter were discouraged by high duties aimed at developing production in
the tropical north of the new Australian federation after 1901.[101] Protection was long maintained in Australia, even though Queensland's coffee

---

[96] Hitch, *Islands*, pp. 45, 115–16; Graham, *Coffee Production*, pp. 66–7.

[97] A. Sarraut, *La Mise en valeur des colonies françaises* (Paris: Payot, 1923), 187–8; Parsons,
"Coffee," pp. 12–21, 18–20.

[98] C. Guy, *Les Colonies françaises: La Mise en valeur de notre domaine colonial* (Paris: Augustin
Challamel, 1900), pp. 228–9; Mauro, *Histoire du café*, pp. 189–93; Robequain, *The
Economic Development of French Indochina*, pp. 194–7.

[99] Grandidier, *Histoire physique*, vol. 4, pp. 73–5.

[100] Chapter 3.

[101] Weightman, *Agriculture in Vanuatu*, pp. 185–6; Haarer, *Modern Coffee Production*,
pp. 388–9.

output reached only some 70 tonnes in 1910, quite insufficient to meet internal needs.[102]

Discriminatory taxation in the Portuguese empire had other economically perverse effects. Given Portugal's limited requirements, the African colonies of Angola, the Cape Verde Islands, and São Tomé e Príncipe sent coffee to Lisbon only because of measures protecting the monopolistic Portuguese steamer company, the Empreza Nacional de Navegação. Most of this coffee had to be reexported, at considerable cost, harming rather than stimulating colonial economies. Much Angolan coffee was thus smuggled into the internationally guaranteed Congo Free Trade Zone, which included a part of northern Angola in which Portuguese tariffs did not apply.[103]

Spain and Italy were no more successful. Coffee from the Spanish Philippines competed with the more favorably situated colony of Puerto Rico, so that enhanced protection on the Spanish market from 1882 to 1898 failed to prevent the collapse of Philippine exports.[104] Nor did Spanish (Equatorial) Guinea's exports of poor quality *robusta* to Spain rise when Spain lost both Puerto Rico and the Philippines in the 1898 war with the United States, as protective tariffs were not set at a sufficient level. This situation lasted until the Franco regime adopted autarkic policies after 1936.[105] Eritrea was unable to meet its own consumption needs, so that protective duties merely acted as a disguised subsidy to Ethiopian and Yemeni coffee, which was reexported to Italy through Eritrean ports.[106]

Heavy general taxes also contributed to the poor performance of states ruled by impecunious governments. Legal Ottoman Turkish duties on Yemeni coffee exports were fixed at 8 percent ad valorem in the late 1890s, but the real tax burden was much closer to 30 percent. As a result, much coffee was smuggled to the British free port of Aden.[107]

---

[102] Graham, *Coffee Production*, p. 11. These are tonnes of 1000 kilos.

[103] [W.] G. Clarence-Smith, *The Third Portuguese Empire, 1825–1975, a Study in Economic Imperialism* (Manchester: Manchester University Press, 1985), ch. 4.

[104] W. G. Clarence-Smith, "The Economic Dynamics of Spanish Colonialism in the Nineteenth and Twentieth Centuries," *Itinerario* 15, no. 1 (1991): 71–90.

[105] R. Perpiñá Grau, *De colonización y economía en la Guinea Española* (Barcelona: Labor, 1945).

[106] F. Santagata, *La Colonia Eritrea nel Mar Rosso davanti all'Abissinia* (Naples: Treves di Leo Lupi, 1935), pp. 140–7, 155.

[107] A. Grohmann, *Südarabien als Wirtschaftsgebiet, zweiter Teil* (Brünn: Verlag Rudolf M. Rohrer, 1933), p. 86.

The Ethiopian authorities placed a 20 percent export tax and a 10 percent internal tax on coffee, counteracting fiscal concessions intended to encourage production.[108] Liberia, saddled with a large foreign debt and undermined by endemic corruption, was obliged to place its customs under foreign administration in 1908. Export duties on coffee were raised to $1.50 per bushel of hulled coffee and $0.50 per for unhulled coffee, contributing to declining exports in succeeding years.[109]

Conclusion

The impact of *Hemileia vastatrix* was probably the main reason that Africa and Asia fell so far behind the Americas as coffee producers in the last decades of the nineteenth century. However, this needs to be placed in the context of other economic factors, especially if one seeks to understand the bewildering variety of responses to the impact of the fungus or, indeed, differing outcomes in the few areas spared by the disease.

Access to virgin forest was clearly necessary to continue as a successful coffee producer, exploiting the "forest rent" that François Ruf's research has done so much to elucidate. However, not all forests were equally suitable for coffee cultivation. East and Central Africa had much recently opened up forested land that was either quite high or had a marked dry season, or both. These conditions made it easier to combat *Hemileia*, especially when cultivating more valuable *arabica* species. In West Africa, Asia, and the Pacific, forested land was either scarcer or more humid, or both. Alternative crops were thus more attractive in the aftermath of the ravages of *Hemileia* and the collapse of the world coffee price. Government actions to protect markets had a limited impact in broadly free trading conditions, whereas excessive taxation and disturbed political conditions could affect coffee producers quite severely.

Social factors also intervened. Thus, coffee cultivation in Hawaii became a refuge for native Hawaiians and a scattering of immigrants from Japan and the Philippines. They were prepared to grow coffee on marginal lands, accepting a life of drudgery and indebtedness, rather than accept the harsh regimentation of plantation life.[110] Similarly, emigrating into

---

[108] Felcourt, *L'Abyssinie*, pp. 104, 158; McClennan, "Land," p. 73; Graham, *Coffee Production*, p. 99.
[109] Great Britain, Foreign Office, Historical Section, *Liberia* (London, 1919), pp. 45–52.
[110] Oliver, *The Pacific Islands*, p. 192.

the hills to grow coffee was one of the few avenues open to impoverished Vietnamese farmers, if they did not wish to toil in the French rubber plantations of Cochinchina.[111] Such factors should not be ignored, but they need to be recovered with a finer net than is possible in a broad trawl of the kind attempted here.

[111] Robequain, *The Economic Development of French Indochina*, pp. 194–7.

5

The Historical Construction of Quality and Competitiveness

A Preliminary Discussion of Coffee Commodity Chains

Mario Samper K.

Coffee commodity chains serve as a bidirectional link between producers and consumers worldwide, and they also interconnect local processes and those taking place in overseas markets. Historically, there has been an extraordinary diversity in the ways in which cultivation, harvesting, transport, processing, and export of coffee have been organized. Consumption patterns and especially consumer preferences have changed over time in ways that need to be taken into account but whose effect on coffee producers throughout the tropical world varies considerably in accordance with local situations and dynamics.

Coffee farmers' responses to changing external conditions have been far from uniform, and cannot be explained merely as passive reflections of world market trends and fluctuations. This chapter uses the development of Costa Rican coffee production and commercialization, together with brief references to other cases, as a starting point for comparative discussion of interactions between local agroecological, economic, and social conditions, on the one hand, and changes in the international market for this product, on the other.

Special attention is paid to the process by which producers of a given country – in this case Costa Rica – come to produce coffee with certain specific attributes that consumers abroad appreciate and for which they are willing to pay. The Costa Rican coffee commodity chain is compared, in passing, to other ones where "high-quality" coffee is produced and subsequently traded under various arrangements, but with substantial – though, of course, variable – smallholder participation at least in cultivation and sometimes in processing and/or transportation.

The Unity of Production and Consumption

Studies on coffee have tended to discuss production, trade, and consumption as relatively separate issues, pertaining to successive stages in the itinerary by which the seed is obtained, then bought and sold, and ultimately used to make a stimulating beverage. This is reflected in the structure of various general works with chapters on each of these aspects, but not on their interrelations. The same applies to numerous monographs on coffee-producing regions that take the world market into account mainly regarding volume or value of exports from those specific regions, with a cursory look at trends of international supply and demand, as well as certain price fluctuations. We often do not pay enough attention to how, and to what extent, changing external conditions are "internalized" by local economies, where endogenous processes and past history play a decisive role.[1] Nor do we fully realize the degree to which local dynamics may be relatively independent of world market trends and fluctuations, while at the same time having an impact on them.[2]

We tend to take for granted the means by which coffee beans ultimately reach consumers, and how their changing habits and preferences affect the decisions of those who cultivate, process, transport, finance, regulate, and export this tropical product. Conceptually, the unity of production and consumption may be almost self-evident, but historically we need to comprehend how it occurs. We also need to understand what the various cases have in common, and why they differ in certain important respects.

The relatively familiar but diversely understood concept of a "commodity chain" or a "production-consumption chain" invites us to follow the coffee fruit and its bitter seed from farmer to processing mill, sometimes via middlemen, to export firm to international trader to overseas importer, then to wholesale and retail merchant, and finally to consumer. Whatever the terminology and its more specific connotations, the analogy of links in a chain is a useful one, moving beyond mere juxtaposition toward a more integrated perspective on the historical interactions among

---

[1] William Roseberry discusses the importance attached by Cardoso, Faletto, and other Latin American dependency theorists to the "internalization" of external processes, in W. Roseberry, L. Gudmundson, and M. Samper, eds., *Coffee, Society, and Power in Latin America* (Baltimore: Johns Hopkins University Press, 1995).

[2] François Ruf, *Booms et crises du cacao* (Montpellier: Kharthala, 1995) has proposed a model of cocoa production cycles in which local agroecological, technological, demographic, and socioeconomic factors play a crucial role within the broader market- and consumption-related processes of an international commodity.

coffee production, processing, transport, marketing, and final consumption. It may also help us to understand the ways in which consumption has affected production, as well as to appreciate those endogenous processes that respond more to local conditions than to external factors.

The actual existence of commodity chains is open to debate. Some authors believe they are simply an analytical tool, and others point out that production of and trade in a given commodity do not exist in isolation from other productive and commercial activities where participants in one specific chain may also be involved.[3] While recognizing that the concept of a "coffee commodity chain" is constructed for analytical purposes, I would argue that there are certain objective socioeconomic relations and institutional arrangements that do revolve around this specific commodity. Coffee is certainly part of more complex systems of production and exchange, yet since farmers' household consumption of the seed is minimal, and coffee is the main commercial crop on many farms, as well as an export product in most cases, it tends to play an especially important role in rural incomes as well as in regional or national economies. Such was, quite clearly, the case in Costa Rica during its "coffee century," as in various other countries throughout the world over major historical periods, and in some even today.

Systems of Production and Commodity Chains

One obvious limitation of a commodity-oriented approach focusing on coffee is that it tends to underemphasize or even set aside the interactions with other commercial or subsistence crops, which are often quite important for coffee farmers. In the history of Costa Rican coffee production, as in many other countries, polyculture was long the rule, rather than the exception. Complete specialization in coffee production is a relatively recent phenomenon, limited to specific types of farms in certain locations. Relatively remote areas tended to combine coffee with other crops to a greater extent and for longer periods, until improvements in transportation made it possible and cost-effective to bring food crops from elsewhere. In Central America, and typically in El Salvador, this has applied not only to

---

[3] For a brief summary of the former position, see Michel Griffon, "Présentation du séminaire," in CIRAD, *Economie des filières en regions chaudes. Formation des prix et échanges agricoles* (Montpellier: CIRAD, 1990), pp. 1–3, and for the latter, cf. Lawrence Busch, "How to Study Agricultural Commodity Chains: A Methodological Proposal," in ibid., pp. 13–22.

peasant farms, but also to many large estates where part of the workers' remuneration was a simple lunch provided by the hacienda.

Quite often, coffee has been one of two or three purely commercial crops on a farm, a strategy that diversified risk and also facilitated a more even distribution of household or hired labor throughout the year. In Costa Rica, the usual combination has been with sugarcane, which partially overlaps with coffee in terms of the altitudes at which both crops can be successfully planted in the Central Valley. While there is some competition for labor during the coffee harvest, sugarcane cutting can be staggered during the year, thus reducing seasonal peaks in labor demand. Furthermore, price variations for these two crops may offset each other. Some farmers grew coffee and tobacco as their two main cash crops, and more recently there has been a movement toward decorative plants and flower production on formerly specialized coffee farms.

The farmers' objective may not be exclusively or even primarily to obtain the maximum possible coffee harvest. Thus, for example, interplanted bananas or plantain may compete with coffee for soil nutrients, but aside from providing some shade, their crop has a commercial value and can also be used to feed hogs. Low coffee prices induced some farmers to increase the density of plantain, which became their main cash crop until the price of coffee improved. On peasant farms, various types of fruit trees have often been a part of coffee groves, together with tubers, vegetables, medicinal plants, and others. On medium to large estates, specialization within the coffee grove has been greater, and shade has usually been provided by nitrogen-fixing trees that can be regulated by pruning. Especially when prices have been low for several years and prospects of the coffee market become rather pessimistic, some coffee growers plant valuable timber trees instead of legumes, as an investment for the future and a possible alternative to coffee production.

By looking almost exclusively at coffee, we can also forget to inquire about possible associations with livestock raising and other nonagricultural activities on coffee farms. Before motor vehicles, most Costa Rican coffee farms had some pastures where they kept horses, oxen, or mules for transportation, and perhaps dairy cows. On some large coffee farms, beef cattle were also raised for sale in nearby cities. But as land became more expensive in coffee-producing regions, livestock raising tended to migrate toward outlying areas where land was less costly. Peasant coffee farmers, especially in areas outside the Central Valley which were settled between the late nineteenth and mid-twentieth centuries, frequently raised hogs, then sold them locally or took them to urban markets.

In Costa Rica, coffee was the foundation for national agroexport
growth for over a century, but its relative importance for the economy
is today far less significant. In terms of export earnings, its longstanding
rivalry with banana plantations has now given way to highly diversified foreign trade, including traditional and nontraditional agroexports,
as well as manufacturing and service industries. Coffee retains a considerable social significance, partly because a substantial population still
derives a major part of its income from coffee directly or indirectly, but
also because of its sociopolitical and cultural connotations. But the Costa
Rican economy is no longer based on coffee, and will rely on it even less
in the future. Something similar has been happening in several other Latin
American countries, most notoriously in Brazil, which despite being the
world's main producer and exporter, consumes an ever-greater part of its
own production and has a rapidly decreasing market share; coffee plays a
far less important role in its economy than it did during the late eighteenth
to early twentieth century.

Technologies and Social Relations

Coffee commodity chains, like other agroindustrial ones, are dynamic
historical constructs that change over time, in terms of both the technical and the social organization of linkages among cultivation, harvesting,
local transportation, processing, overseas transportation, and distribution abroad. Technological innovations in any phase may substantially
alter the dynamics of other links, both "upstream" and "downstream."
For example, manual depulping machines allowed early-twentieth century
Colombian peasant farmers to produce coffee in remote mountain reaches
from where it would have been extremely difficult to transport cherries in
a few days to centralized processing plants, before their seed underwent
chemical changes detrimental to its quality. At the same time, wet processing by smallholders – as opposed to the drying of cherries – contributed
much to the quality traits associated with mountain-grown, mild-flavored
Colombian coffees, which came to be appreciated by consumers.

In Costa Rica, on the other hand, improvements in transportation facilitated the expansion of supply networks linking numerous small- and
medium-sized farms to the agroindustrial wet-processing plants. Insofar
as fresh cherries could be brought in sufficient amount from somewhat
more distant farms, industrial economies of scale favored larger, better
equipped processing plants, which could process greater quantities in less
time and at lower costs, and this organization of processing also facilitated
quality control.

In Costa Rica, as in Colombia and many other countries, cultivation of coffee was not monopolized by large estates, despite their importance in certain regions and the fact that land tenure was far from egalitarian. The key to control of the coffee business and its grid of social relations was closely associated with how processing was organized: predominantly by the wet method, in central processing plants located either on large farms or in towns and cities, with increasingly technical procedures and attention to quality. Yet such processing also had implications for the manner of harvesting (handpicking only ripe cherries), the development of transportation (first oxcarts, then railroads and trucking), and relations between coffee mill owners and their suppliers of fresh coffee fruit. These "client" networks were not limited to the purchase of cherries, since private credit played a major role in structuring the flow of funds and harvests, especially before nationalization of the banking system in 1949 but even afterward. Interactions between *campesinos* (peasants) and *beneficiadores* (processing mills) in a given place also had other, noneconomic connotations, as shown through interpersonal relations exemplified by *compadrazgo* (Godfatherhood), where symbolic kinship expressed both social hierarchy and reciprocity.

Often viewed as the result of cooperation among economic agents, commodity chains also reflected a delicate and potentially unstable balance of conflicting interests.[4] In the case of coffee, this applied to relations not only among participants in the local export segment, but also between countries that exported and imported this valuable commodity. At times, they have reached agreements to avoid extreme fluctuations of supply and prices; other times, major producers have sought to restrict supply unilaterally to raise prices, although this has invariably invited others to plant more coffee or to intensify their production.

Bargaining power of the various economic agents participating in coffee commodity chains has varied from one period to another. The outcome of conflicts and negotiations among them, as well as government interventions or the impact of an economic crisis, has altered ownership patterns, relative distribution of coffee revenues, degree of vertical or horizontal integration, and overall structure of the commodity chain. For example, the turn-of-the-century crisis made it very difficult to pay back debts, which were then foreclosed. A number of major farms and processing plants thus went from the hands of Central American proprietors to those of

---

[4] See, e.g., Robin Bourgeois and Danilo Herrera, *CADIAC. Cadenas y diálogo para la acción. Enfoque participativo para el desarrollo de la competitividad de los sistemas agroalimentarios* (San José: IICA-CIRAD, 1996).

European creditors. These, in turn, sometimes sold them to countrymen who emigrated to these lands and subsequently maintained close ties with import firms in their fatherlands. This was especially the case of German citizens, who became prominent in the late nineteenth and early twentieth centuries in the coffee sector of Guatemala and Costa Rica. Other devalued and indebted plantations and processing facilities were placed on the local real estate market and a domestic process of centralization ensued. In addition, an as yet undetermined number of smallholders also lost their lands, whether via foreclosures on debts to processing firms or by direct sale to better-off farmers. In late nineteenth- to twentieth-century Costa Rica, such processes of landholding concentration in coffee regions could still be partially counteracted by emigration to settlement frontiers beyond the Central Valley, where coffee farming would develop anew two or three decades later. Ultimately, the gradual end of the coffee frontier made technological intensification crucial for continued growth of Costa Rican coffee production.

Quality Is a Curious Thing

"Good coffee" is a matter of taste, literally and figuratively speaking. Consumers in different places and periods, as well as in different socioeconomic and cultural groups, have preferred various types of coffees, just as they have chosen diverse manners of preparation. Qualities of coffee are a combination of certain measurable traits (such as color, density, chemical composition, humidity, shape, and size of the dry bean); other traits that are best appreciated by connoisseurs and professional tasters (e.g., aroma once roasted and cup flavor); and some intangible features that are nevertheless a factor in consumer preferences: specific brands and national origins, sometimes enhanced by publicity in accordance with exporters' or importers' interests, or a specific type of production ("organic," "green," "bird-friendly") that consumers deem desirable.

Recognition may be awarded to the names of specific farms known to consistently produce coffee with desirable attributes. Some large farmers in Costa Rica have classified their coffees by precise altitudes and locations, harvested and processed them with special care, and exported directly to roasters who contracted supply beforehand.

Preference has often been for coffees from a specific region, the most famous of which is Jamaica's Blue Mountain. In Costa Rica, that distinction was formerly obtained by coffee from Tres Ríos, one of the earlier places of cultivation near the capital city of San José. More recently, Tarrazú came to be considered the ideal zone in terms of altitude, climate, and type of bean obtained. As Gudmundson points out in this volume, this is a dramatic change from the earlier low regard for Tarrazú's coffee. Recently, to avoid possible abuse regarding actual geographical origins of certain coffees, producers as well as processing firms in areas where quality is especially high, such as that of Dota in the region of Los Santos, have sought to guarantee the local origin of all the coffee they process and export.

Roasters, retailers, and consumers have also associated certain generic national as opposed to local origins with especially high qualities. "Mocha" and "Java" are historical examples, which have subsequently acquired very different objective characteristics, and are now terms used for other purposes. Guatemalan, Costa Rican, Colombian, and Kenyan coffees earned longstanding reputations that the international classification system has remunerated accordingly.

When a national origin has been associated with higher quality of coffee from that country, it is worth inquiring how that came to be: Was it simply the more or less objective evaluation of measurable traits or other attributes in blind tasting or did importers and roasters intervene in the social perception of "quality"? How effective have marketing campaigns by exporters and importers been, and since when? These are not questions we can fully answer here, but we should bear them in mind when discussing the historical construction of quality in Costa Rica and as we compare this process with others.

Another relevant point which we cannot resolve in this chapter is that of changing market segmentation, as it pertains to quality and price. In its origins as an exotic product for elite consumption, cost was probably not the most important aspect for nobles, merchants, and intelligentsia. In several respects, coffee subsequently became "the beverage of capitalism," to use the radically appropriate expression of an insightful researcher on the history of coffee marketing and consumption in the United States.[5] In the early stages of its establishment as a working-class beverage during the industrial revolution, and afterward when "coffee breaks" sought to make office workers more alert, price certainly became a very pertinent consideration, and lower-quality seed could find a market. At the same time, social and intellectual elites continued to appreciate certain

---

[5] Michael F. Jiménez, "'From Plantation to Cup': Coffee and Capitalism in the United States, 1830–1930," in Roseberry, Gudmundson, and Samper, eds., *Coffee, Society, and Power*, pp. 38–64.

attributes that they associated with high quality and would usually pay for. This market segmentation was compounded further by blending coffees from various origins by European and North American roasters; then by the development of processes for manufacturing soluble coffees that did not require "high quality" coffees; and more recently by the expansion of nontraditional markets, both in high-income countries where consumers accepted high prices for mountain-grown coffees and in middle- to low-income countries that needed to import coffee but could not pay for the "better" qualities. Therefore, different strategies of producers have been possible, some concentrating on the attainment of the more appreciated characteristics that the market has favored, and others on low-cost production.

Since the mid-nineteenth century, but especially during the first four decades of the twentieth century, many Costa Rican exporters focused on improving quality so as to obtain the best possible price for their coffees. There were others in this country, however, who followed different routes based on cost reduction or on speedier processing to sell their somewhat lesser-grade coffee when prices for all qualities were higher. Clearly, there was a trade-off between quality and production costs, which in some regions favored higher qualities, while in others stressed cost reduction and timing. The former coffee zones were usually at intermediate to high altitudes, and the latter at lower ones where the inherent properties of the seed were less attractive to consumers abroad.

Firms that were vertically integrated from coffee grove to processing to export could adapt both agricultural and agroindustrial production to the objectives of their participation in the international market. Yet even those processing firms that bought all or most of their coffee from local farmers began to set conditions as regards quality of the fruit – especially ripeness – and price differences among qualities became more pronounced. Exporters and agents of wholesale buyers overseas also had clearly defined criteria, quality controls, and price differentials.

Although it improved to the point of obtaining international recognition toward the 1930s, the quality of Costa Rican coffee has been far from uniform. In addition to altitudinal variations, local microclimates and even soil types affected the characteristics of the seed. Not all cherries were harvested with the appropriate ripeness, and even within wet processing there were various methods that yielded different qualities. For example, washing with fresh, clean river water after the cherry has been mechanically depulped is believed to improve the end product, but it is not always done because it requires additional labor and abundant water; subsequent fermentation to remove the mucilage is not always controlled appropriately, and can be accelerated by adding certain substances or substituted by mechanical means, which certainly conserves water and reduces contamination, but may be somewhat detrimental to quality.

It is difficult to ascertain whether the overall quality of Costa Rican coffee has improved or deteriorated over time; perhaps there has been no linear, long-term trend, but rather substantial variations within shorter periods. Processing during the early decades of the nineteenth century was rudimentary, as the whole fruit was sun-dried, then dehusked in stone mortars or by oxcart wheels and oxen hooves, or by adapting rudimentary mechanical devices. It then improved gradually as the wet method prevailed in export-oriented production; ripe cherries were carefully picked; and dry seed was meticulously classified. Nevertheless, persistence of dry processing was reflected in descriptions of "old-type" mills where sun-dried fruit was dehulled, still using stone-laden oxcarts or rudimentary threshing machines in the 1880s, both for domestic consumption and for export (see Tables 5.1 and 5.2).[6]

At the end of the nineteenth century, there were still complaints about the unsatisfactory quality of some of the coffee exported from Costa Rica, while the local press highlighted the fact that the highest quality Costa Rican coffees were always in demand and suffered less price reduction during the turn-of-the-century crisis.[7] However, these coffees had not yet attained the highest prices in a market where the long-standing prestige of certain geographical origins still dominated consumer preferences:

... it is completely dependent on what the buyers understand as "quality" ... the appearance or name of a coffee has an imaginary importance for him. Mocha coffee is the worst one can imagine; yet ultimately it is Mocha coffee, and someone will pay ridiculous prices for it. "Old Government" Java coffee is unwashed, yellow from age, swollen by the humidity it has absorbed, and its aroma is weak, yet they pay high prices for it.[8]

During the subsequent recovery of international prices, Costa Rican and immigrant European coffee processors and exporters seriously bet on quality, and attained positive results. Both in the Roaring Twenties and

[6] See Carlos Naranjo, "El Beneficiado 1890–1930," in *Cuadernos de Historia Aplicada* (Heredia: Universidad Nacional, 2001).
[7] Ibid.
[8] *El Noticiero*, Nov. 14, 1906, p. 1, cited by in ibid., p. 15.

TABLE 5.1. *Costa Rican Coffee Commodity Chain, 1830s–1840s*

Farm-level	Processing	Local trade	Transportation	Overseas trade
Coffea arabica, var. *typica* Usually shadeless or with surrounding trees and plantain Density: c. 2000–2500/ha Area expanded gradually to 4000 or 4500 ha	Artisanal dry processing on small farms; sun-dried on ground; manually dehulled with mortars.	Local and foreign merchants bought hulled, low-quality coffee.	Local: at first mules, then mules and oxcarts. Cart road to Pacific port: *Carretera Nacional* to Puntarenas, built in 1846.	Free trade; downward trend of international price (50% decline 1830s–1840s); short-term crisis in 1848–49. Price of Costan Rican coffee in London market in 1848 was lower than for Rio, Maracaibo, Ceylon, Jamaica.
Annual production grew from several hundred *fanegas* (unit of volume, yields about 100 lb dry seed) in 1830s to 60,000–80,000 in second half of following decade. Productivity/ha. was at first high due to initial fertility and system of cultivation (c. 20–30 *fanegas*/ha; up to 40–50 *fanegas*/ha exceptionally.	Dry-processing on some medium to large farms; dehulling by oxcart wheels or oxen hooves. First wet-method *beneficio* in 1838, with paved *patio*; others in 1840s. Processing capacity of each: c. 2000 *fanegas*/year.	Some *beneficiadores* exported higher-quality parchment coffee, directly or through intermediaries.	To Europe: sailing vessels to Valparaiso and around Cape Horn. Cost of transporting coffee to port: about 12% of FOB price at Puntarenas.	Shipments were small at first, on consignment; credit in kind for imports, payable with coffee sale proceeds. Main destinations (at first through Chile): England, Germany, France

Small coffee groves on larger farms; coffee with other crops on smaller holdings Small groves without shade on larger farms Coffee picking paid first by the day, then by amount Coffee zone: Virilla River basin, then also the valleys of Guarco and Orosi	Manual labor in peasant-farmer *patios*; animal-driven in intermediate *beneficios*; hydraulic force in larger ones to operate depulpers and dehullers.	Local consumption was minimal; chocolate and *aguadulce* preferred.	Storage at port and transfer on lighters to ships was at first a high cost (15–25% of FOB price). Shipping cost about 8% of final price at European port.	Sustained growth of volume exported until 1848 (96,544 qq that year); decrease in following two years. In 1845 there were some 35 exporters. Coffee went from being an experimental crop to become the main item of Costa Rican export trade (5% of value exported in 1833; main export product in 1839; 80% of value of exports in 1843). Costan Rican participation in world trade volume: 0.04% in 1830; 0.2% in 1840; 0.9% in 1850.

TABLE 5.2. *Costa Rican Coffee Commodity Chain, 1850s–1880s*

Farm-level	Processing	Local trade	Transportation	Overseas trade
C. *arabica* var. *typica*; first references to "San Ramon" dwarf cultivar; experiments with C. *liberica*.	Sun-dried coffee hulled with mortars by small-scale farmers; less unpaved *patios* for drying.	Small amounts of lowest grades purchased for local consumption	Oxcarts from farms to processing plants, and from there to Pacific port. Combined railroad and oxcart route to Caribbean port of Limon in 1880s.	Free trade. Prices increased up to mid-1870s due to expanding European consumption; subsequent decline compensated for by international deflation.
Little shade before 1870; then legume and other trees together with *Musaceae* within coffee groves.	Some dry cherry coffee dehusked on medium-sized farms with oxen, oxcarts, or simple equipment; animal-driven threshers with stone wheels to dehusk, wooden wheels to thresh inner membrane.	Owners of *beneficios* bought fresh cherry coffee, exported parchment coffee.		Prices for Costa Rican coffee higher than those for Guatemalan, Rio, and Maracaibo coffees in 1864.
Density of coffee decreased due to interplanted shade; typically 1400–1600/ha, but less in polycultural coffee plots (c. 720–1150/ha)	Major part of harvest is depulped by wet method in *beneficios*, mostly sun-dried but a few mechanical steam-powered dryers near end of period. First machines for polishing and classifying seed. Cleaning with manually operated winnowers. Final selection of dry seed by women working at long tables.			Since 1850, direct trade with Europe; European consignees and some shippers advanced credit (in kind or money) to Costa Rican exporters for purchase of coffee.
Coffee area estimated at c. 15,000–17,000 ha at end of period.				
Annual production: over 100,000 *fanegas* in 1859 and 200,000 in 1867; slower growth in 1870s. Number of farms increased rapidly, up to some 7,500–8,000.		Owners of processing mills made loans to farmers with funding provided by the European importers.	Sail and steamships north along Central American coast, south around Cape.	

Productivity/ha began to decline in older groves of Virilla River basin (near San José/Heredia). High productivity on new lands toward east and west of Central Valley. Problems with ants and *ojo de gallo* (*Mycena citricolor*) in 1880s. Many smallholders and some larger farms in the Virilla watershed began to specialize in coffee. On settlement frontier in N.W. of Central Valley, coffee was combined with several other crops on variously sized farms. Coffee with bananas, livestock, on large farms in Reventazon-Turrialba.

A large *beneficio* could process the coffee delivered by several hundred small farmers.
The number of processing plants (of all types) grew up to some 250 near end of period.

Gradual development of the local habit of drinking coffee, partially displacing chocolate and *aguadulce*.

Cost of internal transportation tripled during 1860s and 1870s; then declined one-third during 1880s due to competition between transport routes toward the Caribbean and Pacific ports. Freight charge by sea was a declining percentage of CIF price in London: 8% in 1850s; 5% or 6% in 1870s and 1880s.

Destinations: England as an entrepot; continental Europe, main consumer market; some coffee to East and West Coasts of the U.S. Volume exported tripled (1885–89 average: 240,000 qq).
Coffee exports accounted for 88% to 90% of total value of Costa Rican exports in 1850s, '60s and '70s; down to 81% in 1883–89 due to banana production.
Costa Rican participation in world coffee market increased from 1.3% in 1851–60 to 2% in following three decades.
76 exporters in 1850 (16 exported 85% of total).

during the recession that followed, fine coffee beans under the recognized
brands of local processors and export firms were sold at comparatively
high prices. Toward 1925, a representative of the Costa Rican coffee sector
in Europe stated that this country's coffee was "one of the most expensive
in the world," and "those of Colombia, Guatemala, and El Salvador can
be bought at much lower prices."[9] Nine years later, an article published in
the official journal of the recently established Instituto de Defensa del Café
stated that prices for Costa Rican coffee were among the highest in the
British market, surpassed only by Jamaican "Blue Mountain."[10] The final
destination for most high-quality Costa Rican coffee at that time was the
German market, where it commanded a high price and there were solid
commercial ties (see Tables 5.3 and 5.4).

During World War II, Costa Rican exports, like those of other Latin
American countries, were redirected toward the U.S. market, which neither recognized nor paid a premium for the finer coffees. Coffee farmers,
processors, and exporters thus became less concerned with quality for
that market, and more with cost reduction. Since then, processing firms
have had two different procedures and qualities: the *chorro americano* and
chorro europeo, depending on whether the coffee went to the Old World
or to North America.

Certain changes in both the agricultural and the agroindustrial phases
have affected the quality of the end product, in Costa Rica as in other
countries. Several of these changes seem to have had moderately detrimental effects on quality, while increasing efficiency or reducing costs:
With the change from *typica* to high-yielding dwarf varieties, there was
an increase in defective beans, and it has been suggested that the quality
of shade-grown is better than shadeless coffee. As labor became more
expensive and scarce for harvesting, and as more immigrant workers
were hired who were used to "milking" the branch rather than picking only ripe fruit, more green coffee was harvested. This trend became
more pronounced as lower prices made selective picking less cost-effective
and new procedures allowed greener fruit to be processed, even if quality suffered. Mechanization of processing may also have harmed quality to a certain extent, although in recent years high-speed electronic

[9] Theodore H. Mangel, cited by Gertrud Peters, "Observatorio histórico de los mercados
   nacionales e internacionales del café. 1900–1960," research paper, Universidad Nacional,
   Heredia, 1998, p. 6.
[10] Ricardo Jinesta, "¿Qué debe hacerse para asegurar el rango del café de Costa Rica en el
   futuro?," in *Revista del Instituto de Defensa del Café* 1, no. 2 (Dec. 1934): 161–5, cited by
   Peters, "Observatorio," p. 11.

color-classification allowed both higher productivity and more uniform grading.

International competitiveness of Costa Rican coffee was built through combining a long-standing concern for quality and ways to lower agricultural and agroindustrial production costs per unit. As labor became more expensive, there was a shift from the strong emphasis on quality during the first four decades of the twentieth century toward higher yields per hectare, harvest-labor productivity, and industrial efficiency to process large volumes at high speeds and then carefully classify the different grades for various markets.

The Costa Rican coffee commodity chain is actually not one but several diverging segments, geared toward different product qualities and consumer markets: The worst and cheapest coffees have invariably been for domestic consumption, and the percentages retained for local consumers have been – not by chance – roughly the same as the proportion of difficult-to-export low-grade coffee produced. The legalized local roasters' practice of mixing coffee with peanut shells and burnt sugar – to add bulk and weight as well as sweetness and dark color – created popular consumption habits that came to prefer bad coffee, and made domestic demand for the pure product rather marginal. Only when prices abroad have been very low, and especially during the more recent crises of the world market, as domestic prices were deregulated, have some firms sold a larger part of their good coffee on the local market, and a growing segment of the population has come to appreciate the higher grade product.

While the export market was oriented mainly toward Europe, quality tended to improve to take advantage of the better prices offered there. As overseas consumers began to purchase ground coffee, and to do so in supermarkets rather than in coffee shops, there was a trend toward prepackaged mixtures of coffee under certain brand names. The appearance of the green or roasted bean became less important, although place of origin continued to be important due to its role in publicity and in consumer preferences.

As the less discriminating U.S. market became more significant toward the mid-twentieth century, processing tended to emphasize cost reduction. In recent decades, there has been an expansion of "gourmet" and "ecological" niche market segments, both in the United States and in Western Europe. Demand has become even more diversified with the rise of coffee consumption both in Japan and – less vigorously – in Eastern Europe, respectively in the upper and lower price/quality ranges (see Tables 5.5 and 5.6).

TABLE 5.3. *Costa Rican Coffee Commodity Chain, 1890s to 1920s*

Farm-level	Processing	Local trade	Transportation	Overseas trade
C. *arabica* var. *typica*; introduction and initial dissemination of *bourbon* cultivar; experimental planting of C. *canephora* (*robusta*) toward end of period.	Wet method dominant and highly concentrated in Central Valley, with various degrees of technification as well as vertical and horizontal integration.	Fresh cherry coffee purchased directly by *beneficiadores*, who obtained funds abroad and lent to small and medium farmers.	Oxcarts to plants and railroad stations. Initial use of motor vehicles in 1920s. Coffee sent by rail to Caribbean port; after 1910 also to Pacific.	Market without joint regulations, but unilateral Brazilian initiatives: three "valorizations" (1907, 1917, 1920) and "permanent defense policy" for coffee in 1920s.
Arabica coffee under shade in varying mix of domestic production units and wage labor farms throughout Central Valley. More specialized coffee farms in Virilla watershed. Coffee with other crops on settlers' farms in Los Santos, Tilaran, Nicoya, San Carlos.	Dry process in some drier or more remote regions, with coffee dried on trees or on ground, for domestic consumption; also stolen from farms and *patios*.	Price setting by owners of processing plants. First open conflicts between producers and *beneficiadores* during the turn-of-the-century crisis.	Steamships across Atlantic and to East Coast of U.S. Internal transportation about 9% of FOB price in 1890s; local freight charge diminished in early 20th century.	Highest price attained in 1894; major crisis from 1897 to 1906; subsequent recovery with short-term fluctuations (WWI, crisis of 1920); Costa Rican coffee lost relative value after 1927.
Beginnings of first modernization of coffee production: regulated legume tree shade, increased use of fertilizer in older	Dissemination of the use of mechanical dryers, cylinder and disk dehuskers, threshers, polishers, and other equipment with motors in main wet-processing plants. Internal combustion engines for power and initial use of electricity for lighting.	A few foreign importers had local representatives to buy parchment from smaller *beneficiadores* who	Ocean freight charges decreased between late 19th and early 20th	Destinations: market for lower-quality coffee on East and West

groves, new pruning systems. Average planting density about 1580/ha.

Coffee area: 20,000 ha toward end of 19th century. Annual production: 470,000 *fanegas* in 1898; fluctuated between 330,000–420,000 *fgas* until 1921 (except for 1914 and 1916); then grew to reach half million *fanegas* in late '20s.

Number of farms: about 8,600 from 1883 to 1893. Productivity declined sharply on older coffee farms in Central Valley (7 or 8 *fanega*/ha vs. average of 10–12), due to loss of fertility, pests, and diseases. Higher yields on new lands brought into production outside Central Valley.

Coffee picking paid by amount harvested, except during turn-of-the-century crisis.

Technologically diverse *beneficios*, from mere *patios* for sun drying to technified production systems. Maximum processing capacity per season remained around 5000 *fanegas*.

220 processing plants in 1920s

did not export directly. Some coffee was purchased by farmers with dry-processing facilities, sold locally.

Coasts of the U.S.; England was the trading center for higher grades; Germany, main market for high-quality coffee imported directly or via England.

Volume exported grew slowly (40% in 40 years);

1925–29 average: 388,000 qq.

Importance in Costa Rican foreign trade declined from 90% to between 35% and 55%.

Costa Rican participation in world coffee market: 1% in 1890s, 1.5% in 1900–1909.

187 main exporters in 1907, 124 in 1915.

Centuries, rose again during WWI

TABLE 5.4. *Costa Rican Coffee Commodity Chain, 1930s to 1950s*

Farm-level	Processing	Local trade	Transportation	Overseas trade
Arabicas: typica, Bourbon, Hibrido Tico (tall, 1940s), and *Villa Sarchí* (dwarf, mid-century). Technological transition with gradual increase in density of plantations and fertilization, under regulated shade, on variously sized farms. Major growth of coffee area (including farms <0.7 ha): 48,000 ha in 1935, 53,000 (est.) in 1950, 83,000 (est.) in 1963. Production fluctuated around 1/2 million *fanegas* until 1955, with a slight downward trend; rapid growth of	Number of private *beneficios* declined: 222 in 1935, some 150 in 1940s, about 124 in late '50s. Greater reduction in central coffee region; some *beneficios* moved to new coffee zones, or new ones were built there. Junta de Custodia (wartime office in charge of managing German property) operated several *beneficios* during WWII. Banco Inter/Nacional operated several processing plants during 1940s and '50s. First steps of cooperative movement. Mechanization increasingly based on internal combustion motors and electricity; centrifuges to eliminate excess moisture; predriers and driers; equipment to save labor moving coffee	Regulated since 1930s by Instituto de Defensa del Café (after 1848, Oficina del Café). System of advance payments upon receival, and final payment after sale overseas. More conflicts between coffee farmers and processors in early '30s, then channeled institutionally. Coffee processed by small *beneficiadores* was bought by local exporters.	Local transportation in oxcarts; also trucks to *beneficios* and from there to railroad stations. Coffee sent by rail to ports on both coasts. Inter-American Highway connected potential coffee zones in southern part of the country: first Pérez Zeledón, then Coto Brus.	Unregulated up to 1930s; U.S. quotas during WWII; subsequent negotiations. Mediocre but guaranteed prices during the WWII; strong postwar demand with high prices until 1956; sharp decline after that year. Destinations: Europe (esp. Germany) main consumer market in 1930s; exports to the U.S. during war; afterward two paths with different qualities and prices.

Export volume unchanged in 1930s–40s; moderate growth in 1950s. Relative weight of coffee in Costa Rican foreign trade grew to 60% in 1930s, then fluctuated within downward trend. Costa Rican participation in world coffee trade: about 1.4% to 1.5% in 1930s, declined during and after WWII to 1% toward 1950; recovered to 1.8% at end of period. Number of export firms declined: 80% of CR coffee was exported by four firms in 1944/45.

Steamships to Europe and the U.S.

Most *beneficiadores* no longer exported directly. State-owned banks channeled funding toward cooperatives and supported technification in 1950s.

within the plant; mechanical separators to partly automate grain selection; first trials of mechanical selection using electronic eyes. Receival networks expanded with improved roads, use of trucks, and construction of wooden *recibidores*. Increasing overlap in areas of influence of the various *beneficios*. Better use of installed capacity by receiving coffee from various regions where it ripens at different times. Some plants received and mixed coffee from various altitudes. Wide range of scales of operation: Most plants had less than 20 workers, but most of the labor force was concentrated in the larger ones. Very small *beneficios* tended to disappear; greater weight of those processing 10–19,000 and 20,000+ *fanegas*.

production after that year, to surpass 1 million *fanegas* in 1959–60. Gradual increase in number of coffee farms (including those <0.7 ha): 25,000 in 1935, 28,000 (est.) in 1950, 35,000 (est.) in 1963. Low yields/ha in 1930s–40s, partial recovery in 1950s (5.3 *fanegas*/ha in production in 1935, 10–11 *fanegas*/ha in prod. in 1955); major differences in yields by regions and by types of productive units. Land settlement and initial expansion of coffee in Pérez Zeledón and Coto Brus. With lower prices during WWII, more green coffee to reduce production costs.

TABLE 5.5. *Costa Rican Coffee Commodity Chain, 1960s to 1980s*

Farm-level	Processing	Local trade	Transportation	Overseas trade
Caturra and other dwarf cultivars became predominant (35% in '79/80, 85% in '88–'89); high densities (7,000/ha); heavy chemical inputs. Average yields increased in '70s to become world's highest; relatively stable in '80s. Higher yields positively correlated with farm size (5.5 MT/ha. under 5 ha., 5.8 to 7.4 on larger farms). Agricultural labor productivity (especially in harvest) multiplied. Area in coffee	Major expansion of areas from which each *beneficio* brought fresh coffee; reduction in number of plants from 119–122 at start of period to a hundred in late '80s. Cooperative *beneficios* processed up to 40% of harvest. Minimum required *rendimientos* (conversion of fresh *fanegas* to dry seed *quintales*) set by regulating agency; profit margins of *beneficios* set by law. Labor-saving technologies applied to process more coffee, cost-effectively, in fewer but larger plants. Average capacity tripled; toward end of period 40 beneficios processed more	Regulated by Oficina del Café, under Ministry of the Economy. New legislation on relations among producers, processing plants, and export firms as of 1961. Separation of coffee processing and roasting for domestic consumption. Vast purchasing networks brought coffee from various regions to	Local transportation mainly by jeep and truck; road network rapidly expanding. *Beneficiadores* had their own trucks, but began to hire transportation.	Regulated until 1989 by ICO for exports to member countries, but growing nonquota market. Destinations: Higher quality coffee exported to W. Europe, gourmet market in the U.S., and Japan; lower grade coffee to other markets. Federation of coffee-producing cooperatives became a major export firm. Vertical integration and concentration of

production stable at about 80,000 hectares during 1970s and in 1984 census.

Annual coffee production: sustained growth since 1960s, 2 million *fanegas* in mid-'70s, roughly 3 million *fanegas* in 1985–86.

Number of farms relatively stable; about 34,000 in 1984.

Strong expansion of coffee growing in Pérez Zeledón as of 1970s.

Sharply defined quality differences according to altitude, climate, and region.

Strong immigration of Nicaraguan harvest workers during 1980s.

than 30,000 *fanegas* each. Major agroindustrial economies of scale, growing labor productivity.

Last stage of processing for export became highly technical, and was increasingly carried out by exporters.

processing plants in central locations.

Local consumption varied as percentage of total production: declined in 1960s, grew until 1982–83, then fluctuated.

Coffee sent by rail and truck to both coasts, then shipped overseas in containers.

export firms with investments in processing.

Declining weight of coffee in the national economy.

Growing participation of Costa Rica in the world market: 1.8% to 2% at the start of this period, 2.2% to 3.3% during 1980s.

TABLE 5.6. *Costa Rican Coffee Commodity Chain, 1990s*

Farm-level	Processing	Local trade	Ship transportation	Overseas trade
90% of coffee trees in 1993–94 were *caturra* or *cattuai*.	Most *beneficios* eliminated fermentation and considerably reduced use of water.	Domestic market (11%) deregulated since '92; four-fifths controlled by three firms. Total number of local roasters: 48 ICAFE became a "non-governmental public entity" as of 1998.	Railways closed down. Trucking throughout domestic network. Local transportation under contracts. Coffee taken to port in containers, whether in bags or bulk. Containerized shipments from both ports to Europe, U.S., Japan, others. 80% of coffee via Caribbean port.	No ICO quotas since '89. Free trade in coffee. Some restrictions later by agreement among coffee-producing countries (ACPC) to support prices.
Renewal of coffee groves in some highly productive zones; decline of coffee production in certain marginal areas.	99 *beneficios* in operation, of which 23 are cooperatives. Some cooperatives with processing plants went bankrupt.			Acute crisis from 1989 to 1993, subsequent recovery, then sharp, speculative fluctuations, recent major drop in prices.
Temporary reduction in use of agrochemicals with low prices, then increase with better prices.	Changes in ownership of private *beneficios*; greater participation by MNCs in local processing firms. Four groups acquired control over processing of 30% of coffee harvested, and national coverage.	Domestic consumption about 10 to 12% of total production. Greater diversity and gradual improvement of coffee sold locally.		Germany, the main importer of Costa Rican coffee (21%), followed by Great Britain and the U.S (13% each).
70,000 *entregadores* (persons who deliver coffee to plants) but only some 40,000 farms. 60% of farms under 5 ha.	Four-fifths of beneficios processed more than 20,000 *fanegas* each; several processed more than 100,000 each.	Costa Rica with highest per capita consumption among coffee producing countries (4.1 kg per year, five-year average)		Greater control over coffee exports by a few MNCs. Seventeen main export firms.
Total area in coffee production: relatively stable at 106,000 ha.	Only one-tenth of *beneficios* carried out the complete process of preparing the grain for export; the rest sent the dry seed to specialized plants.			Brand names once again became important; direct ties between processing firms, exporters, and overseas importers. Small-scale efforts to market organic and other ecological coffees.
Average yields: 33–35 *fanegas*/ha. Heavy reliance on Nicaraguan labor force for harvest.	Some coffee roasted in the country for export.			Costa Rican participation in world coffee market: 3.1% to 3.5%

The Cost of Good Coffee

The higher price paid for certain coffees is related to objective traits and subjective consumer preferences, as well as to higher costs of production and limited supply. Jamaican "Blue Mountain" is perhaps the extreme case in this regard, but "mountain grown" mild washed coffees from specific high-altitude regions are also examples of the above.

Price fluctuations have been moderated for some time by overt or covert agreements among exporters and/or importers, as they were from the establishment of the International Coffee Organization in the early 1960s to the demise of the economic accord in 1989. Short-term climatic factors in a major producing country like Brazil have pushed prices upward temporarily, while speculative buying and selling can make speculative buying and selling more pronounced, as they have done recently. Yet in the long run, the changing costs of supplying what the market demands will tend to prevail.

Nevertheless, coffee supply is neither immediately nor mechanically determined by current prices, as other factors have played an important role. One such factor has been the well-known effect of the delay between planting new coffee areas, often toward the end of a high price period, and the growth of production in subsequent years while prices declined further and further. Yet we must also bear in mind that the expansion of coffee production areas has frequently been associated with peasant-farmer settlement processes that may reflect endogenous dynamics rather than price trends.

Coffees having attributes associated with "high quality" can be produced only in certain places, which are not necessarily the most productive in terms of yields per area. As with some vineyards where grapes for the finest wines may be harvested, such lands and climates are often not the ideal ones for abundant crops. In the case of coffee, it is not fertility but rather altitude, in conjunction with other climatic factors, that seems to have made the difference.

In Costa Rica today, Tarrazú and Dota toward the south, in the mountainous region of Los Santos, and several areas at relatively high altitudes on the volcanic slopes of the Central Valley produce especially "good" coffees, under somewhat suboptimum conditions regarding yields and productivities. Temperature and cloudiness may cause problems with certain fungal diseases, partly counteracted by the elimination of shade trees and use of fungicides. The harvest there tends to be late, and the fruit are slow to mature. Several *pasadas* (pickings) are required, and therefore costs of harvesting are higher.

Average yields in Costa Rica are relatively high compared with other regions of the tropics where "strictly hard bean" *arabica* coffee is grown, but they are obtained with heavy financial investments, and unit costs may be similar or higher than elsewhere.

Differences among species of *Coffea* affect both quality and cost of production. *Robusta* may be cultivated successfully where *arabica* cannot, for example, at lower altitudes and in much warmer climates, thus incorporating vast lowland areas of Africa and Asia. Yields of *robusta* per hectare are substantially higher than for *arabica*.[11] For some countries, planting *robusta* has been a viable strategy, but others – like Costa Rica – focused on quality, opted for mountain-grown *arabica*, and ultimately forbade the planting of other species of *Coffea*.

Historically, disease has been a significant factor in the displacement of *arabica* by *robusta*. Such was the case in the Netherlands East Indies (now Indonesia). Clarence-Smith explains in this volume how *arabica* production came under attack by coffee rust (*Hemileia vastatrix*), and subsequently recovered with *robusta*. The slow spread of coffee rust from one continent or region to another has made cultivation with susceptible species and varieties costly and less productive, even though means were later found to control it to a certain extent.

Some hybrid *arabica* cultivars have been selected for resistance to major diseases, but the effect of new varieties and farming systems has been a mixed one: together with higher yields, it has become necessary to replant coffee groves more frequently. Economic advantages for farmers who modernized successfully using these cultivars are more obvious in terms of total income per hectare than in unit costs. On the other hand, certain dwarf cultivars that seem less susceptible to fungi such as coffee rust nevertheless have raised serious quality concerns among farmers.

Transportation and Transformation

Domestic transportation has at times been an obstacle to the expansion of coffee production in specific regions, despite their potential to produce high-quality coffee. The difficulty and cost of taking the fruit to processing plants made it less attractive for owners of capital to invest in coffee plantations on remote and rugged mountainous lands than, say, in

---

[11] In India, recent data are 760 kg/ha for *arabica*, and 1112 kg/ha for *robusta*. Cf. Sunalimi N. Menon, "Notes Techniques. Interconnection between Post Harvest Processing and the Intrinsic Quality of Coffee," in *Café cacao thé* 36, no. 3 (July–Sept. 1992): 213–22.

livestock raised in more accessible valleys. Instead, peasant settlers entering mountain ranges with lands and climates agroecologically ideal for high-quality coffee found coffee to be a useful commercial crop to supplement their subsistence plantings, even if transportation was difficult and initial processing had to be done on the farm. The classical case in this regard is late nineteenth- and early-twentieth-century Antioquia, in western Colombia, where ranchers dominated the valleys and peasants farmed coffee and subsistence crops and raised hogs in the highlands. A more recent Central American example has been that of Honduras, where expansion of grazing in lowlands apparently pushed peasant farmers into a number of more distant mountainous areas, where transportation was difficult but coffee did quite well. After the mid-twentieth century, smallholder coffee production expanded rapidly in that country, which was formerly dominated by cattle and bananas.

Dried coffee cherries can be kept for longer periods than the fresh fruit, but weight and volume make transportation costly over great distances. It is then preferable to dry-process coffee either on the farm itself or at a nearby plant, as in parts of El Salvador, where local scarcity of water was a limiting factor at harvest time. As is well known, Brazil had opted for dry processing large volumes of lower-grade coffee. There is not much detailed information on dry processing in Costa Rica, perhaps because its existence was officially ignored most of the time, but we do know that where water was insufficient for wet processing and transportation difficult, the dry cherries were processed locally.

Wet processed parchment coffee (*pergamino*) is much lighter than the whole cherries. While the seeds are still covered by the inner skin or shell that gives it the name, the pulp and exterior skin have been removed. The parchment is left on to protect the bean during processing, storage, and transportation. Under appropriate conditions, dry parchment coffee can be kept a longer time without much harm coming to the desirable attributes of the seed. Actually, the parchment protects the seed, and well into the twentieth century, much Costa Rican coffee was exported as *pergamino*, rather than as green coffee (*café oro*).

Given the poor storage and transportation facilities available in the nineteenth century, and even in the early twentieth, parchment did in fact help protect the beans. British importers preferred to thresh it in the United Kingdom, after which they reexported most of it to continental Europe. Gradually, and more rapidly after midcentury, improvements in storage, packing, and transportation as well as the growing importance of the U.S. market – where importers preferred green coffee – made local threshing predominant in Costa Rica and other coffee-producing countries. At first it was done in the existing agroindustrial plants, then in a few highly technically sophisticated plants where wet-processed coffee was polished and classified for export.

Overseas transportation was a major component of costs, and could also affect quality. Sailing ships with Costa Rica's first coffee exports took the Pacific route along South American coast to Valparaíso, from where it was reexported to Europe and, at first, given the Chilean port of origin. Toward 1890, the newly constructed railroad to the Caribbean coast shortened the overseas distance considerably for coffee exports from Costa Rica to Europe and the eastern United States. At the same time, steamships further reduced costs and delays, together with risk of product deterioration from long voyages at sea.

In comparison with previous Central American export crops since colonial times, such as indigo and cochineal, freshly harvested coffee and even the dry bean is a somewhat bulky commodity. Therefore, the sustained extensive growth of coffee cultivation has required – and also facilitated – a continuous expansion and improvement of transportation networks, from farm to processing center to warehouse to port.

Before and Beyond the Coffee Farm

Agricultural production does not take place exclusively on farms, nor only from planting to harvest. The prior origins and itineraries of coffee seed, systems of cultivation, and processing methods are essential to an understanding of the historical development of this commodity chain. In the case of Costa Rican coffee, the original seed of the *typica* variety apparently came from Cuba in the late eighteenth century. The know-how on shadeless cultivation and wet processing had in turn been brought there by emigrant planters from St. Domingue (now known as Haiti), who sought refuge from the storm of revolutionary emancipation in the former French colony. Subsequently, seed of other species of *Coffea* and other varieties of *C. arabica* came to Costa Rica, by various routes, from several parts of the world.

As rural settlement expanded well beyond the Central Valley, Costa Rican farmers in areas where *arabica* did not grow well experimented with other species of *Coffea*: In 1886, *liberica* coffee (from western Africa, possibly by way of Jamaica where it first arrived in 1874) was for sale in the capital city of San José; it was announced as especially appropriate for warm, humid, low-altitude zones. However, the quality of the coffee obtained was unsatisfactory. Since 1908, *canephora*, or *robusta*, seed (from the Belgian Congo, probably also via the West Indies) was locally disseminated on an experimental basis by the Costa Rican Department of Agriculture in the Caribbean coastal lowlands and in the northern plains. As soon as small amounts of this coffee were exported during World War I, the issue of quality became paramount: Shipments containing *robusta* were considered inferior and brought lower prices, so the decision was reached to destroy the experimental plantations.[12]

Quality was also an issue with respect to varieties of *Coffea arabica* other than *typica*: Bourbon, a variety from the island of Réunion, which gained favor in El Salvador, was planted on a small scale in Costa Rica's Central Valley in the early twentieth century. There was considerable debate on whether its quality was similar to that of *typica*, and fear of a fiasco similar to that of *robusta* exports led to measures forbidding its introduction and dissemination. However, in the 1940s a number of tests sponsored by the Central American and Mexican Coffee Federation, together with U.S. importers, put the issue to rest by classifying Bourbon coffees in the same "strictly high grown" category as *typica* harvested in Costa Rica's Central Valley. Immediately, the Costa Rican coffee board, Instituto de Defensa del Café, began to plant large seedbeds and to massively distribute the Bourbon variety.[13]

Shortly thereafter, a mutation of Bourbon coffee with a dwarfing gene led to the appearance and subsequent selection of a smaller yet highly productive variety, named Villa Sarchí after the area of Costa Rica's Central Valley where it was found and where commercial seedbeds were established. It turned out to be very similar to Brazilian *caturra*, which became the dominant cultivar after its introduction in the 1960s. Both responded quite well to high-density plantations with little or no shade, if large amounts of fertilizer were applied together with uniform pruning. Yields per hectare and productivity of labor increased dramatically, and quality of the end product was seemingly unaltered (although several elderly farmers still believe that *typica* yielded better coffee).

Unit costs of production probably did not diminish substantially with the new genetic material and technological package, but neither did they increase notoriously. Long-term agroecological sustainability and energy efficiency of this new system of cultivation may be open to debate, but

---

[12] Carlos Naranjo, "La Modernización de la caficultura costarricense 1890–1950," M.Sc. thesis in history, Universidad de Costa Rica, 1997, pp. 94–104.

[13] Ibid., pp. 103–4.

most Costa Rican farmers adopted the small, high-yielding varieties. However, despite the strong trend toward technological intensification, actual farming systems were far less uniform than one might infer from official recommendations and standardized descriptions.

Processing as a Crucial Link

Coffee mills or *beneficios* that used the wet-processing method were the key component of the Costa Rican coffee commodity chain. "Upstream," they purchased the fresh fruit from a number of small- to medium-sized farmers, to whom they often lent money, usually requiring a commitment to deliver a specified amount of coffee to that *beneficio*, in addition to other guarantees. "Downstream," several plants might supply a single export firm, whether or not they were under common ownership.

The organization of processing affected the structure of production, local transportation, domestic exchanges, and export of coffee. To cite only two examples that differ substantially from the situation in Costa Rica, most coffee estates (fincas) in Guatemala have had their own *beneficio*, and often exported their own coffee. In western Colombia, many small farmers, since the early twentieth century, have depulped and dried their own coffee, which they subsequently sold to local merchants acting as agents of major exporters, or – after 1927 – via the Federación de Cafeteros de Colombia.

Since the mid-nineteenth century, most Costa Rican coffee has been processed by the wet method in agroindustrial *beneficios*. This contributed to better quality, and also led to concentration of control over processing, credit networks for coffee production, and the export business. This is not to say that all Costa Rican coffee was thus processed, nor that all *beneficios* belonged to members of the coffee-exporter elite. At the turn of the century, newspaper reports stated that over half the coffee harvested in this country was poorly processed, and much of that was "dried without previously depulping, and is identical to that of Nicaragua and El Salvador, and suffers the same fate as the coffee from those countries, though not that of coffee from Brazil."[14] Part of Costa Rica's coffee was still dry-processed in the early to mid-twentieth century, and even in the late 1970s this was the prevailing method in certain outlying, rather marginal, coffee zones. However, "natural" coffee beans, from sun-dried cherries, were also produced in the core coffee-producing region, often

---

[14] *La República*, January 29, 1898, p. 3, cited in ibid., p. 41.

from stolen fruit and also from green or defective cherries.[15] The quality of these "natural coffees" was considered very inferior, and efforts were made for it to be sold only in the domestic market, then called the Bolsa del Café de Consumo Nacional.

Up to the mid-twentieth century, most Costa Rican processing centers were located on larger farms in the Central Valley and in a few rather remote coffee-producing regions. Farmers or merchants might take the cherries directly to a nearby *beneficio*, but as competition between the buyers became more intense, in the early decades of the twentieth century, the agents of certain processing firms would go meet the oxcarts that brought coffee toward San José or another major city, and would purchase it in the outskirts, thus preempting other potential buyers. Starting in the 1920s, motor vehicles and road construction facilitated the use of trucks as mobile collection points. Between the 1930s and the 1950s, a growing number of processing and export firms constructed partially overlapping networks of *recibidores,* that is, small wooden structures where fresh coffee fruit was received, measured, and loaded onto trucks every day during the harvest.

The number of *beneficios* grew during the second half of the nineteenth century, but in the course of the twentieth century those numbers first became stable and then decreased after the 1940s as improved transportation made it possible to centralize processing. Supply networks for each coffee mill, which used to overlap locally within the Central Valley, expanded to cover much larger regions, and began to bring coffee from several different parts of the country. Clearly, this altered the structural relations between farmers and processing firms, but also interactions among the latter. Competition for "clients" was often keen, yet at the same time *beneficiadores* sought to coordinate prices offered to farmers, or at least the advances given upon receipt of the fruit, so as to improve their collective bargaining position. Recently, a group of major private and cooperative processing firms signed and publicized a document in which they coordinate their policies on purchase of the fruit, especially regarding degree of ripeness.

Since the late nineteenth century, Costa Rican farmers have been becoming better informed on prices overseas through the local newspapers, which in turn received dispatches via submarine cable, instead of waiting for ships to arrive with news as before. During the turn-of-the-century crisis, coffee producers began to object more vocally to joint price setting

---

[15] Alvaro Jiménez, *Algunas ideas sobre comercialización de cafés naturales y el serio problema del merodeo* (San José: Oficina del Café, 1978).

by the processing and export firms, "who have come together to make war on the poor farmers...there is no doubt that it is a preconceived plan...."[16] Shortly thereafter, the farmers' suspicions were confirmed as the press reported an agreement among the main processing firms in the central coffee-producing region to reduce prices in a concerted fashion. Small farmers in at least one major city reacted by rapidly mobilizing and threatening to let their coffee dry on the tree, and a week later the price paid to them had risen considerably.[17]

At least one attempt was made to eliminate price differentials in favor of coffee farmers in certain specific locations, where quality and recognition abroad allowed exporters to obtain exceptionally high prices. When the processing mills attempted to set a uniform price for all coffees in 1903, farmers in that area mobilized and successfully defended their advantage, while also setting a precedent by questioning the *precio corriente* (the current price paid for coffee on the local market).[18]

In the 1920s, larger farmers and owners of processing plants, grouped in the Chamber of Agriculture, set the domestic purchase price of coffee for all *beneficios*, nationwide. Perhaps more than the price level itself, this joint decision irritated small and medium producers because it effectively stopped them from negotiating better prices for their coffee from one or another coffee mill. In addition to earning those very distinguished gentlemen the sobriquet of "El Trust" de la Cámara de Agricultura (the Coffee Chamber Trust), that decision served as a catalyst for the establishment of an independent association of coffee farmers, which was to play a prominent role in the struggle against unilateral price setting in the following years.[19]

Owners of *beneficios* were perceived by a number of small and medium-sized coffee growers or their spokesmen in early twentieth-century Costa Rica as *"el trust" de los beneficiadores*, or what an economist might call an oligopsonic group. The larger firms certainly did try to set prices among themselves and artificially create a "buyers' market" situation. As the leader of the Asociación Nacional de Productores de Café stated in 1932, when disputes over the local price of coffee were acute and small farmers

---

[16] In "El Café y sus explotadores," 1898, cited by Naranjo, *La Modernización*, p. 43.
[17] Naranjo, *La Modernización*, pp. 47–48.
[18] Ibid., pp. 48–50.
[19] The mobilization and slogans of this movement have been discussed by V. H. Acuña, "La Ideología de los pequeños y medianos productores cafetaleros costarricenses (1900–1961)," in *Revista de Historia*, no. 16 (July–Dec. 1987): 137–59. With respect to the 1921 agreement and subsequent protests, see Naranjo, *La Modernización*, pp. 233–5.

were rallying against the processing firms, some of which had also begun to take lands away from debtors unable to pay back their loans in the midst of that crisis: "The owners of coffee mills have behaved as wolves."[20] However, elite solidarity was sometimes broken by a newcomer or a renegade *beneficiador* seeking to increase his participation in the processing and export business. One might even reinterpret the laws that subsequently regulated relations between coffee farmers and processing firms, and the very creation of the Instituto de Defensa del Café, as legal and institutional measures that not only defused confrontations between those two groups, but also institutionalized price-setting mechanisms and relations among the *beneficiadores* themselves. The government mediated to avoid extreme abuses that might, in turn, cause renewed protests by smaller coffee farmers.

Relations between processing firms and their coffee suppliers were subsequently regulated via institutional channels, but conflicting interests still caused serious frictions in following years. President León Cortés (1936–40), a member of the coffee elite who chaired the Board of the Coffee Institute, confronted the leader of the National Association of Coffee Producers. As Gudmundson discusses in this volume, during the 1940s and '50s there were fewer open conflicts between mill owners and organized smallholders. Despite their opposition, social legislation was passed during World War II by the unique alliance of a more or less "social-Christian" government that had lost elite support, the workers' movement led by an increasingly moderate Communist Party, and the socially progressive hierarchy of the Catholic Church. The banking system was nationalized in 1949 by the more or less "social-democratic" winners of a brief civil war. They had been supported by the coffee elite in their efforts to overthrow the previous government, but their reformist sociopolitical project required breaking the monopoly of that very elite over credit and strengthening the role of the state in the economy. Some of the large farms and coffee mills taken from German citizens during World War II remained under administration by nationalized banks during the 1950s, and in the early '60s were transferred to smallholder cooperatives. The Coffee Institute was also reorganized after the civil war, and became the Oficina del Café. In 1961, after considerable public debate and private negotiations, a new law was passed that modified the regulations pertaining

---

[20] Manuel Marín Quirós, "Discurso ante la Asamblea de Productores de Café, celebrada en el Teatro Júpiter de Guadalupe, en la tarde del domingo 27 de marzo de 1932," in *Revista de Historia*, no. 16 (July–Dec. 1987): 133–6.

to relations among coffee farmers, processing firms, and exporters.[21] Since then, under the international coffee accord, the Coffee Office (now Instituto del Café) played a prominent role in the administration of export agreements, until the breakdown of the international quota system in 1989. In January 1998, the Coffee Institute became a nongovernmental public institution with representation of the various groups involved in cultivation, processing, and export of Costa Rican coffee.

Questions of Quality and Competitiveness

As Topik points out in Chapter 1, the coffee commodity chain became global early on, much sooner than many food crops that continued to be produced, traded, and consumed in local or regional circuits. When Costa Rica began to export coffee, it was for sale in Europe, a demanding and relatively well-supplied market, where it competed with well-established coffees from South America and the West Indies, Asia and the Pacific islands, as well as Arabia. Circa 1830, the main locus of production had already moved from the Old World to the New, and was shifting from the West Indies (specifically St. Domingue) toward the mainland: Venezuela and Brazil were the major producers, coffee was just beginning to expand in Colombia, and Costa Rica was pioneering sustained export-oriented coffee production in Central America.[22]

Coffee was initially planted in Costa Rica on a small scale, not only on peasant farms, as has often been said, but on plots within larger estates. Despite rapid expansion, the area covered by coffee plantations in nineteenth-century Costa Rica was insignificant by comparison with a single region of Brazil, and minor next to Venezuelan production. With Costa Rica's limited resources, it was evident that this country would never be a major player on the world coffee market, and would hardly be able to influence price formation. Instead, it could carve a niche for itself by means of quality, and substantial efforts were directed toward that aim

[21] *Ley no. 2762 de 1°. De julio de 1961 reformada por ley no. 2798. Ley sobre el régimen de relaciones entre productores, beneficiadores y exportadores de café* (San José: Oficina del Café, 1961).

[22] This is not to say that Costa Rica was the first place where coffee was planted in the isthmus. We know that coffee was present well before in orchards elsewhere in Central America, and at least one historical document seemingly refers to some coffee production for trade in the Guatemalan mountains by the mid-eighteenth century: Jaime Villar, "La Tierra templada en América Central," text written in 1744, apparently first published in Venezuela, and republished in *Annales de la Sociedad de Geografía e Historia* 31 (1958): 68–70. I thank José A. Fernández for referring me to this document.

first by export and processing firms, then by individual farmers, and later on by government agencies.

Until the mid-twentieth century, increases in Costa Rican coffee production were primarily based on additional inputs of land and labor. Some technological improvements were made on a number of farms toward and after the turn of the century, which at least slowed down the reduction of yields as fertility began to decline and trees grew older. Eventually, modest improvements in production per hectare were attained in the first half of the twentieth century, but Costa Rican productivity lagged far behind that of El Salvador, renowned for careful cultivation and very high yields.

Processing was crucial for Costa Rican coffee to succeed in European markets, especially after the turn of the century. Labor-intensive harvesting of ripe cherries, quick transportation to central coffee mills, washing, depulping, fermentation, drying, classification, storage, and care in overseas transportation all contributed to ensuring quality, which was the key to competitiveness of coffees supplied by this minor producer to the global coffee commodity chain.

It was only after the mid-twentieth century, specifically in the 1960s and '70s, that cultivation in Costa Rica attained the extremely high average yields that allowed this country's coffee production to continue growing and to be cost-competitive despite scarcity and costliness of both land and labor.[23] Processing technology has also continued to improve, but harvesting of greener cherries as a labor-saving measure may be threatening the high-quality standards of this country's coffee, and one of its strengths in the world market. On the other hand, currently a growing number of producers and processing plants have shown renewed interest in improving the quality both of the coffee fruit harvested and of the processed beans. With this, a strategy that was fruitful for the Costa Rican coffee sector during the early decades of the twentieth century could be followed once again, albeit under new world market conditions.

[23] Recent studies on the Costa Rican coffee commodity chain include Paul Sfez, "La Cadena de exportación del café en Costa Rica," in M. Samper, ed., and P. Sfez, *La Cadena de producción y comercialización del café: Perspectiva histórica y comparada* (San Jose: Pan-American Institute of Geography and History and Universidad Nacional, 2002); Wim Pelupessy, "La Cadena internacional del café y el medio ambiente"; Rafael Díaz Porras, "La Importancia de los modelos teóricos de la competitividad en el comercio internacional del café"; and Marco Sánchez Cantillo, "La Competitividad de la torrefacción de café en Costa Rica," in *Economía y Sociedad*, no. 7 (May–Aug. 1998); and several unpublished research papers of the History Department at Universidad Nacional, Heredia.

PART II

PEASANTS

Race, Gender, and Property

6

Coffee Cultivation in Java, 1830–1917

M. R. Fernando

Java began exporting coffee in the early eighteenth century, under the aegis of the Dutch East India Company (VOC), which introduced coffee to the lucrative European market. Coffee cultivation had a checkered career until the 1830s, when it became part of the system of state control of peasant agriculture known as the Cultivation System (*Kultuur Stelsel*). For well over half a century after 1830, Java produced a substantial portion of the coffee imported by Europe. On the eve of the outbreak of leaf rust (*Hemileia vastatrix*) in the early 1880s, which ravaged Java's coffee groves, the island exported nearly 82 percent of all coffee leaving the Dutch East Indies, which amounted to 18 percent of world coffee exports.[1]

Thereafter, Java's coffee cultivation declined rapidly. Nevertheless, as forced coffee growing had been the bedrock of colonial revenue in its heyday, the Dutch colonial government was understandably reluctant to abolish its monopoly of coffee production and export.[2] By 1917, when the final remains of the monopoly were wound up, the Dutch East Indies produced a mere 5 percent of world production, and accounted for only 2 percent of world exports.[3]

We know little about the impact of coffee cultivation on Java's peasantry in comparison with sugar, the other major commercial crop of the Cultivation System, which profoundly affected every aspect of the

---

[1] D. Bulbeck, A. Reid, and Lay Cheng Tan, *Southeast Asian Exports since the Fourteenth Century* (Singapore: ISEAS, 1998), pp. 150–1.

[2] C. Fasseur, *The Politics of Colonial Exploitation* (Ithaca: Cornell, 1992), pp. 142–61.

[3] Bulbeck et al., *Southeast Asian Exports*, pp. 162 and 166.

economic life of indigenous people.[4] The colonial government left almost
all aspects of coffee production in the hands of peasants, despite some
efforts at modernization in the late nineteenth century. Coffee cultivation
consequently remained outside the close supervision of the administration. This was in striking contrast to sugar cultivation, which was scrupu-
lously managed by colonial officials. Peasants involved in the production
of coffee in Java, as well as in Sumatra, were nevertheless profoundly
affected, to judge from recent studies based on colonial archives.[5]

The aim of this chapter is thus to present an overview of the ways in
which coffee cultivation affected the lives of peasants in Java from 1830
to 1907. During this period, Javanese peasants were forced to produce
coffee on a large scale on behalf of the government, and they made numerous adjustments to comply with these demands. These adjustments,
and their secondary effects, explain much about the mode of operation of
a peasantry engulfed in the production of commercial crops for the world
market.

Compulsory coffee cultivation attempted to make use of the existing
organization of peasant households, but, due to a heavy demand for labor to raise coffee production on large plantations, Javanese peasants
experienced considerable difficulties in integrating coffee into other economic activities. They preferred growing coffee as a minor crop, in or near
their villages. This required much less time and labor, and provided some
flexibility in the allocation of family labor. When and where coffee cultivation proved unrewarding financially, in proportion to the amount of

[4] C. Fasseur, "Organisatie en sociaal-economische beteekenis van de gouvernementssuik-
ercultuuur in enkele residenties op Java omstreeks 1850," *Bijdragen tot de Taal-, Land-,
en Volkenkunde* 133 (1977): 261–93; G. R. Knight, "From Plantation to Padi-Field: The
Origins of the Nineteenth Century Transformation of Java's Sugar Industry," *Modern
Asian Studies* 14, no. 2 (1980): 177–204; R. E. Elson, *Javanese Peasants and the Colonial
Sugar Industry: Impact and Change in an East Java Residency, 1830–1940* (Singapore: Oxford
University Press, 1984).
[5] C. Dobbin, *Islamic Revivalism in a Changing Peasant Economy: Central Sumatra 1784–1847*
(London: Curzon Press, 1983); K. R. Young, *Islamic Peasants and the State: The 1908
Anti-Tax Rebellion in West Sumatra* (New Haven: Yale University Press, 1994); M. C.
Hoadley, *Towards a Feudal Mode of Production. West Java, 1680–1800* (Singapore: ISEAS,
1994); F. van Baardewijk, "Rural Responses to Intensifying Colonial Exploitation; Peasant
Reactions to the Introduction and Intensification of the Forced Cultivation of Coffee
in Central and East Java, 1830–1880," paper presented at the Fifth Dutch-Indonesian
Historical Congress, Lage Vuursche, 1986; M. R. Fernando and W. J. O'Malley, "Peasants
and Coffee Cultivation in Cirebon Residency, 1800–1900," in A. Booth, W. J. O'Malley,
and A. Weidemann, eds., *Indonesian Economic History in the Dutch Colonial Era* (New
Haven: Yale University Press, 1990), pp. 171–86.

labor involved and in comparison with other sources of income, Javanese peasants became indifferent toward it. The decline of coffee cultivation in Java from the 1880s was largely due to this state of affairs.

Java's Coffee Cultivation before 1832

In the eighteenth century, Java supplied a little over 4,000 tonnes of coffee a year, the second largest amount to reach Europe.[6] At that time, almost all coffee was grown in West Java, particularly in the Cirebon-Priangan region, which was well suited for the crop. The VOC persuaded and bullied the indigenous potentates of the region into accepting contractual obligations to supply coffee at fixed prices. Local chiefs then procured coffee from their subjects, who were bound to serve their lords in terms of "feudal" obligations.[7]

With the increasing demand for coffee, people in West Java were forced to relocate themselves near areas suitable for cultivating the crop. Subordinates of lords controlled these communities of coffee planters. A village community consisted of a certain number of manpower units (*cacah*), each accommodating at least four people.[8] Each household was counted as a *cacah*, and its ability to meet the prescribed production quota was a function of the manpower at its disposal. Peasants were not eager to cultivate coffee, as much of the income from growing the crop did not reach them. The cash that trickled down to a household was too insignificant to induce changes in the allocation of labor. In West Sumatra, village communities and households were organized on different principles. Moreover, marketing was not controlled by the VOC, but was in the hands of British and American interlopers. Peasant households thus responded enthusiastically to opportunities to earn cash, among others those offered by the cultivation of coffee in the eighteenth century.[9]

After 1800, when the VOC collapsed and Java came under the direct control of the Netherlands, apart from a brief British interregnum in 1811–16, coffee cultivation attracted a great deal of attention, because of its potential value to the new authorities. Some reforms were introduced to make coffee a more attractive crop for cultivators, mainly, opening marketing to private traders, who were keen to profit from it. Coffee

---

[6] Bulbeck et al., *Southeast Asian Exports*, p. 147. A tonne was 1,000 kilos.

[7] D. H. Burger, *Ontsluiting van Java's Binneland voor het Wereldverkeer* (Wageningen: Veenman, 1939), pp. 3–49; Hoadley, *Towards a Feudal Mode of Production*.

[8] Hoadley, *Towards a Feudal Mode of Production*, pp. 37–45.

[9] Dobbin, *Islamic Revivalism*.

plantations were leased to villages, in return for payment ranging from half to a third of the output, to be paid in kind or money. The remaining beans could be sold to private traders, but the government retained the option of buying coffee at a fixed price.[10] These reforms were part and parcel of a wider economic agenda of creating a "virile yeomanry."[11] With the removal of local chiefs, however, their subordinates became tenants of coffee plantations. They allocated plantations among *cacah* units; collected the product; sold it to Chinese, Arab, or European traders from coastal towns; and pocketed much of the cash.[12]

State Enterprise in Commercial Agriculture after 1832

The life of Javanese peasants underwent a transformation after 1830, when a new policy was introduced, which forced them to set aside a portion of their land or their labor to cultivate a range of commercial crops, on behalf of the colonial state. The state progressively gained a monopsony over many crops, notably, indigo, sugar, tobacco, and coffee. Peasants were compensated at a price fixed by the government. To process the raw materials, the government awarded contracts to European and "Foreign Oriental" manufacturers, who were granted generous loans to set up factories, and who were helped to procure the necessary labor. However, coffee beans did not require the same kind of industrialization as sugar, and were generally exported as they were, after primary processing by producers using the "dry method." A semiofficial firm, the Nederlandsche Handel Maatschappij, handled exports and shipping. Products were then sold at auction in the Netherlands, on behalf of the state.

Crops were generally paid well below world market prices, and hence the state obtained a high profit margin from selling them in the Netherlands. The new policy was financially successful beyond the wildest expectations of Dutch politicians, and it remained in place until the 1870s. At this point, its basic tenets came to be politically unacceptable, and they were replaced by a set of liberal ideas. However, compulsion in the coffee sector lingered on much longer than for other crops.[13]

---

[10] P. H. Van der Kemp, *Java's Landelijke Stelsel 1817–1819 naar Oorspronkelijke Stukken* (The Hague: M. Nijhoff, 1916), pp. 123–65.

[11] G. H. Soest, *Geschiedenis van het Kultuurstelsel* (Rotterdam: H. Nijgh, 1869), vol. 1, pp. 117–47.

[12] R. E. Elson, *Village Java under the Cultivation System, 1830–1870* (Sydney: Allen and Unwin, 1994), pp. 36–7.

[13] Fasseur, *The Politics of Colonial Exploitation.*

Despite the name given to it later by historians, the new economic policy was hardly a "system," but, rather, a bewildering array of local arrangements. Local officials were given a degree of latitude in implementing the basic concept to suit local conditions, which varied greatly from one area to another. Peasant communities made the most of a degree of freedom allowed to them by local officials, who were keen to benefit personally from increasing exports of commercial crops.[14]

Coffee was not initially included among the crops to be produced by peasants under the Cultivation System, but, after a long debate, it was decreed to be a compulsory crop in 1832.[15] This was ostensibly to put an end to abuses that had allegedly become widespread in the coffee sector, due to the ubiquitous influence of private traders.[16] Henceforth, specific peasant communities were to supply the government with coffee at the price of 25 guilders per *pikul* (62 kilos). Two-fifths of this amount, that is, 10 guilders, was initially deducted in lieu of "land rent" (land tax). Another 3 guilders were deducted to meet costs of transportation from the storehouse to the port of export. In areas where "land rent" was not being raised, cultivators were paid at reduced rates.[17]

The Expansion of Coffee Production, 1832–1884

Local officials set about expanding the production of commercial crops with zest, because they were rewarded with a generous premium, in proportion to total output. The cultivation of coffee thus grew considerably after 1832, as numerous coffee trees were planted in many parts of Java. By 1834, the island reportedly had 187,185,108 coffee trees, a little over two-third of them newly planted.[18] As a result of this expansion, Java's production rose significantly (Fig. 6.1).[19] The export figures suggest that the bulk of coffee exported from Indonesia came from Java well into the early 1880s (Fig. 6.2). Most coffee came from the compulsory deliveries,

---

[14] R. Van Niel, *Java under the Cultivation System* (Leiden: KILTV, 1992), pp. 121–53.

[15] Elson, *Village Java*, p. 63. Much of the information from archival sources for the period 1830 to 1870 is reproduced in this excellent study of the Cultivation System, which is my main source of information for this period.

[16] S. van Deventer, *Bijdragen tot de Kennis van het Landelijke Stelsel op Java* (Zalt-Bommel: Noman and Zoon, 1865), vol. 2, pp. 499–528.

[17] Elson, *Village Java*, p. 64.

[18] Ibid., pp. 64–5.

[19] Figs. 6.1–6.3 are based on statistics from P. Creutzberg, ed., *Changing Economy in Indonesia*, vol. 1: *Indonesia's Export Crops 1816–1940* (The Hague: M. Nijhoff, 1977), pp. 105–12.

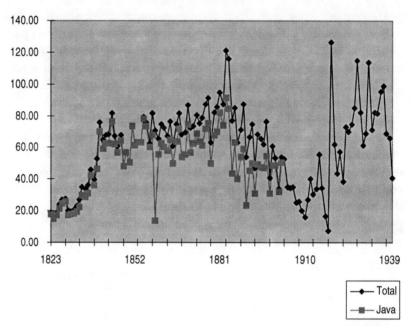

FIGURE 6.1. Coffee production in Indonesia, 1823–1942 (in thousands of tons). *Source:* R. E. Elson, *Village Java under the Cultivation System, 1830–1870* (Sydney: Allen and Unwin, 1994), pp. 64, 65.

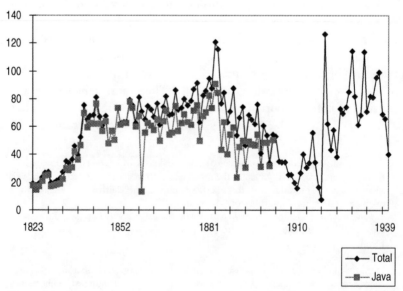

FIGURE 6.2. Coffee exports, 1823–1931 (in thousands of tons). *Source:* Elson, *Village Java.*

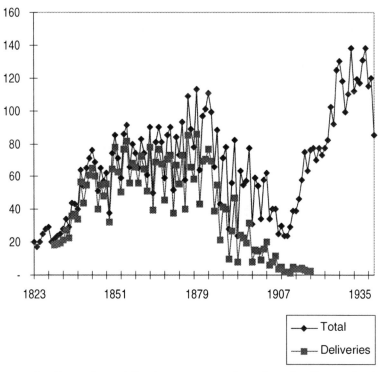

FIGURE 6.3. Compulsory deliveries as a proportion of total coffee production, 1823–1935 (in thousands of tons). *Source:* Elson, *Village Java*, pp. 64, 65.

attesting to the great labor services that the state imposed on peasants (Fig. 6.3).

Once initial expansion came to an end, by about 1840, coffee cultivation settled down to a steady pattern. Peasants gathered as much coffee as possible from existing plantations, as well as hedgerows and forests near their villages, and cared little about maintaining distant coffee plantations, unless forced to do so. There was little expansion in coffee cultivation in the 1840s and 1850s, as far as the number of coffee trees was concerned.[20] By then, much of the land suitable for growing coffee near villages had been occupied, and peasants were forced to go further away to find suitable land. Local officials applied pressure on peasants to maintain existing coffee trees in plantations with more care, to preserve production levels. Thus, plants were supposed to be pruned, fertilized, and protected from wild animals. Any gaps were to be filled with seedlings.[21]

[20] Elson, *Village Java*, pp. 110 and 131.
[21] Ibid., pp. 135–6.

The diminishing area of land suitable for coffee cultivation was regarded as a problem, but officials had to admit that the real problem was the low price paid to coffee growers.[22] It was thus raised from a low point of 8.40 per *pikul* to 13 guilders in 1867. To further encourage peasants, they were allowed to clean and dry coffee in their own villages, instead of having to do so near the storehouses. The practice of deducting the cost of coffee transport from the crop payment was also stopped, and existing plantations could be abandoned where they became unproductive.[23]

In 1872, the specific regulations governing coffee cultivation in Priangan, the foremost coffee growing area in Java, were revised, in order to relieve the pressure on local inhabitants and encourage them to expand production. The revised regulations considerably reduced the amount of work required to maintain the large coffee plantations far away from villages.[24] These reforms helped coffee planters to some extent, and made cultivation slightly more efficient, but they did not arrest the erratic oscillations in coffee deliveries (Fig. 6.2).[25]

The Decline of Coffee Cultivation after 1880

Coffee cultivation in Java declined after 1880, largely as a result of the spread of devastating orange rust (leaf blight, or *Hemileia vastatrix*).[26] Despite numerous efforts on the part of the colonial government to restore coffee cultivation, it failed to rise to its former glory.[27] Production and exports plunged to hitherto inexperienced depths in the last two decades of the nineteenth century (Figs. 6.1 and 6.2).

The colonial government made some effort to inject a degree of technical sophistication into coffee cultivation and modernize it, but with dismal results in the last two decades of the nineteenth century.[28] Coffee

---

[22] J. Kuneman, *De Gouvernements Koffiecultuur* (The Hague: M. Nijhoff, 1890), pp. 23–33.

[23] Elson, *Village Java*, pp. 137–8.

[24] J. W. De Klein, *Het Preangerstelsel (1667–1871) en zijn Nawerking* (Delft: J. Waltman, 1931), pp. 119–29; A. Goedhart, *De Onmogelijke Vrijheid* (Utrecht: Vrijuniversiteit, 1948), pp. 66–90.

[25] Kuneman, *De Gouvernements Koffiecultuur*, pp. 34–41.

[26] W. Burck, *Over de Koffiebladziekte en de Middelen om haar Bestreiden* (Buitenzorg: Gouvernements Drukkerij, 1889).

[27] K. W. Huitema, *De Bevolkingskoffiecultuur op Sumatra* (Wageningen: Veenman and Zoon, 1935), pp. 26–43.

[28] Huitema, *De Bevolkingskoffiecultuur*, pp. 26–43; Kuneman, *De Gouvernements Koffiecultuur*, pp. 119–33; *De Gouvernements-koffiecultuur van 1888 tot 1903* (Batavia: Gouvernementsdrukkerij, 1904); *Koloniaal Verslag*, 1890, appendix TT.

was still a source of revenue, however, and the government only slowly and reluctantly restricted the area subject to its coffee monopoly. The changing political climate in the Netherlands after 1900, which led to the introduction of a colonial policy professedly more keen to promote the well-being of indigenous peoples, hastened the complete abolition of compulsory coffee cultivation in 1917.[29]

Peasants were particularly reluctant to cultivate coffee in large and distant plantations, a task that required a major reshuffling of labor at household level. They preferred to grow coffee in and around their villages on a small scale, in order to supplement their income, especially when returns from coffee were falling, as after the world price collapse of the mid-1890s. The crop was increasingly unattractive to most peasant households, in comparison to other sources of income such as wage labor, small domestic industries, and petty trade. These alternative sources of income became increasingly popular with villagers, as all aspects of indigenous economic life became more commercialized.[30] The colonial state was reluctant to admit that changing indigenous economic life was a factor contributing to a diminishing interest in coffee. To better understand peasant reluctance to cultivate coffee, it is necessary to examine how cultivation of the crop was incorporated into local economies, and especially how coffee cultivation collided with other activities of peasant households.

Coffee Cultivation and the Peasant Economy

In the middle decades of the nineteenth century, coffee was grown in Java according to three different modes: in plantations, in hedgerows, and as an agroforestry crop. Growing coffee in plantations located far away from villages was the most arduous mode of operation for peasants, but the government preferred it, because of its greater short-term productive capacity. To prepare coffee plantations, people were mobilized en masse. They cleared land of shrubs and large trees and ploughed, weeded, terraced, and fenced the cleared land, before planting out. Seedlings were gathered from old plantations, and were aligned in rows between shade trees, each household usually planting around 600. This preliminary work was normally carried out during the dry season, but it continued into the

---

[29] Goedhart, *De Onmogelijke Vrijheid.*
[30] M. R. Fernando, "Growth of Non-Agricultural Economic Activity in Java, 1820–1880," *Modern Asian Studies* 29, no. 1 (1995): 77–119.

early part of wet season. During this initial phase, coffee-planting house-holds were required to stay in temporary shelters near the plantations, to save time and labor.[31]

It is difficult to state with any confidence whether entire households were mobilized, or whether only men were requisitioned for this work, which forced people to stay away from their homes for fairly long periods under strenuous conditions. Growing coffee in plantations located far away from the villages was understandably unpopular, because it kept people away from other economic activities, such as cultivating food crops and domestic industries.

The other modes of growing coffee caused no such problems. People could easily accommodate the work needed to plant coffee as hedgerows or as shrubs in forests subject to minimal clearing (agroforestry). That required much less arduous labor, and women and children could give a helping hand.

Once planting was completed, peasants did not have to work hard on a regular basis, although a large work force was required for harvesting. Little maintenance was required until the coffee trees began to bear fruit, after three or four years. The arduous task was picking coffee beans and carrying them in bags to the villages, where men, women, and children helped to clean and dry them.

Transporting coffee beans to local storehouses, which were not con-veniently located for inhabitants of remote areas, caused great hard-ship. Trekking along footpaths across the mountains carrying heavy bags was difficult, although draught animals sometimes eased the operation. Further irritation was caused by people having to wait many days to de-liver their coffee, due to insufficient personnel and weighing equipment in storehouses and shortages of cash with which to pay them.[32]

The way in which labor was allocated in cultivating coffee varied a great deal from one area to another, depending on local arrangements. These were influenced by ecological and manpower constraints, which appear to have been most severe in the remote upland areas of Java, where coffee was mainly grown. When labor was scarce, the inhabitants of one or several villages usually combined their resources in the initial phase of planting. This was perhaps a practice harking back to before 1830, when the cultivation of coffee was imposed on a village community as a whole. Villages followed this old custom when a heavy workload was involved,

---

[31] Elson, *Village Java under the Cultivation System*, p. 65.
[32] Ibid., pp. 66–7.

spreading the burden more evenly among households. Collective village work might also be a necessity for harvesting. Villagers divided up the area planted in coffee trees between individual households, however, for the purposes of maintenance, which required little labor. This may have reflected the fact that, after 1832, peasant households became the basic units of production of coffee in the eyes of the Dutch authorities.[33]

Peasants could ill afford to be away from their wet-rice fields during the initial phase of preparing land, which partly coincided with coffee planting. The government's insistence on plantations, as against the other two preferred modes of cultivating coffee, thus proved to be a major stumbling block. Coffee came to attract less and less attention as time went by. Aging coffee plantations were rarely replaced, especially when there was little forested land that could be used for this purpose within a tolerable distance from a village. Nor were seedlings planted to fill gaps in aging plantations. Fencing was neglected, and proved ineffective against the ravages of wild animals. Plantations thus yielded fewer and fewer coffee beans per hectare in the 1850s and 1860s.[34]

Peasant households' enthusiasm for coffee also waned when it brought little money in return for a considerable outlay of labor. The method of payment varied from place to place, and depended to some extent on the whim of local officials. Thus, the government made the situation more difficult in 1844, by lowering the purchasing price to 10 guilders per *pikul*, and by imposing a 2 percent overweight charge to compensate for any loss of weight in transit.[35] The payment per *pikul* was subsequently increased, but the contribution to peasants' income depended on a host of factors not taken into consideration when setting the official price. Crop payments for coffee were sometimes handed over to village heads, who found it not too difficult to pocket most of it. However, this was frowned upon by the Dutch, who cited this as a reason for obliging peasants to take their beans to storehouses, where they were paid in person.[36]

The Javanese peasant economy, although centered on production of food crops for consumption, was not a subsistence or natural economy, as often depicted by scholars.[37] Even in the early nineteenth century,

---

[33] Ibid., p. 67.
[34] Kuneman, *De Gouvernements Koffiecultuur*, pp. 42–56.
[35] Elson, *Village Java*, pp. 69–72.
[36] W. G. Clarence-Smith, "The Impact of Forced Coffee Cultivation on Java, 1805–1917," *Indonesia Circle* 64 (1994): 245–50.
[37] Burger, *Ontsluiting van Java's Binnenland voor het Wereldverkeer*.

domestic industries, petty trade, and wage labor were significant.[38] The range and degree of activities for earning money to meet the material needs of households were determined by the amount of resources at their disposal. In the light of the little information available, it is difficult to be precise about the allocation of labor by peasant households. Around 1880, however, a peasant household, in a hilly area of central Java where coffee was grown, earned over 80 percent of its cash income a year from work outside the production of food crops. The bulk of this income, 72 percent, came from selling garden products, grass, timber, and cloths woven by women. Money earned from selling coffee was only 4 percent of total income, a paltry sum in comparison with other sources. However, coffee plantations required 15 percent of the time bestowed on all economic activities. It is not surprising, therefore, that Javanese peasants were reluctant to cultivate coffee and sell it to the government at a low fixed price.[39]

The way in which labor was allocated along gender lines is unclear, but, from the nature of work, it can be safely deduced that work requiring hard manual labor fell on the husband's shoulders. The wife spent some time on food crop production, sowing and planting out rice, weeding, harvesting, and drying paddy, as was usual for women in Java. She also spent a fair amount of time weaving cloth for sale, once again a preoccupation of women. The small amount of labor bestowed upon food crop production resulted from the small size of farms, consisting of an average of 0.04 hectare of wet-rice land, 0.07 hectare of dry land, and 0.03 hectare of yard. In upland areas, rice was cultivated on a small scale on terraced fields and provided only part of the food for local inhabitants.[40]

Coffee-growing areas of Java were different from those in Sumatra, where there was a clearer differentiation between men earning cash and women growing food.[41] In Java, too, men were involved in economic activity to earn money, but they also had to carry out much of the work to produce food crops, and thus could not be away from home for any length of time to deal with coffee. Javanese peasants certainly had a clear sense of the importance of different types of work in terms of their economic value, even if some observers found it naive and out of step with Western notions of the economic value of time and labor.

[38] Elson, *Village Java*, pp. 3–22; P. Boomgaard, *Children of the Colonial State* (Amsterdam: CASA, 1989), pp. 116–34.
[39] Arminius, "Het budget van een Javaansche landbouwer," *Indische Gids* 11, no. 2 (1889): 2174–7.
[40] Ibid., pp. 2174–5, 2181.
[41] Young, *Islamic Peasants*, pp. 146–51.

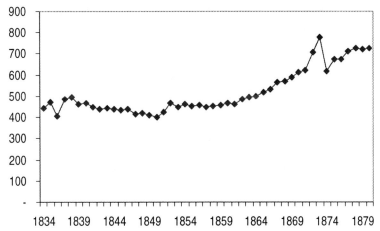

FIGURE 6.4. Number of coffee-growing peasant households in Java, 1834–70.
Source: Elson, *Village Java*, pp. 64, 65.

Although Javanese peasants were disinclined to undertake work that did not bring them adequate financial rewards, they could not give up coffee, because it was a compulsory crop. The Cultivation System was based on the ruler's prerogative to acquire the land and labor of peasants. The number of households forced to cultivate coffee rose throughout the middle decades of the nineteenth century (Fig. 6.4), and much of the increase in the number of coffee-growing peasant households occurred in Central Java (Fig. 6.5).[42]

The effects of compulsion can be seen from the statistics of the number of peasant households obliged to grow coffee, which rose until it amounted to nearly 60 percent of all peasant households on the island. It seems that the government tried to compensate for the rapidly diminishing area of land suitable for cultivation by forcing more people to cultivate coffee. However, there was some regional variation, suggesting local forces at work, with West Java having more coffee growers than Central and East Java, as shown in Table 6.1.

However, in Central and East Java, variations were indicative of a change in domestic economic activities at household level. The majority of peasant households had become accustomed to the use of cash as never before in daily life. To raise their money income, they found it necessary

---

[42] Figs. 6.4–6.6 are based on data from F. Van Baardewijk, ed., *Changing Economy in Indonesia*, vol. 5: *The Cultivation System, Java 1834–1880* (Amsterdam: KIT, 1993), pp. 249–60.

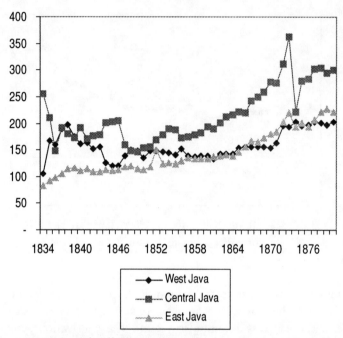

FIGURE 6.5. Number of coffee-growing peasant households in Java by province, 1834–1879. *Source:* Elson, *Village Java*, pp. 64, 65.

to diversify their economic activities outside food crop cultivation. Coffee was for a time a reasonably profitable source of cash, notably, for people who could grow it on a small scale in hedges and forests near their homes. More and more peasants turned to coffee after 1860, but it was a short-lived phenomenon, for the number of coffee-growing households dropped again by 1880. In West Java, in contrast, coffee cultivation remained high but stagnant. This was due to the disenchantment of local inhabitants, who were forced to seek land suitable to grow coffee on plantations, far away from their villages and for no extra payment.

Crop payments to coffee-producing households were subjected to frequent fluctuations during the middle decades of the nineteenth century (Fig. 6.6). The amount of money that coffee planters actually received was dependent on several factors, including soil fertility, the age of trees, and the degree of control villagers could exercise over village officials. Peasants growing coffee in Pasuruan, East Java, found it an exceptionally suitable area for coffee, and thus appear to have benefited more than coffee growers elsewhere.

TABLE 6.1. Impact of Forced Coffee Cultivation on Peasants, 1830–1870

Province	No. peasant house-holds 1836–60	% all peasant house-holds 1836–60	No. peasant house-holds 1840–70	% all peasant house-holds 1840–70	No. peasant house-holds 1850	% of peasant house-holds 1850	No.	%
West Java	159,689	65	161,422	57	134,521	45	139,857	47
Central Java	148,496	32	192,361	40	153,093	39	192,834	31
East Java	97,560	27	111,101	30	113,606	27	133,516	27
Java	405,745	38	464,884	41	401,220	36	466,207	33

Sources: F. van Baardewijk, Changing Economy in Indonesia, vol. 5: The Cultivation System, Java 1834–1880 (Amsterdam: KIT, 1993), pp. 186–93; "Kultuur Verslag" (cultivation reports held in Dutch archives), 1836–51, and Koloniaal Verslag, 1852–71.

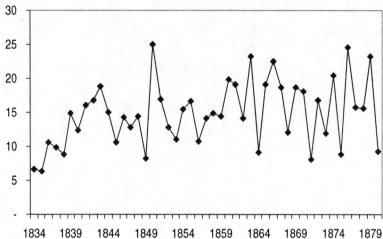

FIGURE 6.6. Crop payment per peasant household, 1834–1879 (in guilders). *Source:* Elson, *Village Java*, pp. 64, 65.

Conclusion

Falling income from growing coffee was evidently a major reason for the crop's decline after 1850.[43] Peasants then began to bestow more time on other economic activities.[44] However, they were still prepared to produce coffee on a small scale, in and around hamlets and in nearby forests, well into the early twentieth century. Peasants also responded to some extent to government efforts to rationalize smallholder coffee cultivation after the onset of *Hemileia vastatrix*. The reforms, however, came too late for most Javanese peasants, who had found greener pastures.

[43] Elson, *Village Java*, pp. 139 and 196.
[44] Fernando, "Growth of Non-Agricultural Economic Activity."

7

Labor, Race, and Gender on the Coffee Plantations in Ceylon (Sri Lanka), 1834–1880

Rachel Kurian

Coffee plantations in Ceylon (Sri Lanka) were developed in the early nineteenth century under British colonial rule, and they were to dominate the economic development of the island until the last quarter of the century. This chapter is concerned with how the ideologies and practices concerning race, caste, and gender differences were incorporated into labor relations on these plantations. It shows how local government policies favored European ownership and helped to sustain differences between the latter and local entrepreneurs. It deals with the recruitment of a "foreign" Indian work force to service the needs of coffee plantations, and how workers were kept isolated from the rest of society. It analyses how race, caste, patriarchy, and indebtedness were used as methods of labor control, both in the recruitment of labor and in the organization of work on the estates. In effect, it is a study of how extraeconomic forms of coercion were effective in promoting the interests of European capitalist production.

The Bias toward European Ownership on Coffee Plantations

British colonial rule in Ceylon coincided with the establishment of industrial capitalism in Western Europe. Parts of Ceylon were occupied by Britain in 1795, but the whole island did not come under British administrative control until 1815. This was the period when the policy of laissez-faire was beginning to be heralded in England as the most effective way of increasing wealth. In addition, there was increasing pressure from London on colonial governments to reduce expenditure. This, together with the emerging commercial ethos of the period and the lucrative prices of coffee in the international market, paved the way for the rapid development of coffee plantations on the island.

Coffee had been grown and exported prior to this period, at the time of Dutch supremacy, being cultivated by the Sinhalese in the Kandyan districts as a garden crop. The "West India system of production," or plantation production of coffee, was introduced by the British, and was associated with predominantly white male management and ownership.[1] This was the outcome of a policy followed by the Ceylon government, which consciously promoted European ownership and management on coffee plantations. The Ceylon government rationalized this policy by emphasizing that Europeans were necessary to "set an example" for others.[2] However, there was a clear vested interest for officials, who wished to develop coffee plantations themselves, and who were initially allowed to do so.

In line with this policy of encouraging European management, specific financial incentives were provided to European entrepreneurs wishing to take up coffee cultivation. This included the availability of cheap land, often in the form of grants, and the exemption from taxes on many items involved in the production of coffee, such as import duties on machinery and land taxes.[3] Local officials, who were involved in developing such incentives, were quick to take advantage of the potential profits from coffee cultivation. Indeed, officials developed most of the early plantations, especially during the 1840s.[4] In fact, Governor Sir Edward Barnes (1824–31) was often referred to as the "pioneer" of the island's planting industry, and it was he who opened up the Grannoruwa estate at Perideniya. Most plantations were private proprietorships, and a principal motivation of planters appeared to be to take advantage of high short-term profits during the coffee boom of the 1840s. The average size of a coffee plantation before 1860 was probably quite small, at about 100 acres or 40 hectares.[5]

---

[1] J. Ferguson, *Ceylon in 1893* (London: J. Haddon, and Colombo: A. M. and J. Ferguson, 1893), p. 64.

[2] SLNA 5/81, Maitland to Castlereagh, Aug. 19, 1808, p. 141. SLNA 4/3 Bathurst to Brownrigg, June 23, 1813, pp. 53ff.

[3] L. A. Mills, *Ceylon under British Rule, 1792–1932* (London: Oxford University Press, 1933), p. 224.

[4] E. F. C. Ludowyk, *The Modern History of Ceylon* (London: Weidenfeld and Nicolson, 1966), pp. 61–2.

[5] D. R. Snodgrass, *Ceylon: An Export Economy in Transition* (Homewood, Ill.: Richard D. Irwin, 1966), p. 23, shows that the average size of coffee land sold to a European between 1833 and 1860 was 97 acres.

The cozy relationship between state and planters was reflected in policy. Local officials in Ceylon were keen to support planters, who pushed for government-sponsored labor immigration. Sir Henry Ward, who became governor in 1855, put forward schemes to help them. These included setting aside money from surplus revenue to create a Cooly Transport Company and a Ceylon Agency, with depots at convenient ports of embarkation. The links between officials and planters often "affected their impartiality in disputes between the planters and plantation labour," resulting in judgments in favor of planters.[6] The European official to whom the villager or worker could present her or his grievances was, in many instances, a planter himself.[7] Records also indicate that judges almost invariably ruled in favor of planters.[8]

Although most planters had little knowledge of cultivation practices, and even less formal training, they were able to prevent competition from local planters. It was only in the 1850s that a systematic effort was undertaken to recruit persons with some degree of farming experience for estates.[9] Local Sinhalese and Tamil entrepreneurs were also involved in coffee cultivation to some degree.[10] However, their cultivation remained almost entirely on a smallholding basis.[11] The relative contributions of estates and smallholders to the coffee industry can be gauged from Table 7.1.

The table shows that while "native" smallholder coffee production also profited from the boom, local people appear to have been less successful than their British counterparts. Clearly, the availability of appropriate and sufficient forested land was an important reason for this, as state policy on land strongly favored European ownership. For local entrepreneurs wishing to develop larger holdings, it would appear that availability of finance was another factor. The minimum cost of setting up a plantation in 1844 was estimated at £3,000, and planters often had to borrow this sum from British-owned banks and agency houses operating in the island. These lending agencies were willing to issue a mortgage for a British

---

[6] S. B. D. de Silva, *The Political Economy of Underdevelopment* (London: Routledge and Kegan Paul, 1982), p. 259.

[7] Ibid., p. 260.

[8] Ibid., p. 262.

[9] D. M. Forrest, "Hundred Years of Achievement," *The Times of Ceylon Tea Centenary Supplement*, July 31, 1969.

[10] M . Roberts and L.A. Wickremeratne, "Export Agriculture in the Nineteenth Century," in K. M. de Silva, ed., *History of Ceylon* (Colombo: University of Ceylon Press, 1973), vol. 3, pp. 94–7.

[11] Snodgrass, *Ceylon*, p. 26.

TABLE 7.1. *Estate and Smallholder Coffee Exports 1849–1886 (Selected Years)*

Year	Estate volume (000 cwts)[a]	Estate unit value (s)[b]	Smallholders volume (000 cwts)	Smallholders unit value	Smallholders volume share (%)
1849	210	33	127	18	38
1850–54	237	44	118	33	33
1860–64	450	54	132	40	23
1870–74	749	82	135	55	15
1880–84	405	91	27	58	6

[a] A cwt is a hundredweight, which is an old British measure equaling 112 British pounds, or 50.80235 kilos.
[b] In British shillings.
Source: D. R. Snodgrass, *Ceylon: An Export Economy in Transition* (Homewood, Ill.: Richard D. Irwin, 1966), p. 30.

planter, but were reluctant to do so in the case of a Ceylonese entrepreneur. Moreover, if they did so, it was generally at a higher rate of interest, making it less profitable for indigenous entrepreneurs than for the British. It was thus the latter, with the help of finance from British-owned sources, who launched large-scale plantations.[12] Thus, from the very beginning, Europeans were favored with regard to ownership and management, and this racial dichotomy became entrenched in the hierarchy on coffee plantations.

A Shortage of Local Labor

The spread of coffee estates in the island was dependent to a large extent on the availability of labor at the appropriate seasons. Attempts to employ local peasants were not successful. Sir Edward Barnes even exempted workers in the Maritime Provinces from compulsory service (*rajakariya*), so that planters might avail themselves of their labor.[13] Following the advice of the Colebrooke-Cameron Commission, *rajakariya* was abolished altogether in 1833. It was hoped that this would free the peasantry to take up work on the plantations, by not having to provide labor for public works. However, this was not to be. The main reason was that coffee plantations did not, in any serious way, disturb the ties of peasants to

[12] Ibid.
[13] G. C. Mendis, ed., *The Colebrooke-Cameron Papers: Documents on British Colonial Policy in Ceylon 1796–1833* (London: Oxford University Press, 1956), p. xxvii.

the land.[14] Thus, the local labor could not be relied on to undertake the coffee picking that coincided with a heavy labor demand in village agriculture.

In addition, local Sinhalese were deterred from joining the plantation work force by relatively low wages, the infrequent and irregular payment of wages, and the bias of officials toward planters.[15] Some Sinhalese performed piecework in the fields, transported goods, constructed buildings, and cleared forests, but they were averse to regular employment on coffee estates. More important, they could not with any certainty be available for coffee picking, which coincided with heavy labor demand in village agriculture.[16] In 1840, the Colonial Secretary of State noted that the "scarcity" of population to service the estates was "a great deficit."[17]

A "Foreign" Work Force for Coffee Plantations

Under these circumstances, planters turned to the relatively close and famine-prone Tamil districts of the Madras Presidency of southern India. There, large numbers of low-caste agricultural workers lived in difficult conditions. Their vulnerability was associated with three phenomena. In the first place, the policies of the British colonial government between 1770 and 1850 resulted in the chronic indebtedness of ordinary villagers to land magnates and city usurers. Second, these regions suffered from episodic famines and deprivation during this period, which particularly affected the lowest castes and classes. Third, bonds of debt continued to exist between landlords and ex-slaves, even after the official abolition of slavery, which occurred in Malabar and most other areas under direct British rule in 1843, and in the princely state of Travancore in 1855. Nor did the Indian Penal Code, which came into force in 1862, reduce the burden of debt for former slaves. The combined impact of these phenomena was "communalized destruction," with the creation of a large pool of

---

[14] L. R. Jayawardena, "The Supply of Sinhalese Labour to Ceylon Plantations (1830–1930): A Study of Imperial Policy in a Peasant Society," Ph.D. thesis, University of Cambridge, 1963.

[15] Silva, *The Political Economy*, pp. 236–73.

[16] I. H. Vanden Driesen, *Indian Plantation Labour in Sri Lanka: Aspects of the History of Immigration in the 19th Century* (Perth: University of Western Australia Press, 1982), p. 3.

[17] SLNA 4/193 Despach, Ansthruther to Colonial Secretary of State, Nov. 24, 1840, London.

pauperized workers, who needed to find some means of survival during abnormally depressed periods.[18]

Kathleen Gough's study on Tanjavur, one of the major sources of labor for Ceylon's coffee estates, reflects many of these pressures on low castes. Her study of the village of Kumbapettai showed that, prior to 1855, most low-caste groups were in a state of bondage. The abolition of slavery did not necessarily provide greater mobility to ex-slaves, for many were Adimai Alukal, belonging mainly to the Pallar and Konar castes, who became *pannaiyal* (debt peons) to landlords. Such ties allowed landlords to retain a sufficient labor force through debt bondage, while it relieved them of the encumbrance of a growing slave population.[19] When laborers were needed for cultivation, landlords operated their authority through debt bondage to retain them in India. When they were not necessary for this purpose, it was in the interests of landlords to allow them to find other work. As the population increased, so did this group of workers, creating a widening pool of casual labor. Indeed, landlords gradually found it less necessary to keep workers in debt, for labor was easily available. Thus, the majority of migrants from Tanjavur were *Harijan,* from the lower castes of non-Brahman peasants. This "coolie" group was particularly affected by agricultural distress, and formed the main pool of labor for estate work in Ceylon.[20]

This was also the case in many parts of Madras Presidency. The *ryot* (owner of land) in the early nineteenth century had attached a certain prestige to the number of workers whom he commanded. After the 1850s, however, many landlords hired out land to cultivators who were rich peasants and usurers.[21] As a result, the *ryot* required less labor for the cultivation of his land. Simultaneously, the increasing monetization of the economy opened up alternative forms of investment. In this situation, landlords found it worthwhile to invest in other areas, such as education and industry, even at the cost of their patronage over workers. By the end of the nineteenth century, the *ryot* found it more remunerative to employ wage workers on a temporary basis at the time of sowing and harvesting,

---

[18] Silva, *The Political Economy,* p. 244.
[19] K. Gough, "Caste in a Tanjore Village," in E. R. Leach, ed., *Aspects of Caste in India, Ceylon and North West Pakistan* (Cambridge: Cambridge University Press, 1962), pp. 119–21.
[20] Gough, "Caste," pp. 131, 184–95.
[21] D. Kumar, *Land and Caste in South India: Agricultural Labour in the Madras Presidency during the Nineteenth Century* (Cambridge: Cambridge University Press, 1965), p. 85; S. Sarkar, *Modern India 1885–1947* (New Delhi: Macmillan, 1983), p. 34.

rather than maintaining a permanent work force. This meant that any agricultural distress had a severely adverse effect on casual workers. As noted by the Collector of Nellore in 1900:

Formerly, the *ryot* with his cultivating labourers was the agricultural unit. The labourers were attached to the soil and looked to their masters for support in good and bad seasons.... The *ryot* has now no anxiety about securing labourers, and therefore no necessity to maintain them in hard times, and has less inducement to do so.... He employs large numbers at the time of sowing and harvest and then dispenses with their services. On the failure, therefore, of a single monsoon, all these labourers who, in former times, would naturally look to and be maintained by their masters, are now thrown adrift without any means.[22]

In spite of these problems, the workers were not always ready to undertake plantation work in Ceylon. It was well known that estate work was arduous and difficult, with little support from the state for the rights of workers. Furthermore, the sea voyage was sometimes difficult, which also discouraged migration to Ceylon. This meant that labor supplies for Ceylon's coffee plantations could not be guaranteed. Given the unpredictability, planters used monetary inducements to get adequate labor, as well as having recourse to extraeconomic forms of coercion, including methods of social control based on race, caste, patriarchy, and debt.

Early Attempts at Encouraging Labor Migration

The first organized attempt at dealing with the recruitment of plantation labor was by the Ceylon Agricultural Society, formed in 1842. The Ceylon Government played an important role in setting up this organization, and Philip Ansthruther, the Colonial Secretary for the Ceylon Government, became its first president. Another attempt was made in 1858 when Ordinance No. 15 was passed by Governor Sir Henry Ward for the specific purpose of "encouraging and improving the immigration of coolies from the South of India." This ordinance created the Immigrant Labour Commission, which attempted to recruit workers with partial funding from the planters.[23]

The commission knew that in spite of problems experienced by low-caste workers in South India, it would not be easy to persuade them to

---

[22] Quoted in D. Wesumperuma, *Indian Immigrant Plantation Workers in Sri Lanka: A Historical Perspective 1880–1910* (Kelaniya: Vidyalankara Press, 1986), p. 93.
[23] Driesen, *Indian Plantation Labour*, p. 70.

work on Ceylon plantations. Clearly, monetary inducement was important in this respect, and between 1851 and 1861 a "Coastal Advance" system of recruitment developed. Recruiters were paid from one to two shillings per head for every migrant they brought, and one pound per month in addition as a retainer. Wages were higher than those available in South India. The commission, for its part, was willing to pay relatively higher rates for "able-bodied" men, with women and youths to be paid at a lower rate.[24]

Migration was usually effected through the *kangany* (recruiter) system. The *kangany* was a man who was given advances by planters to recruit people to come and work on estates. The *kangany* was usually from a relatively high caste, familiar with, and usually originating from, rural South India. He would offer inducements to kinsmen and other people to go to Ceylon and work on a particular plantation. Those willing to do so were given a cash advance, to meet expenses incurred in their journey.

The labor force was subdivided into smaller groups, each under a *silara* (lesser) *kangany*, generally in charge of a kin group. Some workers formed themselves into gangs, ranging from twenty-five to 100 people, and selected from among themselves a leader, also called a *kangany*, who would "conduct their journeys, negotiate their engagements, superintend their labour and receive in return a trifling proportion of their pay."[25] There existed yet another system, whereby a *kangany* would meet potential workers on their arrival from the coast, and undertake to lead them to estates, for which service he received payment.

Workers generally stayed between five and twelve months, and then returned home with their savings, sometimes coming back, or being succeeded by others in the following year.[26] The government took the position that the seasonal cycle of coffee cultivation meant that it was possible for seasonal migration, by and large, to meet the demands of the coffee industry.[27] It was estimated that between 1843 and 1877, an average of 56,000 men, 10,300 women, and 8,000 children came to Ceylon to work on coffee estates.

---

[24] SLNA 2/2644, Dawson to Graham, March 6, 1960.

[25] Much of the material in this and the following paragraphs is from the lucid analysis and description provided in SLNA 3/34 Pt. 1, Tennent to Grey, Despatch No. 6 (misc.), April 21, 1847.

[26] Driesen, *Indian Plantation Labour*, pp. 8, 52.

[27] K. M. de Silva, "Indian Immigration to Ceylon – The First Phase c. 1840–1856," *Ceylon Journal of Historical and Social Studies* 4, no. 2 (1961): 106–37.

Female Labor

Given the problems of migration, most early migrants were men, but planters were keen to encourage female migration for several reasons. An important consideration was lower payment given to women in South India, a reflection of the prevailing patriarchal ideology embodied in the caste system. A comparison of wage rates in several regions sending workers to Ceylon shows that women were paid about half what men received. In 1859, a male worker in Tinnevelly and Madurai received three pence per day, while a woman received about a penny and three quarters.[28] A similar disparity existed in the case of Yangan.[29] Another important consideration was that women from low castes and classes were at the bottom of the Indian hierarchical order, which forced them to accept hard and menial tasks.

In addition, planters felt that if women came with men, there was a greater chance for estates to have a more settled population. The secretary of the Immigrant Labour Commission was thus specifically to ask the agent in India to look for workers who would bring their wives and families with them.[30] The agent, for his part, felt that it would be good to recruit more women, as they were "more steady and regular labourers." Moreover, if men could be induced to bring their wives and children along, it was likely that they would stay for longer periods, rather than returning after a few months' work.[31] Planters were keen to keep workers who had survived the initial period, as mortality at this stage was very high, possibly as much as 25 percent.[32] This was due to harsh conditions on the journey and problems of acclimatization, as well as the work regime. If women were encouraged to migrate, there would be less incentive for men to go home quickly. Additionally, the small proportion of women among the immigrants came to be seen as a great evil, because of a high incidence of sexually transmitted diseases and related problems.

Despite these factors reflecting discriminatory and patriarchal attitudes toward women, which were retained throughout the history of the plantations, the number of women on estates did grow. An increase in destitution and the erosion of patron-client relations in South India contributed

---

[28] SLNA 2/2644, Graham to Hansbrow, March 24, 1859.

[29] SLNA 2/2644, Graham to Dawson, Sept. 20, 1860.

[30] SLNA 2/2644, Dawson to Graham, March 6, 1860.

[31] SLNA 6/2644, Graham to Hansbrow, March 24, 1859.

[32] Colonial Office, CO 54/475, W. G. Van Dort, "Report on the Gampola Civil Hospital," in "Correspondence on the Condition of Malabar Coolies in Ceylon."

to this slow shift in the sex composition of the estate work force. More women began to migrate, and they came to constitute a fifth of migrants between 1843 and 1877.

It is likely that the small number of women led to the provision of sexual services outside stable family relationships. Medical records indicate a very high incidence of sexually transmitted diseases among male workers. The few women on estates, who had to endure dreadful hardships on the journey, were often exposed to illnesses and infections, and had to face sexual abuse from men. Their plight can be perceived from the observations of W. C. Twynam, Government Agent of Jaffna during the initial period of migration. He saw

... miserable gangs of coolies of 1843 and 1845, with one or two women to 50 or 100 men, strangers in a strange land, ill-fed, ill-clothed, eating any garbage they came across (more however from necessity than choice), travelling over jungle paths, sometimes with scarcely a drop of water to be found anywhere near them for miles, and others knee-deep the greater part of the way in water, with the country all round a swamp; working on estates just reclaimed from jungle, or on jungles about to be converted into estates, badly housed, and little understood by their employers....[33]

The Patriarchal and Caste Hierarchy of Labor Control and Management

The workers were slotted into a labor regime that was characterized by a clear sense of differentiation and hierarchy. This was based on color, race, ethnicity, and sex, with little but stylized interaction between the different levels within this pyramid. The overall emphasis was to exert maximum control over the work force and instill respect for those in authority. Women workers were at the bottom of the pyramid, and male domination was enforced at each and every level.[34]

A plantation had clear geographical boundaries, within which there was a strict hierarchy. At the head was the superintendent, or *periya dorai* (big master), the white manager, who governed the estate like a slave plantation in the Caribbean. His word was law, unquestioned within the estate, and this social acceptance was manifested through a series

[33] Colonial Office, CO 54/475, Letter to Colonial Secretary, Henry T. Irving, in "Correspondence on the Condition of Malabar Coolies in Ceylon," p. 16, Enclosure no. 8, Sept. 30, 1869.
[34] R . Kurian, "State, Capital and Labour in the Plantation Industry in Sri Lanka 1834–1984," Ph.D. thesis, University of Amsterdam, 1989.

of rituals and behavior patterns, which emphasized his complete authority. The workers were on no account to look him in the face, and they
were to step out of his way if they met him on a path. No direct words
were to be spoken to the superintendent, and the men were not to lower
their *sarong* (tunic) in his presence. Workers could not use an umbrella or
other forms of apparel that might indicate high status or might lessen the
social and political distance between them and their superiors. This was
reinforced by a qualitative difference in housing and physical comforts.
The palatial bungalow of the superintendent, with its splendid view and
beautiful gardens, was a far cry from the barrack-like line rooms of the
workers, which rarely boasted even adequate water or minimal hygienic
conditions.

Below the *periya dorai* were the *sinna dorai* (small masters), generally
European assistants. They were also provided with a great deal of comfort in terms of housing and perquisites, but lived in a somewhat less
luxurious style than the *periya dorai*. The clear distance between the two
highest levels of authority was significant, for it underscored the importance of differentiation and the unquestioned acceptance of respect for
hierarchy. Below the *sinna dorai* were the estate staff, the *kanakapillai*
(accountant) and others who helped in running the office. These persons
were Tamil-speaking, but did not belong to the same background as the
workers. In many cases, they came from the north or east of Ceylon,
rather than from South India. Referred to as "the staff," they lived in
"quarters," housing that was better than that of the workers but considerably less comfortable than the houses of the *dorai*. The staff handled the
payment of wages and checked weighing and production processes. They
treated the workers as befitted the general principle of conventional estate organization, that is, with little respect and often with a great deal of
arrogance.

The head *kangany* was a key figure in labor relations on the estate.
While his role was technically akin to that of both foreman and recruiter,
his power extended to both planters and workers:

The laborer's lack of access to the estate manager made the kangany the link
between the estate management and the laborers; in the early years, he even
distributed wages on behalf of the employer, and till recently a laborer's notice of resignation required the kangany's endorsement. His ties of caste and
kinship with those whom he recruited gave a moral basis to his authority. He
mediated in their family affairs and was their representative and spokesman in
labor disputes. Combined with this patron-client relationship between the kangany and his labor gang was a creditor-debtor relationship, which place the

laborers in financial bondage to him, and consolidated his leadership. As an intermediary the kangany was not a neutral element but a prop in the power structure of the estate community. In the eyes of the laborers he was effectively their employer.[35]

Laborers were at the bottom of the pyramid, numerically most significant and least remunerated in terms of monetary and physical rewards. However, within the work force there was also a clear hierarchy. The head *kangany* was generally of the highest rank, and the work force was split up into different gangs, each under the authority of its own patriarch, the *silara kangany*. The whole work force was structured so that these divisions tended to enhance what was seen as the "family principle." This meant that the male authority at each level exercised rights on those below him and paid respect to those higher in the hierarchy. Such methods were said to produce the most "satisfactory results" as workers could usually "settle on the estate."[36]

The caste system introduced yet another element in the hierarchy. Brought from India, this can be seen as a kind of racist ideology. Castes were considered to be endogamous groups, traditionally associated with ascribed occupations and ranked hierarchically. Each caste had subdivisions, and a person acquired her or his caste solely through birth. The two castes that were numerically dominant amongst the migrant workers on the estates were the Sudra and the Adi-Dravida.

The caste hierarchy was imported to the Ceylon estates in different ways. In the first place, the *kangany* was usually a man from a relatively high subcaste. As migration took place under his supervision, usually in families or kin groups, the preservation of caste identity was facilitated. Second, when these groups arrived on the estate, they were isolated, having little social contact with the rest of Ceylon society. In 1871, only 3.3 percent of the resident population on the estates were local Sinhalese.[37] Third, the formation of labor gangs under *kangany* and *silara kangany* was based on caste, strengthening both caste and kinship ties. Research has indicated that *silara kangany* groups tended to be homogenous in terms of caste and kinship.[38] Fourth, the estate owners had a vested interest in

[35] Silva, *The Political Economy*, p. 329.
[36] *Ceylon Labour Commission Handbook*, 1935, p. 20.
[37] E. Meyer, "Between Village and Plantation: Sinhalese Estate Labour in British Ceylon," in *Asie due Sud: Traditions et Changements* (Paris: Colloques Internationaux du CNRS, 1979), p. 460.
[38] R. Jayaraman, *Caste Continuities in Ceylon: A Study of the Social Structure of Three Tea Plantations* (Bombay: Popular Prakashan Press, 1975), p. 20.

preserving caste differences, and using the ideology that lay behind it to control workers.

Estate housing and the preparation of food also maintained caste differences. Caste differentiation was respected by management, which in early days would often allocate housing on the advice of the head *kangany*, who would ensure that standards of "acceptable" housing were adhered to. For example, certain castes would not face others, and certain castes would not live with others.[39] Living quarters were often arranged on the basis of caste, because higher-caste people disliked living the same "lines" as people of lower castes. There were also instances recorded of an Adi-Dravida cooking food at a festival, which Sudra participants refused to eat.

Women workers formed the lowest rung of the estate hierarchy, directly under the command of men at every level. Even though they worked for wages, they had little access or control over the money. In most cases, their wages, lower than those of men, were handed via the *kangany* to the male partner, who often used them according to his own needs. Indeed, giving women's wages to men is a practice that has continued until the present day on plantations. Women faced the worst effects of class, social, caste, and sexual oppression. They experienced the negative impact of caste repression and they were subjected to the ideology of male superiority inherent in their social and work circumstances. Most of these women had to bear the brunt of male domination inherent in caste ideology, which was preserved and even reinforced by the process of kin-group migration. Some of them even faced more rigid sexual restrictions in their new setting, as their husbands made attempts to "privatize" their sexuality, something that was less rigidly observed in their traditional background in India. Indeed, it could be argued that the process and nature of the integration into the estate labor force, in kin and subcaste groups, led to a reinforcement of caste ideology and caste power, and to a resulting loss of freedom for women within their community.

Indebtedness and Infrequent Payment as Methods of Labor Control

An important way of controlling workers was through debt. As the money for travel expenses was advanced to the worker, he or she generally began life on the estate in debt. This debt was mediated through the recruiter, the *kangany*, who effected a certain degree of control over the movements

---

[39] Rachel Kurian, *Women Workers in the Sri Lanka Plantation Sector* (Geneva: International Labour Office, 1982).

186 *Rachel Kurian*

of the worker, because the recruiter had lent estate money to the worker. Moreover, since money was advanced through the *kangany*, the worker was "virtually the servant of the *kangany*."[40] Means and levels of payments were such that workers could rarely pay off accumulated debts. In most cases, the worker himself had little idea of the amount of debt he or she had to pay, and was frequently "made responsible for larger sums than he has in fact received or has had expended on his behalf."[41] The debt of the worker was written on a *tundu*, or piece of paper, and it was only after these dues were paid that the worker was "free" to leave employment.

This system was notoriously abused by some planters, who simply refused to issue tickets when they did not want labor to leave their estates.[42] Control over the mobility of estate labor was reinforced by the use of guards.[43] As a recruit was personally known to the *kangany*, he would often be caught in his home village in South India if he ran away, and he or his relatives would be made responsible for paying his debt. I have argued elsewhere that the *tundu* system in practice contained the principle of indentureship, even if it was never formally viewed as such in law.[44]

The Immigrant Labour Commission, primarily interested in recruiting more labor, saw indebtedness as a major factor in hindering labor availability, and it was clear that planters portrayed the *kangany* recruiter as the main culprit. As early as 1859, it noted that the

greatest evil of the system and which doubtless has had the most prejudicial effect on the supply of labour... is the loss which the *cooly* sustains in the extortion practised by the *Canganies* when making advances to him, or in being compelled to make good the advances received by other coolies who may have died on their way to their place of employment.[45]

Nevertheless, planters quite early understood the significance of advances to workers. And while critical of the power enjoyed by recruiters, they also used this system to ensure that the workers were successfully tied to the estate during the peak season of labor demand.

[40] SLNA PF/24, Attorney General to Colonial Secretary, No. 364, Sept. 4, 1897.
[41] *Report and Proceedings of the Labour Commission* (headed by Sir Hugh Clifford) (Colombo, 1908).
[42] K. V. Jayawardena, *The Rise of the Labour Movement in Ceylon* (Durham, N.C.: Duke University Press, 1972), p. 18.
[43] Report of the agent of the government of India 1926.
[44] Kurian, "State, Capital and Labour," p. 93.
[45] *Report of the Immigrant Labour Commission*, Colombo, for half-year ending June 30, 1859.

A feature of labor relations was the infrequency of wage payments, often only two or three times a year. Withholding wages allowed management to have some security for the recovery of advances, while also tying labor to the peak period of coffee production. Moreover, working capital was kept to a minimum. Planters had a limited supply of working capital and obligations of higher priority to meet, such as the purchase of rice and stores. They thus preferred to pay workers as late as possible.[46] A *kangany's* account of such delaying tactics goes as follows:

My old Master was a very good Dorai, but he had a temper and when I came to the office and said that I thought the coolies ought to have some pay, he would, if he were in a good mood give me a cheque for, say, a couple of thousand rupees. And, if he was not, he would tell me to go to the devil! And in that case I would ask him again two or three days later. Now, if I should say, "Dorai, two thousand is not enough," my Master would answer, "all right, you can take a couple of those black pigs!" And if I replied "May God be my witness! two black pigs are not sufficient," he might answer, "Very well then, you can have the pigs and the little red heifer which is in calf by the Australian bull!" And so it was![47]

For nearly a century, there was little attempt to systematize or regulate wage rates, which ranged from four pence to nine pence for a working day of ten to eleven hours in the 1830s and 1840s, and rose to about 10 pence per day in the 1860s.[48] The wage also took a cash and kind form. Most estates supplied rice to the workers, the cost of which was deducted from their salaries. The rice was imported mainly from South India, and in periods of distress its price increased. The plantation workers were cushioned with regard to the availability of rice, as it was a component of the wage. At the same time, the increased cost of the imported rice resulted in a decline in nominal wages on plantations.

The Harsh Life and Work Regime of Laborers, and their Resistance

Workers lived in severe circumstances, suffering from poor health and high mortality. The Assistant Colonial Surgeon estimated that some 350,510 persons, or 25 percent of the total arrivals of immigrant workers, were unaccounted for between 1843 and 1867. In his opinion, a large

---

[46] L. R. Jayawardena, "The Supply of Sinhalese Labour to the Tea Industry in Ceylon," Research Study, Cambridge University, 1960, p. 27 (kindly made available by the author).
[47] A. P. Lanter, "A Planter's Pilgrimage and Some Rum'uns Encountered by the Way. Memoirs of Alfred Hugh Mead 1873–1939," pp. 7–8 (undated memoirs of a Ceylon planter, kindly made available to the author by his great grandson Philip van Ryneveld).
[48] Jayawardena, *The Rise of the Labour Movement*, p. 20.

proportion of these deaths could have been prevented by a more elaborate system of Medical Police, beginning its supervision in the maritime
districts of the Northern Province. Immigrants needed to be accompanied
along the inland routes to their several places of destination, and there
should be a strict enforcement of sanitary laws in cooly lines on coffee
estates.[49] Conditions of work and life on the estates, including whipping
and assault, were harsh, contributing to high mortality.[50]

This state of affairs was compounded by the inadequate medical services available for estate workers. There was constant argument between
the colonial government and planters about who was to bear the expenses
of medical care. Ordinance No. 14 of 1872 was unsatisfactory, and was
replaced by the Medical Wants Ordinance No. 17 of 1880. However,
planters and government had their differences on how the scheme was
to be financed, the latter insisting that the planters should bear the total
costs of the medical scheme. This was violently opposed by planters, who
argued that costs should be borne by the state. The Colonial Office in
London placed pressure on the local colonial government in Colombo,
and Ordinance No. 11 of 1881 was passed, placing a capitation tax, according to the numbers of workers employed on an estate, to finance the
health scheme. In 1882, however, the government agreed to bear half the
costs of medical welfare. Ordinance No. 9 of 1882 imposed a low import
duty on rice in place of the capitation tax.

However, this did not resolve the issue. There were instances when additional medical expenses incurred were taken from the workers, through
profits made on the rice that was issued to them.[51] Minimal attention
was paid to maternity facilities and benefits. The Medical Ordinance of
1872 made provisions for rudimentary medical facilities in the plantation
districts. The maternity benefits provided were two measures of rice and
75 cents in cash per week for four weeks.

The housing provided on estates promoted ill health, as it was very
poor. Workers lived in "line rooms," or barrack-like structures generally
built of stone with metallic roofing, similar to those constructed in other
colonial plantation economies. According to a contemporary planter, the
"coolies" appeared to "prefer smaller houses," which they considered
both "warm and more cosy." In his opinion, rooms of 12 feet by 12 feet

---

[49] Colonial Office, CO 54/475, W. G. Van Dort, "Report on the Gampola Civil Hospital,"
in "Correspondence on the Condition of Malabar Coolies in Ceylon."
[50] Driesen, *Indian Plantation Labour*, p. 10.
[51] Wesumperuma, *Indian Immigrant Plantation Workers*, p. 252.

could hold some twelve workers, as they had "no objection to be packed tolerably close." It is interesting to note the cost implications of this attitude. Each line room cost him five pounds sterling, while the superintendent's bungalow set him back to the tune of 500 pounds sterling.[52] The workers lived in these "line rooms" during their stay on the plantations, and there was little or no change in the housing conditions during the coffee period. Indeed, these barracks still exist on plantations, as housing for the majority of workers.

Women faced the triple burden of harsh work regimes with low pay, household work in difficult conditions with violence within the household, and bearing children without access to proper care. Housing conditions on estates were particularly difficult for women, as they had to do a great deal of work within the household, notably, cooking and cleaning. The difficult experience of women in these conditions was compounded by their lack of privacy and vulnerability to sexual abuse. They were thus undoubtedly more vulnerable to health problems and related mortality.

It would be fallacious to assume that workers meekly acquiesced to and accepted their conditions of work and life. They did resist the controls placed on them, even though they were mainly migrants and government and management practices restricted their possibilities for free movement and association between estates. Under these conditions, worker resistance was ad hoc and at an individual level, employing what Scott has called the "weapons of the weak." Acts of flight, sabotage, and even theft formed part of the "unwritten history of resistance."[53] There were cases when workers simply did not return to the island for work. There was also absenteeism from work and "bolting" from the estates, two forms of resistance that became particularly significant toward the end of the nineteenth century. Formal trade unions and other political organizations did not develop until the twentieth century, when the developing tea and rubber plantations required a more settled work force throughout the year.

Conclusion

As on plantations in other parts of the world, labor relations on Ceylon's coffee estates were hierarchical, with patronage and patriarchy reinforced

---

[52] W. Sabonadiere, *The Coffee Planter of Ceylon* (Colombo: Mees, J. P. Green, 1866, pp. 65–6.
[53] J. C. Scott, "Everyday Forms of Peasant Resistance," *Journal of Peasant Studies* 12, no. 2 (1986): 5–6.

at all levels of production. In the case of Ceylon, the position of women was particularly bad, due in part to the relatively unstructured and unsupervised nature of migration to the island from neighboring South India. Moreover, a special role was attributed to caste differences, which complemented hierarchies based on color, race, and gender in management, division of work, and distribution of benefits on plantations. While extra-economic forms of control over a migratory work force were to be found in tropical estates around the world, caste was limited to areas where Hindu workers migrated, and was particularly salient in Ceylon.

8

Coffee and Indigenous Labor in Guatemala, 1871–1980

David McCreery

Not until after the mid-nineteenth century did Guatemala become an important producer of coffee. The economy had languished during the last years of the colony and those immediately following independence because of political turmoil, locust infestations, and the separation of El Salvador, which produced the captaincy's main cash crop, indigo. In the 1840s and 1850s exports rebounded modestly with cochineal, a red dye made from the bodies of insects that lived on nopal cacti. The dye found a strong demand among domestic and foreign textile producers, and plantations and small holdings flourished around Amatitlán and Antigua, in the southwest of the country. But while cochineal could be very profitable in good years, production was a highly speculative activity, and a short rain shower at the wrong time or an unanticipated cold snap could ruin a year's work. In any event, production involved only a small part of the country and a few thousand workers. Led by the Economic Society of the Friends of the Country, a prodevelopment association subsidized by the government, a few landowners and Indian communities began to experiment with coffee in the 1850s and 1860s, in some places interplanting it with the cochineal. Expectations for the new crop were high.[1]

But transition to coffee proved to be neither swift nor simple. Lessons learned planting coffee in Colombia and Costa Rica did not transfer easily to the soil and climate of Guatemala; several early efforts ended in

[1] On the early history of coffee in Guatemala, see Ignacio Solís, *Memoria de la Casa de Moneda de Guatemala y del desarrollo económico del país*, 6 vol., (Guatemala City, 1979); Julio C. Castellanos, *Coffee and Peasants in Guatemala* (Stockholm, 1985); and David McCreery, *Rural Guatemala, 1760–1940* (Stanford: Stanford University Press, 1994), chap. 6.

disaster. Cochineal had its risks, and markets for natural dyes declined sharply in the 1860s with the appearance of new chemical dyes. But it is always difficult to convince agriculturalists to rip up what they know and essay what they do not, at least until a few pioneers show the way. Capital was in short supply. What was available found a steady demand in trade and commerce, at better rates and better security than that available for the fledgling commodity of coffee. The fact, too, that the new crop took four or five years of investment before it entered full production aggravated capital problems. Early growers had to string together money from family members, commercial credit, and loans backed by collateral such as urban property to finance their first coffee estates (fincas). Once production was under way, they could usually obtain current account financing from merchant houses or loans from foreigners with access to overseas capital at lower rates.[2] But long-term agricultural credit remained hard to obtain and always was expensive. Because so much of it came from foreign-controlled sources, each downturn in the economy, and the resulting foreclosures, put more and more land and production into the hands of non-Guatemalans.

Technology threw up similar obstacles to the expansion of the new crop.[3] Although early exporters such as Costa Rica got by initially with selling dry processed coffee, by the 1860s European markets more and more demanded a quality of product available only with wet processing. This required that growers invest heavily in tanks and drying facilities or be forced to sell their harvest at low prices to processors that had the requisite equipment. Such capital and processing demands favored medium and large estates over family farms, and set a pattern for Guatemalan development quite different from that of Costa Rica or Puerto Rico.[4]

---

[2] Most evident and most successful were Germans: Regina Wagner, *Los alemanes en Guatemala, 1828–1944* (Guatemala City, 1991).

[3] Mauricio Dominguez, "The Development of a Technological and Scientific Coffee Industry in Guatemala, 1830–1930," Ph.D. diss., Tulane University, 1970.

[4] For Costa Rica, see Ciro Flamarión Cardoso, "The Formation of the Coffee Estates in Nineteenth-century Costa Rica," in K. Duncan and I. Rutledge, *Land and Labour in Latin America* (Cambridge, U.K.: Cambridge University Press, 1977); for Puerto Rico, see Laird Bergad, *Coffee and the Growth of Agrarian Capitalism in Nineteenth-Century Puerto Rico* (Princeton: Princeton University Press, 1983); for Colombia, see Marcos Palacios, *Coffee in Colombia, 1850–1970* (Cambridge, U.K.: Cambridge University Press, 1980). For comparison, see Stanley Stein, *Vassouras: A Brazilian Coffee County, 1850–1900* (Cambridge: Cambridge University Press, 1957), and Warren Dean, *Rio Claro: A Brazilian Plantation System* (Stanford: Stanford University Press, 1976). For the sizes of Guatemala estates, see *The World's Coffee: Studies of the Principal Products of the World Market*, no. 9 (Rome, 1947), 136.

To develop large-scale coffee production, Guatemalan growers needed access to unprecedented amounts of the right kind of land. Much of this belonged to Guatemala's majority indigenous population, or so they long had claimed. Although by legal and illegal methods Spanish and creole settlers had appropriated large areas of Indian land during the colonial period, Spanish law nevertheless recognized indigenous rights, as the "ancient lords of the lands of the Americas before [European] conquest,"[5] and repeatedly confirmed village ownership of their community lands (ejidos). Rarely were the boundaries of these possessions adequately surveyed, however, and by the early nineteenth century the countryside was a welter of overlapping claims, of communities, haciendas, small farmers, ranchers, and the state (*baldíos*). In the absence of a widely grown cash crop, such confusions mattered little, but now coffee began to change this, touching off half a century of sometimes violent land conflict.

Apart from the early experiments at Amatitlán and Antigua, of which only the second prospered, coffee developed chiefly in two areas in Guatemala, the western piedmont (the Boca Costa) and the Alta Verapaz, in the northeast of the republic. Traditionally, there had been only a few towns in the lightly inhabited western piedmont, and coffee quickly overwhelmed these, converting many of the inhabitants into workers on fincas owned by outside investors.[6] But much of the Boca Costa was claimed by Indian communities that were located not in the piedmont itself but on the adjacent highlands. This was land they used seasonally to produce "tropical" crops such as cotton, peanuts, and short-season varieties of corn. In a number of cases, however, and over the considerable protests of the communities,[7] the state now confirmed their possession of only a small part of what they said they owned, declaring the rest state-owned *baldíos* and opening it up for sale to would-be coffee growers. Much of the land in the Alta Verapaz suitable for coffee also had community claims, and in some areas Indian villagers had pioneered the crop as an adjunct to their subsistence production. But state and merchant policies assumed the superior efficiency of large-scale, private production over that of the

[5] Archivo General de Centro América (hereafter AGCA), Tierras, 5989 52765.
[6] For an example of the history of the struggles of one such town, see AGCA, Ministerio de Gobernación (hereafter MG), 28564 153 and 157, 28588 135, 28589 234, 28593 120 and 145, and 28595 37 and 39.
[7] The papers of the Jefes Políticos in the AGCA, organized by department and year, hold hundreds of protests for communities about land loss. See the notes for McCreery, *Rural Guatemala*, chap. 8.

communities, and gradually private fincas displaced Indian coffee and corn.

The most serious problem confronting large-scale production of the new export was a general and persistent shortage of labor. Early efforts made do with cochineal workers or women and children recruited from nearby villages.[8] Because coffee labor was seasonal, growers initially needed extra workers for only a few months a year. But as production expanded, and as it more obviously threatened the lands and livelihood of the indigenous population, labor became harder to obtain. Guatemala's place in world markets rested on the high quality of its coffee. This depended on a careful harvest, a process that, as the groves spread up and down the sides of the mountains, could take six months or more. Workers went over the same bushes repeatedly, picking each bean only as it ripened to a perfect red, and then carrying the day's pick to the processing sheds. Guatemalan elites shared in the prejudices of the time that privileged "white" workers and would have welcomed European immigrants to its labor force, but emigrants leaving Europe found North America, Argentina, or even Brazil more attractive. If large-scale coffee was to develop in Guatemala, it would have to do so figuratively and literally on the backs of the Indians.

The indigenous population of the western highlands resisted working on the coffee estates for various reasons. Their colonial experience with forced wage labor (*repartimientos*) had given them a horror of the insects, heat, and diseases they encountered in the hot country.[9] Mortality rates were staggering, and the survivors brought disease back to their home communities. The Indians also remembered the verbal and physical abuses they had suffered at the hands of landowners, foremen, and state agents who treated them as racial inferiors. Although some among the Indians went voluntarily to the lowlands as part of long-distance trade and others made brief visits there to cultivate tropical crops, the indigenous population sought as much as possible to avoid contact with non-Indians and, even more so, to avoid working for them in commercial agriculture.

Daunting, too, for those who hoped to recruit workers was the realization that, in general, the Indians did not need the money offered. The majority still had access to enough land and other resources in their home

---

[8] See the photographs in E. Bradford Burns, *Eadweard Muybridge in Guatemala, 1875* (Berkeley: University of California Press, 1986).

[9] Murdo MacLeod, *Spanish Central America: A Socioeconomic History, 1520–1720* (Berkeley: University of California Press, 1973), chap. 5.

communities to sustain themselves and their families. Their culture defined a limited range of "needs," needs that they could satisfy almost entirely from their own production and through barter exchange.[10] Their money requirements were still small and largely fixed – for example, church fees or state taxes – and usually they could easily meet these by selling some of their agricultural or handicraft production or by wage work nearby. They understood the advantages of higher wages and might seek these out where they became available, but usually only so as to be able to work for less time.[11] Guatemala's Indians in the 1870s and 1880s were not capitalist free workers, in the sense of having only their own labor to sell to support themselves, and most showed a distressing lack of interest in either capital accumulation or opportunities to participate in industrial consumer culture.

Anticipating the wealth possible if they could mobilize enough labor, planters demanded that the state intervene to force the Indians to work the export economy. But because much of the political support for the Conservatives and Rafael Carrera rested in these indigenous communities, the government generally resisted forced labor schemes. In 1871, however, coffee growers were instrumental in the Liberal Revolution of that year and soon held many important posts in the new regime. It should have been no surprise, then, that when the dust settled, the new government turned its attention to the labor question. In November of 1876, the president issued a decree reviving the forced labor drafts[12] – now called *mandamientos* – little used in the half-century since independence. As the system had operated during the eighteenth century, Guatemalan landowners short of workers applied to the Audiencia (the colonial appeals court/administrative council) for a order that required a community or communities to supply a certain number of workers to a landowner for a set number of days or indefinitely.[13] This was wage labor, and the law required employers to pay travel costs and wages in advance, if typically at below market rates. The 1876 presidential decree brought these drafts

[10] Planters and the state were constantly frustrated by the Indians' lack of "civilized needs." E.g., see Antonio Batres Jáuregui, *Los Indios: Su historia y su civilización* (Guatemala City, 1893).

[11] On this phenomenon, see Elliot Berg, "Backward Bending Labor Supply Functions in Dual Economies: The African Case," *Quarterly Journal of Economics* (Aug. 1961): 468–92.

[12] *Recopilación de las leyes de Guatemala* (Guatemala City, 1881), vol. 1, p. 457.

[13] On repartimientos in colonial Guatemala, see Lesley Bird Simpson, *Studies in the Administration of New Spain*, vol. 3: *The Repartimiento System of Native Labor in New Spain and Guatemala* (Berkeley: University of California Press, 1938).

back, and a general labor law the following year refined the system:[14]
Export producers in need of workers might apply for help to a *jefe político*
(departmental governor). If the application was accepted, the jefe would
order a given village to supply a certain number of workers, for two weeks
at a time if job was in the department and a month if outside. These orders could be renewed. Employers paid the workers in advance, including
travel time, and community officials were responsible for selecting those
who would go to fill an order and for making sure that the men arrived
at the right place on time. The Indians loathed *mandamientos* and as individuals and communities did all they could to avoid them. But a long
history of forced wage labor made the drafts "custom" and gave them a
patina of legitimacy.

Mandamientos furnished workers for the export sector, but the system was far from satisfactory. The labor was not cheap. A fundamental
problem was the involvement of the *jefe político*. *Mandamientos* gave him
control over much of the labor in his district, labor he sometimes used
himself or, and more commonly, for which he demanded bribes: "It required a certain courage to confront the departmental boss and ask for
a *mandamiento*. That terrible personage was for the planters something
of a god dwelling in a sanctuary difficult and fearsome to enter and only
accessible to those who made sacks of golden disks sound before the
doors."[15] Employers paid workers' wages as a lump sum in advance, and
some or all of this might be siphoned off by the jefe or by corrupt community officials before it reached the men. Even if the workers received their
pay, *mandamientos* were still forced labor. Most of those drafted worked
resentfully and with little enthusiasm or initiative. Others responded by
refusing to go, by fleeing the community or by escaping from the work
gang on the way to the coast or on the return from from the finca. Because
of the turnover, employers had little opportunity to train the workers in
specialized tasks or to keep those who proved particularly adept.

For the Indians, the *mandamiento* was paid labor but poorly paid, and
the men had little control over where they went or what they did. The
drafts might take them out of their communities just when they needed
to work on their own crops or leave their plantings vulnerable to preda-
tors or bad weather or theft. On the fincas they were exposed to disease
and heat, conditions sometimes aggravated by inadequate housing and
difficult working conditions. Employers frequently tried to keep them at

[14] *Recopilación . . . Guatemala*, vol. 2, pp. 69–75.
[15] *Diario de Centro América* (Guatemala City), Jan. 29, 1919.

work longer than the order provided, typically by assigning them tasks (*tareas*) that could not be completed in the time available. Since *mandamiento* workers brought their own food, they faced serious problems if not allowed a timely return to their villages. Those who complained or resisted were showered with abuse, beaten, or jailed. Many workers died; survivors staggered back to their communities exhausted, perhaps to find their crops ruined and their families hungry or another *mandamiento* order awaiting them.[16]

Mandamientos were satisfactory neither to employers nor to workers, but they survived until at least 1920 because they served an important purpose for the coffee economy. Under the labor law of 1877, and detailed more closely in the 1894 revision, the only practical way an indigenous male could escape being forced into the *mandamientos* was to be able to prove that he had a contract for labor in the export sector. The 1894 law exempted from the drafts: "1. Seasonal workers 16 years or older owning 30 pesos or more for labor . . . ; 2. *Colonos* (resident workers) . . . who owned 15 pesos or more; 3. Indians who could show a contract for at least three months labor on a finca of coffee, sugar cane, cacao, or large-scale banana cultivation."[17] That is, the only viable alternative to repeatedly being sent on *mandamientos* was to be indebted to an export finca. Not only were the *jefe político* and community officials supposed to honor the exemption that such a debt provided, but employers too had a strong incentive to defend the men they had under contract from the forced drafts. As a result, almost every eligible indigenous man, and many women, in the accessible parts of the highlands soon bound themselves to one or more export properties. The search for workers to fill *mandamientos* pushed further and further into the peripheries, in turn forcing more of the population into debt contracts. By the turn of the century, village after village was reporting that there was no one left to be drafted.

The key to the functioning of this debt labor system was the *habilitador* (labor contractor). These men lived or traveled regularly in the highlands, giving out wage advances and signing up workers for the plantations. A few, called *contratistas*, operated independently, contracting men on their own and reselling these obligations to the highest bidder, but most

---

[16] For a typical series of protests against *mandamiento* conditions, in this case the villages of Santa María de Jesus and San Lucas Sacatepéquez against finca Mauricio, see AGCA, Jefe Político, Sacatepéquez, 1886, Santa María, Aug. 20 and 21, 1886, and San Lucas, May 10 and Aug. n.d., 1886, and the responses of the owner E. Lehnoff, June 21, Aug. 23, and Sept. 1, 1886.

[17] *Diario de Centro América*, Feb. 22–24, 1894.

habilitadores were employed by only one or two fincas. They made their money on a per head fee for the men they signed up, as well as a commission on the number of days these men labored on the plantation. Inevitably, there was competition and even conflict among the recruiters in their scramble to contract workers. By law, for example, it was forbidden to sign up a man already obligated to another property, but *habilitadores* did it anyway, blaming the men for any resulting confusion and plunging the fincas into extensive legal battles over the "ownership" of workers. Recruiters dispensed alcohol freely: "There is an unceasing coming and going of labour contractors in Nebaj. And there is rum [*aguardiente*]. The place stinks of it. The rum business and the coffee business work together."[18] Owners of drink shops commonly ran side businesses indebting Indians and forcing them to sign labor contracts. If the men woke up the next morning and resisted going to the coast, the recruiters turned to the local authorities for support, and travelers reported conveys of workers roped together and marched under guard to the coast.

Actually, as evident in the wording of the 1894 law, there were two types of indebted workers. Some of these were *colonos*, men who lived with their families more or less permanently on the fincas and who, in return for access to land for subsistence farming and wages for day labor, submitted themselves to the everyday control of the owner. A few came from the piedmont towns overrun by coffee, and others were ladinos (non-Indians) who migrated from the eastern part of Guatemala, but most were Indians who had abandoned their communities of origin in the highlands to live on the coffee estates. Why would they do this? Some had committed crimes at home or had lost their rights to land because of alcohol abuse or gambling; others were fleeing a bad marriage or tensions in their family. The number of resident *colonos* varied widely among properties and over time, but they were particularly important in the Alta Verapaz.[19] There coffee plantations directly engulfed village ejidos, leaving the Indians the option of fleeing to remote areas or remaining where they were but now as dependent labor. To leave was not easy, given the Indians' commitment to the burial places of their ancestors and their recognition of telluric deities associated with specific mountains and caves. Anyway, if they tried to

[18] Robert Burkitt, "Explorations in the Highlands of Western Guatemala," *Museum Journal* (University of Pennsylvania) 21, no. 1 (1930): 58–59.
[19] Arden King, *Cobán and the Verapaz: History and Cultural Process in Northern Guatemala* (New Orleans: Middle American Research Institute publication no. 37, 1974), and Guillermo Nañez Falcón, "Erwin Paul Dieseldorff, German Entrepreneur in the Alta Verapaz of Guatemala, 1889–1937," Ph.D. diss., Tulane University, 1970.

escape the pull of coffee by settling in an unclaimed area, "somebody buys the land and puts them to work, or else they have to run further away."[20]

More common than *colonos* were *temporalistas*, or temporary workers, who left their villages for two to six months a year to work on the coffee fincas. Whatever their debts, they demanded and got additional wage advances each year from the *habilitador*, who organized them into gangs and dispatched them to the estate as required. Or, rather, he tried to, for the Indians were no more enthusiastic about working off what they owed than they were about *mandamientos*, and they employed similar strategies of resistance. Such difficulties aside, seasonal labor had real advantages for the export sector. Most important, workers supported themselves when not required for labor on the fincas. The employers did not have to provide wages adequate to support the workers and their families year round or fund the reproduction and training of replacement workers, as is the case with free labor. Instead, they paid only for the weeks or months of work they actually needed, and that at wages depressed by the effects of *mandamiento* coercion.

There were costs for the employers, of course. Properties carried on their books the debts of hundreds or even thousands of laborers, tying up capital or forcing employers to borrow the money at interest. Workers died or ran away and their debt might be lost. Overall, the *finqueros* (estate owners) would have preferred a system in which the Indians worked without advances, but the Indians stubbornly resisted this. If they had to work and only a debt protected them from *mandamiento* drafts, they would extract as much money as possible from the estates. The government and employers had the coercive power of the army, the telegraph, and the repeating rifle on their side. But the indigenous population had the numbers and an awareness that without their participation the export economy would collapse.

A relationship in which a minority used actual or threatened violence to coerce work from a majority of the population that they deemed to be culturally and racially inferior was bound to be marked by tension. Elites took it for granted that the Indian was lazy, stupid, dirty, and drunken: "The Indian is a pariah, stretched out in his hammock and drunk on *chichi* [corn beer]."[21] And they found it simplest to assume that he could be motivated only by threats and force. "Chucho" (mutt) they called him, and

[20] Burkitt, "Explorations," 45.
[21] *Diario de Centro América*, April 19, 1892.

foremen routinely slapped and hit workers or threw them in jail or bound them in stocks to punish them for real or imagined infractions. Landowners worked the Indians long hours, assigned them excessive tasks, and cheated them on the weight of coffee they picked or took advantage of the Indians' illiteracy to manipulate their debt records.[22] Small wonder that when Guatemala signed the 1923 Washington Convention that banned the physical coercion of labor, the planters were, briefly, worried.

Much of the abuse was structural and almost unconscious. Because the planters' racism led them to assume that Indians lived in filth, the plantations provided the temporary workers only the flimsiest of housing, often a open shed that crowded them together promiscuously but left the sides open and the inhabitants exposed to the elements. Food, provided by the employer for indebted workers, was routinely inadequate and drinking water polluted or contaminated with fertilizer or chemicals. If the men complained, the foreman told them to "eat shit."[23] Sanitary facilities were poor or nonexistent. Under such conditions, disease, including malaria, dysentery, and smallpox, was rampant, and workers traveling between the coast and the highlands spread sickness over wide areas.[24] When in the interest of increased efficiency or to protect their own health finca owners made improvements, such as digging latrines or vaccinating workers, they commonly nullified much of the possible benefit by failing to explain the changes to Indians they assumed too stupid to understand.

Although most seasonal and *mandamiento* labor was done by men, women worked too in the coffee economy. At first some were recruited for day labor from nearby villages, but as production expanded, women were more likely to become involved in coffee labor as members of male-dominated households. Wives and children commonly worked in the fields with the men to pay off what might be technically the man's debt but which in fact all involved treated as a family obligation. If the man died, employers sometimes sought to force the wife or children to assume responsibility for the outstanding balance.[25] This was against the law, but often family members acquiesced, because it offered them additional advances or,

[22] For a bitter comment on how the Indians were cheated, see *Diario de Centro América*, May 3, 1919.

[23] AGCA, B119.21.0.0 47749 350.

[24] An anthropologist working in the highland community of Chichicastenango during the 1930s reported that there was no disease in the village except malaria, brought by workers returned from the coast: Ruth Bunzel, *Chichicastenango: A Guatemalan Village* (Seattle: University of Washington Press, 1952), 143.

[25] E.g., AGCA, B119, 21.0.0 47751 119.

for *colonos*, because it guaranteed them continued access to land for sub-sistence plantings. In extreme cases, men "sold" wives or daughters to recruiters, taking the advance and leaving the unsuspecting or protesting women with the debt and the labor obligation. Some women, particularly single mothers or widows, contracted with the fincas on their own, to pick the harvest, winnow out bad beans as part of the cleaning process, or cook for the labor gangs. All suffered the threat or fact of sexual harassment, and all were subject to the pressures of labor debts; when it came to work, one woman lamented, we "have equal legal rights with men."[26]

It would be wrong, though, to imagine that indigenous women or men were in all cases simply passive victims. True, they rarely rebelled openly, whether against land incursions or labor demands or abuses by state officials. To do so, particularly after 1871 with the expansion of the state's repressive capacity, was to court destruction. Open defiance was likely to be drowned in blood. There were other, more effective ways to resist. Workers sometimes refused to leave the communities when called to the fincas or sought to delay their departure, and if pressed they could easily evade the *habilitadores*, whether by slipping away to an uninhabited area or fleeing across the border; labor pressures, one official admitted, "provoked a large number of Indians to emigrate to Mexico and British Honduras."[27] The *habilitador* usually had the law and the state on his side, but in the villages he was on his own. Most were themselves too socially marginal to provoke a fuss if they disappeared on a dark night, and both sides knew this, prompting negotiations more often than demands.[28] On the fincas, workers often engaged in foot dragging and sabotage or ran away, prompting owners on occasion to imprison whole gangs at night for fear they might escape.[29]

The most common and most efficient, if not the most dramatic, form of indigenous resistance was the petition.[30] In a tactic perfected during the colonial period, indigenous communities, families, and individuals rained protest documents on local officials, governors, and the president,

---

[26] AGCA B119.21.0.0 47811 106.

[27] Ministerio de Agricultura, *Agricultura-1902*, 41–42.

[28] For the massacre of a number of *habilitadores*, an event that did stir up a violent govern-ment response, see David McCreery, "Land, Labor, and Violence in Highland Guatemala: San Juan Ixcoy (Huehuetenango), 1890–1940," *The Americas* 45, no. 2 (Oct. 1988): 237–49.

[29] For the story of a particularly dramatic escape from a finca, see Juan de Dios Rosales, "Notes on Aguacatán," Microfilm Collection of Manuscripts on Middle American Cultural Anthropology, University of Chicago, no. 24.

[30] Many examples are available in the papers of the *jefes políticos* in the AGCA.

and repeatedly followed these up with personal visits, sometimes going as far as the capital. In these they rehearsed the abuses to which they said the fincas or recruiters or local authorities had subjected them and they begged for official intervention to give them justice. They were, of course, careful to acknowledge that the official to whom they addressed the complaint could not have known of these abuses and as much as they was a victim of corrupt subordinates and rapacious *finqueros*. The recipients of these petitions paid attention. They understood that, if pushed too far, the Indians might resort to violence, and perhaps violence on a massive scale, as they had in the Carrera uprising of the 1830s[31] and in the "War of the Castes" that raged off and on in southern Mexico for much of the century. Yet to appear too ready to give in threatened to compromise state and elite authority. Instead, these petitions generally initiated, or were part of, a negotiating process among the community, the workers, the employers, and the state. Several hundred years of colonial rule had given each side had a generally accurate idea of how much and how far they could push without these negotiations breaking down. Occasionally, misjudgments or misunderstandings occurred, but typically the petitions brought the seasonal workers the promise of a few cents more an hour pay or an order for an employer to end some particularly egregious abuse, together with the stern admonition that the Indians were to report at once to the fincas to fulfill their contracts. Generally, they did, though all were aware that these negotiations could, and probably would, begin again at some time in the not too distant future.

The effects of temporary wage labor on the workers and on their families and communities were complex and contradictory.[32] Men and women

---

[31] R. L. Woodward, *Rafael Carrera and the Emergence of the Republic of Guatemala, 1821–1871* (Athens: University of Georgia Press, 1993).

[32] A number of anthropological studies deal in part with the relationship between finca labor and life in the communities. Among these are Richard Appelbaum, *San Ildefonso Ixtahuacán, Guatemala* (Guatemala: Cuadernos del Seminario de Integración Social Guatemalteca, no. 17, 1967); Bunzel, *Chichicastenango*; Robert Carmack, ed., *Harvest of Violence: The Maya Indians and the Guatemalan Crisis* (Norman: University of Oklahoma Press, 1988); Benjamin Colby and Pierre van den Berghe, *Ixil Country: A Plural Society in Highland Guatemala* (Berkeley: University of California Press, 1969); Ricardo Falla, *Quiché rebelde* (Guatemala City, 1978); Jackson Lincoln, "An Ethnographic Study of the Ixil Indians of the Guatemalan Highlands," Microfilm Collection of Manuscripts on Middle American Cultural Anthropology, University of Chicago, no. 1; Douglas Madigan, "Santiago Atitlán: A Socioeconomic History," Ph.D. diss., University of Pittsburgh, 1976; Maude Oakes, *The Two Crosses of Todos Santos: Survivals of Mayan Religious Rituals* (Princeton: Princeton University Press, 1951); Jean Piel, *Sacabaja: Muerte y resurrección de un pueblo de Guatemala, 1500–1970* (Guatemala City, 1989); James Sexton, ed., *Son of*

who went to the coast were exposed to disease and physical and verbal abuse. They also faced the confusions of deculturation, though the latter was attenuated for temporary workers by the tendency to work in community-based gangs and because of the relatively short time they were gone from their villages. For some workers, the wages gave access to new consumer goods and helped create new "needs," while others accumulated savings and bought land or agricultural equipment. Most commonly, though, the wages and food rations from the fincas went simply to make up for subsistence shortfalls in families in the highland villages, as a growing population now pressed against declining resources. Temporary wage labor allowed the indigenous communities to support populations that would not otherwise have been possible, but it left them vulnerable to any downturn in employment.

Apart from simple subsistence, perhaps the most dramatic effect of the availability of wage labor for families was on generational relations. Young men no longer had to wait years or decades in strict subservience to their fathers in the hope of inheriting rights to land, a relationship traditionally fraught with vast tensions. They could now instead find alternative employment if they wished, or they might be able to accumulate enough money to buy their own land.

As for the communities, temporary wage work on the fincas tended to drain the highland economy of needed labor, sometimes at key moments in the cycles of planting or harvest. It also aggravated problems of disease and alcoholism and the tensions attendant on the increasing socioeconomic differentiation inherent in any newly monetarizing economy. On the positive side, the wages made money more available to the villages, and some of this went to reinforce community institutions such as *cofradías* (religious brotherhoods) or to purchase or litigate land. Most important, it allowed the highlands to sustain a greater population than would have been possible based solely on locally available resources.

Mandamientos persisted in Guatemala until the years immediately after World War I. The collapse of coffee prices in the wake of the "Dance

Tecun Uman (Tucson: University of Arizona Press, 1985); Waldeman Smith, *The Fiesta System and Economic Change* (New York: Columbia University Press, 1977); Charles Wagley, *The Economics of a Guatemalan Village* (Menosha, Wis.: American Anthropological Association Memoir no. 58, 1941); Kay Warren, *The Symbolism of Subordination: Indian Identity in a Guatemalan Town* (Austin: University of Texas Press, 1978); and John Watanabe, *Maya Saints and Souls in a Changing World* (Austin: University of Texas Press, 1992).

of the Millions," together with the effects of the worldwide influenza epidemic and fall of long-time dictator Manuel Estrada Cabrera, provoked a rethinking of the country's labor systems in the early 1920s. A new regime did away with forced wage labor for agriculture,[33] which, in any event, most planters now equated with the extortions of the *jefes políticos*. And an unprecedented debate broke out in the newspapers over the possibilities of abolishing debts and instituting *trabajo libre*, "free labor."[34] These articles did not contemplate free labor in a capitalist sense but, rather, an arrangement in which wage labor would be obligatory for Indians, and now for poor ladinos, too, but in which there would be no advances or debts. Such a system potentially had advantages for all involved, but from the planters' perspective it presupposed a strong vagrancy law and a political regime able to enforce this, neither of which Guatemala had in the early 1920s. Planters and Indians alike were fundamentally conservative, and the state in these years was embroiled in an ultimately unsuccessful attempt at political democracy, so when coffee prices rebounded in 1924 the debate faded and the "custom" of debts reasserted itself.

Problems arose again only after 1929. Guatemala weathered the Depression rather better than did many other primary producers,[35] but a fall in income in the early 1930s prompted coffee planters to again question labor costs and to look for ways to reduce them. Censuses in the 1920s made employers and the state aware of increases in the indigenous population, opening the possibility of an end to labor shortages. After a generation of work in the wage economy, many of Guatemala's Indians, as individuals and as communities, had acquired needs that only cash could satisfy. In 1931–32, they were knocking at the doors of the fincas, only to find no work available. But when reforms came, they were only a half-step. In May of 1934, the dictator General Jorge Ubico ended labor debts and instituted *trabajo libre*, as outlined in the debates of the early 1920s: rural men, Indians and ladinos alike, were free to contract their work as they wished, but those who could not prove that they had access to relatively large amounts of land or who did not practice an exempted profession

[33] Evidence for the end of agricultural *mandamientos* is indirect, as in theory they had been illegal since the 1894 labor law, and the government often denied that they existed; see McCreery, *Rural Guatemala*, 302.

[34] See, esp. the pages of the *Imparcial* (Guatemala City), Guatemala's first modern newspaper.

[35] Victor Bulmer-Thomas, *Political Economy of Central America since 1920* (Cambridge: Cambridge University Press, 1987), chaps. 3 and 4.

or trade were required to work for wages on an export plantation for at least 100 to 150 days a year.[36]

The state backed this up with a tough new vagrancy law,[37] enforced by obligatory identity cards and work records and by police checkpoints and sweeps through the countryside. Despite the law, however, Indians continued to refuse to go to the fincas without advances. The state gave in on this but limited these to what could be worked off in a few months and would not enforce long-term labor debts. The indigenous population welcomed the changes, not the least because they now required that non-Indians as well as Indians work. They valued work and the new law seemed fairer: "When Ubico entered the government, there was a change because he created an article in the constitution which made work sacred."[38] Sales of work papers soon demonstrated an emerging balance between the labor requirements of the export economy and those Indians and ladinos with so little land that they had to seek wage labor.

If they accepted the new law as an improvement over the old one, the Indians nevertheless continued to resist coerced labor. Many hid out and tried to avoid situations where they could be forced to produce their work records: "The survivors were like lizards hidden among the rock, only raising their heads to spy the danger that came in search of more workers."[39] Others bribed local officials to certify land or a profession they did not have or bought falsified papers. Employers made deals to pay the men less than the going wage but to record in their books a greater number of days than they had actually worked. Authorities hoped that the new law would induce emigrants that had taken refuge in Mexico and British Honduras to return, but few did. Those accused of vagrancy sometimes mounted elaborate and successful defenses, and the courts went to surprising lengths to help defendants obtain evidence that might validate their claims.[40]

The new laws brought changes to the communities. One effect was to reverse a half-century trend of ladinos migrating to western highland towns, to exploit recruiting and commercial opportunities stimulated by the rise in available cash. The need for *habilitadores* declined, and *contratistas*, dependent on their indebted clientele, were wiped out. Into

---

[36] Rosendo Mendez, *Leyes vigentes de agricultura* (Guatemala City, 1937), 214–15.
[37] Ibid., 244–47.
[38] Warren, *Symbolism*, 149.
[39] From an unpublished manuscript made available to the author by Prof. Ben Paul.
[40] See the many cases in the Archivo de los Tribunales, presently in the AGCA.

the place of departing ladinos stepped individuals from among the better-off segment of the indigenous population, taking over labor recruiting, managing small shops and trades, and taking advantage of the government's aggressive road-building campaign to set up truck and bus lines.[41] With the fall-off in advances and the growing impoverishment of much of the population, the profits from these activities were less than they had been but were still greater than those available in subsistence agriculture or barter trade, and they too offered exemption from the vagrancy law. The effect was, on the one hand, to "re-Indianize" the local economy in many towns while, at the same time, hastening socioeconomic differentiation among the indigenous population and heightening the possibilities of the conflict such differentiation entailed.

Only with the Revolution of 1944 did elites and the state finally abandon the legal coercion of labor. Indeed, this was one of the first topics the new government took up. The old arguments about the backwardness and laziness of the Indians and their supposed unwillingness to work for wages resurfaced, but times had changed.[42] For one thing, it was now painfully obvious that the population of the western highlands and the Alta Verapaz was rapidly running out of resources. The census of 1950 confirmed this: Almost half of all agriculturalists in the country cultivated two manzanas (one manzana equals approximately 1.7 acres) or less of land, and by the end of the decade estimates were that only 20 to 30 percent of the Indians in the western highlands had access to enough land to support their families.[43]

The young revolutionaries were committed to converting Guatemala to a modern capitalist economy, including free labor, but at a measured pace. They abolished the vagrancy law as a vehicle for labor recruitment[44] but hesitated at further reforms that might affect exports or alienate powerful agriculturally based elites. For example, the government approved unions for urban workers but for not those in the countryside. The hope instead was that land reform would solve rural problems. A first step was a law requiring the rental of unused land. Then in 1952, the new Arbenz regime enacted Decree 900, one of the most sweeping land reforms in the history of Latin America, though one still well within the confines of a capitalist

[41] For a more recent, if unsuccessful, example of such entrepreneurship, see Sexton, ed., *Son of Tecun Uman.*
[42] See, e.g., *El Imparcial*, May 2, 1945.
[43] Appelbaum, *San Ildefonso Ixtahuacán*, 18.
[44] Augusto Zelaya Gil and Manuel Antonio Lucerno, eds., *Resumen de leyes de la República, clasificados y anotados por secretarías* (Guatemala City, 1955), 255.

system. By June of 1954, some 100,000 families had received 750,000 acres as community or individual property, and more land was in the process of being expropriated.[45] The government promised as well credit, roads, and agricultural extension services to make the reform effective. Caught in Cold War tensions, however, the revolution collapsed in the face of an exile invasion backed by the United States and an army coup. White terror rolled back land reform and abolished most labor rights.

The economic conditions evident by 1950 accelerated in the next decades and inequalities accentuated. Population grew almost exponentially, rising from 2.8 million in 1950 to 8.5 in the mid-1980s, so that per capita access to land continued to decline. Under pressure to do something about land shortages, the postrevolutionary governments promoted colonization schemes that settled Indians in the largely uninhabited, and isolated, northern parts of the country. But when in the 1970s it appeared that some of this area might hold important oil reserves, the army moved it and evicted the settlers, adding to the numbers of landless and unemployed seeking work.[46] Anthropologists researching in the western highlands reported that far from having to forcibly recruit workers, it was now sufficient to park a truck in the village plaza and make an announcement over the local radio station to have all the seasonal workers a finca needed.[47] But extralegal coercion had not disappeared, particularly on the export properties where armed guards tried to prevent labor organizing and strikes.

In the cities and towns, death squads murdered hundreds of union leaders and political activists during the 1960s and 1970s.[48] By the late 1970s tensions had become unbearable and strikes erupted in urban areas and on the rural estates, and leftist guerrillas, repressed in the 1960s, reappeared in the western highlands. Guatemala exploded into violence and descended into the horrors of civil war. Fighting had subsided inconclusively by the mid-1980s, but the repression of strikes and labor organizing continued, giving Guatemala one of the worst labor, or simply human, rights record in the hemisphere. Tens of thousands of those displaced by

[45] Jim Handy, *Revolution in the Countryside: Rural Conflict and Agrarian Reform in Guatemala, 1944–1954* (Chapel Hill: University of North Carolina Press, 1994), 94–95.
[46] On violence in the northern settlement areas, see Ricardo Falla, *Massacres in the Jungle: Ixcán, Guatemala, 1975–1982* (Boulder, Colo.: Westview Press, 1994).
[47] Reported to the author by Prof. John Watanabe.
[48] On political violence in Guatemala, see Susanne Jonas, *The Battle for Guatemala: Rebels, Death Squads, and U.S. Power* (Boulder, Colo.: Westview Press, 1991). On the recent situation, see the www.amnesty-usa.org.

the war or the destruction of the highland economy scrambled for survival in the urban "informal sector" or sought work on the coastal coffee, sugar cane, and cotton plantations. Free labor had come to Guatemala.

Coffee is perhaps unique among tropical export commodities in supporting a wide variety of production schemes, from large slave-based plantations to family farms, all of which can be made to be profitable. If in the late nineteenth century Brazil produced enormous quantities of coffee and dominated the market and Costa Ricans found a niche for themselves with a small but high quality output, Guatemala's experience fell somewhere in between. By the turn of the century, the country was the world's fourth largest coffee exporter, but its product was so highly regarded in Europe that much of it was marketed under the names of individual fincas. This ability to combine relatively large-scale production while maintaining high quality was possible because of the availability of tens of thousands of Indians workers, coerced into coffee labor by state power, "custom," and, increasingly after 1930, "needs." This was low-cost but not cheap labor; ranked by productivity Guatemala in the 1910s and '20s fell well behind its neighbors. But the labor was available and did allow Guatemala's elites to export large quantities of high-quality coffee that commanded premium prices on world markets. The process also impoverished the indigenous population and threatened to destroy a centuries-old culture.

9

Patriarchy from Above, Patriarchy from Below

Debt Peonage on Nicaraguan Coffee Estates, 1870–1930

Elizabeth Dore

In Latin America, coffee production involved a wide variety of class relations.* Before emancipation, many laborers on Brazil's plantations were slaves; after abolition most were *colonos*.[1] In the nineteenth century in Costa Rica, Venezuela, and parts of Colombia, coffee was produced largely by extended households on family farms.[2] In Nicaragua, Guatemala, and El Salvador, most coffee was produced on large estates that relied on forced labor drafts and debt peonage.[3] Notwithstanding

---

* Robbie Gray, Donna Guy, Turid Hagene, Colin Lewis, Eugenia Rodríguez, Steven Topik, John Weeks, and reviewers for Cambridge University Press gave me valuable comments on an earlier draft of this chapter. I thank them all.

[1] For an analytical overview of Latin American coffee producing countries, see Steven C. Topik, "Coffee," in Steven C. Topik and Allen Wells, eds., *The Second Conquest of Latin America: Coffee, Henequen, and Oil during the Export Boom, 1850–1930* (Austin: University of Texas Press, 1998), 37–84. For the case of Brazil, see, among others, Warren Dean, *Rio Claro: A Brazilian Plantation System, 1820–1920* (Stanford: Stanford University Press, 1976).

[2] For Costa Rica, see Mario Samper, *Generations of Settlers: Rural Households and Markets on the Costa Rican Frontier, 1850–1935* (Boulder, Colo.: Westview Press, 1990); for Venezuela, see Doug Yarrington, *A Coffee Frontier: Land, Society and Politics in Duaca, Venezuela, 1830–1936* (Pittsburgh: University of Pittsburgh Press, 1997); and William Roseberry, *Coffee and Capitalism in the Venezuelan Andes* (Austin: University of Texas Press, 1983).

[3] For Guatemala, see David McCreery, *Rural Guatemala, 1760–1940* (Stanford: Stanford University Press, 1994); for El Salvador, see Aldo Lauria-Santiago, *An Agrarian Republic: Commercial Agriculture and the Politics of Peasant Communities* (Pittsburgh: University of Pittsburgh Press, 1999); for Nicaragua, Jeffrey L. Gould, *To Die in This Way: Nicaraguan Indians and the Myth of Mestizaje, 1880–1965* (Durham: Duke University Press, 1998); Elizabeth Dore, *The Myth of Modernity: Peonage and Patriarchy in Nicaragua, 1840–1990* (Durham: Duke University Press, forthcoming); and Julie Charlip, *Cultivating Coffee: The Farmers of Carazo, Nicaragua* (Ohio University Press, forthcoming).

great differences in the class character of coffee-producing societies, some similarities in their gendered character are striking.

Gender relations in Latin America's coffee economies arose largely out of a union of nature and culture: the nature of coffee production and the culture of patriarchy. By nature, coffee harvesting was and remains a laborious process of picking and sorting coffee cherries (which contain beans) one at a time. In many times and places this phase of production tended to be women's and children's work, partly because of their purportedly "nimble fingers" and their low-paid labor.[4] Notwithstanding variations in patriarchal cultures and ideologies, there were powerful similarities in the patriarchal character of societies in Latin America's coffee-producing zones.[5]

An older historiography indicated by commission or omission that the labor force in coffee production was predominantly male.[6] Subsequent research overturned that view, demonstrating that women played an important, sometimes predominant, role in the labor process.[7] This chapter

---

[4] For the argument that "nimble fingers" are historically, not biologically, constructed, see Diane Elson and Ruth Pearson, "Nimble Fingers Make Light Work: An Analysis of Women's Employment in Third World Export Manufacturing," *Feminist Review* 8 (Spring 1981): 87–107.

[5] For analyses of patriarchy in Latin America, see inter alia, Elizabeth Dore and Maxine Molyneux, eds., *Hidden Histories of Gender and the State in Latin America* (Durham and London: Duke University Press, 2000); in particular, Elizabeth Dore, "One Step Forward, Two Steps Back: Gender and the State in the Long Nineteenth Century," and Maxine Molyneux, "Twentieth-Century State Formations in Latin America," 3–81; Heidi Tinsman, *Partners in Conflict: The Politics of Gender, Sexuality and Labor in the Chilean Agrarian Reform, 1950–1973* (Durham: Duke University Press, 2002); and "Household *Patrones*: Wife Beating and Sexual Control in Rural Chile, 1964–1988," in Daniel James and John French, eds., *The Gendered Worlds of Latin American Women Workers* (Durham: Duke University Press, 1997), 264–96; Karin A. Rosemblatt, *Gendered Compromises: Political Cultures and the State in Chile, 1920–1950* (Chapel Hill: University of North Carolina Press, 2000); Steve J. Stern, *The Secret History of Gender: Women, Men and Power in Late Colonial Mexico* (Chapel Hill: University of North Carolina Press, 1995); Thomas Miller Klubock, *Contested Communities: Class, Gender and Politics in Chile's El Teniente Copper Mine, 1904–1951* (Durham: Duke University Press, 1998); Susan K. Besse, *Restructuring Patriarchy: The Modernization of Gender Inequality in Brazil, 1914–1940* (Chapel Hill: University of North Carolina Press, 1996); Ann Farnsworth-Alvear, *Dulcinea in the Factory: Myths, Morals, Men and Women in Colombia's Industrial Experiment, 1905–1960* (Durham: Duke University Press, 2000); Gilbert M. Joseph, ed., *Gender and Society: A Special Issue of the Hispanic American Historical Review* 88 (2001).

[6] E.g., Stanley Stein, *Vassouras, a Brazilian Coffee County, 1850–1900: The Roles of Planter and Slave in a Plantation Society* (1958; rpt., Princeton: Princeton University Press, 1985).

[7] Verena Stolcke, *Coffee Planters, Workers and Wives: Class Conflict and Gender Relations on São Paulo Plantations, 1850–1980* (Basingstoke: Macmillan, 1988), and "The Labors of Coffee in Latin America: The Hidden Charm of Family Labor and Self-Provisioning,"

contributes to the growing body of research on gender and class relations in coffee-producing regions by examining the patriarchal character of debt peonage in Diriomo, a municipality in the Department of Granada, in one of Nicaragua's first coffee-producing zones. Diriomo is one of a number of communities on the Meseta de Los Pueblos, a region that spans the coffee-producing districts of Granada, Managua, Carazo, and Masaya. This story of Diriomo is in many respects a history of the large coffee estates and peasant communities in Nicaragua.[8]

Although laws governing patriarchal authority applied to men and women across Nicaragua's social spectrum, patriarchal practices varied widely along lines of class and race.[9] To emphasize the social differentiation of patriarchy, I call planters' patriarchy patriarchy from above, and peasants' patriarchy patriarchy from below. Patriarchy from above was central to the class, race, and gendered character of peonage on Nicaraguan coffee estates. Patriarchy from below contributed to the gendered character of peonage and peasant household production; it tended to push women and children into rather than out of the labor force in the coffee sector in Nicaragua and in other Latin American countries.

The argument is presented in five sections. Section 1 examines patriarchy and its juridical foundations in Latin America; section 2 describes land privatization and debt peonage in Nicaragua, with a focus

---

in William Roseberry, Lowell Gudmundson, and Mario Samper K., eds., *Coffee, Society and Power in Latin America* (Baltimore and London, 1995), 65–93; Lowell W. Gudmundson, *Costa Rica before Coffee: Society and Economy on the Eve of the Coffee Boom* (Baton Rouge, Louisiana, 1986); Heather Fowler-Salamini, "Gender, Work and Coffee in Córdoba, Veracruz, 1850–1910," and Francie R. Chassen-López, "'Cheaper Than Machines': Women and Agriculture in Porfirian Oaxaca, 1880–1911," both in Heather Fowler-Salamini and Mary Kay Vaughan, eds., *Women of the Mexican Countryside, 1850–1990* (Tucson, 1994), 27–73; Michael F. Jiménez, "Class, Gender, and Peasant Resistance in Central Colombia, 1900–1930," in Forrest Colburn, ed., *Everyday Forms of Peasant Resistance* (New York and London: Sharpe Publishers, 1989), 122–50; Gould, *To Die in This Way,* 134–176; and Charles Bergquist, *Labor in Latin America: Comparative Essays on Chile, Argentina, Venezuela, and Colombia* (Stanford: Stanford University Press, 1986), 351–52.

[8] See Charlip, Chapter 10, on the Carazo region. The contrast between the two chapters may reflect the fact that patterns of social change varied significantly within the region, or that she and I interpret social change quite differently.

[9] I adapt Terence J. Byers's terminology for a different purpose; see *Capitalism from Above and Capitalism from Below: An Essay in Comparative Political Economy* (Basingstoke: Macmillan, 1996). Judith Stacey calls the extension of patriarchal rights to peasant men in socialist China "democratic patriarchy" in *Patriarchy and Socialist Revolution in China* (Berkeley: University of California Press, 1983), 12. While there are similarities between my "patriarchy from below" and Stacey's "democratic patriarchy," in my view, "democratic patriarchy" is an oxymoron.

on Diriomo. Section 3 analyzes patriarchy from above, in particular, how patronal practices of protection and violence enhanced planters' class and gendered domination of the peasantry. The racial dimensions of estate-based patriarchy I treat elsewhere.[10] Section 4 investigates patriarchy from below: how male peasants' patriarchal authority allowed them to consign wives and children to debt servitude. Section 5 examines the high incidence of female-headed households in Diriomo, and the extent to which wide-ranging male prerogatives contributed to female peonage and household headship.

1. Patriarchal Laws and Practices

My definition of patriarchy is five-fold.[11] Patriarchy rests on senior male domination over females and subordinate males. Patriarchal authority is constituted through legal, economic, political, social, and sexual rights, privileges, and obligations. Patriarchy assumes different meanings, manifestations, and consequences in the integrated spheres of household, locale, and nation-state. Patriarchy is historically contingent and socially specific: patriarchal practices vary by epoch, class, race, nation, and generation. Finally, patriarchal relations are dynamic: Men and women continually renegotiate patriarchal domination and subordination.

Gender differs from, but is related to, patriarchy. Gender is constituted by and reproduces the material practices and ideologies of male-female difference and inequality, including but not exclusively sexual difference. Like patriarchy, gender roles and relations are historically changing, socially specific, and continually renegotiated. Historians widely regard patriarchy as a – if not the – cause of gender inequalities. They have paid less attention, however, to the role of patriarchy in constituting class and race differences and inequalities.

To understand the gendered and class dynamics of Nicaraguan society, this chapter examines coffee planters' control over the labor, bodies, and wages of male and female peons, and peasant men's control over the labor, bodies, and wages of their wives and children. This double vision of

---

[10] Dore, *The Myth of Modernity*.
[11] This definition draws on Anne Phillips, *Divided Loyalties: Dilemmas of Sex and Class* (London: Virago, 1987), and *Which Equalities Matter?* (Cambridge, U.K.: Polity Press, 1999); Mary Kay Vaughan, "Modernizing Patriarchy: State Policies, Rural Households, and Women in Mexico, 1930–1940," in Dore and Molyneux, eds., *Hidden Histories*, 194–214; Deniz Kandiyoti, "Bargaining with Patriarchy," *Gender and Society* 2, no. 3 (1988): 274–90; and Tinsman, *Partners in Conflict*.

patriarchy – from above and from below – highlights features of Nicaragua's social order that historians have largely ignored.

Patriarchal authority was a foundational principle of the social and juridical order in colonial and postcolonial Latin America. In a number of ways, patriarchy hardened rather than softened after independence in the nineteenth century.[12] Patriarchal laws and practices tended to assume more absolutist forms in the second half of the century, an era characterized by the rise of coffee production. The senior male in every household, from the highest to the lowest (excepting the enslaved), had wide-ranging authority over his wife, children, and other dependents. Latin American family law rested on the principle of *patria potestad* – loosely translated as power of the patriarch.[13] *Patria potestad* legally required a wife to obey her husband, and children to obey their father. The patriarch, the senior male, was guardian and legal representative of every member of his household; he was the state's representative in the family and the representative of household members vis-à-vis the state and public realm. Only the patriarch was empowered to enter into contractual relations and administer property; therefore, he signed contracts for and controlled the property and labor of every member of his household. In addition, family patriarchs had the legal obligation to maintain discipline within the domestic sphere. To this end, patriarchs not only were permitted but were obligated to punish dependents as they saw fit. Although laws proscribed excessive brutality, within limits, patriarchs were masters of their domain, however humble or grand. The framework of Latin American political systems rested on the premise that society was governed at its most basic level by male heads of household.[14]

Paradoxically, liberal reforms enacted throughout the region in the second half of the nineteenth century tended to fortify patriarchal authority in a number of key areas. In many countries, jurists revised civil codes to

[12] Dore, "One Step Forward, Two Steps Back."

[13] For Mexican laws, see Silvia Marina Arrom, *The Women of Mexico City, 1790–1857* (Stanford: Stanford University Press, 1985), 55–96; for Argentine law, see Donna Guy, "Lower-Class Families, Women and the Law in Nineteenth Century Argentina," *Journal of Family History* 10, no. 3 (1985): 318–31. For patriarchy and family relations, see Ann Varley, "Women and the Home in Mexican Family Law," and Donna Guy, "Parents before Tribunals: The Legal Construction of Patriarchy in Argentina," in Dore and Molyneux, eds., *Hidden Histories*, 172–93, 238–61. For patriachy and nation building, see Mark Szurchman, *Order, Family and Community in Buenos Aires, 1810–1860* (Stanford: Stanford University Press, 1988), 190.

[14] The words *patria* (fatherland) and *patriarch/patriarca* (ruler, chief or head of a family) are from the same root.

reinforce a husband's control over his wife's body, labor, wages, and property. And notwithstanding a certain loosening of patriarchal rights over adult sons, an unmarried daughter remained subordinated to paternal authority throughout her father's lifetime – unless legally "emancipated," that is, granted independence by her father. In addition, if adult sons and daughters disobeyed their father, he could call upon the state to enforce his will. In line with constitutional law in the region, Nicaragua's constitution of 1858 suspended a man's rights of citizenship if he suborned his father's authority.[15] In sum, Latin America's legal tradition established the authority of male elders over women and subordinate men. To enforce this principle, constitutions of the new republics invested patriarchs with extensive powers in the domestic and public spheres.

For married women, neither a father's death nor marriage ushered in emancipation, because husbands exercised patriarchal authority over their wives. Legally, wives were in much the same situation as children, especially concerning their property, labor, and lack of personal authority. The equivalence between wives and children was spelled out in the preamble to Nicaragua's civil code of 1867, which stated that, "wives are obliged to submit to the tutelage of their husbands just as in the case of minors."[16]

Patriarchal domination over females was highly differentiated according to two criteria: women's marital status (*estado civil*) and reputation for honor, meaning sexual decency. This essay analyzes the former; the latter – female honor and its place in the reproduction of patriarchal power – I treat only in passing. Yet two aspects of the condition of "female honor" are pertinent here. First, the formal criteria to measure honor and decency varied according to racial ascription in the colonial era, also after independence, although then more informally. Second, a woman's legal rights and privileges rested on "public" perception that she was honorable; in practice, the "public" that passed judgment on a woman's honor was comprised exclusively of patriarchs of the community.[17]

Returning to the relationship between patriarchy and marital standing, for many purposes the death of the husband liberated the married woman

[15] Luis Zuñiga Osorio, "Patria Potestad," tesis para el doctor en derecho, Managua, p. 47. For implementation of laws, see E. Bradford Burns, *Patriarch and Folk: The Emergence of Nicaragua, 1789–1858* (Cambridge: Harvard University Press, 1991).
[16] Zuñiga Osorio, "Patria Potestad," 32–8.
[17] Elizabeth Dore, "Property, Households and Public Regulation of Domestic Life: Diriomo, Nicaragua 1840–1900," and María Eugenia Chaves, "Slave Women's Struggles for Freedom in Colonial Guayaquil," in Dore and Molyneux, eds., *Hidden Histories*. 147–71, 108–26.

from direct male authority – though more within than outside the household. The rights of widows (and of legally emancipated unmarried adult women) were similar to those of adult males. Widows were permitted to administer property, sign contracts, and receive wages. In one important respect, however, widows and single women remained legally subsumed under male authority. In Nicaragua, as elsewhere, no woman was permitted to exercise *patria potestad*, or parental authority. Until the turn of the twentieth century in Nicaragua, and until far more recently in other countries of the region, widows and unmarried women did not have legal authority over their children. In female-headed households, parental authority passed to a senior male, even if he had no kinship tie to the family. The social and legal justification for this practice was that women were child-like, that is, legally constituted as quasiminors; therefore, they were neither eligible nor deemed capable of exercising authority over other human beings. The practical effect of denying women parental authority was that unmarried mothers and widows bore the legal responsibility to feed and support their children but lacked juridical authority over them.

Revisions to Nicaragua's Civil Code in 1904 partially emancipated married women from their husband's authority. Thereafter, wives could administer property and sign contracts without their partner's consent. Nevertheless, women could not exercise authority over their children unless – and here there was some forward movement – the father died or was declared mentally incompetent.[18] An amendment to the civil code finally granted father and mother joint authority over their children in 1940.

Notwithstanding revisions to patriarchal laws, male authority remained embedded in Nicaragua's justice system. Until the late twentieth century, male adultery was legally condoned, so long as a husband's behavior was not particularly flagrant. In the words of one legal scholar, "when the husband kept a mistress discretely outside of his home, and conducted his affairs without public scandal, he suffered no castigation in the law."[19] This tolerance contrasted sharply with the criminalization of female adultery. A wife's infidelity, even the public perception that her behavior was indecent, constituted grounds for divorce. In such cases, judges frequently imposed harsh penalties on women. For instance, when judges ruled that a woman's honor had been violated, frequently they

---

[18] Zuñiga Osorio, "Patria Potestad," 49.
[19] Ibid., 53. The 1904 and 1940 amendments to Nicaragua's civil code granted impunity to male adulterers.

denied the purported criminal access to her children. And in the event she was murdered by husband, father, or brothers, the law allowed the court to grant immunity to the murderers on the grounds that public perception of female indecency brought dishonor to the entire family.

Nicaragua's justice system was in line with regional jurisprudence. Although polygamy was outlawed in Latin America, in many countries polygamists enjoyed extensive de facto legal protection. Adultery laws have far-reaching effects on family patterns in all societies. In Nicaragua, the contradiction between male and female sexual rights inside and outside marriage contributed to normalizing patriarchal practices, including domestic violence against women and children.

Regarding formal political participation, until the mid-twentieth century in many Latin American countries, only propertied, professional, and literate adult males were eligible to vote, hold office, and participate in the formal political life of the nation-state. In Nicaragua, no woman, regardless of class or marital status, could vote or hold national public office until 1954. The framework of legal and extralegal patriarchal authority conditioned the class and gendered character of debt peonage in Nicaragua.

2. Landed Peasants: Debt Peons

The expansion of coffee production unleashed a process of land privatization that created rather than destroyed the landed peasantry in Nicaragua.[20] Before the coffee boom, society in Diriomo was modestly stratified along lines of class, but markedly stratified by gender and race. Notwithstanding disparities in wealth and access to land within the township (*municipio*), virtually all households enjoyed common property rights under the aegis of Diriomo's Indian community (*comunidad indígena*). For most Diriomeños, everyday life rested on self-sufficient household production within a framework of wide-ranging common rights to arable land, waterways, woodlands, footpaths, and pastures.

In consort with the expansion of coffee estates in the nineteenth century, upheavals in land and labor relations accentuated class and gender stratification in Diriomo. Those same upheavals gradually eroded the social significance of racial differences. Around the turn of the twentieth

[20] Gould, *To Die in This Way*, 42–56; Elizabeth Dore, "Land Privatization and the Differentiation of the Peasantry: Nicaragua's Coffee Revolution, 1850–1920," *Journal of Historical Sociology* 8, no. 3 (1995): 303–26.

century, the Nicaraguan government ruled that private property was the only legitimate form of land tenure. To that end, it legally abolished Indian communities and their common property rights. In Diriomo, as in other municipalities in western Nicaragua, the elimination of Indian land rights was the death knell of the Indian community.[21]

The rise of private landed property accentuated peasant stratification; it did not create a class of landless peasants, or rural proletarians. In the early twentieth century, when the class character of Diriomo was becoming more heterogeneous, and the racial character less so, most Diriomeños lived in poor peasant households that survived, sometimes precariously, alongside a stratum of middle peasants. The township's elite was comprised of medium planters; these town fathers ran the municipality and governed everyday life in the community. They were not, however, the "ruling class." The owners of the large coffee plantations on the slopes of the Mombacho Volcano, within the boundaries of the municipality, ruled over rural society. These planters dominated regional politics, and many also figured among the ranks of the country's leading politicians and landowners.[22]

In Diriomo, the rise of coffee gave birth to a new society of landed peasants and large planters who coexisted both parasitically and symbiotically, but more the former than the latter. Peasant self-provisioning might have allowed individual planters to pay misery wages to peons whose survival rested on subsistence agriculture, rather then seasonal wages. However, whatever benefits planters might have garnered from peasant's self-provisioning were more than off-set by the obstacles it threw up to the ability of the planter class to systematically appropriate the labor of the peasantry. For it was peasant's self-sufficiency, more than anything else, that stood in the way of planters raising a large seasonal labor force. Over time, the expansion of coffee estates impoverished many households in Diriomo; nevertheless, until the middle twentieth century, peasant livelihood rested predominantly on family production. This was the coffee planters' dilemma. With peasants engaged in self-sufficient agriculture, planters did not have ready access to an army of temporary workers who relied on seasonal wage labor for basic survival. Consequently, the owners of large coffee estates had to compel Diriomo's self-sufficient peasantry, one way or another, to produce a surplus – in this case surplus labor. From the 1870s to the 1930s and beyond, Granada's

---

[21] For survival of Indian communities, see Gould, *To Die in This Way.*
[22] Dore, *Myth of Modernity.*

planters solved their labor problem through a combination of debt peonage, overt violence, paternalism, and state labor drafts, and largely in that order.

Like Guatemala, the Nicaraguan state enacted laws that forced the rural poor to work in plantation labor.[23] Unlike Guatemala, however, where most workers for coffee estates were conscripted by the state, in Nicaragua most peasants were pressed into plantation labor via debt peonage. Diriomo's municipal government organized labor drafts, but as an exception rather than the rule. Instead of state officials or their adjuncts rounding up peasants and marching them off to pick coffee, as they did in Guatemala, most laborers on the great estates of Nicaragua worked under debt peonage arrangements. In Diriomo, peonage relied on force: the force of state-mandated compulsory labor that underpinned the force of patriarchal authority and debt. The laws requiring all peasants to work on coffee plantations were part of Nicaragua's political landscape, but for the most part these forced labor laws were the backdrop. Personal arrangements between planters and peasants occupied the social and political center stage. Patriarchal arrangements ruled everyday life; they conditioned the consciousness and labor relations of planters and peons in the coffee districts.

Nicaraguan peonage usually involved indebtedness and always involved the machinery of state to make the system work. In Diriomo, planters routinely offered cash advances to peasants who pledged that they or their dependents would work on coffee estates for the entire harvest season and beyond, until the debt was repaid with labor. Most Diriomeños were pushed and pulled into debt peonage through the interplay of forced labor laws, planters' power, and peasant impoverishment. Some 52 percent of Diriomeños between the ages of ten and fifty-five worked in peonage from 1880 to 1915.[24]

3. Patriarchy from Above

Unlike debt peonage in other parts of Latin America, peonage in Nicaragua was more obstacle than precursor of rural capitalism.[25] On

[23] Chapter 8.
[24] Calculated by author from Censo de la población: Diriomo, Año 1883, Archivo Municipal de la Prefectura de Granada (hereafter cited as AMPG), caja 191, leg. X7, fol. 152 (copy kindly provided by Justin Wolfe). Censo Provisional de 1906, and Libros de Operarios, 1880–1915, Archivo Municipal de Diriomo (hereafter cited as AMD).
[25] For the capitalist/protocapitalist nature of Latin American peonage, see Arnold J. Bauer, "Rural Workers in Spanish America: Problems of Peonage and Oppression," *Hispanic*

Diriomo's coffee estates, peonage was part of a class system that rested predominantly on nonmarket patriarchal relations. For about eighty years, from 1870 to 1950, coffee planters appropriated peasants' labor via a complex of gendered rights, obligations, privileges, and coercion. Together this formed a class and gendered system of patriarchy from above. Rather than creating conditions for free wage labor, patriarchy from above postponed them.

This form of patriarchy from above and peonage were relatively new in Diriomo in the 1870s. Before coffee, the everyday life of most Diriomeños was regulated principally by the *comunidad indígena*. Diriomo's Indian community was not egalitarian with regard to gender or wealth; however, its structures of inequality were different from those of ladino-hispanic society. Before coffee revolutionized local landscape and society, the system of patriarchal authority as codified in Hispanic law was largely tangential to the regulation of life in Diriomo. After coffee production set in motion the decline of Diriomo's *comunidad indígena*, patriarchalism was at the center of planter-peon relations. Rather than representing archaic social relations inherited from colonial times, planters' patriarchalism and peonage – patriarchy from above and below – were born out of the upheavals of the coffee era. However, the hispanic tradition of patriarchal laws and customs contributed to legitimating debt peonage in Diriomo. As coffee production and the demand for labor expanded, planters, state officials, and peons endeavored in different ways to rework traditional practices associated with *patria potestad*. Over time, the process of negotiating patriarchal rights and obligations contributed to remaking rural society in Nicaragua's coffee districts.

Occasionally, reconfiguring patriarchy was accomplished purposefully and consciously. The jurists who drafted Nicaragua's forced labor legislation borrowed from the laws and the language of domestic patriarchy to codify planters' legal authority over peons.[26] The new labor laws granted planters patriarchal authorities, both legal and spiritual. Consequently, labor laws invested planters with rights traditionally enjoyed by domestic patriarchs: possibly most important, the right to punish dependents. In addition, traditional patriarchal laws and customs that required subordinate household members to obey senior males were transposed to

American Historical Review 59 (1979): 34–63; and Alan Knight, "Mexican Peonage: What Was It and Why Was It?," *Journal of Latin American Studies* 18 (1986): 41–7.

[26] Ley de Agricultura, Decree of Feb. 18, 1862, Archivo Nacional de Nicaragua (hereafter cited as ANN). Document given to author by the Director of the ANN, Lic. Alfredo Gonzalez before it was cataloged. Hereafter cited as Ley de Agricultura, 1862.

accommodate the new planter-peon relation. Just as the state required family patriarchs to maintain order in their households, it held planters legally responsible to maintain discipline on their estates.

Besides these overt reconfigurations of family patriarchy, the remaking of patriarchy from above was accomplished behind the backs of law-makers and the state. A social process was under way that conflated the traditional power and authority of senior males with those of the new landlord class. In Diriomo, the new language of debt peonage echoed the codes and idioms of *patria potestad* and of the hispanic patriarchal laws and traditions. Soon patriarchal rights and obligations took on roles and meanings beyond their traditional contexts in ladino society, in families, in households, in constitutional law, and in the political discourses of nation building. In Diriomo, the new meanings and understandings of patriar-chal rights and obligations became central features of emerging class and gendered relations of plantation labor.

Patriarchy from above was institutionalized in contractual peonage obligations. Planters' authority over their subordinates, their right to com-mand obedience, and their promises of protection were codified in con-tracts between planters and peons (*matrículas*). The double-sided charac-ter of patriarchy, violence and protection, was explicit in the contractual language of peonage. On the one hand, peons swore "to subjugate them-selves to all of the practices and customs established by their patron" (*que se somete a todo los usos y costumbres establecidos por su patrón*). On the other hand, planters, promised "to provide succor to the peons and ser-vants on their hacienda" (*socorrer operarios y sirvientes de la hacienda*).[27] To facilitate peonage, planters and the state reinterpreted older patriarchal laws and practices to legitimate the new relationships. Peasants promised to submit themselves to the authority of the patriarch; in return, planters assumed patriarchal duties and obligations to protect their peons, their dependents. In Diriomo, peonage rested on a patron-client bond that was not at its heart about market forces.

Texts of debt peons' contracts tended to be formulaic, and as such re-veal more about the legality and expectations regarding patronal rights and obligations and less about everyday practices. However, court records of disputes between patrons and peons shed considerably more light on the patriarchal character of labor practices. Significantly, planters accused

[27] Libros de Operarios, 1879–1905, AMD, Ramo de Agricultura. See, e.g., Contratos de Agricultura, 1905, no. 32, Jorge Cabrera compromete con Sr. Alejandro Mejía, AMD, Sección Alcalde Municipal.

by peons of violating labor laws often defended their honor and reputation for proper seigneurial behavior (*hombría de bien*) by emphasizing their routine patronal practices. Planters described in detail the assistance or succor (*socorro*) they regularly gave peons. According to planters, fiestas on their estates were an important demonstration of patriarchy in practice. A number of planters narrated to Diriomo's courtroom how, at the culmination of festivities, they and their wives personally distributed alcohol (*guaro*), food, clothing, and gifts to the men, women, and children who worked as their peons.[28]

In courtroom contests, planters frequently refuted peons' accusations of malfeasance by trying to turn the peon's version of events upside down. Many planters explained to Diriomo's agricultural judges that although their estate accounts might appear to indicate violations of the labor code, in fact they demonstrated the opposite: the fulfillment of patriarchal obligations. On several occasions, planters and estate administrators explained away, or tried to, what appeared at first reading to be irregular and highly illegal accounting, and in the process they reworked peasants' evidence and re-presented it as proof of the estate's patriarchal practices. For example, responding to charges of withholding wages and generally fiddling his payroll (i.e., his accounting of peons' debts and labor payments), Don Alejandro Mejía explained to the magistrate that the prosecutors' reading of the estate ledgers fundamentally misrepresented both the quantitative and qualitative nature of labor relations on his plantations. Over and above wages paid (or not paid), Mejía said that remuneration to his peons included alms (*limosnas*), food, clothing, and assorted fees paid to priests, pharmacists, herbalists, and doctors for services rendered to peons and their families. These calculations of his patriarchal generosity did not figure, he maintained, in the formal records.[29] General Augustín Avilés, another major planter, told the court that his accounting of wages paid gave a diminished picture of his workers' remuneration: "I give the mozos plenty of money for *guaro*, food, sickness, death, succor and alms," he said.[30]

Notwithstanding planters' sometimes eloquent speeches about their charity, there is considerable evidence that planters regularly billed peons for succor. Disputes about whether patriarchal assistance constituted

[28] Demanda verbal entre Sr. Esteban Sanchez y Don Celedino Borge, March 28, 1889. AMD, Ramo de Agricultura.
[29] Entre Casimiro Ramirez y Don Alejandro Mejía, Feb. 12, 1899, AMD, Ramo de Agricultura, Sección: Juez de Agricultura.
[30] Libro de Condenas, 1881, AMD, Ramo de Agricultura, Sección: Juez de Agricultura.

obligations of the patron or rights of the peon featured prominently in litigation in Diriomo's courtroom. The issue in contention was whether the costs of patriarchal protection and assistance should – legally and legitimately – be added to peons' debts.[31]

Peons accused by planters of breaking the country's labor laws by running away from the estate usually tried to secure legal assistance to defend themselves against patronal charges. However, only middle peasants, those who through downward mobility descended into peonage, generally contrived to pay someone to assist them in court. These more savvy – and once more well-off – peons often testified that their patron had illegally and purposefully extended their servitude by adding fictitious charges to their account or failing to record their debt payments in labor. In these cases, the peon's legal counsel customarily asked the magistrate to subpoena the estate ledgers. In the event, few planters allowed the court to see their account books. However, of those few who permitted this so-called public – but in practice quite private – scrutiny of their payroll, many had billed peons for the patriarchal assistance and gifts they provided. When this practice came to light, peons denounced the abuse, declaring that it was perpetrated behind their backs and behind the back of the law. Regularly, peons' self-defense rested on the claim that succor formed part of planters' patriarchal obligations and peons' customary rights. In negotiating patriarchy, peons interpreted assistance as a gift, not a means of payment or a loan.[32] In sum, planters commonly portrayed assistance to peons as a patriarchal favor; however, assistance and gifts often replaced wages.

If patronal protection frequently was but a veiled form of paying peasants for their labor, Diriomo's planters regularly employed a greater subterfuge. They included in their peons' contracts the explicit proviso that all succor they provided would be added to the original cash the peon had received in advance, and thus increased the labor debt. By writing this amendment into contracts, planters claimed that their practices were neither illegal nor hidden, but formed part of the mutual understanding between planter and peon. However, for their part, peons claimed no knowledge of these so-called mutual understandings. Rather, they claimed the practice was another way that planters tried to portray themselves as benevolent patriarchs, when in effect the practice extended planters' patriarchal rights well beyond the bounds of the law.

[31] Kandiyoti, "Bargaining with Patriarchy."
[32] Luis Cano contra Don Andrés Marcia, Libro de Condenas, 1894, AMD, Ramo de Agricultura, Sección: Juez de Agricultura.

Conflicting testimony in Diriomo's courtroom shows that planters' gifts, cum assistance, played a triple role. Depending on circumstances, they could be a means of bestowing charity and favor, thus cementing a patriarchal relationship between planter and peon; they could be a means of labor payment, and they could be a mechanism for planters to augment peasants' debts. Keeping in mind that debt was the prime method of mobilizing labor in Diriomo, contests over patronal assistance and gifting was a central aspect of negotiating patriarchy from above.[33]

If Granada's planters exaggerated their patriarchal allegiance to subordinates, Diriomo's peons mounted counterclaims regarding patriarchal gifts and favors to justify their own transgressions. In 1900, Don Joaquín Cuadra, one of the largest planters in Granada, ordered Diriomo's rural magistrate to capture debt peons who ran away from his estate or otherwise violated peonage obligations. Concepción Reyes and his son Palomito numbered among the fifty or so fugitive peons rounded up in the dragnet operation. Diriomo's rural police arrested Reyes and son in their fields; they were harvesting corn and beans, the foundation of peasant self-sufficiency. After spending several days in the municipal jail, Reyes told the judge that he had fled the estate because and only after – and this was key to his testimony – Cuadra failed to live up to the promise that he would help the family whenever necessary. Here we see Reyes attempting to turn the tables on his great *patrón*. Reyes's self-defense rested on the claim that it was Cuadra who had violated the patriarchal bargain. In this instance, Diriomo's agriculture judge did not uphold the peasant's reworking of the patriarchal bargain; instead, he declared that Reyes and son were "labor breakers" and he sentenced them to forced labor on municipal public works.[34]

Transcripts from Diriomo's agricultural tribunal shows planters and peons actively engaged in negotiating patriarchy. Planters and peons both broke labor laws consciously and purposefully, and both confected self-serving justifications to cover their transgressions. However, equating planters' and peons' power in these contests would seriously misrepresent the class and gendered character of rural society. On the most basic level, for most peons, their very presence in the courtroom was nonvoluntary and itself a manifestation of the patron's power and ability to coerce.

---

[33] Steve Stern describes a similar process as contesting absolute and contingent patriarchal rights and obligations; *Secret History*, 70–85.

[34] Entre Concepción Reyes y Joaquín Cuadra, Libro de Condenas, May 8, 1900, AMD, Ramo de Agricultura, Seccion Jueces de Agricultura.

Furthermore, planters negotiated patriarchy to tie laborers to their estates, while peons negotiated patriarchy to minimize their bondage. The latter, paraphrasing Eric Hobsbawm, was the way Diriomo's peasants struggled to work the system to minimize its disadvantages.[35]

The mere existence of court records, with their contrapuntal testimonies, points to a measure of shared belief regarding patriarchy from above. In Diriomo, rich and poor, planter and peon subscribed to a morality in which planters bore some responsibility to protect peons, and peons had some grounds to claim patriarchal protection. The divergence or convergence between morality and actuality regarding everyday practices, expectations, and meanings of patriarchy from above was the stuff of planter-peon contestation. The contests to which we as historians figure among the witnesses, scribes, and interpreters, took place in Diriomo's court room. Taking into account the nature of court transcripts, it is difficult to delve beneath the formal edifice of the justice system, with its institutionalized officialdom. It is almost impossible for the historian to glimpse those private negotiations between planters and peons that undoubtedly took place, to see bargains never committed to paper that were part of a world of informal promises made and broken. Nevertheless, the official transcripts demonstrate that negotiating patriarchy was central to the making of debt peonage and, I would add, to its longevity in Diriomo. Negotiating patriarchy was part of a process of constructing the new society in Diriomo, a society that, notwithstanding change, endured for almost a century.

Coffee planters attempted to generate at least a minimum acceptance of peonage by deploying consensual practices. Yet court transcripts point to a systematic gap between planters' promises and peons' expectations of patriarchal protection. This gap was filled, in part, by patriarchal violence. Patriarchal violence was central to the operation of debt peonage on the large coffee estates of Granada. The majority of Diriomo's peasants were bound to the seasonal labor regime, legally or illegally. Laws requiring all peons to pick coffee until the harvest ended, whether or not they were in debt, counted among the legal and at the same time overtly coercive labor measures the government ratified. To complement legal measures, planters routinely deployed illegal means to maintain peons under their thrall. The latter included manipulation of estate ledgers to falsify indebtedness, refusal to permit peasants who had worked off debts to leave the estate, and fabrication of documentation at the conclusion of the harvest

[35] E. J. Hobsbawm, "Peasants and Politics," *Journal of Peasant Studies* 1, no. 1 (1973): 3–22.

to ensure peons were tied to the estate for subsequent year. Many peons caught between conflicting pressures – between the need to cultivate subsistence plots and the real or confected obligations to patrons – ran away from coffee estates. Desertion was by far the most common form of resistance to the labor regime.

When a planter reported a runaway peon, he set in motion the repressive apparatus. Throughout the harvest season, Diriomo's magistrate sent lists of runaway peons (*operarios desertores*) to his counterparts throughout Nicaragua, asking them to capture and return fugitives. After installation of the telegraph, rural magistrates maintained daily, sometimes hourly, contact with one another to capture and repatriate deserters. The telegraph was probably the single most effective instrument of state in Nicaragua's coffee regions, as it was in Guatemala. The telegraph's main use and its effectiveness were not lost on peasants, who routinely cut the lines.

Diriomo's rural police patrolled the countryside to capture deserters. Police chained together the runaway peons they caught and marched them to the municipal jail. There peasants were put in stocks to await the administration of justice.[36] The salary of the magistrates and their rural police was calculated according to the number of fugitives they captured and convicted – thus, personnel of the repressive apparatus were paid by piece rate. This practice was entirely within the law, which spelled out that "expenses incurred in the pursuit, capture, imprisonment and return of delinquent workers will charged to the peon's account" (*cargará en cuenta al peón*), in other words, added to the peasants' debt.[37] By this means, enforcement of debt peonage was financed jointly by the municipal council and the convicted peons.

The officials responsible for enforcing the labor regime, the agriculture magistrates, in the main were themselves coffee planters. As judges, they sentenced runaway peons and other "labor breakers" to two weeks' labor on public works, in the first instance. Ironically, in Diriomo, convicted peons ordinarily worked off their sentences by repairing telegraph lines. Thereafter, the police returned peons to their patron, who administered further punishments, as the law stated, "in keeping with the custom of the estate." Peons feared most these ordeals, which were legal yet outside the law. As the labor code instructed planters to maintain order on

---

[36] Sr. José Esteban Sandoval demanda a Nicolás Mercado y Ramipio Pérez, Libro de Condenas, Dec. 22, 1901, AMD, Rama de Agricultura, Sección Jueces de Agricultura.

[37] Ley de Agricultura, 1862, Art. 32.

their estates by "whatever means necessary," some planters inflicted brutal punishments including floggings and lengthy confinement in small cages under the gaze of the estate's peons.[38]

Peons charged with violating labor laws often complained to Diriomo's agriculture tribunal about the unjust and inhumane treatment they suffered. Pedro Mercado told the court that the planter Alejandro Mejía "caused him extreme suffering."[39] However, testimonial evidence about disciplinary measures according to the "*usos y costumbres del patrón*" for the most part was phrased in general terms. Perhaps peasants resisted recounting details of their indignities in the courtroom, which was, after all, Diriomo's most public space. The courtroom was Diriomo's theater, pulpit, and press room all rolled into one.

In marked contrast to the tenor of court transcripts, fifty years later Diriomeños had lost whatever inhibitions they and their forebears once may have had when describing patriarchal punishments. In the mid-1990s, Diriomeños' oral histories were replete with grisly tales of sanguinary punishments on coffee estates. At the close of the twentieth century, these stories formed a vital core of the historical memory of the lower echelons of Diriomo's society. Men and women who worked as debt peons as late as the 1940s described the ordeals they themselves, their family and friends of present and previous generations, and – with a certain relish – their enemies suffered at the hands of planters. Many Diriomeños recounted in vivid – possibly exaggerated – detail humiliating punishments they said were a standard feature of peonage on the coffee estates of Mombacho.[40]

Significantly, notwithstanding historical memory of planter brutality, I found no record of cases in which peons brought criminal charges against patrons for cruel and unusual punishments. The reticence in written records regarding disciplinary measures, juxtaposed with the plethora of details in oral histories, suggests two contrasting explanations. Either a degree of brutality was routine and taken for granted, with peons, their

---

[38] "Los hacendados o empresarios tiene obligación de celar y impedir que en su finca o labor se cometan desordenes y para ello tiene derecho de usar de todos los medios indespensables y disponibles..." "Landlords are obligated to prevent disorder on their estates. To this end, they have the right to use all means at their disposal." Ley de Agricultura, Art. 15.

[39] Libro de Condenas, May 8, 1900, AMD, Ramo de Agricultura, Sección: Juez de Agricultura.

[40] Interviews with Nestor Sanchez, Teófilo Cano, and Carmen Ramirez, Diriomo, 1991, 1995.

legal counselors, and judges accepting that sanguinary measures were a legitimate part of planters' patriarchal practices, or planters inflicted brutal punishments rarely, and primarily as a deterrent to would-be fugitives, rather than routinely, as retribution for violation of the labor laws.

Whether brutality was habitual or exceptional, violence was overt and part of the system whereby planters ruled the peasantry. The legal and customary basis of planters' authority to punish peons as they saw fit was an outgrowth of patriarchal laws and traditions. Planters' disciplinary power derived directly and indirectly from *patria potestad*, whereby the state vested patriarchs with the authority to maintain order and the obligation to punish dependents. Planters maintained order on coffee estates largely by reconfiguring the patriarchal authority to protect dependents and punish their disobedience. In Diriomo, the patriarchal power of punishment contributed to the class and gendered nature of peonage. Compared with planters' overt forms of discipline and their manipulation of peon's debts, market mechanisms played a minor role in the recruitment and discipline of laborers on coffee estates.

In addition to the gendered relationships of patriarchy and peonage that rested on male-female and senior-subordinate male power relations, landlords exercised patriarchal rights of a different kind. Apparently, some coffee planters expected that the women and girls who worked on their plantations would provide sex, either as obligation or favor. While the issue of planters' sexual license per se was rarely the object of planter-peon litigation, not infrequently male peasants complained to the court of the patron's sexual practices when defending a wife or daughter accused of breaking labor laws. It is probably unsurprising that court transcripts contain few details about the sexual practices of the planter class. Litigation on that score would have required witnesses, testimonies, and all manner of public revelations that husbands and fathers might well have wanted to avoid in Diriomo's close quarters. Instead, peasants' references to planters' sexual practices were worked into testimonies as passing comments, seemingly to disqualify a patron's claims to decency, honor, and benevolence.[41]

Finally, for all practical purposes, widows were the only women legally permitted to speak in Diriomo's courtroom. All other women were represented in court by their patriarch, be he father, husband, or guardian. The fact that most women had no public voice contributed, probably in

---

[41] Demanda verbal entre Sr. Carlos Castillo y Don Andrés Marcia, Jan. 5, 1885, AMD, Ramo de Agricultura.

large measure, to the virtual absence of accusations regarding planters' sexual violations of peasant women.

4. Patriarchy from Below

Patriarchy from above was shored up in several ways by patriarchy from below. Peasant men, in keeping with the laws and customs of *patria potestad*, had the right and the authority to sign up – or consign – their wives and children to the labor regime. This possibility became a reality in part because female participation in plantation labor was codified in agrarian labor laws. Nicaragua's rural labor laws did not discriminate by sex. On the contrary; laws enacted between 1885 and 1910 stated explicitly that "all persons above the age of sixteen, male or female, who possesses property or income valued at less than 500 pesos are required to support themselves by working for a patron."[42] The gendered character of labor law contributed to normalizing the notion that poor females could – indeed, should – be compelled to work in plantation labor.

It is noteworthy that the laws of *patria potestad* created a framework of gendered inequality of rights for the purported objective, among other things, of protecting women. In contrast, agrarian labor laws ratified a gendered equality of forced labor. By institutionalizing a gendered equality of labor obligations for the working poor, agrarian labor laws stood in marked contrast to the laws of patria potestad, and in a sense stood the objective of *patria potestad* on its head. The legalization of female forced labor, combined with the patriarchal authority of peasant men in a context of rural poverty, instead of facilitating male protection of women and children, facilitated male allocation of the labor of their wives and children in the plantation sector.

This contrast between the formal sexual equality of labor law and the formal sexual inequality of family law supports one of the central findings of historians of gender. Although patriarchal law required senior males to protect as well as to patrol their female and male dependents, the protective side of patriarchy was evident more in the higher than in the lower echelons of society. Despite, or in this case because of, the laws of *patria potestad*, poor peasant women were subjected to the harsh realities of debt peonage both alongside male counterparts and in isolation from them.

In Diriomo, the majority of peasants who registered for peonage did so as a family, either male- or female-headed. Consequently, the peasant

---

[42] Ley de Trabajo, Art. 1, *La Gaceta* (Managua), Oct. 3, 1901.

family was the typical labor unit for harvesting coffee. Usually the first step into peonage, both for families and individuals, was the rite of registration. In this ritual, the head of the household appeared before the agriculture magistrate to swear his or her allegiance to the patron. For example,

The widow Josefa Cano, jointly with her five children... swears to Don Agustín Avilés to serve on his haciendas Progreso or Cutierres on the Mombacho Volcano. The family will work as coffee pickers and be paid one "real" for every 6 cartons of coffee cherries [they pick], plus two meals per day. They are obligated to work as soon as they are needed, to remain working for the duration of the harvest and beyond until they have paid off their debt with labor. [Cano] received four pesos in advance. She swears to submit herself and her children to all of the practices and customs established by the patron.[43]

The head of household received whatever cash or wages the family received. However, in the event that a family defaulted on its labor obligation, all its members – including children – were legally responsible for paying off the debt. That fate befell the Gaitan family, whose contract reads,

José Angel Gaitan jointly with [two sons and two daughters] pledge themselves to Don Apolinar Marenco.... If one worker [*operario*] dies, is injured, or for whatever reason is absent from work, the labor debt [*el desquite*] will be assumed by those who are well and able to work [*buenos y aptos para trabajar*]. If the family defaults on its commitment, it will be fined 30 pesos which will be added to the advance and to whatever other monies they receive. Guarantor: Esteban Gaitan. They submit themselves to the work regime and the customs of the fincas.[44]

Soon José Angel Gaitan died and the eldest son was injured; within the year the family defaulted on the peonage arrangement. José Angel's father, the family's guarantor, petitioned the magistrate to release the family from its labor obligations on account of the misfortunes that befell the family. However, Diriomo's magistrate ruled that it was not within his power to annul a legally binding contract.[45]

Family peonage brought large numbers of women and children into the unfree labor regime. This history of debt peonage expands the scope of the classic model of the peasant household as a unit of production and consumption. Usually, this model applies to peasant self-provisioning in

---

[43] Partida no. 325, Lista de Operarios 1879, AMD, Ramo Alcaldia Municipal, Sección Alcalde Municipal.
[44] Partida no. 381, March 16, Matrícula de la familia de José Angel Gaitan con Don Apolinar Marenco, AMD, Ramo Agricultura, Juez de Agricultura, Libro de Matriculas 1886.
[45] Entre Esteban Gaitan y Don Apolinar Marenco, Dec. 22, 1887, AMD, Rama Agricultura, Sección, Jueces de Agricultura, Asuntos, Demandas.

subsistence agriculture. However, in the context of debt peonage, families extended the boundaries of peasant household production to encompass the household's estate labor.

Alongside family peonage, peasant men consigned their wives and children into seasonal or more permanent peonage. Peasant men's legal authority to enroll family members in the labor regime rested on *patria potestad*, in particular, laws that granted senior males the right to sign contracts for and control the labor of their dependents. This manifestation of patriarchy from below resulted in women working in the coffee harvest both within and without the family unit.

In Diriomo, peasant men normally received a cash advance when they signed up their wives and children for peonage. For example, in 1905 the husband of Ramona Zambrano pledged that she would work on the estates of Srs. Eisenstuck and Bahlcke. Zambrano's husband received a cash advance of 20 pesos, and in return his wife swore, "authorized by my husband, who signs this contract, I am obligated to repay with my labor the entire sum plus whatever might be added to it through patronal assistance paid to my husband by working on any of the coffee estates the señores own throughout the Republic. . . ."[46] In common with all married women, Ramona Zambrano was not permitted to sign contracts or receive wages without the written permission of her husband. In the ritual of registration, Ramona Zambrano declared that her wages and whatever else she received by way of patronal assistance would be paid to her husband.

Similarly, José María Marcía received a cash advance of 34 pesos and a sombrero worth six pesos from Don Alejandro Mejía. Marcía pledged that his wife and six-year-old daughter would pick coffee in three coffee harvests or until the debt was repaid.[47] This is another case where a male head of household exercised patriarchal powers to authorize peonage arrangements for his wife and children, and to take their earnings.

This analysis of debt peonage underlines some possible pitfalls in ignoring the gendered character of class relations. In Nicaragua, as in Latin America more generally, patriarchs, including peasant patriarchs, represented all members of their family in the public sphere. As a consequence, in Diriomo, men appeared in lists of peons in greater numbers than their

[46] Matrícula 287, Feb. 4, 1905, Operarios de los Señores Eisenstick and Bahlcke, Hacienda Alemania, AMD, Ramo Alcaldía Municipal.

[47] Matrícula, No. 357, July 28, Operarios de Alejandro Mejía, Libro de Operarios Comprometidos 1879, AMD, Ramo Alcaldía Municipal.

actual participation rate in the debt labor regime. Peasant men pledged not only their own labor; they pledged the labor of dependents. Therefore, at first reading, lists of peons seemed to be mostly men. However, a closer reading, a reading informed by gender, brought to light women and children who were, so to speak, hidden beneath the patriarchal umbrella.

The stories of Ramona Zambrano and Josefa Maltez de Marcía come from the *Libros de Matrículas*, the formal register of peonage contracts. These registers provide few clues as to whether Ramona, Josefa, and other wives went willingly or unwillingly into debt peonage. However, in contrast to the silence of the *Libros de Matrículas*, the archives of Diriomo's agricultural tribunal contain the voices of sons and daughters who contested their father's right to consign them to servitude. For example, the case of Margarita Aguilar versus Don Vicente Cuadra had its roots in 1878, when Enrique Aguilar took an advance from Don Vicente Cuadra and pledged that his thirteen-year-old daughter, Margarita, would work off the debt. Ten years later, and still indebted to Cuadra, Margarita petitioned the judge to annul the arrangement. Her lawyer argued that "since [she] is an adult and free from her father's authority [*patria potestad*], no longer could the court force her to work off her father's debt." Unfortunately for Margarita, Cuadra's lawyer pointed out that unmarried daughters remained subject to their fathers' authority until legally emancipated. Since Enrique Aguilar never liberated Margarita from his patriarchal authority, she remained locked into the labor regime.[48]

By and large, Diriomo's peasant patriarchs were driven by poverty to pledge the labor of their dependents. One father, Victoriano Granera, explained his plight to the judge:

Owing to the poverty that always holds me in the grip of pecuniary difficulties and seeking improvements for my family, whose numerous members I must of necessity feed and support, I consign my legitimate son Eusebio Granera, of about eleven years of age, to work as a debt peon on the finca San Diego.... My son's contribution to household labor has helped me to provide my family's necessities. But despite his youth and good behavior, he is imprisoned by my poverty.[49]

The model of male breadwinner/female housewife clearly is at odds with the gendered allocation of labor within peasant households in

[48] Margarita Aguilar vs. Don Vicente Cuadra, AMD, Rama Agricultura, Juez de Agricultura, Feb. 5, 1888.
[49] Entre José Esteban Sandoval y Marcelino Alguera: una demanda, April 28, 1924, AMD, Ramo Agricultura, Juzgado. This case demonstrates that debt peonage continued in Diriomo after its legal abolition.

Diriomo. That paradigm was based on a 1950s, mostly middle-class and urban, model of the gendered division of labor within families in the United States and Western Europe. While the model was more ideal than real even for the countries it was supposed to fit, overwhelming evidence about family patterns among Diriomo's peasantry points to an entirely different gender/generational distribution of labor. When families were driven to supplement self-provisioning, women and children were often the first to work "off-farm," or more precisely, outside the boundaries of the so-called traditional peasant economy. The family model most in evidence among Diriomo's peon-peasantry turns the 1950s family model on its head. In Diriomo, the necessity to supplement household resources frequently pushed women and children into what passed in Diriomo for the "formal sector": debt peonage. Under these circumstances, peasant men often dedicated themselves to what might be called the "domestic" sphere: self-provisioning.

The manner in which Diriomo's peasants supplemented self-provisioning and thereby sustained their nonmarket economy was similar to the ways that rural households in late twentieth-century Latin America tried to sustain their peasant livelihood. Fieldwork repeatedly demonstrated that when peasant households were threatened with extinction, frequently, daughters were the first to seek outside employment, usually in domestic service and sweatshops (*maquiladoras*).[50] However, social scientists often overlooked the roots of this practice in patriarchal law and custom, whereby senior males had the authority to allocate the labor of dependents as they saw fit. Consequently, in Latin America, women's work outside the household was and remains not so much a question of what wives and daughters "want" or "decide to do" as a question of where authority and power reside in the family and the wider polity.

Returning to nineteenth-century Diriomo, there is one example of a wife who enrolled her husband in the labor regime. In 1882 Vicenta López pledged the labor of her husband, Fernando Acevedo, and received an advance of 13 pesos.[51] This case stands in stark contrast to the patriarchal tradition and is tantalizing for what it does and does not reveal about the gender order. It indicates that the patriarchal system was not

[50] Lourdes Benería and Martha Roldán, *The Crossroads of Class and Gender* (Chicago: University of Chicago Press, 1987), 1–16.

[51] "Vicenta López lo comprometio su esposo Fernando Acevedo con 13 pesos deudando para cortar café a 2 medios por el real, cosecha proxima," Libro de Operarios Comprometidos, Operarios de Alejandro Mejía, 1882, AMD, Ramo Alcaldia Municipal, Sección Alcalde Municipal.

cut from whole cloth. But beyond that, this apparently unique case underlines the need for further research on the gendered nature of debt peonage
in Nicaragua and further afield in coffee-producing countries.

5. Female Headship

The social upheavals that accompanied the coffee revolution left their
mark on household headship in Diriomo. In 1882, some 40 percent of
households in the pueblo were headed by women, and it appears that
marriage was less widespread than it had been a century earlier.[52] Whereas
31 percent of the adult population was single in 1776, some 51 percent was
single in 1883.[53] Although we do not know whether for census purposes
"married" meant in a conjugal union, legal or otherwise, the comparative
data suggest a rise in nonmarrying behavior. Combined with the high
incidence of female-headed households in 1883, we have a very different
picture of peasant society in rural Latin America than the one we have
been routinely offered. The traditional view of the peasant household as
male-headed, extended, with at least two working adults appears not to
have been the norm in Diriomo or, as I have argued elsewhere, in most of
rural Latin America in the nineteenth century.[54]

This evidence suggests a link between the coffee revolution, debt peonage, and disintegration of the patriarchal peasant household. That strong
conclusion merits careful scrutiny, however. Such a premise rests on the
notion that the male-headed household was pervasive in the preceding
historical period. While that might have been the case, as indicated by
a higher incidence of marriage in Diriomo in 1776, I believe the evidence
here remains inconclusive for a number of reasons, not least that the
1776 census was administered by the church, the institution charged with
ensuring that people married. Instead, I offer a weaker hypothesis. It is
possible that the practice of nonmarrying behavior on the part of peasant women was in part motivated by patriarchy. Insofar as patriarchal
laws and customs gave men the authority to sign up wives and children
for debt peonage and appropriate their wages, peasant women may well
have approached marriage with considerable caution. After all, if women

[52] Censo del Departamento de Granada, Año 1882, AMPG, caja 175, leg. 486, fol. 121.
[53] Censo de Diriomo de 1883, AMPG. According to the census, 40 percent of adults were
married, 51 percent were single, and 9 percent widowed.
[54] Elizabeth Dore, "The Holy Family: Imagined Households in Latin American History,"
in Elizabeth Dore, ed., *Gender Politics in Latin America: Debates in Theory and Practice*
(New York: Monthly Review Press, 1997), 101–17.

wanted to, or more likely had to, work in the labor regime (and if their fathers were dead or had emancipated them), women could sign on to debt peonage themselves and receive the cash advance and wages that might, or then again might not, be paid. The image of the female house-hold head usually brings to mind single mothers, the stereotype of recent Latin American policy debates. However, in nineteenth-century Diriomo, widows headed about 35 percent of female-headed households, and single mothers the rest, or 65 percent. In other circumstances, both widows and single mothers might have been subsumed into a male-headed household. It is possible, however, that the dangers and the opportunities of debt peonage, combined with possibilities for female landholding and partici-pation in the cash economy, all aspects of the coffee revolution, gave some peasant women both the motives and the financial wherewithal to remain unmarried.

I propose that the high participation rate of women and children in debt peonage in Diriomo was the result of a combination of four factors: first, agrarian laws that codified sexual equality for the rural poor in the forced labor regime; second, patriarchal laws and customs that gave peasant men the authority to consign their wives and children to servitude; third, the custom of women and children working in the coffee harvest while senior males were responsible for self-provisioning; and fourth, the possibility that patriarchal laws and customs encouraged nonmarrying behavior on the part of peasant women. This last may have contributed to the high incidence of female-headed households and, by extension, to women's need to engage in debt peonage.

This history of the gendered nature of peonage underlines connections between women's economic dependence and male control over female property, labor, and sexuality. In particular, the fact that so many debt peons were women and children and the fact that almost 40 percent of households in Diriomo were female-headed points to the importance of patriarchal power in the development of debt peonage and the unfolding process of peasant differentiation.

In conclusion, the double-sided character of patriarchy contributed to the nature and endurance of labor relations on Nicaragua's large coffee es-tates. Evidence from Diriomo indicates that Nicaragua's rural social order was not a market-driven society overlaid with patriarchal networks and ideologies.[55] Rather, patriarchy in its dual form underpinned economic,

---

[55] Richard Graham argues that patronage was an aspect of Brazilian capitalism. *Patronage and Politics in Nineteenth-Century Brazil* (Stanford: Stanford University Press, 1990).

political, and social life taken together. From above, planters' patriarchy went some way toward constructing consent among the peasantry. To the degree that Diriomo's peasants regarded debt peonage as legitimate, the system relied on peons accepting that superior males had the right to exercise power and authority, but only if they also protected their subordinates. From below, peasant patriarchalism contributed to the heavily female and young labor force on coffee estates. Women and children were drawn into debt peonage less because of market means and more because of patriarchal authority.

10

Small Farmers and Coffee in Nicaragua

Julie A. Charlip

The coffee industry that began in Nicaragua's Carazo region circa 1880–1930 brought significant changes to the country's economy and society, but widespread proletarianization was not one of them. Even as a handful of large coffee growers came to dominate production, financing, and processing, most of the land was still held by the far larger number of small and medium-sized coffee producers. These smaller producers joined in the new coffee economy in the same ways as their larger counterparts: producing and selling coffee, buying and selling land, splintering and amalgamating landholdings, borrowing and lending money. They became active and willing participants who likely viewed the economy in the same way as their richer neighbors. The only aspect of the coffee economy in which smaller growers did not participate in the same ways was in processing and exporting, which became the exclusive and lucrative domain of the largest growers.

The subsistence farming sector, however, did not disappear. In fact, it expanded, thanks to state-guaranteed access to land in the ejidos (territory provided by the state to muncipalities and distributed to the landless for free or at nominal rates). These subsistence farmers were the backbone of the labor force needed only seasonally on the larger coffee farms, where they were sometimes joined by small coffee farmers who needed to earn extra income.

The market for coffee led to the expansion of markets for land, credit, and labor and the commercialization of society, with careful separation of coffee groves from usufruct rights from the land itself – as well as inheritance rights to any of those items – for sale or collateral. Widespread participation in all these markets indicates that *caraceños* readily joined in these transformations.

That is not to say, however, that traditions did not continue. Smaller farmers continued to rely on family labor, larger growers cemented alliances through marriages, and paternalistic relations tempered commercial relations between buyers and sellers, borrowers and lenders. Women exercised more rights, but within the limits of a patriarchal society. Many indigenous people became coffee growers themselves, or put a modern facade on traditional holdings by turning their traditional counsels into ladino organizations and their old communal lands into modern, subdivided ejidos.

This reevaluation of Nicaraguan economic history sheds new light on some of the problems faced by the Sandinistas, whose agrarian reform efforts were led by Jaime Wheelock Román. Wheelock, whose analysis of the proletarianization of the Nicaraguan countryside had become the standard interpretation, expected to find generations of landless workers interested in collective landholding or a guaranteed wage on state farms.[1] Instead, the surprised Sandinistas found that smallholders existed in unexpected numbers and that even the proletarianized or semiproletarianized workers wanted their own plots of land. They found that the campesinos viewed themselves as producers rather than workers, and when given the option of preferential financing arrangements for cooperatives, the majority opted for higher interest rates and their own individual properties. These workers wanted what their ancestors historically had.

The results of this study also differ markedly from those found elsewhere in this volume, particularly Elizabeth Dore's work on nearby Diriomo and David McCreery's study of Guatemala. Some of the differences undoubtedly are dictated by the nature of the sources available to each scholar. To some extent, the difference is one of focus: Dore looks more at conditions for workers, while this study focuses on opportunities for farmers. To some extent, the two chapters taken together show more of the totality of the spectrum of relations during the coffee boom. It is also quite likely that the strength of the indigenous community made a significant difference. In Carazo, there appeared to be more of a willingness to abandon traditional indigenous ways in favor of more commercial interests. As early as the 1850s, indigenous people in Carazo were growing

---

[1] For Wheelock's interpretation, see *Imperialismo y Dictadura* (Managua: Editorial Nueva Nicaragua, 1985).

and processing sugar for the market, and the struggles that would mark
relations between the indigenous and ladino worlds in Matagalpa and
other northern regions of Nicaragua were absent in Carazo.[2] While the
Carazo scenario may not be true of every coffee zone, it is likely that a
close reading of similar documents throughout the coffee-growing world
would find more places that fit this scenario than the old stereotype of
landlessness and proletarianization.

Smaller Farmers and Land

This study focuses on the Department of Carazo, which is located
in Nicaragua's Pacific Zone, bordering the Sierras of Managua. At
950 square kilometers, Carazo is one of the smallest and most densely
populated departments in the country. Originally, the area was a subpre-
fecture of Granada, and it was given departmental status in 1891. Carazo
rests on a high plateau, bordered by the Department of Masaya to the
north, the Pacific Ocean to the south, and the Departments of Managua
to the west, Granada and Rivas to the east. It was in the *caraceño* town
of Jinotepe circa 1848 that Dr. Manuel Matus Torres founded the finca
La Ceiba and began the cultivation of coffee in Nicaragua.[3] The towns
of Diriamba and San Marcos would also become prime coffee areas. In
1926, the Pueblo District, which comprises the departments of Carazo,
Masaya, and Granada, produced 44 percent of the country's coffee. The
Carazo area lacks the steep hills of the Managua district and therefore
allowed "better cultivation and consequently better production both
as to quality and quantity."[4] In short, Carazo is where coffee growing
originated in Nicaragua and remained one of the most important coffee
regions in the country.

By 1877, the export of coffee had made land a valuable commodity,
so much so that the national government created a land registry. The
regulations for the Registro Conservatorio de Bienes Raíces, published

---

[2] For Matagalpa, see Jeffrey L. Gould, *To Die in This Way: Nicaraguan Indians and the Myth
of Mestizaje, 1880–1965* (Durham: Duke University Press, 1998).

[3] For the origins of coffee in Carazo, see Alberto Lanuza Matamoros, "Estructuras socioe-
conómicas, poder y estado en Nicaragua, de 1821 at 1875," graduate thesis, Costa Rica,
164; Paul Levy, *Notas Geográficas y Económicas sobre la República de Nicaragua* (Paris:
Librería Española de E. Denné Schmitz, 1873), xxx; Julian N. Guerrero and Lola Soriano,
Monografía de Carazo (Nicaragua: 1964), and the *Registro Oficial*, No. 60, p. 251, León,
March 14, 1846.

[4] Harold Playter, *The Coffee Industry in Nicaragua* (Corinto, Nicaragua: American Consulate,
1926), 7.

July 16, 1877, were based on two principles: the elimination of secrecy in property transactions by having records open to the public and the clear delineation of property rights.[5] The Registro records show how the land market developed along with the coffee economy. For the purposes of this study, land categories are: minifundios, less than 10 manzanas (one manzana equals 1.7 acres, or 0.7 hectare); small farms, 10–49 manzanas; medium farms, 50–199 manzanas; large farms, 200–499 manzanas; and latifundios, 500 or more manzanas. This is a modification of the conventional classifications of property sizes for Latin America, especially for Central America, which groups together farms of under 10 manzanas, 10–49, 50–499, and 500 and above.[6]

The Registro records show that from 1880 to 1930, there were 1,175 coffee farm sales for which both size and price data were recorded. Some 91 percent of the farms sold were minifundios or small farms, which comprised 40 percent of the area. Medium-sized farms comprised 8 percent of the total, with 32 percent of the area. No latifundios were sold, and large farms amounted to 1 percent in number, 14 percent in area.

Most of the land sold was not incorporated into larger holdings to create large estates and latifundios. A profile of 73 farms that were dismembered gives the general pattern: Originally, 55 percent were minifundios, 21 percent small farms, 8 percent medium farms, 3 percent large farms, and 1 percent latifundios. In the dismemberment process, larger farms tended to split apart, increasing the small farm sector. The 73 farms became 102, but despite all of the fragmentation that took place, the minifundista section did not increase appreciably, accounting for 56 percent of the new farms formed. The small sector rose substantially to 33 percent, and medium farms grew slightly to 10 percent. The small farm sector apparently grew at the expense of the large farms, which declined to 1 percent, and there were no latifundios.

A similar pattern emerges from an analysis of 245 farms that were merged into larger holdings. Among the newly formed farms, 43 percent were small farms. Medium-sized farms were created in 19 percent of the mergers. Of course, larger farms were created: 9 percent became large farms, and 3 percent latifundia. But even minifundios – 26 percent – were the results of mergers.

[5] Norma Maria Tapia Cerda, "Sistema Jurídico Registral Adoptado en Nicaragua," doctor in law thesis, Universidad Centroamericana, Managua, Nicaragua, 1980.

[6] *Diagnostico Socio-Económico del Sector Agropecuario: Carazo* (Managua: Centro de Investigaciones y Estudios para la Reforma Agraria, CIERA, and Ministerio de Desarrollo Agropecuario y Reforma Agraria, MIDINRA, Dec. 1980), 64, 70–1.

The results of these transactions can be seen in the Censo Cafetalero conducted by the Nicaraguan government in 1909. This survey occurred at the end of the administration of José Santos Zelaya (1893–1909), whose government has been credited with fostering the rise of the coffee economy and blamed for dispossessing the Nicaraguan "peasantry." But the census shows that 75 percent of the farms were still held by minifundistas and small farmers. These farms constituted 55 percent of the coffee farm area. The smaller farms were not the most productive, however: The ten largest growers produced 53 percent of the coffee.

Nonetheless, the smaller growers did not constitute a "peasantry" in the traditional sense of small growers whose main interest is in subsistence and who are generally left out of the commercial, export economy. The coffee census shows that the smaller growers planted their land more densely, trying to grow as much coffee as possible. While latifundio averaged 262 trees per manzana and large farms averaged 306, medium farmers averaged 476 trees per manzana, small farmers 574, and minifundistas 793. These were indeed farmers, operating with the same goals as their larger counterparts producing for the market.

In addition to the sale of property, other markets emerged: There were 66 cases documented of inheritance rights being sold. These birthrights were sometimes sold at a considerable discount. In 1901, Diriamba carpenter José Maria Perez sold his rights to the inheritance of his mother, Ramona Perez, for 150 pesos but noted they were valued at 262 pesos.[7]

Not everyone entered this coffee economy, however; others continued in a subsistence economy that not only did not disappear with the growth of coffee but was actually fostered by the national government. The state's goal was most likely the year-round maintenance of a labor pool that would be available during the harvest months. The state fostered this economy by providing ejidal land to the local communities: In 1881, the state gave the town of La Paz six caballerias of farming land and two *caballerías* of pasture land for cattle grazing.[8] In 1886, the residents of the area called Dulce Nombre in San Marcos filed documentation showing their petition for a survey by the state of their ejidal land, which indicated the community had 40 *caballerías* of land. In 1890, the state gave 9.75 *caballerías* to Diriamba and 8.25 *caballerías* to Santa Teresa.

---

[7] *Registro del Inmuebles*, May 8, 1901, no. 60, p. 51.
[8] One caballeria equals 64 manzanas, or 109 acres.

Ejidal lands were also granted to Jinotepe by the state in 1892 and 1900 and to Diriamba in 1892.[9]

The communities, in turn, distributed the land to local residents. Between 1880 and 1930, the Registros de Propiedad in Granada and Jinotepe show 563 cases in which Carazo-area municipalities distributed land in the ejidos by donation, rental, sale, or titling occupied lands. Of these, only forty-three properties, that is, barely 8 percent, ended up with coffee planted on it by 1930. Clearly, the ejidos were not targeted by nascent coffee growers. Instead, the ejidos retained their traditional role: small plots for subsistence agriculture, along with several large landholdings that were most likely cattle ranches.

From 1880 to 1906, some 77 percent of the ejidal land distributed was donated to recipients without charging the fees suggested by law, while from 1907 to 1930, most of the land (62 percent) was rented out. The shift to rentals rather than donations followed a 1906 decree outlawing the sale of ejidal land.[10] While the rental rates varied depending on the time and place, the annual cost was usually nominal. In 1907 in Jinotepe, land rented for 3 pesos per manzana. In 1911 in Rosario, one property rented for 50 cents per manzana and another for 25 cents. In 1916 in La Conquista, land rented for 4 cents per manzana, and in 1919 in La Paz, it rented for 3 cents per manzana.[11] Although some rental properties were quite large, most remained in the category of minifundios, as were the majority of donations.

While the ejidos were the realm of the smallholder, national land, or *terrenos baldíos*, were the domain of large farmers. Of sixty-seven sales from 1878 to 1930, some 56 percent were of 200 manzanas or more and 37 percent of the sales were in the category of 500-plus manzanas, for a total of 28,366 manzanas of land. However, the vast majority of these properties were cattle ranches. Only 21 percent of these properties ended up with coffee planted on them by 1930.

---

[9] *Libro de Propiedad*, Granada, Feb. 8, 1881, no. 34, pp. 17–18; Sept. 26, 1886, no. 389, pp. 271–3; Feb. 25, 1890, no. 94, pp. 53–5; April 18, 1890, no. 295, pp. 169–75; *Libro de Propiedad*, Jinotepe, May 24, 1892; April 3, 1900, no. 74, pp. 80–1; Dec. 19, 1892, no. 553, pp. 78–80.

[10] Managua, June 27, 1906, issued as a clarification of the Agricultural Law of 1902.

[11] *Libro de Propiedad*, Jinotepe, Dec. 23, 1907, vol. 21, pp. 164–5; April 25, 1911, vol. 40, p. 94; Feb. 6, 1911, vol. 21, p. 181; April 1, 1916, vol. 50, pp. 274–5; Aug. 19, 1919, vol. 71, p. 93.

Smaller Farmers and Credit

Smaller farmers needed cash, whether to run their farms or to buy small coffee farms and additional plots of land to expand, and so they resorted to borrowing. The financing of coffee production was frequently the nexus of the smaller grower's relationship with his larger counterpart. However, the small farmer was not simply at the mercy of the banks or the large growers. There were 550 people lending money in Carazo from 1880 to 1930, indicating that anyone with extra cash was willing to lend it and that people were not dependent on a handful of lenders.

There were no bank loans made in Carazo until the twentieth century. The first loan was 150 *pesos fuertes* from the London Bank of Central America Ltd. to Vicente Rodriguez in 1901 for the harvest on his Diriamba farm, Santa Cecilia.[12] From 1880 to 1930, the Anglo Central American Commercial Bank Ltd. made twenty-seven loans in Carazo, and the Banco Nacional de Nicaragua Incorporado made seventy-one. More importantly institutionally was the Compañia Mercantil del Ultramar, which made ninety-nine loans. But private lending was far more important. The Gonzalez family alone made 418 loans during the same period of time.

There were two forms of credit available: the *pacto de retroventa*, a resale agreement, or the *hipoteca*, a mortgage on the farm itself or on another piece of property. Both forms of loan were typically repaid in coffee, usually at a rate established by three of the major coffee purchasers and processors in the region, that is, by the same people providing many of the loans.

The *pacto de retroventa* was the earliest form of money lending to appear in property records. The borrower sold his property to the lender, while retaining usufruct, with the agreement that he could repurchase the property by a certain date. While most common before the turn of the century, the *pacto de retroventa* continued at least through the 1930s. Usually, the agreement stipulated that the borrower/seller could rebuy the property at the same price for which it was sold, that is, without interest. The interest-free loan may seem appealing, but it was interest-free for a reason – it was risky.

The advantage to the lender/buyer was that the property was registered to him or her. If the borrower did not repay the loan, the lender did not need to seek legal recourse to obtain title to the land. Instead, it took the

[12] *Registro de Inmuebles*, Jinotepe, Feb. 16, 1901, no. 42, p. 38. The *peso fuerte* was the official currency until 1912 that was supposedly equivalent to the U.S. dollar.

filing of a new deed to return the property to the seller/borrower. One Jinotepe coffee grower said lenders were commonly "unavailable" when borrowers came to repay. Most of those who borrowed money in *pactos de retroventa* – 66 percent – lost their farms. However, that does not mean that these people then ended up as part of a landless proletariat; 73 percent of them owned other parcels of land. The property registry shows further transactions for only 26 percent of the farms that were not repurchased, which means that these properties were not formally merged with other land that the buyer/lender owned and were not used as collateral for his or her own loans.

In fact, it is possible that the previous owner retained usufruct even after losing title to the property. This possibility is suggested by cases in which property was sold while a *pacto de retroventa* remained in effect. For example, on May 3, 1902, San Marcos housewife Petrona Aguirre sold her three-manzana farm for 200 *pesos fuertes* to Benjamín Zapata, a San Marcos amanuensis, in a *pacto de retroventa*, to be repurchased by March 1903 for 29 fanegas of coffee (a *fanega* was a measure of volume usually equal to 125 pounds). On May 18, 1902, Zapata sold the property, with the *pacto* still in effect, to Camilo Zúniga, a Jinotepe doctor, for 200 pesos fuertes. Zúniga, in turn, sold the property to Antonio Salinas, a Jinotepe farmer, for 200 pesos on June 21, 1902. On May 9, 1903, Vicente Salinas Leiva, apparently Antonio Salinas's heir, resold the property to Petrona Aguirre for 750 pesos. The same day, Aguirre resold the property in another *pacto de retroventa* to Jinotepe farmer Ezequiel Sotelo Navarro for 1,195 pesos. There is no record of the resale; however, the next transaction shows the farm back in Aguirre's hands, as she obtained a *hipoteca* of 163.20 pesos fuertes in May 1906. Aguirre managed to repay the debt in early November 1907, only to enter another *pacto de retroventa* later that month with Pablo Emilio Chamorro for 280 pesos. She never repaid the amount and lost the property to Chamorro in 1909. While awaiting Aguirre's repayment, Chamorro promised to sell the farm to Liberato Valerio Ramos, a Granada farmer, for 40 fanegas of coffee. The agreement noted that Valerio received immediate possession of the property.[13]

Despite the many transactions and changes of ownership that took place over seven years, the property remained in the hands of the original

[13] *Registro de la Propiedad y Derechos Reales*, Jinotepe, May 11, 1902, no. 179, p. 110; May 20, 1902, no. 211, pp. 130–1; Oct. 16, 1902, no. 511, p. 307; May 28, 1903, no. 210, pp. 117–8; May 28, 1903, no. 211, pp. 147–8; *Libro de Propiedad*, Jinotepe, May 22, 1906, vol. 11, pp. 80–1; Nov. 23, 1907, vol. 11, pp. 81–2; April 9, 1909, vol. 11, p. 82, vol. 22, p. 302; May 12, 1908, vol. 22, pp. 302–3.

owner-borrower, Aguirre, until it was passed to Valerio. The intermediate buyers never took possession of the farm themselves, but they were able to buy and sell it, using it as an asset. Clearly, there was an active market in both property and loans. Lending was the more profitable venture, as indicated by the marked preference for repeated sales and loans rather than accumulation of land and concentration of production.

A less risky but more expensive loan was the *hipoteca*, a mortgage that was usually to be repaid in coffee. The terms of the loan tended to differ depending on the size of the property: the larger the landholding, the more advantageous the terms. Minifundistas and small farmers typically paid 2 percent per month, medium-sized farmers paid 1.5 percent, large farm loans were under 1 percent, and latifundistas paid about 1.25 percent. There is no sign of the higher interest rates that Wheelock took to be the norm.[14] There were no loan rates below 1 percent for minifundistas, and only for one of 262 small farmers, while no large farm or latifundio carried an interest rate over 3 percent. However, although larger landowners usually paid lower interest rates, they also paid sales commissions, typically 2.5 percent. And if there was not enough coffee produced to pay back the loan, the remainder could be paid in cash or bank drafts, with a "false commission" of 2.5 percent. Size also mattered for the few loans that called for repayment in work; of these fourteen *hipotecas*, eleven were held by minifundistas, two by small farmers, and one by a medium-sized farmer.

While the largest coffee growers and processors were also the major lenders, the smaller growers had many options for obtaining loans. Of the 550 people who lent money to coffee growers in Carazo from 1877 to 1930, most of them – 73 percent – were Carazo residents. Only 3 percent of the loans came from abroad, and 24 percent were from other Carazo cities. The majority of lenders, 57 percent, lent money only once. Some 90 percent of lenders provided loans on five or fewer occasions.

One striking difference between the *pactos* and *hipotecas* is the default rate. While 66 percent of *pacto* borrowers lost their property, only 28 percent of *hipoteca* borrowers defaulted or sold their property to pay off their debts. The aim of lenders in the *pacto*, then, would seem to be to acquire property, while the aim of *hipoteca* lenders seemed to be the earning of interest profits. The profit motive seems even more clear when the timeliness of *hipoteca* repayment is considered. Cancellation of the loan was late in 63 percent of the *hipotecas* that provided both due date

[14] Wheelock, *Imperialismo y Dictadura*, 86.

and cancellation dates (627 *hipotecas*). While the principal was not paid off for months or even years – most frequently, cancellation was one to two years late – the lender was collecting interest.

Minifundistas were most likely to default on their *hipotecas*: 33 percent defaulted, compared with 26 percent of small farmers, 20 percent of medium-sized farmers and latifundistas, and 7 percent of large farmers. What is most striking, however, is that the vast majority of even the minifundistas were able to repay their loans. Furthermore, in the cases of default, few lenders kept the property to add to their own landholdings. Most resold the farms to small- or medium-sized growers and proceeded to lend them money, continuing the profitable debt cycle.

Smaller Farmers and Processing

Coffee processing in Nicaragua began in a basic, artisanal manner. According to Juan M. Mendoza's *Historia de Diriamba*, circa 1868 there were no steam processing plants or mills driven by animal power; coffee was hulled using wooden piles in boxes made of guanacaste wood.[15]

Few records in the *Registro* provide details about the equipment included on the farms. In the nineteenth century, there were fourteen properties that listed hullers among their equipment. Three of those detailed that the hullers were made of stone masonry (*trillo de cal y canto*), perhaps similar to a simple huller made by the Guatemalan manufacturer Edelman, or perhaps a makeshift device. As early as 1893, José Maria Lacayo had a Gordon pulper on his 160-manzana farm; the British-manufactured equipment was considered among the best. The smallest of the properties with processing equipment in the nineteenth century were Francisco Castro's 30-manzana farm in San Marcos and Salvador Lacayo's Santa Teresa property, which had 30,000 trees planted. Castro, however, also owned the 186-manzana hacienda San Marcos, the 25-manzana Ojo de Agua and the hacienda Promisión, and may have been using the huller at the 30-manzana property for coffee from several farms. Similarly, Lacayo owned several properties. The average size farm with such equipment was 73 manzanas.[16]

In the twentieth century, twenty-two additional properties were described in the *Registro* with processing equipment. Smaller properties

---

[15] Juan M. Mendoza, *Historia de Diriamba* (Guatemala: Imprenta Electra, 1920), 35.

[16] *Libro de Propiedad*, Jinotepe, Nov. 8, 1893, no. 220, pp. 278–9; *Libro de Propiedad*, Granada, March 27, 1890, no. 176, pp. 106–7; *Libro de Propiedad*, Jinotepe, Dec. 21, 1893, no. 213, pp. 335–6.

continued to have basic hulling equipment, while the larger properties were more frequently described as having coffee processing plants
(*maquina de beneficiar café*). The 1909 coffee census surveyed machinery
used on the farms in Nicaragua. In Carazo, they reported eighteen steam-
operated machines and thirty-six operated by "blood," presumably by
human or animal power (Pablo Edelman describes in detail machines requiring cranks to be turned by hand and machines turned by oxen).[17]
There was also one operated by water power. The steam-operated equipment was mostly used on larger farms: eight medium farms, three large
farms, and three latifundios.

It was not until after World War I that Nicaraguan coffee growers began
to modernize the production process. By the 1920s, growers supposedly
were moving toward washing all the coffee because it brought a higher
price on the market. Playter makes that assertion at one point, yet he goes
on to say that the percentage of unwashed or common coffee produced in
1926 was still 60 percent nationwide and 70 percent in Carazo.[18] The high
percentage of dry coffee would seem to further reinforce the argument
that most coffee was indeed produced by small growers. If most coffee
was produced by larger growers, who could afford the expensive wet
processing process, the percentage of wet coffee production would likely
be higher. However, if as much as 70 percent of Carazo's coffee was not
washed, then even some of the larger growers were opting for the dry
method as well. Given the high rate of return on investment, the inferior
method of processing did not seem to hurt their income enough to induce
further investment.

The cost of processing equipment, however, could be prohibitive. In
1864, Pablo Edelman estimated that coffee processing equipment could
run from 860 to 900 pesos, but he also showed that the equipment on
the 50,000-tree Hacienda de Barcéna in Guatemala cost 1,455 pesos. By
1922, when José Robleto died and an inventory was filed of his 50,000-
tree Hacienda San Jorge in San Marcos, the value of his equipment was
listed as 4,600 cordobas (the cordoba replaced the *peso fuerte* in 1912). It
was the high cost of equipment that led 70 percent of Caraceños to bring
their coffee to specialized coffee processors or more commonly to larger
growers, who purchased and processed their coffee. In theory, smaller
growers could borrow money to buy the processing equipment, but what

---

[17] Pablo Edelman, *Apuntamientos sobre el beneficio del cafe y las maquinas en que se ejecuta*
(Managua: Imprenta del Gobierno, 1864).
[18] Playter, *Coffee Industry*, 5, 32.

would they process if they were to pay back their debts with coffee? Would lenders even provide financing for the purchase of equipment that would compete with their own *beneficios* (coffee processing plants)? The larger growers, after all, needed a supply of coffee to pay back their own debts.

For example, Nicasio Martinez Sanz was the owner of the Trilla Castellana, formed in 1905, the earliest citation of a *beneficio* in the registro. In 1907, he estimated the value of the machinery on his property at $11,000, including two water tanks, a bath, a stone masonry patio, and a steam-driven coffee huller with all its accessories.[19] Martinez had his own debts to pay: In 1910 he borrowed 32,100 German marks from Teodoro Tefel, two-thirds of which was to be repaid with coffee, the rest with letters of credit. The coffee was to be *"lavado o trillado de buena calidad mercantil, bien limpio y escogido* [of good commercial quality, washed or hulled, very clean and well selected]." If there was not enough coffee to fulfill the requirement, he would have to pay 1.5 marks for each *quintal* (100 pounds) not delivered.[20] It is no wonder, then, that Martinez Sanz required that the many people who owed him money repay it in coffee, delivered to his *beneficio*.

Although there were not as many coffee processors as money lenders, the smaller farmer did have some choices. The 1923 *Directorio Oficial de Nicaragua* listed four custom processing plants: In addition to La Castellana, there was Santa Rosa in Jinotepe, which belonged to the heirs of Manuel Lacayo; Santa Rosalia, which belonged to Roman and Baltodano, in Diriamba; and the U.S.-owned Compañia Mercantil del Ultramar plant in San Marcos. The directory also listed fifteen proprietors of farms with steam-driven processing equipment, including those belonging to the José Esteban Gonzalez estate, José Ignacio Gonzalez, and Vicente Rappaccioli, three of the region's largest lenders and growers.

In 1926, U.S. Consul Harold Playter estimated that 50 percent of the planters had their own cleaning and processing plants. By 1929, Carazo boasted numerous custom coffee mills: "...the best in the Republic to process this grain to the taste of the producer, ready for export, these mills having powerful machines that cost up to thousands of *cordobas*."[21]

The number of options available to smaller growers, however, was unlikely to translate into better prices for the coffee used to repay their

---

[19] *Libro de Propiedad*, Jinotepe, Sept. 7, 1907, vol. 1, margin notes, pp. 75–6 and vol. 18, p. 90.
[20] *Libro de Propiedad*, Jinotepe, Oct. 11, 1910, vol. 1, p. 76, vol. 19, pp. 95–6.
[21] Playter, *Coffee Industry*, 42–3; Fernando Briceño, "Jefe Político de Jinotepe," in *Memoria de Hacienda* (Managua: Tipografía Nacional, 1929), 267–9.

debts. The loans frequently stipulated that the coffee would be valued at market price at the time of repayment, or the price set by three area merchants. It was unlikely that there was much variation in the price.

Unequal Opportunities

The coffee boom did indeed provide opportunities and create new fortunes, and the three dominant families of Carazo – the Rappacciolis, Gonzalezes, and Baltodanos – all came from humble beginnings. Vicente and Buenaventura Rappaccioli were the illegitimate sons of Macedonia Gutierrez, who earned her living making cigars and selling aguardiente, and Italian immigrant Juan Rappaccioli. In 1890, Buenaventura was one of the founders of Diriamba's first social club, bringing the elites together.[22] And in 1909, the Rappaccioli brothers were the largest landholders in Carazo, with 1,245 manzanas of land and 325,000 trees, worth 1,232,000 pesos. Vicente Rappaccioli served as both a senator and a deputy and was an unsuccessful presidential candidate in 1928.[23]

The Gonzalez brothers, José Esteban and José Ignacio, were behind the Rappacciolis in landholding, at 980 manzanas, but with 766,000 coffee trees, their properties were worth 3,175,000 pesos. Their roots were humble as well: Their grandfather, Román Gonzalez, was the illegitimate son of Juan Gualberto Parrales and an indigenous woman, Bernabela Gonzalez.[24] Juan and Bernabela's son, Francisco, was a successful farmer, so he was able to give his sons, José Esteban and José Ignacio, a base on which to build. José Esteban, known as a great modernizer, brought the first Ford automobile to the region in 1897. It was during José Estéban's administration as mayor of Diriamba that gas lighting was brought to the city, and he was the Liberal party's presidential candidate in 1920. José Ignacio was a medical doctor and surgeon, trained in the United States, as well as one of the most important coffee grower and money lenders in the region. He was a candidate for vice president of Nicaragua in 1916.[25]

The third most important family socially and politically was headed by Enrique Baltodano, an illiterate day laborer who married Dolores Parrales, the daughter of the prominent Francisco de Sales Parrales.

---

[22] Jorge A. Blanco G., *Diriamba* (Managua: Editorial Atlántida, 1938), 37.
[23] Guerrero and Soriano, *Monografía*, 93.
[24] Mendoza, *Historia*, 79.
[25] Ibid., 392–403.

According to Juan Mendoza, Parrales gave his son-in-law work as a carter and some uncultivated land, and Baltodano used it to build a fortune.[26] In 1909, Enrique's sons, Ignacio, Roman, and Moisés, owned 400 manzanas of land worth $500,000. While not the wealthiest of the elites, their political and social influence was great. Moisés was a medical doctor, educated in Paris, and also served as a senator.[27] As late as 1964, the most important fincas in the region still belonged to Buenaventura Rappaccioli, José Ignacio Gonzalez, and Moisés Baltodano y Hermanos.[28]

The majority of coffee growers, of course, did not attain the wealth of these three families. The largest growers acquired the resources to ensure better harvests via higher levels of care in maintenance of their groves and harvesting of their product. The ten largest coffee growers produced 53 percent of Carazo's coffee and owned 49 percent of the coffee land and 46 percent of the trees. Furthermore, 70 percent of producers had no processing facilities, and the processors formed an oligopsony that controlled prices offered for the product; exporters then earned another 30 percent return over their costs through exporting the coffee.

Beyond the division between wealthy coffee producers and the smaller producers were divisions based on gender and ethnicity. Both women and indigenous people found opportunities in the coffee economy. But these opportunities were constrained: Women chafed against patriarchal norms, and indigenous groups found that opportunities awaited those who essentially became ladinos.

Women joined men in the coffee economy as buyers and sellers of property and lenders and borrowers of money. Transactions for which there are complete data show that 10 percent of all loans on coffee properties were made by women, and 21 percent of the borrowers were women. In sales of property, women were the sellers 19 percent of the time, and the buyers in 13 percent of the transactions. The 1909 coffee census showed that 12 percent of all coffee fincas were owned by women. Women frequently acted as legal representatives for their husbands. They occasionally managed their husband's businesses, and one woman even successfully took her husband to court for selling their communally owned property.

But just as frequently, women were restricted by husbands whose wills demanded that widows not remarry, threatening them with loss of custody

---

[26] Ibid., 52–3.
[27] Ibid., 331–2.
[28] Guerrero and Soriano, *Monografía*, 50.

of their children. Fathers set guidelines for children in their wills. And they openly left goods to acknowledge illegitimate children and mistresses, so that coffee wealth that was inherited provided a quasipublic venue in which male freedoms were flaunted and widows were expected to endure. Women also continued in their traditional roles in the reproduction of labor; the average *caraceño* family numbered ten, and the women and children provided labor on their own farms and on larger farms. For elite families, the children were important for intermarriages that linked families. The Rappacciolis, Gonzalezes, and Baltodanos all intermarried.

Women, of course, could not simply become men and gain all their rights and perquisites. Indigenous men could gain the property and voting rights given to all males, if they largely put their indigenous identities aside. This can primarily be seen through the abandonment of the traditional indigenous community. Unlike in the Matagalpa region, there are no documents in Carazo showing the continued existence into the twentieth century of recognized indigenous communities with landholdings. Also in contrast to Matagalpa, there are no records of violent conflicts between indigenous communities and ladinos over land.

There were certainly disputes. In 1865, the indigenous community of San Marcos failed to prevent part of their land being declared *baldío* and sold; in Jinotepe in 1866, the indigenous community succeeded in a similar battle. But several of the indigenous leaders in the San Marcos case simply went on to buy land and become coffee growers themselves. The ready ladinozation does not seem unusual considering that the indigenous people of Jinotepe were already heavily involved in commercial sugar production in the 1850s.[29]

The communities of Rosario and La Conquista appear to have dropped their indigenous status and become ladinoized communities. These were not areas of coffee production, and it seems most likely that indigenous leaders simply became the new municipal officers and distributed ejidal land, putting a ladino veneer on traditional practice.

It appears, then, that no group was systematically excluded from the coffee economy, and that members of all communities found limited degrees of success. They were, of course, required to adapt to the changing

---

[29] Justin Wolfe, "Rising from the Ashes: Community, Ethnicity and Nation-State Formation in Nineteenth-Century Nicaragua," Ph.D. diss., University of California, Los Angeles, 1999, pp. 162–3, 225; Julius Froebel, *Seven Years' Travel in Central America, Northern Mexico, and the Far West of the United States* (London: Richard Bentley, 1859), book I, p. 50.

economic, social, and political institutions. But those institutions were constituted in ways that accommodated traditions: Clientelistic relationships continued in personalized loan agreements, for example, though they now had the legal formality of public documents and interest.

Conclusions

The old stereotypical picture of sprawling latifundios displacing the peasantry and converting them into proletarians is indeed wrong. In Carazo, the majority of land was held by minifundistas and small- and medium-sized farmers: 91 percent of the farms and 40 percent of the area according to *Registro* records from 1880 to 1930, and 75 percent of the farms and 55 percent of the area in the coffee survey of 1909. The records show that many small growers did manage to buy small farms and additional land to expand their holdings, however modestly. And most of the farms that merged into larger properties – 88 percent – still remained in the categories of minifundios, small-, and medium-sized farms.

The 1909 coffee census also shows that these small coffee farmers were not "peasants" with no interest in producing for the market or producing only a little to supplement subsistence. Instead, they were planting densely to maximize their income. They invested in land, they borrowed money, and, when necessary, they sold their labor or hired labor, depending upon their fortunes. Their main concern was still their household, but that household was indeed a business; similarly, even the big growers ran family businesses.

These patterns reveal the complexity of the property structure in the Nicaraguan countryside. It was a fluid and dynamic process, driving some people out of coffee growing while bringing others in. From 1878 to 1904, some 175 people apparently sold the only property with coffee that they owned, and another 102 people with no previous record of owning coffee property were buying such land for the first time.

Meanwhile, those who aspired only to subsistence still had access to the ejidos, and the state continued to provide *baldíos* to the municipalities to meet those needs. The fact that more land was distributed by the state to the municipalities of Carazo than municipal leaders distributed to individuals indicates little land hunger in the region.

Access to land, however, is not the only important issue. The farmers needed credit, and while they found it to be readily available, they also found that the terms were more onerous for smaller growers. Those who undertook *pactos de retroventa* were likely to be those who had little opportunity to get a mortgage: Only 34 percent of those who sold property in *pactos* were also *hipoteca* holders. The terms appear to be better than in *hipotecas*: Most often, no interest was charged, and when it was, the interest rate tended to be lower than in *hipotecas*. But the stakes were higher: *Pactos* were more likely to result in default. However, the lender buyer did not keep the property to add to his holdings. Instead, the property was resold, or perhaps used as an asset while the previous owner remained as a tenant, maintaining the property and producing the coffee.

In the *hipotecas*, smallholders were more likely to be charged higher interest rates and to be paid less for the coffee they used to pay back their loans. However, the data show that with little property, people could borrow a great deal of money and manage to pay it back. Large and small growers defaulted, although the latifundistas probably let go of a losing proposition while holding on to more lucrative haciendas. There were also many more lenders than has been assumed, giving the smaller grower more options in the market. The small grower clearly operated at a disadvantage compared with the larger grower, but was not kept out of the market.

Coffee offered the potential for enormous profits. There is remarkable consistency in the return over costs during this period of time. French engineer Paul Levy estimated the profit circa 1870 at 35 percent; U.S. Consul Playter, drawing on more detailed statistics, estimated 36 percent for a twenty-year average from 1906 to 1926.[30] Levy's estimate includes the costs of establishing the coffee grove over a period of three years. Discounting start-up costs to estimate profits on an already established farm, the profit level rises to 50 percent.

Add to that the interest earned from loans and the profits from exporting the coffee processed in the larger growers' *beneficios*. Exporters earned profits ranging from a low of 9 percent in 1920–21 to a high of 61 percent in 1910–11, with an average of 36 percent for the twenty-year period from 1906 to 1925. Since most processors were also producers, these profits were in addition to profits on production.

However, owning a processing plant was no guarantee of success. Pedro Gomez Rouhaud's plant, El Beneficio de Café de los Pueblos, had been very successful. The property, worth $141,000, included a two-story house; offices and barracks for workers; warehouses to store coffee; patios; tanks; machinery that included a pulping machine, huller, and classifier; and fields planted in grass and in sugarcane. There was even a

---

[30] Levy, *Notas Geográficas*, 465; Playter, *Coffee Industry*, 39.

railroad line that ran through the property to transport the coffee.[31] But he ended up so deeply in debt that when he died in 1932, his heirs had to sell the plant to settle his debts. The buyer was Minor C. Keith, the railroad and banana entrepreneur who founded the United Fruit Company.

It is unlikely, however, that the heirs of Gomez Rouhaud, a Granada attorney, found themselves in the same shoes as the families of smaller farmers. The failure of the Beneficio de Café de los Pueblos meant the loss of an investment, not the loss of the family's life savings or its way of life. For the smaller coffee farmers, the options were much more limited: They could return to subsistence agriculture and/or go to work at the larger coffee farms. Despite all the similarities among the coffee growers big and small, in the last analysis, the risks that they took had very different consequences. And therein lies the difference between the larger and smaller farmers.

---

[31] *Libro de Propiedad*, Jinotepe, Feb. 1, 1930, vol. 101, pp. 35–41; Feb. 13, 1930, vol. 101, pp. 35–43, 70–1.

PART III

COFFEE, POLITICS, AND STATE BUILDING

11

Coffee and the Recolonization of Highland Chiapas, Mexico

Indian Communities and Plantation Labor, 1892–1912

Jan Rus

Introduction

In the mid-1890s, the nascent coffee industry of Chiapas, Mexico, was in crisis.* Encouraged by high prices on world markets, by the Mexican government's offer of vast extensions of fertile land for as little as two pesos a hectare, and by the promise of abundant cheap labor, Mexican and foreign entrepreneurs had planted more than four million coffee trees in the state between the late 1880s and 1895, most of them after 1892. By 1895, some 1.1 million were already in production, with 3.2 million more scheduled to begin bearing by 1899. Millions more were in seedbeds and nurseries, guaranteeing that Chiapas's productive capacity would double by the end of the century, and continue increasing well into the 1900s.

The problem was that this sudden increase in production required a similarly rapid growth in the work force. Most of the new fincas, however, had been planted in the lightly populated mountains of Chiapas's southern Pacific coast, the Soconusco, far from an adequate source of workers. Even so, the planters and their backers, knowing they had five to seven years before their trees matured, had been confident they would be able to mobilize the large, seasonal labor forces they would need well before their first harvests. From the beginning it had been assumed that

* This paper would not have been possible without the generosity of Friederike Baumann, who over the years has shared her documents and deep knowledge of Chiapas's nineteenth- and early-twentieth-century economy, and Thomas Benjamin, who, asked for references on one or two letters from the 1890s, sent his entire file of hand-copied documents from the Porfirio Díaz archive in Mexico City. I have also benefited from comments and suggestions by Steven Topik, George Collier, Jane Collier, Andrés Aubry, Angélica Inda, Alan Wells, Aaron Bobrow-Strain, Charles Hale, Sr., Justus Fenner, and Diane Rus. I am grateful to all.

the necessary workers could be drawn from the densely populated Maya communities of Chiapas's undeveloped Central Highlands. What no one seems to have anticipated was that as late as the mid-1890s arrangements for the transfer of this labor would remain incomplete, that there would still be no highland Indians on any of the Soconusco plantations. As a result, already in 1895 there were barely enough hands available for the harvest. Unless a solution could be found, the relentlessly larger crops expected in 1896 and subsequent years were going to go unpicked and Chiapas's coffee boom would suffocate before it really got started.

To jump to the end of the story, of course Chiapas's coffee plantations did finally secure sufficient highland Indian laborers to pick their rapidly increasing crops. From fewer than 5,000 coffee workers in the entire state in 1895 – virtually all of them plantation residents or year-round workers from nearby villages – the numbers grew until by 1910, counting all regions, there were more than 21,000, some 10,000 of them long-distance Indian migrants from the Central Highlands.

The first purpose of the following pages is to explain how this labor was finally mobilized. Why had no workers from the Central Highlands appeared in the Soconusco through the mid-1890s, and how was the flow finally started? Working through this seemingly straightforward problem leads, in turn, to larger questions about the ways Chiapas's society and economy functioned before coffee, and the ways they had to be reorganized at the end of the nineteenth century to adapt to international markets. Reconstruction of Chiapas's plantation economy and labor systems is just beginning, and so far most studies have focused on periods when the plantations were functioning, established enterprises.[1] As a result, it

[1] Modern studies of Chiapas's labor systems began with Rodolfo *Stavenhagen's Las clases sociales en las sociedades agrarias* (Mexico City: Siglo XXI, 1969) and Henri Favre's *Changement et continuité chez les Mayas du Mexique* (Paris: Éditions Anthropos, 1971). Also see Robert Wasserstrom's *Class and Society in Central Chiapas* (Berkeley: University of California Press, 1983) and Friederike Baumann's account of the formative years of the German coffee plantations ("Terratenientes, campesinos, y la expansión de la agricultura capitalista en Chiapas, 1896–1916," *Mesoamérica* 4 (1983): 8–63). On labor, see Juan Pohlenz, *Dependencia y desarrollo capitalista en la sierra de Chiapas* (Mexico City: UNAM, 1995); Daniela Spenser, *El Partido Socialista Chiapaneco* (Mexico City: Casa Chata, 1988); Mercedes Olivera, "Sobre la explotación y opresión de las mujeres acasilladas en Chiapas," *Cuadernos Agrarios*, no. 9 (Mexico City, 1979); Ana Bella Pérez Castro, *Entre montañas y cafetales: Luchas agrarias en el norte de Chiapas* (Mexico City: UNAM, 1989); and Sonia Toledo, *Historia del movimiento indígena en Simojovel, 1970–1989* (Tuxtla Gutiérrez, Chiapas: Universidad Autónoma de Chiapas, 1996), and *Fincas, poder y cultura en Simojovel* (Mexico City: UNAM, 2002); (José Alejos, *Mosojäntel, Etnografía del discurso agrarista en los ch'oles de Chiapas* (Mexico City: UNAM, 1994); "Dominio

TABLE 11.1. *Indigenous Populations by Department, 1890*

Highland departments		Lowland departments	
Las Casas	39,360	Soconusco	7,872
Simojovel	14,645	Tonalá	0
Chilón	19,514	Tuxtla	8,773
Comitán	32,657	Chiapa	7,416
TOTAL	106,176	La Libertad	6,920
		Mezcalapa	8,162
		Pichucalco	3,302
		Palenque	10,449
		TOTAL	52,894

Note: Simojovel and Chilón were mixed highland-lowland departments, but most indigenous villages were in the highland sections.
Source: Censo General de Población (Mexico DF: Gobierno Federal, 1890).

sometimes seems that they came into being full-blown and remained static. By looking at the rise of the late nineteenth-century plantations in the context of the economic and social systems that preceded them, attending not just to the succession of regimes but to the process of transition, it may be easier to see what changed with the coming of coffee, and to gauge the impact of that change on the lives of those who participated in it.

Labor in Chiapas before Coffee

When the coffee boom began, most of Chiapas's rural labor force – essentially, its indigenous population – lived in just four of the state's twelve departments. These were regions of what might be called "traditional haciendas" in the Central and Northern Highlands (the departments of Las Casas, Simojovel, and Chilón), and the adjacent Eastern Plateau (Comitán) (see Table 11.1). Meanwhile, most investor-driven

extranjero en Chiapas: El desarrollo cafetalera en la Sierra Norte," *Mesoamérica* 32 (1996): 283–98. Finally, in recent years testimonial histories coproduced by indigenous communities in bilingual and native language editions have begun to describe plantation labor from "inside," e.g., in Tzotzil, Jacinto Arias, ed., *Historia de la colonia de "Los Chorros"* (San Cristóbal: SUBSAI, Gobierno del Estado de Chiapas, 1984); Jan Rus et al., *Abtel ta Pinka/Trabajo en las fincas* (San Cristóbal: INAREMAC, 1986), translated as "Migrant Labor on the Coffee Plantations," in John Womack, *Rebellion in Chiapas* (New York: New Press, 1999), 111–18; and in Tojolabal, Antonio Cómez Hernández and Mario Ruz, *Memoria Baldía: Los Tojolabales y las fincas. Testimonios* (Mexico City: UNAM/UNACH, 1992).

TABLE 11.2. *Coffee and Cacao in Production, and Planted but Not Yet Producing, by Department, 1895*

| Department | Coffee trees | | Cacao trees |
	Producing	Planted	Producing
Soconusco	1,000,000	1,000,000	125,000
Tuxtla	(few)	1,000,000	
Mezcalapa	(few)	500,000	
Pichucalco		100,000 (?)	2,500,000
Palenque	(few)	550,000	
Chilón	50,000	75,000	
Simojovel	10,000	90,000	
TOTALS	1,160,000	3,215,000	2,625,000

Source: Gobierno del Estado de Chiapas, *Chiapas, su riqueza, sus ventajas para los negocios* (Mexico City: Oficina de Informaciones de Chiapas, 1895); Ramón Rabasa, *Estado de Chiapas, geografía y estadística: Recursos del estado, sus elementos, condiciones de riqueza, etc.* (Mexico City: Tipografía del Cuerpo Especial del Estado Mayor, 1895); *Boletín Estadístico del Estado*, 1897.

agricultural development was occurring in lowland departments with smaller pools of workers. In addition to the Soconusco, these were found around the western edges of the highlands in Tuxtla, Mezcalapa, and Pichucalco, and in the northeastern jungle of Palenque (see Table 11.2). Through the early years of the boom, prospectuses distributed in Mexico, the United States, and Europe had advertised that coffee in Chiapas offered "enormous possibilities," that the marriage of the fertile tropical soils of the state's lowlands with the plentiful indigenous labor of its highlands was a natural one, sure to enrich planters and their backers.[2] On the basis of such promises, investment had begun flooding into the state in the late 1880s and continued to do so for twenty years.[3]

[2] E.g., Matías Romero, *Cultivo del café en la costa meridional de Chiapas* (Mexico City: Secretaría de Fomento, 1871, revised 1893) (in English in Romero, *Coffee and India Rubber Culture in Mexico* (New York: Putnam, 1898); Ramón Rabasa, *Estado de Chiapas, geografía y estadística: Recursos, condiciones de riqueza, etc.* (Mexico City: Tipografía del Cuerpo Especial del Estado Mayor, 1895); Gobierno del Estado de Chiapas, *Chiapas, su riqueza, sus ventajas para los negocios* (Mexico City: Oficina de Informaciones del Gobierno de Chiapas, 1895); Agustín Farrera, *Excitativa a los hacendados del Estado de Chiapas* (Mexico City: Tipografía de "El Lápiz del Aguila," 1895); W. W. Byam's *A Sketch of the State of Chiapas, Mexico* (Los Angeles: Byam and Cannon, Mexican Land and Mining Brokers, 1897).

[3] Of Chiapas's seven million hectares, just over three were transferred to private hands between 1884 and 1897, the vast majority in the Soconusco, Central Valley, Mezcalapa,

The problem with the development path suggested by the prospectuses, however, was that they had misinterpreted the status of the large native populations of the highlands. Seeing the Indians, who lived in tightly organized, corporate communities within which they spoke their own languages and wore their own distinctive clothing, outsiders – including "*científico*" planners from Mexico City – had jumped to the conclusion that they were unoccupied, "primitive" people, their villages autonomous, self-sufficient societies cut off from the rest of Mexico.[4] All that was needed to take advantage of their labor was to force them out of their supposedly isolated spaces into the money economy.

In fact, however, Chiapas's native communities were managed as labor reserves by local non-Indian elites, just as they had been during the colonial period. Indeed, much Indian labor continued to be requisitioned directly – if illegally – through mechanisms that were in effect a continuation of the colonial *repartimiento* under which communities had been collectively responsible for providing workers to private employers in order to be able to pay their church taxes and tribute to the Crown. As cases from throughout the state, but especially the highlands, attest, still in the 1880s ladino (non-Indian) landowners and merchants were notifying Indian town councils of their labor requirements, paying them a pittance in advance – called an *habilitación*, or "enabling" payment – and then receiving adult male workers as a levy.[5] This system of colonial, caste-like obligation was grudgingly maintained from inside the native communities themselves as the customary price of some measure of internal political

and the northern and northeastern jungle (Moisés De la Peña, *Chiapas económico*, 4 vols. (Tuxtla Gutiérrez, Chiapas: Departamento de Prensa y Turismo, 1951), 335ff; Robert Holden, *Mexico and the Survey of Public Lands ... 1876–1911* (DeKalb: Northern Illinois University Press, 1994), 16ff.). Coffee was the first important commercial crop on this land, and in the most important coffee region, the Soconusco, Germans owned or managed three-quarters of the coffee groves by 1900 (Baumann, "Terratenientes," 15ff).

[4] E.g., Romero, *Coffee and India Rubber*, 74ff.

[5] *Habilitaciones* typically consisted of expense money to get to where the work was to be performed plus the first few days of wages. For the Central Highlands, descriptions of labor requisitioned through native authorities can be found in cases from Zinacantán (*El Espíritu del Siglo*, San Cristóbal, Oct. 16, 1873; microfilm in the Latin American Library, Tulane University, hereafter cited as TU), San Andrés (*Borradores del Secretario*, Jan. 9, 1886, Archivo Histórico Diocesano, San Cristóbal, hereafter cited as AHDSC), and Huistán ("Cartas de parroquias," April 20, 1886, AHDSC). Ironically, although planters in Chiapas in the early twentieth century complained that what the state needed was a system of forced labor like the *mandamiento* in Guatemala, Julio Cambranes (*Coffee and Peasants in Guatemala* (South Woodstock, Vt.: CIRMA/Plumsock Mesoamerican Studies, 1985), 140–1) points out that when the *mandamiento* was being enacted at the beginning of the 1870s, it was Chiapas's "customary" system of obligatory labor that provided the model.

and social autonomy. But it was also enforced by the surrounding non-Indian society, which was prepared to repress – with a ferocity meant to terrify – communities that resisted.[6]

In addition to the direct requisition of Indian labor, Chiapas's landowners had also taken full advantage of the evolving laws of the Mexican republic to cement their control of native workers. As new legislation from 1826 on permitted non-Indian landowners to claim untitled communal lands, for instance, they turned the people of entire villages into their tenants. Reduced to a serf-like status known as *baldiaje*, the original occupants were typically required to work three or four days a month for the new landowners in order to continue occupying their own houses and fields.[7]

Indians were also tied by debt. Indeed, with involuntary labor formally outlawed by the liberal Constitution of 1857, by the start of the 1870s the system of direct requisition of workers was increasingly reconceptualized as a system of debt labor, with the *habilitación*, or wage advance given to a conscripted worker, redefined as a "loan" brokered by his community's government. Such loans appear to have been small – never more than five or ten pesos. Their purpose was to establish an obligation, but they were meant to be repaid in a single stretch of work.[8]

Far from "isolated primitives," then, all of Chiapas's Indians were in fact already spoken for. That most of this potential labor was controlled by the elite of a single extended region – the highlands, consisting of the department of Las Casas and the adjacent mountainous portions of Simojovel and Chilón – had, in turn, over time become a major source of friction between the highland and lowland elites. Following Independence, the landowners, merchants, and bureaucrats of the highlands,

---

[6] Indigenous resistance to, among other things, obligatory labor led to severe repression in the Chiapas highlands in 1848 and again in 1869–70, with more than 1,000 indigenous people in massacres over the course of a year in the latter case (R. W. Wasserstrom, "The Caste War That Never Was: The Tzeltal Conspiracy of 1848," *Peasant Studies* 7, no. 2 (1978): 73–85; Jan Rus, "Whose Caste War? Indians, Ladinos and the 'Caste War' of 1869," in Murdo MacLeod and R. W. Wasserstrom, eds., *Spaniards and Indians in Southeastern Mesoamerica* (Lincoln: University of Nebraska Press, 1968), 127–68).

[7] Rus, "Whose Caste War?," 129–35; Wasserstrom, *Class and Society*, 69ff. Land titles in this period typically listed "*baldíos*" and "*deudas de mozos*" as part of the property, e.g., "Carta de Porfirio Trejo a la Catedral," May 19, 1857, AHDSC. For an extraordinary debate about the legality, if not morality, of this serfdom, with detailed descriptions of cases argued by each side, see *La Voz del Pueblo*, San Cristóbal, July 8, Nov. 30, 1855, Jan. 1, and Feb. 2, 1856, TU.

[8] This new sense of *habilitación* can be found in Romero in 1871 (*Cultivo del café*, 24ff.), and more explicitly in an editorial in *El Espíritu del Siglo, Periódico Oficial*, Oct. 16, 1873, TU.

hoping to "inherit" the rents, taxes, and religious fees of their region's numerous Indians, had favored changing the political regime of the colonial period as little as possible. Siding with the conservatives nationally, they envisaged a centralized state in which power would be concentrated in the hands of seigneurial *criollos* rather than the Crown and Spaniards.

The ambitious ranchers and merchants of the lowland, Central Valley departments of Tuxtla and Chiapa, on the other hand, identified with the liberals nationally. Judging that economic progress in their potentially rich agricultural region depended on the secularization of Church property (more than half of the lowlands' best land), on minimal taxation, and on the free movement of labor, the lowlanders favored breaking up the centralized, colonial order. As they struggled to increase their production after Independence, they soon realized that the most critical of these issues was access to labor. Accordingly, after having favored laws that permitted the privatization of the lands of indigenous communities from the 1820s through the early 1840s (during which time they confiscated the remaining Indian lands in their own region), by the late 1840s they advocated outlawing *baldiaje* and even returning lands to indigenous communities to "untie" the Indian workers of the highlands. Nationally, this division between liberals and conservatives led to repeated coups and rebellions through the 1840s and '50s, and then to civil war from the second half of the 1850s through the mid-1860s. All of these convulsions were felt in Chiapas as well, where armed groups fought each other repeatedly over a period of almost twenty years.[9]

As for the employment of highland Indians during the first five decades of Independence, although both sides of Chiapas's highland-lowland, conservative-liberal divide coveted them, actual demand for their labor through the 1860s does not appear to have been great enough to have disrupted the life of their corporate communities.[10] Small quantities of wheat, corn, sugar, and cattle were generated on the traditional estates of the highlands, mostly for local use and trade within Chiapas. The indigenous labor that produced these goods was essentially unpaid. In official documents, wages for requisitioned workers were reported to be 0.08 to 0.16 pesos per day, but according to many complaints to the Church and press, they were even less than that. And, of course, *baldíos* worked for

---

[9] Rus, "Whose Caste War?," 129ff. Comitan's elite was independent of San Cristóbal's, sometimes an ally, sometimes a rival.
[10] Rus, "Whose Caste War?," 129ff.; Wasserstrom, *Class and Society*, 107ff.; Benjamin, *A Rich Land*, 15ff.

free. Nevertheless, it seems that the actual number of days of obligated agricultural labor, although onerous, was never so much that families could not attend to their own fields and activities.

In addition to agricultural work, Indians were also pressed into service as bearers, or *cargadores*, to carry merchandise back and forth from Chiapas's capital and commercial center, San Cristóbal, to the towns in the north of the state and the Gulf of Mexico port of Villahermosa, Tabasco. Again, however, because of the constant political unrest, because markets were limited, and because the conditions of production in Chiapas itself were so bad (in particular, the lack of credit and infrastructure), transportation needs appear to have been light enough that those who used conscripted Indian labor for cargo bearing seem not to have exploited it to the fullest extent possible before the 1870s.[11]

Mobilizing Workers for Tropical Agriculture, 1871–1892

In the early 1870s, with Mexico's constitutional crises and civil wars finally behind them, Chiapas's landowners and merchants of all regions, seeing the growing prosperity of export agriculture across the border in Guatemala and even in nearby Mexican states such as Yucatán and Veracruz, began casting around for products that might lift their own state out of its chronic lethargy and poverty. As late as 1879, the state government in San Cristóbal was offering property tax exemptions to encourage experimentation with a whole list of possible export crops: indigo, which had been tried during the colonial period; coffee, which was just beginning to be planted, and also wine grapes, flax, and temperate fruits as such apples, none of which were ever grown in commercially significant amounts.[12]

Meanwhile, even before they had figured out what to produce, the state's regional elites were moving aggressively to privatize remaining public lands and legalize their control of at least their own regions' work

---

[11] Production figures for the nineteenth century are unreliable. However, De la Peña, *Chiapas económico*, vols. 3 and 4, provides a product-by-product summary of what figures there are; see also Wasserstrom, *Class and Society*, 107ff. As for commerce and the work of bearers, although travelers in the late eighteenth century reported having to step off trails while caravans of 300 or 400 laden Indians passed (Manuel Trens, *Historia de Chiapas* (Mexico City, 1943), 201), there appears to be no way to quantify either internal trade or the amount of labor involved.

[12] Decree of Nov. 30, 1879, in Angélica Inda and Andrés Aubry, eds., *La Paz de Utrilla, Boletín del Archivo Histórico Diocesano de San Cristóbal*, vol. 4, no. 3 (San Cristóbal: INAREMAC, 1991).

forces. From 853 *fincas* in Chiapas in 1837, the number grew to 3,159 in 1889, some 80 percent of the increase after 1880.[13] All of these new land-holders automatically captured the residents of their new estates through *baldiaje*. At the same time, elites throughout the state, but particularly in the highland departments, intensified their efforts to transform their customary but extralegal control of the labor of indigenous communities into legal, contractual relationships with individual workers. In 1871, the state government enacted a head tax, or *capitación*, under which adult men aged sixteen to sixty were required to pay 0.25 pesos per quarter – the equivalent of two to four days of wages at contemporary rates in the highlands. In indigenous villages, the town councils (*ayuntamientos*) were made responsible for the tax's collection, and if there were shortfalls, the council members themselves could be jailed and fined up to ten pesos each. To ensure compliance, ladino *agentes* named by the departmental govern-ments (the *jefaturas políticas*) were posted in every village to oversee the native *ayuntamientos*.[14] Finally, to seal the transformation of taxes, fines, and administrative control into individual labor obligations, in 1880 a further law mandated that any man who failed to produce a *capitación* receipt on demand was a "vagrant" and could be arrested on the spot and auctioned to potential employers for the value of his unpaid taxes. The same 1880 statute also provided for the registration of workers and their debts with the departmental governments. Once registered, those who attempted to run away without clearing their accounts could be pur-sued by the police on the grounds they had stolen the money they owed their "masters" (*amo* was the word used in the law.) As a further measure to enforce such debts, landowners were made responsible for notifying the *jefatura política* within two weeks of any new workers who took up residence on their estates. If such workers proved to be runaways with outstanding debts, the owners were enjoined to "take responsibility for the resulting damages" – that is, to pay off the workers' accounts with their previous masters.[15]

---

[13] Favre, *Changement et continuité*, 61ff. Note that this is before either the assault on indige-nous ejidos beginning in 1893, which by 1909 would "privatize" more than 50 percent of formerly Indian lands in the department of Las Casas (Benjamin, *Rich Land*, 90), or the greater part of the sale of *terrenos nacionales* to foreign investors by federally chartered land companies (*compañías deslindadoras*) (Holden, *Mexico and the Survey*, 16ff).

[14] Actually, the head tax had existed since Independence, but had been suspended for almost fifteen years during the civil wars of the 1850s and 1860s (Rus, "Whose Caste War?," 137ff).

[15] "Reglamento de policia y buen gobierno," Articles 82–89, "De la vagancia," June 1, 1880, Colección Moscoso, San Cristóbal (hereafter cited as CM); see also Chester Lloyd

The first department to profitably combine postcolonial latifundios
with the new labor laws was Pichucalco in the northwest. By the late
1870s, cacao, which had been a regular, if modest export of Pichucalco before the nineteenth century, was beginning to be grown again. By the mid-
1880s, plantations extending across the border of Chiapas into the state
of Tabasco were providing most of Mexico's chocolate. In the Chiapas
tradition, most work on these estates was performed by Indian laborers,
the majority being Zoques, who had been reduced to *baldiaje* by the privatization of their lands during the 1870s. Under the pressure of the cacao
boom, the amount of work required of such *baldíos* had grown from a
few days a month to five and a half days per week. In exchange, families
were given minimal pay and the privilege of keeping a house and plot of
corn for their own use.

Pichucalco's plantations were also served by indebted workers called
mozos, who did the same work as the *baldíos* but without receiving use of
any land. Most of these hailed from nearby Zoque villages, but there were
also Tzotzil and Tzeltal-Mayas from the highlands. Although, in theory,
the *mozos* had more leeway to negotiate the terms of their employment
than the *baldíos*, in fact, after they had contracted their debts they became
dependent on their *patrones* for a roof and food in a way the "entailed"
baldíos did not.

Meanwhile, at the same time labor requirements increased in
Pichucalco, working conditions worsened. Beginning in the late 1870s,
there were continuous reports of workers being chained at night to prevent them from escaping during periods of peak labor demand, of the use
of stocks and whipping posts, and of beatings administered in the cacao
groves to increase production. Most of all, however, laborers' debts grew.
Workers were scarce in Pichucalco, and by law planters could hire runaways from neighboring plantations by the simple expedient of paying
off their accounts. To forestall such "poaching," the debts landowners
recorded for *baldíos* and *mozos* alike were no longer the relatively small
amounts that had traditionally guaranteed clientship in the highlands. Instead, they had been raised to as much as 500 pesos per man. Everything
the worker and his family consumed, even their tools, was recorded as a
loan, and at the end of each year's work, the amounts owed were regularly

Jones, *Mexico and Its Reconstruction* (New York: Appleton, 1922), 119ff. In 1885, Angel
Pola, a native of Chiapas, presented a detailed description of the legal traps that ensnared
debt workers ("Artículos de Angel Pola," in Gastón García Cantú, ed., *El Socialismo en
México, Siglo XIX* (Mexico City: ERA, 1969), 378–402).

more than the beginning wage advance. Nor did these burdens end with death: If a worker died, his wife and children were forced to assume his obligations.[16]

When labor conditions in Pichucalco were described in the Mexico City press in 1885, they became a national scandal. Saddled with "loans" they had no chance of repaying, forced to work indefinitely without wages on the grounds they were paying off their accounts, and liable to being bought and sold for the value of those same accounts, in practice workers in Pichucalco were the property of their "masters."

While the reputation for the most abusive labor system in Chiapas attached to Pichucalco, however, contemporary testimony suggests that labor practices throughout the heavily indigenous regions of central and northern Chiapas were similar.[17] Wherever the soil and climate permitted, local landowners had begun planting export crops in the 1880s. Since they turned first to their own "tied," *baldío* labor, everywhere this meant sharply increasing demands on local indigenous workers. Certainly, this was true in Simojovel and Chilón, which in addition to their densely populated, highland regions where they adjoined Las Casas, also contained deep valleys to the North and East where tropical exports could be grown. By the mid-1880s, landowners in both departments had vastly expanded their plantings of such "old" crops as sugar and tobacco and, to a lesser extent, cacao, as well as begun experiments with new products such as henequen, rubber, and coffee.[18] By 1892, out of a total indigenous population of slightly more than 34,000 in Simojovel and Chilón (approximately 20 percent of the Indians in the state), more than 20,000 were living on fincas as *baldíos* – a radical shift from just twenty years earlier, when virtually all were still "free" residents of Maya villages.[19] When indebted workers – *mozos*, not *baldíos* – were counted five years later, there were found to be some 1,760 of them as well, accounting with

[16] "Artículos de Angel Pola," 387ff. Similar, if less spectacular, accounts can be found in German sources (Karl Kaerger, *Agricultura y colonización en México en 1900* (1901; reprinted in Spanish, Mexico City: Universidad Autónoma de Chapingo/CIESAS, 1986), 60) and North American ones (Jones, *Mexico and Its Reconstruction*, 119ff.).

[17] Artículos de Angel Pola." For the Central Highlands, from 1885 on, see Trejo, *Apuntes y memoria*; for Simojovel, see Toledo, *Historia del movimiento*.

[18] R. Rabasa, *Estado de Chiapas*, 19ff.; Gobierno del Estado de Chiapas, *Chiapas, su riqueza*, 15ff.; De la Peña, *Chiapas económico*, vols. 3 and 4.

[19] *Censo general de población, 1890* (Mexico City: Imprenta del Gobierno, 1892); "Empadronamiento ... de Julio de 1892," in Rabasa, *Estado de Chiapas*, 112ff.

their families for another 8,800 people.[20] Assuming that adult men were approximately one-fifth of the population, this meant that out of a total of 6,800 men (one-fifth of 34,000) 6,760, or virtually 100 percent, were "tied" laborers.

By any normal economic standard, however, most of the export crops on which the work forces of Simojovel and Chilón labored should never have been planted. Both departments were essentially incommunicado, their agricultural regions so isolated by steep, jungle-covered mountains that even mules had trouble reaching them. The only way to get their products to market was to send them out on Indians' backs over narrow, slippery trails and across dozens of rope suspension bridges to river ports where they could be embarked for the Gulf of Mexico. Since even the most accessible valleys were three and a half to four days' walk from the rivers, the amount of labor consumed in the transportation of goods was almost as much as that involved in their production.[21] Only the superabundance of subject, unpaid labor made such plantations feasible. On the one hand, they made the cost of production itself extremely low (in 1896 it was said that all of the coffee of Simojovel – by that time, some 1,000 hectares – had been planted without any expenditures for labor because *baldíos* had done the work in fulfillment of their rent obligations). On the other, when they did not carry the products out on their own backs, the *baldíos'* and *mozos'* low-paid or free labor provided the margin that made it possible to hire Indian bearers from other regions to do the job.[22]

---

[20] *Boletín estadístico del estado* (Tuxtla Gutiérrez: Imprenta del Gobierno del Estado, 1897). (Note: Through the nineteenth century, references to indigenous workers in Chiapas generally meant adult men. In the Central Highlands communities around San Cristóbal in particular, even in the 1970s women hardly ever left their home communities to work. Both patterns perhaps reflect colonial customs of requisitioning adult male workers.)

[21] Rabasa (*Estado de Chiapas*, 19ff.); Karl Helbig, *Chiapas: Geografía de un estado mexicano*, vol. 2 (Tuxtla Gutiérrez: Gobierno del Estado de Chiapas, 1976), 183; and Prudencio Moscoso, *La arriería en Chiapas* (San Cristóbal: Instituto Chiapaneco de Cultura, 1988), 75ff., 183, all agree that bearers carried loads of between 46 kilos (the standard for coffee) and 50 kilos.

[22] De la Peña, *Chiapas económico*, 363. In 1898, Chiapas's Governor León said that highland Chiapas merchants had explained to him that human bearers were cheaper than mules or wheeled transport because (1) bearers were given wage advances and contracts, which made them personally financially responsible for their loads; (2) they carried their loads more delicately; (3) they did not require salaries for drivers or muleteers; (4) one did not need to worry about feeding them as one did mules; and (5) if a mule died, the merchant lost its value, but had no responsibility if a bearer died or was killed (León to Porfirio Díaz, Dec. 20, 1898, CGPD).

Indians and the Cargo-Bearing Boom of the 1880s and '90s

Because cargo bearing occupied a large proportion of the labor in the highlands as a whole, and involved as well important sectors of the elites of Las Casas, Simojovel, and Chilón, it deserves a closer look.

By 1895, Simojovel and Chilón would have required more than 1,200 full-time bearers just to transport to market products that because they were exported or generated taxes were consistently counted. The exports were coffee, tobacco, henequen, cacao, and rubber, all of which were carried to northern river towns. The taxed product was *aguardiente* – rough cane alcohol – which went to internal markets in Chiapas.[23] In addition, both departments also produced large amounts of other commodities – corn, beans, raw sugars, meat products, eggs, and fruits – in quantities well beyond what was needed for local consumption, with much of the surplus according to contemporary descriptions also carried out on Indians' backs. Meanwhile, there was also a lively bearer-borne trade from San Cristóbal to Chiapas's northern departments and on to the Gulf of Mexico in wheat flour, bread, refined sugars, and preserved meats – a business for which several San Cristóbal *comerciantes* in the 1890s reportedly employed as many as 500 *cargadores* each. Clearly, then, there must have been in the Central and Northern Highlands many more than the 1,200 full-time bearers that would have been required to transport just the verifiable cargos of Simojovel and Chilón.[24] But how many more? 2,000? 5,000? And how many would there have had to be if, as was almost certainly the case, cargo bearing was not a full-time job but half-time or less? Twice as many? More?

Unfortunately, there is insufficient information to answer these questions. Most interregional trade was not recorded, nor have highland merchants' account books been found. Certainly no one kept track of indigenous employment. Then there is the humbleness of the *cargador*'s task

---

[23] Simojovel's exports in 1895 weighed 814.5 tons: 16,770 loads that had to be carried in 3.5 days to Tapijulapa. Chilón's weighed 304.9 tons: 6,611 loads to be carried in four days to Salto de Agua. If a full-time *cargador* worked 200 days per year (100 days outbound, 100 back), the 85,139 outbound man-days for the two departments would have required 850 full-time bearers. As for *aguardiente*, more than 320 full-time bearers, each carrying two 20-liter glass jugs (a 42-kilo load with the containers), would have been required to carry the reported quantities to the nearest markets (*Boletín estadística del estado*, 1897; Rabasa, *Estado de Chiapas*, 19ff., 27ff.; Moscoso, *La Arriería*, 77–92).

[24] Chilón, in particular, produced food well beyond local requirements, perhaps to supply mahogany camps in the northeastern jungle. Cargadores would have been responsible for much of this trade. (The report of merchants with more than 500 *cargadores* is from León to Porfirio Díaz, Dec. 20, 1898, CGPD.)

itself, which was often mentioned by travelers in Mesoamerica, shocked to see humans used as beasts of burden, but never thought worthy of careful description by any local writer.

While it may not be possible to know exactly how many bearers there were, however, some deductions can be made about changes in the demand for them during the 1880s and '90s, and from there about the division of labor among the three highland departments and the labor systems of each. First, from production figures, it appears that more than half of the *baldío* and *mozo* labor of Simojovel and Chilón went just into the production of export goods and sugar for alcohol. When all other commodities are considered, it seems likely that most of the laborers native to the two northern highland departments would have been used locally, in direct agricultural work. Lending support to this conclusion is the fact that by the late 1880s debt laborers from the department of Las Casas were being sent to Simojovel and Chilón to supplement the local agricultural work forces. Indeed, several new villages were created on the edges of fertile sections of Simojovel to house Indians transplanted from Las Casas during this period.[25]

If Simojovel and Chilón had to import workers from Las Casas to fill their demand for agricultural laborers, however, then where did the thousands of *cargadores* come from? It appears that they, too, were mostly Indians from the densely populated communities surrounding San Cristóbal in the Central Highlands. As production in the north grew during the 1880s and '90s, more and more men from Las Casas were drawn into cargo bearing until eventually they constituted a majority in several of the department's largest communities.[26]

This in turn provides clues about Las Casas's labor system. Since according to various censuses and tax counts during the 1890s, there were very few *baldíos* and *mozos* in the department, the men who worked as *cargadores* must have been recruited from their villages via *habilitación/* wage advance contracting.[27] Although by the mid-1880s this customary

[25] Pérez Castro (*Entre montañas*, 66ff.) gives examples of sixteen fincas in Simojovel with resident Tzotzil workers from Las Casas.

[26] According to observers (Byam, *A Sketch*, 21; Rabasa, *Estado de Chiapas*, 29; Gonzalo Aguirre Beltrán and Ricardo Pozas, *La Política indigenista en México* (Mexico City: INI, 1954), 14), most of the adult men of Chamula and Tenejapa, two large communities close to San Cristóbal, as well as a large proportion of the men from Cancuc and the *pueblo* of Chilón, were full-time *cargadores* by the 1890s.

[27] If approximately one-fifth of the population consisted of adult men, there would have been 7,800 potential indigenous workers in the department of Las Casas in 1890 (*Censo general... 1890*; see Table 11.1 above). At most, however, there were only several dozen

contracting had been increasingly disguised by tax and vagrancy laws, what distinguished it from straight contract labor was the lingering flavor of communal obligation derived from *repartimiento*. Instead of the excessive debts that were used to stabilize plantation labor forces in Pichucalco, then, or reduction to *baldío* and *mozo* status as in Simojovel and Chilón, control of Las Casas's work force continued to be exercised, as it had been for generations, through domination of indigenous communities by way of their town councils. Now overseen by ladino officials backed by the state militia based in San Cristóbal – and by the memory of the organized violence that could be unleashed against communities that dared resist – Las Casas's indigenous *ayuntamientos* still brokered and enforced "contracts" that community members were essentially obliged to accept.[28]

As for the profits that could be made on the backs of such *habilitación*-contracted bearers, according to reports from the early 1890s, San Cristóbal's *transportistas*, as the contractors of bearers were known, charged a peso and a half per day for the use of their *cargadores*, of which the shipper received a peso and the bearer half a peso. The bearers were paid, however, only for the days they were actually carrying cargos, so if they did not have loads on the return trip, or had to walk to where they picked up their loads, those days were unpaid. In addition, bearers were expected to buy their own food on the road.[29] In fact, then, the *cargador* usually made less than 25 cents a day, while the *transportista*'s peso per day was free and clear.

To go back to the volume of cargo carried by bearers in the Central Highlands, then, if the amount of labor required to move just Simojovel's and Chilón's export and taxed produce in the mid-1890s was equal to the work of 1,200 bearers each carrying loads for 100 days a year, the profit generated would have come to 120,000 pesos a year. In the context of Chiapas's, and particularly highland Chiapas's, previously austere, somewhat marginal economy, in which highland fincas had been valued for tax purposes at one peso per hectare at the end of the 1880s, this was an enormous profit. By comparison, Chiapas's state budget in the

---

baldíos right through the 1890s (Gloria Pedrero, "Las Haciendas y ranchos sancristo-balenses del siglo XIX," in *San Cristóbal y sus alrededores* (Tuxtla Gutiérrez: Gobierno del Estado, 1984), 99–139), and in 1896 only 973 *mozos* ("peones") (*Boletín estadístico*, 1897).

[28] Rus, "Whose Caste War?," 151ff.

[29] Governor León to Porfirio Díaz, Dec. 20, 1898, CGPD; Pola in García Cantú, *El Socialismo*, 384–5.

mid-1890s came to less than 400,00 pesos a year.[30] Not surprisingly, the
list of San Cristóbal's merchant-*transportistas* came to include many of
the city's most distinguished men: politicians, landowners, and lawyers.
When demand for agricultural laborers around the state began to increase
in the 1890s, they had good economic reasons not to let "their" Indians
be "kidnapped" (*secuestrado*) by the elites of other regions.

"Freeing Indian Workers," Part 1: The Missteps of the Early 1890s

Given the various regimens by which the labor of the highland departments was tied – *baldiaje*, long-term debt (the *mozos*), and customary,
habilitacion obligations – when extensive export agriculture finally began
in the mid-1880s, and then began to draw investment from outside of the
state in the second half of the decade, the new enterprises quickly found
that the state's labor was not mobile, that in each department it had already been claimed by local landowners and merchants. As a result, the
owners of the Soconusco's first great wave of coffee plantations in the late
1880s, for instance, were forced to rely on Indians from across the border in Guatemala as well as on Mexican "Guatemalans," mostly Mam
Indians who had resettled in the mountainous region of Motozintla, just
north of the Soconusco, to clear the forest and plant their crops.[31]

As this Soconusco boom coffee began to mature at the beginning of the
1890s, however, and it became clear both that the local labor supplies were
insufficient and that the large indigenous populations in the Central and
Northern Highlands were not available, the federal government, which
had actively invited Mexicans and foreigners alike to invest in Chiapas's
coffee, finally stepped in.[32] The agent selected to break the blockade on the
movement of highland Indians was Emilio Rabasa, who became governor
of Chiapas on December 1, 1891. Although the son of a well-connected
Central Valley ranching family, Rabasa had graduated from the same
schools in Oaxaca as President Porfirio Díaz and begun a brilliant legal

[30] "Catastro de fincas rústicas del Dpto del Centro," appendix to Manuel Carrascosa,
Informe de gobierno, 1889 (Biblioteca de Na Bolom, San Cristóbal); Benjamin, *A Rich
Land*, 47; *El Hijo del pueblo*, San Cristóbal, Nov. 19, 1911, Archivo General del Estado
de Chiapas, hereafter cited as AGCH.
[31] Baumann, "Terratenientes," 15ff. See also Helen Seargeant's memoir of life on a
Soconusco coffee finca from the late 1880s to the early 1900s (*San Antonio Nexapa*
(Tuxtla Gutiérrez, Chiapas: Gobierno del Estado, 1971), 183–97).
[32] In addition to its interest in economic growth, the federal government also wanted to
develop Chiapas's borderland to secure it against Guatemala (Benjamin, *A Rich Land*,
44, 56).

career in Mexico City. With Díaz behind him, he came to Chiapas as the virtual proconsul of the federal government.

Beyond securing a labor source for lowland agriculture, Rabasa was charged with a whole range of modernizing measures designed to make Chiapas more hospitable to investors: fiscal and customs reform, road and bridge building, and privatization of national and communal land holdings. Within just a few weeks of arriving in the state capital of San Cristóbal, however, he was complaining to President Díaz that the officers of Chiapas's government – in particular, the *jefes políticos* of the departments of the Central and Northern Highlands, but also the heads of the state bureaucracy – were refusing to cooperate with any of these initiatives; in fact, they were actively working against him. So bitter did relations become that by March 1892, convinced the highland elite would never permit a modernization that would decrease its own power, Rabasa was begging Díaz to relieve him. Most of all, he was sure the Indians would never be voluntarily released by "the inhabitants of San Cristóbal, their eternal tormentors [*verdugos*]."[33] Díaz refused his request, however, and insisted he take more energetic steps. He did. On June 15, 1892, he unilaterally moved the state capital from San Cristóbal to Tuxtla Gutiérrez, in Chiapas's Central Valley. Almost simultaneously he decreed that in the future, the *jefes políticos* were to be appointed by the governor instead of elected. He then replaced all of those in the highlands with trusted colleagues from outside of Chiapas, most from Oaxaca. Now, Rabasa declared to Díaz, he could "begin attending to the protection and promotion of the interests of coffee."[34]

From their own letters, the highlanders who resisted Rabasa in 1892 were concerned most of all by his efforts to transfer "their" Indians to the lowlands. In later years, however, they would reframe the conflict as a continuation of the old regional struggle between highlanders and lowlanders and claim Rabasa had acted in bad faith. Rabasa, they would recall, was a native of Tuxtla (although he had never lived in Chiapas as an adult), and his family had always been liberal partisans of their region;

---

[33] Rabasa to Díaz, Feb. 12 and April 4, 1892. The phrase "los habitantes de San Cristóbal han sido sus eternos verdugos" is from Aug. 23, 1892. In the same months Rabasa was asking to be relieved, on March 2, 1892, he asked Díaz for permission to buy 2,500 hectares of Soconusco coffee land from the government at the preferential price of 2 pesos/hectare (the market price by then was 6 to 20 pesos/hectare.) Díaz replied on March 16 that he would "help in any way I can ... " (CGPD).

[34] Rabasa to Díaz, June 9, 15, and Aug. 23, 1892 (CGPD). Decree of Aug. 11, 1892, "Traslación de Poderes," *Periódico Oficial*, Tuxtla Gutiérrez (CM).

surely he had come to the governorship with the intention of harming old conservative, highland enemies.[35]

In fact, Rabasa was very much conscious of the highland-lowland division, but not for the revanchist reasons attributed to him. After the Soconusco, the department of Tuxtla had planted the second highest amount of coffee by the early 1890s and would soon be needing migrant laborers itself. Moreover, Tuxtla's liberal merchants were by this time the major conduit for trade from Chiapas's rich Central Valley and coast, through Oaxaca, to Central Mexico – a trade that allied them with the major commercial houses of Oaxaca, which in the absence of local banks were the main source of credit in Chiapas. Finally, there was the fact that Tuxtla had supported the liberals in the civil wars of the 1850s and '60s – Porfirio Diaz's side – while San Cristóbal had supported the conservatives. If there was to be a contest between the up-and-coming businessmen of Tuxtla and the conservative, clericalist elite of San Cristóbal for Díaz's affection, San Cristóbal's loss was foreordained.[36]

In an attempt to induce highland Indians to become migratory workers, during the five months after he moved the capital Rabasa decreed the sale of their villages' communal holdings, or ejidos, updated the tax rolls to improve collection of the *capitación*, and reinvigorated the 1880 vagrancy laws for those who failed to pay. He also strengthened the public administration and police in rural areas to enforce these new regulations. In addition, he argued that for the Indians to become useful, productive citizens – the kind who would be able to participate in a "free economy of wage workers" – they needed to be educated. Accordingly, he decreed that schools should be founded in the Indian pueblos, their costs to be underwritten by new taxes on the Indians themselves. And finally, to facilitate transportation, he began to improve the state's inventory of roads and bridges – for all of which the Indians were also taxed.[37]

From the first, the highland elite understood that Rabasa's reforms were meant to undermine the traditional order on which their power was

---

[35] M. M. Mijangos to Porfirio Díaz, June 24, 1892, Anonymous to Porfirio Díaz, July 8, 1892, CGPD; Rosauro de J. Trejo, "Causas del odio que el Lic. don Emilio Rabasa tuvo a la Ciudad de San Cristóbal...hasta lograr trasladar los poderes...a Tuxtla," flyer, Aug. 8, 1937, AHDSC.

[36] Benjamin, *A Rich Land*, 37–54.

[37] Decree of Aug. 11, 1892, "División de Egidos," refined by decrees on April 9 and Oct. 26, 1893; decree of Oct. 14, 1892, "La Contribución personal," all *Periódico Oficial*, CM. For Rabasa's explanation, see *Discurso del Lic. Emilio Rabasa...ante la XVIII Legislatura al abrir su primer período...*, 1893, AHDSC. Also Benjamin, *A Rich Land*, 39–54.

founded. Although they complained about all of his measures, in editorials and in letters to Porfirio Díaz they continually returned to the dual themes of restoring the state capital to San Cristóbal and control of the Indians to those who understood the subtleties of managing them. If Rabasa's measures were allowed to stand, they warned, a "caste war" was inevitable. Only when the *indios* knew the power of the state was close by and able to react immediately to the slightest disobedience, they claimed, was there any chance of "... directing, repressing, educating [and] civilizing" them.[38]

While the public debate over control of the indigenous population in the highlands was being phrased in terms of "treating Indians like human beings" versus the need to "make the aboriginal race feel the power of a steady hand," the underlying struggle for economic and political control over them continued. Unfortunately, Rabasa had underestimated the highland elite's tenacity, and his measures to "free" the region's Indians from the supposedly stagnant economies of their communities and force them "to look for work" in the lowlands backfired. Rather than improving labor flows to the lowlands, the new taxes and improved enforcement of vagrancy laws actually facilitated the highland elite's ongoing conversion of its hold on their labor from extralegal, customary conscription into legal contracting based on wage advances. Meanwhile, the sale of the ejidos – which around the state were typically bought by local elites – converted still more village Indians into tenants. As for the new mid- and low-level administrative and police positions, they were generally filled by clients of the local elites, meaning that the state now paid minions of those elites to enforce their hegemony. Even the schools quickly became a means of further indebting rural people through unregulated "taxes" for buildings, teachers, and materials.[39]

Recognizing that the old highland elite was confounding his plans, Governor Rabasa reacted by continuing to replace their officials with his own men. By the time he left Chiapas at the beginning of 1894 (to become federal senator for the northern state of Sinaloa), he was able to report that all of the *jefes políticos* and upper administrators were his appointees, and

---

[38] Vicente Pineda, *Traslación de los poderes públicos del Estado*, 1892 (pamphlet, AGCH).

[39] "Denuncias de terrenos baldíos" (ex-ejidal lands) in the indigenous *municipios* of the highlands appeared regularly in the *Periódico Oficial* from 1894 to 1903; in 1907 there were 329 *fincas rústicas* in the Departamento de Las Casas and the Partido de Chamula (*Periódico Oficial*, Jan. 5, 1907, AGCH), vs. 206 in 1889 (Carrascosa, *Informe de gobierno*). Trejo, *Apuntes y memoria*, 14–15, and Pineda, *Traslación de poderes*, describe the use of taxing power to subjugate labor.

all non-Chiapans. His justification was that in the long run this would set the state on the path to professional, impartial administration. Although it deepened the hostility of the highland elites, however, it had no effect on the mobility of Indian workers.

Finally, at the start of the 1893–94 coffee-picking season, Rabasa himself, faced with his inability to engineer the transfer of workers from the highlands to the new plantations through legal and economic reforms, resorted to directing his *jefes políticos* to "be responsive to the needs" of foreign planters. They, in turn, began requisitioning labor directly from indigenous pueblos and assigning it to the new plantations.[40] At least temporarily, Rabasa had acceded to the system of obligated labor he had come to Chiapas to replace. Unfortunately, the *jefes* could compel labor for villages and plantations only within their own jurisdictions, so the problem of transferring workers from one region to another remained unsolved.

"Freeing Indian Workers," Part 2: The Attack on the Highland Elite, 1894–1897

Between Rabasa's withdrawal from Chiapas in early 1894 and 1896, the federal government tried a different tack to free up highland labor. It was finally beginning to be recognized that the agricultural boom in the Soconusco and the accessible lowland regions west and northwest of the Central Highlands was being echoed in Simojovel and Chilón, and that it was the very dependence of this local boomlet on almost unlimited, virtually unpaid labor that was preventing the movement of workers beyond those two departments and the neighboring department of Las Casas. Rabasa's interim replacement as governor in 1894 therefore undertook to speed road construction from Las Casas to the north on the theory that this would free *cargadores* for other kinds of work, while at the same time allowing the interior regions of Simojovel and Chilón to continue exporting and developing.

Unfortunately, these measures, which were based on the view that trade borne on human backs was an anachronism bound to disappear as soon as there were alternatives, failed to recognize the wealth generated for highland merchants by the *cargadores*. Nor did the attempts by the governors appointed from Mexico City to "free" highland labor take into account the highland elite's investments in land and loans in order to control

[40] Rabasa to Díaz, Dec. 20, 1892, and Jan. 13, 1894, CGPD.

Indian workers – investments that would be worthless if they were to lose the use of the laborers. As an example of this lack of understanding, when Chiapas's next permanent governor, Francisco León, was offered a 30,000 peso bribe in 1896 to *not* build a cart road from San Cristóbal to Chilón (an amount almost twice the 16,400 pesos paid for the 7,400 hectares of one of the largest haciendas in the department of Las Casas in 1891) – a road that would have ended the dependence of the *aguardiente* trade on *cargadores* – he took it as an example of the highland elite's cynical rejection of progress, and reported it as such in an outraged letter to President Porfirio Díaz, rather than interpreting it as the attempt to defend a lucrative economic system that it was.[41]

Part of the reason the representatives of the federal government failed to appreciate the highland elite's resistance to loosening its control of its region's labor was that the *public* debate was carried out not in terms of the actual functioning of the highland economy but on the grounds of its morality. This became clear during the Congreso Agrícola that Governor León (who had taken office on December 1, 1895) called for March 25, 1896. Ostensibly, the purpose of the Congreso was to come to agreement on a range of measures the new administration hoped to undertake to promote Chiapas's agricultural development. Almost immediately, however, debate focused on the real question, which was labor. To the delegates representing Chiapas's lowlands and the foreign planters, the question was one of economic rationality. The capital tied up in debt labor was essentially static. If instead of being given loans, workers were simply paid decent wages, it would cost employers less, and the capital that was freed could be invested in productive activities. Moreover, it would release workers from season to season to go where their labor was most needed – and best paid. For the conservative landowners and lawyers who represented the highland departments, on the other hand, the issue was not economic at all (at least publicly), but a matter of the "civilized race's" "responsibility for Indians' welfare," as well as for the peace and security of the regional society that included Indians and non-Indians alike. Indians, the argument went, would be lost without their communities; they were unprepared to exist in a world of wages and individual rights and responsibilities, and to force them into such a world would be to cast them adrift. By extending them wage advance "loans" through their *ayuntamientos*, highlanders who used Indian labor claimed they strengthened the social and cultural bases of local indigenous society, provided for a

---

[41] León to Porfirio Díaz, Dec. 20, 1898; in an earlier letter (June 15, 1896).

hierarchy of government that eventually connected each local hamlet to the *jefe político* and from there to the state, and paid the worker in a way that entailed a long-term reciprocal relationship with his employer.[42]

As it became clear to Governor León over the weeks of the Congreso that persuasion was not going to be enough to free indigenous labor, behind the scenes he pursued discussions with Porfirio Díaz about other, more direct ways to remove highland workers to the lowlands. Diaz directed him not to outlaw debt labor outright, but if the Congreso ended without the desired result, he gave León permission to redraw the departmental boundaries in the highlands. Accordingly, when the Congreso adjourned on April 22, 1896, without an agreement on "free labor," León, on April 25, unilaterally stripped San Cristóbal of the better part of its hinterland.[43] A new administrative entity, the Partido de Chamula, was created, placing 90 percent of the Tzotzil population of the department of Las Casas under the direct control of the federal and state governments – and the lowland planters.

By itself, however, even this was insufficient to start the flow of workers from highlands to low. For one thing, the native *ayuntamientos*, exercising traditional caution, were slow to cooperate with the *jefe político* of the new *partido*. Accustomed to *habilitación* and still needing to work to feed themselves, members of the communities near San Cristóbal appear to have continued to accept work in the old way from their old masters through 1896. Governor León and the new *jefe político* of the Partido de Chamula, for their part, unable to instate a new tax and administrative apparatus before the fall of 1896, had to watch yet another coffee harvest pass with little or no highland Indian presence on the plantations of the Soconusco.

Meanwhile, the creation of the Partido de Chamula did seal the alienation of the highland merchants and landowners from the state and federal governments. Over the next several years, there were assassination attempts on the governor, rumors of conservative rebels stockpiling

[42] *Documentos relativos al Congreso Agrícola de Chiapas*, Imprenta del Gobierno del Estado, Tuxtla Gutiérrez, 1896, AGCH.

[43] The messenger between León and Díaz was Manuel de Trejo, state treasurer, largest landowner in the Tzotzil *municipios* north of San Cristóbal, and an associate of important Tuxtla-based lowland merchants. The sequence was as follows: letter introducing Trejo (León to Díaz, March 31, 1896); text of approval from Díaz (April 6, 1896); León thanks Díaz for his telegram of instructions on actions following the Congreso (April 8); Díaz approves the Partido de Chamula (April 21), all CGPD. While Díaz approved circumventing those who blocked access to Indian labor, however, he also consistently denied León's proposals to outlaw debt labor.

weapons and conducting military training in the hills above San Cristóbal, other rumors of efforts to incite an Indian uprising, and, finally, the "preventive arrest" of several of the highland's political leaders and wealthiest merchants to stop their supposed plotting.[44] Not until after 1900 was the region again to be fully at peace.

The "Labor Problem" Is Finally Solved: The Arrangement of 1897–1998

It is not clear just what the machinations were that finally started highland workers flowing to the lowlands, and particularly the Soconusco. To some extent, it will probably remain an occult history. However, from the outcome we can make some deductions. By 1897–98, there were greatly increased numbers of indebted workers in the lowlands, including, as in the Soconusco, numbers of debtors far beyond previous local Indian populations.[45] The logical conclusion is that at least some of these workers came from the Central Highlands. In support of this conclusion, Karl Kaerger, a German consultant who visited Soconusco in 1899, wrote of there being Indians "from Chiapas's *altiplano*" in the region by that year.[46]

Unfortunately, 1897–1904 were not good years for coffee in Chiapas. Prices had fallen in 1897 and remained low, and there was a volcanic eruption on the eve of the 1902 harvest that destroyed both that and the next year's crops. As a result, even if the highland labor market had opened to Soconusco coffee growers in 1897, demand for workers was down over the next seven years, making the effect of the change less striking.[47] Labor

---

[44] Benjamin, *A Rich Land*, 66–70.

[45] The indigenous population of the Soconusco, for example, was 7,872 in 1890, meaning some 1,570 men. It can be assumed these were the 1,550 *baldíos* in that same census. In 1896, there were reported to be 2,365 "peones agrícolas" – rural workers of all sorts – resident in the department. When indebted workers in the Soconusco were registered in 1897, however, there were found to be 6,078, with an average debt of 124 pesos each.

[46] Kaerger, *Agricultura y colonización*, 105 ff.

[47] Benjamin (*A Rich Land*, 77) argues that the collapse of world coffee prices before the 1897–98 harvest led the major planters of the Soconusco to begin lobbying the state and federal governments for financial relief in March 1898. Although they were not given the tax breaks they sought, Benjamin suggests that the state government did give them permission to begin using highland debt-labor. This may well be true, although the obstacle to the use of highland workers was not the government but the highland elite. On the other hand, this does seem to be the moment when the coffee planters and state government had their change of heart about agreeing to the sancristobalenses' conditions to use "their" Indians. (It should be noted as well that the low price of coffee after

demand did increase again in 1904, however, and when the working of the contracting system was next described it was a system that finally provided incentives for the highland elite to agree to "sell" its formerly private labor reserve: Labor contractors for the major foreign plantations were now to be paid a salary of 100 pesos per month, as well as a commission (in some cases mounting to one peso per man) for those they contracted. These were excellent wages in an era when laborers made less than 0.50 pesos per day, but they were still finite, subject to a ceiling. Perhaps more important, then, was that the federal government and the mostly foreign planters, who through the 1890s had argued for a system of free labor and fair wages to attract workers, had settled for a system of modified debt labor, a system now administered by the highland elite who had always controlled the Indians. Through labor contractors in San Cristóbal – many working out of the same commercial houses that had formerly organized caravans of *cargadores* – the plantations paid "wage advances" to the workers before they left on the eight-day walk to the Soconusco.[48] There appears to have been almost no control, however, on how this advance was given to the workers, or how it was created. Contractors could thus receive reimbursement in cash from the planters for overpriced goods sold to Indians at their stores, or for imaginary fines created by government officials, or for the "rent" Indians owed on the lands that had been swallowed in highland privatizations.[49] In essence, over the course of just a few decades, the highland elite had managed to transform its "rights" to Indian labor through traditional communal obligations derived from colonial *repartimiento* into monetary terms as debt – debt they often conjured out of nothing. And now they had been permitted to sell that debt to planters in other regions.

The planters, for their part, seem finally to have resigned themselves to the extra burden represented by debt labor – debt that they carried on their books as real loans, as though they would eventually be repaid – just to get the workers they had to have. Within a very few years, however,

1897 may finally have made it unprofitable to pay *cargadores* to transport coffee out of Simojovel and Chilón.)

[48] According to Ricardo Pozas ("El trabajo en las plantaciones de café y el cambio socio-cultural del indio," *Revista Mexicana de Estudios Antropológicos* 12, no. 1 (1952): 31–48), the first Soconusco planter to begin recruiting heavily in the region of San Cristóbal was the German Walter Kahle in 1904. On contractors' pay, see Kaerger, *Agricultura y colonización*, 105, and Hipólito Rébora, *Memorias de un chiapaneco* (Tuxtla, Chiapas: Serie Histórica Regional, 1982), 50.

[49] Trejo, *Apuntes y memoria*, 31; Rébora, *Memorias*, 49ff.; Arias, *Historia de la colonia de "Los Chorros."*

the contradictions between debt contracting and their own finances became obvious. Since planters in the Soconusco needed migrant laborers only three to six months a year, and since they wanted them to return voluntarily in the future, they were wary of garnishing their wages to recoup the debt as landowners did in places like Simojovel and Chilón, where they controlled the workers' villages. The Soconusco planters had little choice about this: Their plantations were more than 150 miles and two mountain ranges away from the highlands. Across that distance, with no police or administrative structure they could count on to compel workers to complete their contracts, if the planters confiscated their workers' wages or treated them poorly, not only would they flee, but they would not return in subsequent years. As a result, although the planters would have preferred not to use debt labor, once they had started they felt compelled to be lenient about recouping their loans. Indeed, at the same time, they were also trying to win their debt-laborers' loyalty by paying the highest wages available to Indians in Chiapas (up to 0.50 pesos per day), and often providing free meals.[50]

Meanwhile, the overhang of debt represented by the accumulated unrepaid "wage advances" eventually became a serious burden. From 1904 through 1909, the price of coffee remained low, driving many planters to the edge of bankruptcy in part because they were unable to service the debts they themselves had contracted to cover the wage advance loans originated by their hiring agents. The planters' collective struggle to get control of hiring, wage advances, and the workers' debt that began with the hybrid debt-labor/wage-labor system of this period continued for three more decades.[51]

If the governments of the indigenous communities – the *ayuntamientos* – appear to have been cautious about cooperating with the new *jefe político*

---

[50] Kaerger, *Agricultura y colonización*, 104, reported in 1900 that those with debts received 0.50/day, those with no debts 0.625/day; while Rébora (*Memorias*, 49) says workers were paid 0.40/day around 1905 – but that this pay was nominal because it was in tokens (*fichas*) good only at the plantation store. For wages in other departments, see *Documentos relativos*, 109.

[51] Seargeant, *San Antonio Nexapa*, 372. The state attempted to control the process of *habilitación* contracting in 1907 with the "Ley sobre Contrato de Peones" of Nov. 23, 1907, which required the registration of all contracts with the *jefe político*, to be paid for by a tax added to the accounts of the Indians who were contracted (*Legislación del trabajo del estado de Chiapas, 1900–1927* (Tuxtla Gutiérrez, Chiapas: Gobierno del Estado, 1975), 19ff.). The next year the mostly German planters formed the Unión Cafetera del Soconusco to try to get control of contracting themselves, limiting debt to 60 pesos, agreeing not to compete with each other for workers, and keeping common records of debt (Benjamin, *A Rich Land*, 84).

of the Partido de Chamula in 1896, by 1902–3 they had been reorganized to reflect the new compact among lowland planters, the state government, and the old highland elite. By this time, the ladino *agentes* who oversaw the indigenous *ayuntamientos* had all been appointed by the *jefe político* of the Partido de Chamula and were responsible to him. Supported by detachments of rural state police (*rurales*), they oversaw tax collection and labor contracting. In this they were assisted in the indigenous *municipios* by new "constitutional" authorities (a municipal president, judge (*síndico*), councilmen (*regidores*), and scribes) who were functional Spanish-speakers and whose election also depended on the approval of the *jefe político*.[52] These "legal" governments functioned parallel to the "traditional" *ayuntamientos* of colonial officers. Concentrated in the hands of the *jefe político*, the purpose of this entire centralized administrative structure was to guarantee the flow of workers to the lowlands. According to contemporary denunciations, in addition to aggressively collecting all of the authorized taxes among its indigenous constituents, the *jefatura política* of Chamula levied numerous irregular contributions of its own. These included, among other things, extraordinary exactions for the construction of its own headquarters, the payment of ladino officials' travel expenses, the purchase of brass instruments for a band – and then the construction of jails and the cost of feeding those who were imprisoned for nonpayment of taxes. All of these amounts, in turn, promptly turned into debt for the purpose of wage-advance/debt contracting. The *jefatura* was also relentless in chasing down runaway workers and tax delinquents, using the new constitutional municipal officers to pursue them all the way to their thatched houses in the mountains.[53]

The system worked. From the 1904–5 harvest on, the Mayas of the Central Highlands were Chiapas's principle source of seasonal, long-distance migrant labor. By 1909, on the eve of the Revolution, it was estimated that the region provided two-thirds of the seasonal work force in the Soconusco – 10,000 men, or by that time more than 80 percent of all the Indian men in the old department of Las Casas.[54]

---

[52] By the early 1900s, the constitutional governments of most "indigenous" *municipios* (e.g., six of eight in the Partido de Chamula) were actually in the hands of ladinos, small populations of whom had begun settling in native pueblos in the 1880s to farm ex-*baldío* and ejido lands, manage small stores, and control labor contracting.

[53] Trejo, *Apuntes y memoria*; Jan Rus, "Contained Revolutions: Indians, Ladinos and the Struggle for Highland Chiapas, 1910–1925," ms.

[54] Benjamin, *A Rich Land*, 89–90.

The Highlands Recolonized

If Chiapas had been a state of largely self-contained regions, each almost sovereign in its isolation as late as the 1880s, by the early 1900s all had been subordinated to the state and federal government and reorganized to suit the interests of export agriculture. In the process, San Cristóbal and the Central Highlands, which had been the leading region in the older, "traditional" economy and politics, became dependent politically on the merchants of Tuxtla and economically on the planters of the Soconusco and the lowlands. Although the highland elite had been pressured to cede the use of its principal resource, however – tens of thousands of Indians – it had, finally, managed to extract from the state a compromise system of labor contracting under which its role as the rightful gatekeeper of highland labor was recognized. If the highland Indians were to participate in the coffee boom, the highland elite would share in the profit.

What of the impact of these changes on indigenous people? Despite all of the high-sounding rhetoric about "preserving traditional communities" versus "free labor," highlanders and lowlanders, Mexicans and foreigners, finally saw them most of all as a resource, a labor pool to be "tapped." If to secure the laborers that coffee required it was necessary to compromise with the highland elite, eventually the Porfirian state was willing to do so. As a result, far from freeing indigenous laborers, coffee led to their recolonization, locking them into controlled communities and dependence on one form or another of seasonal, migrant labor for seven more decades – until the coffee plantations themselves began to fail in the 1970s.

As for the reaction of the indigenous people themselves to the transition of 1897–1904, the available evidence is ambiguous. Whereas before the late 1890s most highland Indians had worked as agricultural laborers in their own region or as *cargadores*, jobs that were ill-paid and that caused great physical suffering, after 1904 if their debts were sold to a Soconusco plantation – a foreign-owned one, in particular – they were able to make 0.50 pesos per day plus rations, more than double their previous wages. According to testimonies, they were also treated better than in other regions and occupations. As a result, many seem to have returned voluntarily to the "good" plantations year after year. This is not to say that these enterprises were not exploitative and even harsh, however, and here is where the element of ambiguity enters. Although we find no indigenous complaints about conditions in the Soconusco itself during the period from 1900 to the Mexican Revolution, during these same years the

planters themselves complained continually to the government to agricultural researchers, and to their foreign creditors that a large percentage of
their workers fled before they had finished their contracts. Indeed, some
claimed that the proportion of "early departures" reached two-thirds of
the work force in the years leading up to 1908, when the German planters
joined together to share data on wage advances and debt and refused to
hire those who had absconded in the past.[55] Were the workers simply
taking advantage of the planters' inability to enforce contracts, or were
they rebelling against the work itself? The question remains unanswered.

Meanwhile, the Indians resisted mightily the system of labor contracting in the highlands and the new political and administrative structures
in which it was embedded. They complained about them to anyone who
would listen – clergy, journalists, and sympathetic government and judicial
officials – leaving a wealth of documents about the highland, contracting side of coffee plantation labor that contrasts starkly with the slight
data about their experience on the plantations themselves.[56] Nor did their
dissatisfaction stop at complaints. By the end of the decade of 1900–10,
indigenous people in many communities of the Central Highlands had
become profoundly alienated from their appointed, constitutional officers and traditional *ayuntamientos* alike. In one of the opening episodes
of Mexico's decade of Revolution, in the winter and spring of 1910–11,
contract laborers, *baldíos*, and *mozos* in the Tzotzil communities north of
San Cristóbal overthrew both sets of officials. The ladinos among them
fled, but scores of Indians who had collaborated with the *jefes políticos* and
labor contractors, along with their families and supporters, were tortured
and beheaded.[57] Whatever the people of the highlands may or may not
have felt about the Soconusco plantations, when they had a chance to express themselves about debt labor, forced contracting, and the penetration
of their communities, the outbursts were terrifying.

This leads to a last question about the organization of the Central Highlands communities themselves after their recolonization. Before the 1870s,
labor contracting had been conducted through a customary adaptation

[55] "Exposición de la Colonia Alemana Cafetera de Soconuzco, sobre la cuestión de la
servidumbre para el cultivo de las fincas," typescript, 1900 (?), courtesy of Friederike
Baumann.
[56] E.g., Trejo, *Apuntes y memoria*, 15ff.; *La Voz de Chiapas*, Feb. 7, 1907, and *La
Libertad del Sufragio*, May 18, 1911, San Cristóbal newspapers, AGCH; Rus, "Contained
Revolutions."
[57] Benjamin, *A Rich Land*, 106ff.; Prudencio Moscoso, *Jacinto Pérez "Pajarito," último líder
chamula* (Gob. del Estado de Chiapas, 1972); Gossen, *The Four Creations*, Text 68.

of the colonial *repartimiento*. Native *ayuntamientos* stood as gatekeepers of their communities' labor, protecting community members from indiscriminate contracting and obliging the non-Indian world to acknowledge the communities' existence. Even if the barrier represented by the *ayuntamientos* was sometimes more symbolic than real, those who used Indian labor could eventually be called to account for abusing the rules. As labor demands increased from the mid-1880s on, however, the elders who composed the *ayuntamientos* soon proved unable to fulfill their old gatekeeper roles. On the contrary, as they themselves were obligated to apply new tax and vagrancy laws and attend to increasing demands by ladinos who wanted debts and contracts enforced, they were subverted into becoming agents of their communities' own exploitation. The internecine violence at the start of the Revolution, where those who had "sold their brothers out" were killed, represented an attempt by the communities to reassert control over their own territory and labor. But the old labor-brokering function of native governments was never completely restored. Instead, after the Revolution, the state itself intervened, establishing a series of "Indian affairs" agencies, official labor unions, and eventually indigenous bosses to act as brokers between the indigenous workers and the planters and their contractors. Once they had been incorporated into the system of lowland production at the turn of the twentieth century, the highland indigenous communities never escaped their status as a resource closely managed by the state.

12

Comparing Coffee Production in Cameroon and Tanganyika, c. 1900 to 1960s

Land, Labor, and Politics

Andreas Eckert

Neither Cameroon nor Tanganyika ever belonged to the most important coffee producers in Africa, let alone in the world.[1] However, coffee was crucial to the economic, social, and cultural transformation of some African societies during the first half of the twentieth century. In this chapter, I compare the Kilimanjaro region of Northern Tanganyika and the highlands of West Cameroon, giving special consideration to two basic factors of production: land and labor. These two regions were centers of coffee production in colonial times, and kept this role after independence. The chapter aims to demonstrate how both internal factors and external political and economic interests led to specific land and labor patterns.

The production of a crop such as coffee for the international market imposes certain common conditions on agricultural economies, notably, for the combination of land, labor, and capital. In much of colonial Africa, there was a complex shift from communal land ownership, albeit often with individual usufruct, to individual ownership. Agricultural

---

[1] From 1885 to 1918, the two territories were under German colonial rule. After 1918, German East Africa, minus Rwanda and Burundi placed under Belgian mandate, was called Tanganyika and administered by Britain as a mandate of the League of Nations, and later the United Nations. Tanganyika gained its independence in 1961 and formed a union with Zanzibar in 1964 as the United Republic of Tanzania. In 1918, the larger eastern part of Cameroon became a mandate administered by France, achieving independence in 1960. Britain administered the smaller western mandate of Cameroon, of which the northern sector elected to join Nigeria in 1961, while the southern sector was reunited with formerly French Cameroon.

commercialization during the colonial period stimulated individual claims to land, and land sales, in many African communities. The expansion of cash crops also had a strong influence on changing patterns of land use. Since coffee is a permanent crop, in many regions land was no longer used for two or three years before being abandoned, but was occupied on a permanent basis. Crop production often led to large-scale recruitment of nondomestic labor and provided new opportunities for accumulation. In other words, the expansion of coffee farming was accompanied by the commercialization of land and labor.

Unlike cocoa, mainly grown by Africans, coffee was also planted by Europeans in some parts of the continent, especially where the more valuable *arabica* species was grown. Besides the usual conflicts, centered on access to labor and to land suitable for specific crops, conflicts between European and Africans over coffee reflected colonial ideologies of superiority and paternalism.

The two main ethnic groups considered here, the Chagga of Tanganyika and the Bamiléké of Cameroon, differed greatly in their social structure. However, their involvement in coffee was quite similar, partly because of similarities in geographical and economic contexts. During the twentieth century, both societies had high population densities and suffered from pressure on land, aggravated by the presence of European planters. Coffee and politics were intertwined from the moment that the crop became sufficiently well established to generate a substantial income. Both African chiefs and the colonial administration wanted to control coffee affairs, while African and European farmers struggled over access to land and labor. In both cases, coffee changed the balance of relationships at the household level, altering "traditional" land rights and politicizing the land question. Thus, the two cases may represent important elements of a general pattern of African crop production in areas with significant European participation.

Coffee on Mount Kilimanjaro, Tanganyika

Situated on a major trading route, and attractive because of the allure of its snow-capped peaks and pleasant climate, Kilimanjaro has been visited by outsiders since the second half of the nineteenth century. There are numerous accounts of its scenery, people, politics, and economy, written by explorers, naturalists, colonial administrators, historians, political scientists, and anthropologists from outside the region, as well as by some

prominent Chagga themselves.[2] The people now designated as Chagga
were divided into small, autonomous chiefdoms in the nineteenth century, and therefore early accounts frequently speak of each as a separate
people. The names of the chiefdoms subsequently became geographical
names for the various parts of the mountain. There are important dialec-
tal differences between the languages spoken in the eastern, central, and
western regions.[3]

In the mid-nineteenth century, the Chagga were prosperous cattle keep-
ers and horticulturalists.[4] They grew beans, maize, eleusine millet, and
various vegetables, but the basic staples were many kinds of banana. They
also kept a few cows, goats, and sheep in their household enclosures. The
Chagga were organized into two or three dozen autonomous chiefdoms,
politically divided into three hierarchical levels, each progressively more
inclusive, namely, patrilineages, districts, and chiefdoms. All were cross-
cut by age grades. The chief's power was founded in large part on the
support of male age sets. Ideally, the chieftainship passed to the first-born
son of an incumbent, but if the new chief proved to be unpopular with
the warrior age set, it could unseat him and install the next eldest brother.
There was no paramount chief of all the Chagga, thus no central government. Some chiefdoms were more powerful than others, however, and
dominated groups of lesser allies.

As to land and labor, modern commercial practices did not exist. Land
was not a commodity. There was no market in land, and no acknowledged
variability of price, but, rather, a number of conventions about land trans-
fers. The Chagga distinguished between *hamba* (singular *kihamba*; plural *vihamba*), permanently held and inheritable cultivated plots usually

---

[2] C. Dundas, *Kilimanjaro and Its people* (London: Witherby, 1924); K. M. Stahl, *History of the Chagga People of Kilimanjaro* (The Hague: Mouton, 1964); S. Geiger Rogers, "The Search for Political Focus on Kilimanjaro: A History of Chagga Politics, 1916–1952, with Special Reference to the Cooperative Movement and Indirect Rule," Ph.D. thesis, University of Dar es Salaam, 1972; J. Samoff, *Tanzania: Local Politics and the Structure of Power* (Madison: University of Wisconsin Press, 1974); S. F. Moore, *Social Facts and Fabrications: "Customary" Law on Kilimanjaro 1880–1980* (Cambridge: Cambridge University Press, 1986); S. F. Moore and P. Purritt, *The Chagga and Meru of Tanzania* (London: International African Institute, 1977); *Tanganyika Notes and Records*, no. 64 (1965) (special issue on Kilimanjaro).

[3] Moore, *Social Facts*; Moore and Purritt, *Chagga and Meru*; D. Nurse, *Classification of the Chaga Dialects* (Hamburg: Buske, 1979). Chagga is spelled in many different ways. The forms the Chagga themselves use are Wachagga (plural) and Mchagga (singular), but in English the prefix is usually dropped.

[4] The best synthesis on Chagga precolonial society and economy is Moore, *Social Facts*, pp. 20–91.

planted with bananas, and *shamba*, plots planted with annual crops. *Shamba* tenure was temporary, though annually renewable until fallowing was necessary. A chief could call up his people for corvée labor as he saw fit. Corvée obligations included house building for the chief, defensive work, and work in the banana groves and millet fields.[5]

The history of the Kilimanjaro area seems to have consisted of a long sequence of small wars. The chiefdoms fought, settled their differences, and fought again. These wars were not disputes over land in its productive sense. In the nineteenth century, there was no shortage of land, and each chiefdom had more land than it could use productively, for labor was the scarce resource. It seems very unlikely that arable lands were taken or occupied in these wars. Raiding was for other purposes, probably to achieve or avoid political domination and to gain tribute and control over trade routes.[6]

Nineteenth-century Kilimanjaro was not an isolated, divided, inward-looking society, but has to be understood in terms of the wider political geography and history of East Africa. The area was commercially significant long before colonial rule. There were economic relations within and among the Chagga chiefdoms on the mountain slopes, there were contacts between the mountain and the areas immediately surrounding it, and there were relations between Kilimanjaro and the coast. The Chagga sold slaves and ivory and, probably more important, provisioned caravans. In the second half of the century, hundreds of men came to the southern slopes of the mountain all year round. The Chagga stocked caravans with food and beasts for the journey inland to Lake Victoria and points south or provided supplies for the return journey to the coast. This must have required a marked increase in food production, probably managed through the chief's powers over collective labor and by individual households.

All in all, the political and economic situation of the Chagga must have been reshaped by participation in external trade. This was not separated from the domestic economy nor segregated from local politics. The physical security of every household must have been intermittently threatened by raiding. The need for soldiers and for corvée labor for defense and food production required a considerable degree of organization. Chiefly

---

[5] The most important source on the precolonial Chagga is probably the German Lutheran missionary Bruno Gutmann, e.g., *Dichten und Denken der Dschagganeger* (Leipzig: Evangelisch-Lutherische Mission, 1909), and *Das Recht der Dschagga* (Munich: Beck, 1926). For Gutmann, see J. C. Winter, *Bruno Gutmann 1876–1966* (Oxford: Clarendon Press, 1979). See also Dundas, *Kilimanjaro*, and Stahl, *History*.

[6] Moore, *Social Facts*, p. 21.

office, and all that surrounded it, was transformed by monopolizing major forms of trade, assembling and redistributing wealth, calling on corvée labor, and commanding the warrior age grade. As Moore puts it: "It was raid or be raided, conquer or be conquered, once ivory, human beings, and cattle had become important items of exchange in impersonal transactions. Every Chagga household must have been involved, directly or indirectly."[7] When the Germans put an end to the slave trade and war, and when ivory trade caravans stopped coming through the region, the Chagga were ready for some other way to enter external markets. Coffee provided them with an opportunity to do so, and they seized it.

By the end of the German period, "every Chagga institution had been buffeted by the changes the Germans brought to the mountain. From the marriage bed to the public arena everything was disturbed and shaken."[8] In the early period, some of the force of German authority was extended to Chief Marealle of Marangu. In his heyday, up to 1904, the Germans made him chief of all of eastern Kilimanjaro. He became something of a maker of subordinate chiefs himself, and had a tremendous effect on internal Chagga politics. Marealle used his office to extract enormous numbers of cattle from subject chiefdoms, as tribute for himself and for Marangu. Marealle's activities were the most extreme example of the persistence of competition between chiefdoms for dominance over territory on Kilimanjaro in colonial times, although competition now occurred in the arena of administrative reorganization. Neither warfare nor alliance but the direct or indirect favor of the colonial government was the new source of power.[9]

Backed by the colonial presence, chiefs willing to cooperate with the Germans occupied new roles, which came to stimulate coffee growing. In particular, chiefs acted as labor recruiters and tax collectors. Men were mobilized to construct buildings and roads for the government and to work on settler lands. Pressed by hut taxes imposed from 1898 onward and by labor obligations that could be bought off with cash, as well as tempted to buy cattle, the Chagga were rapidly drawn further into the cash economy. First, they sold their labor. Then, little by little, following

---

[7] Ibid., p. 37.
[8] Ibid., p. 95. For German rule in Tanganyika, see J. Iliffe, *A Modern History of Tanganyika* (Cambridge: Cambridge University Press, 1979), chs. 4–7, and *Tanganyika under German Rule 1905–1912* (Cambridge: Cambridge University Press, 1969); J. Koponen, *Development for Exploitation; German Colonial Policies in Mainland Tanzania, 1884–1914* (Hamburg and Helsinki: LIT and Finnish Historical Society, 1995).
[9] Moore, *Social Facts*, pp. 96 ff.

the example of the missionaries, they began to plant coffee bushes in their banana gardens.[10]

The cultivation of coffee started slowly, and did not deeply affect Chagga society under German rule, though the ground was laid for dramatic changes after the First World War. Indigenous varieties of *robusta* had long featured in indigenous regional trade in the Lake Victoria area, although its cultivation, for example, in Bukoba, had not been extensive. No drink was made from it, as coffee beans were simply chewed for refreshment on journeys and in certain rituals.[11] There are conflicting accounts as to the introduction of *arabica* coffee, but it seems that Holy Ghost Fathers, Catholic missionaries, started planting it in the coastal area of Bagamoyo in 1877. From there, it was taken to hinterland mission stations, including Kilimanjaro, where the first mission stations were founded in 1891.[12] After an unpromising start at Kiloma mission, trees survived, and all mission stations on the mountain adopted the crop. At the Kibosho mission, for instance, the number of coffee plants increased from about 700 in 1900 to some 5,000 in 1910.[13]

It is not entirely clear how coffee planting spread among Kilimanjaro Africans, and what part missionaries played. It seems that the Holy Ghost Fathers were "reluctant to help the Chagga to grow coffee," but did distribute seedlings.[14] Fumba, chief of Kilema, was on record as coming to the station for some in 1901. Some dissident European colonists also provided seedlings. In Marangu, an Italian settler is said to have assisted chief Marealle's advisor Mawalla to plant coffee in 1902.[15] Additional support for Chagga coffee planting came from the settler-trader E. Th. Förster, "a peculiar mixture of the social idealist and the shrewd businessman."[16] Förster initially thought that mass production by Africans was "perfectly compatible with our great patriotic interests," although he later veered toward a more orthodox "master settlement" line. In any case, he distributed seedlings and bought Chagga coffee.[17] Among his

[10] Ibid., pp. 95 ff.

[11] T. S. Jervis, "A History of the Robusta Coffee in Bukoba," *Tanganyika Notes and Records* 8 (1939): 47–58.

[12] J. A. P. Kieran, "The Origins of Commercial Arabica Coffee Production in East Africa," *African Historical Studies* 2 (1969): 51–67; Koponen, *Development*, pp. 202f.

[13] Kieran, *Origins*, pp. 59–61.

[14] Ibid., p. 61.

[15] Geiger Rogers, "Political Focus," p. 165; Koponen, *Development*, p. 434f.

[16] Winter, *Gutman*, p. 53.

[17] E. Th Förster, "Die Siedlungen am Kilimandjaro und Meru," *Zeitschrift für Kolonialpolitik, Kolonialrecht und Kolonialwirtschaft* 9 (1907): 516–53, 728–43; and "Negerkulturen und

closest cooperators was Joseph Merinyo, who later recollected having begun to grow coffee in 1907. He was to become chief organizer of coffee planting among the Chagga during the 1920s.[18]

The first noteworthy commercial *arabica* farmers were a handful of chiefs and entrepreneurs, mainly, *akida*, or local agents of the colonial state.[19] In contrast, the general feeling among ordinary peasants was that coffee took too long to come into bearing to be worth the effort. By 1907, they had, at most, only a few dwarf holdings. "What has been achieved so far cannot be called people's cultivation but chiefs' cultivation," complained a writer in the settler press in 1909. According to this observer, coffee growers came from "the more intelligent, propertied class, such as chiefs and *akidas*," who alone possessed enough cattle and land.[20] Access to nonhousehold labor was another important factor.

However, new individual cultivators continued to appear. Coffee cultivation became most widespread at Marangu, whose chief Marealle was reported in 1909 to have made preparations to plant 15,000 coffee trees.[21] Mawale, a former *akida*, had actually planned 9,400 in 1913. At Mamba, the most successful farmer of ordinary rank, "a Christian called Davidi who had almost no help except his wife," possessed about 2,000 trees in 1912.[22] In 1913, a colonial investigator found six African farmers in Marangu and Mamba alone with over 1,000 trees, and many more with several hundred trees.[23] Cultivation also spread to Machame, Moshi, and the Shira Plateau. British officials in the 1920s estimated that the total number of coffee trees planted by Chagga at the end of German rule ranged from about 14,000 to over 88,000.[24]

The emergence of Chagga coffee growers complicated the labor situation on Kilimanjaro. In other regions with severe labor shortages, the government introduced the labor card system, beginning in the Usambara

Plantagenanbau am Kilimandjaro," *Deutsch-Ostafrikanische Zeitung*, Aug. 21, 1909. See also Koponen, *Development*, p. 435.

[18] J. Iliffe, "The Age of Improvement and Differentiation (1907–1945)," in I. N. Kimambo and A. Temu, eds., *A History of Tanzania* (Nairobi: East African Literature Bureau, 1969), p. 136. For Merinyo, see below.

[19] Iliffe, *Modern History*, pp. 209f. for *akida*.

[20] Förster, "Negerkulturen"; Koponen, *Development*, p. 435.

[21] Geiger Rogers, "Political Focus," p. 165.

[22] Koponen, *Development*, p. 435, quoting a German administrator in Moshi.

[23] J. Franke, "Zur Veränderung der wirtschaftlichen Verhältnisse bei den Dschagga am Kilimandscharo unter den Bedingungen der deutschen Kolonialherrschaft 1885–1916," *Jahrbuch des Museums für Völkerkunde zu Leipzig* 32 (1980): 189f.

[24] *Report on Tanganyika Territory to the League of Nations 1925*, p. 53, for the higher estimate, which seems to be correct. For other estimates, see Koponen, *Development*, p. 436.

Mountains in 1907. Every Usambara cultivator, except for government employees, had to obtain an official labor card. Its thirty squares were ticked off according to the number of days worked by the holder for European employers, including missionaries, at wages "normal in the locality." If a card was not filled within four months, the holder could be ascribed to public works, at less pay or none at all.[25]

For fear of violent Chagga reactions, the government delayed the introduction of this system in Kilimanjaro until 1912. However, troops were stationed there in 1908, to round up those refusing plantation employment and make them labor instead on public works.[26] Chagga coffee farmers were apparently exempted from plantation labor, but they were prohibited from employing other Chagga on the same terms as European employers. A missionary noted in 1913: "There are really industrious cultivators in the area who lay out small coffee plots for themselves and would enlarge these if they had more land and workers. At present they are almost entirely dependent on the help of their wives, who have quite sufficient to do without this." He suggested that such farmers be allowed to employ laborers "on the same conditions as other employers," meaning workers filling in their labor cards.[27] Not surprisingly, the district official turned down the suggestion. All available labor was needed for booming settler cash crop production, including much coffee.[28]

Land shortages and conflicts were not yet central problems at the end of the German period. In 1914, the Kilimanjaro area had only 105 to 115 male European settlers, who held 24,644 hectares of land, including 2,267 hectares that belonged to the missions.[29] Governor Rechenberg banned all further European settlement on Kilimanjaro in 1911 until a native reserve could be created "to protect the Chagga tribe... against uprooting and proletarianisation."[30] The most important stretch of cultivable land thus remained in Chagga hands. It consisted of a highland belt, about seventy miles long and five to eight miles wide, which ran at an altitude of 3,500 to 5,000 feet above sea level.[31] A good deal of

[25] Koponen, *Development*, pp. 400 ff.
[26] Iliffe, *Modern History*, p. 153.
[27] Quoted by ibid., p. 155.
[28] R. Tetzlaff, *Koloniale Entwicklung und Ausbeutung. Wirtschafts- und Sozialgeschichte Deutsch-Ostafrikas 1885–1914* (Berlin: Duncker and Humblot, 1970), pp. 117–55, for general information on European plantations.
[29] Geiger Rogers, "Political Focus," p. 171.
[30] Iliffe, *Modern History*, p. 144.
[31] David R. Brewin, "Kilimanjaro Agriculture," *Tanganyika Notes and Records* 64 (1965): 115.

this belt was suitable for coffee. Although the spread of coffee cultivation eventually changed the significance of land holding and Chagga land law, that transformation was not fully felt until well into the British colonial period. "The three decades of German colonial rule were just a beginning."[32]

Few early British colonial officials foresaw that coffee growing would soon create complex conditions, under which political and economic issues, both local and territorial, would become irrevocably intertwined. Chagga chiefs with different interests and positions, a rising Chagga counterelite, and a bitterly vocal group of white settlers came increasingly into conflict by the late 1920s. More than any other factor, the revival and rapid extension of Chagga coffee cultivation after the First World War determined the shape and nature of these conflicts.[33] After the British took charge, the cultivation of coffee increased steadily. Combined with a great growth of population, this produced a gradually intensifying shortage of land. From about 110,000 in 1900, the population increased to 289,000 in 1948 and 351,000 in 1957.[34] Kilimanjaro became a rural area with an urban density of population.

By the late 1920s, pressure on land had developed to such an extent as to worry British officials, as well as many Chagga. In 1929 a district officer from Bukoba, A. W. M. Griffith, was engaged to make a survey of the local land situation. He was to give attention both to indigenous customary rules and to the problem of land shortage, with an eye to determining whether land registration was possible. Griffith reported that the buying and selling of land was not yet permitted, and that the chiefs were against allowing it. In 1927, the chiefs had even gone so far as to appeal to the governor to ask him to prohibit commercial land transactions. This implies that the sale of land for cash had actually begun. The chiefs had good reason for their position on the matter: According to Griffith, "the control of all land which is not in beneficial occupation is tending to become a perquisite of the chief."[35] Chiefly prerogative, which in precolonial times was essentially an administrative control over unused and unoccupied land, had been converted into something more like a personal interest.

[32] Moore, *Social Facts*, p. 103.
[33] The following paragraphs draw heavily on Geiger Rogers, "Political Focus," pp. 234ff., and Moore, *Social Facts*, pp. 110ff.
[34] S. P. Maro, "Population and Land Resources in Northern Tanzania; The Dynamics of Change, 1920–1970," Ph.D. thesis, University of Minnesota, 1974.
[35] Rhodes House Library, Oxford (henceforth RHL), MSS.Afr. S.1001: A. W. M. Griffith, Chagga land tenure report, 1930, pp. 63, 88; Moore, *Social Facts*, p. 111.

Coffee had made unoccupied land valuable, and population growth had made it scarce. Even so, chiefs did not dare seize land once it had been planted with coffee.

A basic tenet of Chagga law was that a man who developed bush land, by planting trees in it, acquired a permanent interest in it. Bananas were the initial plant around which this doctrine was formulated. Then the rule was easily transferred to coffee and other tree crops.[36] Chiefs were now using their privileges of allocating unused land to give plots to their innumerable sons and other kinsmen. In essence, one could make out four large-scale processes relating to land use during the British period. First, open plots, earlier used for grazing in the populous *hamba* belt, progressively came into cultivation. Second, as more and more banana-growing lands were filled with coffee bushes, and the population continued to increase, the proportion of the diet involving produce from *shamba*, land used for annual crops, must have become larger. Third, *shamba* lands were gradually converted into *hamba* lands, permanently held and inheritable cultivated plots, as more and more households moved down the mountain. Fourth, a growing number of more prosperous landowners held scattered plots.[37]

Coffee and politics were intertwined on Kilimanjaro from the mid-1920s, when the Chagga coffee crop became large enough to generate a substantial aggregate income. Both Chagga chiefs and the colonial administration wanted to control coffee affairs. Over time, revenues from the taxation of coffee growers, eventually through a direct tax on coffee, came to swell the funds of the Kilimanjaro district treasury. During the British colonial period these funds were, to a great extent, expended locally on public institutions and public works, eventually putting Kilimanjaro's facilities far ahead of those of many other parts of Tanganyika. Moreover, legislative, administrative, and executive action repeatedly reorganized marketing and production.

The rapid development of the coffee crop was both a spontaneous growth from earlier beginnings and the result of government policy to encourage Africans to grow cash crops. Around 1920, a number of Chagga farmers began to clean and prune their neglected coffee trees and

[36] On Chagga land law, see Moore, *Social Facts*, and Moore and Purritt, *Chagga and Meru*.
[37] Moore, *Social Facts*; Michael von Clemm, "People of the White Mountain: the Interdependence of Political and Economic Activity amongst the Chagga in Tanganyika, with Special Reference to Recent Changes," D.Phil. thesis, Oxford University, 1962; Michael von Clemm, "Agricultural Productivity and Sentiment on Kilimanjaro," *Economic Botany* 18 (1964): 99–121.

eventually expanded their plots. District Commissioner Charles Dundas retrospectively noted: "...on taking a count I found that no less than 125,000 trees were being cultivated by natives, to say nothing of scores of thousands of seedlings which were readily purchased by Europeans. Further enquiry revealed that the profits of this cultivation unencumbered by wage bills, were such that it was becoming increasingly popular. I had no doubt in my mind that with visible evidence on every side the native not only could grow coffee, but could do so with profit, the cultivation was bound to become more general. That this assumption was justified is proved by the returns of 1922 when a further 50,000 trees were planted. In the following years no less than 300,000 were planted all of which were obtained from native seed beds."[38]

In 1922, Joseph Merinyo, who generally accompanied Dundas on his mountain tours, requested permission to start a nursery to supply interested farmers with coffee seedlings. Dundas agreed to the plan and seed was purchased from a European farmer in Arusha, where the price was considerably lower than in Moshi. This further increased Merinyo's prestige and reputation among the Chagga, and placed him in the forefront of coffee growers.[39] A nursery was established just above Merinyo's home near the site where the first Central School of Kilimanjaro was to be built in 1925. It soon attracted the attention of other Chagga chiefs, who requested that seed be obtained for them.[40]

D. C. Dundas played an important, though not decisive, role in the birth, early advancement, and organization of the Chagga coffee sector between 1922 and 1925. Once he had appreciated the extent to which the Chagga had already progressed by their own initiative and endeavor, Dundas saw, as did the Director of Agriculture with whom he conferred, that coffee was well suited to the needs of a people hard-pressed for land. Because it could be grown in the shade of the staple crop, bananas, it was an ideal crop for Kilimanjaro. In his Annual Report for 1922, he lauded the "remarkable keenness" of Chagga coffee farmers, pointing out that Chagga coffee was often equal in quality, if not superior, to that of neighboring Europeans. He asserted, not without a degree of competitive

[38] Tanzania National Archives, Dar es Salaam (hereafter TNA), 13060/203–204, p. 5, A. L. Pennington, Report on the KNPA, quoting from an original report by Dundas. See also Geiger Rogers, "Political Focus," p. 239.

[39] On the smaller coffee production of the neighboring Meru and Arusha regions, see T. Spear, *Mountain Farmers; Moral Economies of Land and Agricultural Development in Arusha and Meru* (Oxford: James Currey, 1997), pp. 139ff.

[40] Geiger Rogers, "Political Focus," p. 237.

pride, that he saw "no reason why the Wachagga should not cultivate a total of 36,000,000 trees," a number "equivalent to the total coffee cultivation of Kenya colony."[41] Dundas moved quickly to suppress forced plantation labor on Kilimanjaro, albeit much more slowly in regard to compulsory labor for chiefs and government. Not surprisingly, he became very unpopular with European settlers.[42]

Coffee growing divided the Chagga. Rombo, on the eastern slopes, was too dry for optimum production, and so supplied labor when other Chagga ceased to work for Europeans. Certain chiefdoms adopted coffee more enthusiastically than others. Differentiation among individuals also resulted. In 1930, only one man in three grew coffee. Of those who did, 96 percent owned less than 1,000 coffee trees, normally planted among the bananas in their *hamba* lands. The remainder, probably less than 500 men, owned nearly a hectare or more of coffee, often growing it in distinct plantations with hired labor.[43] These "emerging capitalists," in Iliffe's words, belonged to two groups. On the one hand, there were chiefs, who inherited large landholdings and commanded tributary labor in the early 1920s. Shangali Ndesuru, retired chief of Machame, was among the largest growers in 1932, with 12,682 trees.[44] On the other hand, there were educated Christians, such as Joseph Merinyo. Christians had access to European aid and were often receptive to change, while some planted coffee on spare *hamba*.

Soon land conflicts among the Chagga emerged. Coffee farmers rarely acquired land allotted by chiefs. Instead, they encroached on their neighbors' uncultivated land, enclosed and cultivated what was theoretically communal pasture, and opened new land to free *hamba* for coffee. Around 1927, they began to buy and sell land, demanding written titles and claiming that freehold tenure was a Chagga "tradition."[45] As land values increased and the law became a lottery, ambitious men realized that unless they claimed a piece of land immediately, none would be left. Disputes multiplied in local courts.[46] The Provincial Commissioner noted: "One

---

[41] TNA 1733, Annual Report Moshi District 1922, pp. 17–18.

[42] TNA 3864/2, Dundas to Chief Secretary, re Letter from the Kilimanjaro Planters Association (KPA) to the Secretary of State for the Colonies, dated June 12, 1924; Geiger Rogers, "Political Focus," p. 241.

[43] RHL, MSS.Afr. S.1001, A. W. M. Griffith, Chagga land tenure report, 1930; Iliffe, *Modern History*, p. 275.

[44] Iliffe, *Modern History*, p. 275.

[45] RHL, MSS.Afr. S.1001, A. W. M. Griffith, Chagga land tenure report, 1930; Clemm, "White Mountain"; Iliffe, *Modern History*; Moore, *Social Facts*.

[46] Iliffe, *Modern History*, p. 275; Maro, "Population," p. 174.

interesting feature of the Court work of the Moshi District is the great number of suits connected with claims for land. Prior to the introduction of coffee, the issues in regard to such claims were fairly clear cut, but the establishment of this valuable economic crop has resulted in considerable complications."[47]

At the same time, antagonism between Chagga and European farmers increased, as soon as it became obvious that the Chagga were making far more than a casual stab at growing coffee. Under the encouragement of Dundas, and the energetic and somewhat authoritarian supervision of Merinyo, Chagga farmers planted, pruned, and prepared their coffee for market. European planters, whose coffee plantations were surrounded by native *hamba*, watched the spread of Chagga coffee with alarm and began to express increasing anger. The formation of the Kilimanjaro Planters Association in 1923 gave the local settlers a forum in which to air their opinions and hear grievances. Agitation against Chagga coffee cultivation, initiated at the local level, was echoed in the European press at the territorial level and reinforced by interests sympathetic to settlers in Kenya and London.[48]

More generally, there was profound unease about emerging African rural capitalism, which was seen "not only as socially and politically dangerous but as somehow improper for Africans, like guitars or three-piece suits."[49] Even Dundas was skeptical. He wrote, "The aim has been to promote coffee growing as a peasant cultivation, each one working his plot by his own industry with the help of his women and children, so that a class of native employers is not evolved, or at any rate is restricted to a small number comprising only prominent persons. A plantation of 500 trees may with careful attention to their cultivation yield from 250 shillings up to 500 shillings per annum, which is as much as the ordinary native can make proper use of."[50] More specifically, settlers argued that the Chagga were incapable of growing *arabica*, despite obvious evidence to the contrary. They claimed that Chagga plots would be full of pests and diseases, which would spread to their own plantations. They also

---

[47] TNA, 19415, Annual Report Northern Province, 1939, p. 6. See also Moore, *Social Facts*, p. 154.
[48] See Geiger Rogers, "Political Focus," pp. 252ff.
[49] J. Iliffe, *The Emergence of African Capitalism* (London and Basingstoke: Macmillan, 1983), p. 37.
[50] Public Record Office, London, CO 691/70/379, Native Coffee Cultivation on Kilimanjaro, May 12, 1924.

alleged that theft of European coffee would continue, and that Chagga coffee would be of inferior quality.[51]

The real issue was labor. Without African workers, readily available on acceptable terms, European enterprises were doomed. The ability to grow coffee only exacerbated Chagga reluctance to work for settlers. They even resisted laboring for the colonial government, though they worked energetically for their own chiefs. The Chagga themselves probably experienced a labor shortage during the coffee harvest. When several chiefs raised objections to the use of child labor by settlers, the Provincial Commissioner commented that they probably wanted to use child labor at home.[52] A report for 1928 mentions that the chiefs of Marangu and Himo forbade children to pick settler coffee, because they wanted them to pick native coffee.[53]

Despite divergent interests, Chagga shopkeepers, traders, and coffee producers were successful in forging an alliance against South Asian competitors, of such importance as commercial intermediaries elsewhere in East Africa. One crucial factor here was the overlapping activities of many Chagga individuals who acted, for instance, as both traders and planters.

Cooperatives also played an important role. In January 1925, fifteen Chagga coffee planters formed the Kilimanjaro Native Planters' Association (KNPA) "to protect and promote the interests of the native coffee growers on the mountainside." Although sympathetic British administrative officers helped to create this organization, it was primarily based on local African initiative.[54] Joseph Merinyo soon became president. In 1926, the KNPA boasted 7,000 members. It was a parallel, nonchiefly, nongovernmental organization, with the whole mountain as its constituency. Its history has been extensively treated elsewhere, so that a brief summary suffices.[55] As the KNPA grew wealthier and came to have more members,

---

[51] TNA, 13060/203–234, Pennington Report, 4; Geiger Rogers, "Political Focus," p. 256.

[52] Moore, *Social Facts*, p. 122.

[53] Ibid. See also TNA, 10902, Northern Province Half-Yearly Report for Period Ending June 30, 1928, p. 9.

[54] TNA, 20378, Memorandum of Association, n.d.; R. J. M. Swynnerton and A. L. B. Bennett, *All about KNCU Coffee* (Moshi: Moshi Native Coffee Board, 1948), p. 11. See also S. Geiger Rogers, "The Kilimanjaro Native Planters Association: Administrative Responses to Chagga Initiatives in the 1920s," *Transafrican Journal of History* 4 (1974): 94–114.

[55] Geiger Rogers, "The Kilimanjaro Native Planters Association" and "Political Focus"; Moore, *Social Facts*; Iliffe, *Modern History*; G. Erdmann, *Jenseits des Mythos: Genossenschaften zwischen Mittelklasse und Staatsverwaltung in Tanzania und Kenia* (Freiburg: ABI, 1996), pp. 72ff.

chiefs began to see it both as a political competitor and as a repository of wealth that they wanted to control. Colonial officials, in their turn, attempted to bring the KNPA under administrative control. After intense struggles and debates, the KNPA survived as a separate body and was not, as planned, taken over by a new central council of chiefs. However, the collapse of the coffee price in 1929 brought about the collapse of the KNPA.[56]

The KNPA was dissolved, reorganized, and replaced by the Kilimanjaro Native Cooperative Union (KNCU).[57] Although coffee brought renewed prosperity for a while, there was another sudden price fall in 1934–35, and the KNCU could not even cover payments already advanced to growers. Rioting broke out in several chiefdoms, and the buildings of a few local branches of the KNCU were destroyed. Some leaders of the anti-KNCU movement were arrested, sentenced by the courts, and even deported. The Native Coffee Ordinance of 1937 established Native Coffee Boards as part of the administration. They were empowered to order all "native" coffee to be sold to them or to any agency they might designate. In November 1937, the Moshi Native Coffee Board was established, and it designated the KNCU its agent. Further dissent was averted, because coffee prices rose by 30 percent from mid-1938, and the mood changed. Indeed, the KNCU emerged stronger than ever.

The cash crop boom of the early 1950s dominated the postwar period. Between 1948 and 1954, Kilimanjaro coffee prices rose from £328 to £582 per tonne.[58] A British administrator noted in 1951: "Coffee is bringing great wealth to the Chagga and, inevitably, inflation on the mountain, and fewer Chagga than ever are prepared to go out and work. For despite land shortage the Chagga are economically independent and with internal trade and transport on the mountain in their hands, cash tends to circulate from hand to hand instead, as elsewhere in the Territory, of rapidly passing into the hands of non-native traders."[59]

On Kilimajaro, evidence of unequal land distribution abounded. P. M. Njau, a Chagga politician, identified three classes living on *hamba*

[56] TNA, 26034, Report P. C. Northern Province to Chief Secretary, Aug. 25, 1931; Geiger Rogers, "Kilimanjaro Native Planters Association," pp. 103ff.
[57] RHL MSS.Afr. s.1047, Lionel A. W. Vickers-Haviland, Note on the KNUC and its organization, March 31, 1937; on the KNUC, see, esp., Geiger Rogers, "Political Focus," pp. 509ff.; Erdmann, *Jenseits des Mythos*, pp. 79ff.; Iliffe, *Modern History*, pp. 279–81; Swynnerton and Bennett, *KNCU Coffee*. See also D. M. P. McCarthy, *Colonial Bureaucracy and Creating Underdevelopment: Tanganyika 1919–1940* (Ames: University of Iowa Press, 1982), ch. 8.
[58] Iliffe, *Modern History*, p. 453. This is a metric ton of 1,000 kilos, or 2,204.6 pounds.
[59] RHL MSS.Afr. s.1461, P. H. Johnston, Notes on the Moshi District, n.d. [1951].

lands in 1949: those who simply lived there, those who sought paid work every month, and those who wished to have large grain farms as their own property.[60] One researcher found that "a very few Chagga, probably mostly members of ruling clans ... have single holdings of considerable size – 20–40 acres of coffee; 50–100 acres of lowland maize fields; 200–2,000 acres of grazing land."[61] A survey of Machame chiefdom in 1961 showed that the size of *hamba* varied from less than 4,000 square meters to four hectares, the average being slightly over one hectare.[62] At the other extreme, 6,615 Chagga were reckoned to be landless in 1949, although most of them, Iliffe suggests, were young men awaiting an inheritance.[63] At the end of the colonial period, land on Kilimanjaro was mortgaged, sold over the owner's head by foreclosing creditors, and used as a security for government loans.[64] In 1946 already, the Chagga Council formally declared that a *hamba* "is a freehold property with which the owner can do whatever he likes."[65]

Part of the income from coffee was invested in children's education. Chagga coffee farmers sent 90 percent of their children to school in 1956.[66] They went to Lutheran, Catholic, or Native Authority primary schools, which dotted the mountainside. Quite a few Chagga children went to government secondary schools and to Makerere College.[67] This became more marked after Thomas Marealle, the highly educated grandson of the famous chief Marealle I, was elected as paramount chief of the Chagga in 1952.[68] Land and coffee played an important role in his

[60] TNA, 5/584, Njau, Kilimanjaro Union, n.d. [July 1949]. See also Iliffe, *Modern History*, p. 458.
[61] Quoted by Iliffe, *Modern History*, p. 458; see also TNA 5/20/16, Memorandum, District Commissioner Moshi, Sept. 11, 1953.
[62] Clemm, "Agricultural Productivity," p. 104. See also Roy Beck, *An Economic Study of Coffee-Banana Farms in the Machama Central Area, Kilimanjaro District, Tanganyika 1961* (Dar es Salaam: USAID Mission to Tanganyika, 1963).
[63] Maro, "Population," p. 130.
[64] RHL, MSS.Afr. s.1001 (2), T. F. Figgis, A Report on the Present State of Chagga Land Tenure Practice, 1958.
[65] Quoted by Iliffe, *Modern History*, p. 459. See also Clemm, "White Mountain," ch. 15. On the land problem in Kilimanjaro immediately after 1945, see also RHL MSS.Afr. s.592, Sir Mark Wilson, Report of the Arusha-Moshi Lands Commission, Jan. 15, 1947.
[66] Iliffe, *Modern History*, p. 445.
[67] See TNA, 5/9/19, Education Tabora School; TNA 5/9/I, List "Tanganyika Students at Makerere College from Moshi District," 1954.
[68] On Marealle, see A. Eckert, "'I do not wish to be a tale teller': Afrikanische Eliten in British-Tanganyika. Das Beispiel Thomas Marealle," in A. Eckert and G. Krüger, eds., *Lesarten eines globalen Prozesses; Quellen und Interpretationen zur Geschichte der*

campaign. He promised that he would do away with the coffee tax, that Chagga *hamba* would be safer, and that more land would be provided for all.[69] Coffee revenues were partly invested in the construction of new schools and in scholarships for younger Chagga. Coffee even played an important role in Marealle's eventual fall. Declining coffee prices, along with other factors, fueled a campaign against him in the late 1950s, which ended in his loss of the paramountcy on the eve of Tanganyika's independence.

Coffee Growing among the Bamiléké of Cameroon

The Grassfields, today divided between the Bamiléké region of Francophone Cameroon and the neighboring Bamenda region of Anglophone Cameroon, served for centuries as a source of slaves for the Atlantic trade and as a labor reservoir for parts of the Bight of Biafra. The slave trade does not seem to have depleted the population, since slaves were mostly insiders, rather than being captured through destructive raiding and warfare.[70] However, land became a scarce resource in several Bamiléké chiefdoms, as only enclosed areas constituted a safe environment for women to grow food crops without being kidnapped. Thus, large stretches of arable land were not utilized.[71]

The term Bamiléké is a twentieth-century construct.[72] For a long time, most Bamiléké identified only with their particular chiefdoms and were often barely able to understand one another's dialects. A Bamiléké ethnic consciousness emerged in the course of the colonial and early postcolonial era, although the genesis of such an identity has not yet been adequately studied. Today nearly a million Bamiléké are estimated to live in a little over 2,000 square miles. There are around a hundred chiefdoms, differing greatly in size. They federate unrelated descent groups under the

europäischen Expansion (Hamburg and Münster: LIT, 1998), pp. 172–86; Geiger Rogers, "Political Focus"; Clemm, "White Mountain."

[69] Geiger Rogers, "Political Focus," p. 891.

[70] J.-P. Warnier, "Histoire du peuplement et genèse des paysages dans l'ouest camerounais," *Journal of African History* 25 (1984): 395–410; J.-P. Warnier, "Traite sans raids au Cameroun," *Cahiers d'Etudes Africaines* 29 (1989): 5–32.

[71] J. H. B. den Ouden, "Incorporation and Changes in the Composite Household: The Effects of Coffee Introduction and Food Crop Commercialization in Two Bamiléké Chiefdoms," in C. Presvelou and S. Spijkers-Zwart, eds., *The Household, Women and Agricultural Development* (Wageningen: H. Veenmann and Zonen BV, 1980), p. 45.

[72] The term is probably mentioned for the first time in *Deutsches Kolonialblatt* 16 (1905): 501. See also Institut des Sciences Humaines, Yaoundé (hereafter ISH), P1 GEA III 642, Département de la Ménoua. Hypothèse sur l'origine et signification du mot Bamiléké, March 29, 1944.

leadership of a council of clan and lineage elders, or ward heads, presided over by a first among equals, variously called *fon* or *mfe*, glossed as "chief" or "king." In the past, chiefs exercised considerable control over the lives of their subjects, whether at home or further afield.

The idiosyncratic social structure of the Bamiléké has long fascinated social scientists.[73] Bamiléké society is highly stratified and inegalitarian, but, despite social hierarchy and chiefly power, people demonstrate a striking degree of individual dynamism. That said, the success of a minority of men has been made possible only by disinheriting younger men and by employing women as an agricultural work force without formal remuneration. The few men who have achieved success have done so at the expense of the majority of junior migrants. The driving force in Bamiléké economic dynamism is the power of male household heads, especially chiefs, to compel younger men to postpone marriage and sexual gratification until a late age or, in many cases, forever. To marry and gain authority, junior lineage members must work hard to accumulate wealth. In so doing, they exploit those in a lower position on the social ladder, which, until the dawn of the twentieth century, included selling them into slavery.

High population density, acute scarcity of land, a lack of promotion prospects, and chiefly abuses in recruiting labor are among the factors that have contributed to an increasingly rapid rate of emigration. Especially since the 1930s, young migrants have headed for southern plantations and towns. In the period between around 1930 and around 1950, over 100,000 people are estimated to have left their homelands.[74] In independent Cameroon, the Bamiléké have displayed business dynamism

[73] See, esp., J.-P. Warnier, *L'Esprit d'entreprise au Cameroun* (Paris: Karthala, 1993). To mention only a few others among an armada: R. Delarozière, "Les Institutions politiques et sociales des populations dites Bamiléké," *Etudes Camerounaises* 25–28 (1949); C. Tardits, *Contribution à l'étude des populations bamiléké de l'ouest Cameroun* (Paris: Berger-Levrault, 1960); J. Hurault, *La Structure sociale des Bamiléké* (Paris: Mouton, 1962); J. H. B. den Ouden, "In Search of Personal Mobility: Changing Interpersonal Relations in Two Bamiléké Chiefdoms," *Africa* 57 (1987): 3–27; E. Rohde, *Chefferie Bamiléké – Traditionelle Herrschaft und Kolonialsystem* (Hamburg and Münster: LIT, 1990); Ch.-H. Pradelles de Latour, *Ethnopsychoanalyse en pays bamiléké* (Paris: E.P.E.L, 1991); D. Malaquais, *Structures du pouvoir: Architectures du pays bamiléké* (Paris: Karthala, 2002).

[74] For a general outline, see J.-L. Dongmo, *Le Dynamisme Bamiléké*, 2 vols. (Yaoundé: Ceper, 1981); R. Joseph, *Radical Nationalism in Cameroon* (Oxford: Clarendon Press, 1977); Jean-Claude Barbier et al., *Migrations et développement: La Région du Moungo au Cameroun* (Paris: ORSTOM, 1983); Warnier, *L'Esprit d'entreprise*. On Bamiléké rural entrepreneurship in the Mungo region, see A. Eckert, "African Rural Entrepreneurs and Labour in the Cameroon Littoral," *Journal of African History* 40 (1999): 109–26.

across the whole country.[75] Their rise from a subordinate position has created resentment and is a critical source of interethnic tensions.[76]

Volcanic soils make the Bamiléké region very fertile, and propitious for growing a wide variety of crops, notably, coffee, tea, maize, cocoyams (taro), potatoes, groundnuts, plantains, bananas, and assorted vegetables. The highlands are also suitable for raising pigs, goats, poultry, and dwarf cattle.[77] During the German period, coffee production was small, for it was grown with little success by a few German planters in the humid coastal areas.[78] In the western highlands, German economic interests were weak. Concession companies, such as the Gesellschaft Nordwest-Kamerun, played a minor role, and there was no evidence of coffee growing.[79]

During the first decade after the First World War, which ended German rule in Cameroon, the French promoted African rural capitalism. This was to achieve an effective *mise en valeur* of their mandate, since the former German plantations were in the British mandate.[80] French enthusiasm for cash crop planting also derived from the assumption that it would lead to the *embourgeoisement* of a significant number of Cameroonians, who would constitute a social anchor for French rule.[81] In the Bamiléké region, in particular, French economic policy was far from clear. The central problem was conflicts arising from the scarcity of land. On

---

[75] D. Miaffo and J.-P. Warnier, "Accumulation et ethos de la notabilité chez les Bamiléké," in P. Geschiere and P. Konings, eds., *Itinéraires d'accumulation au Cameroun* (Paris: Karthala, 1993), pp. 33–69.

[76] See, among others, J.-F. Bayart, *L'Etat au Cameroun* (Paris: Presse de la Fondation Nationale de Sciences Politiques, 1979); A. Mehler, *Kamerun in der Ära Biya* (Hamburg: Institut für Afrikakunde, 1993); M. Krieger and J. Takougang, *African State and Society in the 1990s: Cameroon's Political Crossroads* (Boulder and London: Westview, 1998).

[77] P. Capot-Rey et al., *Les Structures agricoles de l'ouest du Cameroun oriental* (Yaoundé: Ministère de l'Agriculture, 1968).

[78] H. R. Rudin, *Germans in the Cameroons 1884–1914* (New York: Greenwood, 1968), pp. 273f.

[79] K. Hausen, *Deutsche Kolonialherrschaft in Afrika: Wirtschaftsinteressen und Kolonialverwaltung in Kamerun vor 1914* (Zürich and Freiburg: Atlantis, 1970); J. Ballhaus, "Die Landkonzessionsgesellschaften," in H. Stoecker, ed., *Kamerun unter deutscher Kolonialherrschaft* (Berlin: VEB, 1968), vol. 2, pp. 99–179.

[80] Walter Herth, "Mise en valeur' und Weltwirtschaftskrise: Koloniale Entwicklungspolitik in Kamerun unter französischer Herrschaft, 1916–1938," unpublished thesis, Zürich University, 1988.

[81] Archives Nationales, Section Outre-Mer, Aix-en-Provence (henceforth ANSOM), Série géo., C.31, Dos.293, Letters Governor Marchand to Colonial Minister, June 18 and Oct. 29, 1923; Joseph, *Radical Nationalism*, pp. 126f.; J. Guyer, "The Food Economy and French Colonial Rule in Central Cameroon," *Journal of African History* 19 (1978): 577.

the one hand, improved medical care led to rapid population growth, causing higher population densities. On the other hand, the commercialization of agriculture caused changes in the accessibility of land for individuals.

In his annual report addressed to the League of Nations, the Chef de Circonscription of Dschang, Chapoulie, outlined a dramatic situation in 1925. In every chiefdom between Dschang and the Noun Valley, sections of the population were going to starve due to land scarcity. The physical appearance of the people indicated whether or not a region provided enough land for an individual: "We notice that the indigenous people of those chiefdoms with plentiful land usually are strongly built, full of muscles ... whereas natives of chiefdoms suffering from scarcity in land are in poor health, ailing, ... often deformed."[82]

Aside from an increasing willingness to stand up for their claim to land, if necessary in a colonial court, many Bamiléké chose the "exit option." Demographic statistics indicate that by 1937, nearly 30,000 Bamiléké, or about one-twelfth of the total population, had left to make a living, either in the neighboring Mungo region or in the cities of Douala and Yaoundé. The French administration reacted between 1925 and 1945 by resettling Bamiléké in less populated neighboring areas, albeit with little success.[83]

Coffee has been the single most important export highland crop since its introduction in the mid-1920s, but this aggravated the land problem.[84] Between 1927 and 1933, the French administration opted for growing coffee by integrating it into existing smallholder production in the Bamiléké area. As the Chef de Circonscription of Dschang put it in 1929, these should be "small individual farms, exclusively run by family

---

[82] ANSOM, AFOM, C.928, Dos.2903, rapport annuel à la SDN, Dschang 1925, ch. 6. See also Archives Nationales, Yaoundé (henceforth ANY), APA 11804/F, Rapports de Tournées, July 19–26 and Aug. 12–22, 1936; ANY APA 11809/E, Rapport de tournée, March 21 to April 28, 1938.

[83] E. Rohde, "'Projet Rive Gauche du Noun': The Miscarriage of Bamiléké Settlement Projects under French Administration in Bamoun (Cameroon)," in R. Debusmann and S. Arnold, eds., *Land Law and Land Ownership in Africa: Case Studies from Colonial and Contemporary Cameroon and Tanzania* (Bayreuth: Bayreuth African Studies, 1996), pp. 203–21.

[84] E. Rohde, *Grundbesitz und Landkonflikte in Kamerun: Der Bedeutungswandel von Land in der Bamiléké-Region während der europäischen Kolonisation* (Hamburg and Münster: LIT, 1997), pp. 111–80 and passim. See also N. M. Mbapndah, "Grassfield Chiefs and Political Change in Cameroon, c. 1884–1966," Ph.D dissertation, Boston University, 1985, pp. 144–222. The following paragraphs owe much to these monographs. My thanks go to E. Rohde and D. Malaquais for drawing my attention to relevant archival sources and unpublished manuscripts.

labor."[85] Chapoulie also tried to transform so-called customary land rights into individual rights, through registration and the issuing of land titles.[86] Smallholder coffee production proved to be extremely successful. In 1931 alone, Bamiléké growers obtained more than 300,000 *arabica* plants from the government coffee nursery in Dschang.[87] In addition, an unknown number of plants were stolen or privately grown. For a time, many Bamiléké were gripped by "coffee euphoria," and French administrative reports regularly mentioned the "unbridled enthusiasm of the indigenous planters."[88]

From 1933, the colonial authorities introduced a number of restrictive ordinances to control or even deter mass involvement in coffee cultivation, although coffee output continued to rise.[89] Official explanations for this abrupt change in coffee policy included the fear that Africans might not manage their farms properly. This could spread plant diseases, with disastrous consequences. Already in 1930, French agronomists feared that unrestricted coffee growing would have negative effects on the quality of the crop, because of greater susceptibility to infestation, and asked for control and regulation. Moreover, the French argued that uncontrolled coffee cultivation could lead to a reduction in the production of food crops, with the attendant risk of food shortages, hunger, and even famine. In its annual report to the League of Nations in 1935, the colonial government emphasized this alleged danger, stating that "... the question of food... remains of prime importance to the mandatory power."[90]

The restriction of coffee production was also stressed in administrative correspondence, often accompanied by a paternalistic discourse, alleging that the authorities were protecting the Bamiléké farmer against himself. One agricultural report stated: "Left on his own, the Bamiléké peasant would cover the land with coffee plants. As his agricultural knowledge is not yet sufficient, these farms, poorly maintained, would constitute a

[85] ANY, APA 11978, Procès verbal de la 2ème session du Conseil de Notables pour l'année 1929, Nov. 11, 1929. See also Rohde, *Grundbesitz*, p. 128.
[86] ANY, APA 11978, Procès verbal de la 2ème session du Conseil de Notables pour l'année 1929, Nov. 11, 1929.
[87] ANY, APA 11825/H, Subdivision Dschang, Rapport trimestriel: 1er trimestre 1930; Rapport annuel à la SDN 1931, p. 46.
[88] ANY, APA 11825/H, Subdivision Dschang: Rapport trimestriel: 1er trimestre 1930. Bulletin agricole. See also Rohde, *Grundbesitz*, p. 130.
[89] N. M. Mbapndah, "French Colonial Agricultural Policy, African Chiefs, and Coffee Growing in the Cameroun Grassfields, 1920–1960," *International Journal of African Historical Studies* 27, no. 1 (1994): 41–58.
[90] *Rapport Annuel à la SDN 1935*, p. 61.

reservoir of diseases. The results would be the complete destruction of the coffee trees as well as famine."[91] The aim was now to leave coffee cultivation mainly in the hands of a small elite of European settlers and African chiefs and notables. The rest of the Grassfields population was to grow food crops to provision the major towns and other areas where food was in short supply. Finally, given the manpower of the Grassfields, the region was to serve as a labor reservoir for both private and public enterprises.

In the early 1930s, European growers in the Grassfields and in the neighboring Mungo region began to realize that they could not compete on favorable terms with African farmers. The increase in cash cropping implied a shortage of labor, especially in the thinly populated Mungo region. Thus, European farmers began to put pressure on the colonial administration to restrict the number of Africans who took up coffee farming. They had some success. To be sure, African production of *arabica* rose from 4.5 percent to 30 percent of the total for Dschang and Noun between 1934 and 1941, that is, from 4.7 tons to 534 tons. However, this was still well below the 1,300 tons of coffee produced by a handful of Europeans in the Noun region in 1941. That said, the less lucrative production of *robusta* remained in the hands of Bamiléké farmers, who produced 97 percent of the 306 tons of *robusta* produced in the subdivisions of Bafang and Bangangté in 1941.[92]

European coffee planters enjoyed limited success in recruiting labor, despite their recourse to the *indigénat* system. This legal code relating to persons of "native status," technically, *sujets* rather than *citoyens*, permitted French administrators to both try cases and impose summary disciplinary punishment. In Cameroon, as elsewhere in French Africa, the *indigénat* became a wide-ranging instrument in the hands of officials to employ "natives" as they saw fit, sometimes for European plantations.[93] Workers, usually put off by scanty pay and distressing working conditions on European plantations, were simply conscripted into work gangs by the administrators and local chiefs.[94]

---

[91] ANY, APA 12039, Région Bamiléké, Rapport Annuel 1945, p. 14. See also Rohde, *Grundbesitz*, p. 133.

[92] ISH, P1 CHA, Rapport semestriel 1934, p. 19; ANY, APA 11742, Rapport annuel 1942; Rohde, *Grundbesitz*, p. 135.

[93] R. L. Buell, *The Native Problem in Africa*, vol. 2 (New York: Macmillan, 1928).

[94] Joseph, *Radical Nationalism*, pp. 122f.; Barbier et al., *Migrations*, pp. 85ff. More generally, see Léon Kaptué, *Travail et main d'oeuvre sous régime français, 1916–1952* (Paris: Harmattan, 1986).

In 1933 and 1935, the French administration issued two decrees: for the registration of coffee farms and for the regulation of coffee cultivation. All owners of coffee farms were requested to report to the nearest agricultural station and to provide details about their farms. The information required included the location and condition of the farms, the number of coffee trees planted, and the variety and age of trees on farms and in nurseries. Thereafter, any persons who wanted to cultivate coffee had to submit certain specifications and details about the planned farms and could begin work only with the express permission of the divisional officer. Any violations of the above prescriptions were punishable in terms of the *indigénat* code.[95] The French administration was quite strict in enforcing these measures. Thus, a number of coffee farms were destroyed because they had been set up without permission.[96]

Through this coffee policy, the French hoped to create a landed Bamiléké bourgeoisie, consisting mainly of chiefs already integrated into the administrative system. The French therefore provided such chiefs with economic privileges, granting them preferential concessions for coffee plantations. Chiefs were thought to be more qualified and capable of using specific techniques of coffee growing. As one report put it, "According to various experiences made in this region until today, the Bamiléké is not yet prepared to master the difficult cultivation of Arabica... only chiefs should be authorized who are intelligent enough to understand and active enough to supervise."[97] More important, however, was the fact that the administration linked the allocation of coffee licenses to two preconditions: availability of labor and access to land.[98] With a few exceptions, only chiefs and notables met these criteria. Thanks to polygynous marriages, they had access to a sufficient number of wives as workers, and they had the possibility of recruiting various subalterns to plant and prune.

Moreover, chiefs were able to convert their traditional right of allocating land into land ownership, sanctioned by French law. A decree of August 20, 1927, provided for recognition of customary rights of land

[95] *Rapport annuel à la SDN 1933*, 194ff.; *Rapport annuel à la SDN 1935*, 176ff. There were also later decrees, e.g., in *Journal Officiel du Cameroun*, 411, June 1, 1937, pp. 441ff. See also ISH, P1 CHA, Note sur la Circonscription de Dschang, Rapport semestriel par Chapoulie 1934, p. 16.

[96] See, e.g., ANY, APA 11804/A, Rapport de tournée, Sept. 10–18, 1937.

[97] ANY, APA 11621/B, Chef de Circonscription Dschang to Chef Subdivision Dschang, May 28, 1932.

[98] ANY, APA 10044, Rapport annuel, Dschang, 1933. See also Rohde, *Grundbesitz*, pp. 136ff.

(*constatation*), which was intended to be a "preliminary stage" of the "Europeanization" of African modes of land ownership. It was supplemented by a decree of July 21, 1932, providing for full French legal registration of landed property. The biggest coffee farms, often numbering from 5,000 to 15,000 trees and covering more than five hectares, belonged almost exclusively to chiefs or notables.[99]

Chiefs thus misused their traditional powers, together with the new authority delegated to them by the French, to monopolize land for their individual economic enjoyment. They tended to interpret local customary law in their favor, and often considered vacant land within their chiefdom to be their private property.[100] Moreover, chiefs often met their labor needs with unpaid forced workers. To run a large-scale coffee farm, a planter had to be politically well connected to be able to attract laborers from their own farms and protect them from being drafted into other kinds of obligatory work. Because of the great powers given to chiefs, and the emphasis placed on manifestations of agricultural progress, people with political links were able to employ the rural population on their plantations without cash remuneration. Mathias Djoumessi, chief of Foréké-Dschang, was the exception confirming the rule. In 1937, he became the first chief in the region to pay workers on his coffee farms. Because he offered relatively high wages, he successfully attracted labor at the expense of the administration.[101] However, most chiefs kept *prestataires* before and after the ten days' work owed to the government, and used their *auxiliaires* on the plantations when there was no other work for them to do. Moreover, they were able to keep a permanent labor force of men, who were escaping recruitment or the extortion of their own chiefs and European farmers by taking refuge as clients of another chief.

No single issue more sorely tested the relationship between the colonial administration, chiefs, and the rest of the population in the immediate post–World War II period than the struggle to eliminate colonial restrictions over the cultivation and marketing of coffee.[102] One Bamiléké

---

[99] ANY, APA 10087/A: Rapport de tournée, Oct. 27 to Nov. 12, 1941, Annex, 1–6; ANY, APA 11809/B, Rapport de tournée, August 1938, p. 7.

[100] M. O. Laurent, "Pouvoirs et société dans le pays Bamiléké: La Chefferie Bamiléké face au changement social dans la région de Banka-Bafang," unpublished thesis, University of Paris V, 1981.

[101] Mbapndah, "French Colonial Agricultural Policy," p. 57.

[102] Philippe Darge, "Le Café au Cameroun (Production, Commercialisation, Problèmes Humains)," mémoire, Ecole Nationale de la France d'Outre-Mer, Paris 1958/59 (in ANSOM, FM 3Ecol/142/d8).

smallholder declared, "I want to be authorized to plant coffee, in order to allow myself to buy a helmet and new wives," a quote that summarizes the aspirations of many peasants in the Grassfields around 1945.[103] In 1948, progressive Bamiléké politicians founded the Coopérative de Production de Collecte et de Vente, a coffee marketing cooperative, as an important step in this struggle. De jure, French coffee legislation remained in force until 1955. On the ground, however, officials started to liberalize coffee production earlier. In 1951, for instance, they granted 6,717 licenses for the creation of small coffee farms of 500 *arabica* trees in Mbouda subdivision.[104] Between 1947 and 1959, the area in coffee increased from 4,593 to 28,015 hectares.[105]

This "second coffee boom" accelerated a number of important changes, notably, by reinforcing the individual ownership of land. Chiefs and lineage heads became extremely reluctant to allocate land to others, in order to preserve sufficient space for their own coffee farms. The earlier interest of a chief in linking individuals to him by giving them a plot of land was replaced by the desire to make money by growing coffee.[106]

The main victims of these transformations were young men and women. For young males, it became extremely difficult to establish themselves as coffee farmers, because they had no access to land. In many chiefdoms, mixed-cropping now gained acceptance, with coffee and food crops in the same fields. Women did all the work, including picking coffee, but kept only the income from selling food crops.[107] However, as the space reserved for coffee was gradually extended at the expense of food crops, it became more difficult for women to supply the household with food. Regular complaints in local newspapers went unheard.[108] Neither young males nor women simply accepted their marginalization. Both groups were among the main supporters of the radical nationalist party, Union des Populations du Cameroun. During the civil war in the Bamiléké area,

[103] ANY, APA 12039, Région Bamiléké, Rapport Annuel 1945, Situation Politique, 3. See also Rohde, *Grundbesitz*, p. 159.
[104] E. Noubissi, "La Caféiculture dans la Menoua, 1930–1960: Esquisse d'une analyse historique," M.A. thesis, University of Yaoundé, 1988, p. 107; Rohde, *Grundbesitz*, p. 163.
[105] Dongmo, *Le Dynamisme*, vol. 1, pp. 130–2.
[106] Jan B. H. den Ouden, "Changes in Land Tenure and Land Use in a Bamiléké Chiefdom in Cameroon, 1900–1980: An Historical Analysis of Changes in Control over People," in *Essays in Rural Sociology in Honour of R. A. J. van Lier* (Wageningen: Agricultural University, 1981), pp. 171–261.
[107] Ibid.
[108] *Le Bamiléké* 12 (April 1956): 8. See also Rohde, *Grundbesitz*, p. 176.

between 1958 and 1962, they took part in burning a number of coffee farms.[109]

Conclusion

The two cases presented here are variations on a larger theme of African coffee farming in areas of high population density and intense European competition. Coffee started as a "chief's crop" and remained such for a long time, but smallholder production gradually expanded. In the Bamiléké area, especially, the colonial administration, pushed by white farmers, then imposed a policy that favored chiefs and notables. Moreover, many chiefs were able to manipulate their privileged access to land and labor for cash crop production. Due to dense population, land scarcity, and the enthusiasm for coffee, Europeans regularly alleged that food security was under threat, even though the evidence for this was slight or nonexistent. Another aspect of the story, only briefly mentioned here, is that many significant political associations and leading individuals of the late colonial period had their roots in coffee cooperatives, which were created to defend local African interests. Finally, the history of coffee in the Kilimanjaro and Grassfields regions provides some important general insights into colonialism in Africa. It highlights problematic interrelationships among the colonial state, white settlers, and local elites. Coffee also provides excellent examples of the ways in which cash crop production led to the privatization of land rights and the development of land and labor markets.

[109] For the UPC rebellion, see Laurent, "Pouvoirs"; Malaquais, *Structures*; Joseph, *Radical Nationalism*.

13

Smaller Is Better

A Consensus of Peasants and Bureaucrats in Colonial Tanganyika

Kenneth R. Curtis

The town of Bukoba has seen better days. Located on the shore of Lake Victoria in the northwestern corner of Tanzania, Bukoba has suffered from years of civil war in neighboring Uganda and Rwanda and from decades of neglect by the distant government in Dar es Salaam. Following German rule from 1889 to 1916 and a British mandate to 1961, this small town was exceptionally prosperous at independence, as were the Haya farmers in the surrounding countryside.[1] Bukoba was the largest coffee-producing region in the country, and investments in trade and education seemed to auger well for the future. Fate has been unkind to Bukoba since 1961. Its coffee economy now supports a tedious status quo of just getting by, rather than a dream of sustained development. Farming is carried out on a small scale by many peasant families, and few have the resources to supply modest inputs that could make a difference to coffee output, such as pumps, fertilizers, and pesticides. This type of small-scale, undercapitalized, market-oriented agriculture is one of the principal legacies of colonialism in rural Africa.

This chapter emphasizes the ability of Haya to make their voices heard and influence the way that coffee was integrated into their society. For all the tensions in the relationship between colonial state and peasants, there was an underlying consensus. The basic unit of coffee production would remain small; outsiders, whether European or South Asian, would not be

---

[1] In this chapter, Bukoba District encompasses what are now the Bukoba and Muleba Districts. A hundred years ago, Haya was a derisive name for island-dwelling fishing folk, but it is well accepted today. The correct forms are Muhaya (person), Bahaya (persons), Buhaya (place), and Luhaya (language).

allowed to invest in production; and land and labor would not themselves be transformed into easily marketable commodities.

Coffee and Scale of Production

Before examining the local dynamics that led to a regime of smallholder coffee production in Bukoba, some of the broader context is needed. One of the most striking features of coffee production is the wide variety of land and labor systems that have developed in various parts of the world to supply ever-increasing demand. In some regions, such as parts of Latin America, coffee has been produced on large estates. Labor systems on these estates have varied, from relatively relaxed seigneurial systems to harsh regimes of state-backed capitalist extraction. In other areas, and characteristically in Africa, coffee has been produced on a small scale. It has been incorporated into the agricultural systems of peasant farmers, who have relatively secure access to land and who rely principally on family labor.

Though the scale of coffee production varies widely, the tendency is toward small-scale production, everything else being equal. What might not be equal in a given situation is a political and social environment in which plantation production is preferred by an elite that is willing and able to use force to sustain it. One explanation for the macroeconomic preference for small and scattered production units is market volatility. Since there is relatively little to be gained by vertical integration, it makes sense for the coffee industry to spread risk widely and push it down to the lowest level. Peasants who grow coffee certainly suffer when market prices tumble, but they do not necessarily face the ruin of estate producers in the same situation. Coffee also needs more than just raw labor. Intensive and knowledgeable cultivation can increase yields, giving smallholders a potential advantage over estates. Whatever the reasons, it seems that coffee is usually produced on estates only where the labor is coerced.[2]

In colonial Africa, such coercion was unlikely to be forthcoming. European capital had little interest in agriculture, and systems of labor coercion were most often established to supply labor for mines or the construction of transport infrastructures. Only in exceptional cases

---

[2] These general points were taken from notes of discussions held at the "Coffee Production and Economic Development, 1700–1960" conference, held at St. Anthony's College, Oxford, September 10–12, 1998.

was significant capital investment necessary for agricultural development to take place. Crops that required significant on-site processing, such as sisal and sugar, demanded capital investment and a considerable scale of production. However, for most other commercial crops, notably, cocoa, cotton, and coffee, incorporation into peasant farming made economic sense.

Economics were not the only factor at play. Particularly in Eastern and Southern Africa, harsh regimes of labor coercion supported plantation agriculture, when European settlers used their political influence to create legal systems that guaranteed them access to cheap labor. Apart from the use of force, most developed in South Africa, settlers had other means of skewing the labor market in their favor. Southern Rhodesia's marketing boards paid higher prices for estate-grown maize than for its African-grown equivalent. As in Latin America, where rural oligarchies also enjoyed privileged access to the state, government intervention could support plantation production even if other economic factors argued against it.

Whatever the political situation, Africans were never free to ignore the mandate of commercialization. Taxes had to be paid in cash, and there were few ways to get it. Whatever strategies they employed, there was usually one central concern: to reproduce the peasant household. Generally speaking, the favored method was cash cropping. Planting cash crops, in addition to staple food crops, did not preclude the pursuit of off-farm income. A son might be sent for seasonal work on a plantation or educated to join the lower ranks of the colonial bureaucracy. A husband or wife might engage in small-scale trade. However, the definition and retention of the peasant smallholding was the key. With the introduction of cash crops, property rights became more central, even if they were contested and adjudicated in terms of "custom." The colonial state was usually comfortable with this peasant agenda, as rural social stability was its primary goal. British "indirect rule" codified this emphasis, with its socially and economically conservative apparatus of "native authorities" and "customary law." Local self-sufficiency in food and finance, achieved by peasant production of export crops, fitted the pattern perfectly.

Even if peasants and bureaucrats could agree on the basic shape of the rural political economy, conflict between them was nevertheless endemic. Questions of what to grow, and how to grow it, generated constant undercurrents of tension, and occasional open revolts. The crop that caused most distress and conflict was cotton. It was low in value, labor-intensive, and hard on the soil. At the opposite extreme were cocoa and coffee. Their advantages to peasant producers were numerous. Once established, perennial crops had relatively light labor demands. The prices that African producers received during the 1920s were good, and this was the time when most decisions were made about which commercial crops to establish. Cocoa production was more demanding, involving the clearing of virgin forest, the formation of consortia to pool resources, and the hiring of labor.[3] Coffee required less forethought. One of its main appeals was that it could be interplanted among existing crops. In those parts of East Africa where plantains were the staple food, coffee could be easily incorporated into an existing agricultural cycle. Problems would appear later, such as the roller coaster of international price fluctuations and an inability to expand production beyond an early plateau. Declining soil fertility jeopardized yields of the subsistence crops with which coffee shared the earth, and the spread of disease could increasingly be combatted only through the use of expensive imported chemicals. In the establishment phase, however, cocoa and coffee were usually the peasant's best options, the first most common in West Africa, and the second in East Africa.

To exercise the coffee option, it was best for Africans to have local European allies. Here the missionary factor was important. East African mission stations were often established in areas where the Europeans had the best chance of good health, notably, cool highland areas. So the strongest mission presence was often in the best areas for growing coffee. The missions needed to meet their own immediate expenses, and coffee was a convenient way to do so. Missionaries were also likely to encourage their converts to take up coffee planting on their own, as the Victorian model of "Christianity and Commerce" held sway. Industry, thrift, and "civilized behavior" could be fostered through market-oriented farming.

On the other side were the European settlers, who were just as likely to oppose the spread of coffee cultivation among Africans. The excuse given was usually disease. African farms, like Africans themselves, were "dirty," and disease could spread to "clean" European farms. However, there were also material issues at stake. It has generally been conceded that African farmers were more efficient producers than European settlers. The latter could survive economically only through state subsidies and restrictions on African output. Moreover, African peasant prosperity meant

---

[3] Polly Hill, *Migrant Cocoa Farmers of Southern Ghana* (Cambridge: Cambridge University Press, 1963); Sara Berry, *Cocoa, Custom and Socio-Economic Change in Rural Western Nigeria* (Oxford: Clarendon Press, 1975).

higher wage rates. In areas where settlers aspired to dominate coffee production, such as Rhodesia, the Ivory Coast, and the central highlands of
Kenya, African coffee growing was restricted. In Tanganyika, settlers were
less successful in restricting African production. As shown in Andreas
Eckert's chapter, Mount Kilimanjaro was the main site of conflict. The
local British administration, while basically sympathetic to settlers, was
not willing to jeopardize an already established and profitable African
coffee industry.[4]

In Bukoba District, coffee found an ideal niche, as *robusta* was indigenous to the area. *Arabica* was introduced to Haya farmers by missionaries, and taken up by some growers, but the familiar *robusta* continued
to dominate coffee growing in colonial times. Though the trees themselves were considered by Haya tradition a royal monopoly, roasted coffee beans were, and still are, offered at all levels of society to guests as a
token of hospitality. A modest beginning with coffee exports to the world
market was made under German rule. With the advent of British rule,
South Asian traders became more numerous and carried the world market
further into the countryside. Links were established with Bukoba town,
import-export houses in Mombasa (Kenya), and the international coffee
market. A strong missionary presence encouraged coffee, and there were
no settlers to oppose it. *Robusta* coffee was easily interplanted with the
plantains that formed the core of Haya agriculture. After a brief postwar
slump, world coffee prices soared throughout the first decade of British
rule. Kerosene lamps, zinc roofs, and bicycles all made their appearance,
but school fees and inflated bride-wealth payments were two of the most
common uses for after-tax cash. The Haya were indeed fortunate, considering the forced labor, forced cultivation, and alienation of land to settlers,
which were the lot of other Africans.

However, that was not the end of the story. A parallel can be drawn
between political and economic spheres in early colonial life. Politically,
the British acted to preserve "tradition," keeping the local kings (*bakama*)
as chiefs and incorporating them into the colonial administrative structure
as "Native Authorities."

The British also codified and legitimized "customary law," and used
the "tribe" as their basic administrative unit. In reality, continuity with
the past was much less evident than rapid political change. Under the
cover of tradition, the most basic relations of power in African life were

[4] Susan Rogers, "The Kilimanjaro Native Planters Association: Administrative Responses
to Chagga Initiatives in the 1920s," *Transafrican Journal of History* 4 (1974): 94–114.

being transformed. Similarly, in the economy, the smooth transition to a coffee-plantain complex allowed a seeming continuity with the past. The general layout of the farms did not change, nor did basic labor patterns. The commercialization of the economy, however, was altering Haya society in fundamental ways. While both British and African participants in the colonial system legitimized their strategies by reference to continuities with the past, references to "custom" and "tradition" were actually the language in which they expressed their concerns about rapid and systematic change. Haya society was fraught with tension. Typical of a society in flux, generational and gender relations were a favorite topic of discussion, particularly, the tendency of women and youth to exploit new ideas and opportunities under colonialism to reject "customary" hierarchical relationships.

The dominance of peasant smallholder production in Bukoba was not in question, but that left many details to be negotiated between key players in the rural colonial economy: peasants, colonial officials, native authorities, landlords, tenants, and coffee traders. Tensions between them could be more than routine, for British interference in Haya agriculture twice led to significant revolts. Moreover, conflict between landlords and tenants created anger similar in kind, if not in devastating violence, to that in neighboring Rwanda. In spite of such strains, however, no one seemed interested in carrying agrarian capitalism to its logical conclusion: a thorough transformation of land and labor into commodities. This essential consensus also has to be explained.[5]

[5] The following account draws heavily on my doctoral dissertation, "Capitalism Fettered: State, Merchant and Peasant in Northwestern Tanzania, 1917–1960," University of Wisconsin, 1989. A basic bibliography for colonial coffee in Bukoba would include: Ralph Austen, *Northwest Tanzania under German and British Rule: Colonial Policy and Tribal Politics, 1889–1939* (New Haven: Yale University Press, 1968); S. K. S. Bakengesa, "An Historical Survey of the Coffee Industry in Bukoba District, 1932–1954," M.A. dissertation, University of Dar es Salaam, 1974; Karl-Heinz Friederich, "Coffee-Banana Holdings at Bukoba: The Reasons for Stagnation at a Higher Level," in H. Ruthenberg, ed., *Smallholder Farming and Smallholder Development in Tanzania* (Munich: Weltforum, 1968), pp. 177–212; T. S. Kalikawe, "The Nyarubanja Land Tenure System and Its Impact on the Growth of Coffee in Bukoba," B.A. thesis, University of Dar es Salaam, 1974; Jorgen and Karen Rald, *Rural Organisation in Bukoba District, Tanzania* (Uppsala: Scandinavian Institute of African Studies, 1975); Priscilla Reining, "The Haya: The Agrarian System of a Sedentary People," Ph.D. dissertation, University of Chicago, 1967, and "Haya Land Tenure: Landholding and Tenancy," *Anthropology Quarterly* 35 (1962): 58–72, and "Land Resources of the Haya," in D. Brokensha, ed., *Ecology and Development in Tropical Africa* (Berkeley: University of California Press, 1965), pp. 217–45; and Charles Smith, "Agrarian Commoditization and Changed Social Relations: The Case of the Haya," Ph.D. dissertation, Essex University, 1982.

Consensus: The Creation of a Yeoman Peasantry

To say that coffee was ideally suited to Bukoba as a colonial cash crop is not to say that the massive coffee planting that took place in the first decade of British administration (1918–1928) was a "natural" occurrence. As in much of the rest of rural Africa, official coercion was initially more important than market forces. However, after a phase of coerced planting, Haya agriculturalists took to coffee with great enthusiasm.

When the British arrived in Bukoba, they found a fairly diversified local economy in which the export sector played a significant role. Coffee was an established commercial crop, but did not overshadow other exports. For the new British administration under D. L. Baines, this economic status quo was inadequate. Baines correctly saw that the export potential of Bukoba was still largely untapped. He decided to concentrate all his efforts on coffee, and coffee exports in 1921 were four times higher than they had ever been under the Germans. In 1919, Baines ordered the *bakama*, who were being incorporated into the colonial state, to establish nurseries for coffee seedlings, and then to distribute coffee trees to their subjects and make sure that they were properly planted. Over the next three years Baines's campaign of coerced coffee planting took on the appearance of a crusade.

Success was largely due to the cooperation of Francis Lwamgira. A man of royal lineage, he had provided invaluable assistance to the Germans and would become, as secretary of the Bakama Council, the most powerful African bureaucrat in the local British administration. Lwamgira toured the district with Baines and convinced both peasants and Native Authorities that the British were serious about securing their compliance. Millions of seedlings were planted between 1919 and 1924, and it was these trees that supplied virtually all of the coffee exported from Bukoba before the Second World War. They came to be known as the *bisibu ba Lwamgira*, Lwamgira's coffee trees.[6]

By the late 1920s, however, no observer would have guessed that any external stimulus had been necessary, such was the enthusiasm of farmers for coffee. By 1924, coffee had become absolutely dominant in the Haya economy. The value of land and labor, and the demand for them, soared, and other forms of commerce were all but forgotten. The 1920s came to be known as the *otandibatira*, the age of "do not tread on my land or

---

[6] Rwamishenye District Office (henceforth RW), E.3/313S.K. Zahoro to *Engoma ya Buhaya*, "Omumwami Gwa Buhaya," 1958?

my coffee."[7] Bukoba coffee became the territory's most valuable peasant export, and Bukoba's Central Native Treasury the richest financial institution of any Native Authority.[8]

Mass enthusiasm resulted from the high price of coffee on the world market in the early 1920s. After a trade slump in 1920 had all but killed commerce in the district, a rapid recovery in the terms of trade meant that the trees planted under the direction of Baines were coming into bearing from 1923 to 1927, just when world demand was reaching a peak. Imported goods flooded into Bukoba. Bark cloth, still the dominant form of dress in the German period, was completely displaced by imported cottons. A visiting official commented in 1923 that he had "never seen a better dressed crowd in all of Africa."[9]

Thirty years later, Joseph Mwikila looked back on his boyhood days with a sort of astonished nostalgia: "When the Germans left Bukoba we were selling coffee and chilies.... When the English came they said we should leave the chilies and just sell coffee. Ten years after the English arrived our country became amazingly rich. The money rained down on us. There was so much money we started to go crazy. At that time we had a famine, but people did not even know it since they had money to buy food. People ate maize porridge, rice, and wheat cakes, people bought bicycles, they built stone houses with tin roofs, and if someone could not find enough things to do with all his money he could lend it to people or use it to help his friends.... We all lived like chiefs and started to wear clothes of European style. No one bothered to acknowledge the peace and prosperity of those days. They built the Mugana church. We lived without war. The Englishman was as sweet as honey. He was a blessing like a fat cow.... Hospitals were built. Schools were started. I was only young at that time, but I already wore a shirt, and shorts, and a white robe [*kanzu*] split down the side so people could see the shirt and the shorts."[10] Mwikila was perhaps guilty of the elder's tendency to exaggerate the golden years of his youth, but there is no question that in the 1920s coffee became a sort of madness in Bukoba, and that demand for imported commodities surged.

---

[7] John Iliffe, *A Modern History of Tanganyika* (Cambridge: Cambridge University Press, 1979), p. 281.

[8] Tanzania National Archives (henceforth TNA), 215/77/A/1, Bukoba District Annual Report for 1927.

[9] TNA, 215/77/11, Bukoba District Annual Report for 1923.

[10] RW, E.3/4, Joseph Mwikila to *Engoma ya Buhaya*, 6/17/54.

A crucial factor generating peasant enthusiasm for coffee was the ease with which it could be integrated into the existing crop cycle. Like the plantains that formed the staple of Haya diet, coffee trees were planted in *bibanja*, intensely productive, mulched, and fertilized areas immediately surrounding hilltop villages. The *bibanja* already supported a two-tiered agricultural system, with plantains above and annual crops below. To plantains and beans, farmers now added a third and intermediate layer, *robusta* coffee. Establishment of coffee in the dry and infertile grasslands (*rweya*) was extremely difficult, requiring both great labor and the application of much manure. Grassland fields were thus planted in annual crops, tended by women, and subject to much less stringent definition of land rights. Another important advantage of integrating coffee into existing plantain plantations, therefore, was that it conformed to the sexual division of labor. As a marketed crop, coffee was a man's prerogative. Had it been planted in the grasslands, the men would have had to either surrender control over it to women or breach their traditional focus on the *bibanja* by undertaking work in the open grasslands under the hot sun.

In later years, agricultural experts decried interplanting coffee and plantains as dangerous to the success of both. They alleged that the early emphasis on quantity, rather than quality, led to coffee trees being too closely spaced in the *bibanja* for adequate yields.[11] More ominous was the progressive decline in plantain yields, first noticed in the late 1930s. From an administrative point of view, the problem with interplanting was that it made it difficult for officials to supervise cultivation practices. Colonial administrators consistently complained that the Haya saw their coffee trees as a "wild orchard crop," harvested but otherwise uncared for.[12] Much as they would have liked to change this attitude, it was difficult to regulate the agricultural practices of tens of thousands of peasant growers. It would not be long before political tensions would arise from official attempts to correct "mistakes" made in the early 1920s.

In the short term, however, the emphasis on peasant control over coffee trees on existing *bibanja* created a public acceptance of the new crop that no other policy could have attained. In 1927, the District Officer noted that a strong yeoman peasantry had now been created: "The result of the abolition of forced labor (one month for the Chiefs in addition to

---

[11] TNA, 38526/12, DA to MANR, Nov. 9, 1948; TNA, 29585/II/545b, Executive Officer BNCB, "Replacement of Old Coffee Trees," June 16, 1952; A. E. Haarer, *Modern Coffee Production* (London: Leonard Hill, 1962), p. 55.

[12] TNA, 25777/I/29, DA to CS, May 14, 1938.

calls by the Government) together with the discontinuation of tribute and the prohibition of forcible eviction from shambas [farms] is clearly visible in the growth of a spirit of independence and self-respect amongst the peasant class of the District."[13] Most Haya were free peasants, who could proclaim "I've got mine" and defend their rights of land ownership and their freedom to cultivate their *bibanja* as they pleased.

The archetypal pattern of peasant economy in Bukoba was now established. Coffee was widely distributed among tens of thousands of *bibanja*, each occupied by a peasant family relying on plantains for subsistence and coffee for cash income. Most labor was done by the family, the man and his wife, or wives, cooperating in the maintenance of the *kibanja*, the women alone working on the annual crop fields in the grasslands. The security of the peasant on his land was very strong. Even before the planting of commercial coffee, the permanent nature of *bibanja* holdings had created a much stronger attachment to particular plots of land than was usual in Africa. Now that coffee had made this valuable land even more highly prized, peasants devoted themselves assiduously to the maintenance of their claims in the spirit of *otandibatira*. The newly established Native Courts proved the most popular of all the colonial institutions in the district, as peasants flocked to them to have their land disputes settled. So valuable had *kibanja* land become that generations of neighbors, even brothers, would fight year after year in the courts over "the smallest piece of plantain land, the width of a native footpath."[14]

This was a stable pattern of "middle peasant" commodity production in which hired labor played a minor role, and it was nearly impossible for a peasant to lose land. Peasant land security resulted from both indigenous proclivities and colonial policy. Both territorial policy and local "customary law" operated to guarantee the security of peasant usufruct. Operating from a paternalistic ideology that argued for the "protection" of Africans from unscrupulous (read "South Asian") traders, colonial law made it very difficult for a "nonnative" to recover any kind of debt from an African, and impossible for Africans to mortgage land as a means of raising capital. Under these conditions, there were no *kulaks* (rich peasants) worthy of the name, and no rural proletariat of landless peasants to give colonial officials nightmares. In Sara Berry's phrase, it was a system of "exploitation without dispossession," an economy ideally suited to the conservative, stability-oriented administrative structures of indirect

---

[13] TNA, 215/77/A/1, Bukoba District Annual Report for 1927.
[14] TNA, 11884/I/73, PC Bukoba, March 22, 1929.

rule.[15] The basic pattern survived through the world depression, a near famine during the Second World War, and the wild and ebullient 1950s, the age of high coffee prices and nationalist politics. In fact, it even survived President Julius Nyerere's attempt to impose collectivized agriculture in the 1970s.

This basic pattern of land security and socioeconomic stability did not indicate the absence of conflict. Here, as elsewhere, "the colonial period in Africa was...a time of intensified contestation over custom, power and property."[16] Indeed, the Bukoba District was notorious within Tanganyika for the volatility of its local politics. In 1937, and again in 1953, significant peasant rebellions against colonial authority took place, each time bringing to the surface the latent tensions inherent in the compromises between British and Haya, and amongst the Haya themselves, which sustained indirect rule. Three issues surfaced: relations between landlords and tenants, competing interests in coffee marketing, and, most insistently, peasant resistance to colonial agricultural intervention. Each crisis tested the limits of "custom" and "tradition" as the focal point of African political discourse.

Twaiyanga, Nyarubanja, and Control of Markets

Indirect rule was partly a British strategy to control and contain political change in Africa through localization and tribalization, but Africans could use its structures for their own purposes. British officials were frequently frustrated by the limitations thus placed on their power. In Bukoba, the spread of coffee had created a basic self-sufficiency in both food and cash within each peasant household, which made subsequent attempts to intervene in the productive decisions of Haya farmers much more difficult. The lesson was learned the hard way in 1937, when an attempt to promulgate and enforce new rules governing coffee cultivation met with a blanket refusal to cooperate. The episode is remembered in Bukoba as "*Twaiyanga!*" ("We Refuse!").

British agricultural officials were upset with what they saw as the unsanitary conditions of Haya coffee farms. To the official mind, the interplanting of coffee and plantains had been a regrettable marriage of convenience. The fact that *robusta* markets reacted more to price than to quality,

---

[15] Sara Berry, *No Condition is Permanent: The Social Dynamics of Agrarian Change in Sub-Saharan Africa* (Madison: University of Wisconsin Press, 1993), ch. 6.

[16] Berry, *No Condition,* p. 8.

because *robusta* was used primarily as a cheap blend for bulk coffee, meant that official concerns with cleanliness and quality were not reinforced by market trends. The instincts of agricultural bureaucrats were constantly frustrated by their lack of control over peasant producers. Bukoba was thus an excellent example of what Ralph Austen calls "peasant-étatist" regimes in colonial Africa, distinguished from "regimes of competitive exploitation" marked by land alienation and strict labor control.[17]

"Coffee Rules" had been issued before 1937, but the *bakama* showed little enthusiasm for enforcing them. With the administration fully committed to implementation, the Agriculture Department ordered chiefs to undertake inspections of peasant farms and to imprison or fine those found to be in contravention of the rules. The rules can be paraphrased as follows: (1) plantations may not contain weeds, long grass, or woody plants other than coffee; (2) fallen cherries must be picked up every day and, if diseased, burned or buried; (3) no maize may be planted in the *kibanja*; (4) when ordered by the Agriculture Department, plantains in a coffee plot are to be removed or thinned; (5) all diseased coffee trees are to be destroyed; (6) trees must be at least three spaces apart, and if they are more than six, a seedling must be planted between them; (7) no new planting can be done unless the Agricultural Officer is satisfied that the grower's present trees are properly maintained; (8) when diseases are noticed they must be reported immediately; (9) the possession of underripe and overripe coffee is prohibited; (10) coffee must be dried off the ground on mats; (11) coffee may not be sold until it is thoroughly dry; (12) it is illegal to be in possession of hulled coffee containing extraneous matter.[18] Some chiefs proved reluctant, and the Agriculture Department intervened, but when officials began to tour the district in February 1937, they were met by spear-wielding peasants shouting *Twaiyanga!* – "We refuse to allow you on our farms!"

Rumors spread that the real intention of the government was to burn down trees and force people into wage labor, a suspicion fueled by the rule allowing Agriculture Department officials to order the destruction of plantain plants.[19] The Agricultural Officer reported that he had been accused of personally introducing coffee disease into the Haya region, so that the peasants would be ruined and forced to work for white settlers,

[17] Ralph Austen, *African Economic History* (London: James Currey, 1987).
[18] TNA, 19222/11, "Instructions to Coffee Growers," 1936?
[19] TNA, 215/1445/10, DC Bukoba to PC Lake, March 8, 1937; TNA, 19222/11, "Instructions to Coffee Growers," 1936?

who planned to come and take their land.[20] In the official view these rumors were spread by partisans of the dissident African Association, who had "seized upon the shortcomings of the Chiefs to foment discord and sedition among the people."[21] As usual, the reference to a minority of "agitators" drew attention away from the real grievances that had brought about a spontaneous surge of peasant politics. The fear of losing their land to settlers and being reduced to wage laborers, while unjustified in this instance, shows how tenaciously protective African farmers could be of their peasant status.

It was the district administration that had caused the Coffee Rules to be passed, and the Agriculture Department that had insisted on their enforcement, but it was the chiefs who were singled out for attack.[22] When one chief attempted to explain the rules, he was publicly "flouted and jeered."[23] Francis Lwamgira, the man on whom the British had relied to get the Haya farmers to plant coffee in the first place, reported that he had to retreat when an angry crowd "threatened to cut [him] into pieces."[24] Throughout the month of February, armed resistance to inspection teams was common, and large crowds gathered whenever an attempt was made to bring to court those who had either broken the rules or resisted the trespass on their *bibanja*.

The District Officer responded with frustrated paternalism: "I compared the Government and the Native Authorities to the father of a family and pointed out that the father had on occasion to give orders to his children which were not liked by some of them. . . . If any child flouted his father he was punished and, if he continued to be obstinate, he was driven out. Government and the Native Authorities occupied exactly the same position in relation to the people."[25] The protestors refused to accept this definition of themselves as wayward children. Their demands were simple: leave us to cultivate our *bibanja* in the way we think best, and do not punish those who speak for us.[26]

Nevertheless, the tactic of arresting and deporting identifiable leaders was effective, and by April of 1937 enthusiasm for confrontation was being replaced by fear of retaliation. On one level it would seem that

---

[20] TNA, 215/1445/24, DO Bukoba to PC Lake, March 8, 1937.
[21] TNA, 215/1445/1, DO Bukoba to PC Lake, Feb. 18, 1937.
[22] TNA, 215/1445/10, DO Bukoba to PC Lake, March 8, 1937.
[23] TNA, 215/1445/48, ADO Bukoba to DO Bukoba, March 8, 1937.
[24] TNA, 215/1445/24, DO Bukoba to PC Lake, March 8, 1937.
[25] Ibid.
[26] Ibid.

Twaiyanga had achieved nothing. The administration refused to withdraw the Coffee Rules, for it could not allow the dangerous precedent of public agitation leading to a change in official policy. The peasantry had, however, won a minor victory. When the dust settled, the Agricultural Inspectors were still empowered to enter plantations, but they were unlikely to do so. There was now much less emphasis on punishment, and more on education and propaganda. The local bureaucracy had come to realize the political costs of agricultural intervention.

It only took fifteen years for this lesson to be forgotten. In 1953 the Agriculture Department, concerned that the spread of the plantain weevil would put the subsistence of the district in jeopardy, undertook a new campaign of agricultural coercion with the same political effect as in 1937. The *bikonya* (plantain stem) legislation of 1953 mandated that older plantain plants, vectors of disease, should be uprooted. Most important, it authorized inspectors to trespass without warning on *bibanja*, to ensure that the orders were carried out. When peasants were told to uproot the very source of their livelihood, they reacted, as in 1937, by saying "*Twaiyanga!*"

In the 1950s, "word of mouth remained the most important form of political communication."[27] That was certainly true in this case. The lines of communication between the district authorities and the peasant farmers were so poor that rumor had no trouble jumping into the breach. From a peasant perspective, an attack on their plantains was a threat to their very lives. As in 1937, they became suspicious that the ultimate goal of the new legislation was to drive them off their land altogether. At the same time as the order for the uprooting of plantains was being enforced, European surveyors appeared in the district.[28] The idea of land alienation in the densely settled parts of the district was never even remotely considered by the administration, but it was believed that this was the opening of a new European offensive to reduce people to wage slavery. The climax of the *bikonya* campaign came when the police fired tear gas at a protest meeting. It was said that the crowd had been "bombed," in the same manner as ex-soldiers had described their experiences of war.[29]

This time, simple repression was not enough to put the political genie back into the bottle. The rise of territorial nationalism made it impossible

[27] Iliffe, *Modern History*, p. 532.
[28] Bukoba District Archives (henceforth BA), L.5/77/21, Mwami of Rwagati to DC Bukoba, March 26, 1956.
[29] G. R. Mutahaba,"Background to Nationalism in Buhaya," 1966, p. 4. Typescript found in the Tanzania National Archives.

to localize the effects of the Agriculture Department's miscalculation. The Bukoba rebellion came just as Julius Nyerere was about to organize the Tanganyika African National Union, the party that came to power at independence. Nyerere used the tear gas incident in Bukoba to argue at the United Nations for an end to the British mandate over Tanganyika.

Resistance to coercive agricultural legislation united virtually all Haya farmers in a common cause, but the simple picture of a peasantry bound together in equality is not quite accurate. While the smallholding pattern of mixed coffee and plantain cultivation was dominant, a minority of peasants were subject to a tenancy system known as *nyarubanja*. It was a "traditional" institution, but one which took on radically different characteristics with commodification. While most Haya peasants had achieved an unprecedented independence, others could be seen as laboring under a "feudal form of tenure" that forced them to hand over a portion of their surplus to landlords.[30]

Nyarubanja simply means "a large plantation." The precolonial institution seems to have involved the right of a *mukama* to give up his own rights to tribute in labor and kind from a group of contiguous *bibanja* and cede them to a particular member of the royal clan. The recipient gained rights not only over the land itself but over the peasants settled on it.[31] From the villagers' standpoint, there was not much to choose between paying tribute directly to the *mukama* or offering goods and services to his local representative. In fact, there was a potential advantage to rendering labor tribute locally, for the *nyarubanja* holder might act as patron and protector in times of civil strife.

Equality between free peasants and *nyarubanja* tenants ended around the turn of the century. The *bakama*, especially those who were most confident of German backing, began to create *nyarubanja* estates for *themselves*. Previously, the *bakama* had not themselves been *nyarubanja* landlords, for the payment of tenant dues and royal tribute had been mutually exclusive.[32] Now they were actually receiving double tribute from part of the population. After 1926, when the British colonial government converted the chiefs' rights to tribute into cash salaries, the gap between tenants and nontenants widened considerably. Each peasant household paid taxes,

[30] TNA, 215/77/17, Bukoba District Annual Report for 1925.
[31] Public Records Office, London, CO691/104/29491/4, W. F. Gowers to W. C. Bottomley, Nov. 5, 1929.
[32] TNA, 7794/11/8, J. L. Woodhouse, "Nyarubanja," Sept. 5, 1924.

from which the native authorities' salaries were paid, but only *nyarubanja* tenants were forced to continue with "tribute," which now increasingly took the form of cash payments derived from coffee income. What had once been a reciprocal system of patronage and deference was now a purely commercial relationship. As the coffee economy developed, the *nyarubanja* tenants felt their inferior position ever more sharply. The legitimacy of the system was hotly contested.

The British decided to encode *nyarubanja* in colonial "customary law," fully conscious of the political implications. They were aware that the tenancy system that had developed since the German period was fundamentally different from the precolonial one, and that "the cloak of Native Custom" had been misused "to satisfy the Sultans' and landlords' greed."[33] They were also aware that the double jeopardy of taxes and tribute was hard to justify by reference to "tradition." The District Officer in 1928 was ready to scrap the whole system. He argued that the best way forward was to oversee the development of "a free nation of peasant proprietors, or peasants holding directly from the state."[34] His advice was overruled by officials more concerned with assuring the cooperation of the *bakama* in indirect rule. Though only about 10 percent of Haya farmers were governed by *nyarubanja*, it remained the most fertile source of rural conflict throughout the colonial period.

Along with the general political ferment surrounding the *Twaiyanga* episode in 1937 came renewed appeals for the abolition of *nyarubanja*. Though the British had become aware that some chiefs were cheating their tenants and illicitly creating new *nyarubanja* estates, they could not take the side of the peasants, as the prestige and legitimacy of their administrative system was at stake. During the next episode of open political tension, the resistance to the plantain regulations of the early 1950s, the nationalists called the whole "native authority" system into question and pointed to *nyarubanja* as a prime example of chiefly malfeasance. *Nyarubanja* became part of a larger public debate about the relative status of aristocrats (*Bahinda*) and commoners (*Bairu*), as defined by the old clan system. There were calls for the abolition of such distinctions, and some dangerous indications that bitterness of a Rwandan type had entered some people's thinking. Hans Cory, the government sociologist who had codified Haya "customary law," and who therefore had a strong vested interest in preserving *nyarubanja*, admitted that majority opinion

---

[33] TNA, 215/77/14, Bukoba District Annual Report for 1924.
[34] TNA/11884/I/26, DO Bukoba, "Comments on the Nyarubanja Rules," 1928.

was in favor of eliminating it altogether.[35] In the end, the colonial government handed the issue over to the semidemocratic local government it had created in 1956, and a compensated end to *nyarubanja* was accomplished.

The volatility of the issue was perhaps surprising, given the few people involved and the modest nature of the burden placed on tenants. Nor was landlordism the issue, per se. Those with surplus land often made it available to tenants, with arrangements varying from payment of rent in cash to the establishment of patron-client relations. The problem with *nyarubanja* was that it contradicted the peasant sense of justice. It is true that *nyarubanja* in its twentieth-century form was a colonial creation that was difficult to legitimize with reference to "tradition," but the ability to assert freedom from state interference in the productive life of the homestead was also a colonial creation. To coffee-growing taxpayers, salaried chiefs could be seen as employees as well as monarchs. To that peasantry, *nyarubanja* was a reminder of what could happen if they were subject to arbitrary political authority on their own farms. The fight against *nyarubanja* was, then, a form of resistance more subtle than but not dissimilar to *Twaiyanga*. In both cases, the sanctity of the peasant homestead from arbitrary outside interference was the underlying issue.

Another contested aspect of Bukoba's coffee economy was its marketing system.[36] Beans from the coerced planting campaigns of the late 1910s and early 1920s flooded the market in the mid-1920s, and a marketing system evolved spontaneously to handle them. South Asian merchants dominated the import-export trade of Bukoba, linked by family and community affiliation from the smallest rural shop through Bukoba town to Mombasa. The concentration of South Asians in trade and the professions was a matter of preference and skills, but also of colonial laws that made it difficult for them to gain access to agricultural land. With a very few exceptions, such as a sugar plantation in a remote and lightly populated corner of the Bukoba District, South Asian capital was kept out of agriculture.

The pattern of South Asian trade was common in East Africa, whereas Bukoba was exceptional for its thousands of African petty traders. Known

---

[35] Hans Cory and M. M. Hartnoll, *Customary Law of the Haya Tribe* (London: Cass, 1945).
[36] Ken Curtis, "Cooperation and Co-optation: The Struggle for Market Control in the Bukoba District of Colonial Tanganyika," *International Journal of African Historical Studies* 12, no. 3 (1992): 505–38.

as *wachuruzi,* or "tricklers," they relied on advances from South Asian traders to buy the coffee crop and bring it to marketing centers. A few managed to move on to larger operations, opening shops themselves, working through their own networks of trade subordinates, and extending credit to peasants in anticipation of the harvest.

Rather than congratulating Haya merchants on their entrepreneurial enthusiasm and business acumen, the British administration reacted with alarm to this system. Part of the problem was the distrust of credit, characteristic of colonial paternalism: "In spite of the value of our exports and imports which are quite enough to guarantee a prosperous trading community the system upon which trade is based is rotten in the extreme. From beginning to end it rests upon credit only, generally at usurious rates of interest. Borrowing from Peter to pay Paul seems to be the keynote and often borrowing more from Paul to pay Peter himself."[37]

It also perturbed bureaucratic minds that the free market refused to support the colonial sanitation fetish. Traders were so anxious to buy coffee that they paid little or no attention to quality, encouraging such officially proscribed procedures as drying the beans on the ground rather than on raised mats. Because *robusta* coffee was used in blends, and increasingly for cheap instant coffee, both trader and farmer were in fact reacting logically to the demands of the world market.

What most disturbed officials about the relative success of African traders in Bukoba was the awkward political relationship it created between merchants and chiefs: "The unsatisfactory feature presented by the petty traders lies in their tendency to organize themselves as an association. They have recognized leaders in every village and the latter have sometimes endeavored to act independently of the native authorities and have claimed a special recognition in administrative matters."[38] African traders, many of them Muslims in a majority Christian area, were not the simple "tribesmen" loyal to their "traditions" on which indirect rule was predicated. They represented an alternative source of patronage, which could potentially undercut chiefly authority. To use Mahmood Mamdani's terminology, the traders, like the Western-educated Haya with whom they often cooperated, were "subjects" of indirect rule because of their status as Africans. However, their professional role and self-image transcended

---

[37] TNA, 215/77/A/4, Bukoba District Annual Report for 1926. D. M. P. McCarthy analyzes colonial rule in Tanganyika in *Colonial Bureaucracy and Creating Underdevelopment: Tanganyika, 1919–1940* (Ames: Iowa State University Press, 1982).
[38] TNA, 1733/5:53, Bukoba District Annual Report for 1923.

the "decentralized despotism" of indirect rule and made them aspire to
the alternative civil society of "citizens."[39] The traders confirmed official
fears by taking a leading role in politics, in the Bukoba Haya Union in
the 1920s, in the African Association in the 1930s, and in the Tanganyika
African National Union in the 1950s.

To the officials backing the 1937 Coffee Rules, it seemed obvious that
marketing reform was also essential. In most other parts of Tanganyika,
a government-organized marketing plan went hand in hand with official encouragement of commercial crops. "Organized markets" were the
norm, and Bukoba's freestyle capitalism the exception. In the other major
coffee-growing region, around Mount Kilimanjaro, an African marketing association had been formed in the 1920s, only to be taken over and
turned into a government-mandated monopoly in 1932.[40] By the time
marketing reform was seriously considered in the late 1930s, however,
Twaiyanga had so poisoned the political atmosphere that it was thought
best to stick to the status quo.

The political courage to reform the marketing of Bukoba's coffee came
during the Second World War. Emergency conditions allowed the creation
of a government marketing board, with price-fixing authority. Africans
accepted artificially low prices during the war, but were less tolerant when
the war was over. In 1950, peasants discovered that the marketing board
was making huge profits by holding local prices down, while selling at
rapidly escalating world market prices. Out of the resulting political crisis
emerged the Bukoba Native Cooperative Union (BNCU).

The BNCU began in 1953 with talented Africans in its administration
and substantial legitimacy among farmers. However, by 1960, it was clear
that the BNCU, with its local monopoly guaranteed by the government,
merely represented another aspect of the state's attempt to "capture"
coffee. Like other such organizations in the late colonial period, it was
a "cooperative" only in name. Since there was no other legal means of
selling coffee, it was not a free association of producers. In fact, colonial
cooperatives had much more in common with socialist parastatals of the
1970s, and were really their progenitors.[41] Frustrated in attempts to assert
control over coffee production, the colonial and postcolonial states were
all the more anxious to monopolize marketing.

[39] Mahmood Mamdani, *Citizen and Subject: Contemporary Africa and the Legacy of Late Colonialism* (Princeton: Princeton University Press, 1996).
[40] Rogers, "The Kilimanjaro Native Planters Association," pp. 94–114.
[41] Andrew Coulson, *Tanzania: A Political Economy* (Oxford: Clarendon Press, 1982).

African traders clearly had a different agenda. Even when they lost the battle over legal marketing, they continued to frustrate government and cooperative officials through black market activities and through their continued importance as village-level creditors and alternative sources of patronage. However, no matter how conflictual the relationship between private traders and cooperative bureaucrats, the switch from private to state-sanctioned cooperative marketing did not change a situation in which commercial profits were unlikely to be invested in agriculture. In this respect, African merchants and cooperative bureaucrats were no different from their South Asian counterparts.

No colonial official sent to Bukoba would have considered it a quiet post. In each of the instances considered above, conflict was endemic. Looking back, it only took one generation for the destabilizing effects of coffee on Haya society to render indirect rule obsolete. But the basic consensus forged during the coffee boom of the 1920s endured, and informed all of these debates. While they might disagree on details, Haya peasants and British administrators were resistant to the development of markets in land and labor.

Conclusion: Late Colonial Continuities

Even when Tanganyika officials finally decided, at the eleventh hour of colonial rule, that capital should be made available for African agricultural investment, their heart was not in it. The impetus actually came from the Colonial Office, which was itself responding to events in Kenya. There, it had been decided by 1955 that agrarian capitalism should be encouraged as a response to the Mau Mau rebellion. The Swynnerton Plan called for the consolidation of farms and the registration of titles, an end to restrictions on African production of such crops as coffee and tea, and state-funded investment in African agriculture.

Nothing as thoroughgoing was envisioned for Tanganyika, but the African Development Loan Fund initiated in 1956 was a step in a new direction. The African Loans Fund Officer who arrived to oversee the program was responsible for the entire Lake Province, but he spent most of his time in Bukoba, since "there [was] far more loan work [there] than in all the other districts put together."[42] Because the aim was long-term agricultural investment, the loan process started with an application to the Agriculture Department, which made an initial judgment of the merits

---

[42] BA, L.50/51/165, AO West Lake to DC Bukoba, Jan. 22, 1957.

of the potential borrower. Most of the thousands of applications that flooded in had nothing to do with farming, however. One man asked for a 1000 shilling advance because he wanted "to go into business." Another applied for 30,000 shillings so that he could buy a bus.[43] Apparently, this new source of cash was regarded by many Haya as supplementary to pre-existing credit sources, which had been geared to trade and simple subsistence, not increased productivity in agriculture. "The public," complained the Deputy Provincial Commissioner, "misunderstands the program."[44] The intended link between credit and agricultural investment was a new one. Unlike trade and the salaried positions to which education might lead, land and labor were not generally thought of in monetary terms.

In a letter to the program office in Dar es Salaam, the Loan Funds Officer, frustrated at the lack of proper applications, described how a successful loan might be made. In doing so, he identified the social target of the program, the "small farmer who has proved on some 2–3 acres that he is a good farmer." He should be someone who had saved something from the "halcyon days of good profits," 1953–55, and had a good house to secure the loan.[45] In other words, the search was for the yeoman peasant. If the applicant was too poor, he would be likely to put the windfall into consumption rather than agricultural investment. If the applicant was too rich, he would have his own resources for capital investment in agriculture, and would therefore not need the loan.[46]

There were many cases when the applicant was deemed too rich for a loan. Applicants with trading licenses were always turned down, and this group would include many relatively prosperous farmers. One such applicant was told, "If you wish to develop your farm you should use the profits from your shop."[47] Those coffee producers who had the best security, the most land, and perhaps the best chance of breaking through to a higher level of productivity through capital inputs and hired labor were systematically excluded from the loan program. The use of wage labor was, in the loan officer's opinion, a further indication of the reluctance of Haya men to do their own hard work. The Deputy Provincial Commissioner agreed: "Agricultural loans here ought to be confined to the extension of cultivated holdings in cases where it is not the intention of the applicant

[43] BA, L.50/51/183, Shabani Ismaili to DC Bukoba, April 6, 1957; BA, L.50/51/198, Laurenti Melchioroles to DC Bukoba, June 18, 1957.

[44] BA, L.50/51/188, DPC West Lake to Chairman ALFC, Dar es Salaam, May 1, 1957.

[45] BA, L.50/51/143, AO Bukoba to DPC West Lake, Feb. 10, 1956.

[46] BA, L.50/51/188, DPC West Lake to Chairman ALFC, Dar es Salaam, May 1, 1957.

[47] BA, L.50/51/19, AO Bukoba to Raphael Bishota, July 23, 1955.

merely to employ extra labour to do work he could do himself. Bahaya men do not normally undertake much agricultural labour themselves, and I do not consider the scheme should be used to allow them to continue this habit."[48] Such attitudes betray an almost instinctive hostility to the development of agrarian capitalism.

Colonial instincts were not too far out of touch with African ones. For the typical Haya man, the basic *kibanja* landholding represented the ultimate security of his family, and in a wider sense the defining element in his status in the community. Holding at least an acre or two of good plantain and coffee land was therefore of fundamental importance. A successful man, however, would never limit his economic enterprises merely to farming. Even in precolonial times, all but the most dependant of tenants would have had other political, craft, or ritual specializations beyond the *kibanja*. In the colonial period, this tendency persisted. A man was by definition poor if his farm represented his only form of livelihood. Service in the state bureaucracy and petty trading continued to afford alternative opportunities. What capital there was to invest flowed into these off-farm activities. Colonial officials were frustrated by Haya reluctance to focus solely on agriculture, but their own disinclination to promote the capitalization of agriculture actually reinforced Haya attitudes. Trade and education continued to absorb most of whatever surplus they had to invest.

In fact, the strategy of Haya peasants is common in Africa. Except when territorial political power is associated with large-scale landholding in areas of white settlement or former white settlement, Africans prefer to keep access to land a fluid matter for negotiation, rather than a simple matter of the market. In Africa, latifundia are hard to establish and difficult to maintain. Though the status quo established in Bukoba in the 1920s was far from traditional, all parties to the negotiations used references to "tradition" and "custom" to legitimize their positions. Contrary to indirect rule ideology, the power of the state in the Haya kingdoms was never just a matter of "traditional rules" governing functionalist political systems. Power was always a matter of negotiation.

In Bukoba, it was *nyarubanja* that brought conflicting interpretations of tradition to bear on colonial land tenure practices. Public antipathy to the colonial version of *nyarubanja* arose from the unfairness of the system. It seemed entirely arbitrary that some farmers were paying "tribute," which looked increasingly like "rent," when most of their fellows had achieved

[48] BA, L.50/51/188, DPC West Lake to Chairman ALFC, Dar es Salaam, May 1, 1957.

an unprecedented prosperity and sense of control over their own affairs. It was such a blatant abuse of "tradition" as a means of legitimizing greed that it became a lightning rod, representing all the uncomfortable compromises of indirect rule.

The history of the coffee trade in Bukoba points in the same direction. The biggest profits to be made were in commerce, and some Africans broke through from petty coffee trading to more substantial enterprises, but traders were specifically excluded from politics under indirect rule, since they were seen as a threat to the authority of the chiefs. Nor was there any strong tendency to turn commercial capital into agricultural investment. In contrast, traders frequently acted as creditors to coffee farmers. Apart from earning interest, these could also be social investments. Rather than invest in things, even land, there was good reason in the uncertain atmosphere of rural Africa to invest in people.

In Bukoba, as in much of Africa, colonial bureaucrats and African peasants, though operating on radically different sets of cultural expectations, had essential principles in common. While the money economy was to be actively developed, political and social institutions should be shielded from the effects of commodification. When it came to land, smaller was, indeed, better. The small *kibanja* as the focal point of rural production conformed to both British and Haya expectations of how social stability could be squared with the radical economic changes brought about by coffee production and participation in the world economy.

Today, many societies, even those that were once masters in the colonial game, are concerned with their decreased ability to shield themselves from the full effects of the market in areas of life previously governed by other rules, institutions, and ethics. It is ironic that the history of the means by which rural Africans sought to benefit from the market, while at the same time using "tradition" as a means of defense against its uglier aspects, is a story of contemporary relevance.

14

On Paths Not Taken

Commercial Capital and Coffee Production in Costa Rica

Lowell W. Gudmundson

Much of the recent scholarship on the history of coffee in Central America has explored the distribution over time and space of small family-based cultivation, particularly in Costa Rica, Nicaragua, and El Salvador. Beyond the question of documenting the at times surprisingly wide distribution of these small-scale production units, researchers have also sought to understand the processes by which peasant or family farms were consolidated or fragmented over time and the reasons for such varied outcomes. From one extreme of dramatic impoverishment and dependence of the minifundista/semi-proletarian, to the other extreme of wealthier smallholders who employed their impoverished fellow villagers, these treatments of coffee's social history have tended to focus on a wide range of issues. Among these, commercial and financial relations between producers and merchant/processors and the always polemical topic of labor recruitment and coercion have been particularly relevant.

While no very broad agreement has yet been reached on a common nature of smallholding in Central America's coffee economy and its evolution over time, three general conclusions seem clear enough: first, some form of small holding survived, however impoverished and embattled, even in the more inhospitable contexts. While Williams no doubt provides the most copious evidence throughout the region, book-length works by McCreery for Guatemala and Lauria-Santiago for El Salvador and articles by Samper for El Salvador and by Charlip and Dore for Nicaragua have all made it clear that even in the cases long thought paradigmatic of estate-based coffee development, small holding has a complex and important history yet to be fully understood.[1]

Second, formally similar social relations of production developed in vastly different fields of social power, with correspondingly great variation in merchant/processor power over producers or in the ability of these two groups to coerce labor. Virtually all recent studies have shown how vastly power relations and social structure differed over various generations, despite the survival of seemingly comparable production and land tenure regimes. In this regard, the studies by Paige and by Gudmundson on twentieth-century class formation, differentiation, and politics are perhaps the most detailed.[2] The chapters in this volume by Rus, McCreery,

[1] Robert Williams, *States and Social Evolution: Coffee and the Rise of National Governments in Central America* (Chapel Hill: University of North Carolina Press, 1994), contributed enormously to this approach by documenting the existence of different land tenure regimes with coffee *within* each Central American nation, and not just across national cases. For other authors that have recently contributed to this topic, see Jeffery M. Paige, *Coffee and Power: Revolution and the Rise of Democracy in Central America* (Cambridge: Harvard University Press, 1997); Mario Samper, *Generations of Settlers: Rural Households and Markets on the Costa Rican Frontier, 1850–1935* (Boulder: Westview Press, 1990); "El Significado social de la caficultura costarricense y salvadoreña: Análisis histórico comparado a partir de los censos cafetaleros," in Héctor Pérez Brignoli and Mario Samper, eds., *Tierra, café y sociedad* (San José: FLACSO, 1994), 117–225; and "In Difficult Times: Colombian and Costa Rican Coffee Growers from Prosperity to Crisis, 1920–1936," in William Roseberry, Lowell Gudmundson, and Mario Samper Kutschbach, eds., *Coffee, Society and Power in Latin America* (Baltimore: Johns Hopkins University Press, 1995), 151–80; David McCreery, *Rural Guatemala, 1760–1940* (Stanford: Stanford University Press, 1994); Aldo Lauria-Santiago, *An Agrarian Republic: Commercial Agriculture and the Politics of Peasant Communities in El Salvador, 1823–1918* (Pittsburgh: University of Pittsburgh Press, 1999); " 'That a Poor Man Be Industrious': Coffee, Community and Agrarian Capitalism in the Transformation of El Salvador's Ladino Peasantry, 1760–1900," in Aviva Chomsky and Aldo Lauria-Santiago, eds., *Identity and Struggle at the Margins of the Nation-State: The Laboring Peoples of Central America and the Hispanic Caribbean* (Durham: Duke University Press, 1998), 25–51; and "Land, Community, and Revolt in Indian Izalco 1860–1900," *Hispanic American Historical Review* 79, no. 3 (1999): 495–534; Julie Charlip, "At Their Own Risk: Coffee Farmers and Debt in Nicaragua, 1870–1930," in Chomsky and Lauria-Santiago, eds., *Identity and Struggle*, 94–121, and " 'So That Land Takes on Value': Coffee and Land in Carazo, Nicaragua," *Latin American Perspectives* 26, no. 1 (1999): 92–105; Elizabeth Dore, "La Producción cafetalera nicaragüense, 1860–1960: Transformaciones estructurales," in *Pérez Brignoli and Samper, eds., Tierra, café y sociedad* (San José: FLACSO, 1994), 377–436; "Land Privatization and the Differentiation of the Peasantry in Nicaragua's Coffee Revolution, 1850–1920," *Journal of Historical Sociology* 8, no. 3 (1995): 303–26; and "Property, Households, and Public Regulation of Domestic Life: Diriomo, Nicaragua, 1840–1900," *Journal of Latin American Studies* 25 (1997): 591–711; and Lowell Gudmundson, "Peasant, Farmer, Proletarian: Class Formation in a Smallholder Coffee Economy, 1850–1950," in Roseberry et al., eds., *Coffee, Society and Power*, 112–50.

[2] Paige, *Coffee and Power*; Gudmundson, "Peasant, Farmer, Proletarian." Studies of El Salvador represent perhaps the most inhospitable case for the survival of smallholding,

Dore, and Charlip certainly suggest the extraordinary variety of social and political outcomes from Chiapas through Costa Rica, where not even in the larger scale farming regimes was small holding among the rural laboring population seriously threatened with extinction by coffee's rise to dominance.

Recognition of substantial regional diversity in coffee production in Costa Rica dates from Carolyn Hall's pioneering work of the early 1970s, if not earlier.[3] Hall brilliantly contrasted a Central Valley (Cartago through Alajuela) regime of small-holding producers provisioning large-scale processors, who also produced coffee on many small and medium plots that never came to dominate the countryside, with the eastern valley fringe area in Turrialba, where large-scale land ownership and production went along with processing from very early on and persisted every bit as tenaciously as its smallholder cousin to the west. Dual misfortunes befell this analysis, however. Its regional discernment often fell by the wayside with readers and interpreters who tended to see value above all else in its seeming proof of the national heritage and contemporary reality of pervasive small holding, rather than in its detailed analysis of both Turrialba's distinct system and the entrepreneurial histories of leading producer-processor figures and their anything but egalitarian experience with coffee. Moreover, successive analysts have done little to explore subregional differences within the Central Valley-west regime of small-holding often presumed to be far more homogeneous in its origins and historical trajectory than may have been the case.

Third, these variations did not correlate with national scale cases so much as microregional environmental and political factors. Where an earlier generation tended toward national comparisons, today most contrasts are drawn without such clear reference to national boundaries. While Paige's framework of "elite narratives" and self-image remains entirely national, perhaps only the work of Samper comparing Costa Rican and Salvadoran experiences, with some very surprising findings of similarities up to at least the 1930s, could be said to retain this earlier framework, pioneered by Torres-Rivas in the 1960s and by Cardoso in the 1970s. Today, whether in Williams's work or that of several other specialists, each of the five isthmian nations would appear to have regional or subregional

---

but even there both Lauria-Santiago and Samper document its importance throughout the coffee economy.

[3] Carolyn Hall, *El Café y el desarrollo histórico-geográfico de Costa Rica* (San José: Editorial Costa Rica, 1976).

variations in cultivation schemes and the relative weight of small holding, especially early on. Nowhere is this contrast made more clear than in the studies by Dore and Charlip in this volume of virtually contiguous regions of Nicaragua.[4]

The intensively researched work on small holding in Costa Rica's coffee economy attempts to deal with both winners and losers among the peasantry. However, either the more or less explicit choice of research focus or the regional settings themselves often predisposed that literature to a "best case scenario."[5] In such contexts, it was all too easy to believe one understood the reasons for the political and economic triumph of wealthy smallholders both before and after the mid-twentieth century: They were simply so prosperous and successful as to "require" their political representation and success; the pervasive tautology in the social sciences of explaining success as its own cause. And just such a story of upward social mobility and political ascendancy is easy enough to document in places like San Ramón or Naranjo in western Alajuela, or Santo Domingo and San Isidro in Heredia, areas of widespread immigrant and resident peasant access to some of the most fertile lands early on in the coffee expansion.

The larger, comparative purpose of this chapter, however, will not be to continue this exercise in peasant capitalist boosterism. Rather, in Costa Rica, long thought a virtual limit case of smallholder resilience and success in coffee production world-wide, we focus on a veritable local worst-case scenario, an area of vastly lower soil fertility, longer term settlement, and more unequal access to land of any quality. In Desamparados-Tarrazú, south of the capital of San José, smallholders also survived and eventually joined with their wealthier brethren elsewhere in the coffee economy

---

[4] For the classic studies, see Ciro F. S. Cardoso, "The Formation of the Coffee Estate in Nineteenth-Century Costa Rica," in Malcolm Deas, Clifford T. Smith, and John Street, eds., *Land and Labour in Latin America* (Cambridge: Cambridge University Press, 1977), 165–202, and Edelberto Torres Rivas, *Interpretación del desarrollo social centroamericano* (San José: EDUCA, 1975).

[5] In effect, both the geographic cases studied so far, Santo Domingo and San Isidro de Heredia (Gudmundson) and western Alajuela (Samper and Torres Hernández), and the studies of the cooperative movement (Winson, Raventós, and Cazanga) were predisposed to find the most successful farmers. See Margarita Torres Hernández, "Los Campesinos de San Rafael de Heredia, 1830–1930: De usufructuarios comunales a propietarios privados," licenciatura thesis in History, Universidad Nacional de Costa Rica, 1991. Anthony Winson, *Coffee and Democracy in Modern Costa Rica* (London: Macmillan, 1989); Ciska Raventós, "Desarrollo económico, estructura y contradicciones sociales en la producción del café," *Revista de Historia* 14 (1986): 179–98; and José Cazanga, *Las Cooperativas de caficultores en Costa Rica* (San José: Editorial Universidad de Costa Rica, 1987).

in building a vibrant producers' cooperative movement *after* the 1948 Revolution that so favored them. However, their route to that triumph involved overcoming a more dominant large estate owner and processor group, and a substantially more polarized and impoverished social structure than was the case in other, neighboring districts.

The data presented in this chapter begins by outlining the now familiar processes of subregional differentiation in land tenure systems in the nineteenth and early twentieth centuries and the triumph of producer cooperatives in the Central Valley after the mid-twentieth century. But then it will problematize the story by asking why it was that coffee processors and merchants, nearly always relatively large producers themselves enjoying manifest predominance, showed so little interest in or capacity to transform productive relations and land tenure systems, as in Desamparados and its surrounding hamlets. Just how was it that the mighty smallholders managed to gain the upper hand in their century-long and often bitter struggle when all the outward signs would have seemed to point to their defeat? With probate and census records, as well as century-long merchant account book information from the district's preeminent producer, processor, and lender, the German immigrant Von Schroter family, we explore the implications of commercial-smallholder symbiosis and conflict as they were experienced in one of Costa Rica's more densely settled and socially polarized coffee districts.[6] Such an analysis will not only shed light on local historical development in the twentieth century, but perhaps also suggest maximal or limit-case levels of price share incentives for household producers of coffee in Latin America and beyond during this time period.

A Tale of Two Villages: Different Bases for Similar Outcomes

To the north of the capital of San José, in Santo Domingo de Heredia and in its contiguous settlement frontier of San Isidro during the second half of the nineteenth century, it was possible to document the consolidation of an extremely dynamic group of mid-sized coffee producers even before their political triumph in 1948.[7] Even though this large and varied group was ever more the minority of the rural population as the twentieth century

---

[6] The Von Schroter enterprise data come from notes taken by Carolyn Hall in 1971 and shared with me in photocopy form. My thanks to her for such generosity and to the Von Schroter family for recognizing the historical value of the data.

[7] The first half of this comparative study of two early, centrally located Costa Rican coffee districts was published some time ago. Gudmundson, "Peasant, Farmer, Proletarian."

advanced, it continued to dominate coffee bean production. The group maintained its both symbiotic and antagonistic relationship with the three or four large-scale processors in the area. But the process described above took place in an area of unequaled conditions of remarkable soil fertility for coffee, among the highest nationwide, and with a modest population density.

Desamparados, on the other hand, offered a very different panorama. South of the capital and surrounded by the colonial Indian villages of Aserrí on one side and Curridabát on the other, Desamparados was faithful to its name ("the abandoned ones") in constituting the first and largest suburb of San José for the poor in general and the mulatto population in particular. It was an area of earlier settlement and greater population density during the entire coffee century (1850–1950), as well as more broken terrain, with a soil fertility little more than half that of Santo Domingo.

Where Santo Domingo and San Isidro in Heredia increased from just under 9,000 inhabitants in 1927 to just over 10,000 in 1950, Desamparados itself increased from just under 10,000 to over 15,000, and Tarrazú from 5,700 to nearly 7,500. The mountains of Tarrazú served as an escape valve for agrarian migrations, just as San Isidro did for Santo Domingo, but in a much larger, more distant, and topographically and ecologically varied area.[8] In effect, Tarrazú was for Desamparados what both San Isidro and the west of Alajuela province had been for Santo Domingo: areas of attraction/expulsion for excess population as the coffee expansion progressed. In both areas, the movement out of colonization zones was every bit as intense as the earlier movement in. By 1950, between 40 and 45 percent of the population born in any of these areas resided elsewhere, with net emigration figures of fully 40 percent for San Isidro and nearly 55 percent for Tarrazú.

Wealth distribution was somewhat more unequal in Desamparados than in Santo Domingo, even among the ranks of the propertied. The percentage of adult males in the 1927 census listed in the *jornalero*, or laborer, category ranged from a low of 49 percent to a high of 75 percent in Desamparados's surrounding hamlets, with a district-wide figure of 63 percent compared with 62 percent for Santo Domingo. In Desamparados, 31 percent said they worked on their own account,

---

[8] All of the subsequent uses of population, coffee, and land tenure survey data come from the following sources; Dirección General de Estadística y Censos, *Censo de Población de 1927; Censo de Población de 1950; Censo Agropecuario de 1955;* and for coffee holdings in 1935, *Revista del Instituto de Defensa del Café* 5 (1937).

TABLE 14.1. *Structure of Coffee Production, Landed Property, and Population Distribution, 1935*

District	No. of owners	No. of farms	Land area (in manzanas)		Population on coffee farms (%)	No. of processing plants
			Total	Coffee		
Desamparados	1,173	1,219	7,748	3,515	47	5
Tarrazú	542	552	13,014	1,974	51	6
Santo Domingo	854	910	2,436	1,826	58	5
San Isidro	442	595	1,522	1,040	51	1

Source: Revista del Instituto de Defensa del Café (San José, 1937, results of the Coffee Census of 1935).

compared with 21 percent in Santo Domingo. Further suggesting a somewhat greater concentration of land and operations, however, only 6 percent of Desamparados's males declared themselves employers (*dueños* or *patronos*), versus 17 percent in Santo Domingo.

This can be explained in part by the weight of the few but large foreign owners, the Von Schroters in particular (see Tables 14.1 and 14.2). Of the nearly 1,200 coffee farmers in Desamparados in 1935, the twelve (1 percent) foreign owners held fully 14 percent of the land in coffee, and nearly half of the total farm area was planted in coffee. Comparable figures for Tarrazú were 542 owners of coffee lands (barely 15 percent of the total farm land area in this settlement zone was then in coffee), where the lone foreign owner farmed only 27 manzanas (one manzana equals 0.7 hectares) in coffee. In Santo Domingo, there were only six foreign owners among 854, holding just under 5 percent of the land planted in coffee, while in San Isidro three foreign owners held just over 6 percent of such lands, although in both of these cases something like 70 to 75 percent of arable lands were planted in coffee. The situation of strong foreign ownership was unique to Desamparados in the Central Valley, to some degree comparable only to the eastern area of Turrialba, where foreigners controlled up to a third of all coffee lands.

Probate records also suggest marked inequality among local property holders themselves, with a few large owners often with little coffee planted and several different crops beyond pasture and cattle herds.[9] The vast

[9] Probate records for these districts were gathered in 1986 while reviewing perhaps 3,000 of the over 10,000 such files organized by both local and district administrative criteria as "Mortuales" in the Archivos Nacionales de Costa Rica (ANCR) in San José. Common surnames in these areas were used as predictors of likely residents when reviewing the

TABLE 14.2. *Modernization and Foreign Ownership of Land in Coffee, 1935*

District	Average yield[a]	% of land fertilized	Average yield[a]	% of land unfertilized	Average yield[a]	No. of foreign owners	Land in coffee (in manzanas)	% of all land in coffee
Desamparados[b]	4.95	22.3	7.57	77.7	4.59	12	493	14.0
Tarrazú[b]	5.99	27.9	10.16	72.1	5.60	1	27	1.4
Santo Domingo	9.43	18.3	12.70	81.7	8.68	6	84	4.6
San Isidro	6.61	18.2	8.60	81.8	5.78	3	65	6.3
National average yield[a]		7.57						

[a] *Fanegas*/manzana.
[b] The figures for 1935 include both organic and chemical fertilizers. In 1955 in these two districts only 90 of 896 coffee farms used chemical fertilizers.

Source: See Table 14.1.

majority of the 352 probate inventories found between 1840 and 1942 were for the Desamparados region rather than for upland Tarrazú. However, even lowlander, settled society tended toward landed wealth holders whose farms were mixed crop enterprises much more often and later than in the more monocultural Santo Domingo–San Isidro. Median holdings for both men and women decedents remained throughout in the one- or two-hectare range, with cases of holdings in excess of 40 hectares very infrequent if not unknown. Nearly all of the district's heirs faced the division of estates the land area of which did not exceed 10 hectares, and with the exception of the Von Schroter estate of 638 hectares in 1906, even a 50-hectare estate would have been thought of as "large-scale" and quite a rarity in the local context.

Whatever the levels of inequality among Desamparados's native sons, however, they cannot be remotely compared to the case of the Von Schroters. When the probate inventory of don Luis Otto Von Schroter was processed in 1906, it listed goods and rights valued at more than twenty-five times the total of the next wealthiest local decedent over the entire century of coffee culture![10] An estate valued at more than 500,000 pesos and claiming rights in properties of more than 600 hectares, however much of it undeveloped, simply had no comparison in the preceding or following half-century in Desamparados.

Desamparados and Tarrazú were characterized by a more mixed agriculture, combined with lower yield and grade coffee production, outside of a few favored upland pockets in the area. More than half the land was used for noncoffee crops and activities, and as much as 75 to 85 percent in the more remote areas at higher elevation in Tarrazú (Frailes, Patarrá, San Cristobal, Rosario), while in Santo Domingo and San Isidro de Heredia, two-thirds to three quarters was planted in coffee. Coffee yields were half to two-thirds those of Santo Domingo, and they were first raised with the use of both organic and chemical fertilizers in the larger farms, whether in Desamparados or Tarrazú (see Tables 14.1 and 14.2). While only 20 to 30 percent of farms used any type of fertilizer in 1935, those that did enjoyed a 50 to 90 percent increase in average yields. However, as late as 1955, only 10 percent of coffee farms in Desamparados-Tarrazú reported using any chemical fertilizers, the single

largest, most undifferentiated administrative units (e.g., "San José" or "Heredia"). I was able to locate 430 files for Santo Domingo/San Isidro de Heredia and only 352 for Desamparados/Tarrazú. The period 1900–20 is somewhat overrepresented in terms of probate documents for Desamparados-Tarrazú for unknown reasons.

[10] ANCR, Mortuales, Juzgado Segundo de San José, No. 9789 (1906).

TABLE 14.3. *Agrarian Structure of Desamparados and Its Surrounding Hamlets, 1955*

District	All farms	Average size[a]	Coffee farms	Average size[a]	Average yield[b]	Farms with wage workers (%)
Desamparados	85	5.4	80	3.6	6.5	78
San Miguel	254	10.5	232	3.5	4.7	43
S. Juan Dios	63	6.0	63	3.9	3.9	62
San Rafael	117	10.7	115	4.9	4.6	72
San Antonio	42	6.1	42	3.6	6.5	84
Frailes	140	13.5	133	3.3	5.8	54
Patarrá	102	14.3	91	3.9	5.1	64
San Cristobal	84	17.3	45	1.9	4.5	34
Rosario	99	10.8	95	3.0	3.8	51

[a] In manzanas.
[b] *Fanegas*/manzana.
Source: Archivos Nacionales de Costa Rica, ANCR Microfilm rolls 35, 36, 40 of the Censo Agro pecuario, 1955, carried out by the Dirección General de Estadística y censos.

greatest contributor to rapidly rising yields in that period. The leading role played early on by large farms in the introduction of fertilizer use did not prove revolutionary. It was not until the coops began their own program of state-financed modernization after the 1960s that their use became generalized.

The leading role one might have imagined for large farms owned by processors was not in evidence in labor relations, either. Even in central Desamparados in 1955, fully 22 percent of coffee farms subsisted with no wage workers whatsoever, and the surrounding villages counted between 16 and 66 percent of farms in this relatively autarchic category of householder self-sufficiency and productive marginality (see Table 14.3). Among the region's 986 coffee farms, the largest employer of salaried workers reported seventy-eight employees, while the largest employer of presumably family, or dependent, "nonsalaried," labor listed twenty-four individuals (see Table 14.4). Just over a third of farms region-wide reported employing no salaried workers, while three-quarters had fewer than five, and under 10 percent of farms employed ten or more salaried workers. Nearly half of all farms employed fewer than five workers of any kind (family and salaried combined), and fewer than one-fifth employed ten or more of any kind. Clearly, however widely distributed the poverty and however highly concentrated existing technical and

TABLE 14.4. *Number and Percentage of Farms Employing Workers in Desamparados-Tarrazu, 1955*

No. of workers	Total		Salaried		Nonsalaried	
	no.	%	no.	%	no.	%
0	7	1	357	36	79	8
1–4	454	46	389	40	798	81
5–9	359	36	162	16	101	10
10+	166	17	78	8	8	1
Highest	97		78		24	
No. of cases	986	100	986	100	986	100

Source: See Table 14.2.

productive advancements were by midcentury, these had not translated into an effective process of full proletarianization, modernized coffee production, or estate-driven land tenure concentration.

After their victory in the 1948 Civil War, the strongman José Figueres Ferrer and what would become the National Liberation Party (referred to as *liberacionistas*) supported the embryonic coffee producer cooperative movement. Following Figueres's election as president in 1953, abundant resources from the recently nationalized banking system flowed to coffee coops. These policies had an unprecedented impact in the coffee districts of the Central Valley and beyond. The use of chemical fertilizers was generalized by the 1970s, and both San Isidro de Heredia and Tarrazú became two of the most productive seedbeds of cooperativism, as well as strongholds of *liberacionista* electoral support.

Commercial Capital and the Nontransformation of Coffee Production

Luis Otto Von Schroter, the family patriarch and one of the largest coffee holders in central Costa Rica, brought more funds with him to Costa Rica than were owned by all of his neighbors combined. His probate records revealed sums more than twenty-five times greater than the second largest fortune recorded in the district. How did he invest his funds and what were their long-term effects? The surprise in this case is the fact that he did not overturn the local system of estate production. Instead, he concentrated on owning a few haciendas and many more isolated plots, combined with the provisioning of finance and processing services to a multitude of more humble neighboring producers. One would have expected the transformation of local coffee culture by means of haciendas rather than small plots. Low yields, the rapid proliferation of farms too small to fully employ family members year round, the growth of an impoverished laboring population, and the concentration of chemical fertilizer use on the few large haciendas would seem to have been an invitation to the concentration of coffee production and processing. But the history of the Von Schroter family helps explain why that did not happen.

The founder of the Von Schroter family in Costa Rica arrived in 1852 to collect credits owed to the English commercial house Joy. Otto Von Schroter found he needed to be even better at local politics than at debt collection, since the sums to be collected were soon to become intertwined with the interests of the English-educated physician and eventual president José María Montealegre. Von Schroter found himself collecting for a firm whose interests benefited briefly from presidential favor, since the president's wife was a member of the Joy family (Sofía Joy Redman). Tact and political intrigue, as much as any diligence in debt collection, contributed to Von Schroter's rapid rise to prominence as a coffee producer, processor, and lender in the country he resided in off and on from 1871 to 1895. When he died in 1905 at age eighty, his wife inherited goods valued at half a million pesos.

An analysis of both the probate inventory and the family company's account books reveals activities based much more on coffee financing, processing, and trading than on cultivation itself. Figure 14.1 contrasts coffee produced on Von Schroeter estates with that grown by others in the total of *fanegas* processed and exported by the Von Schroters over a ninety-year period. With the partial exception of the period following World War I, when the firm produced virtually none of its own coffee, the century-long pattern was one of estate cultivation of no more than 10 to 20 percent of all the coffee they processed for export and sold abroad. And this on the part of one of the largest growers of the time!

Much of the property declared in probate by the family patriarch was unimproved land in neighboring mountainous tracts, but the heart of the enterprise could be found in the complex of several coffee haciendas with three or four attached processing plants, together with a multitude of rights to small properties of less than five manzanas each. Nearly all of these properties were located in the area of Curridabát-Desamparados-Aserrí, just south of San José, although he also owned a *beneficio* in La Uruca north of San José. Given his and other major processors' level of dependence on third-party harvest supplies and their commercial profit

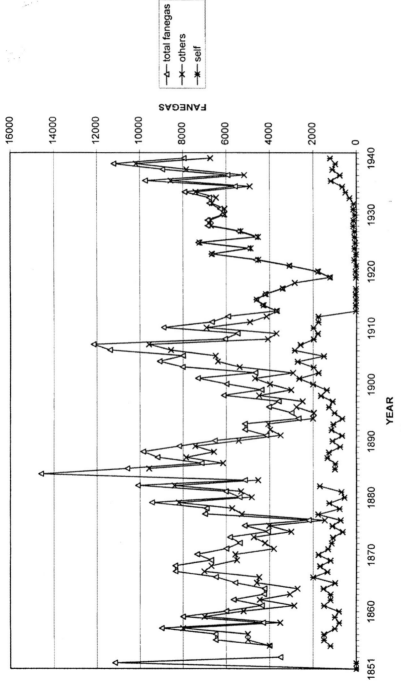

FIGURE 14.1. Coffee production by source, Von Schroter, 1851–1940.

possibilities, it is understandable that Von Schroter avidly financed and purchased coffee grown by small holders in practically all of the communities surrounding San José and even as far east as Cartago.

The haciendas owned by Von Schroter were, at one time or another: La Pacífica (San Francisco Dos Ríos/San Antonio), Lagunilla (Curridabát), Cañas (San Juan de Díos), San Miguel (S. M. de Desamparados), La Constancia (San Antonio), and La Eva y La Raya (Desamparados). Nearly all these *haciendas* were supposedly sold between 1906 and 1913.[11]

Some of the haciendas, such as La Pacífica, were purchased already formed from other large growers. Others, like La Raya and San Miguel, the only two that remained part of the enterprise through the difficulties of the First World War, were expanded after purchase. La Raya was purchased between 1875 and 1880 and grew from some 24 manzanas to between 100 and 120 before its seizure as German property during the Second World War and its break up and sale as urban lots in the 1950s. San Miguel was purchased around 1930 and was converted from pasture to coffee during the following decade. Outside of these two cases of territorial expansion, the pattern was one of purchase and sale among a small group of large processors (Florentino and Teodosio Castro, the Montealegres, the Lindo Brothers, etc.) of already formed haciendas of relatively stable size. When urbanizing centrally located properties after 1950, or selling others as a consequence of the damage caused by Irazú volcano's eruptions in 1963–65, the resulting funds often were invested in the growing Pacific coastal cattle industry rather than in coffee production.

The behavior of these large coffee investors took place in a context of prior peasant possession of most of the land. The peasants' surplus could be captured more effectively through commercial activities such as processing, exporting, and financing of coffee and retailing imported goods in their family dry goods stores. These most centrally located lands

[11] The frequent absences in Europe of those responsible for the enterprise, as well as their vulnerability in the face of anti-German political campaigns, make questionable any claims of representativity for the firm's experience overall. Even though their own family's trade was predominantly with London, the Von Schroters and other German nationals in Costa Rica would be threatened with expropriation during World War I and would actually lose their properties during World War II. These properties were then given or sold to politically well-situated local interests, both private firms and cooperatives, with very little concern for proving any Nazi sympathies among those under attack. Thus, I have chosen to concentrate my attention not on the firm's strategies so much as on its less controversial commercial practices; that is, the source of coffee to be processed (Fig. 14.1) and the relative prices on both sides of the Atlantic (Fig. 14.2).

came to have a higher monetary value than land in virtually any other coffee-producing nation. The marked preference of the London market for Costa Rican coffee and premium prices paid by them meant that exports were overwhelmingly concentrated in that market until at least the 1930s. In effect, when the enormous difficulties and costs involved in any attempt at dispossessing smallholders were combined with the equally enormous profits possible in the processing and commercialization of the bean, the challenge of transforming coffee's traditional forms and relations of production was more often than not politely declined by large processors before 1950. This Herculean task would fall to a state-financed coffee producer coop movement after the mid-1950s, leading to some strikingly small farm sizes even after modernization and consolidation of holdings had been accomplished by the 1970s.

Lessons of Capital's Abdication and Peasant to Farmer Differentiation

The Von Schroters, just as other major processors, had many reasons to consider theirs a great success story. Prior to the 1930s, they ruled with little in the way of serious challenge on the local political front. However, their basic source of profit and power – the triple finance operations of crop-lending, harvest processing, and foreign sales – remained their Achilles' heel as well. This was made plain to them in political terms, first rather politely with state pricing board intervention in the depths of the Depression in 1933, and then much more painfully during the 1950s and 1960s with the consolidation of the coops and their alternative financing and processing channels. Facing this truly systemic challenge and the loss of their direct political dominance after the 1940s, those who hoped to avoid the eventual fate of the Von Schroter family (virtual disappearance from the coffee elite's "front ranks") would be forced into a vastly more competitive stance as financiers and processors. Moreover, they would eventually undertake their own version of modernized, large-scale production of coffee in formerly remote regions into which cultivation expanded very rapidly after an extensive system of all-weather roads was built in the 1960s and 1970s.

The fate of the Von Schroters and their fellow processor elites also suggests some larger comparative lessons. When commercial capital fails to undertake a thorough modernization of production processes this does not mean the inevitable decline of the activity it once dominated. Nor can one assume that producers trapped by this commercially exploitive system and incapable of transforming it would become impoverished. At

the same time, state intervention in favor of producers did not inevitably
lead to the collapse of the export sector by making it into the tax base and
cash cow of profligate urban modernizers, as has so often been asserted
for African cases in the twentieth century.

Thus, two analytical controversies based on Costa Rica's curious history with coffee, and especially large-scale capital's seeming abdication
of any radically transformative role during the first half of the twentieth
century, may well be of considerable comparative interest. First, what
are the upper limits to peasant cum farmer participation in the profits of
export agriculture when facing oligopolistic commercial capital as a key
bottleneck and mediator? Second, who or what brings about the historical transformation of peasant to farmer differentiation when commercial
capital fails to play the leading role in this regard? In this second case, in
other words, what weight should we assign, historically, to "initial conditions" and what to the historical agency of social and political forces
bent on remaking such conditions?

Thanks to the Von Schroter data, one can engage in some fairly
well-informed speculation as to the sources and levels of profit of the
processors/exporters, as well as their evolution over the period prior to
the development of cooperatives. Looked at from the opposite angle, it allows us to estimate maximal levels of producer share of foreign (London)
wholesale sales price, since both average prices are given in the account
books, although in local and foreign currencies (which we have converted). In Figure 14.2, one can see that, on average over the first half
of this century, Costa Rican producers supplying the Von Schroter enterprise may have received something on the order of 40 to 60 percent of their
wholesale sales price in London. If Costa Rican success is to be looked at
as something of a limit case, then these might prove useful benchmarks
for future comparative studies in other nations or regions in the world
coffee economy at this or other points in time.

This impressively egalitarian distribution roughly parallels another recent estimate made by the Costa Rican scholar Jorge León Sánchez.[12] In
his extraordinarily rigorous study of nineteenth-century factor prices and
returns, León Sánchez documents the continuous decline in the costs of
transport (by both land and sea, but especially the latter) and insurance in
the last twenty or thirty years of the century, as well as offering a detailed
study of the evolution of coffee prices and their social distribution. His

[12] Jorge León Sánchez, *Evolución del comercio exterior y del transporte marítimo de Costa Rica,
1821–1900* (San José: Editorial Universidad de Costa Rica, 1997), pp. 102–6, 337.

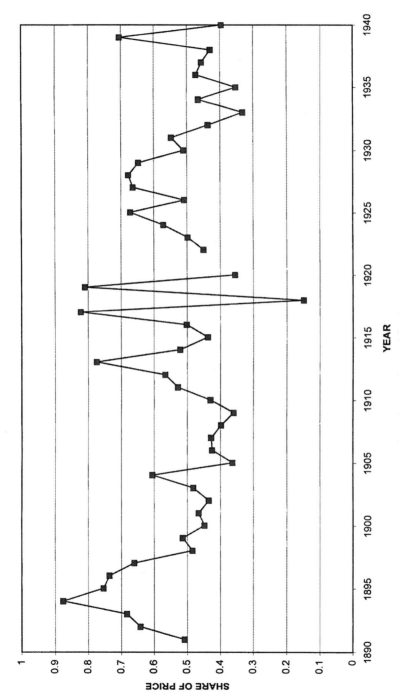

FIGURE 14.2. Estimated producer's share of final price, Von Schroter, 1891–1940.

estimates of returns to producers during the nineteenth century ranged from a low of 29 to a high of 63 percent of the final London sales price, or from 41 to 76 percent of the total if London merchant commissions were discounted. This compares with a range of 3 to 15 percent received by Costa Rican merchants and 17 to 45 percent taken by London merchants responsible for placing the coffee in the wholesale market. The Von Schroter data do not clarify what prices in London mean exactly, but most likely they reflect their own sales prices rather than the final market price of coffee once in the hands of London brokers and agents. However comparable these data sets, they no doubt understate the overall profit potential for processor-exporters with third party coffee, based not on one but three related activities: finance, processing, and export.

León Sánchez notes that processors charged, generally speaking, between 10 and 15 percent of the coffee processed in exchange for their processing services, traditionally defined as the 10–15 pounds of dehusked and dried coffee obtainable in excess of the *quintal*, or 100 pounds, to be returned to the grower from each *fanega* of freshly picked beans delivered to the processor's plant. (Advance payments at interest by the processor to the grower during the year to finance the crop production were based, as well, on the number of *fanegas* to be harvested and delivered.) After the 1948 Revolution, this charge was limited by law to 16 percent, but more important, both the provision of operating loans by the National Banking System and the growth of coop processing plants began to cut into traditional sources of profit. In the case of Von Schroter, this processing charge oscillated between 10 and 20 percent over the entire century, reaching the extraordinary level of 35 percent only once, in 1862.

An even greater source of controversy, and potential profit, was the practice of "grading" of coffee quality in advance of sale for substantially different prices abroad. Nowhere was this more subject to arbitrary practice than in the remote villages of Tarrazú, then the pariah of coffee producers and today its newfound "standard of quality"! Regardless of what we may estimate to be the relationship between average prices at home and abroad, one will never know for certain what the differences may have been between what local producers were told met the highest quality standards, and thus were paid for at higher prices, and what processors were able to obtain for the same coffee abroad. Both grading and physical measurement ("shorting" or "topping off" the baskets for the volume measurement – the *fanega* – not to mention converting to a processed weight measurement – the *quintal*) led to endless conflicts over appropriate and accurate standards for delivered/returned coffee and are among the most deeply ingrained aspects of rural folklore in Costa Rica. Therefore, we hesitate to assert any terribly reliable measure of profit given the repeated weighing, measuring, and grading involved.

When León Sánchez estimated that producers received between 60 and 75 percent of the gross income earned by coffee exports, versus our own Von Schroter data estimate of 40 to 60 percent, it is important to keep in mind that both calculations reveal substantial variation over time. The "best" times for local producers, in terms of both price levels and their share of final price, were the decades of the 1890s and the 1920s, while the "worst" were 1900–1905 and the early to mid-1930s.[13] Relative prosperity appeared to allow for greater social distribution of profit, probably owing to more intense processor-exporter competition in search of product with which to respond to external demand and price signals. Bad times, on the other hand, led to less processor-exporter competition and more caution, falling most heavily on the backs of direct producers.

The economic power of the processors faced serious challenges with the price boom following the First World War. It was precisely at the start of the 1920s that the Processors' Committee of the Chamber of Agriculture's Coffee Commission tried to formally set a common or fixed price (of 34 *colones* per *fanega*) for coffee to be paid by all processors, something they had sought, unsuccessfully, since the preceding century.[14] This attempt to formally limit competition in harvest purchases failed miserably, just as it did again at the end of the decade. Failure was due not only to opposition from producer groups but to more competitively aggressive processors themselves, such as Sánchez Lépiz of Heredia.[15]

The pressures on profit margins for processors were notable well before the law of 1933 that created the Institute for the Defense of Coffee and tried, for the first time, to publicly regulate relations between producer and processor. They would increase dramatically, however, after the emergence of coop processing plants in the 1960s. And it can be seen as something of a tribute to the theoretical flexibility and political skills of the coops' founders that they sought essentially to spur precisely this competitive behavior within the new context of a real if minoritarian coop finance and

[13] Exchange rate instability in the 1890s makes calculations of share distribution somewhat suspect for that decade, and the disruptions of the First World War make any calculations for 1915–20 similarly questionable.

[14] Carlos Alberto Naranjo Gutiérrez, "La Modernización de la caficultura costarricense, 1890–1950," master's thesis, Universidad de Costa Rica, 1997, pp. 233–6.

[15] Ana Virginia Arguedas Chaverri and Martha Ramírez Arias, *La Actividad cafetalera y el caso de Julio Sánchez Lépiz* (San José: Universidad Estatal a Distancia, 1990), pp. 128–35.

processing capacity, rather than replace a private oligopoly with a public monopoly and risk the loss of their very income gains in the process.

In assessing the impacts of these mid-twentieth century policies, one inevitably must deal with the weight of initial historical conditions inherited from the nineteenth century, as well as the subsequent actions of the very commercial capital interests undermined but hardly annihilated by the coop reforms. However much one may marvel at the skill and wisdom of certain *liberacionista* political leaders in overcoming both opposing oligopolists *and* the understandable tendencies within their own movement toward triumphalism and statist dominance of the economy, success is never its own explanation.

Robert Williams has recently advanced a particularly compelling model of socioeconomic and political evolution of Central America's coffee zones, based essentially on the structures, experiences, and patterns of behavior of the first historical stage of cultivation in each subregion.[16] What he refers to as "path dependence" is tied very closely to local or municipal political institutions developed with the birth of coffee culture that were made into national ones over the next two generations or so. Few historians of the nineteenth century may feel comfortable rejecting this kind of expression of faith in our explanatory power, but such an analytical framework seems to me problematic for this case.

If one were to explain the experience of Desamparados-Tarrazú based fundamentally on its initial or mid-nineteenth-century historical conditions, there would probably be little hope of recognizing, much less predicting, what emerged after the mid-twentieth century. The political control exercised by those at the pinnacle of San José's elite, as well as the distinctive roles of both commercial capital and foreign ownership in the area during the nineteenth and early twentieth centuries, would have led us to expect an agrarian "path" substantially different from that found in Desamparados-Tarrazú.

These initial conditions of inequality and lack of autonomy did not lead to an inevitable modernization based on commercial capital's dominance nor to an estate-driven land consolidation, similar to what did in fact take place to the east in Turrialba, for example, not even with the infusion of the vast – in local terms, at least – Von Schroter fortune. National politics and its complex contest of new and old social actors and regions seems to have played a critical role in counteracting strong local tendencies early on toward both landed concentration and proletarianization.

[16] Williams, *States and Social Evolution*.

The weight of the nineteenth century may have been enormous, but in Desamparados-Tarrazú, at least, the weight of mid-twentieth-century innovations counted for even more.

Processors and exporters may have had to lick their wounds following the 1948 Revolution (which brought the *liberacionistas* to power) and the rise of the coops, but they were hardly without resources or new strategies. Indeed, the success of the coop movement was predicated on private capital and former enemies responding competitively in ways that favored direct producers in either situation. Gertrud Peters and Jeffery Paige have recently made major contributions to our understanding of this regrouping of large-scale producers and processors after the rise of *liberacionista* coops in the 1950s and 1960s. Large-scale producers regrouped and sought to retain clients not only via price competition and ancestral loyalties, but particularly by developing their own coffee lands and processing capacity in new and formerly remote areas.[17]

Both Peters's "enterprise strategies" and Paige's histories of "megaprocessors" help to shift the focus away from immutable initial conditions and from the "happy ending" literature so typical of many *liberacionista* treatments of 1948, the coop movement, and their legacies today. And yet their narratives at times appear to be developing in something of a social and economic vacuum. Worse yet, their inevitable and laudable focus on outlying areas of new coffee production can make colonization zones seem like the new bastions of hierarchy and polarization, a veritable staging ground for commercial capital's late twentieth-century counterattack against its midcentury betrayal.

Rather than considering these areas as essentially reclaimed by the traditional coffee interests, a far better hypothesis is that it was precisely in these new sites of conflict where the fate of cooperativism's struggle with the old model of private processing was decided in the 1960s and 1970s. As Seligson and Edelman have eloquently shown for the South Pacific region and its new coffee zone of Coto Brus, there, too, nonprocessor producers disputed the process by which land was claimed, often times successfully.[18] It was precisely these colonization areas, characterized by both substantial inequality in land tenure and outmigration from

---

[17] Paige, *Coffee and Power*; Gertrude Peters Solórzano, "Historia reciente de las grandes empresas cafetaleras, 1950–1980," in *Historia, problemas y perspectivas agrarios en Costa Rica*, Número especial, *Revista de Historia* (1985): 241–63.

[18] Marc Edelman and Mitchell Seligson. "Land Inequality: A Comparison of Census Data and Property Records in Twentieth-Century Southern Costa Rica," *Hispanic American Historical Review* 74, no. 3 (1994): 445–91.

relatively early on, that offered the best conditions for the rise of cooperativism: widespread coffee cultivation but within a mixed agriculture involving essentially all farming families, controlled by local, resident "rich farmers" without neighboring or resident processors. These two groups' relations, in the view of the farm families, at least, were chronically embittered owing to long distances, low prices, and lack of competition among processors buying their too often uniformly low-grade coffee.

Certainly, the experience of Tarrazú itself strongly suggests just such a dominant rather than merely contestatory role for resident coffee-growing farm owners. Its own modernization and dramatic increase in productivity between 1950 and 1980 was led by medium-sized farmers employing both terracing conservationist techniques and chemical fertilizers for the first time, under the direction of local extension agents tied to the nationalized banking system and the coops themselves.[19] This was a movement based not so much on an impoverished if egalitarian coffee peasantry, perhaps typical of some older areas like Desamparados, but on a new and contradictory local inequality capable of supporting a movement led by property-holding "*fuerzas vivas*" (a widespread euphemism in Costa Rica for the local or municipal "gentry") far above the level of both their poorer neighbors and their lowlander kin and forbearers.

San Marcos de Tarrazú, the district headquarters for the uplands, was home to one such coffee producer cooperative. Founded relatively late, in 1960, it enrolled some 1,247 members by 1973, some 1,167 in 1978, and 907 in 1980. By 1971, the coop members' subscription of some 330,000 *colones*, along with some state-provided funds, allowed it to loan nearly one million *colones* (over $100,000) to its members. Nonfarmers could also be shareholders, but decision making, as in virtually all of these organizations, was concentrated in the hands of a board of directors chosen from among the leading farmers, and the administrator they hired to run the firm on a daily basis. The 1,559 shareholders in 1978 had subscribed nearly three million *colones* and the coop was processing and selling nearly 16,000 *quintales* of its members' coffee crop.[20]

[19] For the modernization of cultivation process since 1950, see Wilson Picado U., "La Expansión del café y el cambio tecnológico desigual en la caficultura de Tarrazú, Costa Rica, 1950–1998," master's thesis, Universidad Nacional, 2000.
[20] ANCR, Ministerio de Trabajo y Seguridad Social, "Cooperativas," no. 60 (Cooperativa de Caficultores de Tarrazú R.L., 1973). See Deborah Sick, *Farmers of the Golden Bean: Costa Rican Households and the Global Coffee Economy* (Dekalb: Northern Illinois University Press, 1999), pp. 76–82, for a particularly clear description and analysis of this

Ironically, today some of the highest-quality, most expensive coffee is grown in microregions of Tarrazú, while prior to the 1960s all coffee grown in both Desamparados and Tarrazú was routinely assigned a lower quality and price, in part based on arguments of poor soil conditions and in part on higher transportation costs. Producer resentment of this uniformly discriminatory pricing among private processors played a key role in the rise of the producer coop movement and its processing plants in the 1960s and 1970s.

Although not active in the local coop in Tarrazú, the *liberacionista* strongman José Figueres and his leadership role offers an especially illustrative case of a successful farmer from precisely such a "close-in" colonization area (his farm, La Lucha, was located in the uplands of San Cristóbal), just as with San Isidro de Heredia. Indeed, the entire Figueres family provides an example not only of the key role of outlying regions in coffee's "march to democracy," but also of the importance of political-ideological commitments and historical calculations based on them rather than a rigidly linear "path dependence" on initial conditions. Both José María Figueres Ferrer and his brother Antonio, sons of a Catalán immigrant, were raised between San Ramón de Alajuela (yet another early center of coffee cooperativism) and the capital. They attended high school in the capital and worked closely in partisan politics with Francisco Orlich, the son of Croatian immigrants and later one of the few large coffee processors in San Ramón.[21]

Both Figueres brothers had extensive experience administering large agricultural properties with numerous laborers. One brother focused on building a cooperative and *liberacionista* movement, after seizing power by force of arms in 1948 and subsequently being twice elected president by landslide margins. The other brother followed a substantially different path, acquiring large coffee estates in the eastern region of Turrialba. There he moved forcefully to evict hundreds of tenant farmers and to modernize cultivation with wage labor and chemical fertilizers.[22] Needless to say, his historical contributions have not been highlighted by his brother's

pattern of control of the coops in a contemporary colonization zone further south in Costa Rica.

[21] Arturo Castro Esquivel, *José Figueres Ferrer: El Hombre y su obra (Ensayo de una biografía)* (San José: Imprenta Tormo, 1955), ch. 1, pp. 13–22. My thanks to Brunilda Hilje for pointing out to me that Orlich's family origin was Croatian rather than Catalán.

[22] See Antonio Manuel Arce, "Rational Introduction of Technology on a Costa Rican Coffee Hacienda: Sociological Implications," Ph.D. diss., Michigan State University, 1959, for material on Antonio Figueres in Turrialba.

partisan allies in advancing the Social Democratic agenda dominant in
Costa Rican politics for nearly half a century. In Turrialba, it seems, commercial capital had neither a tradition nor any intention of abdicating its
transformative leadership role, whatever the costs in terms of bitter social
conflict.

Options, both personal and historical, may be severely limited by "initial conditions," by the weight of history, by one's experience, and by
one's family and friends, but they exist and have manifestly important
consequences as well. Whether as militantly committed to the vision of a
Costa Rica of small farmers as José Figueres or not, processors such as
Francisco Orlich could actually rise to prominence within *liberacionismo*
once they understood and accepted the new rules of the game. But when
brothers part company as radically as the legendary politician José and
the obscure businessman Antonio, paths diverge not only personally but
historically. Each profoundly influenced the subsequent development of
peripheral, colonization zones and coffee production therein, but in ways
neither predictable on the basis of initial conditions nor assignable a priori
to the smallholder or commercial capital camp. Some lead and innovate;
others conform and prosper; still others make all the wrong choices.

Conclusion

While I am certainly not in favor of biography as history, nor as a mor-
alizing enterprise thinly disguised as the former, invoking the example
of the Figueres brothers amounts to a modest plea for the relevance of
both politics, broadly defined, and individual choice in the moral science
of history. And I must vehemently insist on the relevance of the twentieth century.[23] If we hope to find the origins of Costa Rica's modicum of
success in creating a somewhat more equitable modernization of coffee
production, we would do well to keep a powerful focus on the twentieth
century and to place coffee's geographic periphery at its very center.

Costa Rican smallholders were able to achieve an enviable share of the
world price for coffee under a technologically backward system dominated by commercial capital, thanks in large part to rapid outmigration

[23] Deborah Yashar's study, *Demanding Democracy: Reform and Reaction in Costa Rica and
Guatemala, 1870s–1950s* (Stanford: Stanford University Press, 1997), makes a powerful case for the crucial differences in mid-twentieth-century coalition politics between
Guatemala and Costa Rica, even though she may needlessly exaggerate the two countries' political similarities in the nineteenth and early twentieth centuries in highlighting
their subsequent divergence.

and expansion of the area under cultivation. More tellingly, they were later able to implement a radical modernization project that revolutionized productivity levels after the mid-1950s, *without* permanently displacing their private processor adversaries but rather by restructuring a vigorously competitive regime of mixed public/private sector pricing and finance. These changes did not, however, overturn the decidedly antismallholder "eastern" regime of Turrialba, powerful testimony to the relevance of subnational or regional differentiation characteristic of the recent literature throughout Central America.

What that literature has failed to emphasize sufficiently, and what we have sought to explore above, are the related dialectics of initial conditions and political choices (path dependence), on the one hand, and national-level politics and regional and subregional class structures, on the other. We have argued, in particular, that both national-level processes and colonization zones have transformative capacities that may lead in relatively unpredictable directions in the twentieth century. Recognizing regional and subregional variation behind the mask of stereotypical "national" images of coffee production has been a key advance in the Central American literature of the past two decades. Linking regions and structures, dynamically and multidirectionally, to national political processes and outcomes would seem a worthy analytical challenge for the next decade or two.

15

Coffee and Development of the Rio de Janeiro Economy, 1888–1920

Hildete Pereira de Melo

Introduction

Brazil has had the world's most successful coffee economy since the middle of the nineteenth century. This chapter evaluates the impact of the coffee economy on the development process of Rio de Janeiro state.[1] This analysis studies the effects of the expansion of coffee exports as the *"staple"*[2] sector in the meaning of Watkins, Baldwin, and Hirschman linkage effects.[3] Unlike in most other coffee countries, coffee exports in Brazil triggered a vigorous process of industrial development, first in the city and state of Rio de Janeiro then in a more pronounced fashion in the city and state of São Paulo. We are concerned with the reasons why coffee in Rio de Janeiro after the abolition of slavery in 1888 more closely resembled the development of other coffee economies than the spectacular

---

[1] Unless specified otherwise, in this chapter Rio de Janeiro refers to what today is the Rio de Janeiro state. Statistics then aggregate the old Município Neutro (later Distrito Federal) and the old Rio de Janeiro state.

[2] This approach was inspired by a suggestion made by Wilson Suzigan in his book *Indústria Brasileira – Origem e Desenvolvimento* (São Paulo: Editora Brasiliense, 1986). See also Roberto B. Martins, "A interpretação do Crescimento com Liderança das Exportações: Modelos Teóricos e a Experiência Brasileira," in *A Moderna História Econômica*, C. M. Pelaez and M. Buescu, coords., (Rio de Janeiro, APEC, 1976); Jonathan Levin, *The Export Economies* (Cambridge: Harvard University Press, 1960).

[3] M. H. Watkins, "A Staple Theory of Economic Growth," *Canadian Journal of Economics and Political Science* 29 (May 1963); Robert Baldwin, "Patterns of Development in Newly Settled Regions," *Manchester School of Economics and Social Studies*, 24 (May 1956); A. O. Hirschman, *Estratégia do Desenvolvimento Econômico* (Rio de Janeiro: Editora Fundo de Cultura, 1961), and *Essays in Trespassing: Economics to Politics and Beyond* (Cambridge: Cambridge University Press, 1981).

(and unusual) income-multiplying effect it had in São Paulo.[4] To fully understand Brazil's participation in the world coffee economy, one has to study regional and subregional diversity.

Economic development could be seen as a diversification process of economic activities around an export-led productive basis; the leading products determine the dynamism of economic growth. This interpretation of export-led growth centers on the dynamism induced in the economy by incomes generated in the export sector. They stay in the capital circuit by their capacity to stimulate investments in their productive chain, both upstream and downstream, and on the income brought about by the expansion of exporting activity. Watkins, following Baldwin, treated this issue in the recently colonized countries of Canada and Australia; for these, a more equal income distribution originating from small, family-type land plots expanded the domestic markets, raising the level of production. This approach appears less attractive for a "plantation"-type land tenure system such as the one present in the Rio de Janeiro case. Watkins himself alerts us that in this case the result will be unequal income distribution and, in consequence, a smaller domestic market. The purpose of mixing the Watkins and Hirschman approaches is that this allows the analysis of success or failure in the establishment of relationships between export growth and the diversification of the economy.

This chapter measures these impacts in the *fluminense* (Rio de Janeiro state) coffee economy, analyzing its developments; from its production process, it tries to identify which activities linked to the staple sector were stimulated along the productive chain. Given the impossibility of estimating technical input-output matrix coefficients for these years, we

---

[4] This is not to say that Rio de Janeiro did not industrialize. The population of Rio de Janeiro state grew in the average at 1.35 percent per annum between 1872 and 1920. The city of Rio de Janeiro (Federal District) had a population growth of roughly 3.04 percent per annum in the same period (IBGE, Anuário Estatístico, 1939/40). Capital accumulation took form in trading houses, banks, and the nascent national industries. Between 1885 and 1895, forty-seven cotton-weaving mills were established in Brazil; of these, twelve were in the Rio de Janeiro state and in the Federal District. The Rio de Janeiro (state and city) mills comprised 25 percent of cotton-weaving mills of Brazil, with 50 percent of the looms. In 1907, the Federal District had 30.2 percent of the gross industrial product, and the Rio de Janeiro state had 7.6 percent. Eulália M. L. Lobo, *História do Rio de Janeiro (do capital comercial ao capital industrial e financeiro)*, 2 vols. (Rio de Janeiro: IBMEC, 1978). What happened was that industries were concentrated in the city of Rio de Janeiro; e.g., in 1919 the Distrito Federal had 1,541 industrial establishments, while Rio de Janeiro state had only 454. By comparison, São Paulo state had then 4,145, and Brazil 13,336 (IBGE, 1920 Census).

used the methodology proposed by Willumsen and Dutt (1991).[5] These authors note that coffee production has weak intersectoral linkages. In the coffee economy, four well-defined stages should be distinguished, which represent distinct phases of the social division of labor: the rural activities of (1) Cultivation, comprising sowing, weeding, pruning, and harvesting, and (2) bean processing on the farm, comprising de-husking, fermenting, washing, and drying; and the urban activities of (3) selection, packaging, and shipping for domestic and foreign trade, as well as (4) coffee bean roasting for final consumption.[6]

The present work has followed this approach in analyzing the coffee economy of Rio de Janeiro. It has classified as backward linkage effects those originating from chemical industry, trade, and transports and which represent significant technical coefficients for industrial diversification. At the turn of the twentieth century, there was little if any use of chemical fertilizers, tools, machines, and other material inputs on coffee plantations in Rio de Janeiro. Forward linkage effects of coffee production concern bean processing (cleaning, selection, and sacking). Regarding final demand effects, Hirschman has suggested that these should be measured by the distribution of the economic value added, including fiscal revenues. Once again, we had recourse to the composition of coffee value added done by Willumsen and Dutt. These authors show that the main components of this value for coffee were the capitalist surplus (profits, land rent, interests) and wages. Profits in the coffee economy corresponded to landed capital (plantations) and commercial capital. In the slavery phase, there was a greater symbiosis between these capitals, but the entry of foreign capital in controlling coffee exports in the 1890s, together with changes in the transport system, the heavy indebtedness of planters, and coffee expansion toward more distant lands in the north, led to greater separation between these fractions.[7] This separation was facilitated by

[5] Maria J. Willumsen and Amitava K. Dutt, "Café, Cacau e Crescimento Econômico do Brasil," *Revista de Economia Política*, São Paulo, vol. 2, no. 3 (43), (July/Sept. 1991).

[6] In the period under study, roasting was largely done by final consumers themselves; there was some commercial roasting, mostly by bakeries and artisanal roasting firms.

[7] Joseph E. Sweigart, *Coffee Factorage and Emergence of Brazilian Capital Market 1850–1888* (New York and London: Garland, 1987), 226. Letter from the English firm E. Johnston and Co., in 1903:"... cheapening in all manners product handling. In time, passing over factors and buying in the hinterland will be our salvation." Cited by Edmar Bacha and Robert L. Greenhill *150 Anos de Café* (Rio de Janeiro: Marcellino Martins and E. Johnston, 1992), 187. The importance of coffee trade in the world economy attracted foreign capital, and in 1899/1902, approximately nine-tenths of Brazilian coffee exports were controlled by foreign firms, and just six firms were responsible for three-fifths of the total.

the institutional gap between the state of Rio de Janeiro and the shipping port in the city of Rio de Janeiro, the federal capital, which was in another jurisdiction and controlled sector trade and financing. This subdivision of the territory into two institutional spaces was also an important element for analysis of fiscal linkage effects. As these comprise the share of income appropriated by the state and its use in promoting growth of other activities, in the *fluminense* case this institutional division weakened their impact on the Rio de Janeiro state economy.

The March of Coffee in Rio de Janeiro

Rio de Janeiro was the matrix of the development of the Brazilian coffee economy, its ascension and apogee comprising the period from 1820 through 1890.[8] In subsequent decades, the dynamism of the coffee economy moved on to the lands of São Paulo and Minas Gerais.[9] In the 1850–1920 period, coffee was the leading export, from both Brazil and Rio de Janeiro. In the first decade of the twentieth century, Brazil controlled around 70 percent of the world coffee supply. Until the abolition of slavery (1888), Rio de Janeiro exercised national and world leadership as coffee producer and exporter. But coffee was already provoking an economic revolution in the state of São Paulo, turning it into the wealthiest region of the country. In 1885, coffee exports through Santos harbor represented roughly 40 percent of Brazilian coffee, approaching the Rio de Janeiro exports, which had reached their top volume in 1882.[10]

In the 1880s, coffee plantations spread throughout the province of Rio de Janeiro. The northern districts were a pioneer zone where coffee was

[8] See Antônio Delfim Netto, *O problema do Café no Brasil* (São Paulo: FEA/USP, 1959); Sylvio F. Rangel, "O café no Estado do Rio de Janeiro, sua origem e influência na vida econômica e social da terra fluminense," in *O Café no segundo centenário de sua introdução no Brasil* (Rio de Janeiro: Departamento Nacional do Café, 1934), vol. 1, p. 161; Stanley J. Stein, "Aspectos do Crescimento e Declínio da Lavoura de Café no Vale do Paraíba 1850–1860," *Revista de História da Economia Brasileira*, Ano I, June 1953, no. 1, and Stein, *Vassouras – Um município brasileiro do café, 1850–1990* (Rio de Janeiro: Editora Nova Fronteira, 1990); Gilberto Ferrez, *Pioneiros da Cultura de Café na Era da Independência* (Rio de Janeiro: Instituto Histórico e Geográfico Brasileiro (IHGB), 1972).

[9] See Sylvio F. Rangel, "O Café," Notícia Histórica in *O Brasil suas Riquezas Naturaes – Suas Indústrias*, Centro Industrial do Brasil (CIB), vol. 2, 1908, and "O café no Estado do Rio de Janeiro," p. 161.

[10] See Bacha and Greenhill, *150 Anos de Café*, and Hildete Pereira de Melo, "O Café e a Economia do Rio de Janeiro 1888/1920," Ph.D. thesis, Instituto de Economia/ Universidade Federal do Rio de Janeiro (UFRJ), 1993.

Hildete Pereira de Melo

TABLE 15.1. *Number of Coffee Trees on Rio de Janeiro Coffee Plantations*

	1883	% state	1920	% state	Growth rate 1883–1920 (% per annum)
Southern Paraíba Valley (Barra Mansa, Barra do Piraí, Petropolis, Paraíba do Sul, Resende, Santa Theresa, Valença, Vassouras)	33,569,543	65	31,922,034	20	−0.14
Central Plateau (Bom Jardim, Cantagalo, Duas Barras, São Francisco de Paula, Macaé, Nova Friburgo, Santa Maria Madalena, Sumidouro)	10,568,000	20	35,105,720	23	3.30
Coastal Lowlands Araruama, Capivari, Barra de São João, Iguaçú, Itaboraí, Maricá, Rio Bonito, São João Marcos	1,503,000	3	3,487,435	2	2.30
Northern Zone (Campos, São Fidelis, Cambuci, Itaocara, Santo Antônio de Pádua, Itaperuna)	6,277,000	12	85,068,235	55	7.30
TOTAL	51,917,543	100	155,583,424	100	3.01

Sources: IBGE, Censuses 1872, 1890, 1920, passim, and C. F. van Delden Laerne, *Brazil and Java: Report on Coffee Culture in America, Asia and Africa to H.E. the Minister of the Colonies* (London: W. H. Allen, 1885), pp. 188–91.

entering; in the Central Plateau, coffee was in full production; and the southern Paraíba River Valley was a zone of decline, where the crop was regressing (see Table 15.1). By the turn of the century, coffee plantations had reached the state frontiers; by 1920, some 55 percent of coffee plantations were located in the north, and 23 percent in the Central Plateau; the remainder was distributed between the southern valley and coastal lowlands. Between 1900 and 1920, coffee plantations in the north had grown at the surprising rate of 7.3 percent per annum, close to the growth rate of the most dynamic area of São Paulo State.[11] However, around 1900 this expansion had reached the geographical limits of the frontier, which represented an obstacle to the profitability of the coffee business in the region. From the point of view of production, coffee could expand to neighboring lands in Minas Gerais, but this was another political territory. The logic of capital prevailed and coffee invaded these lands; the Mata Mineira became a rich coffee-producing region, subordinate to Rio de Janeiro. The closing of the Rio de Janeiro frontiers in the second decade of the twentieth century also meant that the formation of new coffee plantations would be a costly operation, because the soils were poor, exhausted by other crops, including old coffee plantations; these latter required greater care and labor than new coffee trees. In contrast to western São Paulo, coffee production in Rio de Janeiro was costly in terms of both chopping down forests and planting new coffee trees. By this time, Rio de Janeiro was the third national producer. But if it had been an independent nation at the time of the first world war, Rio de Janeiro state would still have been the world's third largest coffee producer.

As the land was not virgin, but planted with old coffee trees, there was less possibility for the laborers to grow beans, corn, and manioc; this increased wage costs for the planters to attract a work force.[12] Since farm credits were unavailable, rather than facing high monetary expenditures in the long-term investment of planting new coffee trees or switching crops, planters chose to prolong the lives of existing coffee trees.[13] The crisis was more acute in the southern valley of the Paraíba River; this region had been the cradle of the coffee expansion and had the oldest plantations; by 1920 it had only 20 percent of coffee trees of the state, as Table 15.1 shows.

By 1920, the main coffee-producing states were São Paulo, Minas Gerais, Rio de Janeiro, and Espírito Santo. The signs of the Rio coffee economy crisis are evident in Table 15.2. Espírito Santo plantations had nearly reached the production level of Rio de Janeiro, while São Paulo and Minas Gerais were much ahead of Rio. An interesting aspect, which

[11] See Sérgio Milliet, *Roteiro do Café e Outros Ensaios*, 4th ed. São Paulo: Hucitec/ Pró-Memória (INL), 1982), p. 61.

[12] Coffee is a permanent crop; until the early twentieth century, a coffee tree took from four to six years until production, and had a productive life of forty years. Until production started, other crops might be cultivated in the spaces between the young coffee plants; the produce was marketed by laborers, generating additional revenue.

[13] An identical situation occurred in the Mata region of Minas Gerais. See Ana L. D. Lanna, *A Transformação do Trabalho* (Campinas: UNICAMP/CNPq, 1988), cap. III.

TABLE 15.2. *Brazil – Principal Coffee Producing States in 1920*

	Production in million sacks[a] (average 1917–20)	Productivity	
		Sacks/ha[b]	Sacks by 1000 trees
São Paulo	7,873	7.7	9.6
Minas Gerais	2,473	3.8	5.0
Rio de Janeiro	820	4.2	5.2
Espírito Santo	772	5.0	6.7
Bahia	148	2.0	3.0
Brazil	12,086	5.5	7.1

[a] One sack weighed 60 kg.

[b] One hectare (ha) equaled 2.471 acres.

Sources: Constantino C. Fraga, "Resenha Histórica do Café no Brasil," in *Agricultura em São Paulo*, Boletim da Divisão Econômica Rural, São Paulo, 10 (1): 15; Anuário Estatístico do Café, 1939/41, D.N.C., Rio de Janeiro.

sustains our slow decline hypothesis for coffee plantations in Rio de Janeiro, is shown by productivity data (Table 15.2). Old coffee plantations of Rio had slightly better productivity than those of Minas Gerais, both by hectare and by tree. This higher productivity probably resulted from the expansion, between 1910 and 1920, of coffee plantations into the new fertile lands of the northern *fluminense* region, especially in the municipios of Itaperuna and Santo Antônio de Pádua, the last lands to be brought into the coffee economy of the state.[14] The share of this zone in the state's production explains the behavior of the average productivity. Espírito Santo plantations had indices close to the national average, which was pulled upward by the fabulous productivity of São Paulo "purple soils."[15]

Backward Linkage Effects: Transport and Commerce

Rio de Janeiro Railroads

The construction of the state's railway system was one of the largest linkage effects of export activity in Rio de Janeiro. Brazil had not only the largest rail network of any coffee-exporting country in the world, but until about 1890 the largest rail network in Latin America. Railways replaced mule caravans in the transport of coffee; the most evident effect on the coffee economy was the reduction in transportation costs, to which

[14] IBGE, Census 1920.
[15] See M. Etesse, "A cultura cafeeira no Brasil," *Revista do Instituto do Café* (Rio de Janeiro), Ano VII, Jan. 1932.

TABLE 15.3. *Kilometers of Railroad in Operation in Major Coffee-Producing States of Brazil, 1873–1936*

Province/state	1873	%	1883–84	%	1905	%	1919	%	1936	%
São Paulo	254	22	1,457	26	3,790	23	6,615	24	7,330	22
Minas Gerais	–		662	12	3,843	23	6,619	24	8,038	22
Rio de Janeiro	510	45	1,706	30	2,661	16	2,794	20	2,810	8
Espírito Santo	–		–		336	2	609	2	773	2
Brazil	1129		5,708		16,782		28,128		33,521	

Source: IBGE, *Estatísticas Históricas do Brasil* (Rio de Janeiro: IBGE, RJ, 1987), p. 412; José Luiz Baptista, "O surto ferroviário e seu desenvolvimento," in *Anais* Terceiro Congresso da História Nacional, vol. VI (Rio de Janeiro: IHGB, 1942).

greater cargo security was added. Coffee railroads were built alongside the old mule trails. Newly opened lands, distant from ports, now became economically viable.[16]

The national railway system evolved as shown in Table 15.3; note that coffee-producing provinces (states in the Republic) accounted for roughly 80 percent of coffee production by the end of the nineteenth century. In 1873, Rio de Janeiro still enjoyed the apogee of its coffee economy and possessed 45 percent of Brazil's working railroads. In the next fifteen years Rio de Janeiro's hegemony in coffee production continued, but the state of São Paulo already showed signs of great dynamism: Her railway system's growth rate between 1873 and 1905 was 8.8 percent a year. By 1888, Rio de Janeiro's railroads were 30 percent of the national system, but their growth in the period had fallen to 5.3 percent a year. The lesser dynamism is also due to the smaller size of the state: Coffee and sugar plantations were already completely connected by the railway system.

Railway investment in Rio de Janeiro was concentrated between 1860 and 1900.[17] Rails went where coffee income ensured the company's

[16] See Basílio de Magalhães, "Os caminhos antigos pelos quaes foi o café transportado do interior para o Rio de Janeiro e para outros pontos do Litoral fluminense," in *Minas Gerais e o Bicentenário do Cafeeiro no Brasil – 1727/1927* (Belo Horizonte: Secretaria de Agricultura de Minas Gerais, 1929); Odilon N. de Matos, *Café e Ferrovias* (São Paulo: Editora Alfa-Omega, 1974); Richard Graham, *Grã-Bretanha e o Início da Modernização no Brasil 1850–1914* (São Paulo: Editora Brasiliense, 1973); Almir C. El-Kareh, *Filha Branca de Mãe Preta: A Companhia da Estrada de Ferro Dom Pedro II, 1855–1865* (Petrópolis: Editora Vozes, 1980).

[17] This railway investment was largely subsidized by the state through interest guarantees that ensured to investors 7 percent interest on the estimated railway cost. This guarantee was good for the duration of the concession (from 50 to 90 years), tax exemptions for

TABLE 15.4. *Rio de Janeiro Railway System, 1885, Working and under Construction*

	Extension (km)	Capital (contos de réis)	Ownership regime
City of Rio de Janeiro			
Pedro II	832	952,453	Public (central)
Rio do Ouro	69	1,165	Public (central)
Corcovado	4	400	Private national
Northern	71	2,000	Foreign
Rio de Janeiro State			
Grão Pará	92	4,000	Private national
Cantagalo	309	10,861	Public (province)
Carangola	188	6,000	Private national
Ramal Cantagalo	86		Private national
União Valenciana	63	1,080	Private national
Macaé/Campos	104	8,000	Private national
Sto. Antônio Pádua	93	–	Private national
Sta. Isabel do Rio Preto	75	3,800	Private national
Pirahyense	56	3,000	Private national
Barão de Araruama	41	800	Private national
Campos/ S. Sebastião	18	600	Private national
Comércio/ Rio Flores	27	790	Private national
Rezende/Areas	28	2,200	Private national
Bananalense	12	810	Private national
São Fidélis	15		Private national
Vassourenses	6		Private national
Rio Bonito/Jutanahyba	9		Private national

Source: C. D. Ribeiro Pessoa, Jr., *Estudo Descritivo das Estradas de Ferro do Brasil* (Rio de Janeiro: Imprensa Nacional, 1886).

profitability and in turn stimulated greater productivity of capital invested in coffee (see Table 15.4). Of the railroads built in Rio de Janeiro, only the Pedro II road had a different history, with the massive presence of the imperial government in its development. The others formed a web of small branch lines and medium-sized lines, organized by the agrarian and commercial capital (coffee and sugar) of exporting regions. When the Republic was proclaimed in 1889, Rio de Janeiro had more than 1,700 kilometers of working railways. The main one was then called the Pedro II (later

importing tracks and equipment, plus leave to explore the land adjoining the rails. See Steven Topik, *A Presença do Estado na Economia Política do Brasil de 1889 a 1930* (Rio de Janeiro: Record, 1987), pp. 94–6, and William R. Summerhill, "Market Intervention in a Backward Economy: Railway Subsidy in Brazil 1854–1913," *Economic History Review* 51, no. 3 (1998).

Central do Brasil), which served the Southern Paraíba Valley and linked
the state with São Paulo and part of Minas Gerais. The most dynamic
coffee zone, the northern region, was criss-crossed with many railroads
(Cantagalo, Carangola, and Macaé/Campos) built by coffee and sugar
cane growers of the region. The arrival of tracks led to the growth of a few
villages and towns around railroad stations, while other towns, distant
from the tracks, dwindled. For example, the prosperous city of Vassouras
suffered a setback when the rails were turned away from its commercial
center. In the north of the state, several rail junctions spawned urban
nuclei: Miracema, Porciúncula, Santo Antônio de Pádua, and Itaocara.

Flávio Saes concludes in his analysis of the performance of São Paulo
railroads that monopoly and constant rail expansion were important elements in the prosperity of enterprises.[18] These features were also valid for
Rio de Janeiro. When rail expansion declined at the end of the nineteenth
century, as state frontiers became an immovable hurdle, operational costs
rose, and a rate war broke out.[19] Numerous companies entered a situation of chronic deficit. The process of decline led to the merging of branch
lines with the Central do Brasil, in the Paraíba Valley, and the formation of
Leopoldina Railway in 1898 from railroads built in the Central Plateau,
in the north, and Minas Gerais. Thus, by the turn of the century, two large
companies remained, Central do Brasil and Leopoldina Railway, controlling the Rio de Janeiro railways; the much vaunted presence of English
capital had been limited to a loan to Pedro II and to the controversial
buy-out of the northern branches to form Leopoldina Railway.[20]

The railway system of Rio de Janeiro (and of Brazil) did not stimulate the development of the local metal-mechanical industry. The material
used, from rail to engines and carriages, was mostly imported; but by
1920, one-third of the wagons used by federal railroads was locally made.
However, this was basically an artisanal production.[21] Engines were re-
paired, but there was only one unsuccessful attempt to manufacture them.
On the positive side, however, repair shops created by the companies
trained specialized manpower such as lathe operators and mechanics, essential for future industrial development. The metal-mechanical complex
of Três Rios (Rio de Janeiro state) had its origin in these machine shops.

[18] See Flávio Azevedo Marques de Saes, *A Grande Empresa de Serviços Públicos na Economia Cafeeira* (São Paulo: Hucitec, 1986).
[19] Law no. 157 of 1894 allowed transport firms freedom in fixing their tariffs.
[20] See Edmundo Siqueira, *Resumo Histórico da Leopoldina Railway e Cia* (Rio de Janeiro: Editora Carioca, 1932).
[21] See Topik, *A Presença do Estado*, 94–6.

Carriage making, for passengers and cargo, grew very slowly despite the stimulus given by the federal railways procurement policy to give precedence to national producers.[22]

It may be argued the building of the railway system modernized the Rio de Janeiro economy; since local construction firms were hired for civil works, local producers for construction materials appeared.[23] These enterprises also increased the training of Brazilian technicians and engineers, who acquired experience in railway management. Nonetheless, the railroad's linkages were certainly far fewer in Rio de Janeiro state than in São Paulo state.

The railway system also reinforced the power and wealth of the plantation elite of Rio de Janeiro; the harbor city of Rio de Janeiro was especially favored by the opening up of the hinterland. This pioneering integration of the Rio de Janeiro economy also contributed, later on, to weaken its industry as it later became exposed to competition from São Paulo's manufacturers. Network expansion toward the Central Plateau and north of the state consisted of small lines and branches. This led to multiple companies favored by regional topography, dominated by rounded hills shaped like half-oranges at middle altitude (around 250 meters), and without large flat expanses, in contrast to the São Paulo plateau. The irregular relief did not impede railway development, although it may have contributed to dispersed ownership. This fragmentation also led to operational problems such as diversity of gauges and rolling stock, which rapidly made these small branches obsolete and difficult to maintain, increasing the operational cost of the firms and leading to low economies of scale. The end result was the concentration of the transport system in two large companies (Central do Brasil and Leopoldina Railway), which served both the state of Rio de Janeiro and the city of Rio de Janeiro (Federal District).

Coffee Trade

As the nineteenth turned to the twentieth century, the world coffee trade went through large changes, and Brazil dominated world supply. The crop

---

[22] From 1910 the federal policy favored national equipment procurement, but this failed to lead to the installation of a metal-mechanical complex in Rio de Janeiro or even in Brazil.

[23] According to Colin Lewis, local subcontractors played a larger role in Brazilian railroad construction than in Argentina. "Railways and Industrialization: Argentina and Brazil, 1870–1929," in Christopher Abel and Colin Lewis, eds., *Latin American Economic Imperialism and the State: The Political Economy of the External Connection from Independence to the Present* (London: University of London/Latin American Studies Monograph Series no. 13, Athlone Press, 1985), pp. 190–230 and 218.

had expanded from the Rio de Janeiro state to lands in São Paulo, Minas Gerais, and Espírito Santo; plentiful land and the increase in international prices favored this expansion and integration of the commercialization process. This was also helped by the establishment of regular steamship lines and the submarine cable. The cable connected Brazil with the world so that exporters were able to hedge risks from the volatility of the world market and to influence this market.[24]

After harvesting, drying, and processing via the dry method, coffee left the *fazendas* (plantations) and went straight to the harbor at first, and later to the nearest railroad station. Transportation from the *fazenda* to the station was via oxcarts, although a few plantations built small branch lines connected with the main railway trunk line. At the station, the coffee was weighed and embarked to Rio de Janeiro city within a week. The principal figure at this stage was the factor, who received the beans on consignment and was responsible for the unloading and storage at the Rio de Janeiro harbor.[25] These middlemen initially represented *fazendeiros* (planters) in selling coffee, but they soon started supplying other consumption goods for farms. These activities grew. The figure of the middleman in coffee trade ceased to be a mere representative of the *fazendeiro* as consignee in the coffee business; the factor came to play an important role in the distribution and financing of coffee activities in Rio de Janeiro.[26]

The first factorage houses were created by traders of the Recôncavo da Guanabara (towns at the far end of Guanabara Bay) and by traditional trading firms of the Court at Rio de Janeiro city. The factor, or *comissário*, who at first concerned himself only with coffee sales, started to intervene in the financing of the crop. As coffee exports grew in answer to the growth of world demand, regional production had to expand. Before the abolition of slavery in 1888, this implied larger amounts of capital to buy slaves, to extend coffee plantations, and to operate existing plantations. To satisfy these demands, *fazendeiros* started to go to factorage houses in charge of

---

[24] See Bacha and Greenhill, *150 Anos de Café*, 173–4; Antônio Delfim Netto, *O problema do café no Brasil*, p. 7.

[25] See Robert Greenhill, "The Brazilian Coffee Trade," in D. C. Platt, ed., *Business Imperialism* (London: Oxford University Press, 1978).

[26] On the role of coffee factors, see the following works: Sweigart, *Coffee Factorage*, and Marieta de M. Ferreira, "A crise dos comissários de café do Rio de Janeiro," M.Sc. thesis, Universidade Federal Fluminense, 1977; Pedro C. De Mello, "Os Fazendeiros de Café e o Mercado de Capitais, 1871/88," *Estudos Econômicos*, São Paulo, IPE/Universidade de São Paulo (Jan./April 1984).

coffee sales and ask them for advances and loans to operate until the harvest. It was at harvest time that *fazendeiros* had more expenses (processing and transportation);[27] as these activities had to be paid in cash, business expansion required greater amounts of capital to be successful. Factors started dealing with the banking system to obtain credit for planters, in an extremely close relationship where personal and family ties between farmers and factorage houses were mingled.[28]

This connection was so strong that Joseph Sweigart concludes that it was hard to distinguish a coffee planter from a factor. "Coffee farmers were in most cases silent partners of factorage houses of Rio de Janeiro. These ties worked both ways: farmers owned factorage houses and commissioners bought coffee plantations."[29] Our work does not study the role of factorage in financing coffee export activities, as this role was more active under the Empire; in the First Republic factorage houses went under, in a slow and profound crisis as they were replaced by banks and public agencies.

The second link in the coffee trade chain was the packer; this was a middleman between the factor (closely linked to the planter) and the exporting houses. Packers bought large lots of coffee from distinct provenances and blended several kinds of beans, of both good and inferior types, to adapt the product to the preference of foreign buyers.

Last in the trade chain came the exporters. In 1870, the *Jornal do Commércio* published a listing of export houses of Rio de Janeiro; this had roughly a hundred large businesses and ninety small ones. It was initially a very dispersed trading structure. Railroad development then shortened

---

[27] C. F. van Delden Laerne, *Brazil and Java: Report on Coffee-Culture in America, Asia and Africa* (London: W. H. Allen, 1895), made an interesting discrimination of these expenses on page 217. Affonso E. Taunay, Historia do Café no Brasil (Rio de Janeiro: Departamento Nacional de Café, 1939/1941), pp. 472–3, citing comparative studies by Sylvio F. Rangel, distinguishes coffee farm costs in Rio de Janeiro and in São Paulo; transportation costs were slightly higher in São Paulo, export taxes lower in Rio de Janeiro, and sales commission was 3 percent, equal in both regions. Farm costs in Rio de Janeiro were lower than in São Paulo, because of less intensive care and lower salaries.

[28] Count Avellar (First President of the Coffee Trade Center of Rio de Janeiro 1901–4) thus defined those ties: "I do not exaggerate in telling you that the great coffee plantations in Brazil were made by the factorage trade of Rio and Santos. In a country lacking farm credit, how could one expect that banks would finance production in the hinterland, giving them resources that commissioners furnished them, inspired most often by personal coefficient[?]" The Coffee Trade Center of Rio de Janeiro was created by the factors of Rio de Janeiro to resist the concentration process of coffee trade led by exporting houses, but it was powerless to reverse the situation. See O Jornal, Oct. 10, 1927.

[29] Sweigart, *Coffee Factorage*, p. 226.

distances and brought this structure, with its many middlemen, into a competitive market. Factors tried to do away with packers, while exporters started traveling inland to concentrate all trade operations in their own hands. This concentration was also favored by the monetarist economic policy of Joaquim Murtinho, finance minister of President Campos Salles (1898–1902), which provoked bankruptcy of national banks and accelerated the integration and concentration of the coffee trade, through the absorption of packers by exporters and the disappearance of factors. Thus, in 1918 the *Brazilian Review* named 137 exporting firms for the whole of Brazil, with a strong presence of European and North American firms; the predominance of foreign firms is explained not only by the size of their home markets, but also by financing facilities in their native markets. There was a movement toward concentration at first, and then fragmentation. Thus, in 1874 the largest exporter accounted for 9.0 percent, and the five largest firms for 38 percent of the total coffee embarked through Rio de Janeiro, Santos, and Vitória (after 1904). By 1904, the respective shares had risen to 23 percent and 64 percent. In 1920, the largest exporter controlled 14 percent and the five largest 43 percent of coffee shipments. This process affected the whole coffee economy of Brazil.[30]

In this trade chain, factors were engaged in production and were affected by all the misadventures of cultivation as well as by fluctuations in crop yield and prices. On the other hand, packers and exporters, especially the latter, were concerned only with intermediating international exchanges. Agriculture and commerce worked in tandem in managing the coffee export business, even though exporting houses had more room to maneuver in the production/trade circuit (see Table 15.5). This occurred mainly because of their advantages in arbitraging exchange rate fluctuations between buying coffee from planters (in national currency) and shipping it abroad.

The stagnation of coffee production in Rio de Janeiro weakened the position of the old factorage houses of the city of Rio de Janeiro that had diversified their activities. From 1900 on, bankruptcies and moratoria multiplied among countless creditors and debtors.[31] However, the trade chain of Rio de Janeiro eventually transferred a sizable share of the coffee surplus to the commercial capital of Rio de Janeiro city. The coffee economy of the north and the Central Plateau, which featured mostly small planters, had neither the production structure of the big coffee plantations

[30] Bacha and Greenhill, *150 Anos de Café*, pp. 193, 389–90.
[31] Taunay, *A História do Café*, Tomo 9, p. 243.

TABLE 15.5. *Major Exporter Houses of Rio de Janeiro and Santos in 1898/1899*
(1,000 sacks)

	Rio de Janeiro			Santos	
1	Arbuckle (USA)	546	1	Naumann Gepp (U.K.)	973
2	J. W. Doane (USA)	375	2	Arbuckle (USA)	870
3	Ed. Johnston (U.K.)	301	3	T. Wille (Germany)	781
4	McLaughlin (USA)	211	4	Goetz, Hayn	756
5	Ornstein (Austria)	190	5	E. Johnston (U.K.)	757
6	Hard Rand (USA)	181	6	J. W. Doane (USA)	615
7	K. Valais (France)	166	7	Hard Rand (USA)	433
8	Aretz	130	8	K. Valais (France)	456
9	Norton Megaw (U.K.)	107	9	Aretz	347
10	Levering (USA)	107	10	Augusto Leuba	214

Source: Brazilian Review, several years.

that had existed in Rio state under slavery nor their relationship of mutual trust between planter and factor. As a rule, these growers sold their coffee in the villages and towns of their region. From these regional centers the coffee was sold to the city of Rio de Janeiro, where the trading structure and the banking system were installed. This was one of the reasons why the income-multiplying effect in the Rio de Janeiro state economy was so much smaller than in São Paulo. The northward expansion led to a clear separation between rural and commercial capital in the Rio de Janeiro plantations.[32] Coffee development in the north of the state took place under this new, unfavorable trade environment, leading to a slow-down of regional growth, although the city of Rio de Janeiro, still the second largest city in Latin America behind only Buenos Aires, did experience a healthy industrialization.

Last, we must stress the importance of the Rio de Janeiro harbor in Brazilian foreign trade. It was the uncontested leader until the advent of the Republic, which also coincided with the supremacy of Rio de Janeiro's coffee economy in the Brazilian scene. The city of Rio de Janeiro as national capital, marketplace, and redistribution center reflected the dynamism of export-led economy, and by 1870 it accounted for more than one-fourth of all the interprovincial trade.[33] This trading entrepot tradition remained; in 1920 the Rio de Janeiro harbor still serviced about

[32] See Stein, *Vassouras*, ch. 4.
[33] Steven Topik, "Metrópoles Macrocéfalas: Uma comparação entre a Primazia do Rio de Janeiro e a cidade do México entre 1800 e 1910," *Dados, Revista de Ciências Sociais*, IUPERJ/Vértice, vol. 34, no. 1 (1991): 63.

46 percent of Brazil's import trade. The importance of the coffee business plus public administration in its role as federal capital also made the city an important financial center; by the end of the nineteenth century the city of Rio de Janeiro held two-thirds of Brazil's bank assets and was the seat of the only stock market in the country.[34]

Forward Linkage Effects: Coffee Processing

Forward linkage effects in the coffee economy are restricted to bean processing in cleaning and selection, as well as roasting. After harvesting and measuring, coffee was transported to the farm yards where processing operations began. Stimuli to encourage the use of machines for coffee processing had been present in the coffee economy since the slave traffic had been outlawed in 1850.[35] These were relatively simple operations. The major innovation was the use of waterproof yards for the drying of beans plus mechanical husking and continuous feeding machines to prepare the beans prior to selling. The use of mechanical huskers and the construction of drying yards represented considerable investments, which only large planters could afford, but which were compensated by the 50 percent higher price obtained by beans thus treated.

During the later half of the nineteenth century, several machines were used for the preparation of coffee beans (see Table 15.6). Rio de Janeiro planters were pioneers in their use, starting with the "Concassor" husker of José Ribeiro da Silva, later perfected and renamed "Congresso," which received the ribbon of honor at the 1881 exposition. To rid beans of impurities, the old sieves were replaced by the Duprat blowers (made by Van Erven e Irmãos, farm managers for the Baron of Nova Friburgo in Cantagalo); bean sifters were implemented that sorted by size and weight;

---

[34] See Maria Bárbara Levy, "O capital usuário e o capital financeiro," *Revista Brasileira de Mercado de Capitais* (Rio de Janeiro) IBMEC, no. 7 (Jan./April 1977), and *A indústria do Rio de Janeiro – Através de suas sociedades anônimas Esboços de História Empresarial* (Rio de Janeiro: Editora da UFRJ, 1994); Gail D. Triner, "British Banking in Brazil during the First Republic," in Annals of the Second Brazilian Congress of Economic History and Third International Business History Conference, Brazilian Association of Researchers in Economic History (ABPHE), Niterói/RJ, October 1996; Anne Hanley, "Suprising Development: Bank Lending and Profitability in São Paulo, 1884–1920," in Annals of the Fourth Brazilian Congress of Economic History and Fifth International Business History Conference, Brazilian Association of Researchers in Economic History (ABPHE), São Paulo, September 2001.

[35] "Introduction of machines and tools that can make the farmer's work more productive," Report of the President of Rio de Janeiro Province, May 2, 1854, pp. 14–15.

TABLE 15.6. *Agricultural Machines by Brazilian Provinces in 1881*

Machine type	Rio de Janeiro	Minas Gerais	São Paulo	Espírito Santo	Total
Traditional					
Pestle mill	186	167	33	9	396
Water pestle	4	2	5	2	13
Modern					
Lidgerwood	138	78	41	2	259
Brazileira	11	4			15
Ferreira de Assis	4	11			15
Concassor	11	6		3	20
Aperfeiçoada	17	5	4		26
Congresso	17	2			19
Triumpho	6	12	1		19
Arens Irmãos		6			6
Hargreaves		2	5		7
Taunay and Telles	1				1
Duprat	6				6
Other	32	26	13		71
Nondeclared	141	50	28	2	221
Subtotal	574	371	130	18	1,093
Unknown origin					52
TOTAL					1,145

Source: Centro da Lavoura e Comércio, *Breve Notícia sobre a Primeira Exposição de Café do Brazil* (Rio de Janeiro: Typographia e Lytographia de Moreira, Maximino e Cia., 1882), no. 5.

and mechanical dryers, the most famous of which was designed by Luiz Goffredo E. Taunay and Augusto Carlos Silva Telles, replaced sun drying with steam.[36]

Documents from the 1881 National Industry Exposition that took place in the city of Rio de Janeiro suggest that there was interest in promoting changes to the traditional mechanical operating processes of the coffee economy. However, artisan crafts embedded in a slave-owning relationship were unable to compete with the English machine industry, which already in the '80s easily supplied the demand of the coffee plantations

[36] *Pareceres da Imprensa, Agricultores, Profissionais, etc sobre o invento dos engenheiros Luiz Goffredo E. Taunay e Augusto Carlos da Silva Telles, membros do Instituto Politécnico Brasileiro* (Rio de Janeiro: Typographia e Lytographia de Moreira, Maximino, 1881). See Almir P. Freitas Filho, "Tecnologia e Escravidão no Brasil: Aspectos da Modernização Agrícola nas Exposições Nacionais da Segunda Metade do Século XIX (1861–1881)," *Revista Brasileira de História* (São Paulo) 11, no. 22 (March/Aug. 1991).

(see Table 15.6). Imported Lidgerwood machines provided all operations: husking, sifting, and grading, and were the most widespread implements on coffee *fazendas* after the traditional pestle mills. The development of this semiartisanal manufacture took place mainly in the city of Rio de Janeiro, which was then hegemonic in coffee growing.[37] By the turn of the century, all modern equipment was being made in Brazil; the Lidgerwood firm dominated the market with two plants in the state of São Paulo (São Paulo City and Campinas), together with Arens company with a plant in Jundiaí (São Paulo). A few national producers also started making coffee equipment, such as Martins Barros and Amaral, but their industries were short-lived, as were the artisan efforts of Rio de Janeiro.

Rio de Janeiro's demand for coffee machinery was probably supplied by São Paulo factories. In the 1907 Industrial Census, we find no reference to production of these modern machines either in Rio de Janeiro City or elsewhere in the state. This was true even though Rio de Janeiro plantations used this equipment. By the Second Coffee Exposition of Brazil, in 1883, some 70 percent of the Rio de Janeiro plantations used the machines for coffee processing; this figure was close to that found in São Paulo.

The last phase (roasting) in that period was an artisanal activity, since coffee was often roasted by final consumers themselves. But in Brazilian urban centers this was done by bakeries and a few small roasting firms. In Rio de Janeiro City, the 1907 Industrial Census done by the Centro Industrial do Brasil counted in the Federal Capital 145 bakeries with 571 workers and 14 coffee roasting firms with 213 workers. These were artisanal firms, with just 63 horsepower in motor power and 1.200:000$000 milréis in capital.[38]

Final Demand Linkage Effects

Until Abolition, the coffee economy of Rio de Janeiro basically depended on slave labor. An 1887 estimate points to 145,880 slaves in coffee-growing regions of the state.[39] Most of these slaves worked on coffee

[37] Rio de Janeiro had the following machine makers in the 1880s: Frederico Vierling and Co., Van Erven, Arens, Hallier, Alegria, Hargreaves, Prince and Aspinal, Correia da Rocha and Co., Oficina Mecânica Industrial, Taunay and Telles and Manoel F. de Castro Nascimento. Almir P. Freitas Filho, "A tecnologia agrícola e a Exposição Nacional de 1881," *Revista Latino-Americana de Historia da Ciencia e Tecnologia* (QUIPU), México (Jan./April 1992): 88.

[38] Eulália M. L. Lobo, *História do Rio de Janeiro*, pp. 487, 572, 577.

[39] Based on the Report of the President of the Province of Rio de Janeiro dated Sept. 12, 1887. See also Hebe M. M. de Castro, "Os libertos e o mercado de trabalho rural

plantations, while a smaller contingent was in sugarcane plantations around Campos. The signing of the Abolition Law ("Lei Áurea") in May 1888, at the beginning of the coffee harvest, did not disorganize coffee production. Coffee production statistics indicate that there were no harvesting losses from emancipation, unlike the sharp decline that sugarcane plantations around Campos suffered. Since international coffee prices were high, it paid to hire labor for coffee harvesting. The opposite happened to sugarcane; sugar prices were low, so sugar mills stopped operating.[40] Early in 1888, farmers of the northern region, then the coffee frontier of the state, had countless meetings to design a labor strategy for defining wages and establishing disciplinary rules for farm labor.

In the formation of the labor market for the coffee economy of Rio de Janeiro, two types of labor relations were dominant: *métayers*, or fixed farm workers under a sharecropping system, and hired temporary labor to execute seasonal tasks. Coffee production by small plot owners appears to have been absent in Rio de Janeiro, in contrast to what happened in the Mata Mineira region of Minas Gerais state or in Costa Rica and Nicaragua, as Gudmundson and Charlip show in this volume. The coffee economy of Rio de Janeiro state had large producers, but their properties were fragmented. *Fazendas* had between 100 and 200 *alqueires* (roughly 250 to 500 hectares) on the average. Reasons for this fragmentation (compared with the enormous plantations of São Paulo) included the constant need to incorporate newer, more distant land, as well as easier slave surveillance on smaller plantations.[41] Coffee arrived in Minas Gerais lands after 1850, and by 1880–90 this area still produced only

pós-emancipação," Niterói, V Encontro Regional de História, Associação Nacional dos Professores Universitários de História (ANPUH), September 1992, and "Beyond Masters and Slaves: Subsistence Agriculture as a Survival Strategy in Brazil during the Second Half of the Nineteenth Century," *Hispanic American Historical Review* (August 1988).

[40] Our assertion is based on the observation that differences among coffee time series in Brazil are due to the fact that some of them refer to harvest data while others refer to coffee exports; given coffee warehousing, production in a given year could differ from exports that same year. Whatever the source, no coffee harvesting losses or export setback can be detected between 1888 and 1889. On slavery and coffee in the Province of Rio de Janeiro, see also Hélio O. Portocarrero de Castro, "Viabilidade Econômica da Escravidão no Brasil: 1880–1888," *Revista Brasileira de Economia* (Rio de Janeiro) (Jan./March 1973), and Pedro C. de Mello, "Aspectos Econômicos da Organização do Trabalho da Economia Cafeeira do Rio de Janeiro, 1850–1888," *Revista Brasileira de Economia* 32 (Jan./March 1978); on sugarcane plantations, see G. De Carli, *A evolução do problema canavieiro fluminense* (Rio de Janeiro: Irmãos Pongetti Editores, 1942).

[41] See Célia M. L. Muniz, "Os donos da terra – Um estudo sobre a estrutura fundiária do Vale do Paraíba Fluminense no século XIX," M.A. thesis, Universidade Federal Fluminense, Niteroi, 1979, pp. 136–9.

half as much as Rio de Janeiro and São Paulo. The occupation of lands in southern Minas Gerais happened mostly under the Republic. The Republic had passed a law granting states the right to legislate about state lands in their territories. In Minas Gerais, squatters in state lands had more time to regularize their occupation; this partly explains the smaller size of properties in its coffee region.[42]

In sharecropping (*meiação*), the *métayer* planted and cared for the trees, then harvested and dried the beans; the beans were divided between the *métayer* and the owner then or after husking. This practice was adopted in all municipalities of the state of Rio de Janeiro, alongside with fixed contracts for executing previously defined tasks, which were paid upon conclusion. According to the contemporary report by journalist Arrigo Zetirry,[43] wages paid for these tasks were the same as in São Paulo; the fact is confirmed by Thomas Holloway.[44] These tasks were normally associated with forming new coffee plantings on the estate itself. Fixed workers dwelt on farms and cared for the fields, being allowed to plant corn and beans in areas put aside by the owner or interspersed between coffee trees on some farms. The coffee harvest was shared (in equal shares or in a 1:2 ratio, according to verbal contract) by the sharecropper and the land owner, after discounting owner's expenses for bean processing and transportation. Labor on coffee plantations remained practically dependent on freedmen; from Zetirry's reports it may be inferred that 50 percent of the workers came from freed slave families. The scope of this chapter does not allow a closer analysis of work conditions, which varied considerably. What is clear is that in Rio state, former slaves and poor farmers, not European immigrants as in São Paulo, made up the bulk of farm labor. In this sense, labor relations were more similar to those in Minas Gerais and Central America than to São Paulo's immigrant *colono* system.

The declining production of Rio's coffee economy did not require immigrants, although successive attempts were made by the government of the state to do so. These failed, either because the financially strapped

---

[42] See Lígia M. Osório Silva, "A questão da terra na Primeira República," in Sérgio S. Silva and Tamás Szmrecsányi, eds., *História Econômica da Primeira República* (São Paulo: ABPHE, Editora Hucitec/FAPESP, 1996). Also see Lanna, *A Transformação do Trabalho.*

[43] The analysis of post-Abolition labor relationships in Rio de Janeiro farms is based on the chronicles published in 1894 in the *Jornal do Commércio* by Arrigo Zetirry.

[44] Thomas Holloway, "Condições do Mercado de Trabalho e Organização do Trabalho nas Plantações na Economia Cafeeira de São Paulo, 1885–1915 – Uma análise Preliminar," *Estudos Econômicos*, IPE/USP, São Paulo, vol. 2, no. 6 (1972): 159.

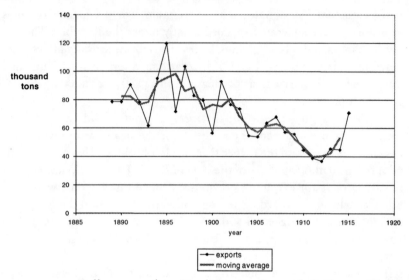

FIGURE 15.1. Coffee exports from Rio de Janeiro. *Source:* A. E. Taunay, *História do Café no Brasil*, vol. 10, tomo 2 (Rio de Janeiro: Departamento Nacional de Café, 1939–41), pp. 312 and 317.

state could not afford to subsidize the travel and setup expenses for the colonists or because of the limited fertile lands for coffee growing. With no expanding frontier, and no change in cultivation and processing techniques, farming in Rio was not attractive enough to compete with São Paulo in bringing settlers. Figure 15.1 shows the decline of coffee exports, which implied less demand for coffee laborers.

This declining trend of coffee exports from Rio de Janeiro meant that there was no structural pressure for the growth of the rural labor market. The modest growth is made explicit in Table 15.7. The maturity of coffee trees in northern plantations, associated with the recovery of sugarcane plantations, resulted in regional growth almost double that of the state average; the exceptional performance of the coastal region is also related to the same causes. During this period, the state attempted a policy of agricultural diversification,[45] and even managed to increase its exports of rice, beans, manioc flour, potatoes, meat, vegetables, and fruits to Rio de Janeiro city on top of its traditional supply of sugar; however,

---

[45] On the issue of the attempt to diversify Rio's agriculture, see Sylvia Padilha, "Da Monocultura à Diversificação Econômica – Um Estudo de Caso: Vassouras 1880/1930," Ph.D. diss., Universidade Federal Fluminense, Niteroi, 1977.

TABLE 15.7. *Rural Labor in the Coffee and Sugarcane Regions of Rio de Janeiro*

	1882	Growth rate (% per year)	1887	Growth rate (% per year)	1920
Southern Paraiba Valley	75,586	−5.59	56,693	0.73	71,985
Northern	38,198	−5.12	29,369	3.77	99,453
Central Plateau	32,484	1.14	34,374	1.88	63,645
Coastal	39,291	−8.32	25,444	2.99	67,368
TOTAL	185,559	−4.70	145,880	2.23	302,451

Sources: Report by the President of the Province of Rio de Janeiro of Sept. 12, 1887; C. F. van Delden Laerne, *Brazil and Java* (1885), pp. 100, 101, 188, 190, and the IBGE, 1920 Census.

this diversification was not enough to reverse the overall declining trend.[46] Growth of food crops was blocked by the form the transition from slavery took in Rio de Janeiro, with no division of rural property and with a mass of impoverished laborers, particularly former slaves, with no resources to buy land. The Rio de Janeiro agrarian elite succeeded in imposing an alternative to the dramatic spread of coffee in São Paulo, Espírito Santo, and later Paraná that resembled the move to staples agriculture of equally declining Minas Gerais: The Rio elite preserved its patrimony by way of extensive cattle raising or coffee plantations as long as government price support policies sustained the coffee price, complemented by food crops for the Federal District.

Last, fiscal linkage effects had differentiated impacts on the state of Rio de Janeiro and the city of Rio de Janeiro (formerly, the Federal District). Coffee, as the main item in Brazilian exports, was heavily taxed both by the Imperial and by the Republican states. Public revenues generated in this export activity both allowed the policy of sustaining coffee prices after 1906 and financed transport infrastructure and immigration to Brazil, important issues for Brazilian development by the end of the nineteenth century. In the Empire, the fiscal system was very centralized and the revenues of the Union were four times larger than provincial revenues.[47] The decentralization undertaken by the Republic attenuated that concentration; even so, federal revenues remained 40 to 50 percent

---

[46] On this policy, see Sônia R. Mendonça, "A Primeira Política de Valorização do Café e sua Vinculação com a Economia do Estado do Rio de Janeiro," Master's thesis, Universidade Federal Fluminense, Niteroi, 1977.

[47] See N. Leff, "A Emergência do Estado Desenvolvimentista Brasileiro: o final do século 19," *Estudos Econômicos*, IPE/USP, vol. 13, no. 3 (Sept./Dec. 1983): 632.

TABLE 15.8. *Per Capita Public Revenues (in mil-réis)*

Year	Rio de Janeiro (RJ)	Federal District (DF)	Average RJ+DF	São Paulo	Minas Gerais
1900	8,606			18,688	4,046
1905	6,630			24,703	3,453
1907	7,694	32,656	18,372	17,825	5,600
1910	7,690	56,189	28,472	13,290	4,945
1915	9,212	39,631	22,209	20,389	7,321
1920	13,694	49,355	29,014	37,954	9,489

Source: IBGE, Separata do *Anuário Estatístico*, 1939–40, Ano 5, vol. 1, *Séries Estatísticas Retrospectivas* (Rio de Janeiro, 1986), pp. 3–15, 119–28.

larger than the total revenues of the states. The state of Rio de Janeiro did not gain by the change to federalism, given the relative stagnation of the coffee-exporting business, which was its main source of revenue. The weight of this problem can be seen in the fall of coffee revenues in the period: In the early 1890s, they accounted for 70 percent of all the state's revenues; after 1910, they fell to around 30 percent.[48]

The Federal District (city of Rio de Janeiro) had a different issue: its government was appointed by the Union, with its own budget, which was further reinforced by the concentration of federal bureaucracy in its jurisdiction. This led to a substantial concentration of income in the capital city from fiscal revenues. The Federal District had per capita public revenues four to five times greater than the state of Rio de Janeiro, and substantially higher than São Paulo state (see Table 15.8). Besides the relative stagnation of coffee production in Rio de Janeiro, another problem corroded the state finances: farmers from Rio de Janeiro and Minas Gerais shipped their products through the Rio de Janeiro harbor. This led to linkage effects that took place in the city of Rio de Janeiro, outside state boundaries, besides rendering tax evasion possible when this was in the farmers' interests.

Conclusions

The process of diversification of economic activities experienced by the Rio de Janeiro economy from 1850 to 1920 was due to the expansion of coffee exports. Coffee production was the most significant event in the economic history of Rio de Janeiro. Growth of coffee exports led

[48] See Hildete Pereira de Melo, "O Café e a Economia do Rio de Janeiro," pp. 201–12.

to development of railways and created towns along the rail lines, such as Paraíba do Sul, Barra do Piraí, Miracema, Santo Antônio de Paduá, Porciúncula, and Itaocara. The population of Rio de Janeiro state grew in the average at 1.4 percent per annum between 1872 and 1920. The city of Rio de Janeiro (Federal District) had a population growth of roughly 3.0 percent per annum in the same period. Capital formation took form in trading houses, banks, and the nascent national industries. Between 1885 and 1895, forty-seven cotton-weaving mills were established in Brazil; of these, twelve were in the Rio de Janeiro state and in the Federal District. The Rio de Janeiro (state and city) mills constituted 25 percent of Brazil's cotton mills, with 50 percent of the looms. In 1907, the Federal District had 30 percent of Brazil's gross industrial product, and the Rio de Janeiro state had 7.6 percent.

The march of coffee through the Rio de Janeiro lands, from south to north of the Paraíba do Sul River, peopled the province, created wealth, but exhausted the soil, leaving in its wake destruction of forests and soil. The coffee economy in its movement toward higher profits demanded a depleting technique; where it passed the soil was exhausted. Slaves first, then settlers and small farmers lived in penury, leading a life with little resources or support. To this perverse side, it should be added that great riches were accumulated along this trajectory.

From 1850 until the turn of the century, the capital generated in the coffee economy built railroads, revolutionizing the means of transport of the society. Rails created the regional unit because they ensured the shipping and the profitability of agricultural production, changed the terrain of the state into arteries through which goods and wealth flowed, and consolidated the firm position of the city of Rio de Janeiro as economic center for the whole region.

The chronicle of the decline of coffee in Rio de Janeiro is shown in the slow but definite agony of that crop, from the first republican decades to the coffee eradication policies pursued by the federal government in the 1930s. This trajectory of crisis hid the relative profitability of the coffee business, which allowed the Rio de Janeiro planters to keep their lands and later convert their former coffee plantations into a low-yield cattle economy.

The coffee economy in Rio de Janeiro did not have the capacity for capital accumulation enjoyed by São Paulo. First, institutional separation between the city of Rio de Janeiro, the privileged port for the region, and the interior of the state concentrated the whole coffee trade structure in the city of Rio de Janeiro. This stimulated conspicuous consumption in the capital city, harming the process of capital accumulation on coffee plantations. Second, the end of frontier expansion in the 1890s and the large number of old plantations in the state restricted the possibilities for manpower absorption. The continuation of coffee exploitation was carried out by former slaves and their offspring under a sharecropping regime that employed them as resident farm workers and temporary hires. The Rio de Janeiro elites, soon after Abolition, tried settlement policies; but the lack of space for expansion, combined with the attractive urban market of the Federal Capital and the greater appeal of São Paulo's fertile fields, condemned these attempts to failure. When compared with the greatest international coffee success story, São Paulo's, Rio de Janeiro state's experience with coffee appears to be a tragedy despite its seven decades of prosperity and even worldwide leadership. But when the perspective is expanded to include the Federal District, Rio de Janeiro city, and one takes into account the growth of major cities (see above), factories, public utilities, one of the largest harbors in Latin America, and a dense rail system, coffee seems to have been much kinder to Rio de Janeiro state than to the great majority of other coffee-producing countries.

Conclusion

New Propositions and a Research Agenda

Steven Topik and William Gervase Clarence-Smith

Our goal at the end of this enterprise is to propose bounded generalizations that are sensitive to variation and that avoid essentialized categories. Coffee was not an all-powerful master that demanded that its subjects follow a specific life-style and mindset. Our findings are often made in opposition to grand theories, such as dependency and modernization, and we are thus cautious about putting forward alternative models, especially at a time when comprehensive metanarratives are suspect. However, we also believe that we should not lapse into the nihilistic belief that every case is unique, every time different. We have to start with empirical work, based on realistic and historically sensitive categories. From these we can inductively create generalizations, which can allow us to attempt deductive reasoning.

Despite our stress on variation and agency, we believe that useful conclusions can be drawn from all this, stimulating comparisons that look for patterns as well as for differences. Indeed, we hope that this volume might even help guide a minister of development in a contemporary coffee-producing country. He or she would consider consulting producers' associations, pickers' organizations, women's groups, ethnic clubs, processors, marketing boards, commercial intermediaries, internal transporters, exporters, and shippers, rather than dictate a "one-size-fits-all" policy from above. Such an enlightened minister would see that variation is determined not just by happenstance and contingency, and that local conditions and experiences affect the forces and consequences of production.

The studies in this book thus lead us to suggest ten new propositions about the relationship between coffee and the societies that produce it.

They are marked by considerable ambiguity and uncertainty, because coffee production relied on many different and complex labor and tenure systems, technologies, credit arrangements, and political regimes. We recognize that none of these propositions is in any sense an iron-clad law, and that societies change over time. Our hope is, rather, that these new propositions can be helpful in thinking broadly about the consequences of this specific export crop across four continents and many islands, and will thus stimulate new research. Such new work will undoubtedly lead other scholars to put forward further refinements and amendments.

1. Size of Holdings

In many parts of the coffee world, including much of Latin America, the latifundium was not the norm, even in Brazil. Melo's chapter shows that medium and small producers predominated in the Brazilian state of Rio de Janeiro, where coffee cultivation began earlier than in São Paulo. Chapters by Rus, Gudmundson, Samper, McCreery, Dore, and Charlip all demonstrate how widespread small holdings were in Central America, where communal lands remained entrenched in some areas, often held by Amerindian communities. A similar situation arose in Puerto Rico and even in other parts of Brazil.[1] Many smallholders were able to hold on to communal property in Africa and Asia, and obtain more land, including some under freehold or similar tenures.

Where large estates did exist, their historical origins were complex, and they often did not function as single units. Nowhere were estates simply a colonial legacy, even if some *sesmarias* (colonial land grants) in Brazil provided the foundations for early coffee *fazendas*. Moreover, the nineteenth-century land grab was patchy.[2] Demesne production was far from automatic. Tenancy prevailed in parts of Central America and Brazil, because latifundistas were unable to subject labor to centralized control.[3] Decentralization meant that the *colonos* on large-scale plantations in

---

[1] Fernando Picó, *Amargo café* (Rio Pedras: Ediciones Huracán, 1981); João Heraldo Lima, *Café e indústria em Minas Gerais* (Petrôpolis: Editora Vozes, 1981).

[2] Eduardo Silva, *Barações e escravidão* (Rio de Janeiro: Editora Nova Fronteira, 1984); Darell Levi, *The Prados of Brazil* (Athens: University of Georgia Press, 1987); Samuel Z. Stone, *The Heritage of the Conquistadors* (Lincoln: University of Nebraska Press, 1990).

[3] Michael Jimenez, "Traveling Far in Grandfather's Car," *Hispanic American Historical Review* 69, no. 2 (1989): 185–220.

São Paulo bore an uncanny resemblance to Colombian smallholders, in terms of effective control over production decisions.[4] Indeed, big Paulista *fazendas* evinced much the same fragmentation of effective control over production decisions, as well as subsistence orientation, that we find presented in chapters by Eckert and Curtis on Cameroon and Tanzania.

Certainly, most coffee landlords should not be considered a rural elite in the dualistic sense adopted by Barington Moore, who counterpoises agriculturalists to an urban bourgeoisie. Landlords in continental Latin America diversified their holdings and invested in urban areas. They were not simply parochial planters, and their attachment to the land did not make them any less bourgeois than the Europeans whom modernizationists and Marxists alike wanted them to emulate.[5] Indeed, recent studies have demonstrated the fluidity of Europe's agricultural-commercial divide.[6]

Colonial rulers sometimes encouraged the emergence of coffee estates in Africa and Asia, although, in his chapter on Tanganyika, Curtis notes, "In Africa, latifundia are hard to establish and hard to maintain." Estates in Africa and Asia were usually the product of temporary colonial policies that privileged settlers, or companies, shortly after colonial conquest. Unlike in Latin America, such estates were normally run as centralized units, under the direct control of a European planter or manager, and the high cost of this type of operation contributed to their lack of economic success over the long term. European holdings in Ceylon (Sri Lanka) and Madagascar, analyzed in chapters by Kurian and Campbell, are good examples of such coffee estates, which were also particularly significant to the economies of Angola, Kenya, Indonesia, East Timor, and

---

[4] Thomas Holloway, *Immigrants on the Land: Coffee and Society in São Paulo, 1886–1934* (Chapel Hill: University of North Carolina Press, 1980); Verena Stolcke, *Coffee Planters, Workers, and Wives: Class Conflict and Gender Relations on São Paulo Plantations, 1850–1980* (New York: St. Martins, 1988); Steven Topik, "Ze Prado e Juan Valdez, Representações do cafeicultor," *Revista Brasileira de Historia* 15, no. 29 (1995): 157–72.

[5] Lowell Gudmundson, "Lord and Peasant in the Making of Modern Central America," in Evelyne Huber and Frank Safford, eds., *Agrarian Structure and Political Power: Landlord and Peasant in the Making of Latin America* (Pittsburgh: University of Pittsburgh Press, 1995), pp. 151–76.

[6] David Blackbourn and Geof Eley, *The Peculiarities of German History* (Oxford: Oxford University Press, 1984); Francois Furet, *Penser la Révolution française* (Paris: Gallimard, 1978); Theodore Koditschek, *Class Formation and Urban-Industrial Society: Bradford, 1750–1850* (New York: Cambridge University Press, 1990); Peter Cain and A. G. Hopkins, *British Imperialism* (London: Longman, 1993).

New Caledonia.[7] To a lesser degree, they also occurred in Côte d'Ivoire, Cameroon, São Tomé, Congo, India, Vietnam, Laos, and the South Pacific, as noted in the Clarence-Smith chapter. In Liberia, however, the coffee plantocracy consisted of black settlers, former slaves repatriated to Africa from the Americas.[8]

At the same time, African and Asian smallholders did not remain frozen in some timeless precolonial past. The spread of coffee and other cash crops was accompanied by a marked trend toward the privatization and accumulation of land. Even if holdings generally remained modest in size, especially when compared with Latin America, these African and Asian "kulaks" were heralds of modernity, in both social and political terms. Their educated sons would often abandon the land for a career in the cities or as traders.[9] Examples of this upward social mobility can be found in the chapters by Eckert and Curtis, where chiefs were men with a foot in two cultural worlds, both bearers of past social models and representatives of a new rural bourgeoisie.

Systems of land tenure broadly categorized as "feudal," rather than communal or capitalist, could also be the basis for larger coffee units in Africa and Asia, as long as the term feudal is not taken to reflect the detailed reality of medieval Europe. In West Java and southern Ethiopia, for example, lords exercised control over large areas of land, including the right to levy tribute in coffee.[10] However, production decisions were generally decentralized, lying in the hands of their "vassals."

[7] David Birmingham, "The Coffee Barons of Cazengo," *Journal of African History* 19, no. 4 (1978): 523–38; Paul Mosley, *The Settler Economies: Studies in the Economic History of Kenya and Southern Rhodesia, 1900–1963* (Cambridge: Cambridge University Press, 1983); Robert McStocker, "The Indonesian Coffee Industry," *Bulletin of Indonesian Economic Studies* 23, no. 1 (1987): 40–69; William G. Clarence-Smith, "Planters and Smallholders in Portuguese Timor in the Nineteenth and Twentieth Centuries," *Indonesia Circle* 57 (1992): 15–30; J. Parsons, "Coffee and Settlement in New Caledonia," *Geographical Review* 35, no. 1 (1945): 12–21.

[8] M. R. Akpan, "The Liberian Economy in the Nineteenth Century: The State of Agriculture and Commerce," *Liberian Studies Journal* 6, no. 1 (1975): 1–25.

[9] John Tosh, "The Cash-Crop Revolution in Tropical Africa: An Agricultural Reappraisal," *African Affairs* 79 (1980): 79–94; Ralph Austen, *African Economic History, Internal Development and External Dependency* (London: James Currey, 1987), ch. 6; R. E. Elson, *The End of the Peasantry in Southeast Asia* (London: Macmillan, 1997).

[10] Mason C. Hoadley, *Towards a Feudal Mode of Production: West Java, 1600–1800* (Singapore: Institute of Southeast Asian Studies, 1994); Charles McClennan, "Land, Labour and Coffee: The South's Role in Ethiopian Self-Reliance, 1889–1935," *African Economic History* 9 (1980): 69–83.

2. Economies and Diseconomies of Scale

"Bigger is better" proved to be an illusion in coffee cultivation, and the size of holdings thus tended to diminish steadily during the twentieth century, as in Nicaragua.[11] In interwar Costa Rica, the distribution of land under coffee was more equal than that of other crops.[12] In Indonesia, this represented a return to the norm, following artificial Dutch attempts to stimulate a European planter class from 1870 to 1900.[13] The Green Revolution, which began at different times in different places, has allegedly reversed this trend, but it may be too early to tell.

Access to land was rarely the key ingredient for success, for capital and labor were the scarce factors of production, and this told against large producers.[14] Whereas big planters required much initial capital to pay for tools, machinery, workers, transportation, and processing, *minifundistas* needed no funds. Instead, they relied on self-provisioning family labor, tools that they already possessed for food production, and the "forest rent" derived from virgin lands. Where wild coffee grew spontaneously in Africa, the need for labor was further reduced. Harvesting was the labor bottleneck, but if family labor was insufficient, smallholders employed sharecroppers, which avoided the need for working capital, or called on mutual help associations. Capital was the end product of the process, in the form of coffee trees that could be mortgaged or sold for discretionary social spending.[15]

Moreover, compared with large landowners, smallholders usually returned higher yields per hectare, per unit of capital, and per laborer, all other things being equal. Charlip's chapter shows that larger growers in Nicaragua were more likely to go bankrupt than smaller ones. Political influence and access to credit were better explanations for large-scale production than superior coffee-growing techniques.

---

[11] Elizabeth Dore, "La Producción cafetalera nicaraguense, 1860–1960," in Héctor Pérez Brignoli and Mario Samper, eds., *Tierra, café y sociedad* (San José: FLASCO, 1994), p. 404.

[12] Mario Samper, "In Difficult Times: Colombian and Costa Rican Coffee Growers from Prosperity to Crisis, 1920–1936," in William Roseberry et al., eds., *Coffee, Society and Power in Latin America* (Baltimore: Johns Hopkins University Press, 1995), pp. 173–6.

[13] McStocker, "The Indonesian Coffee Industry."

[14] Verena Stolcke, *Cafeicultura. Homens, mulheres e capital (1850–1980)*, trans. Denise Bottmann and João Martins Filho (São Paulo: Editora Brasiliense, 1986), p. 189; Margarita Nolasco in *Café y sociedad en México* (Mexico D.F.: Centro de Ecodesarrollo, 1985), p. 42.

[15] C. Blanc-Pamard and François Ruf, *La Transition caféière, côte est de Madagascar* (Montpellier: CIRAD, 1992).

Although coffee was one of the few major world crops in which cultivators in the "south" determined standards of production, this owed little or nothing to mechanization of cultivation. The Prussian agronomist Franz Dafert said of the Paulistas, considered the most advanced coffee growers of his time: "[A]ccustomed to the easy and unworried life of the rich domain of torrid lands, they have not the least idea of the hard work of the great European crops."[16] High yields per hectare in Brazil were due to the natural fertility of virgin soils and not to modern agricultural methods or cutting-edge technology. Samper shows that Costa Rica began investing in higher-quality beans only in the 1930s. Native smallholders realized the highest quality beans were grown in Central America and Colombia, but the key to this success was quality control in picking, sorting, and processing.[17]

Primary processing was a better candidate for economies of scale, at least when the "wet method" prevailed. This consisted of washing the pulp off fresh cherries, and was more common in Latin America than in Asia and Africa, and on estates than on small holdings. In much of Africa and Asia, as in parts of Colombia, processing was by the simpler "dry method," which produced beans of slightly lower quality, but generally at much lower cost. Cherries were dried and processed in rudimentary hand-powered mills or simply with the mortars and pestles employed for staple food grains.[18] Even when *beneficios* were set up to process large numbers of beans by the "wet method," capital was probably more important than technology for increasing profit levels. Processors often operated more as bankers and exporters than as industrialists, asserting local monopsonic power rather than profiting from high productivity.

Economies of scale showed up in transport, with the spread of railroads, trucks, and steamers, but these economies accrued to the economy as a whole, and not to particular types of producer. Steamers were the cheapest technology, directly available to small islands and production zones along navigable rivers, although islands often suffered from restricted forested land suitable for expanding coffee production. Railroad networks were particularly dense in south eastern Brazil, with more

[16] Franz Dafert, *Principes de culture rationelle du café au Bresil* (Paris: Augustin Challand, 1900), p. 41. See also Jacobo Gorender, *A burguesia brasileira* (São Paulo: Editora Brasiliense, 1981); Topik, "Ze Prado."
[17] We thank Lowell Gudmundson and Mario Samper for this keen observation.
[18] J. de Graaff, *The Economics of Coffee* (Wageningen: Pudoc, 1986), pp. 42–7.

miles of track than all of Africa and all of Asia outside India in 1890. Continental Africa acquired railroads later and less abundantly.[19] Moreover, whereas animal transport was common in Asia and Latin America, Africa could benefit from this often forgotten technology only in the few areas free from deadly tsetse-borne trypanosomes, such as Ethiopia. Human carriers thus remained vital for transport for decades, delaying and limiting the spread of coffee cultivation in Africa. Humans also continued to be used as beasts of burden in certain Central American coffee economies, as discussed in Rus's chapter on Chiapas.

3. The Impact of the Moving Frontier

Coffee was a everywhere a frontier crop eating the forest, even though institutionalized frontier democracy rarely developed.[20] Even in relatively densely populated Java, the main coffee "gardens" of the nineteenth century were up in the forested mountains, as shown in Fernando's chapter. Similar situations occurred in parts of Latin America with large pre-Colombian populations, as in Central America, although, even when coffee was planted close to existing populations and farmlands, it was almost always extended at the expense of the forest. Coffee thus favored lands that Spanish colonialism had largely left to indigenous peoples.[21]

However, these forests were never empty or unclaimed, as was previously believed. The development of a coffee pioneer front always displaced indigenous peoples or subsumed them into a new coffee economy. As William Roseberry eloquently noted: "Despite the frontier character of much of coffee expansion,...most of the 'wildernesses' into which coffee farmers moved were already encumbered by people, overlapping and competing claims to land, conceptions of space, time, and justice – in

---

[19] Austen, *African Economic History*, pp. 126–9.
[20] Catherine LeGrand, *Frontier Expansion and Peasant Protest in Colombia, 1830–1936* (Albuquerque: University of New Mexico Press, 1986), pp. 87–9.
[21] J. C. Cambranes, *Coffee and Peasants in Guatemala: The Origins of the Modern Plantation Economy in Guatemala 1853–1897* (Stockholm: Institute of Latin American Studies, 1985), pp. 61–84; Jeffrey Gould, "El Café, el trabajo, y la comunidad indígena de Matagalpa, 1880–1925," in Pérez Brignoli and Samper, eds., *Tierra, café y sociedad*, pp. 279–376; Hector Lindo-Fuentes, *Weak Foundations, the Economy of El Salvador in the Nineteenth Century, 1821–1898* (Berkeley: University of California Press, 1990), pp. 88–93; Robert Wasserstrom, *Class and Society in Central Chiapas* (Berkeley: University of California Press, 1983), pp. 107–70.

short, 'history'...and these encumbrances shaped their respective coffee economies even as the regions were transformed by the move toward coffee."[22]

Moreover, there were enormous opportunity costs incurred of an ecological nature, for this could easily turn into the crudest form of primitive accumulation. Once the Atlantic forest of Brazil had been cut down and the fertile land denuded, the coffee frontier simply moved inland.[23] Melo discusses the consequences for Rio state when the frontier was exhausted. This was not only a botanical tragedy but an economic one as well. No one ever calculated the depreciation or replacement costs of the forest and soil, which proved to be difficult or impossible to renew. Brazilian *fazendeiros*, rather than building for tomorrow, were splurging on their children's inheritance. Madagascar faced the same kind of problem, where undercapitalized Réunionais settlers struggled to make ends meet, as suggested in Campbell's chapter. In Java, the washing away of unconsolidated volcanic ash soils on mountain slopes was worsened by the ignorance and cupidity of Dutch officials, seeking to benefit personally from increasing the acreage of coffee in "regular gardens" on clear-felled land. The catastrophic consequences for sugar and rice irrigation systems in the plains were one reason for deciding to put an end to the Cultivation System.[24] This type of ecological disaster was the all too frequent companion of the expansion of cash crops around the tropical world, but coffee, as a "forest-eating" mountain plant, was potentially one of the most dangerous of all to the environment

Destructive coffee cultivation was not found everywhere, although the reasons for differing approaches to "biological capital" remain to be fully elucidated. Where forest land was scarce, labor relatively abundant, and local attitudes favored conservation, types of agroforestry developed in which coffee cultivation became permanent, or almost permanent, part of the landscape. This was noted in Clarence-Smith's chapter for Mysore in India and indigenous "forest coffee" in eastern Java and reported for parts of Central America as Gudmundson and Samper discuss for Costa

---

[22] William Roseberry, "La Falta de Brazos: Land and Labor in the Coffee Economies of Nineteenth-Century Latin America," *Theory and Society* 20, no. 3 (1991): 359.

[23] Warren Dean, *With Broadax and Firebrand* (Berkeley: University of California Press, 1995).

[24] William G. Clarence-Smith, "The Impact of Forced Coffee Cultivation on Java, 1805–1917," *Indonesia Circle* 64 (1994): 241–64; Robert W Hefner, *The Political Economy of Mountain Java: An Interpretive History* (Berkeley: University of California Press, 1990).

Rica. In some regions of Africa, gathering of wild coffee also preserved the forest, including stands of *arabica* in Ethiopia.

4. Monoculture and Polyculture

Coffee was very rarely a monoculture, if only because self-provisioning by workers was an important means of keeping down costs. Even on the *fazendas* of São Paulo, arguably the largest in the world, resident workers, or *colonos*, earned as much as 80 percent of their income by growing food and raising livestock. In Java under the Cultivation System, as shown in Fernando's chapter, peasants grew coffee for a proportion of their time fixed by the administration, but were expected to be mainly producers of rice and other foodstuffs. In Guatemala and Chiapas, workers retained their highland subsistence plots while migrating down to the coffee lands for the harvests.

Coffee not only coexisted with other crops but was often in a symbiotic relationship with them. Indeed, Mario Samper's chapter makes the insightful observation that a limitation of a commodity-oriented approach, focusing on coffee, is that it tends to obscure the interactions with other commercial or subsistence crops, which are often quite important for farmers. He recommends thinking of a "coffee complex," rather than just coffee alone. Marco Palacios has also noted that coffee in Colombia was not monocultural.[25] The use of other crops for shade, such as bananas, cocoa, or rubber, is not agronomically optimal from the point of view of getting the most coffee beans per tree. However, it has the advantage of spreading risks deriving from pests and market fluctuations, thus possibly maximizing income per hectare and improving the quality of the coffee. Thus, Afro-Cuban smallholders in Oriente carefully altered their mix of coffee and cocoa trees, according to changing prices for each commodity.[26]

Techniques of mixed cropping were taken to great lengths in Indonesia. Small Dutch planters in central Java, often of mixed blood, developed complex crop associations that were scornfully dismissed by modernizing officials as veritable "grocers' shops." After the shock of the disastrous *Hemileia vastatrix* plague, which wiped out their *arabica* in the 1880s, they replanted with *robusta*, cocoa, rubber, nutmeg, kapok, cola, and black

[25] Marco Palacios, *El Café en Colombia, 1850–1970* (Mexico D.F.: El Colegio de México, 1979), p. 93.
[26] I. A. Wright, *Cuba* (New York: Macmillan, 1910), pp. 447–8, 460.

pepper, in all sorts of complicated combinations.[27] Similarly, smallholders in southern Sumatra grew dry rice for a couple of years, harvested *robusta* for four years, and then uprooted the coffee trees to allow rubber trees to grow properly.[28]

5. The Nature of the Labor Force

Indigenous peoples on Latin America's coffee frontiers have received considerably more attention of late, as Amerindians have been removed from the category of the exotic to be seen as a special sort of peasant. Ethnic definitions and identities are considered to be socially and historically constructed, rather than biologically determined. Amerindians are recognized as able members of the modern world who have constructed their own social space with limited resources. They did not drag their feet to remain "traditional," or some sort of essentialized *Indio*, but maintained values and practices that differentiated them from the rest of the rural peasantry or proletariat. As shown in the chapters by McCreery and Rus on Maya cultivators, they were able to maintain their culture even as they worked the *cafetales*, despite planter attempts to push them off their land and government attempts to erase them as a census category – which was rather successful in Costa Rica, El Salvador, and Nicaragua. However, they also faced internal fissures.

The salience of local cultures is no novelty for students of Africa and Asia, but there has been a tendency to see them in a more positive light. Ethnicity is now examined as a resource rather than a curse, prompting a reevaluation of what was once seen as a major stumbling block along a centrally defined route to national progress. The chapters by Eckert and Curtis delineate the elaboration of local cultures in the midst of coffee booms in Tanzania and Cameroon, where indigenous peoples were able to shape colonial regimes to a surprising degree, while fighting each other over the definition of "custom." In Kurian's chapter, the vexed question of caste raises its head in the context of Tamil Nadu, where its influence on labor exports to coffee estates remains unclear.

Everywhere, the central part played by women and their children in coffee economies is being increasingly recognized. Even when women did

---

[27] W. Roepke, *Cacao* (Haarlem: H. D. Tjeenk Willink and Zoon, 1922), pp. 2–4.
[28] B. H. Paerels, "Bevolkingskoffiekultuur," in C. J. J. van Hall and C. van de Koppel, eds., *De landbouw in de Indische archipel* (The Hague: W. van Hoeve, 1946–50), vol. 2b, pp. 112–13.

not directly work in agriculture, their unpaid role in self-provisioning and social reproduction underpinned the profitability of coffee cultivation.[29] Rachel Kurian shows that in Ceylon, hierarchy was "based on color, race, ethnicity, and sex." Women workers were "at the bottom of the pyramid, and male domination was enforced at each and every level." In Nicaragua, Elizabeth Dore also finds the pervasive influence of patriarchy in law and in practice at the beginning of the coffee boom. However, women there may have gained economic independence over time. She finds women in 40 percent of the cases to be heads of households. "Family morality" was as important as economic calculations in determining female availability for labor, and morality was a changeable concept. The struggle for land incited by the expansion of Nicaragua's coffee economy led to a transformation of rural tenure and the role of women in it, as the local state began playing a much larger role in adjudicating issues of family morality.[30] Julie Charlip reveals substantial activity by women as lenders and borrowers. Detailed studies by Gudmundson and Samper suggest that family inheritance strategies muted class antagonisms in Costa Rica while privileging males.[31]

The employment of children requires more attention. Generally speaking, coffee is a crop that needs less heavy and regular work than sugar, and some tasks were seen as particularly suited to children, such as harvesting the coffee cherries closest to the ground, picking up windfalls, or chasing away birds. Demand by south eastern Brazilian planters for child slaves in the nineteenth century, as sugar declined and coffee expanded, may have played a role in the puzzling increase of exports of children from Equatorial Africa.[32] At a later stage, Paulista planters also preferred to employ European immigrants with numerous offspring.[33] The demand for child laborers led Nicaraguan and Costa Rican municipios to provide easy access to land to fix families in the coffee zones for use during the harvests.

[29] Verena Stolcke, "The Labors of Coffee in Latin America," in Roseberry et al., eds., *Coffee, Society and Power*, pp. 65–94.

[30] Elizabeth Dore, "Property, Households and Public Regulation of Domestic Life: Diriomao, Nicaragua, 1840–1900," *Journal of Latin American Studies* 29 (1997): 591–611.

[31] Lowell Gudmundson, *Costa Rica before Coffee* (Baton Rouge: Louisiana State University Press, 1986); Mario Samper K., *Generations of Settlers* (Boulder, Colo.: Westview Press, 1990).

[32] David Eltis, *Economic Growth and the Ending of the Transatlantic Slave Trade* (Oxford: Oxford University Press, 1987), p. 175.

[33] Holloway, *Immigrants on the Land*.

6. Workers and Revolution

The extent to which coffee can be viewed as a revolutionary force de-
pends not only on these more complex analyses of workers, but also on
new views of coercion, whether through slavery, forced labor, vagrancy
laws, or debt peonage. The meaning of coercion in Latin America has
been turned on its head recently, notably, by the argument that debt peonage was less of a primary constraint on workers than the return to
old-fashioned forced labor on Spanish colonial lines.[34] Indeed, extraeconomic coercion may have been a sign of the vitality of Guatemala's
Mayan indigenous communities, since they were self-sufficient enough
to not need work on fincas. The move to more regular wage labor thus
marked the triumph of planters over land-hungry Maya peasants.[35] In
Soconusco, Mexico planters were obliged to advance payments to recal-
citrant Maya and other indigenous peoples to induce them to seasonally
migrate for the harvest, and often lost their advances when workers absconded.[36] Whether capitalist bosses paying wages treated their workers
better is uncertain, although wage laborers might enjoy more bargaining
power. Conditions in Mexico certainly improved noticeably after a coffee
pickers' union was established in 1937.[37]

Even Brazilian slaves are now often viewed as "proto-peasants" rather
than "proto-proletarians." They had some rights and bargaining power,
and the ability to accumulate money, sometimes to purchase their own
freedom.[38] That Brazilian planters used many methods besides brute force
to coax labor out of slaves is suggested by the fact that the abolition of

---

[34] Arnold Bauer, "Rural Workers in Spanish America," *Hispanic American Historical Review*
59, no. 1 (1979): 34–63; Alan Knight, "Mexican Peonage: What Was It and Why Was
It," *Journal of Latin American Studies* 18 (1986): 41–74.

[35] David McCreery, "Wage Labor, Free Labor and Vagrancy Laws: The Transition to
Capitalism in Guatemala, 1920–1945," in Roseberry et al., eds., *Coffee, Society and Power*,
pp. 206–31.

[36] Friederike Bauman, "Terratenientes, campesinos y la expansión de la agricultura cap-
italista em Chiapas, 1896–1916," *Mesoamerica* 4, no. 5 (1983): 8–63; Karl Kaerger,
Landwirtschaft und Kolonisation im Spanishchen Amerika, vol. 2: *Die Südamerikanischen
Weststaaten und Mexiko* (Leipzig: Duncker and Humblot, 1901).

[37] Jan Rus, "The Comunidad Revolucionaria Institucional," in Gilbert M. Joseph and Daniel
Nugent, eds., *Everyday Forms of State Formation* (Durham, N.C.: Duke University Press,
1994), pp. 268–9.

[38] Jacob Gorender, *O escravismo colonial* (São Paulo: Atica, 1978); Stuart Schwartz, *Slaves,
Peasants, and Rebels: Reconsidering Brazilian Slavery* (Urbana: University of Illinois Press,
1992); Mark Turner, ed., *From Chattel Slaves to Wage Slaves: The Dynamics of Labor
Bargaining in the Americas* (Bloomington: Indiana University Press, 1995).

slavery was succeeded by a variety of social relations, such as the *colonato* (resident immigrant family labor), sharecropping, and renting, but little extraeconomic coercion.[39] On the other hand, Clarence-Smith reminds us that European nations that prided themselves as beacons of liberty, such as Belgium, the Netherlands, France, and Portugal, retained forms of coerced labor in their colonies for decades after slavery was abolished in the Americas.

Such labor systems, which existed throughout the coffee world, represented an intermediary arrangement between coercion and wages, although this should not be considered to be a discrete peasant mode of production. As McCreery notes, "the peasant is part of a larger social, economic, and political system usually structured to extract rent, labor, and product from him on exploitative terms. It follows that there can be no 'peasant mode of production.'"[40] Many coffee workers before 1930 fell into this middle ground, in which they were by turns, or even simultaneously, smallholders, renters, tenants, sharecroppers, and day laborers. They filled numerous niches and received much of their compensation in nonmonetary forms, such as usufruct. Workers were frequently migratory, with the Maya of Guatemala and Chiapas among the most ambulatory.[41]

Whereas peasant agency used to refer to the ability of peasants to resist the forces of capitalism, it has come to mean their ability to adapt to capitalism. Varieties of land tenure and labor arrangements, as well as ethnicity and gender, accentuated social fissures and impeded joint action. Political responses varied widely in the face of similar circumstances, but smallholders were generally reluctant to organize along class lines with workers. The greater preponderance of smallholders in the coffee lands of Africa and Asia, especially as the twentieth century progressed, made this particularly clear in the Old World.

[39] George Reid Andrews, *Blacks and Whites in São Paulo, Brazil, 1888–1988* (Madison: University of Wisconsin Press, 1991); Hebe Maria Mattos de Castro, *Ao sul da historia* (São Paulo: Ed. Brasiliense, 1987); Holloway, *Immigrants*; Stolcke, *Coffee Planters*; Nancy Naro, *A Slave's Place, A Master's World* (London: Continuum, 2000).

[40] David McCreery, *Rural Guatemala, 1760–1940* (Stanford: Stanford University Press, 1994), p. 5. See also William Roseberry, *Coffee and Capitalism in the Venezuelan Andes* (Austin: University of Texas Press, 1983), pp. 192–208.

[41] John M. Watanabe, *Maya Saints and Souls in a Changing World* (Austin: University of Texas Press, 1992), pp. 142–8; Rigoberta Menchu, *Me llamo Rigoberta Menchu, testimonio*, with Elizabeth Burgos Debray (Havana: Casa de las Americas, 1983); Jan Rus, *Abtel ta pinka...Trabajo en las fincas, platicas de los Tzotziles sobre las fincas cafetaleras de Chiapas* (San Cristobal de las Casas, Chiapas: Taller Tzotzil, INAREMAC, 1990).

Recent studies thus do not portray the *cafetales* as breeding grounds for revolutionaries in Latin America.[42] In Brazil, São Paulo was one of the most politically conservative states while coffee dominated, even revolting against the populist regime of Getúlio Vargas.[43] Chiapas was late in taking part in the Mexican Revolution, and the forces of revolution came from without.[44] Elsewhere in Mexico, the finca workers of Veracruz do not seem to have been a major constituency of the Agraristas.[45] Nicaragua underwent a socialist revolution because of the weakness of the coffee planting class, not because coffee exacerbated social contradictions.[46] The Arbenz "revolution" in Guatemala issued from the cities and was extended by politicians to the countryside, where support was insufficient to sustain the regime.[47] The one true social revolution generated by harsh conditions on coffee plantations was in Haiti (1791–1804), which was both a war for national liberation and a slave rebellion. However, the society that ensued was marked by inequality, authoritarianism, and poverty and lost its role as the world's leading coffee producer.

Coffee small holders and workers participated in anticolonial struggles in Africa and Asia, but rarely envisaged any greater revolutionary aim than to reclaim land filched by European planters. The endeavor was not to overthrow the bourgeoisie but more to join it across the race line. Land alienation was the root cause of Kenya's bloody Mau Mau insurrection, with landless laborers on European estates at the core of the struggle, but the regime that finally emerged in independent Kenya was notoriously conservative.[48] Similarly, Campbell's chapter shows how coffee smallholders were central to the bloody 1947 revolt in Madagascar against French officials and settlers. The "coffee kulaks" of Angola were another group who fought to get land back from European usurpers but

[42] Jeffery M. Paige, *Coffee and Power: Revolution and the Rise of Democracy in Central America* (Cambridge: Harvard University Press, 1997).
[43] Joseph Love, *São Paulo in the Brazilian Federation* (Stanford: Stanford University Press, 1980).
[44] Daniela Spenser, *El Partido Socialista Chiapaneca* (Mexico D.F.: CIESAS, 1988); Thomas Benjamin, *A Rich Land, a Poor People: Politics and Society in Modern Chiapas* (Albuquerque: University of New Mexico Press, 1989).
[45] Heather Fowler-Salamini, *Agrarian Radicalism in Veracruz* (Lincoln: University of Nebraska, 1978).
[46] Robert G. Williams, *States and Social Evolution: Coffee and the Rise of National Governments in Central America* (Chapel Hill: University of North Carolina Press, 1994).
[47] Cindy Forster, "Campesino Labor Struggles in Guatemala," in *Identity and Struggle at the Margins of the Nation-State* (Durham: Duke University Press, 1998), p. 218.
[48] Gavin Kitching, *Class and Economic Change in Kenya: The Making of an African Petite Bourgeoise, 1905–1970* (New Haven: Yale University Press, 1980).

proved hostile to the Marxist government after independence.[49] The long and unsuccessful struggle by coffee and cocoa producing Bakweri to regain their ancestral lands around Mount Cameroon was another example of such limited aims.[50] At the same time, chiefs' power and "customary" rights were sometimes the target of resistance by small farmers, as shown in the chapters by Eckert and Curtis.

7. Merchants and Coffee Economies

The growing emphasis on smallholders has brought a renewed interest in merchants, without whom the development and maintenance of coffee pioneer fronts based on small farmers would have been inconceivable. Merchants are now seen in a more positive light, as providers of vital services, rather than as parasitic usurers. Credit was not the key to the relationship, as smallholders rarely required much, if any, capital to set the productive forces in motion. If they became indebted, it was more to finance social expenditure of a discretionary nature. Rather, merchants purchased crops at competitive prices, as they were rarely in monopsonistic positions. They also provided planting material, tools, and information on techniques of production and markets.[51] These home truths about merchants had been proclaimed long before by Peter Bauer, but his was a lone voice crying in the wilderness, at a time when marketing boards were all the rage.[52]

The distribution of mercantile communities around the tropical world was broadly clear by the nineteenth century, although much research is still needed on this topic. The great import-export firms that handled coffee were mostly North European, especially Scottish, Dutch, and Hanseatic German.[53] As for rural purchasers of cash crops, the lands to the east

[49] William G. Clarence-Smith, "Class Structure and Class Struggles in Angola in the 1970s," *Journal of Southern African Studies* 7, no. 1 (1980): 109–26.

[50] William G. Clarence-Smith, "Plantation versus Smallholder Production of Cocoa: The Legacy of the German Period in Cameroon," in Peter Geschiere and Piet Konings, eds., *Itinéraires d'accumulation au Cameroun* (Paris: Karthala, 1993), pp. 187–216.

[51] Gareth Austin and Kaoru Sugihara, eds., *Local Suppliers of Credit in the Third World, c.1750–c.1960* (London: Macmillan, 1993).

[52] P. T. Bauer, *West African Trade: A Study of Competition, Oligopoly and Monopoly in a Changing Economy* (London: Routledge and Kegan Paul, 1963).

[53] Robert G. Greenhill, "Merchants and the Latin American Trades: An Introduction," in D. C. M. Platt, ed., *Business Imperialism 1840–1930: An Inquiry Based on British Experience in Latin America* (Oxford: Clarendon Press, 1977), pp. 119–97; J. T. Lindblad, *Foreign Investment in Southeast Asia in the Twentieth Century* (Basingstoke; Macmillan, 1998).

of the Cape of Good Hope were the stamping ground of Asians, especially Chinese, Indians, and Muslim Arabs. South Chinese merchants were dominant in Southeast Asia's coffee lands, with Hadhrami Arabs as their main competitors.[54] In the coffee zone of Western India, Gujarati traders from further north were at the fore.[55] Gujarati merchants also exercised great influence over the major coffee economies of East Africa, although Hadhrami Arabs were significant in the Red Sea.[56]

In contrast, the lands to the west of the Cape of Good Hope were largely the preserve of Europeans and Christian Arabs. "Syrians," mainly Christians from Lebanon and Palestine, as well as from Syria proper, were the chief mercantile community in West Africa. They were also prominent in many Latin American coffee zones, especially São Paulo, Colombia, and parts of Central America.[57] Among the Europeans, the North Portuguese were at the fore in Brazil and Angola, whereas Germans predominated on the Pacific coast of Latin America, together with a scattering of North Italians, Basques, Catalans, Provençaux, Corsicans, Swiss, and others.[58]

Merchants were unlikely to acquire coffee lands from smallholders in Africa and Asia, although European estates might fall into their hands

[54] William G. Clarence-Smith, "Hadhrami Entrepreneurs in the Malay World, c. 1750 to c. 1940," in Ulrike Freitag and William G. Clarence-Smith, eds., *Hadhrami Traders, Scholars and Statesmen in the Indian Ocean, 1750s to 1960s* (Leiden: E. J. Brill, 1997), pp. 297–314.

[55] Anirudha Gupta, ed., *Minorities on India's West Coast: History and Society* (Delhi: Kalinga Publications, 1991); T. J. Mohamed, *The Gujaratis, a Study of Socio-economic Interactions, 1850–1950* (Delhi: Deputy Publications, 1990).

[56] William G. Clarence-Smith, "Indian Business Communities in the Western Indian Ocean in the Nineteenth Century," *Indian Ocean Review* 2, no. 4 (1989): 18–21; Janet Ewald and William G. Clarence-Smith, "The Economic Role of the Hadhrami Diaspora in the Red Sea and Gulf of Aden, 1820s to 1930s," in Freitag and Clarence-Smith, eds., *Hadhrami Traders*, pp. 281–96; Chapter 2.

[57] Albert Hourani and Nadim Shehadi, eds., *The Lebanese in the World: A Century of Emigration* (London: Centre for Lebanese Studies and I. B. Tauris, 1992); Ignacio Klich and Jeffrey Lesser, eds., *Arab and Jewish Immigration in Latin America: Images and Realities* (London: Cass, 1998); Nancie L. González, *Dollar, Dove, and Eagle: One Hundred Years of Palestinian Migration to Honduras* (Ann Arbor: University of Michigan Press, 1992); R. Bayly Winder, "The Lebanese in West Africa," *Comparative Studies in Society and History* 4, no. 3 (1962): 296–336.

[58] William G. Clarence-Smith, *Cocoa and Chocolate, 1765–1914* (London: Routledge, 2000), ch. 5; A. da Silva Rego, *Relações luso-brasileiras, 1822–1953* (Lisbon: Panorama, 1966); K. Trümper, *Kaffee und Kaufleute: Guatemala und der Hamburger Handel, 1871–1914* (Hamburg: LIT Verlag, 1996); P. J. Eder, *Colombia* (London: Fisher and Unwin, 1913); William G. Clarence-Smith, "Capital Accumulation and Class Formation in Angola, c.1875–1961," in David Birmingham and Phyllis Martin, eds., *History of Central Africa* (London: Longman, 1983), vol. 2, pp. 163–99.

through debt. Most traders, especially at higher levels, were foreign, and colonial regimes tended to prohibit the transfer of indigenous land to non-natives to settle debts. Men of straw could be used, but in contrast to Latin America, merchants had an aversion to acquiring rural land, which increased their risks and reduced the liquidity of their assets. Little plots of land acquired from smallholders on a haphazard basis were also difficult to consolidate into proper estates. Moreover, these particular foreigners were exterior to both local cultures and colonial patronage networks, and thus found it difficult to mobilize labor.[59]

The relation between merchants and large Latin American landowners, currently undergoing reexamination, was somewhat different. As planters defaulted on their loans – a frequent occurrence – merchants came to own many coffee groves. The great social prestige and political power derived from land ownership may have counterbalanced the disadvantages. At the same time, merchants were less culturally alien from their host societies in Latin America and more integrated into local power and status structures, often through marriage.[60]

For all the hold that merchants had over Latin American coffee economies, there was no foreign takeover. Although numerous merchants were born abroad, as indicated in chapters by Gudmundson, McCreery, and Samper, they generally worked with locally accumulated capital. They were immigrants with good connections to overseas markets, rather than foreign investors, and they frequently became part of the national elite. Moreover, some merchants and processors were native-born, especially at lower levels. Thus, Charlip's chapter indicates surprisingly substantial smallholder participation in the capital and land markets of Nicaragua.

8. Coffee Elites as Bearers of Progress

In a twist on conventional wisdom, smallholders and their commercial allies are increasingly being seen as more responsible for modernization than great planters. The push for land registration, together with the call for the provision of banks and modern forms of transport, were often more insistent in areas where small growers predominated. Even when large landowners also pressed for such changes, they were not necessarily the "coffee actors" who made most effective use of them.

[59] Austin and Sugihara, *Local Suppliers of Credit*.
[60] Lois J. Roberts, *The Lebanese Immigrants in Ecuador, a History of Emerging Leadership* (Boulder: Westview Press, 2000).

In São Paulo, there was a marked contrast between attitudes of growers and merchants. Planters concerned themselves little with rural property rights, mortgage registries, foreclosure laws, or wage labor. They fought against the institutionalization of land rights, because these might limit the arbitrary private power of planters. Though interested in banks and transport, the *fazendeiros* exploited and ultimately destroyed banks and the stock market in an enormous speculative scandal in the 1890s. It was thus merchants, primarily concerned with conditions in the ports, who were the principal purveyors of bourgeois property rights, as well as standard weights and measures.[61] We must caution, however, that the distinction between planter and merchant was often fuzzy because many growers also doubled as traders, exporting not only their own production but also servicing neighboring smaller growers.

In Colombia and Central America, the institutionalization of land rights was often more common among smaller producers. Even very small land sales, and loans secured on land, were registered in Rio de Janeiro state after slave emancipation, as in parts of Central America.[62] Many smallholders in Colombia and Central America sought titles to communal or ejido lands to protect them from appropriation by large-scale landowners, even if they were not always successful in this endeavor.[63] As Williams notes, "If a single economic transformation was associated with the development of the coffee economy it was toward privately titled properties with much more clearly delineated boundaries than was true before coffee's introduction."[64] The rise of coffee exports in Central America also correlated quite closely with the opening of banks and the building of railroads.[65]

"Traditional" rulers in much of Africa, and in restricted parts of Asia, at times preferred established land rights that favored their privileged

---

[61] Eugene Ridings, *Business Interest Groups in Nineteenth-Century Brazil* (Cambridge: Cambridge University Press, 1994); Steven Topik, "Brazil's Bourgeois Revolution?," *The Americas* 48, no. 2 (1991): 245–71.

[62] Castro, *Ao sul da historia*; Geraldina Portillo, "La Tenencia de la tierra en el Departamento de La Liberdad, 1897–1901," and Aldo Lauria Santiago, "La Colonización del Volcan de San Vicente, El Salvador, 1860–1900," both unpublished papers, Tercer Congresso Centroamericano de Historia, San José CR, July 18, 1996; Chapter 10.

[63] LeGrand, *Frontier Expansion*, pp. 167–70; Aldo A. Lauria-Santiago, *An Agrarian Republic: Commercial Agriculture and the Politics of Peasant Communities in El Salvador, 1823–1914* (Pittsburgh: University of Pittsburgh Press, 1999), pp. 230–3.

[64] Williams, *States and Social Evolution*, p. 237, notes.

[65] Hector Lindo-Fuentes and Lowell Gudmundson, *Central America, 1821–1871; Liberalism before Liberal Reform* (Tuscaloosa: University of Alabama Press, 1995), p. 47; Williams, *States and Social Evolution*, p. 193.

position, rather than new bourgeois titles. As the chapters by Eckert and Curtis show, officials often backed such social groups, because they preferred to limit the cost of governing by administering their subjects through "organic" rulers. After the First World War, colonial powers also sought to deflect the growing nationalist challenge by supporting traditional rulers. Hence, officials sought to avoid changes in local social relations. However, the maintenance of old forms of land tenure clashed with a discourse of modernization initiated by colonialism itself. Furthermore, a general process of commodification and monetarization sprang from the levying of taxes in cash, and successful smallholders wished to acquire private title to land. Even chiefs were uncertain which way to jump and tried to combine the best of both worlds.[66]

Estate owners in Africa and Asia certainly saw themselves as resolute modernizers "shouldering the White Man's burden," but there are good grounds for doubting this theatrical self-perception. Planters pressed consistently for banks, transport improvements, and agricultural research stations, but only as long as the cost was borne by indigenous smallholders, as in Kenya, or the metropolitan taxpayer. They usually held freehold title to their land, although the Dutch issued only long leases in Indonesia after 1830. Overgenerous concessions of vast blocks of forest from the state were not conducive to an active land market, as settlers and companies used their land reserves to block the expansion of indigenous smallholders. Attitudes toward labor were even less progressive. Enterprises were typically burdened with heavy debts and very high running costs, because they borrowed huge amounts and spent extravagantly on "scientific" cultivation and expensive white expatriates. They were thus short of working capital to pay workers and resorted to precapitalist coercion when they could get away with it, especially in the colonies of France and the southern European powers.[67]

9. Coffee and Manufacturing Industry

The relationship of coffee to manufacturing has receded as a concern for historians of Latin America, and the studies in this book have rarely explored the industrial multiplier effects of coffee exports. Indeed, what

---

[66] Anne Phillips, *The Enigma of Colonialism: British Policy in West Africa* (London: James Currey, 1989).
[67] William G. Clarence-Smith, "Cocoa Plantations in the Third World, 1870s–1914: The Political Economy of Inefficiency," in John Harriss et al., eds, *The New Institutional Economics and Third World Development* (London: Routledge, 1995), pp. 157–71.

stands out from an initial look at countries that have concentrated on coffee production is that they have tended to remain poor. Still, as Hildete de Melo demonstrates, the coffee trade played a large role in building the infrastructure of Rio de Janeiro city and state. Although the spectacular growth of São Paulo came to overshadow the Rio region, Rio still had one of the densest rail networks and largest cities in Latin America. A large financial sector emerged. Factories also arose, though mostly because of coffee's consumption and fiscal linkages rather than forward or backward linkages of coffee production. It could be argued that diversification into other crops has been a precondition for any measure of success. More widely, economists have come to doubt the centrality of industrialization to development, as the West's industrial sector has declined dramatically in relative terms. However, São Paulo's prosperity has arguably been due in large part to industrialization, and this leaves open the question of whether industrialization was based on the proceeds of coffee exports, as Warren Dean argued decades ago.[68] Countries did not have to choose either coffee exports or industrialization, as the most strident *dependentistas* suggested. Brazil, Colombia, and El Salvador were able to enjoy a substantial degree of both. Brazil today is still the world's leading exporter of coffee and is the world's eighth largest economy, while coffee's share of GDP and exports has fallen sharply. Brazil is now, according to *The Economist*, the second *least* trade-dependent economy in the world.[69]

For scholars of Africa, the question of the relationship of coffee exports and industrialization remains more alive than for those working on Latin America or Asia, given that many African countries have witnessed an increased dependency on a small range of primary exports since independence, among them, coffee. The dramatic failure of import substitution industrialization under tariff barriers has led to a resurgence of interest in less protectionist models of industrialization, building on export receipts. For East Africa, in particular, the potential of coffee remains tantalizing.

The case of Angola is both instructive and dramatic. Under late Portuguese colonialism, the territory became Africa's largest exporter of coffee, mainly produced on estates owned by Portuguese settlers. It simultaneously became one of the most industrialized regions of Africa, as estate owners reinvested considerable amounts of coffee profits into

[68] Warren Dean, *The Industrialization of São Paulo, 1880–1945* (Austin: University of Texas Press, 1969).
[69] The Economist, *Pocket World in Figures, 2001 Edition* (London: Profile Books, 2001), pp. 22, 30, 45.

manufacturing, especially in and around Luanda.[70] All that crumbled after 1975, due to the chaotic flight of Portuguese settlers, an unending civil war, ill-judged Marxist economic policies, and the "Dutch disease" effects of an overvalued currency. Angola almost ceased to export coffee, and factories lay in ruins or limped along at a fraction of their capacity.[71]

10. Coffee Planters and Liberal National States

The extent to which planters created politically peaceful "coffee republics" in Latin America has been repeatedly questioned, and the existence of authoritarian colonial regimes in the Old World indicates in the clearest way possible that there was no necessary link between coffee and democracy. Latin American coffee planters proved quite disunited, and national planters' organizations developed in most countries only after the First World War. Planters were divided partly by different scales of production and relations to the means of production, and partly by competition for labor and capital. They also split in their political allegiances, for producing an export crop did not automatically lead to the adoption of liberal views. Many were Conservatives, particularly in Brazil and Colombia.[72] The same was true of Central America.[73]

The extent of planter power has also been brought into question. Although a case has often been made for *fazendeiro* rule in São Paulo, smaller subsistence and coffee growers exercised a good deal of political influence. In Costa Rica, Samper points out, instead of coffee growers, it was *beneficio* owners who employed their "triple monopoly" of credit, processing, and marketing to control the state.[74] In both Costa Rica and Nicaragua, the chapters by Dore, Charlip, and Gudmundson indicate that political power remained fragmented, and that smallholders were

---

[70] Clarence-Smith, "Capital Accumulation."

[71] Margaret J. Anstee, *Orphan of the Cold War: The Inside Story of the Collapse of the Angolan Peace Process* (New York: St. Martin's Press, 1996).

[72] José Murilo de Carvalho, *Teatro de sombras* (São Paulo: Vertice, 1988); Frank Safford, "Agrarian Systems and the State: The Case of Colombia," in Evelyne Huber and Frank Safford, eds., *Agrarian Structure and Political Power: Landlord and Peasant in the Making of Latin America* (Pittsburgh: University of Pittsburgh Press, 1995), pp. 111–49.

[73] Williams, *States and Social Evolution*; Lindo-Fuentes and Gudmundson, *Central America*; Dore, "La Producción cafetalera nicaraguense"; Ralph Lee Woodward, Jr., *Rafael Carrera and the Emergence of the Republic of Guatemala* (Athens: University of Georgia Press, 1993); Jeffry Paige, "Coffee and Power in El Salvador," *Latin American Research Review* 28, no. 3 (1993): 7–40.

[74] Mario Samper, "El Significado de la caficultura," in Pérez Brignoli and Samper, eds., *Tierra, café y sociedad*, p. 128.

influential in politics. Coffee planters did not even dominate politics in Chiapas, for Rus's chapter notes that the highland *hacendados,* producers of corn, wheat, sugar, and cattle, continued to rule the state. Moreover, apparent political differences, such as Costa Rica's democracy versus El Salvador's authoritarian oligarchy, diminish upon closer inspection.

The weakness of planter power meant that coffee republics had limited capacity and penetration, particularly during the early years of export boom. In Central America, municipal governments and ejidos rather than the national government were initially the most important institutions. In the countryside, private landowners of all kinds ruled for the most part. The national state's largest role was not in distributing land to large-scale *finqueros* nor in directly providing labor but, rather, in providing troops and police to prevent organized opposition to private appropriation.

Nonetheless, coffee states played an important role in the wider accumulation process, notably, in marketing. Mostly, they oversaw international links by borrowing money abroad, attempting to maintain the value of currency, and promoting transportation and communications improvements. As Topik discusses, the Brazilian state, while remaining true to liberalism in its rhetoric, intervened to a considerable degree, going so far as to take control of the international market for coffee.[75] Indeed, the British economist Rowe noted, "Brazilian coffee has been subjected to artificial control of a more thorough, prolonged and deliberate character than any raw material of major importance."[76]

Other Latin American states, together with planter organizations, came to play a fundamental role in marketing, though the extent to which this was public is open to debate. Samper refers to El Salvador's Asociación Cafetalera as "a private state within a not very public state."[77] The same was often true for Colombia's Federación de Cafeteros, which became a branch of the Colombian government in the 1940s.[78] Coffee did not necessarily create either an instrumental or an autonomous state. Indeed, even within the same country, the export elite's control of the state and the state's participation in the coffee sector varied over time.

---

[75] Steven Topik, "L'Etat sur le marché: Approche comparative du café brésilien et du henequen mexicain," *Annales, Economies, Societies, Civilisations* 46, no. 2 (1991): 429–58.

[76] J. W. F. Rowe, *Studies in the Artificial Control of Raw Material Supplies: Brazilian Coffee* (London: London and Cambridge Economic Service, 1932), p. 5.

[77] Samper, "El Significado," p. 212.

[78] Robert H. Bates, *Open-economy Politics: The Political Economy of the World Coffee Trade* (Princeton: Princeton University Press, 1997), p. 89.

Marketing boards, of a much more clearly public nature, formed the single greatest direct intervention by the state in the coffee economies of Africa, and one that proved singularly disastrous in its effects. Late colonial regimes, which inaugurated the system, were perhaps keen to protect small farmers from volatile world market prices.[79] However, postcolonial governments shamelessly exploited the boards as a punitive form of taxation and a source of immense patronage and corruption. Indeed, many an African state was arguably brought to its knees by killing the golden goose, removing all incentives from farmers to do anything except smuggle their crop to where they could get a decent price for it.[80]

This worst-case scenario was not always witnessed, and Côte d'Ivoire became the classic case of prosperous coffee and cocoa cultivators taking power at independence, creating an African version of a "coffee republic." Félix Houphouët-Boigny, the president, was both a chief and a "kulak," and he rose to power by heading an association of smallholders. The state marketing board (Caisse de Stabilisation) was less interventionist than elsewhere, and left room for "Syrian" and other traders. Policies on land privatization, labor immigration, and transport were tailor-made to generate an immense boom in coffee and cocoa production, and the political stability and democracy enjoyed by Côte d'Ivoire came to be the envy of much of Africa. However, the whole system rested on the reckless destruction of virgin forest, and the regime collapsed when the president died and the forest ran out.[81] Kenya provides another, albeit more ambiguous, example of the same kind.[82] Ethiopia under Haile Selassie might even be a candidate for a kind of "coffee empire," until the regime fell victim to one of the most radical Communist insurrections on the continent.[83]

Most Asian coffee producers were decolonized in the aftermath of the Second World War, and were thus able to avoid the dubious benefits of colonial marketing boards, although Socialist countries such as Vietnam developed their own versions. Where relatively free marketing systems

---

[79] Bauer, *West African Trade.*
[80] Robert H. Bates, *Markets and States in Tropical Africa: The Political Basis of Agricultural Policies* (Berkeley: University of California Press, 1981).
[81] J.-P. Chauveau and E. Léonard, "Côte d'Ivoire's Pioneer Fronts: Historical and Political Determinants of the Spread of Cocoa Cultivation," in William G. Clarence-Smith, ed., *Cocoa Pioneer Fronts since 1800: The Role of Smallholders, Planters and Merchants* (London: Macmillan, 1996), pp. 176–94; Bastiaan A. den Tuinder, *Ivory Coast, the Challenge of Success* (Baltimore: Johns Hopkins University Press, 1978).
[82] Kitching, *Class and Economic Change in Kenya.*
[83] Richard Pankhurst, *The Ethiopians* (Oxford: BLackwell, 1998).

persisted, as in Indonesia, the coffee sector performed quite well.[84] However, coffee was nowhere of such importance as to dominate the economy of an entire country, especially as the Asian "economic miracle" began to lead to rapid industrialization, so that "coffee republics" were out of the question.

A Research Agenda

To stimulate research on the past, and thus inform the "coffee actors" of the present and future more effectively, we should not be locked into assuming that what happened in the coffee fields of São Paulo must also have happened in Ceylon or Tanzania. More direct comparisons between widely dispersed coffee economies should yield a rich harvest.

It is clearly important to re-create the lived lives of individual actors in coffee economies, including the women and children who have remained invisible for so long. Their existence embraced far more than picking coffee cherries, and we need to understand the broader structures that enhanced or restricted their freedom of action. Today's coffee workers sometimes have less independence of movement than in the past, despite greater rural democratization.

At the same time, we have to historicize not only the human actors in the drama but the set and props as well, and we thus need to pay closer attention to the production process itself. We also need to bear in mind the evolving nature of the world coffee market. As Topik points out, the nature of demand, the sort of coffee, the degree of institutionalization, communications, and transportation all have changed over time, with important implications for the participants in the global coffee commodity chain. For example, the twentieth-century decline in the scale of holdings, at least until after the onset of the Green Revolution, may augur a greater concentration of wealth, rather than a more equal spread of incomes. Current *Coffea* varieties require greater capital, since they are planted more densely, preclude other crops, and demand more fertilizer and pesticides. Hence, a small finca today may be more of an agroindustrial enterprise than a large hacienda at the turn of the century, which dedicated only a small area to coffee. On the other hand, the precipitous fall in coffee prices since 1989 has led producers to pay less attention to the quality of their beans and has encouraged greater production and use of lower-quality *robusta* beans.

[84] McStocker, "The Indonesian Coffee Industry."

We should also think statistically over the long term, and we hope that the statistical appendix by Mario Samper and Radin Fernando provides a good basis for such an approach. Individual counterexamples do not nullify broad, consistent trends. Statistics may appear arid at first sight, but they are a fertile ground for the production of new and excitingly different questions about historical process. Piecing together long series of figures is a service that historians can render to economists.

Although governments have played increasingly important roles in coffee economies, national borders should not dictate the frontiers of generalizations and analysis. There has been much variation within countries, as well as similarity among them. Regional histories and cultures need to be interwoven with those of nation-states and the wider world. Similar economic impulses have had substantially different outcomes in different contexts. The local and the global need to complement one another.

To examine the internalization of the external, we also need to better understand the external. Too often the international price of coffee is considered to be the only exogenous variable, and one that cannot be changed effectively by coffee producers. In reality, internal decision making is constrained by the policies of other growers, associations such as the ICO, agricultural research, primary and secondary processing technology, world transportation, segmentation of the market, roaster oligopsonies, and the cost and availability of capital. By understanding the development of the international coffee economy, scholars can come to appreciate that differences in local production systems may make little difference to the international masters of the trade. They may be less signs of local autonomy and independence than evidence of local irrelevance from a global perspective. So many coffee sources are available that roasters roam the globe choosing whatever is most beneficial to them. To fully appreciate the local coffee economy, we need to understand its function in the global economy, as well as its local ramifications.

Overall, to fully appreciate the importance of the new insights that have been developed recently, social, economic, and cultural history need to come together. By understanding how demography, geography, local history, indigenous peoples, labor systems, gender, cultural understandings, and family morality create a plethora of responses to the same capitalist world economy, we unmask *Homo economicus,* giving her and him innumerable human faces. Such apparently social questions as ethnic, gender, religious, and family practices should be part of economic equations, together with labor and tenure systems. Nor can politics be considered an exogenous variable.

There is a lot of history in your cup of coffee. It not only keeps us awake, but it can also enable us to see and understand this world and how its many parts have developed and interrelated over the centuries. By following the "life cycle" of coffee across the centuries and the continents, from bean to cup, we can illuminate many of the factors that have made our world as it is today.

Appendix

Historical Statistics of Coffee Production and Trade from 1700 to 1960

Mario Samper and Radin Fernando

Introduction

The goal of this statistical chapter is to summarily present reliable time series on production, volume of net exports and net imports, as well as selected information on prices from the beginning of the eighteenth century to 1960. The information provided here is part of a larger data set, abbreviated for publication. We sought to provide a relevant selection for those interested in the history of coffee-producing regions of the world, of the international coffee commodity chain, and of consumption trends. General readers may find the abridged tables helpful in terms of clarity, while specialists will perhaps appreciate the detailed annual data. We hope that these tables and the broader database from which they are derived will be improved on in the future through our collective efforts, as we continue to explore sources and share information.

This endeavor has been a cooperative project at several levels. The initiative came out of the conference on "Coffee Production and Economic Development, ca. 1700–1960," held at Oxford in 1998. The two coauthors subsequently undertook this task with the enthusiastic support of the editors, who generously contributed their own data and expertise. William G. Clarence-Smith supplied information on a number of African and Asian cases, and Steven Topik on Brazil; both offered relevant suggestions and valuable feedback. Several other researchers also provided data and source references for the historical cases with which they are familiar. We especially thank Carlos Alfaro, Gwyn Campbell, Elizabeth Dore, José A. Fernández, David Geggus, Rachel Kurian, Hildete Pereira

TABLE A.1. *Coffee Exports, 1712–1821 (metric tons, five-year averages)*

	Java	Surinam	Jamaica	Brazil
1712–1716	1.08			
1717–1721	20.60			
1722–1726	822.80			
1727–1731	1728.20	174.34		
1732–1736	1677.40	614.40		
1737–1741	1461.20	1867.73	28.18	
1742–1746	1593.00	1423.15	15.84	
1747–1751	1381.00	1654.22	18.33	
1752–1756	1512.40	2423.21	33.54	
1757–1761	1521.40	4745.33		52.68
1762–1766	1731.00	6160.37		50.21
1767–1771	1896.40	6130.98	105.70	47.95
1772–1776	2284.00	7615.47	359.93	44.20
1777–1781	1819.40	6355.17	206.20	
1782–1786	2197.20	6117.64	577.44	
1787–1791	1678.40	5143.20	817.21	
1792–1796		1855.38	2,431.19	
1797–1801		622.89	5,012.45	481.69
1802–1806		2382.54	9,976.82	348.24
1807–1811		3024.09	11,642.17	374.58
1812–1816		1363.20	11,050.26	1,507.87
1817–1821		3187.83	8,525.03	6,124.10

Sources: Brazil: 1741, 1750, 1756–77, 1796–1802, 1806–16: Teixeira de Oliveira (1984), pp. 208–10, 237, table 1 (includes only exports from Brazilian regions to Portugal and geographical coverage varies, so data do not reflect all Brazilian exports in those years); 1817–19 (sum of several regions to Portugal, and from Rio de Janeiro to all destinations): Teixeira de Oliveira (1984), table 1, and Thurber (1883), p. 135; 1820 (only Rio de Janeiro): Thurber (1883), p. 135; 1821 (for all Brazilian exports): Rodrigues da Cunha (1992), table 1.6 (material supplied by Steven Topik and Hildete Pereira de Melo). *Jamaica*: 1737–56, 1768–78, 1782–1821: Rodriguez (1961). *Java*: 1712–80, 1783–94, 1803, 1808–10: Bulbeck et al. (1998), tables 5.1, 5.2B. From 1724 to 1794, coffee purchased by VOC; for 1803, 1808–10, and 1822, coffee production of all Java. *Surinam*: 1724–1821: van Stipriaan (1993); pp. 429–33, data supplied by William G. Clarence-Smith; Ukers (1935).

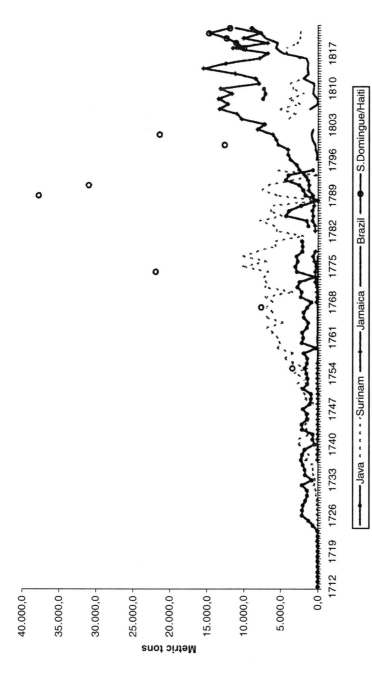

FIGURE A.1. Annual coffee exports, 1712–1822, in metric tons. *Sources*: Brazil, Jamaica, Java, and Surinam: See Table A.1. Saint Domingue/Haiti: Izard (1973), p. 208; Moral (1961), pp. 20, 91; Tarrade (1972), pp. 34 and 747; exports from Saint Domingue to France, supplied by David Geggus; data for 1772, 1774–78, 1781, 1784–87 contributed by David Geggus, compiled from various primary sources. Accuracy may vary, and volume smuggled is unknown.

TABLE A.2. *British Net Coffee Imports, 1701–1810 (metric tons, five-year averages)*

1701–1705	242.0
1706–1710	108.7
1711–1715	406.5
1716–1720	123.2
1721–1725	372.0
1726–1730	258.8
1731–1735	161.1
1736–1740	336.3
1741–1745	120.5
1746–1750	154.4
1751–1755	220.6
1756–1760	41.1
1761–1765	176.6
1766–1770	84.9
1771–1775	302.2
1776–1780	−176.8
1781–1785	169.5
1786–1790	638.4
1791–1795	775.4
1796–1800	1,789.0
1801–1805	823.9
1806–1810	9,968.9

Source: Schumpeter (1960), table 18. The last average is for three years, 1806–8, and imports were exceptionally high in the latter year.

de Melo, Gustavo Palma, Simon D. Smith, Michel Tuchscherer, Jean C. Tulet, and Robert Williams.

Scope of Statistical Survey

There is a great deal of statistical information on various aspects of the coffee industry, much of which is buried in archival sources and unpublished research material inaccessible to us. We set ourselves a modest target of compiling, inasmuch as feasible, a reasonably complete and reliable set of statistics on amounts harvested and traded, as well as international prices of coffee from 1700 to 1960. We have relied on material already published and some unpublished research work made available to us by our colleagues or obtained from primary sources through our own research.

TABLE A.3. *Prices of Coffee in Amsterdam, 1733–1812*
(guilders per pound, five-year averages)

	Java	Mocha	Surinam	S. Domingo
1733–1737	0.69	0.99	0.61	
1738–1742	0.47	0.62	0.37	
1743–1747	0.59	1.07	0.53	
1748–1752	0.65	0.85	0.55	
1753–1757	0.57	0.85	0.46	
1758–1762	0.49	0.89	0.37	0.37
1763–1767	0.52	0.99	0.40	0.41
1768–1772	0.60	0.88	0.53	0.51
1773–1777	0.44	0.79	0.32	0.28
1778–1782	0.50	0.89	0.51	0.48
1783–1787	0.54	1.02	0.47	0.45
1788–1792	0.68	0.75	0.57	0.52
1793–1797	0.77	0.86	0.73	0.70
1798–1802	1.14	1.25	0.92	0.89
1803–1807	1.03	0.99	0.99	0.94
1808–1812		2.12	1.96	1.98

Source: Posthumus (1946), vol. 1, pp. 75–79 (material supplied by William G. Clarence-Smith).

This body of information is incomplete for some variables and years in specific cases. We avoided filling the gaps through statistical extrapolation or other procedures commonly used to estimate aggregate figures at the expense of local, year-by-year precision. However, we did include the more reasonable aggregate estimates for each major variable, as a means both to assess the coverage of our own data and to identify overall trends as well as changing orders of magnitude.

While we cannot enter here into an in-depth methodological discussion, we must say that there are major discrepancies among various authors' estimates of world production, exports, and imports, as can be seen in Tables A.5 to A.7. While original sources are the same for certain periods, they differ in others, and since information is often incomplete, gaps are filled in by various means: repetition of data or use of averages from previous years, interpolation and extrapolation, or simply making rough estimates based on more or less reasonable assumptions. Definitions also vary from one country or period to another, so aggregate time series sometimes combine disparate data.

Overall exports and imports rarely match, partly because information derives from very different sources of information in the countries

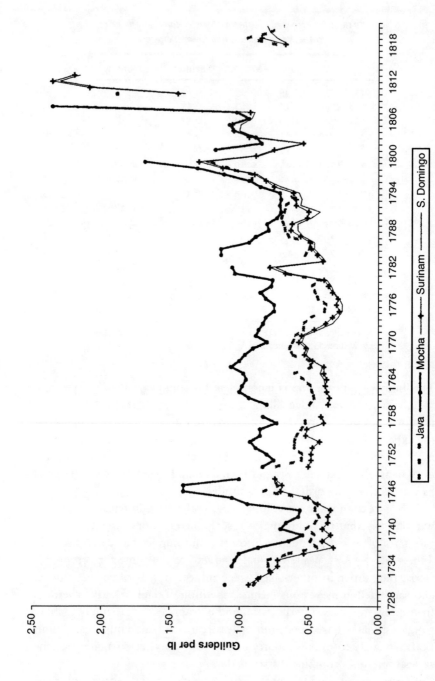

FIGURE A.2. Annual prices of coffee in Amsterdam, 1728–1821, in guilders per pound. *Source:* See Table A.3.

TABLE A.4. *World Coffee Production Estimates, 1856–1960 (thousands of metric tons, five-year averages)*

	(A)	(B)
1856–1860	326.40	324.70
1861–1865	315.60	314.70
1866–1870	408.00	407.81
1871–1875	426.00	426.76
1876–1880	512.40	510.50
1881-1885	600.96	600.91
1886–1890	538.32	550.80
1891–1895	634.08	650.40
1896–1900	888.36	868.80
1901–1905	1,032.36	979.20
1906–1910	1,152.24	1,076.40
1911–1915	1,180.20	1,129.20
1916–1920	1,179.96	1,083.60
1921–1925	1,437.12	1,280.40
1926–1930	1,983.96	1,775.96
1931–1935	2,341.44	2,172.70
1936–1940	2,330.76	2,260.14
1941–1945	1,820.52	1,765.38
1946–1950	2,237.52	2,056.52
1951–1955	2,598.96	2,498.36
1956–1960	3,681.48	3,521.00

Sources: (A) 1856–1960: Rodrigues da Cunha (1992), table 1.1 (material provided by Steven Topik and Hildete Pereira de Melo); (B) 1856–83: van Delden Laërne (1885), p. 462; 1884–1928: Daviron (1993), table 19; 1929–60: FAO (1961), table IA.

that ship and receive coffee. The distinction between exportable production and coffee that is actually exported becomes more significant after the late nineteenth century, and valorization schemes involving retention or destruction of coffee complicate matters. Amounts purchased by international traders and actually imported into various countries also vary.

Estimates of production often differ from, and are sometimes lower than, export data. This is primarily due to the fact that production data refer to the harvest year, which in turn varies from one country to another, while trade information is usually supplied for the calendar year. However, this is not always the case, and in certain countries the information

TABLE A.5. *World Coffee Export Estimates,*
1851–1960 (thousands of metric tons,
five-year averages)

	(A)	(B)
1851–1855	289.21	
1856–1860	319.05	
1861–1865	324.51	
1866–1870	403.57	
1871–1875	439.21	384.45
1876–1880	472.75	413.88
1881–1885	585.53	529.80
1886–1890	534.43	492.51
1891–1895	620.71	585.24
1896–1900	800.55	808.62
1901–1905	980.83	890.06
1906–1910	1,055.75	851.76
1911–1915	1,101.64	1,092.18
1916–1920	1,056.76	1,056.76
1921–1925	1,277.21	1,277.21
1926–1930	1,443.89	1,443.89
1931–1935	1,549.01	1,549.01
1936–1940	1,614.94	1,623.34
1941–1945	1,320.00	1,389.60
1946–1950	1,844.40	1,843.20
1951–1955	1,945.96	1,929.60
1956–1960	2,352.41	2,335.20

Sources: (A) 1851–1960: Rodrigues da Cunha (1992), table 1.6 (material provided by Steven Topik and Hildete Pereira de Melo); (B) 1871–1912: Lewis (1978), table A.10 (dates in the original source are listed here as the previous year, since they refer to the agricultural year ending in the one listed by Lewis; this is mentioned by the author in Appendix III and was corroborated by comparison with other sources); 1913–28: Wickizer (1943), table 5; 1929–60: Junguito and Pizano (1993), table III-1.

was first supplied for harvest years, and then for calendar years. Furthermore, data on production proper were often nonexistent before the late nineteenth or early twentieth century, so they were often inferred from and sometimes confused with export data.

Clearly, caution must be exercised in short-term correlations and similar analyses, although the information is useful to perceive approximate magnitudes and general trends.

TABLE A.6. *World Coffee Import Estimates,*
1851–1960 (thousands of metric tons,
five-year averages)

	(A)	(B)
1851–1855	289.21	
1856–1860	319.05	
1861–1865	324.51	
1866–1870	403.57	
1871–1875	439.21	420.12
1876–1880	472.75	479.04
1881–1885	612.39	588.84
1886–1890	616.74	581.52
1891–1895	648.00	653.16
1896–1900	815.94	798.12
1901–1905	951.78	954.48
1906–1910	1,008.95	1,051.08
1911–1915	1,021.04	1,144.92
1916–1920	1,055.72	1,005.36
1921–1925	1,256.42	1,237.68
1926–1930	1,422.11	1,388.76
1931–1935	1,554.68	1,434.60
1936–1940	1,564.13	1,555.08
1941–1945	1,195.70	1,309.92
1946–1950	1,729.57	1,799.88
1951–1955	1,933.73	1,911.24
1956–1960	2,343.24	2,316.96

Sources: (A) 1851–1960: Rodrigues da Cunha
(1992), table 1.7 (material provided by Steven
Topik and Hildete Pereira de Melo); (B) 1871–
1960: Daviron (1993), table 22.

Data included here on physical volumes cover total production, net exports, and net imports of coffee. These variables were understood and treated as follows.

Production: As far as possible, we included data on total production as opposed to exports. In some cases there was a clear distinction, while in others the difference was negligible. A few coffee-producing countries did not export at all in certain periods. Secondary-source data purported to refer to production may in a number of cases actually refer to exports, while rough estimates of local consumption are sometimes used by others to infer production levels; when this was clearly the case and we were not able to determine actual production, we excluded that information. We have not adjusted export figures by estimating local consumption to

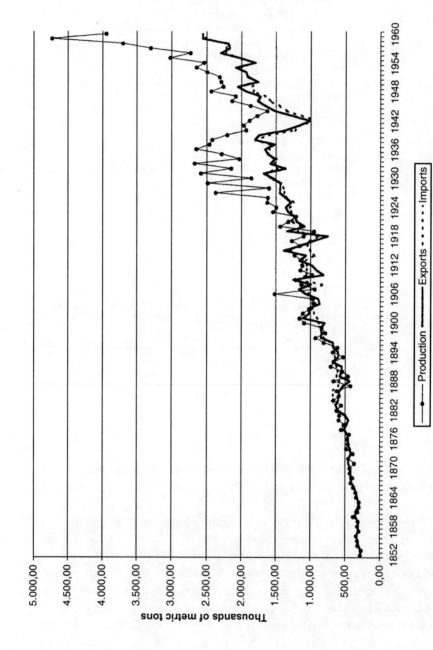

FIGURE A.3. Annual world coffee production, exports, and imports, 1852–1960, in thousands of metric tons. *Source:* Rodrigues da Cunha (1992), tables 5 to 7.

TABLE A.7. *Central American and Mexican Coffee Production, 1881–1960*
(thousands of metric tons, five-year averages)

	Costa Rica	El Salvador	Guatemala	Honduras	Nicaragua	Mexico
1881–1885	14.96	9.34	18.18	1.56	4.08	6.72
1886–1890	11.96	7.68	17.40	1.92	4.13	5.52
1891–1895	12.06	11.58	28.56	1.80	5.66	13.20
1896–1900	16.50	13.20	29.16	1.14	5.94	24.49
1901–1905	15.41	25.86	31.74	1.20	8.40	31.67
1906–1910	13.36	27.36	35.06	1.04	7.98	44.68
1911–1915	11.53	26.23	36.84	1.09	9.00	45.10
1916–1920	9.28	27.00	40.92	1.15	9.96	34.56
1921–1925	14.89	40.57	43.10	1.19	15.10	42.36
1926–1930	19.58	52.94	42.64	1.42	14.14	51.18
1931–1935	22.52	57.26	52.90	1.66	14.16	48.32
1936–1940	23.50	67.56	54.08	1.20	15.18	57.56
1941–1945	23.02	63.02	54.82	2.38	12.56	54.25
1946–1950	22.10	65.82	54.58	8.46	14.92	58.01
1951–1955	27.20	69.24	63.18	15.78	21.80	80.90
1956–1960	50.48	91.82	84.42	20.24	23.56	105.83

Sources: Springuett (1935), table "World Coffee Production"; FAO (1961), table IA; Hernández (1996).

TABLE A.8. *Caribbean Coffee Production, 1881–1960 (thousands of metric tons, five-year averages)*

	Cuba	Dominican Republic	Haiti	Jamaica	Puerto Rico
1881–1885			30.82	5.52	11.78
1886–1890			26.16	5.94	18.86
1891–1895			28.56	6.78	16.56
1896–1900			25.79	5.10	11.58
1901–1905			23.74	5.16	8.16
1906–1910			22.74	3.96	8.32
1911–1915			26.24	3.72	10.86
1916–1920			27.19	3.66	10.26
1921–1925			29.60	4.34	10.62
1926–1930			31.88	3.72	2.54
1931–1935	28.38	18.00	30.80		
1936–1940	29.20	23.72	22.32		
1941–1945	30.02	19.80	21.68		
1946–1950	30.06	22.72	36.52		
1951–1955	36.44	29.18	37.46		
1956–1960	39.40	33.88	27.96		

Sources: Springuett (1935); FAO (1961), table IA; Ukers (1935).

TABLE A.9. *South American Coffee Production, 1881–1960 (thousands of metric tons, five-year averages)*

	Brazil	Colombia	Ecuador	Venezuela
1881–1885	347.88	6.47	1.50	36.67
1886–1890	306.67	10.78	2.10	35.98
1891–1895	360.95	19.51	2.64	42.72
1896–1900	608.60	26.78	2.40	51.48
1901–1905	752.93	35.05	2.52	43.20
1906–1910	879.19	37.06	2.40	43.42
1911–1915	866.69	56.96	2.76	60.84
1916–1920	807.17	78.42	3.00	60.54
1921–1925	902.70	127.62	3.20	59.40
1926–1930	1,311.62	161.10	7.80	56.40
1931–1935	1,424.83	222.52	10.04	55.08
1936–1940	1,319.24	269.36	13.82	56.72
1941–1945	760.90	330.54	12.98	38.98
1946–1950	931.20	345.00	14.92	41.36
1951–1955	994.14	380.46	25.24	48.36
1956–1960	1,619.38	451.12	37.62	53.32

Sources: Di Fulvio (1947), table 1.3; Junguito and Pizano (1991), table I-1; FAO (1961), table IA.

TABLE A.10. *Asian Coffee Production, 1881–1960 (thousands of metric tons, five-year averages)*

	Ceylon	India	Indonesia	Malaya	Portuguese Timor	Yemen
1881–1885	18.59		109.48		1.64	
1886–1890	6.14		77.62		1.43	
1891–1895	3.11		73.24	0.19	1.00	
1896–1900	2.00		74.39	1.31	0.19	
1901–1905			65.79	3.12	0.68	
1906–1910	0.15		50.05	1.12		
1911–1915			65.15	0.58		
1916–1920			88.64			
1921–1925			86.29			
1926–1930			116.09			
1931–1935		15.90	120.83			4.66
1936–1940		15.86	119.30			4.10
1941–1945		19.08	68.94			9.04
1946–1950		21.00	27.42			5.62
1951–1955		26.68	58.31			4.40
1956–1960		44.90	77.55			5.46

Sources: Bulbeck et al. (1998); Springett (1935); Graham (1912), p. 11 (only data on production, as other figures in this table refer to exports); FAO (1961), table IA.

TABLE A.11. *African Coffee Production, 1931–1960 (thousands of metric tons, five-year averages)*

	Cameroon	Congo (Belgian, Zaire)	Ethiopia	Kenya	Madagascar	Tanganyika	Uganda
1931–1935	0.70	10.62	17.74	14.60	14.49	13.54	5.46
1936–1940	3.68	24.40	9.30	16.68	32.68	14.58	14.90
1941–1945	5.42	29.22	11.08	13.08	23.50	14.12	19.74
1946–1950	6.82	30.46	20.80	9.30	26.26	13.88	28.06
1951–1955	11.28	37.22	41.56	17.80	42.80	17.72	45.80
1956–1960	26.28	72.26	51.28	30.14	50.33	23.86	90.86

Sources: FAO (1961), table IA; data for Madagascar supplied by Gwyn Campbell.

arrive at production levels, as there are few reliable figures on actual consumption for exporting countries throughout most of the period.

Net exports: These were defined as volume of total exports minus imports. Overall coverage of exports is more complete, as many countries kept better records of coffee entering international trade. A few countries that produced and exported coffee also imported some in specific periods. When they exported more than they imported, such countries were listed as net exporters of the difference. Official export figures may understate actual amounts of coffee shipped from a country at a given time for several reasons, including contraband, tax evasion, and insufficient records, especially when it was exported from ports in neighboring countries. Ethiopian and Yemenite coffee exports, for example, are very difficult to segregate from others going through Aden; an indeterminate amount of West Indian coffee was sold without going through official channels in colonial times, and there is little information about early trade in coffee among African or Asian countries.

Net imports: This information basically reflects total import volumes minus reexports. While total and net imports are similar in many countries, several of the major importers also reexported large quantities of coffee, so the difference there is quite significant. Such is the case of the Netherlands especially in the eighteenth century, Great Britain throughout the nineteenth century, and the United States since the latter part of that century. On the other hand, a number of countries that imported coffee were also producers, and some imported variable amounts either in alternate periods or at the same time that they exported some of their own coffee. When such countries imported more than they exported, they were included as net importers of the balance.

424 *Mario Samper and Radin Fernando*

TABLE A.12. *Annual Central American, Mexican, and Hawaiian Coffee Exports,*
1832–1960 (thousands of metric tons)

	Costa Rica	El Salvador	Guatemala	Honduras	Nicaragua	Mexico	Hawaii
1832	0.02						
1833	0.04						
1834							
1835							
1836							
1837							
1838							
1839							
1840							
1841	0.65						
1842	0.76						
1843	1.15						
1844	2.27						
1845	3.03						0.00
1846	3.77						0.00
1847							0.01
1848							0.02
1849							0.01
1850							0.09
1851							0.01
1852	3.07					0.01	0.05
1853	3.63					0.13	0.02
1854						0.04	0.04
1855	3.25					0.02	0.04
1856	3.82					0.00	0.03
1857	4.14					0.01	0.14
1858	2.78					0.04	0.03
1859	4.99					0.29	0.04
1860	4.14		0.06			0.23	0.02
1861	5.19					0.00	0.02
1862	4.96					0.42	0.07
1863	3.98		0.82			0.01	0.06
1864	5.18	0.22			0.04	0.00	0.02
1865	6.19				0.10	0.24	0.14
1866	8.34					0.42	0.04
1867	9.20				0.20	0.42	0.06
1868	9.38					0.14	0.04
1869	9.38					0.12	0.15
1870	11.56	2.67	3.44		0.19	0.24	0.19
1871	8.33				0.57	0.86	0.02
1872	11.59					0.93	0.02

TABLE A.12. *(continued)*

	Costa Rica	El Salvador	Guatemala	Honduras	Nicaragua	Mexico	Hawaii
1873	9.20		6.76			1.33	0.12
1874	10.78	3.86	7.26			1.25	0.03
1875	4.84	3.99	7.35			2.47	0.08
1876	11.18		9.31			3.27	0.07
1877	8.36		9.43			2.96	0.06
1878	11.59		9.40			4.40	0.06
1879	10.70		11.32		1.60	4.79	0.03
1880	7.93	7.53	13.01		2.05	6.45	0.05
1881	11.24	6.59	11.69		2.13	7.88	0.01
1882	7.41	8.10	14.02		3.32		0.00
1883	9.20	9.36	18.15		2.48		0.01
1884	16.63	9.06	16.68		3.28		0.00
1885	9.15	13.47	23.37		3.20		0.00
1886	9.04	3.64	23.79		3.29		0.00
1887	13.08	6.00	21.50		3.11		0.00
1888	10.31	6.60	16.46		4.00		0.00
1889	12.81	7.20	24.81	0.19	3.82		0.02
1890	15.39	14.97	22.84		5.16		0.04
1891	14.14	14.53	23.56		4.15		0.00
1892	10.80		22.08				0.01
1893	11.44	15.90	26.87				0.02
1894	10.78	7.20	27.85				0.09
1895	11.09	5.99	31.39				0.05
1896	11.72	10.80	31.03				0.12
1897	13.87	9.00	34.25				0.15
1898	19.49	6.00	37.47		4.71		0.33
1899	15.37	22.20	38.15		4.58		0.37
1900	16.06	18.00	33.11				0.15
1901	16.57	19.84	30.67		5.88		
1902	13.75	18.88	35.11				
1903	17.33	26.35	26.26		8.36		
1904	12.58	34.16	29.38		9.80		
1905	18.05	28.04	36.78		9.12		
1906	13.77	28.43	31.04		8.80		0.56
1907	14.47	25.55	49.99		8.48	14.16	0.65
1908	8.98	25.05	25.43		9.34	21.46	0.89
1909	12.03	28.73	39.99		8.42	26.69	1.23
1910	14.40	28.05	30.14		11.86	18.68	1.57
1911	12.64	29.36	35.13		7.54	18.86	
1912	12.24	26.49	32.80	0.32	6.08		
1913	13.02	28.39	39.71	0.24	11.83	20.95	

(continued)

TABLE A.12. *(continued)*

	Costa Rica	El Salvador	Guatemala	Honduras	Nicaragua	Mexico	Hawaii
1914	17.72	34.18	37.71	0.54	10.21		2.03
1915	12.21	30.04	35.18	0.12	9.01	22.69	1.71
1916	16.84	35.26	39.68	0.24	10.31	25.08	1.41
1917	12.27	35.75	41.00	0.36	8.31	23.57	1.16
1918	11.45	35.55	35.50	0.12	11.43	13.61	2.62
1919	13.96	32.59	40.67	0.84	15.07	17.40	1.65
1920	14.00	41.60	42.62	0.48	6.86	5.95	1.16
1921	13.34	27.92	42.42	0.12	13.39	13.73	2.26
1922	18.62	42.48	42.43	0.36	8.75	24.91	1.67
1923	11.09	41.41	43.40	0.90	13.52	16.38	1.38
1924	18.21	48.18	40.28	0.84	17.75	15.89	1.63
1925	15.35	31.62	43.94	0.78	10.67	23.65	
1926	18.25	49.92	42.30	1.20	17.43	21.07	
1927	16.15	35.70	52.02	1.44	10.11	26.09	
1928	18.84	52.37	43.54	2.34	17.56	31.58	
1929	19.70	46.80	43.90	1.60	13.20	29.90	
1930	23.50	58.60	56.70	1.80	15.30	30.70	
1931	23.00	54.60	36.10	1.10	15.80	27.30	
1932	18.50	36.70	45.60	1.60	8.10	20.00	
1933	27.80	56.20	35.20	1.90	13.70	41.30	
1934	19.10	49.90	48.40	1.90	14.70	37.80	
1935	24.20	50.10	40.40	1.10	18.50	31.60	
1936	21.30	49.40	50.60	1.50	13.10	42.80	
1937	26.50	67.60	47.00	2.50	15.80	35.10	
1938	25.00	53.80	49.00	1.20	14.30	35.10	
1939	20.20	55.80	43.80	1.90	17.40	39.10	
1940	18.70	56.50	41.50	1.40	15.30	25.70	
1941	21.50	41.80	43.40	0.90	12.70	27.90	
1942	20.70	53.10	56.10	2.20	12.70	21.80	
1943	24.20	56.40	49.80	2.00	12.00	34.40	
1944	18.80	63.10	51.30	1.90	13.10	35.70	
1945	21.80	57.70	51.30	2.70	12.30	35.70	
1946	15.70	48.20	49.70	3.80	11.80	33.30	
1947	19.90	62.60	55.80	2.60	10.00	32.90	
1948	23.50	60.30	48.50	3.20	14.50	31.50	
1949	16.60	74.60	54.80	6.20	6.80	49.00	
1950	16.90	69.30	54.90	6.00	21.00	46.10	
1951	18.60	65.90	50.90	8.20	16.10	51.50	
1952	21.20	66.90	60.40	8.30	18.90	52.20	
1953	27.90	65.90	56.60	11.20	18.80	74.10	

TABLE A.12. *(continued)*

	Costa Rica	El Salvador	Guatemala	Honduras	Nicaragua	Mexico	Hawaii
1954	18.70	62.20	52.80	9.30	17.10	66.70	
1955	28.30	71.80	58.40	8.90	22.80	83.50	
1956	22.80	64.50	62.50	11.90	16.90	74.00	
1957	29.50	83.20	61.80	10.40	22.00	88.80	
1958	46.20	80.50	71.40	11.30	22.90	78.80	
1959	43.30	83.00	83.10	15.30	16.30	74.40	
1960	46.60	0.00	104.00	0.00	22.50	83.00	

Sources: **Costa Rica**: 1832–33, 1843–46, 1852–53, and 1855–1928: Williams (1994), table A-1; 1841–42: Obregón (1997); 1929–60: FAO (1961), Table III A. **El Salvador**: 1864, 1870, 1875, 1881, 1885, 1890–91, 1895, 1901–28: Williams (1994), table A-1; 1874/75: Ukers (1935); 1880: Lauria (1999), table 2; 1882/83 to 1884/85, 1886/87 to 1889/90, 1893/94 to 1894/95, 1896/97 to 1900/1: Duque (1938), p. 2424; 1929–60: FAO (1961), Table III A. **Guatemala**: 1860, 1866, 1876: Ukers (1935); 1873–1928: Williams (1994), table A-1; 1929–60: FAO (1961), Table III A. **Nicaragua**: 1864–65, 1867, 1870–71: Velázquez Pereira (1992), data supplied by Elizabeth Dore; 1879–91: Radell (1964), table I; 1898–99, 1901–28: Dirección General de Estadística y Censos (1961), p. 52, data provided by Elizabeth Dore; 1904–28: Williams (1994), table A-1; 1929–60: FAO (1961), Table III A. **Honduras**: 1889: República de Honduras (1893), information supplied by Robert Williams; 1912–28: Williams (1994), table A-1; 1929–60: FAO (1961), Table III A. **Mexico**: 1852/53 to 1881/82: van Delden Laërne (1885), p. 412 (we entered the data for 1852/53 as 1852, and so forth); 1907–11: Graham (1912), p. 47; 1913–28: Bynum (1930), table 21 (these are net exports, as Mexico was also importing some coffee at that time); 1929–60: FAO (1961), Table III A. **Hawaii**: 1845–1900: Schmitt (1977), p. 551–52, data supplied by William G. Clarence-Smith; 1906–10: Graham (1912), p.11; 1914–24 from Bynum (1926), table 677.

The data on production, exports, and imports are provided in thousands of metric tons of dry seed, except for the period before 1820 when volumes were low and hence are given in tons. As far as possible, we sought to use green coffee equivalents, but up to the nineteenth century information on some countries may actually be for parchment coffee, which can weigh up to 20 percent more than peeled or "green" dry coffee seed.

While we have not included trade value series, the international price series seemed indispensable. Eighteenth-century prices are in guilders due to the major importance of the Dutch import and reexport trade. With respect to the nineteenth and twentieth centuries, we focused on New York prices in U.S. dollars, to facilitate comparisons. A deflation index was used to convert current into constant prices.

The tables have been organized to cover two main periods, with some variations due to data coverage and the spatial organization of coffee production, consumption, and trade: the "long" eighteenth century, extending from the late seventeenth to the early nineteenth centuries, and

TABLE A.13. *Annual Caribbean Coffee Exports, 1823–1960 (thousands of metric tons)*

	Cuba	Dominican Republic	Guadeloupe	Haiti	Jamaica	Martinique	Puerto Rico
1823	12.55		1.30	16.49	9.22	0.64	
1824	9.92		1.47	21.67	12.55	0.95	
1825	12.05		1.17	18.04	9.64	0.80	
1826	19.96		0.42	16.26	9.23	0.50	
1827	22.52		0.98	24.31	11.68	1.01	
1828	14.45		1.02	21.77	10.08	0.83	
1829	19.53		1.19	19.56	10.09	0.97	
1830	20.23		1.13	20.79	10.10	0.61	
1831	23.97		0.91	19.87	6.38	0.38	
1832	23.05		0.96	24.06	8.99	0.61	
1833	28.87		0.66	15.47	9.01	0.52	
1834	20.44		0.89	22.75	8.04	0.62	
1835	15.93		0.54	23.67	4.80	0.30	
1836	18.12		0.73	18.42	6.10	0.46	
1837	24.00		0.48	15.10	4.55	0.28	
1838	17.44		0.70	24.39	6.15	0.51	
1839	21.94		0.44	18.55	4.52	0.24	
1840	24.12		0.52	22.58	3.30	0.33	
1841	13.89		0.34	16.70	2.92	0.15	
1842	22.49		0.41	19.94	3.20	0.38	
1843	18.36		0.34		3.34	0.13	
1844	13.95		0.42		3.24	0.29	
1845	6.29		0.29	19.05	2.28	0.09	
1846	9.20		0.36		2.74	0.08	
1847	10.49		0.18		2.91	0.14	
1848	7.81		0.17		2.58	0.09	
1849	9.87		0.19		1.56	0.20	
1850	5.85		0.18		2.33	0.07	
1851	6.47		0.22		2.54	0.11	
1852	8.32		0.24		3.23	0.10	5.16
1853	4.98		0.25		2.29	0.12	5.25
1854	5.75		0.16		2.72	0.04	5.11
1855	5.33		0.32		2.57	0.08	6.19
1856	5.28		0.20	17.24	1.51	0.02	4.79
1857	2.15		0.32		3.22	0.06	5.05
1858	2.04		0.14		2.38	0.02	4.19
1859	3.19		0.48		2.45	0.03	6.02
1860	8.34		0.25		2.98	0.05	7.22
1861	7.57		0.33		3.07	0.01	
1862			0.22		2.54	0.01	5.71

TABLE A.13. *(continued)*

	Cuba	Dominican Republic	Guadeloupe	Haiti	Jamaica	Martinique	Puerto Rico
1863	2.08		0.41		3.85	0.03	7.58
1864			0.22		2.46	0.01	7.29
1865			0.45		2.90	0.04	8.60
1866			0.14	25.29	3.55	0.01	6.77
1867	1.73		0.36		2.84	0.02	8.72
1868	1.20		0.33		3.97	0.07	7.28
1869	1.80		0.35		2.14	0.04	7.14
1870	0.97		0.26		4.46	0.02	7.90
1871	0.26		0.28		2.50	0.01	9.44
1872	0.01		0.46		4.31	0.01	8.33
1873	0.03		0.38		3.27	0.00	11.72
1874	0.02		0.28		4.68	0.01	8.06
1875	0.09		0.28		3.24	0.00	11.87
1876	0.04		0.47	23.72	3.92	0.01	9.45
1877	0.02		0.40		4.32	0.01	7.19
1878	0.01		0.61		4.27	0.00	7.73
1879	0.02		0.29		4.91	0.00	13.85
1880	0.01		0.35		4.62	0.01	9.90
1881	0.00	0.64	0.51		4.47	0.01	21.40
1882	0.06		0.55		3.37	0.01	13.35
1883	0.01		0.43		4.29	0.00	16.83
1884			0.30		2.46	0.00	11.68
1885	0.00		0.45		4.10	0.00	21.37
1886	0.00		0.34		2.79	0.00	16.53
1887			0.36	37.81	2.87	0.00	12.37
1888		0.67	0.47	25.91	5.03	0.00	23.01
1889			0.50	25.51	4.30	0.00	17.11
1890			0.39	26.70	3.73	0.00	19.64
1891			0.42	30.77	3.84	0.00	18.66
1892			0.65	31.87	4.42	0.00	21.18
1893			0.48	26.29	4.94	0.00	22.02
1894			0.53	33.92	4.49	0.00	22.59
1895			0.48	21.44	4.83	0.00	18.00
1896			0.69	32.88	4.29	0.00	26.29
1897			0.67	30.35	3.38	0.00	23.18
1898			0.68	27.73	4.34	0.00	
1899			0.79	32.46	5.60	0.00	

(continued)

TABLE A.13. *(continued)*

	Cuba	Dominican Republic	Guadeloupe	Haiti	Jamaica	Martinique	Puerto Rico
1900		1.79	0.52	26.16	4.25	0.00	
1901			0.66	28.99	4.36	0.00	
1902			0.73	21.53	5.24	0.00	
1903			0.75	21.97	5.48	0.00	
1904			0.52	27.39	4.07	0.00	
1905				29.05	2.62		
1906		1.32		31.01	4.10		17.58
1907		1.55		28.73	2.79		15.99
1908		1.85	1.03	18.60	4.79		12.92
1909		0.70		35.74	3.74		20.51
1910		2.06			4.44		15.39
1911					3.05		
1912					4.55		
1913		1.05	0.94	27.97	2.96		2.28
1914		1.83	0.65	39.57	4.05		2.32
1915		2.47	0.62	17.61	3.23		1.46
1916		1.73	0.86	21.88	3.35		1.80
1917		1.09	0.50	22.52	2.61		1.71
1918		2.29	0.97	19.00	4.64		1.27
1919		2.21	0.38	48.50	3.74		1.49
1920		0.62	0.80	33.16	2.10		1.21
1921		0.94	0.77	22.19	3.28		1.06
1922		2.36	0.60	28.37	3.21		0.76
1923		1.40	0.53	35.56	3.92		0.99
1924		2.23	0.76	29.17	2.64		1.08
1925		2.67	0.98	30.52	5.28		1.19
1926		4.31	0.59	35.40	3.37		0.88
1927		4.09	0.82	28.47	4.15		0.36
1928		4.54		40.82	4.01		0.06
1929		5.50		28.60	2.98		
1930		4.80		34.30	3.12		
1931		5.10		26.30	4.16		
1932	6.10	6.40		23.20	4.03		
1933	3.30	11.80		41.70	4.46		
1934	1.20	9.60		34.00	3.24		
1935	1.80	8.90		19.00	3.44		
1936	2.20	14.60		36.10	4.72		
1937	6.70	11.00		24.80	3.44		
1938	6.80	8.40		25.10	4.29		
1939	8.50	14.10		29.30	3.79		

TABLE A.13. *(continued)*

	Cuba	Dominican Republic	Guadeloupe	Haiti	Jamaica	Martinique	Puerto Rico
1940	6.70	8.60		16.20	2.66		
1941	4.40	12.10		22.60	2.08		
1942	4.90	7.80		18.10	2.41		
1943	5.90	10.60		25.80	1.90		
1944	7.20	8.60		23.10	2.18		
1945	2.30	17.70		30.00	2.55		
1946	0.00	10.40		24.80	1.01		
1947	0.00	9.10		22.40	1.60		
1948	0.00	11.50		22.90	1.40		
1949	0.70	14.40		33.20	1.23		
1950	0.20	12.90		23.40	1.69		
1951	0.00	14.20		25.00	1.34		
1952	0.00	26.30		32.50	1.36		
1953	0.00	20.10		22.30	1.56		
1954	0.00	23.90		31.00	2.10		
1955	4.10	24.40		19.60	2.66		
1956	20.00	26.40		31.10	2.43		
1957	11.40	21.70		19.40	1.54		
1958	7.20	25.80		32.80	1.25		
1959	3.00	21.90		21.90	1.34		
1960	0.00	28.80		23.70			

Sources: *Cuba*: 1804–59: Oficina Internacional de las Repúblicas Americanas (1902), pp. 43–44; 1860–61, 1863, 1867–83, 1885–86: Pérez de la Riva (1944); 1932–60: FAO (1961), table III A (Cuba was a net importer in other years). *Dominican Republic*: 1881, 1888, 1900, 1909: Ukers (1935); 1906–8, 1910: Graham (1912), p. 10 ("Santo Domingo"); 1913–28: Bynum (1930), table 19; 1929–60: FAO (1961), table III A. *Guadeloupe*: 1818–1904: Légier (1905), data supplied by William G. Clarence-Smith; 1908: Ukers (1935); 1913–27: Bynum (1930), table 20. *Haiti*: 1818–42: Ardouin (1853–60), vol. 10, pp. 53–54, 238, information contributed by William G. Clarence-Smith; 1856, 1866, 1876: Ukers (1935); 1887/88 to 1909/10: Graham (1912), p. 54; 1913/14 to 1928/29: Bynum (1930), table 16. *Jamaica*: 1823–1959: Rodriguez (1961) (from 1871 to 1908 the years were agricultural, coffee-harvest years; the year 1908–9 was eliminated due to the change to calendar years thereafter). *Martinique*: 1818–1904: Légier (1905); Martinique was a net importer of coffee from 1913 to 1923. *Puerto Rico*: 1852–97: Bergad (1983); 1906–10: Graham (1912); 1913–28: Bynum (1930), table 17 (years running from July 1 to June 30 of the following year).

TABLE A.14. *Annual South American Coffee Exports, 1823–1960*
(thousands of metric tons)

	Brazil	Colombia	Ecuador	Peru	Surinam	Venezuela
1823	13.56				3.42	
1824	16.44				3.15	
1825	13.44				2.10	
1826	19.08				1.92	
1827	25.80				1.56	
1828	27.12				2.78	
1829	27.54				1.48	
1830	28.80				3.01	
1831	32.94				1.49	
1832	43.02				1.23	
1833	67.23				1.57	
1834	62.73	0.16			1.10	
1835	60.66	0.00			1.08	
1836	58.86	0.24			1.64	
1837	61.77	0.33			1.33	
1838	74.46	0.47			0.94	
1839	81.48				1.18	
1840	78.66	0.66			1.73	
1841	78.06	0.00			0.97	
1842	84.21				0.79	
1843	89.55	1.14			1.31	
1844	91.98	1.23			0.98	
1845	97.44	1.44			0.85	
1846	123.30				0.15	
1847	141.81				0.35	
1848	133.38				0.71	
1849	106.77				0.31	
1850	118.14				0.38	
1851	144.66				0.15	
1852	143.01				0.68	
1853	136.80				0.28	10.33
1854	159.60	2.06			0.36	10.03
1855	181.29	2.13			0.23	11.67
1856	181.26	2.48			0.51	12.25
1857	167.07	2.86			0.12	9.98
1858	153.45	3.29			0.23	11.76
1859	157.77	3.88			0.26	13.20
1860	182.85				0.17	9.13
1861	179.73	0.16			0.07	12.63
1862	136.68	0.00			0.18	11.91
1863	124.20	0.24			0.14	9.32

TABLE A.14. *(continued)*

	Brazil	Colombia	Ecuador	Peru	Surinam	Venezuela
1864	139.47	0.41			0.09	13.64
1865	152.43	4.67			0.12	9.51
1866	167.79	4.10			0.01	12.35
1867	201.54	6.20			0.01	14.68
1868	220.89	3.80			0.02	16.89
1869	207.51	0.81			0.01	18.46
1870	208.26	6.40				
1871	236.61	8.01				
1872	226.71	7.36				34.27
1873	188.13	10.36				31.08
1874	198.81	4.56				35.72
1875	217.80	3.46			0.00	32.85
1876	208.80	2.22				29.12
1877	221.88	4.61				28.70
1878	262.41	4.67				25.13
1879	225.66	4.10				
1880	188.34	6.20				33.63
1881	232.23	3.80				42.80
1882	323.04	3.99				40.08
1883	360.09	6.40				38.71
1884	346.62	8.01				40.44
1885	350.22	7.36				39.06
1886	345.33	10.36				41.72
1887	283.89	4.45				43.10
1888	206.64	3.43				50.47
1889	335.16	2.22				43.17
1890	306.54	4.61			0.00	50.83
1891	322.38	4.66				
1892	426.54	6.46				40.73
1893	318.42	6.65				57.57
1894	334.92	20.26				12.49
1895	403.20	21.50				52.22
1896	404.64	28.52				47.37
1897	567.78	27.56				51.54
1898	556.02	31.89				53.36
1899	586.26	23.23				48.20
1900	549.30				0.19	38.50
1901	885.60					42.27
1902	789.42					33.00
1903	775.62					56.96
1904	601.50					39.44

(continued)

TABLE A.14. *(continued)*

	Brazil	Colombia	Ecuador	Peru	Surinam	Venezuela
1905	649.26	30.06				42.81
1906	837.96	38.16	2.65	0.61		43.00
1907	940.80	34.08	1.14	0.84		40.91
1908	759.48	36.42	3.77	0.73	0.14	46.93
1909	1,012.86	42.42	3.42	0.33	0.18	42.63
1910	583.44	34.20				37.16
1911	675.48	37.98				55.25
1912	724.80	55.92				60.86
1913	796.08	61.26	3.69	0.53	0.21	62.81
1914	676.20	61.92	2.98	0.33	0.37	50.82
1915	1,023.66	67.80	2.32	0.59	0.53	63.43
1916	782.34	72.66	3.23	0.11	0.77	44.82
1917	636.36	62.82	2.67	0.06	0.73	34.12
1918	445.98	68.94	3.49	0.04	0.00	82.38
1919	777.78	101.04	1.69	0.16	3.67	44.35
1920	691.50	86.64	1.59		0.98	37.35
1921	742.14	140.76	6.15		1.51	62.16
1922	760.38	105.90	4.07	0.16	2.17	45.66
1923	867.96	123.66	5.60		2.91	56.51
1924	853.56	132.96	5.79	0.09	2.23	52.26
1925	808.92	116.82	4.11	0.31	1.89	48.22
1926	825.06	147.24	6.07	0.44	2.07	43.04
1927	906.90	141.42	5.87	0.72	2.31	43.70
1928	832.86	159.60	9.15	0.98	3.46	60.41
1929	856.90	170.15	7.30	0.80		64.40
1930	917.30	190.38	9.40	0.70		47.10
1931	1,071.10	182.02	8.30	2.10		56.00
1932	716.10	191.14	8.00	2.40	3.25	49.20
1933	927.60	199.61	7.00	1.90		34.10
1934	848.80	185.05	14.40	4.10		45.60
1935	919.70	226.13	12.50	2.20		53.60
1936	851.20	236.53	13.80	3.10		61.60
1937	727.40	250.67	14.10	2.90		41.70
1938	1,026.80	256.42	13.70	2.50		35.90
1939	989.90	224.32	12.90	3.40		27.40
1940	722.70	269.03	14.60	1.50		28.80
1941	663.10	176.16	11.80	3.10		44.60
1942	436.80	260.78	6.10	0.40		35.60
1943	606.70	317.70	12.30	0.70		29.20
1944	813.30	297.89	14.50	2.00		20.10

	Brazil	Colombia	Ecuador	Peru	Surinam	Venezuela
1945	850.30	311.67	10.70	2.50		28.20
1946	930.30	339.70	7.60	0.90		40.50
1947	889.80	320.30	10.40	0.80		30.80
1948	1,049.50	335.30	19.50	0.90		35.90
1949	1,162.10	324.60	10.30	0.90		22.00
1950	890.10	268.30	20.20	0.80		18.60
1951	981.50	287.60	16.60	2.20		18.90
1952	949.30	301.90	20.00	2.60		30.30
1953	933.50	397.90	18.30	4.70		44.10
1954	657.00	345.20	21.00	4.60		26.00
1955	821.70	352.00	23.10	6.80		30.80
1956	1,008.30	304.20	24.50	7.10		23.50
1957	859.20	289.40	29.00	11.10		28.20
1958	772.90	326.40	30.20	17.30		35.60
1959	1,046.20	384.80	23.80	19.90		28.20
1960	1,009.10	356.30	32.40	0.00		0.00

Sources: Brazil: 1821–1928: Rodrigues da Cunha (1992), table 1.6; 1929–60: FAO (1961), table III A. *Colombia*: 1834–99, 1929–45: Samper (1948), table 22; 1905–28: Junguito and Pizano (1991), table I-5, p. 22; 1946–60: FAO (1961), table III A. *Ecuador*: 1906–9: Graham (1912), p. 10; 1913–28: Bynum (1930), table 5; 1929–60: FAO (1961), table III A. *Peru*: 1906–9: Graham (1912), p. 10; 1913–19, 1922, 1924–28: Bynum (1930), tables 7 and 8; Peru was a net importer in 1920–21 and 1923. *Surinam*: 1823–1869: van Stipriaan (1993), pp. 429–33, material contributed by William G. Clarence-Smith; 1890, 1900, 1908–9, 1932: Ukers (1935); 1913–28: Bynum (1930), table 24. *Venezuela*: 1853–67: van Delden Laërne (1885), pp. 414–15; 1868/69, 1869/70, 1872/73 to 1878/79, 1880/81 to 1890/91, 1892/93 to 1928/29: Ardao (1984); 1929–60: FAO (1961), table III A.

the period from 1823 (or a later date, as appropriate) to 1960. Actual timespan for different regions and countries reflects the availability of information for different parts of the world in each period as well as changes in the locus of production and international trade.

In the early eighteenth century, as supply for the world market shifted from the original Arabian export center toward southern and eastern Asia, especially the Netherlands East Indies, production there grew rapidly and was especially well documented. Once the main source of supply shifted again after midcentury, toward the Caribbean plantations, data refer basically to exports, but local consumption was minimal, so the difference between production and exports was often negligible.

As continental Latin America, and especially Brazil, came to supply most of the world's coffee in the course of the nineteenth century, data on

TABLE A.15. *Annual Asian Coffee Exports, 1823–1960 (thousands of metric tons)*

	Ceylon	India	Indonesia	Malaya	Portuguese Timor	Yemen
1823			18.71			
1824			16.26			
1825			18.12			
1826			22.95			
1827			26.11			
1828			26.86			
1829			19.09			
1830			18.77			
1831			20.11			
1832			21.59			
1833			25.59			
1834			31.78			
1835			31.53			
1836	5.62		32.55			
1837			41.75			
1838			37.24			
1839			49.19			
1840			70.72			
1841			61.25			
1842			63.51			
1843			61.94			
1844			74.56			
1845			62.08			
1846			56.16			
1847			63.18			
1848			49.10			
1849	17.17		55.03			
1850	16.41		50.74			
1851	14.63		73.95			
1852	20.73	3.57	64.01			
1853	16.41	3.65	66.57			
1854	22.05	3.36	67.15			
1855	24.54	4.18	84.75			
1856	22.30	4.62	81.59			
1857	26.87	2.78	71.17			
1858	28.25	5.30	78.86			
1859	30.58	6.51	67.37			
1860	32.26	8.67	64.04			
1861	31.14	9.75	73.14			

TABLE A.15. *(continued)*

	Ceylon	India	Indonesia	Malaya	Portuguese Timor	Yemen
1862	30.53	9.55	70.20			
1863	41.00	12.12	66.05			
1864	33.33	14.69	74.87			
1865	47.20	15.74	61.35			
1866	45.06	8.00	71.51			
1867	44.10	15.05	78.76			
1868	51.16	21.68	65.30			
1869	51.06	16.37	74.28			
1870	51.51	15.34	83.11			
1871	48.52	25.77	69.04			
1872	36.98	19.10	70.05			
1873	50.19	18.65	76.74			
1874	35.56	15.89	12.72			
1875	50.24	18.97	18.78			
1876	35.00	15.45	17.49			
1877	47.09	15.17	18.86			
1878	31.85	17.39	16.64			
1879	41.86	18.34	17.19			
1880	33.22	18.80	85.54			
1881	22.96	17.68	94.50			
1882	23.57	18.07	87.28		1.37	
1883	13.36	17.31	105.98		1.76	
1884	15.80	16.68	100.07		1.19	
1885	15.80	18.85	60.28		1.31	
1886	11.18	18.82	73.82		2.07	
1887	9.04	13.91	51.72		1.05	
1888	7.01	18.56	62.51	0.05	1.67	
1889	4.42	12.18	73.39	0.12	1.27	
1890	4.42	11.86	38.75	0.05	1.10	
1891	4.47	15.84	55.99	0.06	1.14	
1892	2.13	15.07	62.02	0.00	1.12	
1893	2.79	14.16	38.81	0.19	0.77	
1894	1.63	14.29	58.79	0.25	0.75	
1895	3.56	14.78	56.38	0.27	1.19	
1896	1.17	10.71	54.41	0.40	0.28	
1897	0.97	11.43	65.24	0.78	0.02	
1898	0.66	13.72	35.90	0.00	1.53	
1899	0.97	14.29	54.92	0.00	1.90	

(continued)

TABLE A.15. *(continued)*

	Ceylon	India	Indonesia	Malaya	Portuguese Timor	Yemen
1900	0.56	12.52	51.04	2.65	0.64	
1901	0.51	12.96	32.93	3.06	1.38	
1902	0.56	13.67	52.37	3.56	1.08	
1903		14.80	52.77	3.78	0.74	
1904		16.75	35.00	3.30	0.68	
1905		18.30	34.27	1.92	0.65	
1906		11.59	34.77	1.95	0.12	
1907		12.41	25.40	1.16	1.13	
1908		15.34	25.77	1.10	1.07	
1909		11.82	20.12	0.82	0.81	
1910		13.83	15.83	0.68	0.65	
1911		12.25	26.83		0.62	
1912		13.56	38.38		0.60	
1913		13.20	28.94		0.72	
1914		18.13	32.26		0.50	
1915		10.17	53.30		0.48	
1916		8.10	33.70		0.36	
1917		12.93	16.72		0.00	
1918		8.35	7.36		0.14	
1919		16.69	124.17		0.09	
1920		8.80	62.24			
1921		13.64	43.69			
1922		8.83	57.36			
1923		10.17	36.61			
1924		10.63	72.98			
1925		13.16	69.73			
1926		5.56	74.42			
1927		14.21	84.80			
1928		12.95	114.53			
1929		5.20	81.81			3.80
1930		15.80	61.51			4.10
1931		9.50	68.58			4.50
1932		8.70	113.80			4.90
1933		8.80	71.02			4.50
1934		8.60	81.87			4.20
1935		8.00	81.47			5.20
1936		13.60	95.21			4.50
1937		6.50	98.86			3.30
1938		7.10	68.96			4.50
1939		8.50	65.87			5.60

TABLE A.15. *(continued)*

	Ceylon	India	Indonesia	Malaya	Portuguese Timor	Yemen
1940		2.70	40.53			2.60
1941		4.30	50.00			3.20
1942		4.20				9.10
1943		3.10				14.20
1944		1.30				9.00
1945		1.50				0.00
1946		4.80				7.00
1947		2.30				6.30
1948		0.00	2.34			6.30
1949		3.40	5.17			8.70
1950		3.80	13.30		1.40	7.20
1951		1.00	23.61		0.80	7.90
1952		2.20	18.41		1.40	9.00
1953		2.80	32.90		1.40	8.00
1954		10.30	36.93		0.90	7.20
1955		3.60	23.17		0.90	8.40
1956		7.50	57.37		1.10	7.50
1957		13.60	50.96		1.30	7.60
1958		15.00	27.22		1.70	2.80
1959		15.50	38.94		1.90	4.60
1960		0.00	42.19		1.20	4.10

Sources: Ceylon: 1836: Ukers (1935); 1849–1902: Peebles (1982), supplied by William G. Clarence-Smith. Export data after 1903 are not included here, as Ceylon became a net importer. *India*: 1852/53 to 1879/80: van Delden Laërne (1885), pp. 456–57 (1852/53 became 1852, and so forth); 1880/81 to 1913/14: "Statement of the Trade of British India," data provided by William G. Clarence-Smith; 1914–28: Bynum (1930), table 26; 1929–60: FAO (1961), table III A. *Indonesia*: 1823–79: Bulbeck et al. (1998), table 5.4 (Java, Sumatra, Menado, and Makasar; no data for some of the islands in certain years); 1880–1941, 1948–52: Bulbeck et al. (1998), table 5.5A (change of sources for original tables may be related to different magnitudes and possible variation of coverage); 1953–60: Bulbeck et al. (1998), table 5.5B. *Malaya*: 1888–1906: Bulbeck et al. (1998), table 5.5A; 1907–10 (Federated Malay States; no data for Perak in 1919): Graham (1912), p. 10. *Portuguese Timor*: 1882–1916, 1918–19: Bulbeck et al. (1998), table 5.5A; 1950–60: FAO (1961), table III A. *Yemen*: 1929–60: FAO (1961), table III A.

TABLE A.16. *Annual African Coffee Exports, 1870–1960 (thousands of metric tons)*

	Angola	Cameroon	Congo (Belgian, Zaire)	Ethiopia	Ivory Coast	Kenya	Madagascar	Tanganyika	Uganda
1870	0.21								
1871	0.25								
1872	0.45								
1873	0.36								
1874	0.18								
1875	0.15								
1876	0.35								
1877	0.24								
1878	0.31								
1879	0.74								
1880	0.41								
1881	0.34								
1882	0.86								
1883	1.47								
1884	1.41								
1885									
1886									
1887									
1888	5.62								
1889	6.93								
1890	8.30								
1891	7.45								
1892	7.38								
1893	9.81								
1894	6.96								
1895	11.07								
1896	7.86								
1897	7.36								
1898	7.97								
1899	8.52								
1900	6.98								
1901	5.40								
1902	5.63								
1903	5.38								
1904	6.00							0.41	
1905	4.94							0.64	
1906	5.14		0.07					0.74	0.01
1907	4.01		0.07					0.63	0.01
1908	5.25		0.04					1.01	0.01
1909	4.47		0.01			0.01		0.91	0.01
1910	6.14		0.01			0.03		1.00	0.09
1911	4.67					0.06		1.18	
1912	4.13					0.10		1.58	
1913	5.10				0.01	0.15	0.09	1.06	
1914	4.46				0.00	0.28	0.26		
1915	4.00				0.01	0.39	0.44		
1916	3.20				0.03	0.30	0.60		
1917	4.19				0.03	0.83	0.05		
1918	4.21		0.04		0.03		0.32		
1919	6.15		0.14		0.11	3.58	1.44		

TABLE A.16. *(continued)*

	Angola	Cameroon	Congo (Belgian, Zaire)	Ethiopia	Ivory Coast	Kenya	Madagascar	Tanganyika	Uganda
1920	3.87		0.08		0.02	5.32	1.22		
1921	5.08		0.00		0.01	4.95	1.23		
1922	10.30		0.24		0.06	3.90	1.50		
1923	6.03		0.12		0.11	6.95	2.33		
1924	8.83		0.17		0.09	7.92	2.96		
1925	12.60		0.22		0.05	7.36	3.36		
1926	9.34		0.20		0.12	7.05	2.77		
1927	10.01		0.24		0.25	10.49	5.03		
1928	9.83		0.54		0.24	10.58	4.03		
1929	8.80	0.00	0.90	13.70		6.80	3.02	9.00	2.10
1930	11.80	0.00	1.50	14.10		15.80	6.67	11.70	2.50
1931	11.80	0.00	3.00	18.10		12.50	11.35	9.40	3.60
1932	9.50	0.10	5.50	25.20		14.00	13.58	11.50	4.40
1933	12.00	0.50	8.60	16.30		13.10	15.25	12.90	5.10
1934	12.00	0.80	12.50	22.50		9.50	14.34	15.00	7.80
1935	11.70	1.40	13.40	19.80		17.60	15.53	18.90	6.40
1936	21.90	2.00	17.40	14.60		20.70	25.00	11.20	11.60
1937	18.80	2.60	17.40	13.00		13.90	21.21	12.80	13.10
1938	18.90	4.30	22.50	5.40		17.40	41.20	14.70	14.20
1939	20.70	5.30	24.90	3.40		17.20	30.92	16.90	17.40
1940	15.80	4.20	19.50	1.50		8.70	20.16	15.90	18.20
1941	14.20	0.10	26.00	1.50		12.60	22.35	13.90	20.60
1942	19.50	6.60	27.90	10.80		12.50	1.14	15.10	17.50
1943	23.90	8.60	31.30	11.90		7.10	12.37	11.10	20.50
1944	23.80	5.10	21.70	13.30		6.20	45.34	15.80	19.50
1945	30.90	6.70	33.10	15.90		7.60	26.91	14.70	20.60
1946	46.50	5.90	27.10	15.10		8.50	22.33	10.10	31.90
1947	44.00	5.60	37.30	15.60		9.70	29.03	11.50	21.40
1948	53.40	7.30	30.50	15.30		14.20	19.94	12.60	38.40
1949	46.40	8.20	31.40	22.30		7.50	25.63	12.10	24.30
1950	37.60	7.70	33.20	18.70		10.20	41.56	15.10	32.40
1951	64.40	8.70	35.40	30.30		10.10	30.52	16.70	44.30
1952	47.70	9.20	30.90	21.60		17.20	41.31	18.90	40.10
1953	71.60	10.90	33.90	43.10		13.60	36.23	14.30	35.30
1954	45.80	11.40	34.40	31.20		10.80	41.49	19.70	36.90
1955	57.90	13.90	43.70	41.80		19.70	47.74	18.80	75.60
1956	84.00	17.80	51.10	30.90		27.10	52.49	22.00	62.60
1957	72.20	16.90	66.00	50.20		22.60	48.21	18.40	85.40
1958	77.30	26.50	69.40	39.00		25.40	44.00	22.60	80.00
1959	89.00	29.50	93.40	45.10		26.30	40.60	19.80	89.80
1960	87.30	0.00	0.00	0.00		28.20	43.62	25.50	118.70

Sources: *Angola* (*"Banana" in 1870s*): 1870–84: van Delden Laërne (1885), pp. 460–61, only exports to Rotterdam; 1888–1913: Mesquita (1918), p. 46; 1914–25: Bynum (1930), table 34; 1926–28: Marques (1962), p. 174, Azevedo (1958), p. 256 (data from the latter two and from Mesquita provided by William G. Clarence-Smith); 1929–60: FAO (1961), table IIIA. *Cameroon*: 1929–60: FAO (1961), table IIIA. *Congo* (*Belgian*): 1906–10: Graham (1912), p. 11; 1918–28: Bynum (1930), table 41; net importer from 1913 to 1917. *Ethiopia*: 1929–60: FAO (1961), table IIIA. *Ivory Coast*: 1913–28: Bynum (1930), table 38. *Kenya*: 1909–19: Waters (1969), pp. 47 and 51; 1920–28: Kamuya Maitha (1969), appendix A; 1929–60: FAO (1961), table IIIA. *Madagascar*: 1913–18: Bynum (1930), table 38, and Bynum (1926), table 64; 1919–60: data provided by Gwyn Campbell, see Chapter 3. *Tanganyika*: 1904–13: Tetzlaff (1970), p. 133, data supplied by William G. Clarence-Smith; 1929–60: FAO (1961), table IIIA. *Uganda*: 1906–10: Graham (1912), p. 11; 1929–60: FAO (1961), table IIIA.

TABLE A.17. *Annual Coffee Imports into the United States,*
1823–1881 (thousands of metric tons)

	(A)	(B)		(A)	(B)
1823	16.78		1853	90.26	84.39
1824	17.69		1854	73.48	68.15
1825	20.41		1855	86.63	79.45
1826	16.78		1856	107.05	101.44
1827	22.68		1857	109.31	98.27
1828	24.95		1858	85.73	79.15
1829	23.14		1859	119.75	111.96
1830	23.14	17.40	1860	91.63	82.58
1831	37.19		1861	83.46	80.70
1832	41.73		1862	55.79	51.26
1833	45.36		1863	36.29	33.93
1834	36.29		1864	59.87	57.99
1835	46.72		1865	48.08	38.25
1836	42.64		1866	82.10	79.05
1837	39.92		1867	84.82	84.93
1838	39.92		1868	112.94	94.79
1839	48.53		1869	115.21	119.82
1840	43.09	39.14	1870	106.60	106.71
1841	52.16		1871	144.24	144.24
1842	51.26		1872	135.62	135.54
1843	42.19		1873	132.90	133.30
1844	73.03		1874	129.28	129.40
1845	48.99		1875	144.24	146.04
1846	60.33		1876	154.22	154.72
1847	71.21		1877	150.59	150.43
1848	68.49		1878	140.62	140.56
1849	74.84		1879	171.46	171.39
1850	65.77	58.87	1880	202.76	202.69
1851	69.40		1881	206.38	206.47
1852	88.00				

Sources: (A) 1823–81: Rodrigues da Cunha (1992), table 1.7; (B): 1830, 1840, 1850: Ukers (1935), p. 529; 1853–65: van Delden Laërne (1885), p. 466; 1866–81: Lock (1888), table M, p. 134.

TABLE A.18. *Coffee Imports Retained for Domestic Consumption in Europe and the United States, 1884–1899 (thousands of metric tons)*

	United States	Austria-Hungary	France	Germany	Great Britain	Italy	Russia
1884	230.72	35.43	67.77	110.88	14.63	16.25	8.27
1885	244.61	36.62	68.23	117.89	14.83	23.55	7.71
1886	243.68	37.52	68.18	127.91	14.33	10.83	7.48
1887	227.17	31.83	63.71	101.62	13.31	14.24	5.19
1888	185.32	34.43	67.86	114.42	13.87	14.00	6.35
1889	254.53	34.63	65.11	112.99	11.04	13.50	5.86
1890	222.34	35.03	67.77	117.88	12.70	13.95	6.38
1891	231.81	35.53	70.00	125.35	13.01	13.79	5.72
1892	285.62	36.62	71.70	121.78	12.80	13.81	6.47
1893	250.11	35.93	68.90	121.94	12.04	12.59	6.83
1894	248.15	37.22	69.65	122.10	12.04	12.20	6.66
1895	291.77	37.92	72.16	122.14	12.45	11.97	6.55
1896	259.76	39.42	75.03	129.63	12.40	12.58	6.29
1897	328.66	41.01	77.31	136.11	12.40	12.96	7.59
1898	386.33	43.51	79.24	152.95	12.52	13.36	8.12
1899	363.68	41.81	81.25	155.81	13.21	14.16	8.34

Sources: Oficina Internacional de las Repúblicas Americanas (1902), p. 68.

TABLE A.19. *Annual Western Hemisphere Coffee Imports, 1913–1960*
(thousands of metric tons)

	United States	Argentina	Canada	Chile	Cuba	Paraguay	Uruguay
1913	389.60	14.79	7.60	5.03	11.38	0.12	0.00
1914	450.19	14.01	6.89	3.47	8.02	0.06	0.00
1915	478.57	16.41	7.30	5.09	9.64		1.92
1916	511.68	14.91	8.62	4.91	8.80	0.06	1.98
1917	573.59	17.00	8.14	5.63	12.51	0.18	2.22
1918	490.01	22.03	6.89	6.95	11.80	0.12	2.39
1919	566.23	17.00	9.28	3.35	10.54	0.18	1.86
1920	564.67	17.60	7.90	5.69	20.18	0.12	2.39
1921	591.26	18.50	9.82	1.74	13.53	0.12	2.28
1922	550.36	21.08	9.76	4.91	8.74	0.12	2.22
1923	626.10	20.48	10.06	5.21	16.88	0.12	2.34
1924	626.22	25.33	10.00	4.25	9.76	0.12	2.39
1925	575.71	20.10	9.40	5.00			2.20
1926	513.51	23.30	10.90	4.00			2.30
1927	643.51	24.50	11.60	4.40			2.40
1928	656.31	24.50	12.30	5.60			2.30
1929	666.40	24.80	11.40	5.00	8.40	0.20	2.30
1930	712.40	25.40	13.00	5.20	5.50	0.30	2.50
1931	784.40	22.90	14.30	4.80	0.80	0.10	2.20
1932	673.60	17.60	14.70	3.30		0.10	2.30
1933	712.60	23.30	14.80	1.20		0.20	2.10
1934	685.90	18.40	14.70	2.50		0.10	1.80
1935	791.30	22.00	15.10	3.40		0.20	2.00
1936	785.50	22.30	18.40	3.10		0.20	2.30
1937	766.30	22.70	17.40	3.70		0.20	2.20
1938	897.00	27.70	19.60	3.40		0.20	2.80
1939	905.00	25.10	20.80	4.40	0.20	0.30	2.30
1940	926.50	25.30	18.70	5.70	3.30	0.30	3.00
1941	1,018.60	34.50	25.00	6.80		0.20	1.40
1942	777.70	22.80	20.30	10.20		0.20	2.90
1943	992.50	26.80	26.80	7.80		0.40	3.00
1944	1,178.60	35.00	43.60	8.20		0.60	3.90
1945	1,222.90	30.40	24.80	9.00	2.70	0.40	3.50
1946	1,237.30	35.30	38.40	11.40	6.90	0.70	3.90
1947	1,105.50	34.80	23.30	9.70	8.00	0.30	3.10
1948	1,239.40	45.50	39.70	2.40	1.00	0.50	3.70
1949	1,311.60	22.70	44.50	15.50		0.50	3.60
1950	1,101.20	28.80	37.60	6.60	5.70	0.10	3.30
1951	1,211.80	29.10	40.10	4.30	2.80	0.20	3.10
1952	1,207.60	23.50	44.30	3.80	3.40	0.10	2.60
1953	1,251.50	29.60	48.80	5.20		0.10	3.50
1954	1,012.00	33.70	43.30	5.50		0.10	3.30
1955	1,163.60	28.20	46.90	6.70		0.10	3.60
1956	1,257.80	27.60	49.80	4.70		0.10	3.50
1957	1,228.60	35.10	50.10	5.90		0.10	3.20
1958	1,178.40	39.70	53.70	5.50			3.00
1959	1,360.20	19.00	60.90	6.40		0.10	4.80
1960	1,322.10	25.80	59.70	5.50		0.10	3.00

Sources: 1913–24: Bynum (1926), table 2; 1925–28: International Institute of Agriculture (1947), pp. 370; 1929–60: FAO (1961), table IIA. Data for 1960 are FAO estimates in several cases.

exports from the subcontinent became more abundant and reliable due to the importance of this item in foreign trade. Information on production proper is scant for most Latin American countries in the nineteenth century, although there is some for specific regions of Brazil after midcentury. Information on imports into Europe and the United States improves in the latter half of this century.

From the late nineteenth to the mid-twentieth century, as production expanded into new areas and the international market underwent major changes, data on coffee were gathered and published more systematically. Information on production up to 1929 probably combines estimates based on exports with actual production figures, while subsequently the distinction was explicit in statistics for most countries.

Detailed information on production, exports, and imports was entered on spreadsheets for all individual countries where available. For purposes of publication, we excluded those for which we had only isolated figures, with the primary exception of Saint Domingue during the period in which it was the main coffee producer and exporter (see Fig. A.1). We also left out or regrouped those countries that produced or traded only small amounts, for economy of space.

All spreadsheets and tables are available for researchers and institutions on a cooperative basis, with the request that any correction be reported directly and that additional information is sent to us, whether as spreadsheets or photocopies, to expand and improve this collective database.*

When there was more than one time series available for a given country and period, we gave preference to original data and to secondary literature that listed and assessed the original sources over publications that made only general references to sources or did not cite them. We also preferred specific, reliable sources for individual countries when there was reason to believe that their quality was superior to that of the more general sources.

The most complete and consistent time series were used for each country. When there were overlaps and obvious discrepancies, the reliability of the two series was checked if possible against other sources. If one series followed another, before using them we sought to ensure that the information was in fact comparable and that orders of magnitude in both were reasonable.

---

* Requests, additional information, and corrections may be addressed to Mario Samper, ich96@racsa.co.cr, P.O.: Human Sciences Institute, Apartado 503-3000, Heredia, Costa Rica. Subsequent versions of spreadsheets will be made available to contributing colleagues on request.

TABLE A.20. *Annual European Coffee Imports, 1913–1960 (thousands of metric tons)*

	Austria	Belgium	France	Germany	Great Britain	Italy	Netherlands	Scandinavian countries	Spain	Switzerland
1913	59.40	42.33	115.26	167.47	16.70	28.32	52.93	265.42	15.15	11.56
1914	72.81		116.40		18.44	28.02	14.13	60.59	13.71	10.84
1915	89.39		138.49		42.69	39.94	31.55	114.18	15.99	13.17
1916	45.21		152.92		58.14	48.98	21.91	129.03	16.41	19.76
1917	8.14		163.64		21.97	44.61	14.13	80.71	17.60	9.52
1918			136.15		6.59	51.61	3.59	61.79	16.35	10.24
1919			208.66		22.09	36.40	41.91	100.41	19.16	10.18
1920	2.63	36.76	145.97	41.19	12.39	30.18	43.23	126.99	22.03	10.30
1921	5.27	37.96	153.46	103.88		47.90	31.49	183.27	21.85	14.31
1922	4.37	37.42	172.98	36.76	40.24	47.24	33.17	157.41	18.68	13.23
1923	6.05	40.65	175.49	38.68	14.97	48.08	31.07	132.80	24.37	12.81
1924	7.90	38.98	170.46	55.38	14.49	46.94	37.84	154.66		14.67
1925	6.80	39.60	168.10	90.40	22.50	42.20	40.30	195.40	19.40	10.90
1926	8.60	39.80	154.20	104.90	11.40	43.70	31.90	191.90	20.30	13.20
1927	8.30	41.20	159.00	123.90	20.60	45.70	34.20	224.40	24.00	13.30
1928	8.30	39.60	161.50	135.10	16.80	47.70	35.60	235.21	21.50	12.50
1929	9.40	38.70	170.00	148.10	13.90	46.90	33.50	242.40	23.90	13.30
1930	9.00	47.10	178.00	154.00	19.00	45.30	36.00	254.30	26.50	13.70
1931	9.80	56.60	193.90	155.50	17.80	43.80	40.20	257.30	22.20	15.30
1932	7.50	49.70	186.90	129.70	21.40	40.80	38.40	230.30	22.00	19.80
1933	5.10	39.70	196.40	129.70	16.00	39.90	48.80	234.40	26.10	11.60
1934	5.40	47.60	176.30	150.70	15.30	39.30	34.40	239.70	26.70	13.70
1935	5.30	48.80	188.50	147.60	12.50	40.40	32.70	233.20	23.80	18.60
1936	5.20	51.90	186.50	155.10	14.20	31.80	31.10	232.20	13.90	15.10

Year										
1937	5.20	45.40	185.30	177.70	14.50	37.90	36.50	266.60		13.50
1938	8.10	46.50	186.30	197.40	14.20	36.00	45.50	293.10		17.30
1939		54.40	164.10	120.70	26.70	24.30	40.20	211.90	1.20	22.10
1940		27.40	137.90	22.90	56.30	16.40	11.90	107.50	6.10	14.20
1941		0.10	36.30	18.90	6.20	0.50		25.60	8.00	5.70
1942			25.10	12.50	22.50	0.20	0.10	35.30	14.10	10.40
1943			7.90	1.40	40.50			41.90	13.00	12.50
1944			0.40	1.40	38.20			39.60	17.40	6.80
1945		26.80	46.70		42.90			42.90	10.60	14.40
1946		62.80	66.50		33.30	15.80	18.30	67.40	10.50	18.50
1947		88.70	81.30		44.80	30.20	20.20	95.20	18.20	14.90
1948	0.50	80.00	71.10	10.50	51.30	47.90	20.90	130.60	18.00	25.30
1949	4.10	69.60	87.50	26.30	51.80	56.40	24.00	158.50	7.30	18.30
1950	4.80	54.60	149.60	26.50	38.90	52.80	19.00	137.20	7.10	25.30
1951	5.10	49.40	150.80	40.80	42.60	53.30	16.00	152.70	5.20	19.80
1952	4.50	51.40	160.40	57.80	40.60	61.00	19.40	178.80	4.10	18.20
1953	4.40	50.90	163.60	80.90	25.30	66.70	28.30	201.20	4.90	19.10
1954	4.80	42.70	168.60	109.00	29.50	69.50	28.30	236.30	7.40	19.10
1955	5.70	45.10	184.20	125.40	30.80	72.40	31.20	259.80	9.10	17.90
1956	7.30	57.80	182.20	142.80	43.50	75.70	40.90	302.90	12.60	22.30
1957	8.10	47.10	181.50	165.40	43.70	77.70	38.40	325.20	12.30	21.90
1958	9.00	48.30	189.00	175.30	41.80	81.40	42.80	341.30	12.50	23.00
1959	9.80	53.70	196.50	208.00	51.40	84.10	50.30	393.80	17.90	26.80
1960	12.20	61.10	197.10	214.60	55.20	99.20	53.60	422.60	17.60	29.80

Sources: 1913–24: Bynum (1926), table 2; 1925–28: International Institute of Agriculture (1947), pp. 362–63; 1929–60: FAO (1961), table IIA. Data for 1960 are FAO estimates in several cases.

TABLE A.21. Annual African, Asian, and Australian Coffee Imports, 1913–1960 (thousands of metric tons)

	Algeria	Australia	British Malaya	Ceylon (Sri Lanka)	Egypt	Japan	Sudan	Union of South Africa
1913	7.90	1.44		0.72	6.29	0.12		12.15
1914	7.36	1.38		0.66	5.93	0.12		11.62
1915	7.30	1.38		0.72	8.50	0.12		14.31
1916	7.60	1.50		0.72	7.54	0.12		12.63
1917	8.02	1.08		0.84	7.13	0.24		13.17
1918	6.89	1.26		0.84	6.95	0.24		20.96
1919	9.16	0.90		0.66	7.07	0.30		7.07
1920	7.42	0.90		0.84	10.24	0.30		12.57
1921	8.44	1.38		1.02	9.40	0.36		13.23
1922	8.08	1.32		1.02	9.82	0.48		13.47
1923	9.58	1.44		1.02	10.18	0.54		14.91
1924	8.80			1.02	11.02	0.84		13.89
1925	9.30	1.70	8.60	1.20	7.80	0.80	4.20	13.20
1926	8.20	1.40	8.40	1.10	9.50	1.10	3.20	12.60
1927	9.60	1.60	8.40	1.40	10.00	1.30	3.70	13.40
1928	10.70	1.50	6.40	1.30	8.10	1.30	3.80	12.10
1929	12.00	1.70	6.10	1.50	9.50	1.80	4.00	12.90
1930	12.60	1.50	6.10	1.30	9.60	1.90	6.20	13.10
1931	13.80	1.30	5.40	1.90	7.50	2.30	4.20	14.30
1932	13.70	1.40	5.30	1.00	7.30	2.80	4.20	11.20
1933	14.00	1.90	6.20	1.40	8.50	2.40	4.90	12.90
1934	13.20	1.50	6.30	1.30	6.60	2.90	6.30	12.20
1935	14.20	2.10	8.00	1.60	7.90	3.40	7.60	14.20

1936	15.40	1.80	7.90	1.10	7.20	5.70	7.80	14.10
1937	14.60	1.90	8.40	1.50	7.70	8.60	6.30	13.60
1938	15.70	1.90	9.90	1.30	9.00	4.50	8.20	16.80
1939	13.30	2.60	10.60	1.60	6.30	1.40	6.60	17.20
1940	15.50	3.50	11.70	1.30	7.00	3.40	7.70	15.20
1941	6.50	4.20	11.10	1.20	7.80	1.50	9.50	24.00
1942	5.70	8.10		0.40	7.60		8.80	25.50
1943	2.00	6.70		1.40	10.40		8.00	23.70
1944	13.70	5.60		1.10	11.00		8.10	32.20
1945	12.90	6.10		0.40	11.80		13.00	29.90
1946	14.00	3.00	8.90	1.70	13.10		8.30	23.40
1947	14.80	3.60	7.90	1.10	9.90		9.00	23.70
1948	14.40	3.60	13.80	1.50	10.50		11.30	23.40
1949	7.90	3.60	10.10	0.90	9.60		7.30	19.50
1950	20.00	3.20	2.10	0.80	5.80	0.30	5.70	16.90
1951	21.10	3.50	2.10	0.60	5.30	1.30	5.80	11.90
1952	19.20	1.80	4.60	0.60	4.90	1.90	6.80	11.80
1953	20.50	4.20	4.10	0.50	4.80	2.50	6.10	11.20
1954	20.90	3.80	0.20	0.40	4.50	2.50	4.40	11.50
1955	22.20	4.60	3.40	0.60	3.70	4.00	5.40	10.90
1956	27.30	7.00	5.80	0.80	4.60	5.00	7.60	11.20
1957	27.30	6.30		0.60	3.40	5.50	8.20	11.00
1958	27.30	7.40	4.60	0.80	5.80	6.40	4.10	10.80
1959	29.70	10.10	7.60	1.00	3.90	8.10	8.00	11.20
1960	30.30	11.20	5.00	1.30	5.50	10.70	6.40	11.60

Sources: 1913–24: Bynum (1926), table 2; 1925–28: International Institute of Agriculture (1947), pp. 376–77, 382–83, and 387; 1929–60: FAO (1961), table IIA. Data for 1960 are FAO estimates in several cases.

TABLE A.22. *Current Prices of Coffee Imported into the United States,* *1821–1960 (current U.S. cents per lb)*

	Average price	Rio 7 to N.Y.	Santos 4 to N.Y.	Colombian to N.Y.	Java to N.Y.	*Robusta* to N.Y.
1821	21.10					
1822	20.88					
1823	17.73					
1824	13.33					
1825	11.48	17.00				
1826	10.55	15.00				
1827	9.03	14.25				
1828	9.30	12.94				
1829	8.80	12.34				
1830	8.08	11.13				
1831	8.25	11.25				
1832	10.08	12.58				
1833	10.68	12.38				
1834	10.78	11.50				
1835	10.38	11.92				
1836	10.18	11.50				
1837	9.53	10.63				
1838	8.80	10.50				
1839	9.08	10.88				
1840	9.03	10.13				
1841	8.80	10.00				
1842	7.65	8.38				
1843	6.50	7.30				
1844	5.95	6.50				
1845	6.05	6.80				
1846	6.05	7.10				
1847	5.60	7.00				
1848	5.45	6.10				
1849	6.60	6.90				
1850	8.05	10.60				
1851	7.95	9.00				
1852	7.55	8.50				
1853	8.30	8.75				
1854	8.80	10.10				
1855	8.90	9.90				
1856	9.10	10.80				
1857	9.35	11.00				
1858	9.50	10.40		12.00	16.13	
1859	10.10	11.30		11.90	14.79	

TABLE A.22. *(continued)*

	Average price	Rio 7 to N.Y.	Santos 4 to N.Y.	Colombian to N.Y.	Java to N.Y.	Robusta to N.Y.
1860	10.95	12.00		13.90	16.15	
1861	11.20	14.01		15.40	18.38	
1862	11.90	23.01		24.30	27.50	
1863	12.25	31.18		31.90	37.04	
1864	11.75	42.49		41.60	49.10	
1865	11.35	20.65		21.30	25.82	
1866	11.05	18.66		19.40	26.08	
1867	10.50	17.24		17.70	24.75	
1868	9.90	15.73		16.40	23.41	
1869	10.00	15.82		17.50	23.02	
1870	10.05	16.33		17.50	21.19	
1871	11.25	15.91		16.20	21.29	
1872	13.85	18.42		18.20	21.30	
1873	17.15	19.99		20.50	23.63	
1874	17.55	21.08		20.90	26.68	
1875	16.25	19.01		20.50	26.71	
1876	16.45	17.97		17.00	21.57	
1877	16.50	19.72		18.90	23.82	
1878	14.65	16.51		15.50	22.48	
1879	13.00	14.85		14.70	24.14	
1880	13.00	15.12		15.50	22.63	
1881	11.25	10.58		12.10		
1882	9.10	8.83		10.50		
1883	8.75	9.26		11.00		
1884	8.75	9.26		10.10		
1885	7.90	8.09		10.50		
1886	9.15	11.43		10.40		
1887	12.35	14.60		10.60		
1888	13.50	14.03		16.00		
1889	14.50	14.70		13.50		
1890	16.49	17.90		15.40		
1891	15.51	16.70		17.10		
1892	17.00	14.30		16.90		
1893	15.20	17.20		18.80		
1894	15.55	16.50	16.60	16.60		
1895	14.65	15.90	15.60	16.00		
1896	12.85	12.30	13.00	15.70		
1897	9.30	7.90	7.40	13.50		
1898	7.00	6.30	6.40	11.50		

(continued)

TABLE A.22. *(continued)*

	Average price	Rio 7 to N.Y.	Santos 4 to N.Y.	Colombian to N.Y.	Java to N.Y.	*Robusta* to N.Y.
1899	6.60	6.00	6.10	8.60		
1900	7.05	8.20	9.00	7.00		
1901	6.94	6.50	6.00	10.80		
1902	6.54	5.90	5.50	10.70		
1903	6.80	5.60	5.40	10.50		
1904	7.55	7.80	7.30	11.30		
1905	8.35	8.30	7.10	10.80		
1906	8.25	8.10	7.90	10.60		
1907	7.75	6.60	6.40	11.20		
1908	7.55	6.30	6.40	11.50		
1909	7.70	7.80	7.50	11.00		
1910	9.10	9.50	8.50	15.20		
1911	11.80	13.40	13.30	16.70		
1912	13.55	14.60	14.80	15.60		
1913	12.45	11.10	13.17	15.60		
1914	10.35	8.20	11.46	15.60		
1915	9.60	7.50	9.57	14.50		
1916	9.85	9.36	10.55	14.20		
1917	9.55	8.95	10.16	12.90		
1918	11.55	9.91	12.71	16.40		
1919	19.50	17.84	24.78	27.70		
1920	19.50	11.50	18.62	21.50		
1921	10.70	7.25	10.00	15.50		
1922	12.90	10.12	14.12	17.40		
1923	13.50	11.37	14.50	18.80		
1924	17.50	17.25	21.00	25.50		
1925	22.30	20.25	24.25	27.90		
1926	21.60	18.00	22.12	28.50		
1927	18.50	14.62	18.50	25.10		
1928	21.30	16.37	23.00	27.30		
1929	20.40	15.75	21.87	22.80		
1930	13.10	8.62	12.87	17.20		
1931	10.10	6.12	8.67	15.60		
1932	9.10	8.00	10.67	11.40		
1933	7.90	7.75	9.00	10.50		
1934	8.80	9.75	11.12	13.70		
1935	7.60	7.12	8.87	10.30		
1936	7.70	7.37	9.75	11.30		
1937	8.90	8.85	11.00	11.60		
1938	6.90	5.20	7.60	11.00		
1939	6.90	5.36	7.30	11.70		

TABLE A.22. *(continued)*

	Average price	Rio 7 to N.Y.	Santos 4 to N.Y.	Colombian to N.Y.	Java to N.Y.	*Robusta* to N.Y.
1940	6.20	5.35	7.10	8.40		
1941	7.90	7.86	11.10	14.70		
1942	12.00	9.37	13.40	15.90		
1943	12.40	9.38	13.40	15.90		
1944	12.50	9.38	13.40	15.90		
1945	12.70	9.38	13.40	16.20		
1946	17.20	12.35	23.10	22.50		
1947	24.00	14.17	26.70	30.10		18.44
1948	25.00	14.49	22.30	32.60		18.23
1949	27.20	18.70	31.70	37.60		24.65
1950	44.72	37.71	50.50	53.30		40.22
1951	50.53	45.65	54.20	58.70		47.20
1952	51.28	48.86	54.00	57.00		45.11
1953	52.70	51.14	58.00	59.80		48.41
1954	65.68	62.98	78.90	80.00		60.44
1955	52.18	43.37	57.10	64.60		41.82
1956	51.17	44.46	58.10	74.00		35.97
1957	49.82	44.21	56.90	63.90		37.44
1958	43.89	40.54	48.30	52.30		38.91
1959	35.65	33.38	36.90	45.20		29.66
1960	34.34	34.14	36.60	44.90		22.22

Sources: **Average price**: Rodrigues da Cunha (1992), table 1.8. *Rio 7 into N.Y.*: 1825–42: Thurber (1883), table 4, average low and high prices for Fair to Prime Rio Coffee in New York, in bond; 1843–60: Williams (1994), table A-1, Fair to Prime Rio; 1861–1960: Rodrigues da Cunha (1992), table 1.8, Rio 7. **Santos 4 into N.Y.**: Rodrigues da Cunha (1992), table 1.8, Santos 4. **Colombian into N.Y.**: 1858–1900, 1902–30: Junguito and Pizano (1991), table I-4; 1901, 1931–60: GRECO (2002). *Java into N.Y.*: Thurber (1883), table III. **Robusta into N.Y.**: International Coffee Organization (1989).

The information included here is only as good as the sources listed for each table, and its use for specific countries or regions should take into account the characteristics and shortcomings of those sources. It is also incomplete partly because of our own limited access to sources, despite the valuable contributions of a number of colleagues. This can, to a certain extent, be resolved through a concerted and protracted effort. However, certain information was never gathered, has not survived, or is of such poor quality as to be misleading.

While we sought to ensure overall compatibility of the data for different regions and periods, users should ascertain comparability for specific cases, in terms of criteria followed and factual precision.

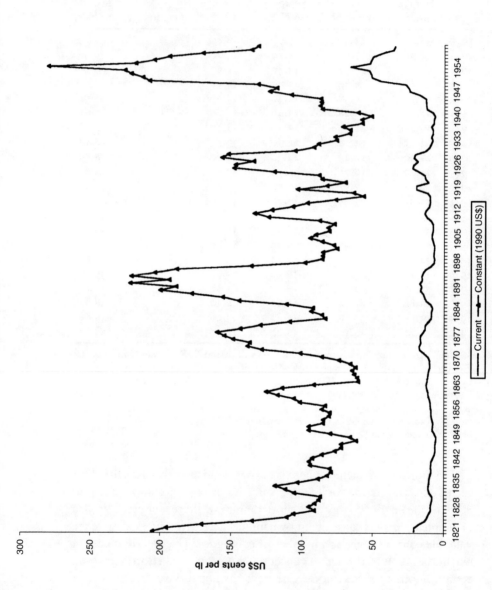

FIGURE A.4. Annual average current and constant prices of coffee imports into the United States, 1821–1960, in U.S. cents per pound.

TABLE A.23. *Constant Prices of Coffee Imported into the United States, 1821–1960 (1990 U.S. cents per lb)*

	Average price	Rio 7 to N.Y.	Santos 4 to N.Y.	Colombian to N.Y.	Java to N.Y.	Robusta to N.Y.
1821	205.39					
1822	195.53					
1823	170.86					
1824	135.00					
1825	110.61	163.80				
1826	105.81	150.44				
1827	91.44	144.30				
1828	95.19	132.45				
1829	91.01	127.62				
1830	88.10	121.36				
1831	87.14	118.83				
1832	105.30	131.42				
1833	111.57	129.33				
1834	118.87	126.81				
1835	103.01	118.29				
1836	88.62	100.11				
1837	82.24	91.73				
1838	79.43	94.77				
1839	80.45	96.40				
1840	94.32	105.81				
1841	94.97	107.92				
1842	92.63	101.47				
1843	86.05	96.64				
1844	76.72	83.81				
1845	72.37	81.34				
1846	72.37	84.93				
1847	61.78	77.23				
1848	65.99	73.86				
1849	79.91	83.54				
1850	95.15	125.29				
1851	95.10	107.66				
1852	85.18	95.90				
1853	84.96	89.57				
1854	80.90	92.85				
1855	80.33	89.36				
1856	86.05	102.13				
1857	83.63	98.39				
1858	101.42	111.03		128.11	172.20	
1859	105.56	118.10		124.37	154.58	

(continued)

TABLE A.23. *(continued)*

	Average price	Rio 7 to N.Y.	Santos 4 to N.Y.	Colombian to N.Y.	Java to N.Y.	Robusta to N.Y.
1860	116.90	128.11		148.39	172.41	
1861	124.95	156.30		171.81	205.05	
1862	113.61	219.68		231.99	262.54	
1863	91.45	232.77		238.14	276.51	
1864	60.45	218.60		214.02	252.60	
1865	60.91	110.82		114.31	138.56	
1866	63.05	106.47		110.69	148.81	
1867	64.35	105.66		108.48	151.68	
1868	62.21	98.84		103.05	147.10	
1869	65.75	104.02		115.06	151.36	
1870	73.91	120.09		128.70	155.84	
1871	85.92	121.51		123.72	162.60	
1872	101.11	134.47		132.87	155.50	
1873	128.03	149.23		153.04	176.41	
1874	138.29	166.11		164.69	210.23	
1875	136.73	159.95		172.49	224.74	
1876	148.48	162.20		153.44	194.69	
1877	154.55	184.71		177.03	223.11	
1878	159.84	180.13		169.11	245.27	
1879	143.42	163.83		162.17	266.32	
1880	129.07	150.12		153.89	224.68	
1881	108.45	101.99		116.64		
1882	83.66	81.18		96.53		
1883	86.02	91.03		108.14		
1884	93.42	98.87		107.83		
1885	92.28	94.50		122.65		
1886	110.79	138.40		125.93		
1887	144.26	170.54		123.82		
1888	155.86	161.98		184.72		
1889	177.74	180.19		165.48		
1890	199.62	216.69		186.42		
1891	188.45	202.91		207.77		
1892	221.15	186.03		219.85		
1893	193.42	218.87		239.23		
1894	220.30	233.76	235.18	235.18		
1895	203.43	220.79	216.62	222.18		
1896	188.14	180.09	190.34	229.87		
1897	135.60	115.19	107.90	196.84		
1898	97.98	88.18	89.58	160.97		
1899	85.86	78.05	79.36	111.88		
1900	85.36	99.28	108.97	84.75		
1901	85.21	79.81	73.67	132.60		

TABLE A.23. *(continued)*

	Average price	Rio 7 to N.Y.	Santos 4 to N.Y.	Colombian to N.Y.	Java to N.Y.	*Robusta* to N.Y.
1902	75.28	67.91	63.31	123.16		
1903	77.51	63.83	61.55	119.68		
1904	85.78	88.62	82.94	128.39		
1905	94.26	93.70	80.15	121.92		
1906	90.22	88.58	86.39	115.92		
1907	80.71	68.73	66.65	116.64		
1908	81.54	68.04	69.12	124.20		
1909	77.21	78.21	75.20	110.30		
1910	87.48	91.33	81.71	146.12		
1911	123.26	139.97	138.93	174.44		
1912	133.19	143.51	145.48	153.34		
1913	121.02	107.90	128.02	151.64		
1914	106.32	84.23	117.72	160.25		
1915	96.16	75.13	95.86	145.24		
1916	76.10	72.31	81.51	109.71		
1917	56.61	53.05	60.23	76.47		
1918	63.38	54.38	69.75	89.99		
1919	102.79	94.04	130.62	146.01		
1920	82.28	48.52	78.57	90.72		
1921	69.46	47.06	64.92	100.62		
1922	85.75	67.27	93.86	115.66		
1923	87.80	73.95	94.30	122.27		
1924	119.17	117.47	143.00	173.65		
1925	147.68	134.10	160.59	184.77		
1926	146.81	122.34	150.34	193.71		
1927	133.79	105.73	133.79	181.52		
1928	156.23	120.07	168.70	200.24		
1929	151.78	117.18	162.72	169.64		
1930	104.80	68.96	102.96	137.60		
1931	91.53	55.46	78.57	141.37		
1932	88.22	77.56	103.44	110.52		
1933	75.57	74.14	86.09	100.44		
1934	76.49	84.75	96.66	119.08		
1935	66.38	62.19	77.47	89.96		
1936	65.98	63.15	83.55	96.83		
1937	71.20	70.80	88.00	92.80		
1938	57.49	43.33	63.32	91.65		
1939	57.62	44.76	60.96	97.70		
1940	50.95	43.96	58.35	69.03		
1941	60.39	60.08	84.85	112.37		

(continued)

TABLE A.23. *(continued)*

	Average price	Rio 7 to N.Y.	Santos 4 to N.Y.	Colombian to N.Y.	Java to N.Y.	*Robusta* to N.Y.
1942	85.58	66.82	95.56	113.39		
1943	87.06	65.86	94.08	111.63		
1944	86.42	64.85	92.64	109.93		
1945	86.65	64.00	91.43	110.53		
1946	107.23	76.99	144.01	140.27		
1947	122.57	72.37	136.36	153.72		94.17
1948	117.55	68.13	104.85	153.29		85.72
1949	130.62	89.80	152.23	180.56		118.37
1950	207.31	174.81	234.10	247.08		186.45
1951	212.21	191.72	227.62	246.52		198.23
1952	220.48	210.08	232.17	245.07		193.95
1953	224.72	218.07	247.32	255.00		206.43
1954	279.41	267.92	335.65	340.33		257.12
1955	217.12	180.46	237.59	268.80		174.01
1956	203.78	177.06	231.38	294.70		143.25
1957	193.08	171.34	220.52	247.65		145.10
1958	169.56	156.62	186.60	202.05		150.32
1959	135.27	126.66	140.01	171.51		112.54
1960	130.30	129.54	138.88	170.37		84.31

Sources: See Table A.22. *Average price*: Rodrigues da Cunha (1992), table 2.10. Other prices deflated to 1990 U.S. cents per pound of coffee using factor of last column in Rodrigues da Cunha (1992), table 2.10.

It is our earnest hope that this modest contribution will be improved on through a collaborative, critical, and ongoing process, to strengthen the historical foundations for broader comparative discussions on this major tropical crop, significant agroindustrial product, valuable international commodity, and stimulating beverage.

References for Appendix Tables and Figures

Ardao, Alicia. 1984. *El café y las ciudades en los Andes venezolanos.* Caracas: Academia Nacional de la Historia.

Ardouin, Beaubrun. 1853–60. *Études sur l'histoire d'Haïti.* Paris: Dezobry et E. Magdeleine.

Azevedo, João Maria Cerqueira de. 1958. *Angola, exemplo de trabalho.* Luanda: Edição do autor.

Bergad, Laird W. 1983. *Coffee and the Growth of Agrarian Capitalism in Nineteenth Century Puerto Rico*. Princeton: Princeton University Press.

Bulbeck, David, Anthony Reid, Lay Cheng Tan, and Yiqi Wu. 1998. *Southeast Asian Exports Since the 14th Century: Cloves, Pepper, Coffee, and Sugar*. Leiden, Canberra, and Singapore: KILTV Press, Research School of Pacific and Asian Studies, ANU, and Institute of South Asian Studies.

Bynum, Mary L. 1926. *International Trade in Coffee*. Washington: U.S. Department of Commerce.

Bynum, Mary L. 1930. *The World's Exports of Coffee*. Washington: U.S. Department of Commerce.

Daviron, Benoît. 1993. "Conflit et coopération sur le marché international du café: Une analyse de longue periode." Ph.D. dissertation, École Nationale Supérieure Agronomique de Montpellier.

Di Fulvio, Antonio. 1947. *The World's Coffee*. Rome: International Institute of Agriculture, Studies on the Principal Agricultural Products on the World Market, No. 9.

Dirección General de Estadística y Censos, Nicaragua. 1961. *El café en Nicaragua*. Managua: Dirección General de Estadística y Censos.

Duque, Juan Pablo. 1938. "Costa Rica, Nicaragua, El Salvador y Guatemala. Informe del Jefe del Departamento Técnico sobre su viaje de estudio a algunos países cafeteros de la América Central." In *Revista Cafetera de Colombia*, 7, no. 102.

FAO. 1961. *La economía mundial del café*. Rome: FAO.

Graham, Harry C. 1912. *Coffee: Production, Trade, and Consumption by Countries*. Washington: U.S. Bureau of Statistics, Department of Agriculture.

GRECO. 2002. *El crecimiento económico colombiano en el siglo XX*. Bogotá: Banco de la República y Fondo de Cultura Económica.

Hernández Navarro, Luis. 1996. "Café: La pobreza de la riqueza/La riqueza de la pobreza." Paper presented at the 1st Sustainable Coffee Congress. Washington: Smithsonian Migratory Bird Center.

International Coffee Organization. 1989. "Precios indicativos, valores unitarios y precios al por menor. Series a largo plazo." WP Agreement No. 15/88 (C) Rev. 2, February 22.

International Institute of Agriculture. 1947. *The World's Coffee*. Rome: FAO.

Izard, Miguel. 1973. *El café en la economía venezolana del XIX. Estado de la cuestión*. Valencia: Vadell Hermanos.

Junguito, Roberto, and Diego Pizano, coordinators. 1991. *Producción de café en Colombia*. Bogotá: Fedesarrollo, Fondo Cultural Cafetero.

Junguito, Roberto, and Diego Pizano, coordinators. 1993. *El comercio exterior y la política internacional del café*. Bogotá: Fedesarrollo, Fondo Cultural Cafetero.

Kamuya Maitha, Joseph. 1969. "Coffee Production in Kenya: An Econometric Study." Ph.D. dissertation, University of New York at Buffalo.

Lauria, Aldo. 1999. *An Agrarian Republic: Commercial Agriculture and the Politics of Peasant Communities in El Salvador, 1823–1914*. Pittsburgh: University of Pittsburgh Press.

Légier, Émile. 1905. *La Martinique et la Guadeloupe, considérations sur l'avenir et la culture de la canne, la production du sucre et du rhum, et les cultures secondaires dans les Antilles Françaises*. Paris: Bureaux de la Sucrerie Indigène et Coloniale.

León, Jorge. 1997. *Evolución del comercio exterior y del transporte marítimo de Costa Rica 1821–1900*. San José: Editorial Universidad de Costa Rica.

Lewis, W. Arthur. 1978. *Growth and Fluctuations 1870–1913*. London: George Allen & Unwin.

Lock, Charles. G. W. 1888. *Coffee: Its Culture and Commerce in All Countries*. London and New York: E. & F. N. Spon.

Marques, Walter. 1962. *Problemas do desenvolvimento econômico de Angola*, 2 vols. [Luanda]: Junta de Desenvolvimento Industrial.

Mesquita, João. 1918. *Dados estatísticos para o estudo das pautas de Angola; Exportação pelas alfândegas do Círculo e do Congo nos anos de 1888 a 1913*. Luanda: Imprensa Nacional.

Moral, Paul. 1961. *Le Paysan Haitien (Étude sur la vie rurale en Haïti)*. N.p.: G. P. Maisonneuve & Larose.

Obregón, Clotilde. 1977. "El comercio cafetalero de Costa Rica. Primera mitad del siglo XIX." Paper submitted at the 3d Central America History Congress, San José, Costa Rica.

Oficina Internacional de las Repúblicas Americanas. 1902. *El café: Historia, cultivo, beneficio, variedades, producción, exportación, consumo, etc., etc.* Washington: Oficina Internacional de las Repúblicas Americanas.

Peebles, Patrick. 1982. *Sri Lanka: A Handbook of Historical Statistics*. Boston: G. K. Hall & Co.

Pérez de la Riva, Francisco. 1944. *El café: Historia de su cultivo y explotación en Cuba*. Ed. Jesús Montero. Havana.

Posthumus, N. 1946. *Inquiry into the History of Prices in Holland*, vol. 1. Leiden: E. J. Brill.

Radell, David. 1964. *Coffee and Transportation in Nicaragua*. Berkeley: Department of Geography, University of California at Berkeley.

República de Honduras. 1893. *Primer Anuario Estadístico, 1889*. Tegucigalpa: Tipografía Nacional.

Rodrigues da Cunha, Mauro. 1992. "Apêndice estatístico." In Edmar Bacha and Robert Greenhil,*150 Anos de café*. Rio: Marcellino Martins & E. Johnston Exportadores Ltda.

Rodriguez, D.W. 1961. *Coffee: A Short Economic History with Special Reference to Jamaica*. Ministry of Agriculture and Lands, Commodity Bulletin No. 2.

Samper, Armando. 1948. *Importancia del café en el comercio exterior de Colombia*. Bogotá: Federación Nacional de Cafeteros de Colombia.

Schmitt, Robert C. 1977. *Historical Statistics of Hawaii*. Honolulu: University Press of Hawaii.

Schumpeter, Elizabeth Boody. 1960. *British Overseas Trade Statistics 1697–1808*. Oxford: Clarendon Press.

Springuett, Leslie E. 1935. *Quality Coffee*. New York: The Spice Mill Publishing Co.

"Statement of the Trade of British India." From *Parliamentary Papers, House of Commons Sessional Papers*, London, various years.

Tarrade, Jean. 1972. *Le commerce colonial de la France à la fin de l'Ancien Régime*. Paris.

Taunay, Affonso de E. 1945. *Pequena historia do café no Brasil* (1727–1937). Rio de Janeiro: Departamento Nacional do Café.

Teixeira de Oliveira, José. 1984. *História do café no Brasil e no Mundo*. Rio de Janeiro: Livraria Kosmos Editora.

Tetzlaff, Rainier. 1970. *Koloniale Entwicklung und Ausbeutung: Wirtschafts- und Sozialgeschichte Deutsch-Ostafrikas, 1885–1914*. Berlin: Duncker und Humblot.

Thurber, Francis B. 1883. *Coffee from Plantation to Cup*. New York: American Grocer Publishing Association.

Ukers, William H. 1935. *All About Coffee*. New York: Tea and Coffee Trade Journal Company.

van Delden Laërne, C. F. 1885. *Brazil and Java: Report on Coffee-Culture in America, Asia and Africa*. London: W. H. Allen & Co.

van Stipriaan, Alex. 1993. *Surinaams Contrast: Roofbouw en Overleven in een Caraïbische Plantagekolonie 1750–1863*. Leiden: KITLV Uitgever.

Velázquez Pereira, José Luis. 1992. *La formación del Estado en Nicaragua, 1860–1930*. Managua: Fondo Editorial Banco Central de Nicaragua.

Waters, Alan R. 1969. "The Cost Structure of the Kenya Coffee Industry." Ph.D. thesis, Rice University.

Wickizer, V. D. 1943. *The World Coffee Economy with Special Reference to Control Schemes.* Stanford, Calif.: Food Research Institute, Stanford University.

Williams, Robert. 1994. *States and Social Evolution: Coffee and the Rise of National Governments in Central America.* Chapel Hill and London: University of North Carolina Press.

Index

Abdalî sultanate, 58, 59
absenteeism, *see* resistance by workers
Abû Arîsh, 57, 59
abuse of workers, *see* corporal punishment; sexual abuse
Abyssinia, *see* Ethiopia
account books, 183, 221–5, 339
addiction, 44, 49
Aden, 51, 54, 57–62, 65, 117, 423
Adi-Dravida caste, 184–5
Adimai Alukal caste, 178
adulteration of coffee, 41–3, 135
Adulteration of Food Acts, Britain, 42
advertising and brands, 40–2, 44, 46, 126–9, 134–5; *see also* grading of coffee; quality of coffee
Africa: credit, 401, 403; cultivation, 2–3, 5, 22, 31, 76–7, 102–4; exports, 11, 97–8, 100; labor, 8, 34, 286–7, 313–16, 403; land, 286–7, 313–16, 333, 386, 398, 401, 403; marketing, 15, 97–8, 314; processing, 390; taxation, 115, 314, 403; transport, 313, 391
African Association, 324, 330
African Development Loan Fund, 331
age of bearing of coffee trees, 35, 70, 107, 112, 192
age grades, 288, 290

agents, *see* intermediaries in importing countries
aging of coffee trees, 92, 104, 107, 153, 167, 365
Agraristas, Mexico, 398
Agricultural Credit Union, 84
agricultural extension services, 207, 308, 322–6, 356
agricultural research, 8–9, 10–11, 28, 85, 92, 403, 409
Agriculture Department, Tanganyika, 323–6, 331–2
agroforestry, 15, 106–7, 163, 166, 170, 392–3
agronomy, *see* agricultural research
Akwapim, 113
Alajuela, 337, 340
alcoholic beverages, 5, 87, 198, 203, 221, 269, 270; *see also* beer; wine
Alexandria, 53, 56, 62, 64
Algeria, 60, 80, 448–9
Alta Verapaz, 193–4, 198, 206
Amaral company, 377
Amatitlán, 191, 193
Amazon, 106
Amerindian peoples: general, 13, 15, 391–2, 394; Mesoamerica, 9, 191–208, 216–17, 219, 237–8, 249–50, 258–85, 340, 386, 394; South America, 32

transaction costs, 26
transplanting, 86
transport and communications, 13,
  29, 32–4, 36–7, 124, 130–3, 136–42,
  144–6, 385, 390–1, 406, 409; *see
  also* animals; bicycles; camels;
  canoes; carts; harbor installations;
  inland waterways; motor vehicles;
  mules and horses; oxen; porters;
  railroads; roads and bridges;
  shipping; telegraph
Travancore, 177
Treaty of Rome, 98
Três Rios, Brazil, 369
Tres Ríos, Costa Rica, 41, 126
tribes, 316, 322; *see also* ethnicity
Trieste, 97
Trilla Castellana estate, 247
Triumpho machines, 376
tropics, 1, 2, 6, 11, 14
tsetse flies, 391
tundu system, 186
Tunis, 53
Tûr, 51
Türkshe Bilmez, 57
Turrialba,133, 337, 341, 354, 357–8,
  359
Tuxtla, 259, 260, 263, 273–4, 283
Tuxtla Gutiérrez, 273
Twynam, W. C., 182
Tzeltal people, 266
Tzotzil people, 266, 278, 284

Ubico, Jorge, 204–5
Udayn, 61
Uganda, 2–3, 6, 98, 103, 106, 109,
  312, 423, 440–1
Ukers, William, 45
Union des Populations du Cameroun,
  310
unions, *see* trade unions
United Fruit Company, 253
United Kingdom, *see* Britain
United Nations, 326
United States: colonial expansion, 2,
  31, 111, 115–16, 117, 207;
  consumption of coffee, 31, 37–8,

42–8, 127–8; credit and investment,
  247; education, 248; imports, 37,
  39, 56, 61–2, 69, 76, 115–16, 133–5,
  140–2, 159, 423, 442–4; marketing,
  37, 39–42, 47, 61, 374; prices, 37,
  39, 44–5; roasting, 42–8, 128;
  taxation, 37
United States Federal Department of
  Agriculture, 42, 44
United States Federal Trade
  Commission, 45
urbanization, 8, 37, 91, 115, 205–7,
  303, 305, 348
Uruguay, 444
Usambara, 109, 292–3
usufruct rights, 236, 242, 286, 321,
  397
usury, *see* credit; debt peonage

vagrancy laws, 204–6, 271, 274–5
Valais, K., 374
Valença, 364
valorization, *see* Brazil, prices
Valparaíso, 130, 146
Van Erven e Irmãos company, 375
Vanuatu, 103, 116–17
Vargas, Getúlio, 398
Vassouras, 364, 369
Vatomandry region, 86–7
vegetables, 123, 288, 304, 380
Venezuela, 7–8, 33–4, 40, 65, 130,
  132, 152, 209, 422, 432–5
Veracruz, 264, 398
vertical integration, 43, 128
Vichy regime, 89
Vienna, 62
Vietnam: consumption of coffee, 116;
  cultivation, 1–3, 36, 65, 104, 106,
  107, 118–19; exports, 71; labor, 71,
  119; land, 11, 119, 388; marketing,
  116, 407
"Villa Sarchí" coffee, 138, 147
Villahermosa, 264
Virilla valley, 131, 133
Vitória, 373
V.O.C., *see* Dutch East India Company
volcanic eruptions, 279, 348

LaVergne, TN USA
18 December 2009
167439LV00003B/7/A